ANATOMY FOR ARTISTS

A visual guide to the human form

Words by Jahirul Amin | Photography by Robin Bharaj
Artwork by Charlie Pickard unless otherwise stated
Scientific proofread by Kirsten Clift MSc, BSc. (KCProofreading)

3dtotalPublishing

3dtotalPublishing

Correspondence: publishing@3dtotal.com
Website: www.3dtotal.com

First published in the United Kingdom, 2020, by 3dtotal Publishing.

Reprinted in 2021

Address: 3dtotal.com Ltd, 29 Foregate Street, Worcester, WR1 1DS, United Kingdom.

Soft cover ISBN: 978-1-912843-10-7
Printing & binding: Leo Paper Products Ltd. www.leo.com.hk

Visit www.3dtotalpublishing.com for a complete list of available book titles.

Managing Director: Tom Greenway
Studio Manager: Simon Morse
Lead Designer: Fiona Tarbet
Lead Editor: Samantha Rigby
Editor: Philippa Barker
Designer: Joseph Cartwright

FSC www.fsc.org MIX Paper from responsible sources FSC® C020056

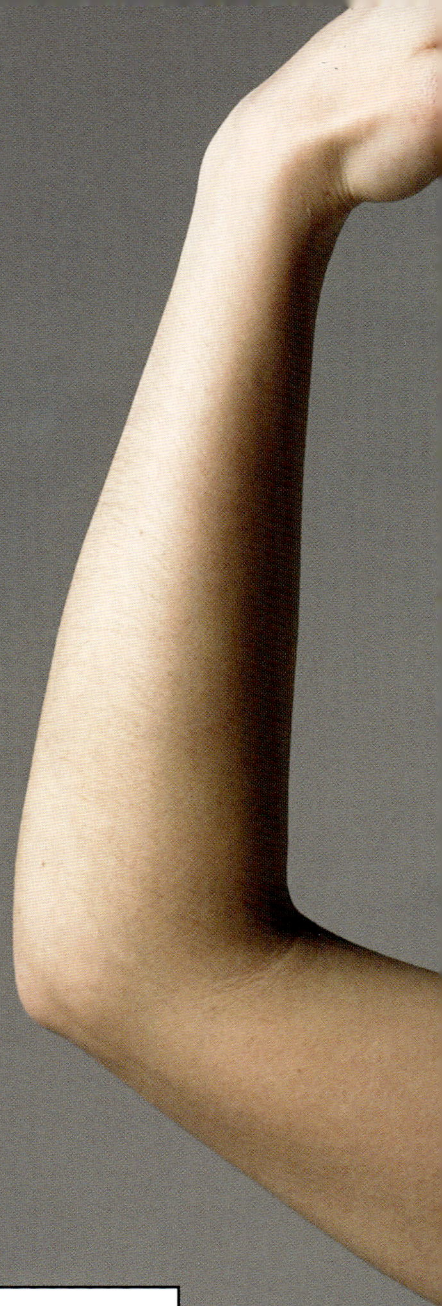

ONE TREE PLANTED FOR EVERY BOOK SOLD

OUR PLEDGE

From 2020, 3dtotal Publishing has pledged to plant one tree for every book sold by partnering with and donating the appropriate amounts to re-foresting charities. This is one of the first steps in our ambition to become a carbon-neutral company with carbon-neutral publications, giving our customers the knowledge that by buying from 3dtotal Publishing, they are working with us to balance the environmental damage caused by the publishing, shipping, and retail industries.

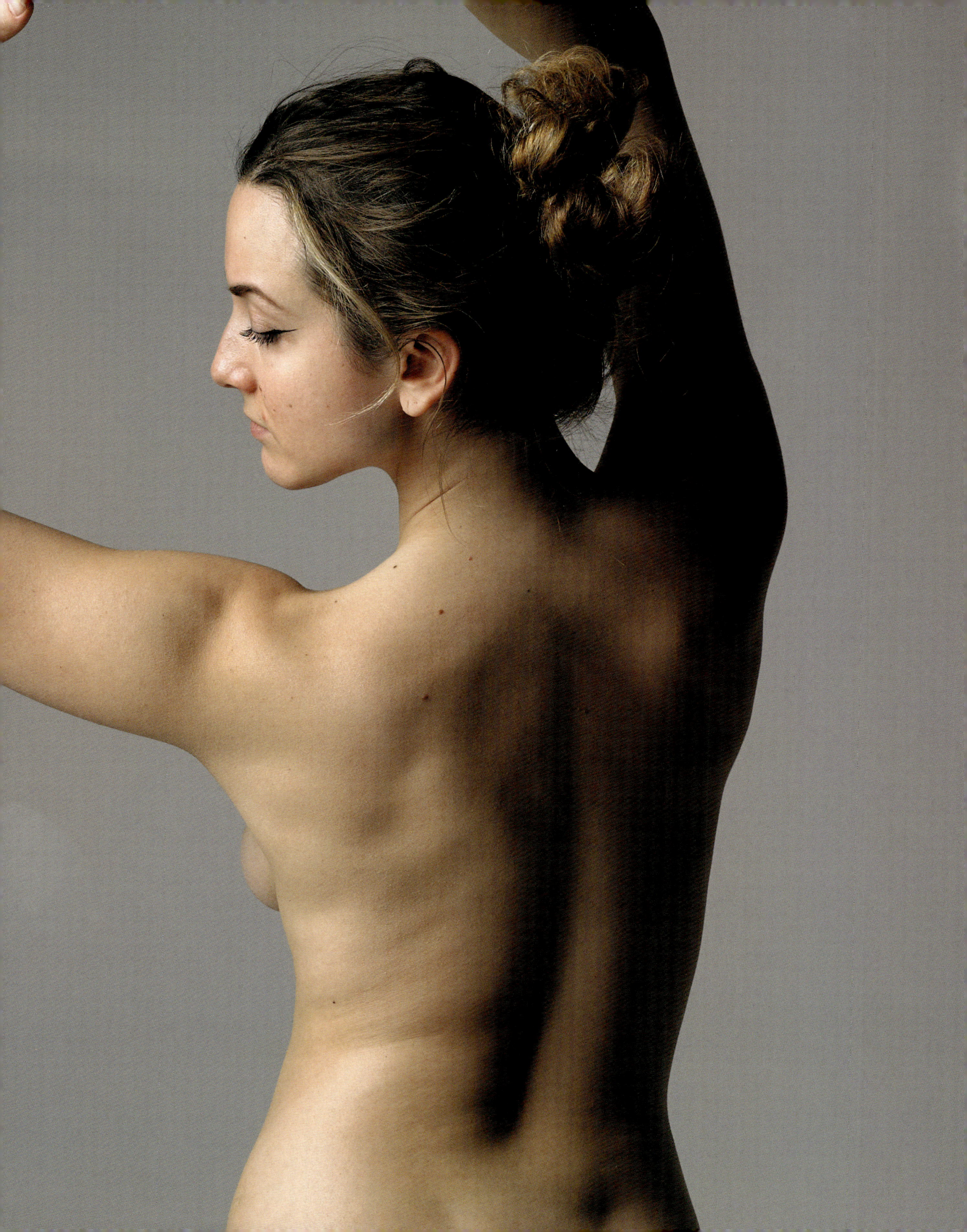

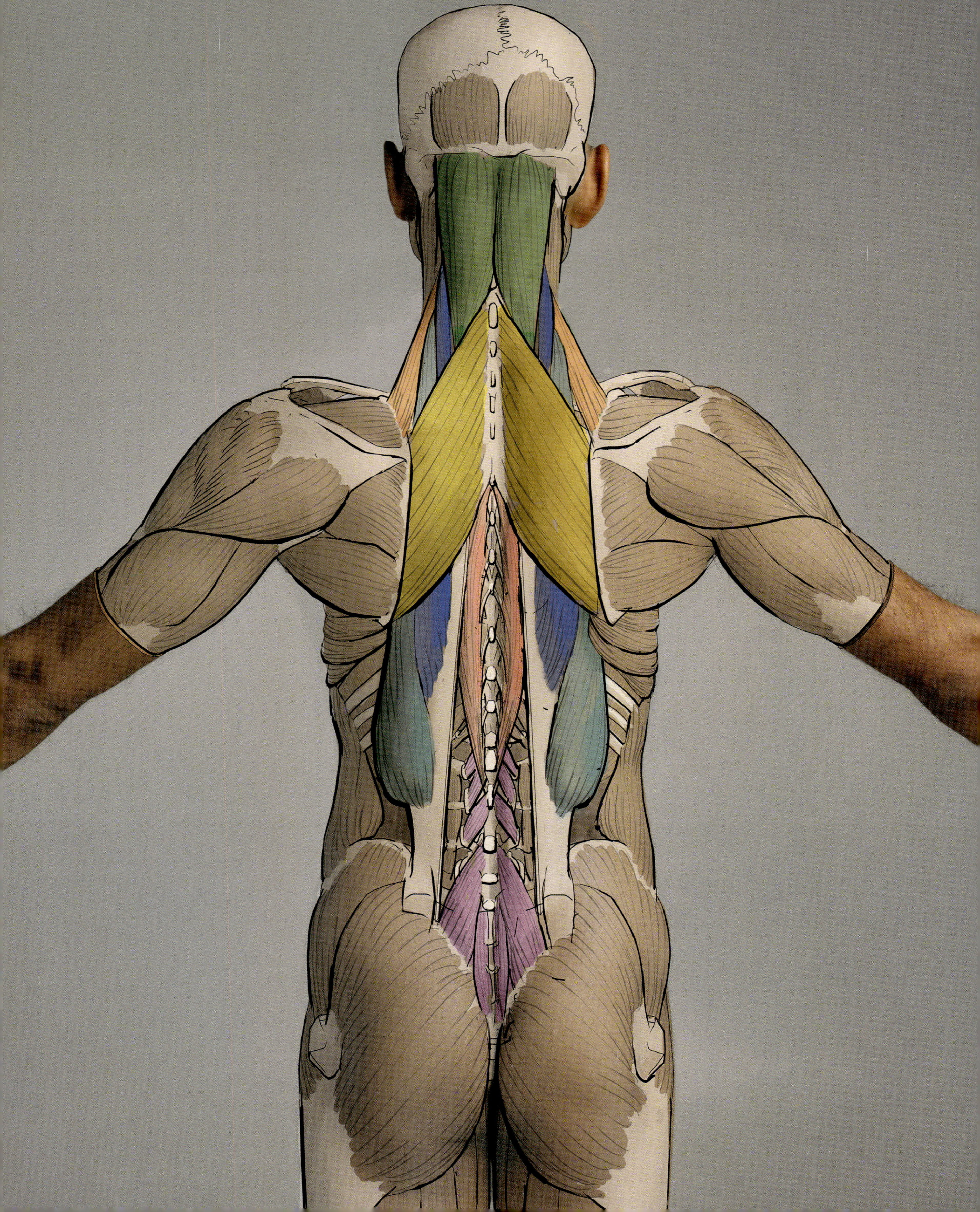

CONTENTS

Foreword

Jacob Hankinson
Artist & instructor

The elements that help to forge a work of figurative art are dizzying. Contour, form, gesture, planes, and design (to name just a few) all play vital roles in creating believable and aesthetically pleasing figures, and yet these alone are not enough to ensure that a work of art will be successful. As an instructor, I frequently see artwork with flowing gesture, well-constructed form, and sharp designs that fall short of their potential — or worse, fall completely flat. These otherwise beautiful drawings are marred by one crucial missing element, an element that both the beginner and experienced draftsman have an unfortunate tendency to overlook. What is this Achilles' heel that causes so many artists to stumble? It is, in fact, the heel itself and all the muscle, sinew, and bone that connect us.

Anatomy is much more than simply memorizing the names and locations of our various parts. It is a way of understanding how we move through the world, a way of perceiving the people around us with a new perspective and sense of wonder. It is a way of looking at a person and being able to recognize every bump, line, and protrusion, and how each one helps us to function. It is a way of using knowledge — not of art, but of ourselves — to breathe life into our work and imbue it with a soul.

Knowledge of human anatomy is essential not only to those striving for realism, but to those whose work requires imagination and invention. It is what divides the amateur from the professional, and the professional from the master. Any number of common errors — hands without discernible wrists, misshapen rib cages, deformed feet, and lumpy legs — can be ascribed to a lack of anatomical knowledge. The difference between drawing a knee that looks believable and a knee that looks like it met with an accident is a simple matter of knowing the bones and their functions; further study will allow an artist to move beyond creating figures that look merely believable to creating figures that appear ready to leap off the page. Of course, anatomy alone isn't a panacea, but combined with diligent study and practice of the core principles of art, it can remedy many of the issues that plague aspiring and professional artists alike.

Having access to high-quality learning materials is critical to an artist's success; after all, we can only learn as well as we are taught. When it comes to anatomy, it is important that the text both clearly explains and clearly shows the forms, functions, and myriad varieties of the human figure — male and female, young and old, stocky and athletic, and everything in between. This book wonderfully distills those complexities into a visually pleasing and easy-to-follow guide. As both a student and teacher, I have amassed a large collection of anatomy books and can safely say that this is among the best I have seen. Not only does it cover joint mechanics, body types, and asymmetry, but it contains a wealth of images and illustrations to learn from as well. I certainly wish I had owned a copy when I was an aspiring artist struggling to teach myself how to draw, and I am sure that this book will be one you reach for again and again in your studies.

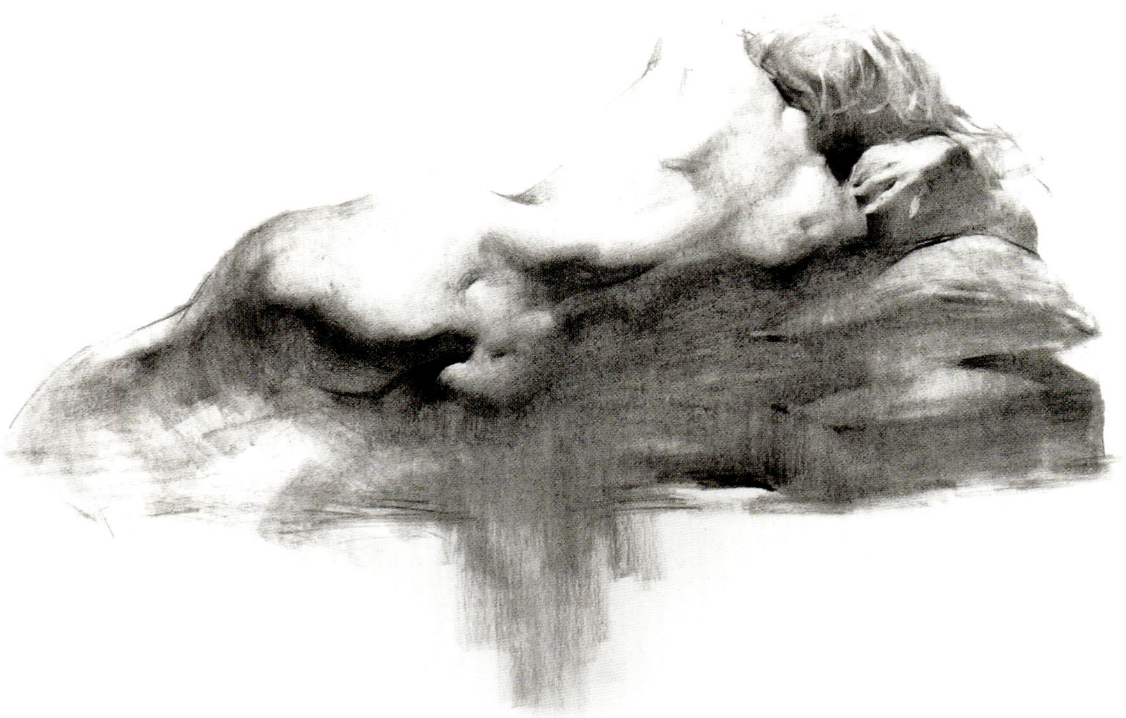

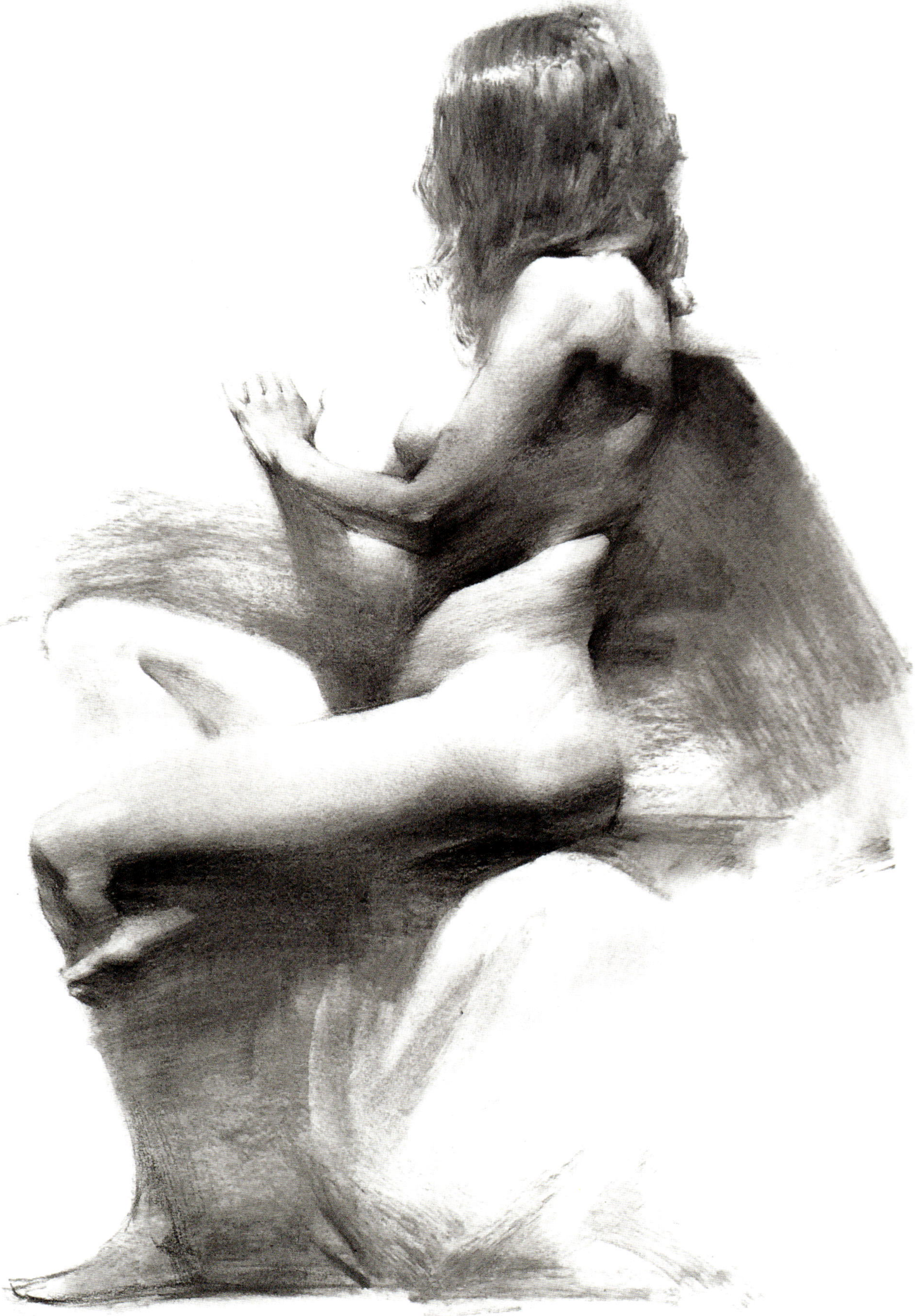

Introduction

HISTORY OF ANATOMY

As visual artists, our aim is to create images that are emotive and believable, whether these are photo-real or stylized, 2D or 3D, still or moving. Further to this, and especially when working on character-based designs, we want to sell the idea that the character on the page or screen is a living, breathing entity. Both 2D and 3D artists need to show that their character has structure, shape, and form to create an illusion that the marks on the page or the vertices on screen have an underlying skeleton to support the body and muscles to drive motion. Audiences are consciously, or subconsciously, aware when things look and move unnaturally. They may not know why, but as soon as there is some doubt in their mind about credibility, the illusion is broken.

Before studying the skeleton, muscles, and tendons of the human form, it is interesting to look back through history to see how our knowledge of anatomy has evolved over time.

Translated from the Greek word *anatomē*, meaning "dissection," anatomy is the study of all things living, from human to animal to plant. It is unclear as to when the first studies of the human form were carried out, but there is evidence to suggest anatomical examination predates the mummification practices of the Ancient Egyptians.

The Greeks continued mankind's fascination with the human form, but many had to restrict their practices to the dissection of animals as it was soon forbidden to use human subjects. Unsurprisingly, this resulted in many strange theories. During this period, Hippocrates (c. 460–370 BCE), known as the Father of Medicine, developed the Hippocratic Oath, a pledge to practice medicine honestly, which is still used by physicians today. Herophilus (c. 335–280 BCE) was another scientist who, along with Hippocrates, became a founder of anatomy. Herophilus was known as the Father of Anatomy and many see him as the greatest anatomist of the ancient times, challenged only by Vesalius in the 16th century.

During the Roman Empire, the theories and practices of Galen (c. 130-210) gained much attention and would dominate medical science for centuries to come. His experience ranged from treating gladiator wounds to becoming the personal physician to many emperors. His dissection of animals, including pigs and macaque monkeys, led to understandings that still hold up today, such as the formation of urine in the kidney and the workings of the peripheral nervous systems.

The next major period of development came during the Renaissance movement. Leonardo da Vinci (1452–1519) dedicated part of his life to the anatomical study of the human form, animals, and plants. His studies filled sixty notepads and he produced over 500 diagrams. He was the first to create a scientific diagram of the fetus *in utero* and his skills, not only as an artist but an engineer, pushed him to understand the mechanics of human movement and what we now call biomechanics. Da Vinci's research led to what has been referred to as the first robot in human form: Leonardo's Robot (1495). By viewing the human body as a kind of machine, he was able to replicate this through the use of levers and pulleys to make his robot sit, stand, and move its arms.

In 1543, Andreas Vesalius (1514–1564), who many would call the Father of Modern Anatomy, released *De Humani Corporis Fabrica Libri Septem (On the Fabric of the Human Body in Seven Books).* Based on his Paduan lecture series, the book was a visual tour de force of the human body. Through a collection of highly detailed illustrations based on human dissections, Vesalius was able to correct the majority of misconceptions that had been passed down from the age of Galen. Though Galen's research was derived from the dissection of animals, Vesalius' attempts to state the now obvious were

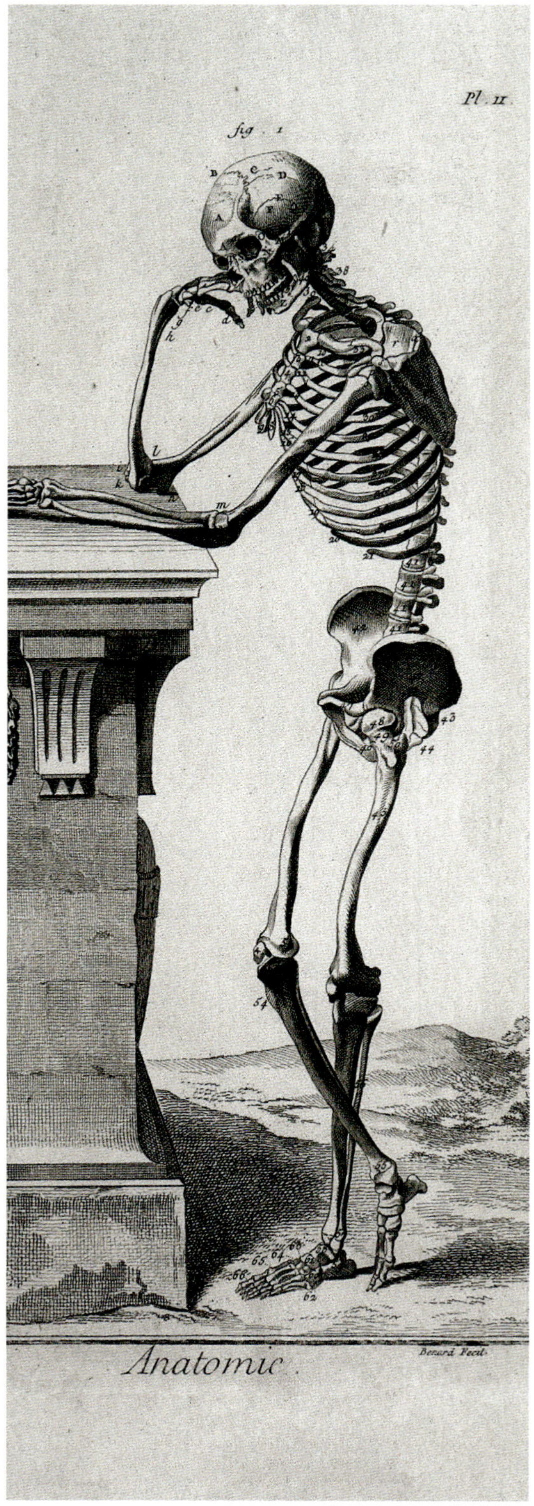

Lateral view of a human skeleton, leaning against a tomb, after Vesalius. Engraving by Benard, late 18th century, after a woodcut, 1543.

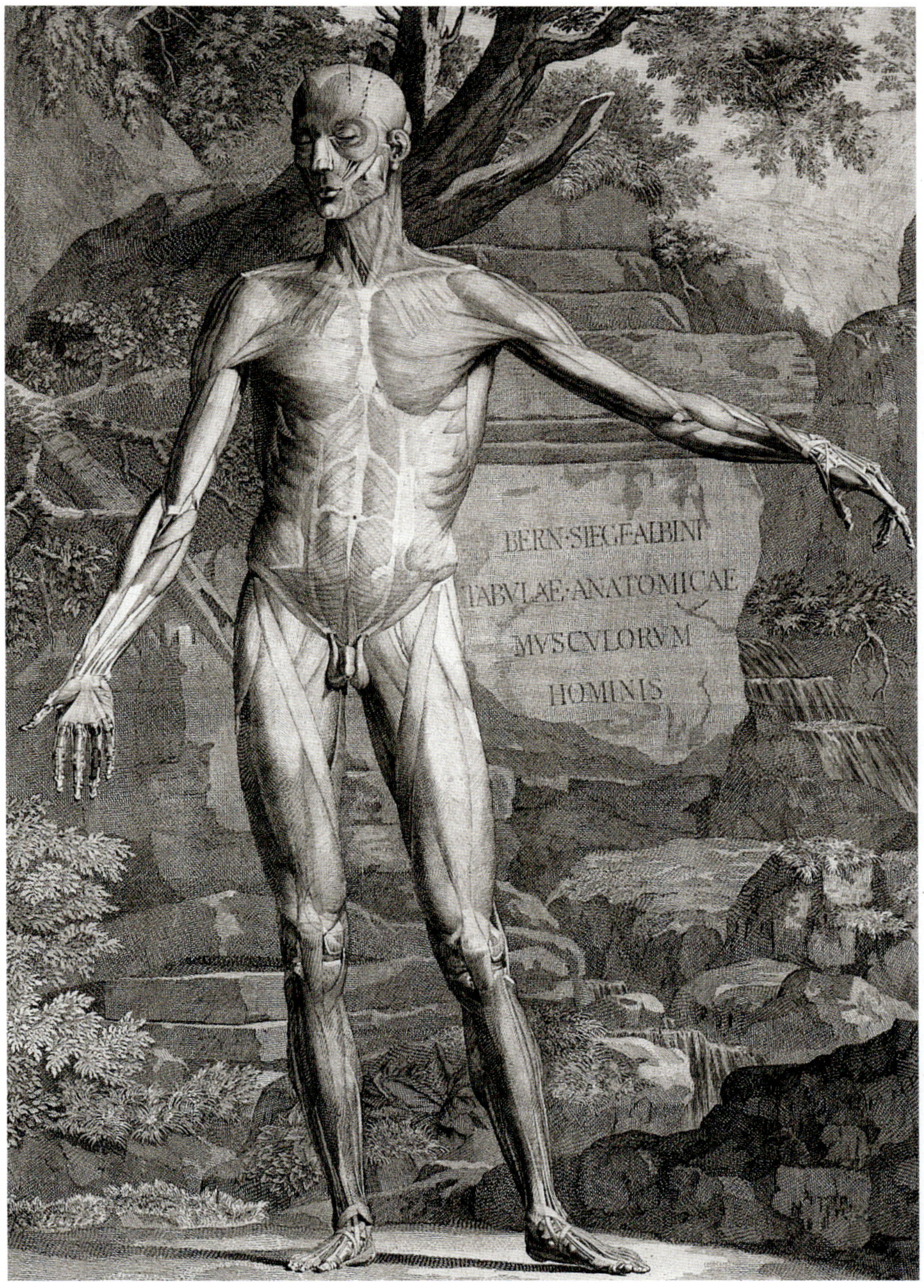

From Tables of the skeleton and muscles of the human body, 1749.
Bernhard Siegfried Albinus, 1697-1770.

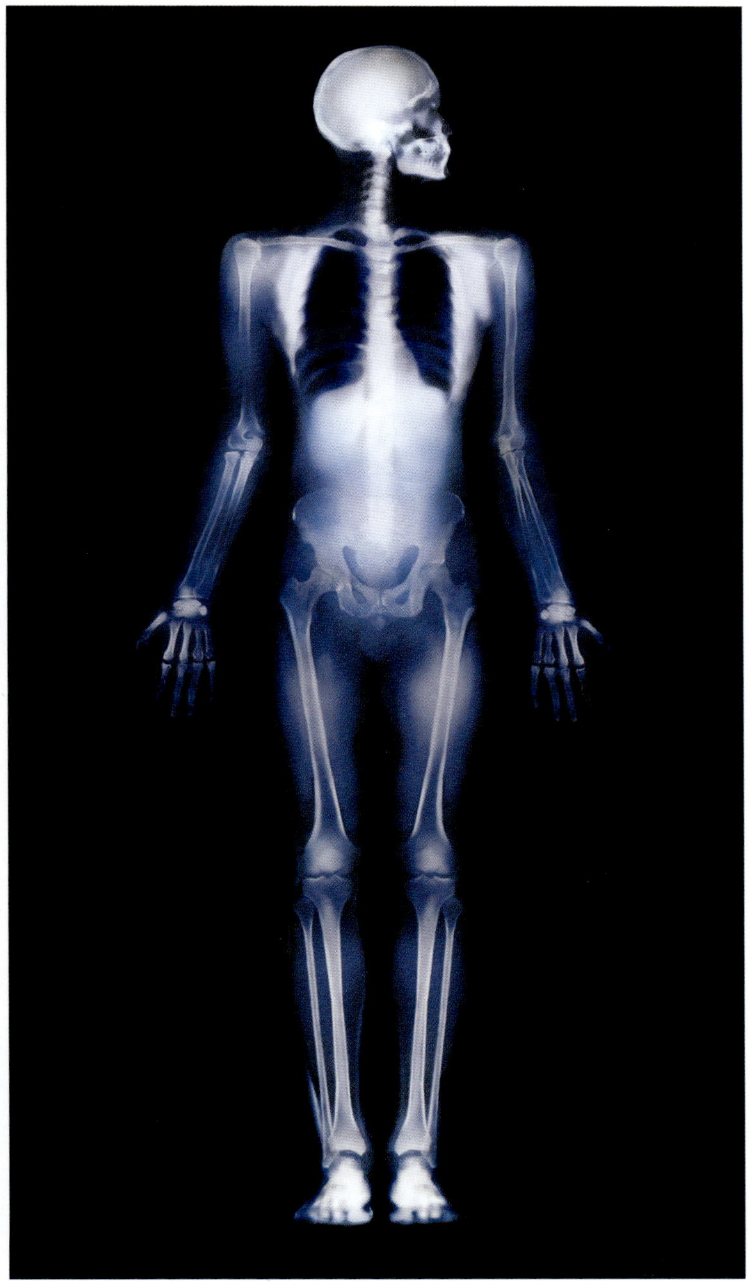

X-ray of the human body, an illustration by Charlie Pickard.

not met favorably by the establishment of the time. Nevertheless, through his dissections of the human body and its organs he was able to shed new light on anatomy.

Moving on to the 17th century and beyond, William Harvey's (1578–1657) *Exercitatio Anatomica de Motu Cordis et Sanguinis in Animalibus* (*An Anatomical Exercise on the Motion of the Heart and Blood in Animals*) solved the puzzle of blood circulation which Vesalius had been unable to achieve. Additionally, Bernhard Siegfried Albinus' (1697–1770) *Tabulae Sceleti et Musculorum Corporis Humani* (*Tables of the Skeleton and Muscles of the Human Body*) increased scientific accuracy through the techniques employed to illustrate the dissected body. Anatomists such as Henry Gray (1827–1861) followed, leading to modern times where advances in technology, such as MRI scans and X-rays, allowed for an ever deeper understanding of the human construction.

THE ANATOMICAL POSITION

Before delving into the skeleton and muscles of the body, it is important to familiarize yourself with the anatomical position. This will allow you to understand the orientation and position of the different body parts through the vocabulary commonly used in reference to anatomy. Think of the anatomical position as the coordinate system for a map; once you figure out your north from your south, it is easier to get from A to B.

In the anatomical position, the body is erect with the head facing forward. The feet are around six inches apart and the toes are facing forward. The arms are down to the side with the palms facing forward and the thumbs pointing outward. This is also known as the supine anatomical position, whereas if the body was lying on its back with palms flat on the ground, it would be in the prone anatomical position.

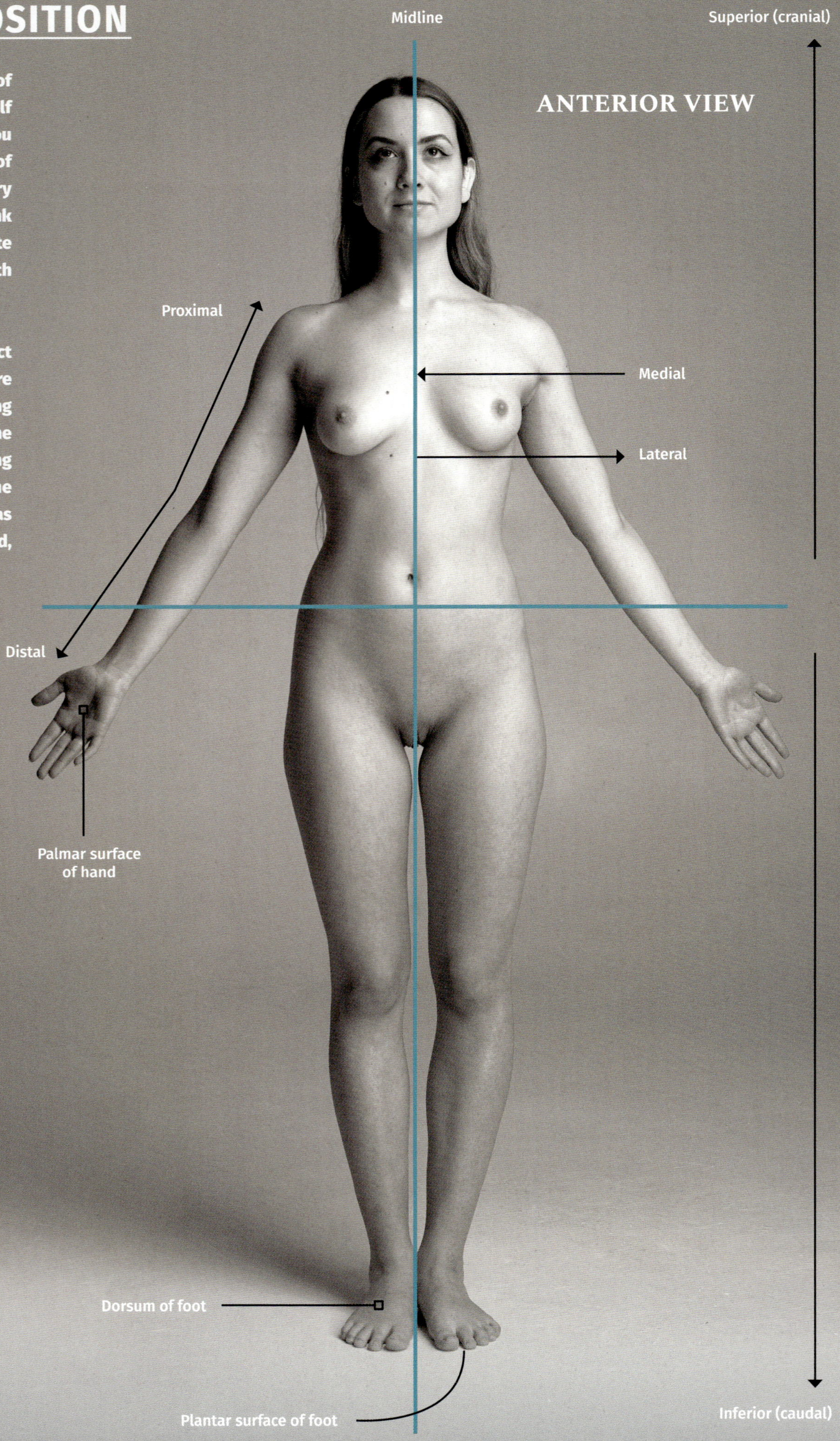

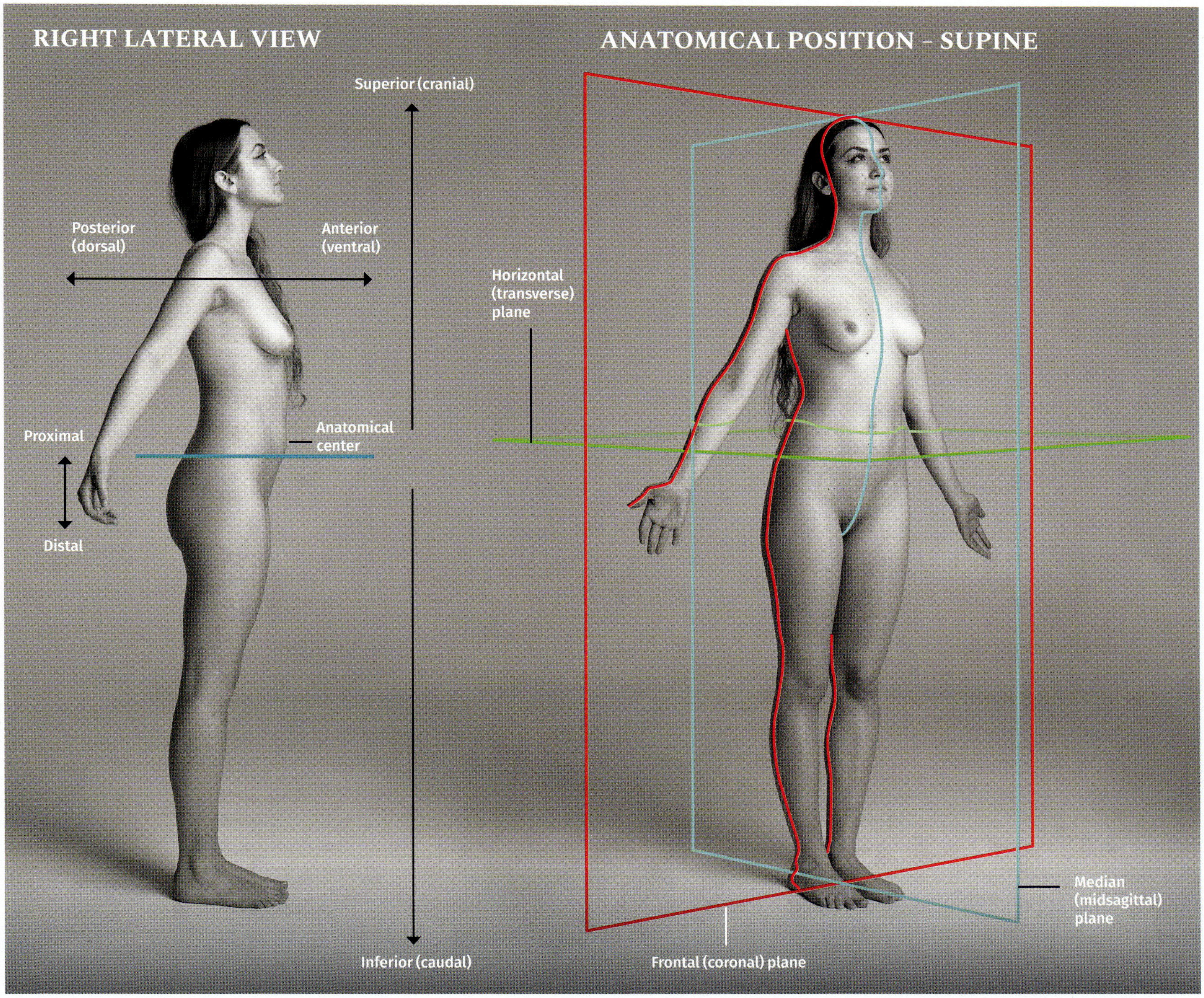

Here is a list of terms related to the anatomical position:

- **Frontal (coronal) plane:** This plane divides the body into front and back portions.
- **Horizontal (transverse) plane:** This is a horizontal plane that runs perpendicular to both the frontal and the median planes.
- **Median (midsagittal) plane:** This plane divides the body into equal right and left halves.
- **Posterior (dorsal):** Toward the back.
- **Anterior (ventral):** Toward the front.
- **Superior (cranial):** Toward the head.
- **Inferior (caudal):** Toward the feet.
- **Proximal:** Near the trunk.
- **Distal:** Away from the trunk.
- **Medial:** Toward the median plane (near the middle of the body).
- **Lateral:** Away from the median plane (away from the middle of the body).
- **Anatomical center:** The point on the body where the frontal, horizontal, and median planes meet so that parts of the body can be referred to as anterior or posterior, or superior or inferior (for example) of this point.

For example:

- The spine is at the posterior (dorsal) side of the body.
- The humerus is lateral (to the side away from the median plane) of the sternum.

ANTERIOR VIEW

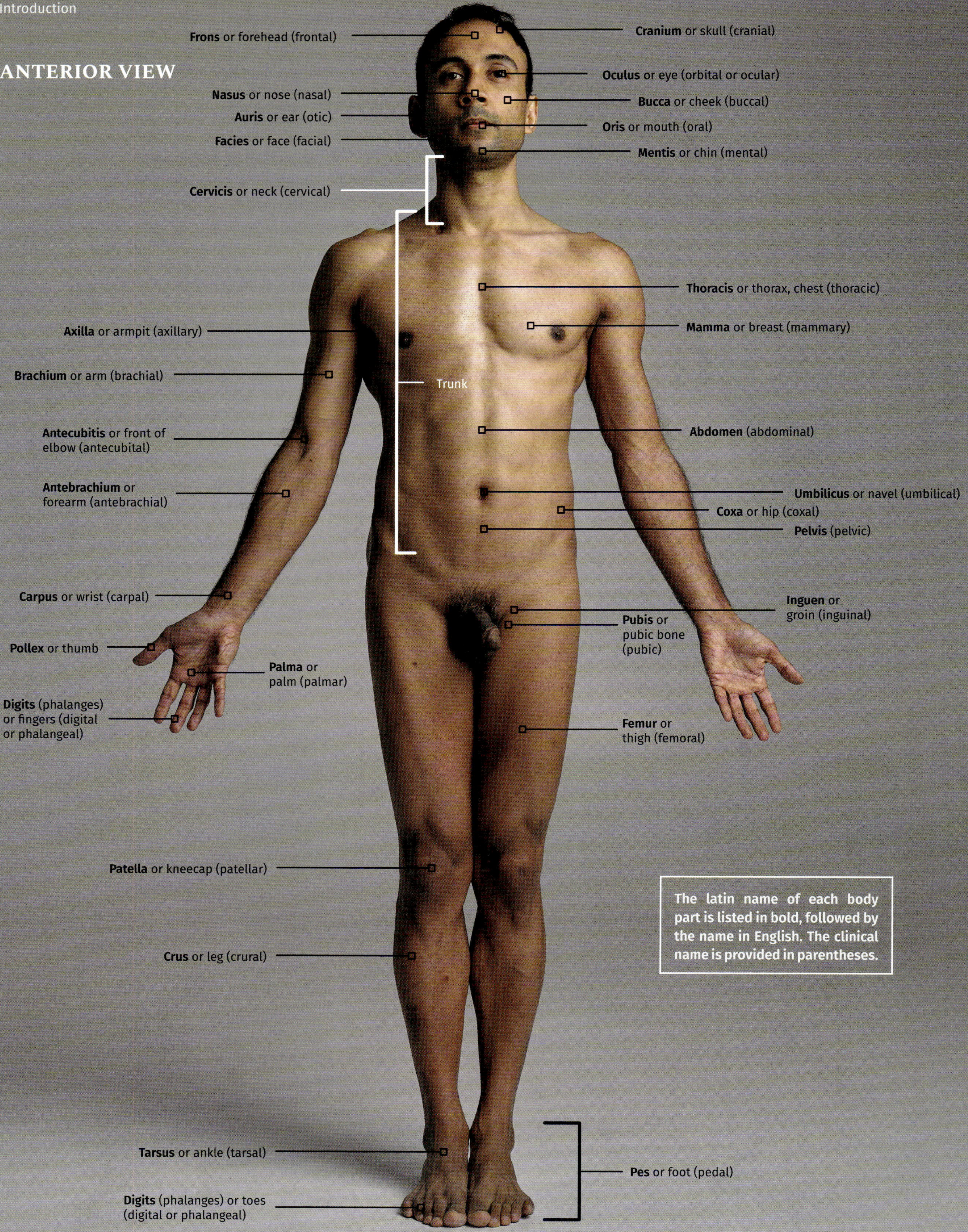

The latin name of each body part is listed in bold, followed by the name in English. The clinical name is provided in parentheses.

POSTERIOR VIEW

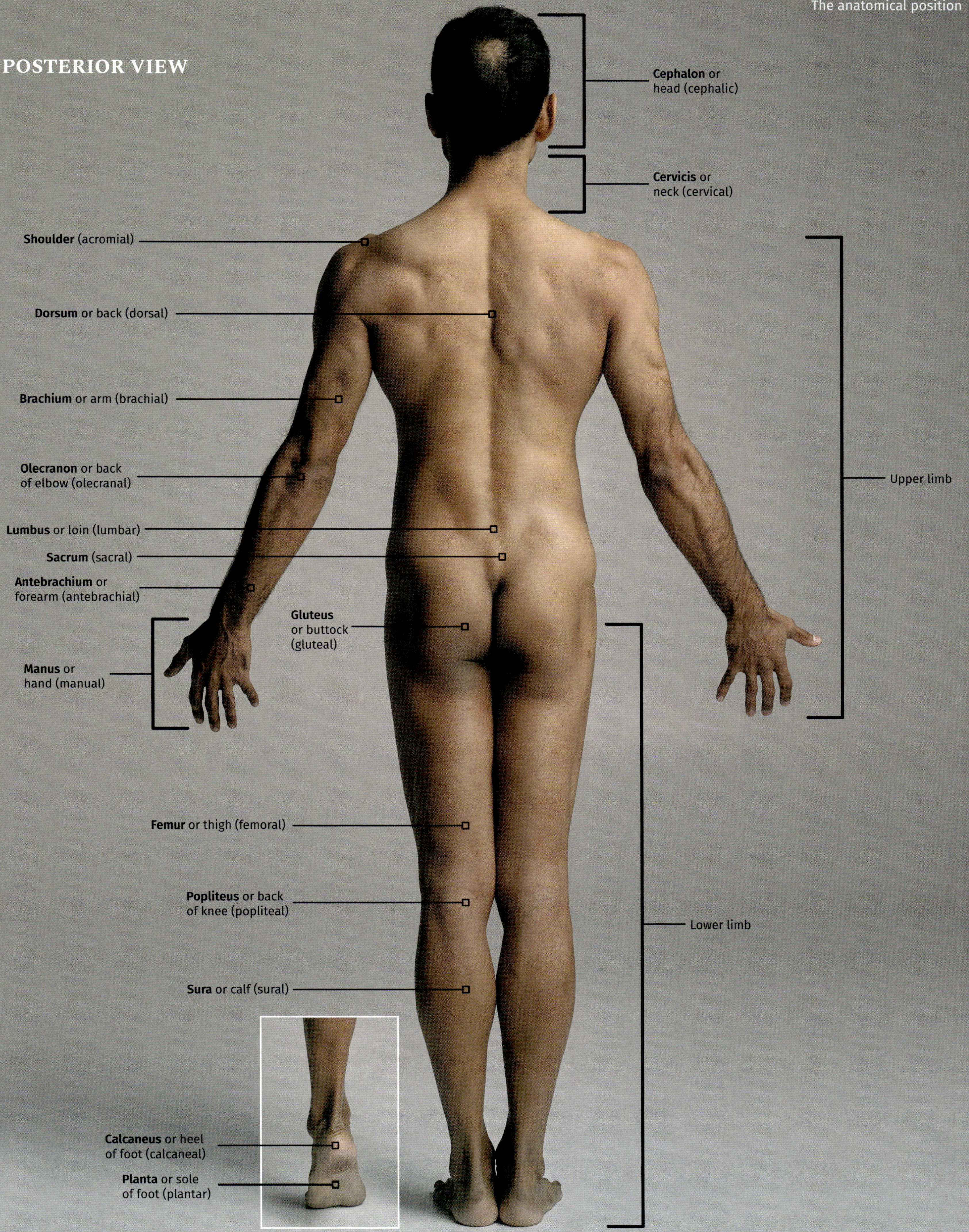

SKELETAL RIGHT LATERAL VIEW

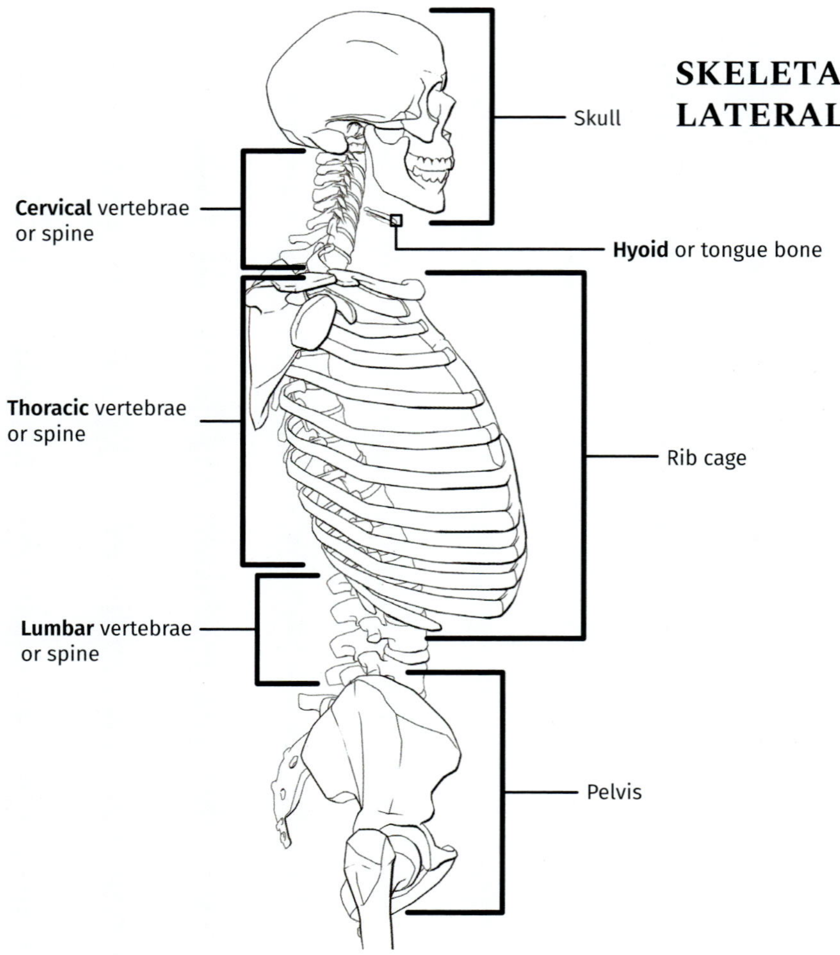

Using terminology

Taking a closer look at the naming of the landmark that is the anterior superior iliac spine will illustrate how having an understanding of terminology can be very useful. (Skeletal landmarks are explored further in **The skeleton and the bony landmarks**, page 28.)

If you break down the name of the landmark, the anterior superior iliac spine, you have anterior (ventral), superior (above), iliac (of the iliac crest), and spine (a bony projection). The name tells you that this is a bony projection on the iliac bone, and the fact that the name includes anterior and superior tells you that there must also be a posterior (opposite to anterior) and an inferior (opposite to superior). Along with the **anterior superior iliac spine** (ASIS), there is also the **anterior inferior iliac spine** (AIIS), the **posterior superior iliac spine** (PSIS), and the **posterior inferior iliac spine** (PIIS).

SKELETAL ANTERIOR VIEW

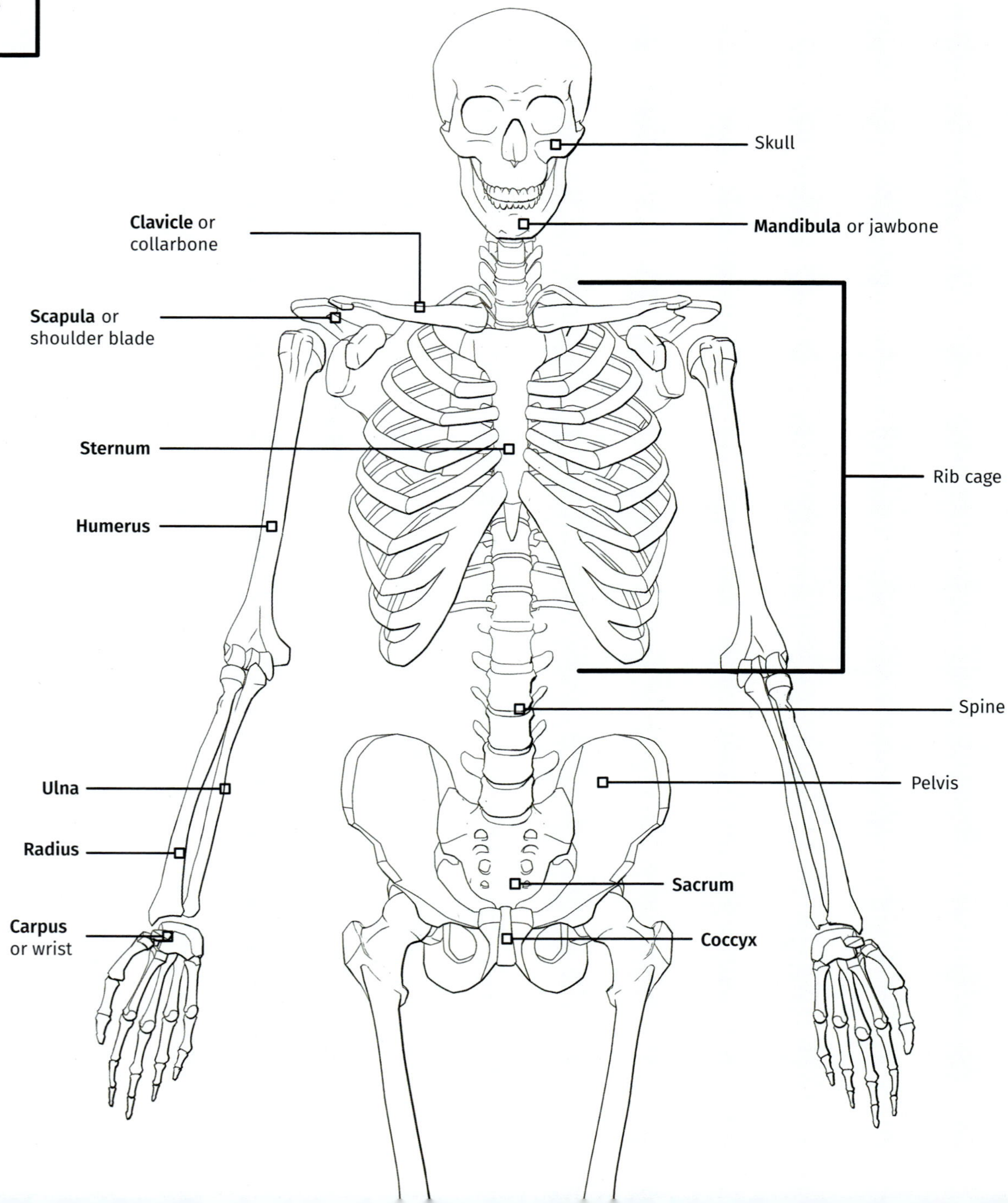

Movement

It is also beneficial to learn the terms relating to different types of movement that are used throughout. Over the next few pages are some of the most frequently used terms.

Extension

- Increasing the angle between two joints. For example, straightening the arm.

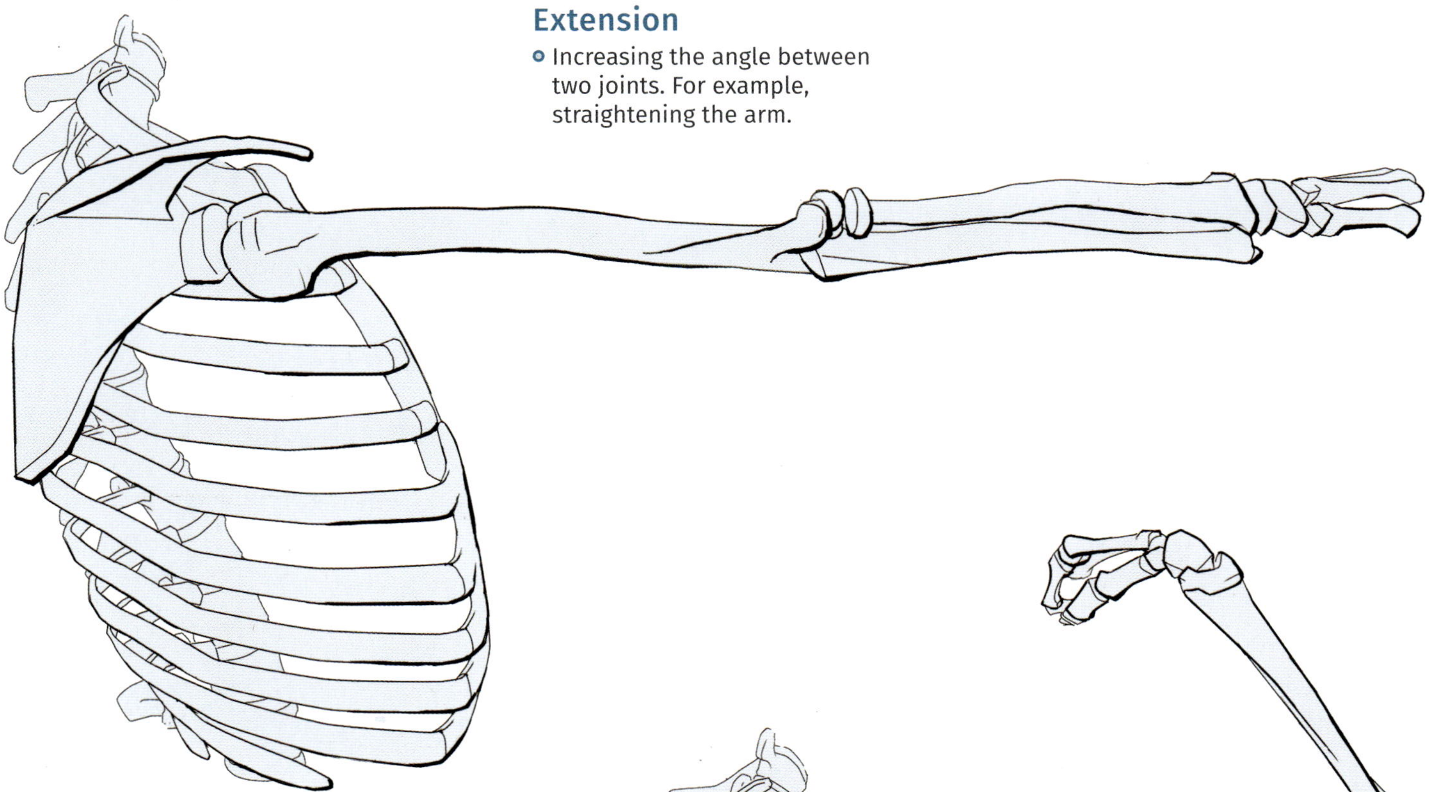

Flexion

- Decreasing the angle between two joints. For example, bending the arm.

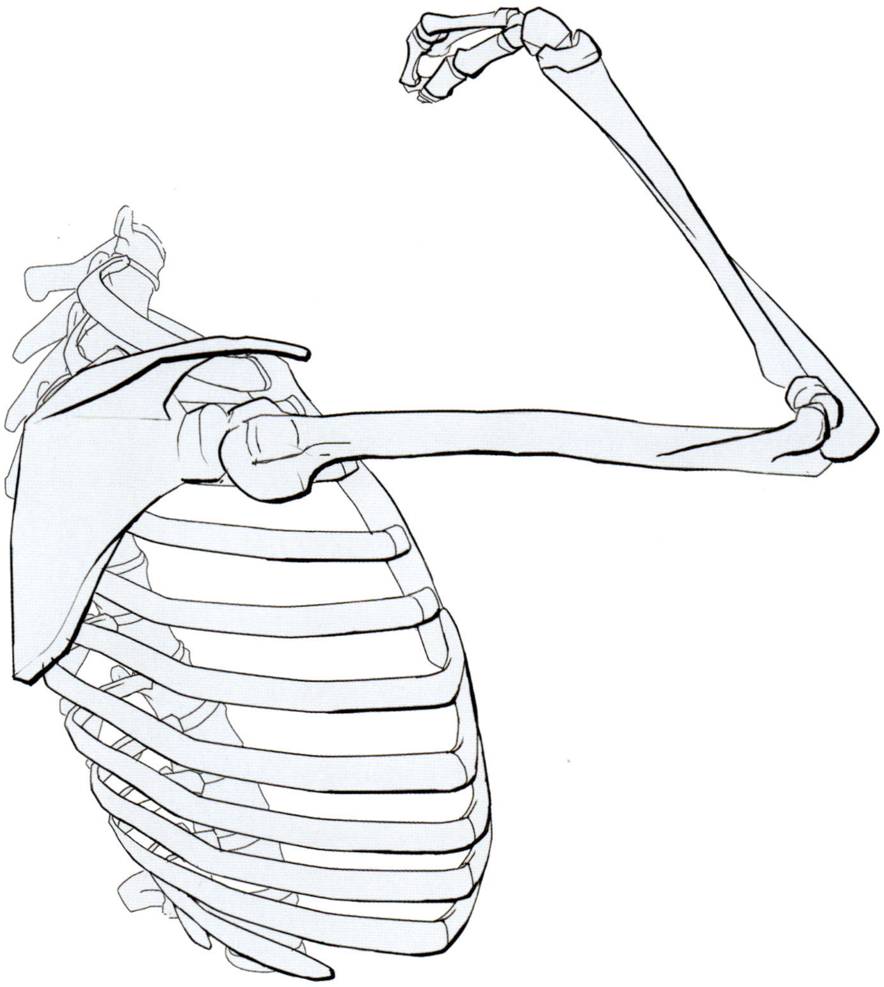

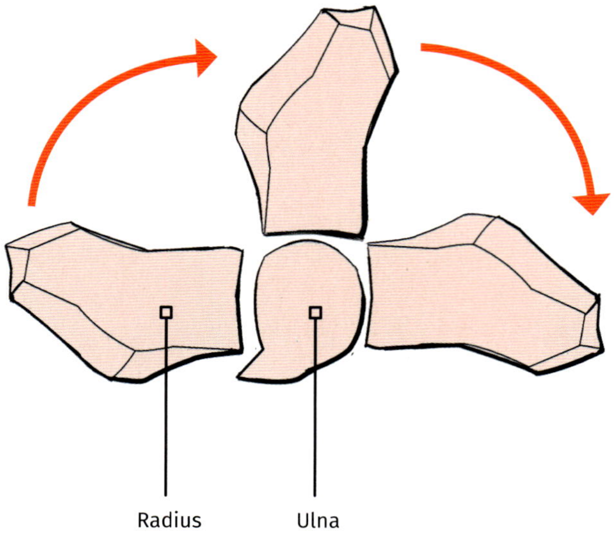

Supination

- Rotating the forearm so the palm faces upward.

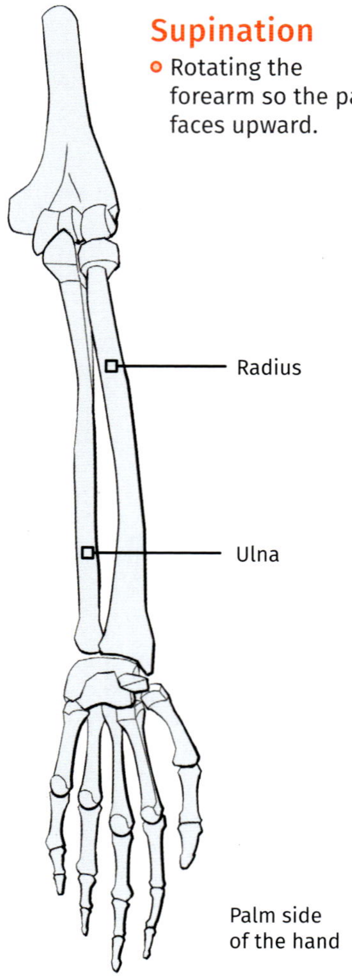

Pronation

- Rotating the forearm so the palm faces downward.

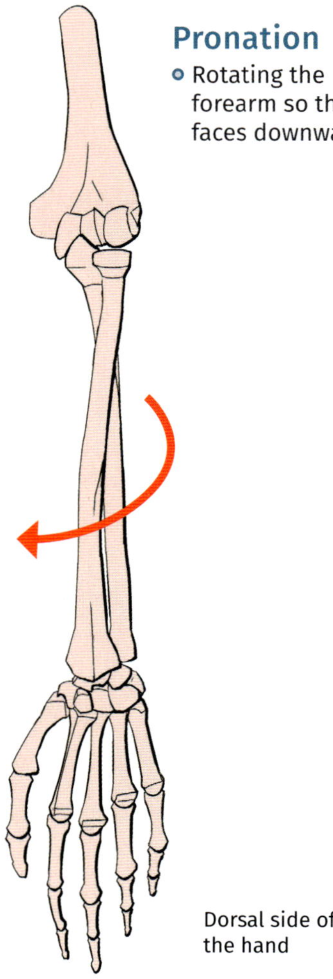

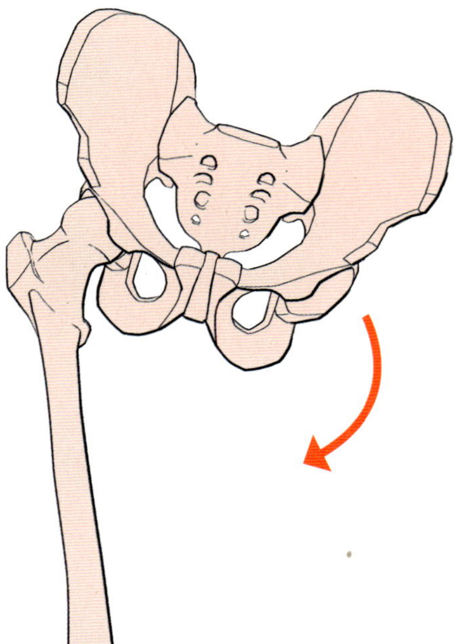

Adduction

- Moving toward the medial plane of the body. For example, moving your leg inward or bringing your fingers together.

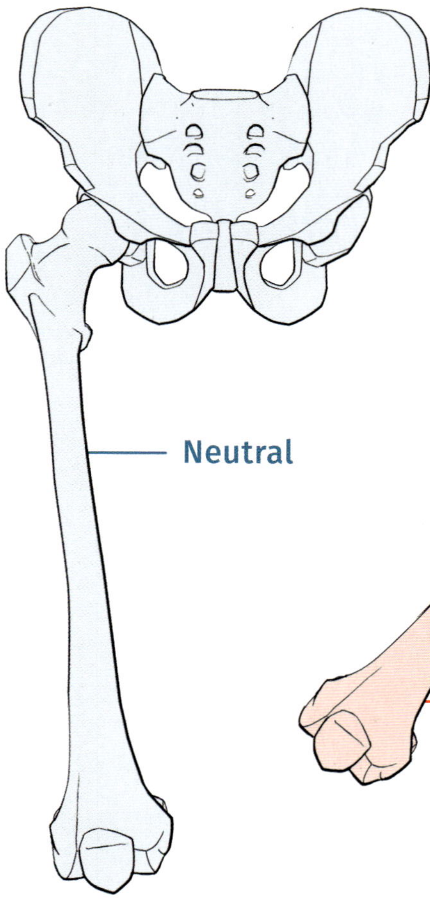

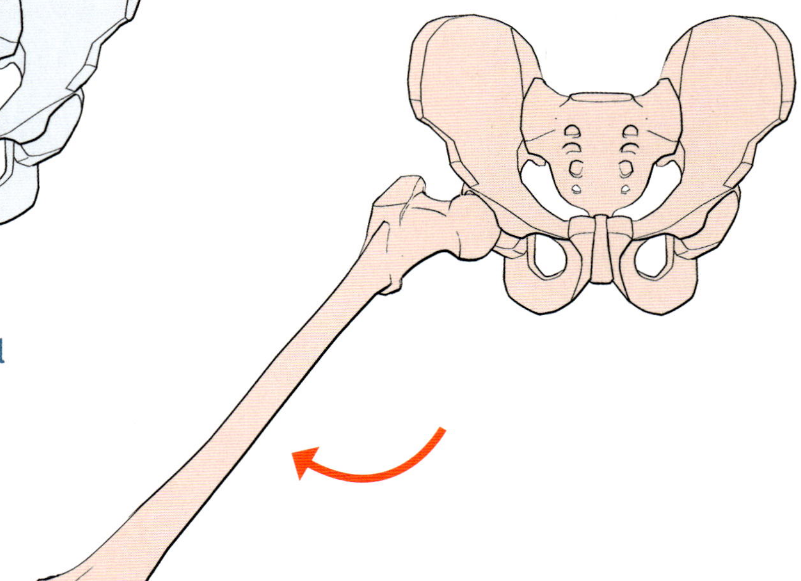

Abduction

- Moving away from the medial plane of the body. For example, raising the leg or arm to the side.

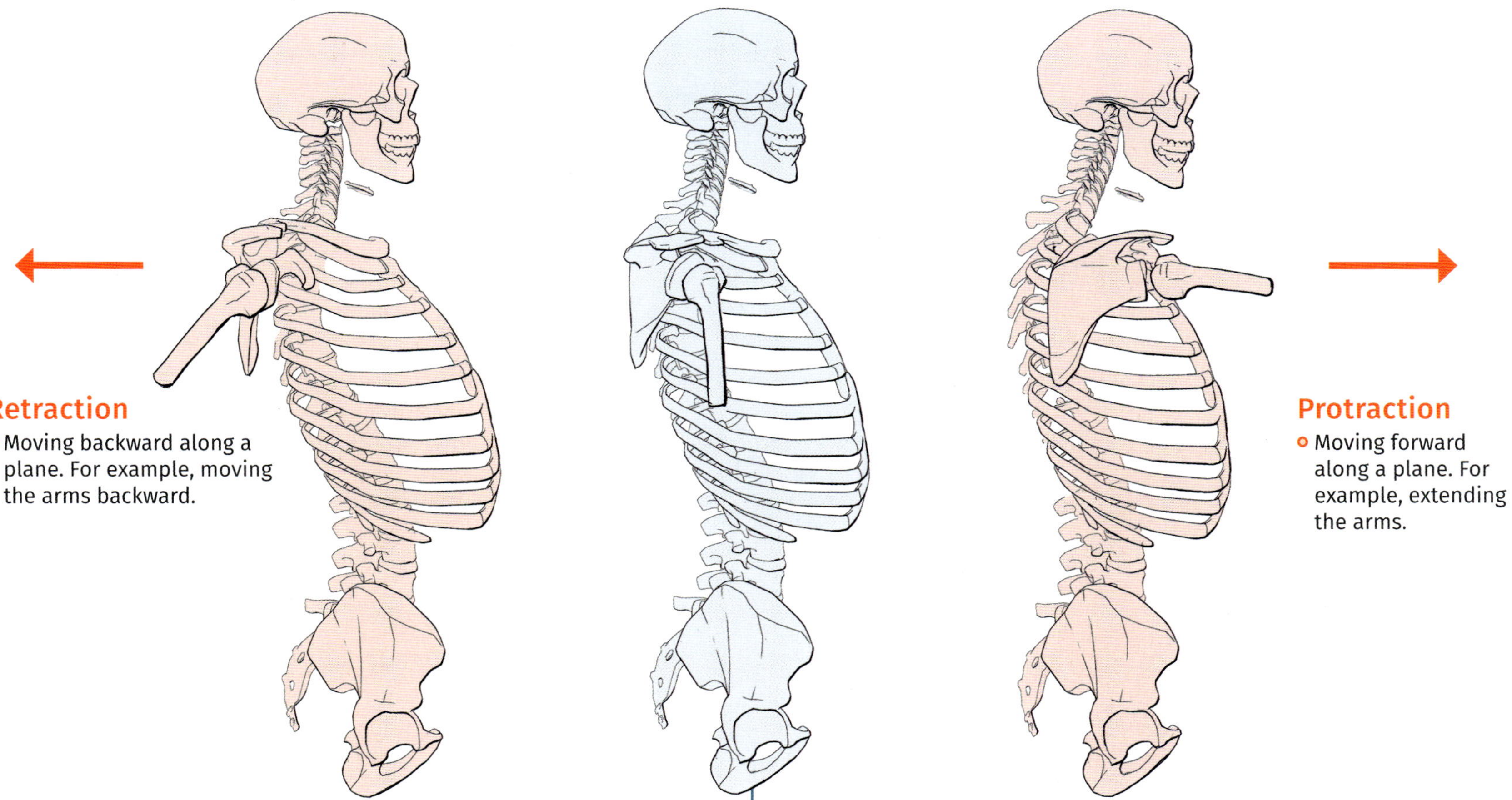

Retraction

- Moving backward along a plane. For example, moving the arms backward.

Protraction

- Moving forward along a plane. For example, extending the arms.

Neutral

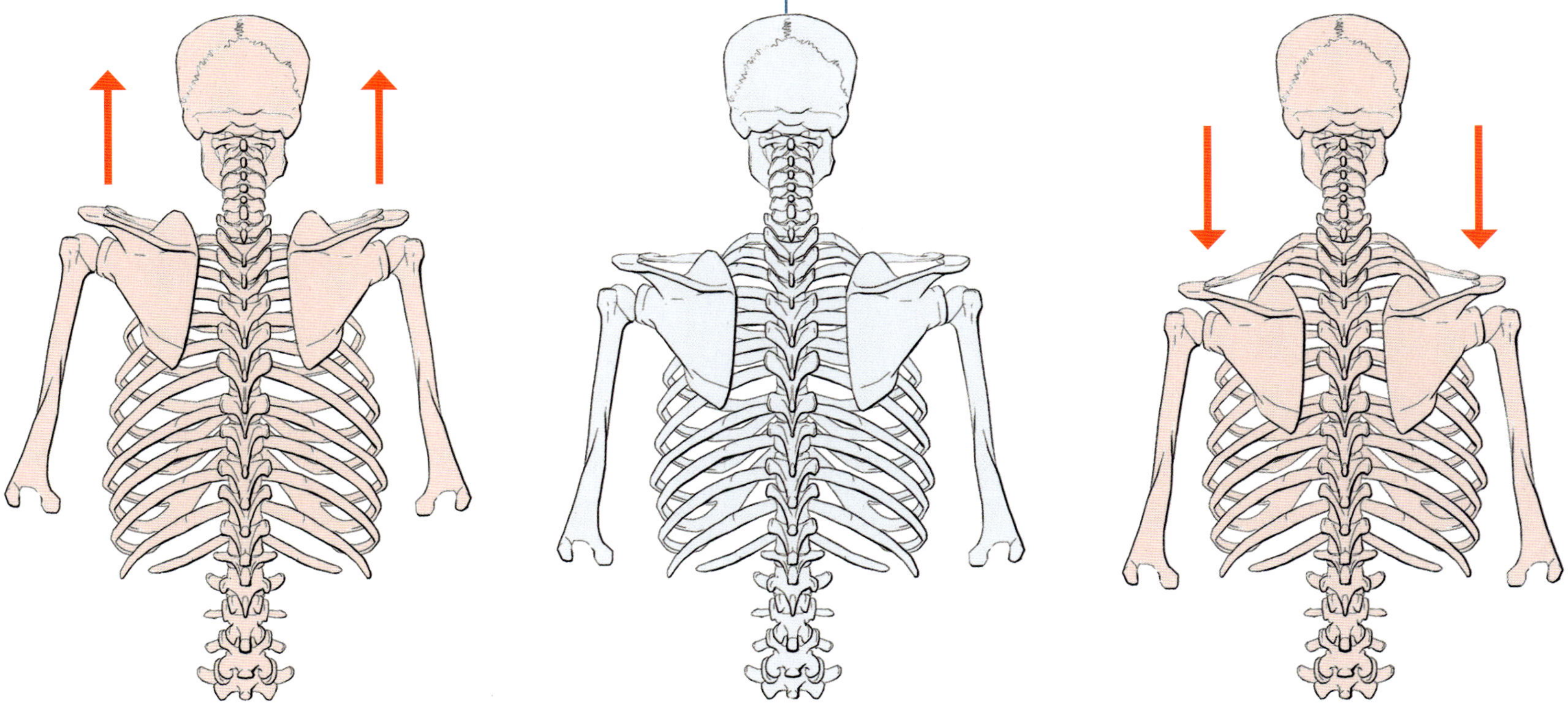

Elevation

- The upward movement of part of the body. For example, raising the shoulders.

Depression

- The downward movement of part of the body. For example, lowering the shoulders or the jaw.

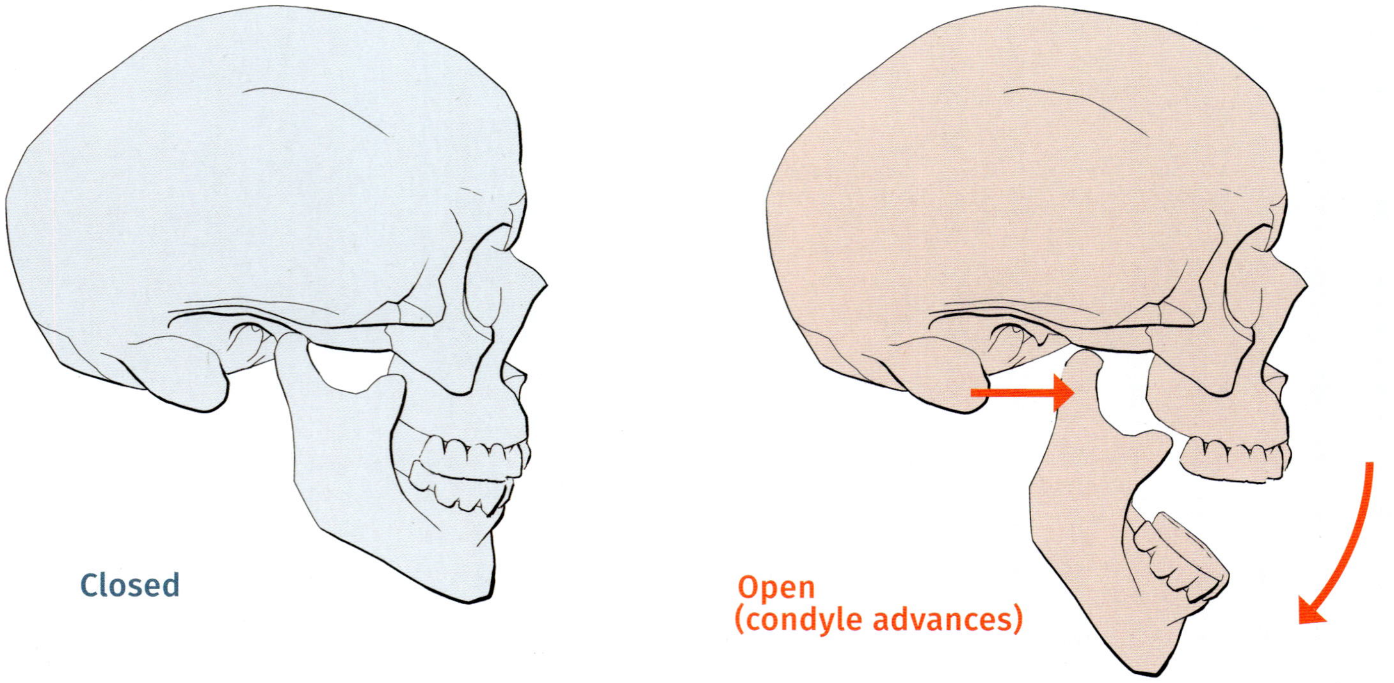
Closed
Open
(condyle advances)

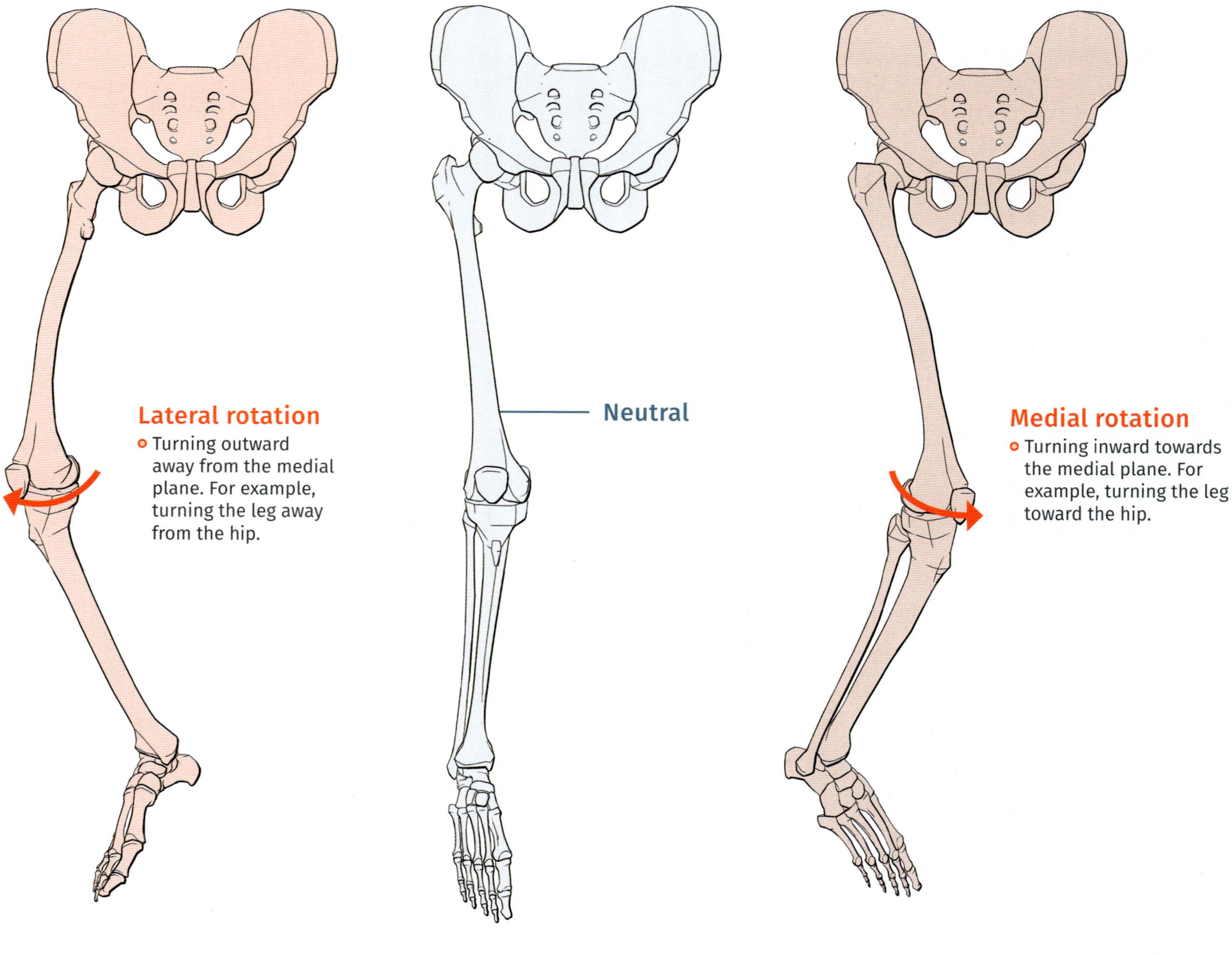
Lateral rotation
Turning outward away from the medial plane. For example, turning the leg away from the hip.
Neutral
Medial rotation
Turning inward towards the medial plane. For example, turning the leg toward the hip.

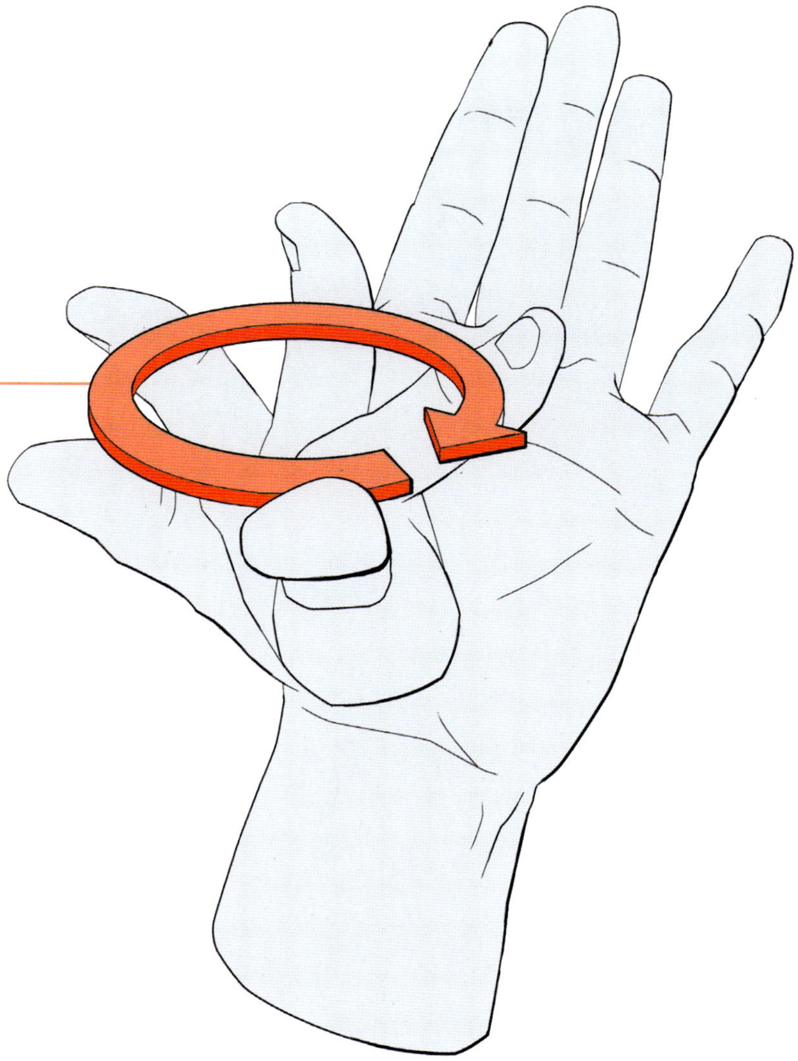

Circumduction:

- Circular motion created by a combination of flexion, extension, abduction, adduction, medial, and lateral movement.

Opposition

- Bringing the tips of the thumbs and the fingers together.

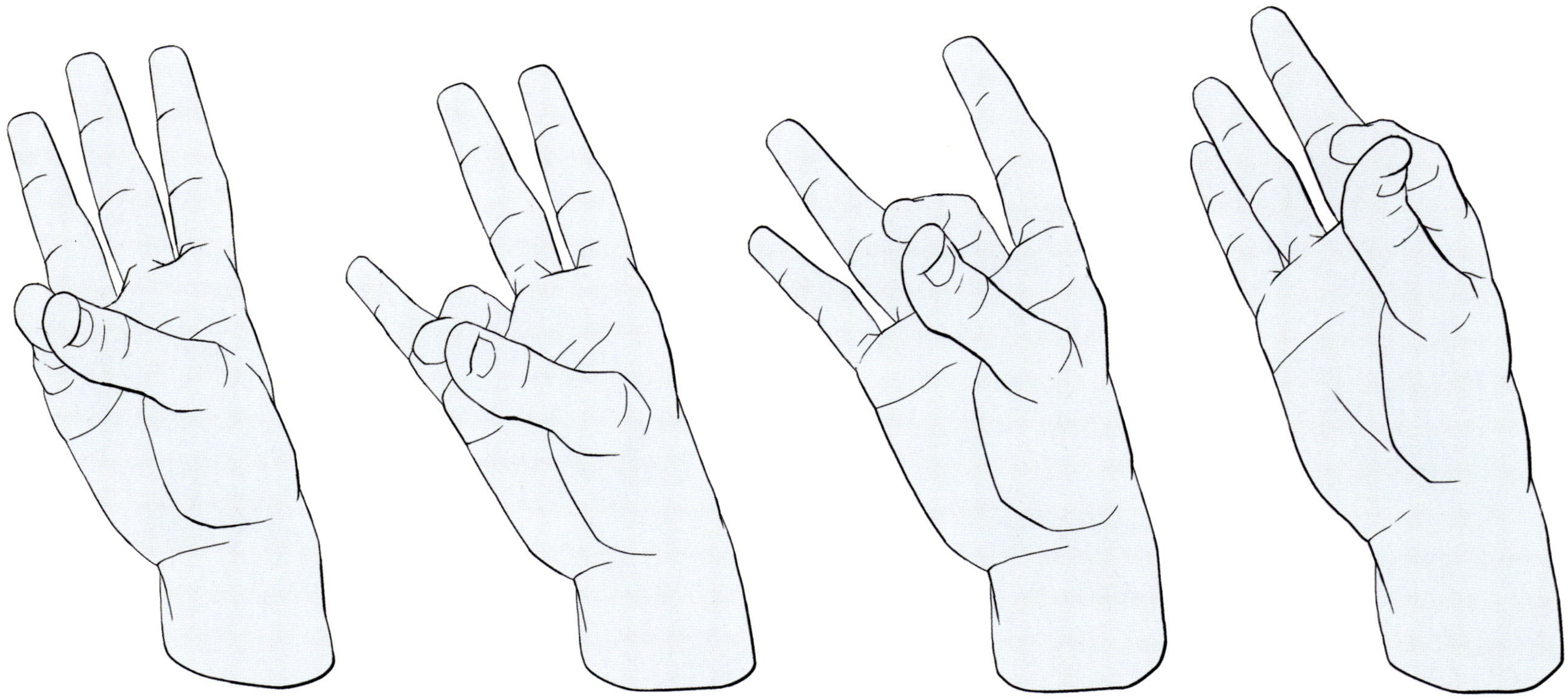

JOINT MECHANICS

Now that you have a solid coordinate system for understanding the body, you can move on to the mechanics of the joints. Understanding these mechanics will allow you to create a framework in which your characters look, deform, and articulate in a believable manner.

So, what is a joint? Put simply, a joint is the point where two or more bones meet. The human skeleton is connected and held together by these joints, with the exception of the hyoid bone in the neck, which is held in place by a set of muscles grabbing onto it from multiple directions. Joints allow for the articulation of the skeleton, giving you the ability to bend, stretch, twist, and so on. Joints can be divided into three main types: fibrous, cartilaginous, and synovial.

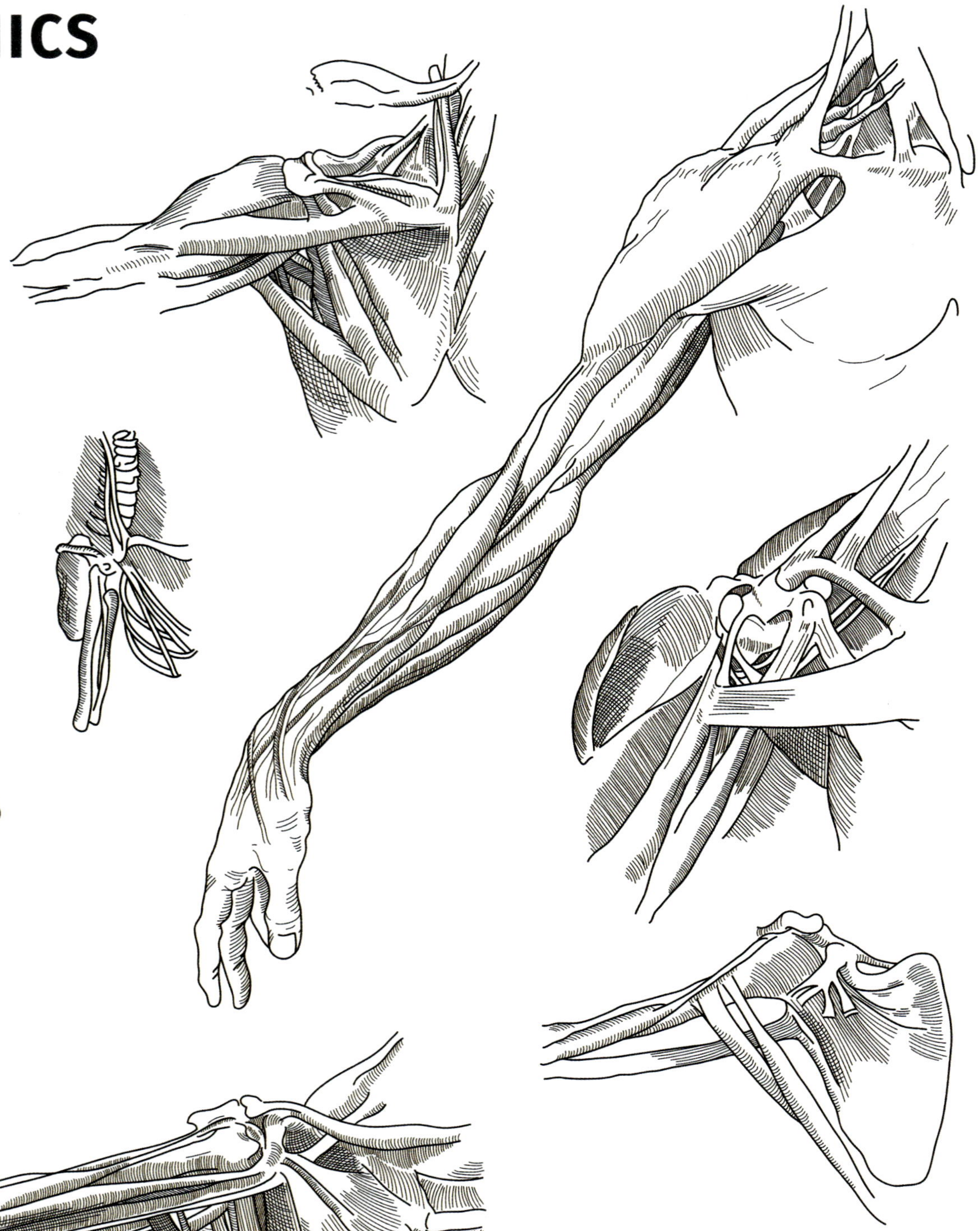

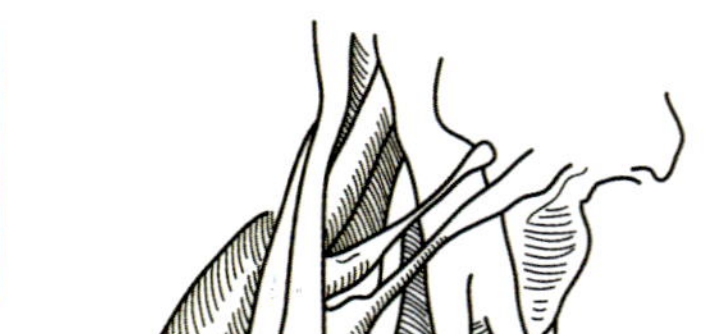

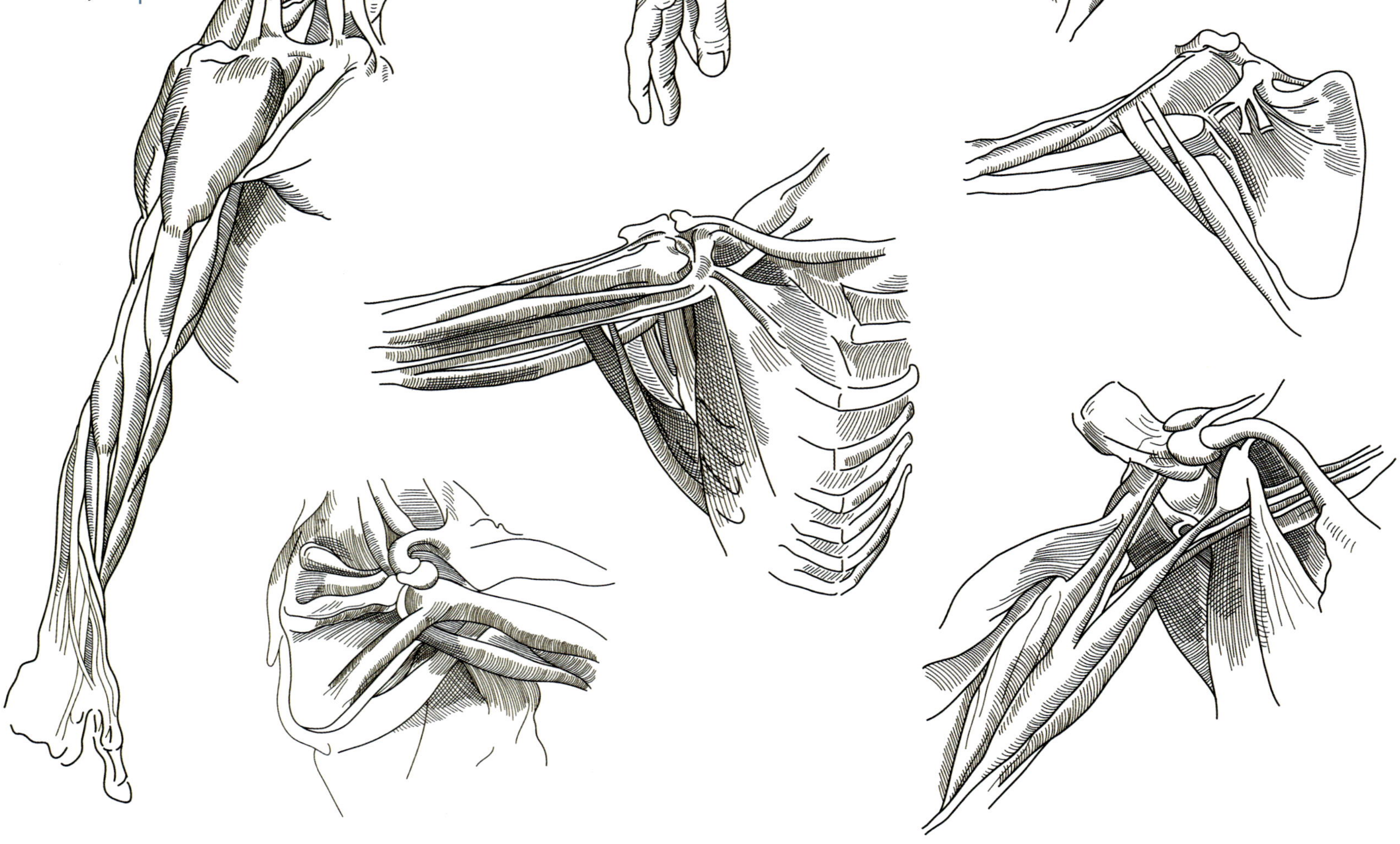

Leonardo da Vinci sketches of shoulder joint anatomy.

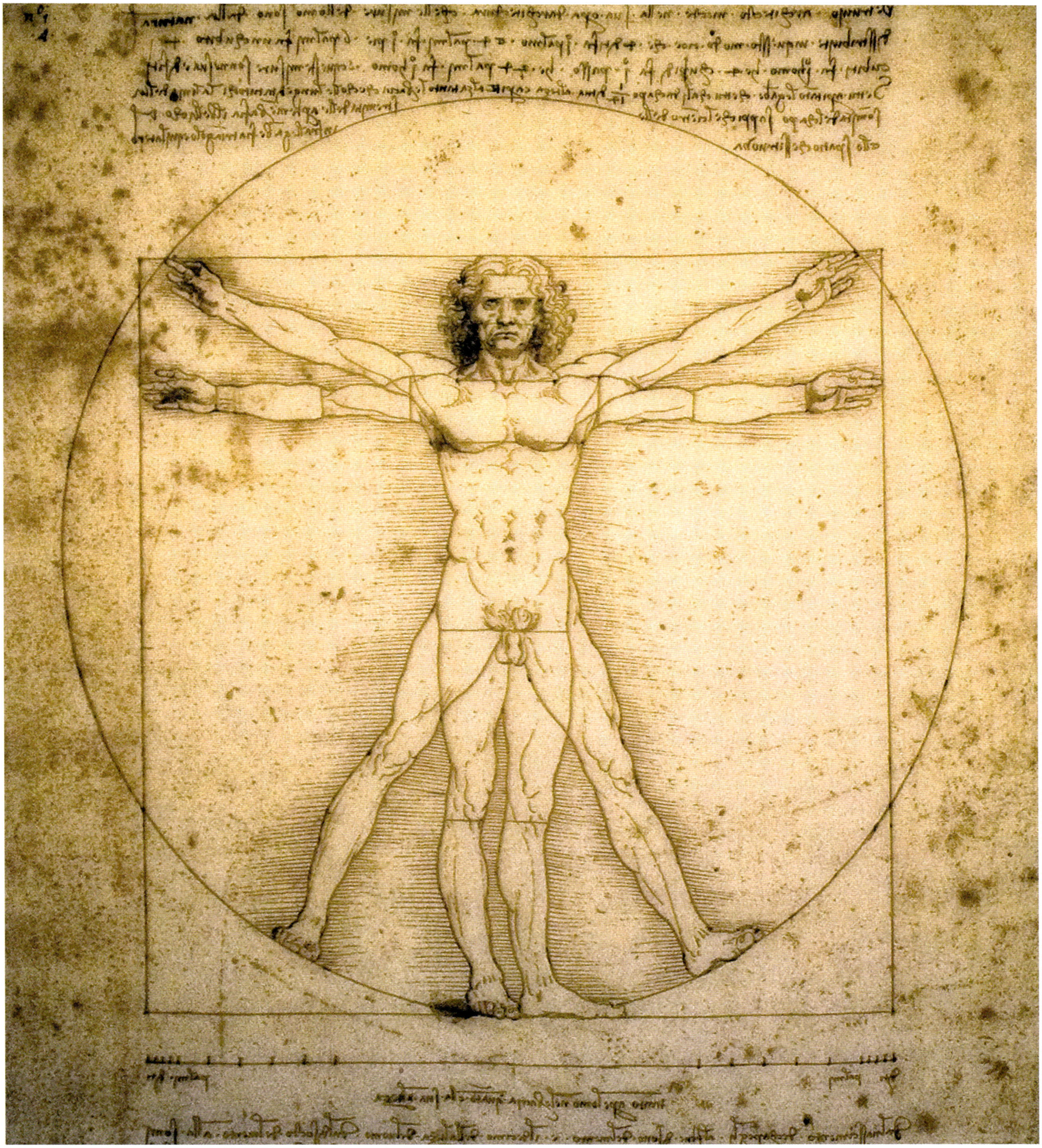

Vitruvian Man drawing by Leonardo da Vinci.

Fibrous joints

Fibrous (synarthrodial) joints, of which there are three types (**sutures**, **syndesmosis**, and **gomphosis**), act as connectors between bones without allowing for any movement. They are also referred to as immovable joints. Examples of fibrous joints include the interosseous membrane between the radius and ulna in the arm, as well as the sutures that connect the many bones of the skull.

Cartilaginous joints

Cartilaginous (synchondrosis and symphysis) joints allow for minor movement of the bones and can be found in areas such as the costal cartilage (cartilage which attaches the ribs to the sternum of the rib cage), between the pubic symphysis, and between each of the spinal vertebrae.

Synovial joints

The final set of joints, and the ones that will be of the most interest here, are the **synovial (diarthrosis) joints**. These joints allow for movement and are the most common type of joint found in the body. They share some common characteristics as noted below:

- **Synovial cavity:** The space in between two bones. This space is filled with synovial fluid that nourishes the articulating cartilage, lubricates the bones, and acts as a shock absorber, evenly distributing the forces acting upon the joints.
- **Articulating surfaces:** Two bones that come together will have surfaces that are able to mate. One end will be concave (female) and the other convex (male). Both ends are covered by a layer of thick articular cartilage (made from hyaline, a glass-like translucent cartilage), which acts to reduce friction and aid in shock absorption.
- **Joint (articular) capsule:** This seals the space by surrounding the synovial joint, holding it together and helping to contain the synovial fluid.
- **Ligaments:** The fibrous tissue connecting bone to bone.

There are six types of synovial joints, each with their own characteristics:

- Ball and socket
- Saddle
- Condyloid
- Hinge
- Pivot
- Gliding

The next section will take a closer look at each one in turn.

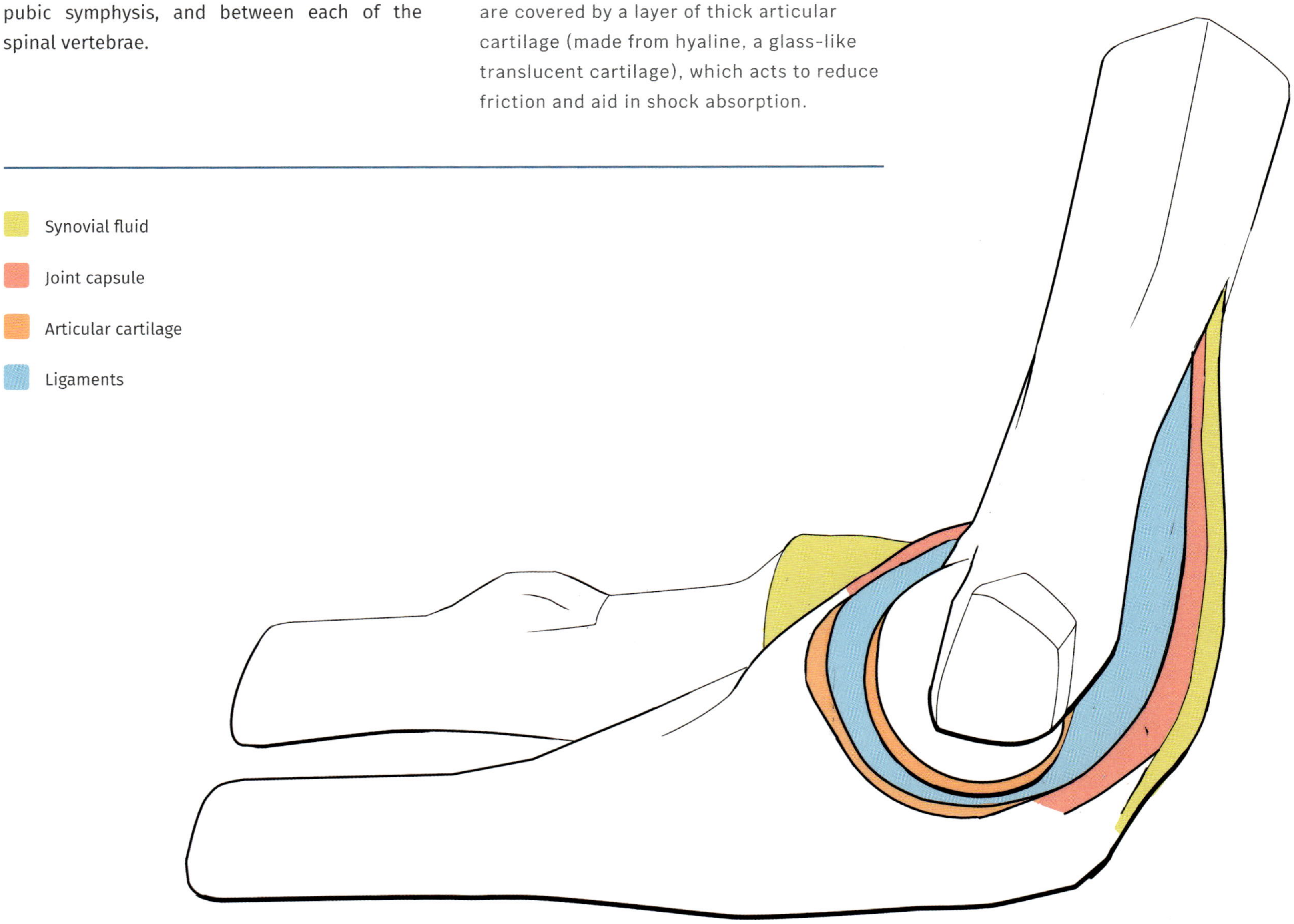

Ball and socket joints

The **ball and socket** is a **triaxial joint**, allowing for articulation with three degrees of freedom, thus making it the most mobile of the synovial joints. It allows for flexion and extension, abduction and adduction, and medial and lateral rotation. When the motion is combined, it creates circumduction. Mechanically, you could compare the joint to a spherical convex surface paired with a concave cup. Examples of this in the human form can be found at the glenohumeral (shoulder) joint and the acetabulofemoral (hip) joint.

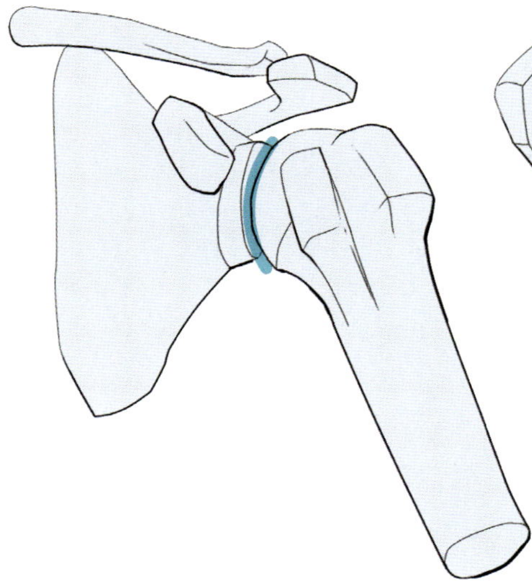

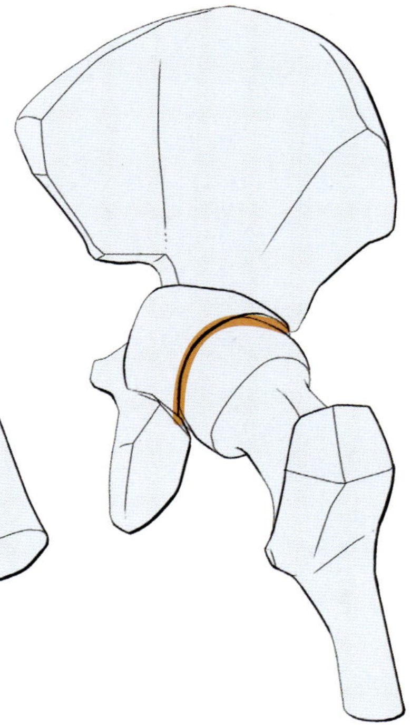

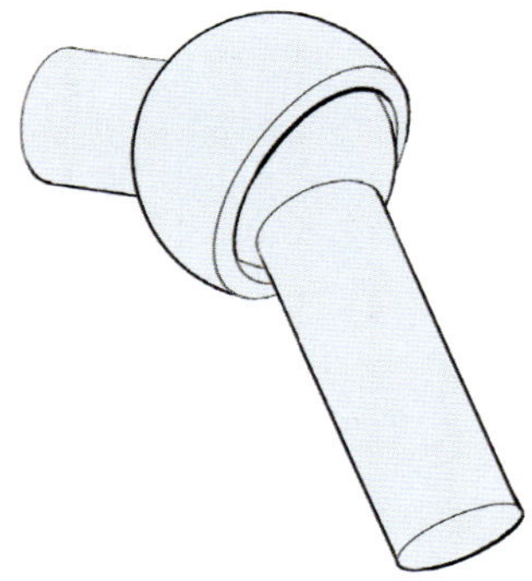

Glenohumeral joint

Acetabulofemoral joint

Saddle joints

Saddle joints are **biaxial**, allowing for two degrees of freedom. The saddle joint of the thumb (the first carpometacarpal) allows for flexion and extension, abduction and adduction, opposition, and some circumduction. The sternoclavicular joint (between the clavicle and the manubrium of the sternum) is also considered a saddle joint, allowing for protraction and retraction, elevation and depression, and also rotation. Saddle joints are convex in one direction and concave in the other. Think of a horse rider sitting on a saddle and you have the working of a saddle joint.

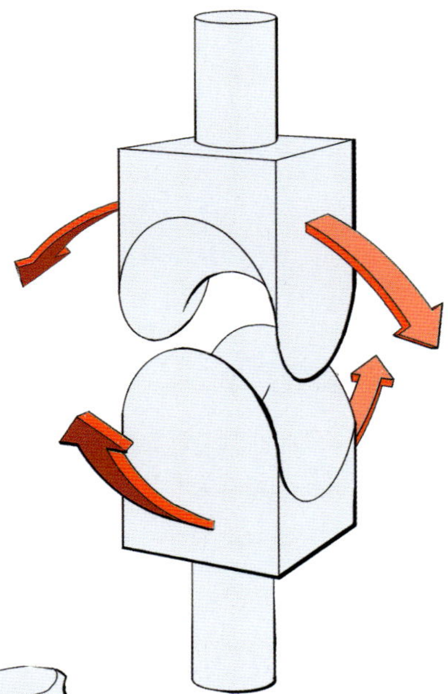

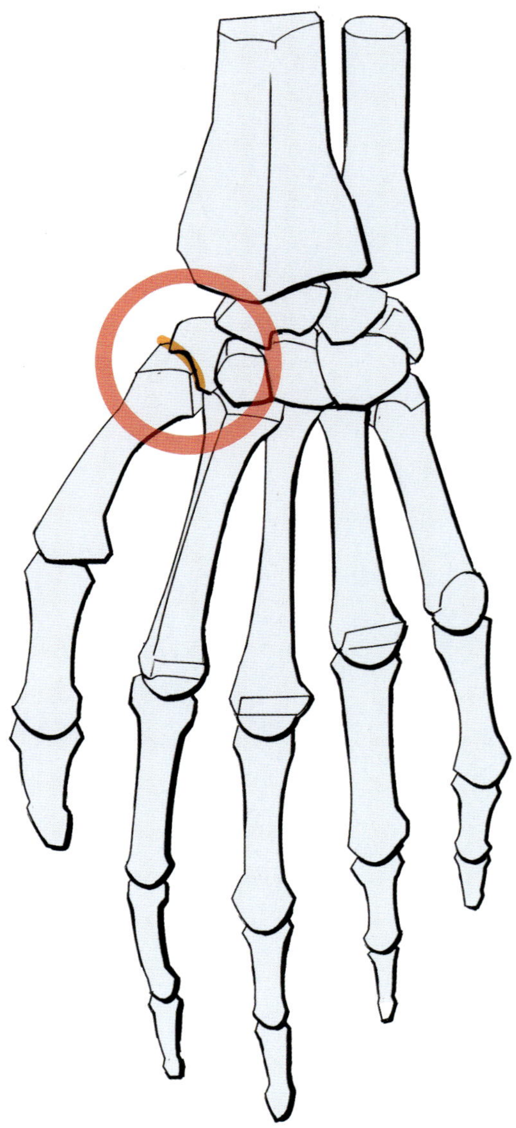

Sternoclavicular joint

Saddle joint of the thumb

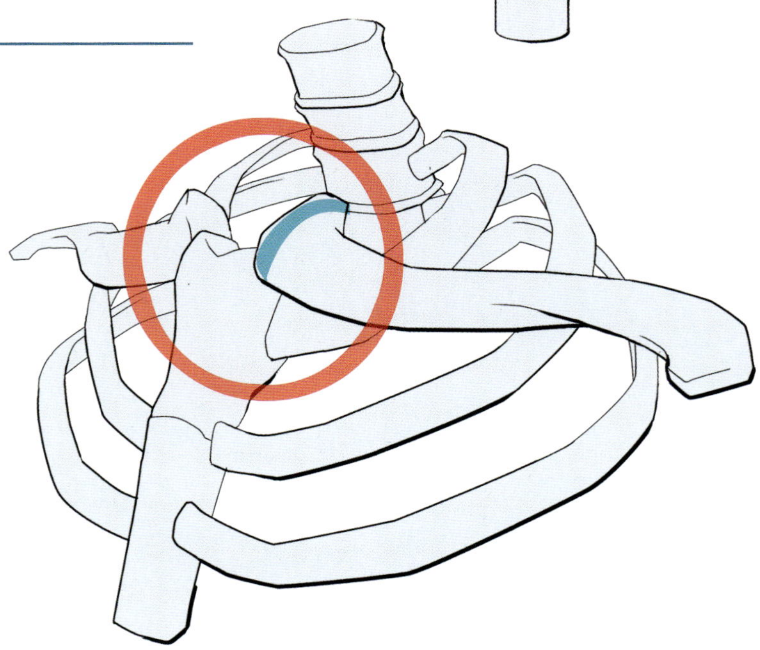

Condyloid joints

This type of joint allows for two degrees of freedom – flexion and extension, abduction and adduction – and is considered as **biaxial**. The joint consists of an oval head that sits inside an elliptical cavity and permits circular-like motion, but is a lot more restricted than a ball and socket joint. The radiocarpal joints (in the wrists) are an example of a condyloid joint, as are the metacarpophalangeal joints (in the hands).

Radiocarpal joint

Metacarpophalangeal joints

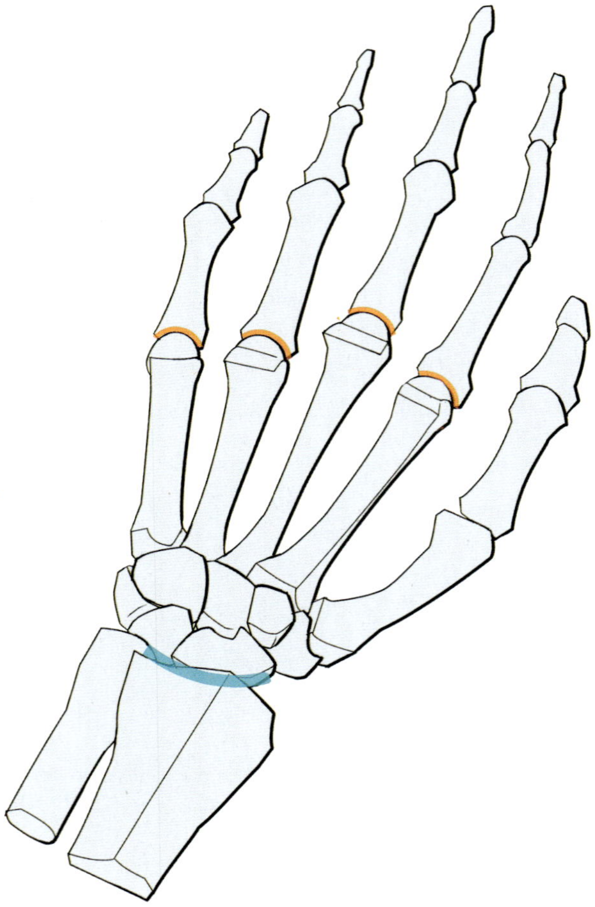

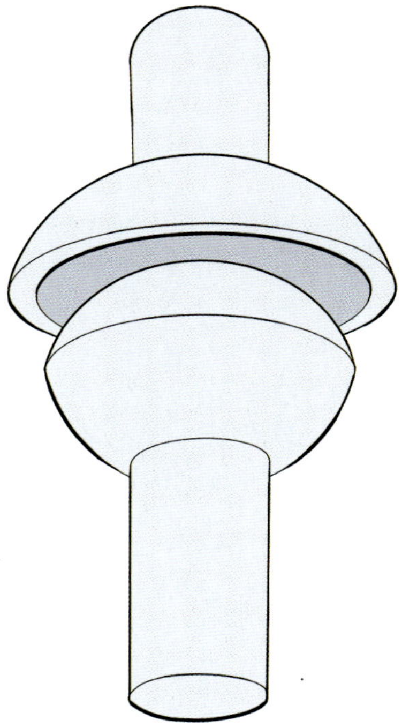

Hinge joints

This joint resembles the workings of a door hinge, as it only allows motion with one degree of freedom, resulting in flexion and extension. This type of joint is regarded as an **uniaxial joint** and examples are found in the humeroulnar (elbow) joint and the interphalangeal (finger and toe) joints.

Humeroulnar joint

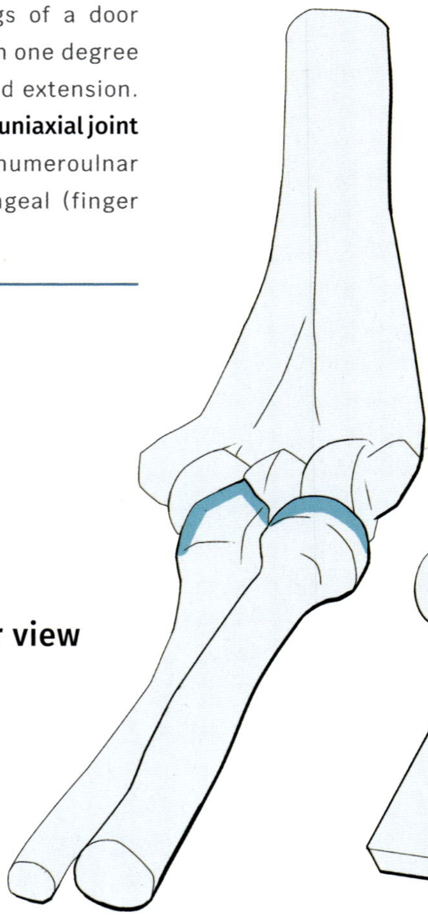

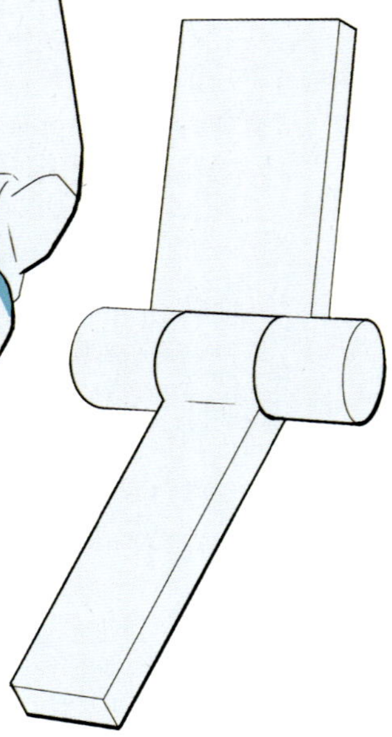

Anterior view

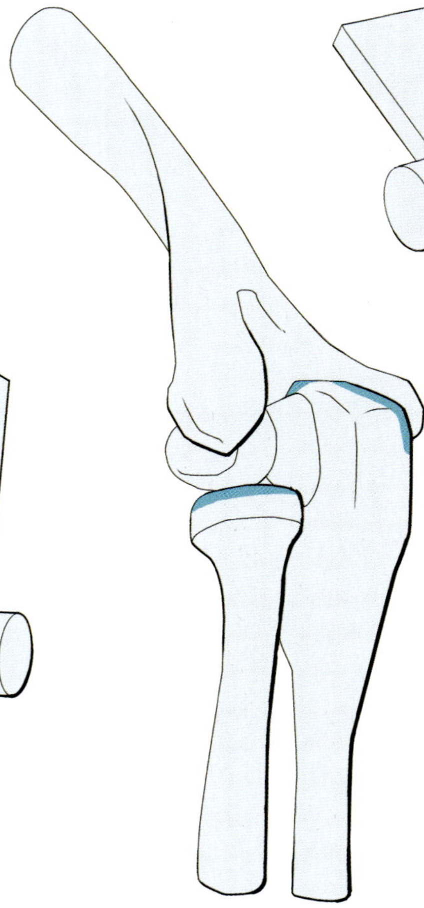

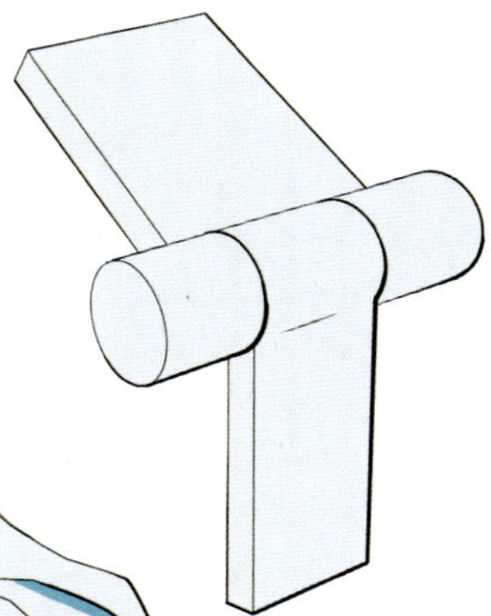

Posterior view

Pivot joints

This is a **uniaxial joint**, which only allows for motion in a single plane. The pivot joint allows one bone to rotate around another. An everyday analogy would be a door knob. The proximal and distal radioulnar joints are good examples of this type of joint in the human body, the pivoting allowing for pronation and supination of the forearm.

- Proximal radioulnar joint
- Distal radioulnar joints

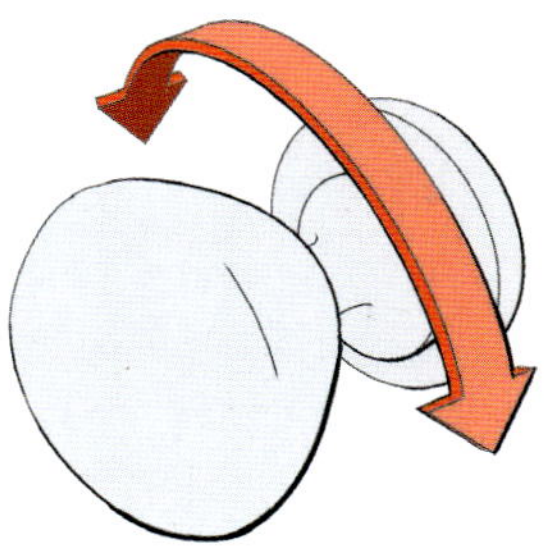

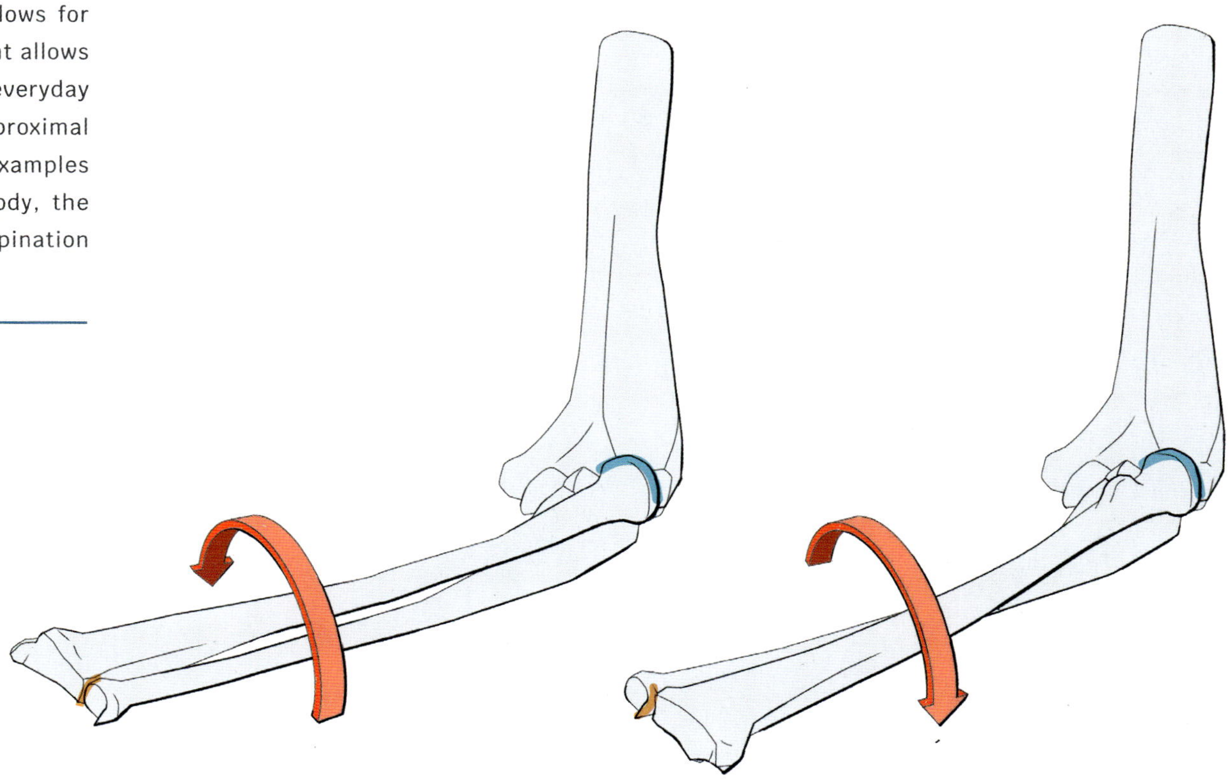

Gliding joints

Gliding joints are considered as **nonaxial** (only very limited movement possible) and have a variable amount of freedom. The bones are generally flat, with some having a slight curvature to them. They allow for the articulating surfaces of two or more bones to slide over one another and examples can be found at the wrist and ankle. Waving your hand side-to-side uses the gliding radiocarpal joints.

- Radiocarpal joint

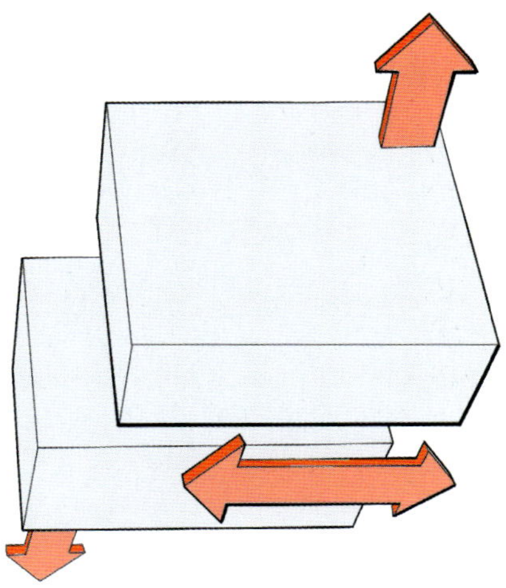

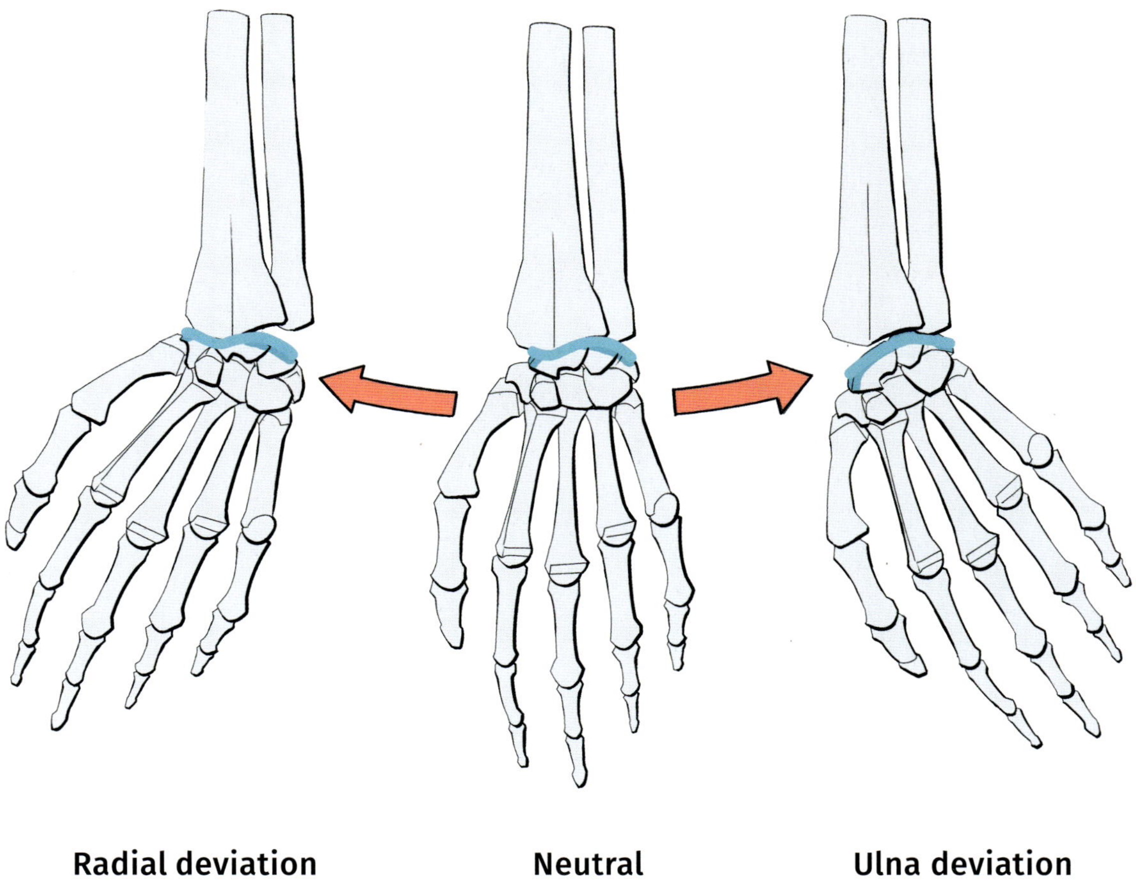

The knee

The knee is a unique piece of functional engineering. Although it is mainly considered to be a **hinge joint**, it also has characteristics of a **condyloid joint**. The two condyles (the round, prominent ends) of the femur meet their counterparts on the tibia and when the leg is bent, the condyles of the femur do not simply hinge, but also roll back slightly, allowing the patella to slide into the open cavity between the condyles of the femur and the tibia. However, whereas a standard condyloid joint allows for flexion and extension, adduction and abduction, and circumduction, the knee only allows for flexion and extension with a degree of rotation.

- Femur
- Patella
- Knee joint
- Fibula
- Tibia

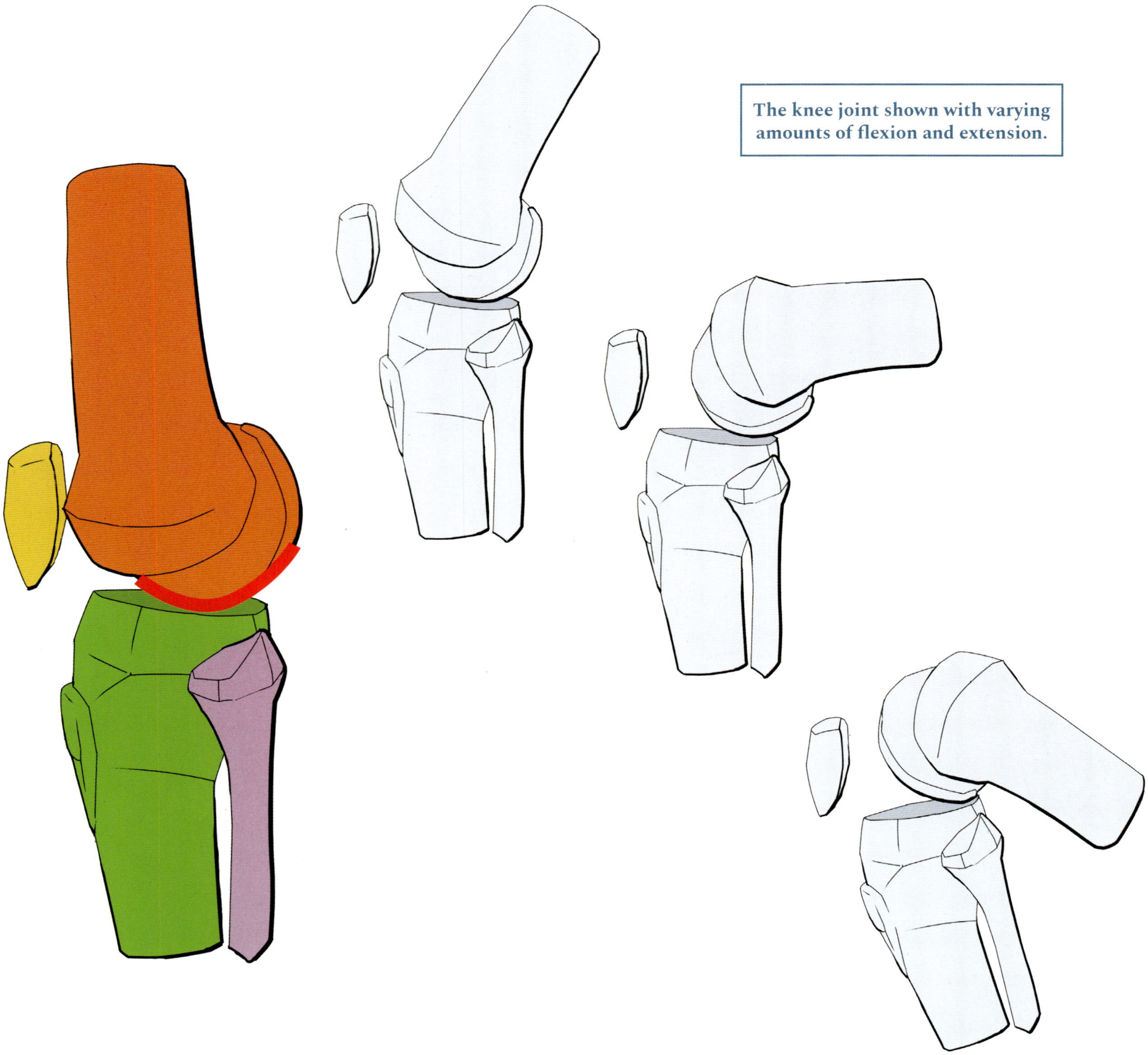

The knee joint shown with varying amounts of flexion and extension.

The scapulohumeral rhythm

The **scapulohumeral rhythm** describes the relationship between two of the joints in the shoulder – the **scapulothoracic joint** and the **glenohumeral joint** – during the elevation of the humerus. The scapulothoracic joint is a "floating joint" that allows the scapula to glide over the contours of the posterior thoracic wall.

During the first 30 degrees of the abduction of the arm, the glenohumeral joint of the humerus will rotate in the scapula's socket (or glenoid fossa). At this stage the scapula will remain still with the medial border of the scapula parallel to the cervical column. If you abduct the arm any further, the scapula will persist in the movement. With the arm abducted an extra 60 degrees, making a total of 90 degrees, the scapula will have rotated 30 degrees. This results in a 2:1 ratio of movement between the humerus and the scapula when the arm is raised between 30 and 90 degrees. Once the arm is elevated to 90 degrees, the glenohumeral joint is locked in its socket. To elevate the arm any further, the clavicle has to pivot, along with the scapula, allowing the arm to rise to a total of approximately 180 degrees.

Glenohumeral joint

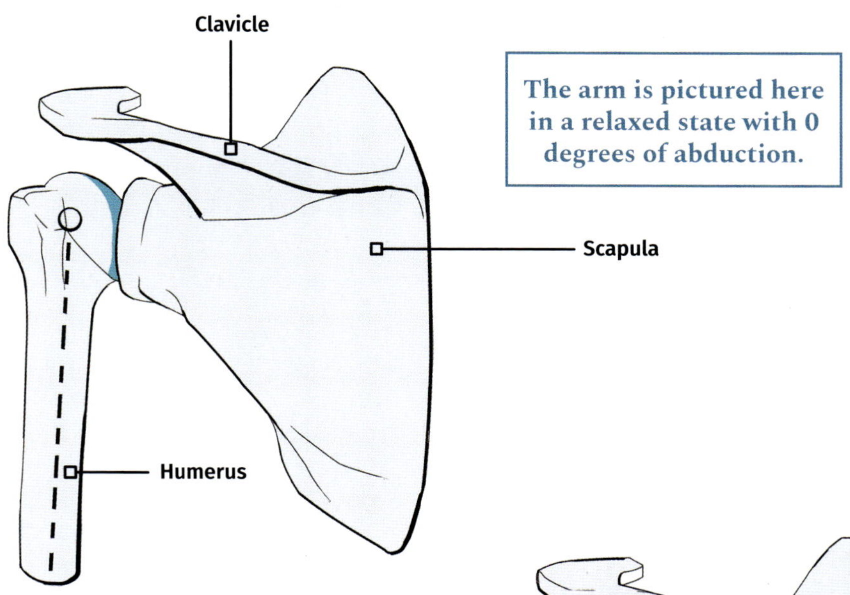

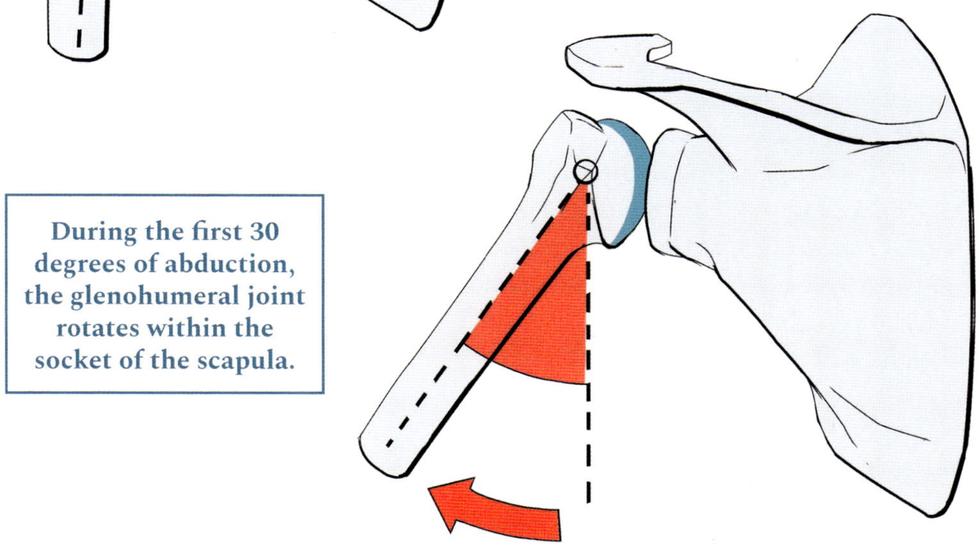

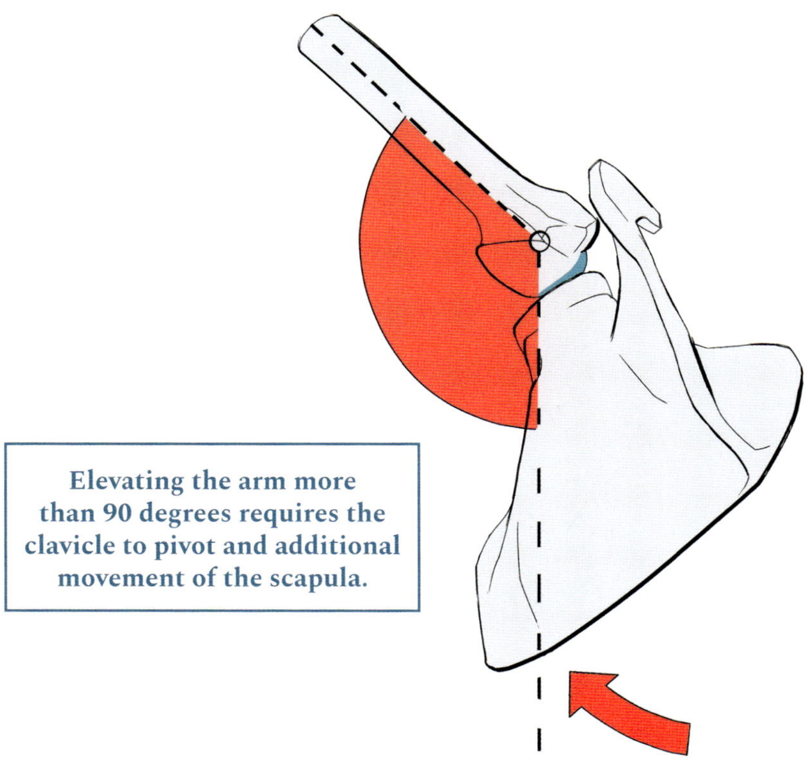

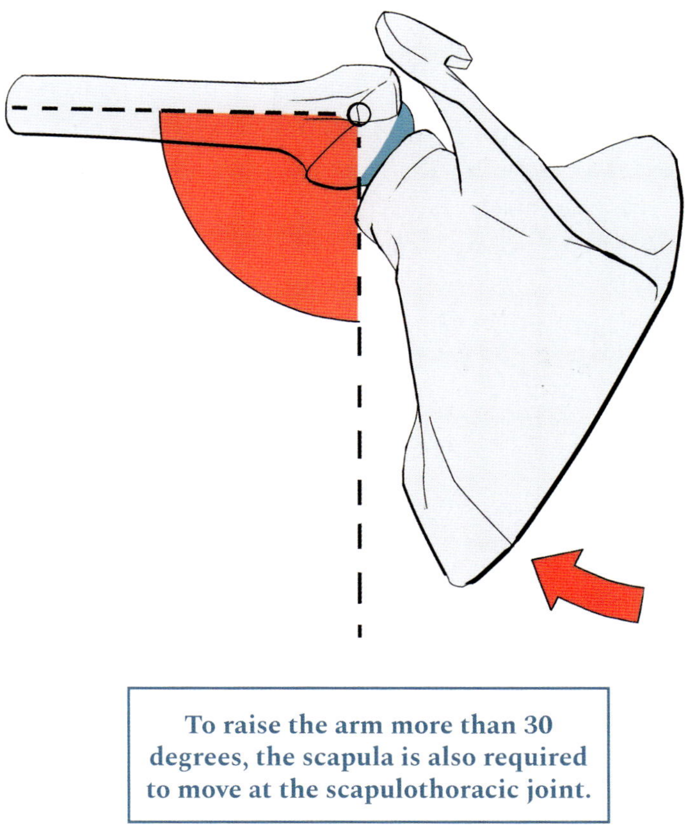

The skeleton and the bony landmarks

Following in the footsteps of Bernhard Siegfried Albinus and da Vinci, it can be helpful to start by looking at the skeleton before working your way outward. The human skeleton, made up of the axial skeleton and the appendicular skeleton, is the framework that supports the body, while the muscles provide the power to drive the skeleton. Unlike muscles, the shapes of the bones are pretty consistent from person to person, as are the skeletal landmarks. Also known as bony landmarks, these are areas on the surface of the skin where the underlying bone sits close to the surface and is palpable. These landmarks can be both felt and seen, and therefore are extremely useful when trying to determine the position and orientation of the bones. By communicating these landmarks to your audience, who will already be subconsciously aware of them, you are on the way to creating the illusion of believable anatomy.

By adulthood, a human will have around 206 bones (we are born with approximately 300, but some fuse as we age). To go through every bone would be an overload of information, so instead this section will mainly focus on the bones that are visible on the skin's surface. Communicating that your characters have this underlying structure will help to portray them as living, breathing organisms.

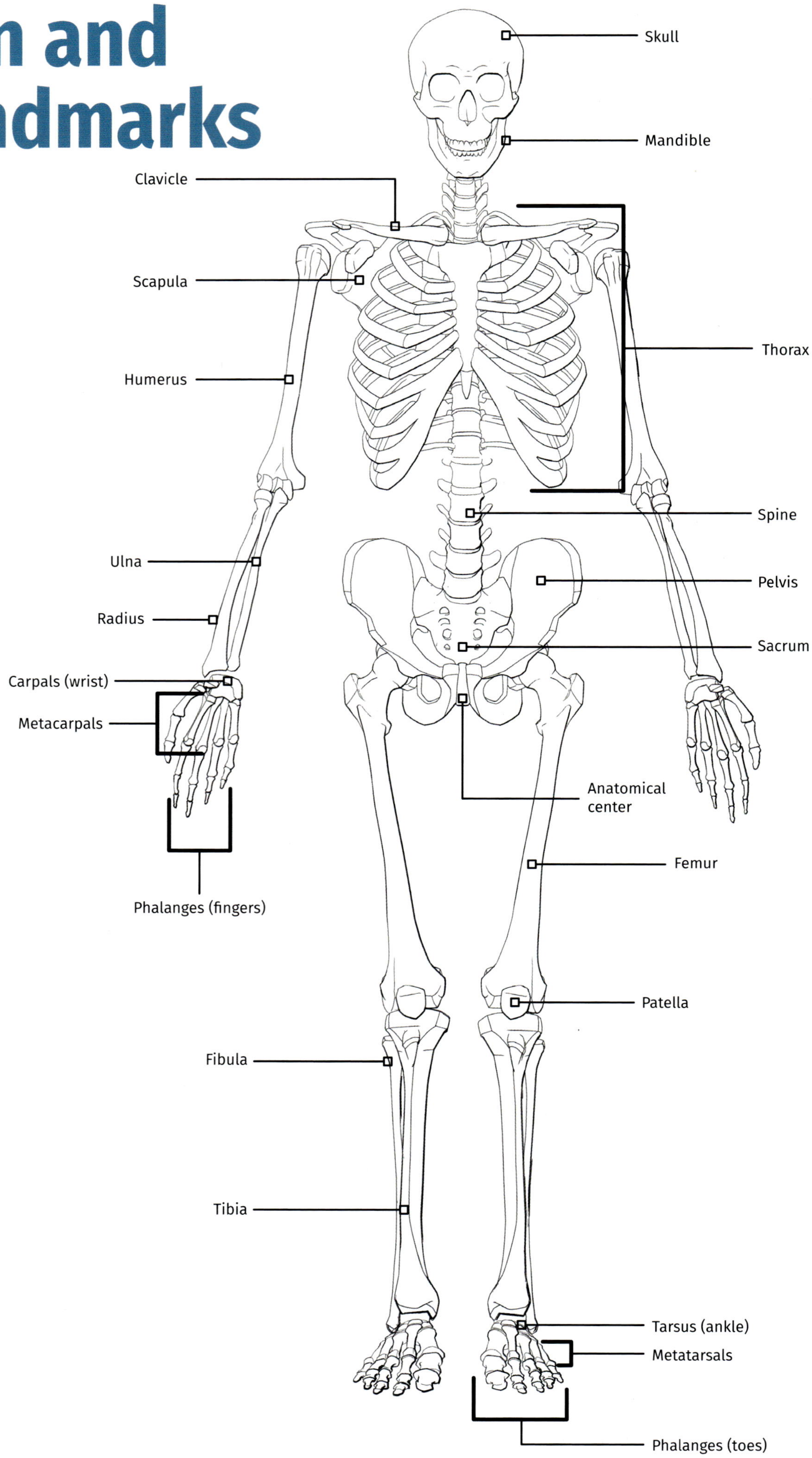

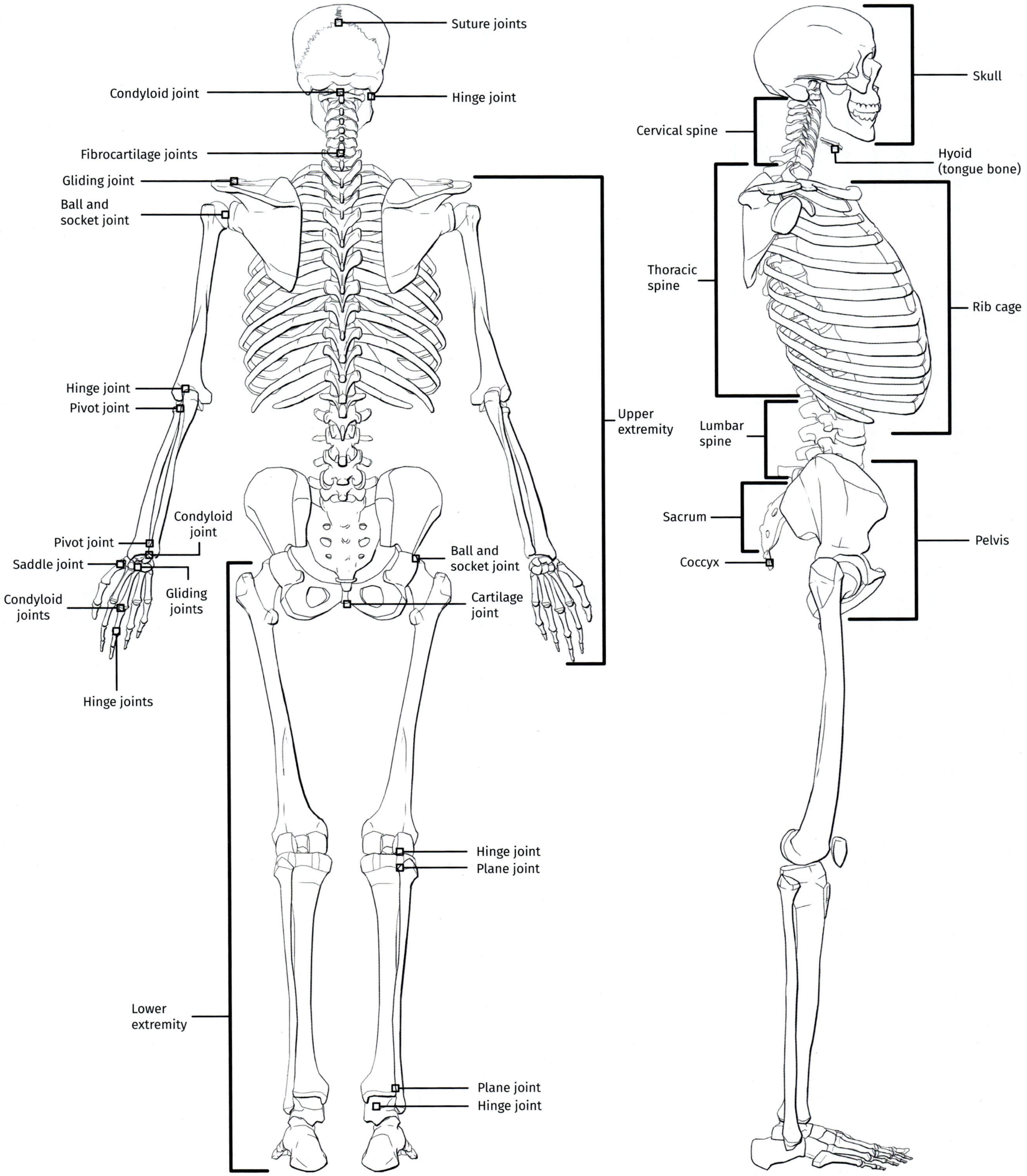
Suture joints
Condyloid joint
Hinge joint
Fibrocartilage joints
Gliding joint
Ball and socket joint
Hinge joint
Pivot joint
Upper extremity
Condyloid joint
Pivot joint
Saddle joint
Condyloid joints
Gliding joints
Hinge joints
Ball and socket joint
Cartilage joint
Hinge joint
Plane joint
Lower extremity
Plane joint
Hinge joint
Skull
Cervical spine
Hyoid (tongue bone)
Thoracic spine
Rib cage
Lumbar spine
Sacrum
Coccyx
Pelvis

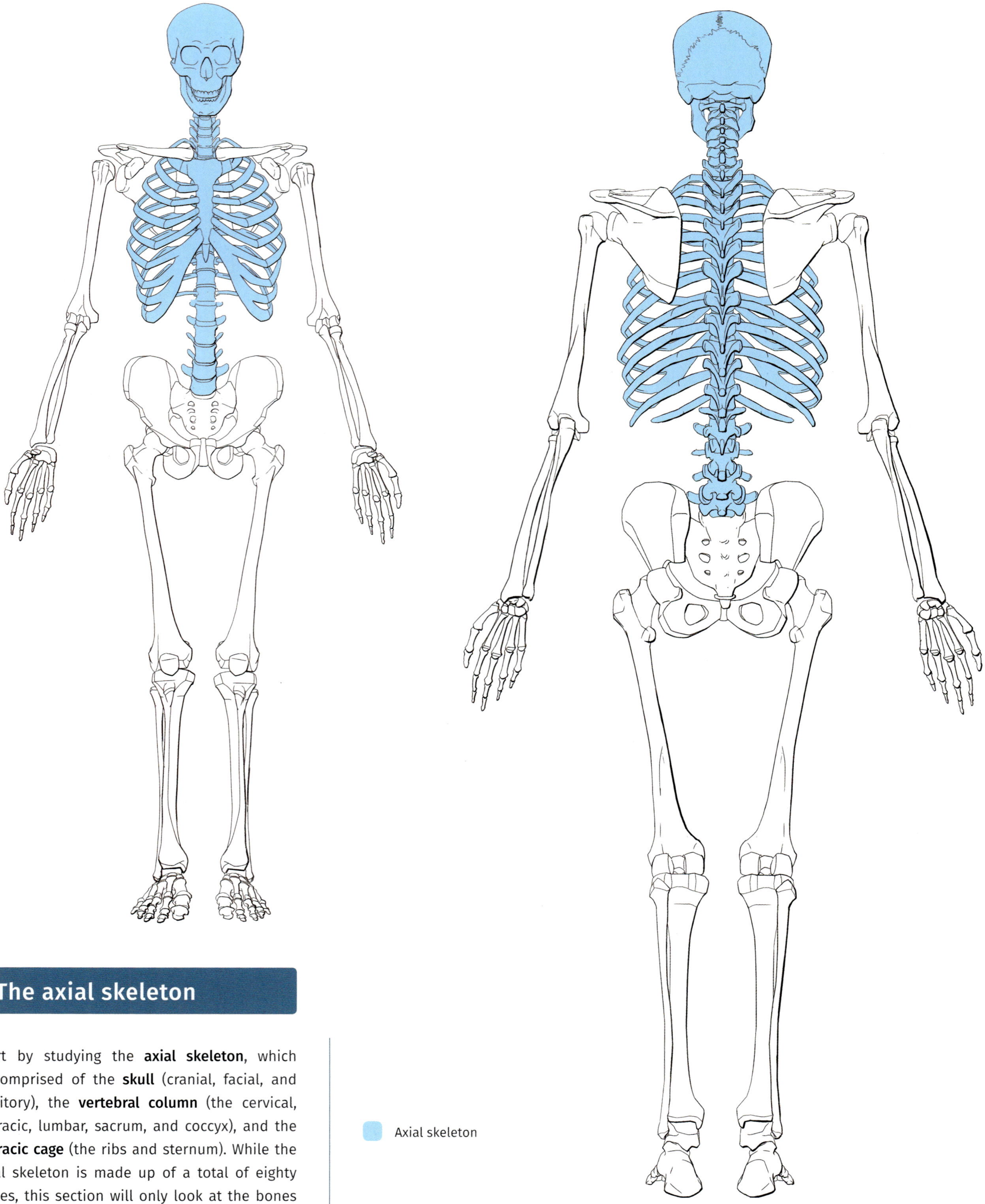

The axial skeleton

Start by studying the **axial skeleton**, which is comprised of the **skull** (cranial, facial, and auditory), the **vertebral column** (the cervical, thoracic, lumbar, sacrum, and coccyx), and the **thoracic cage** (the ribs and sternum). While the axial skeleton is made up of a total of eighty bones, this section will only look at the bones that push against the surface of the skin.

Axial skeleton

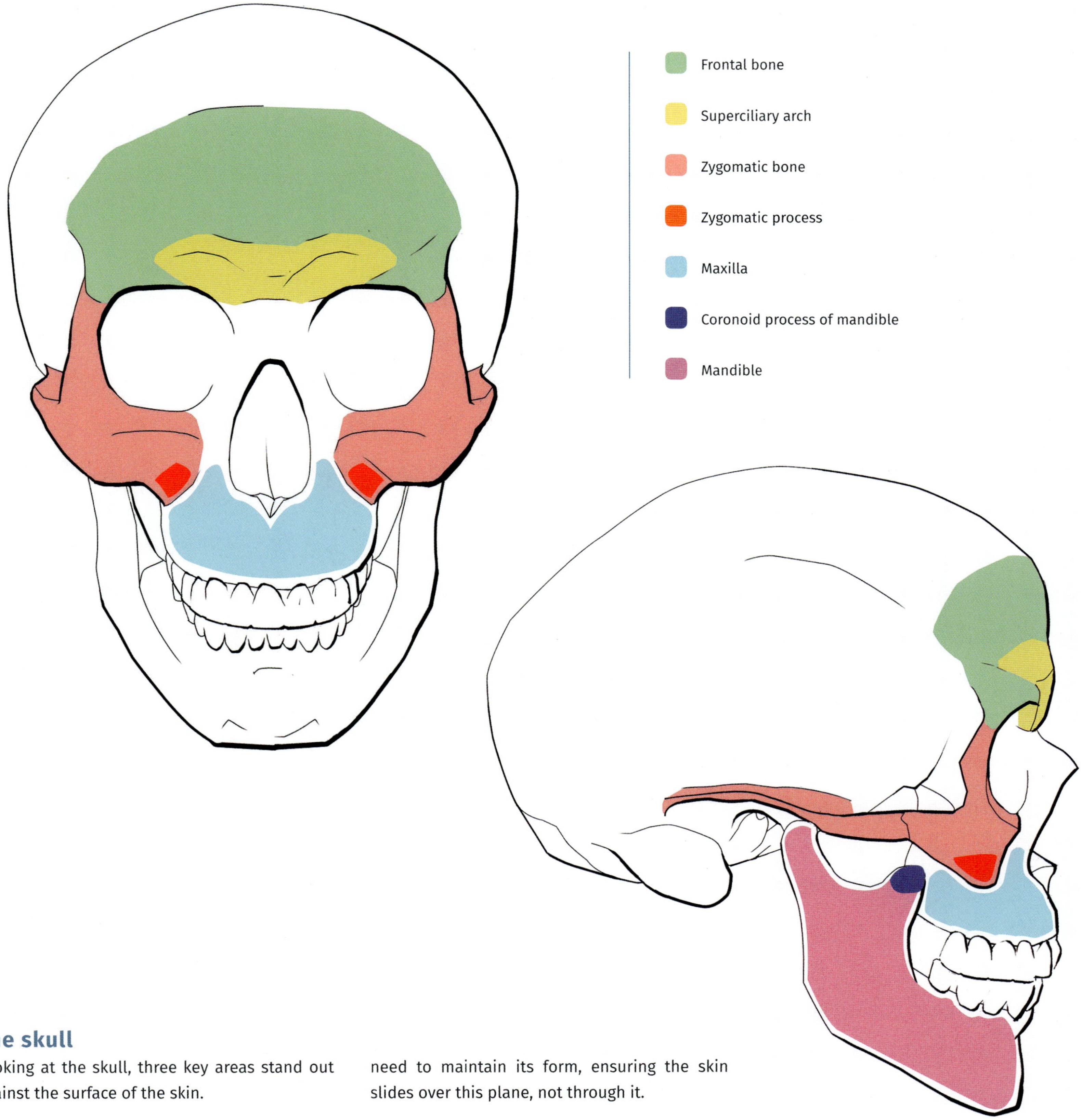

The skull

Looking at the skull, three key areas stand out against the surface of the skin.

Firstly, the **zygomatic bone.** This creates the frontal plane of the face and is covered by a layer of fat. As age takes hold, this layer begins to sag, revealing more of the bone. Weight can also play a factor in its visible appearance.

When drawing the forehead, it is also important to remember that the **frontal bone** exists. You need to maintain its form, ensuring the skin slides over this plane, not through it.

The **superciliary** arch helps to define a character's form, especially in profile. The arch is more prominent in males due to the high levels of testosterone released during puberty. In females the area is usually fairly smooth, but with high levels of testosterone introduced artificially, the same effect will also become evident.

The vertebral column

Moving down to the **vertebral column**, this is comprised of twenty-four **vertebrae** separated by **intervertebral disks** (seven **cervical** - C1 to C7, twelve **thoracic** - T1 to T12, and five **lumbar** - L1 to L5), after which there is the **sacrum** (five fused vertebrae) and the **coccyx** (tailbone).

- Cervical
- Thoracic
- Lumbar
- Sacrum
- Coccyx

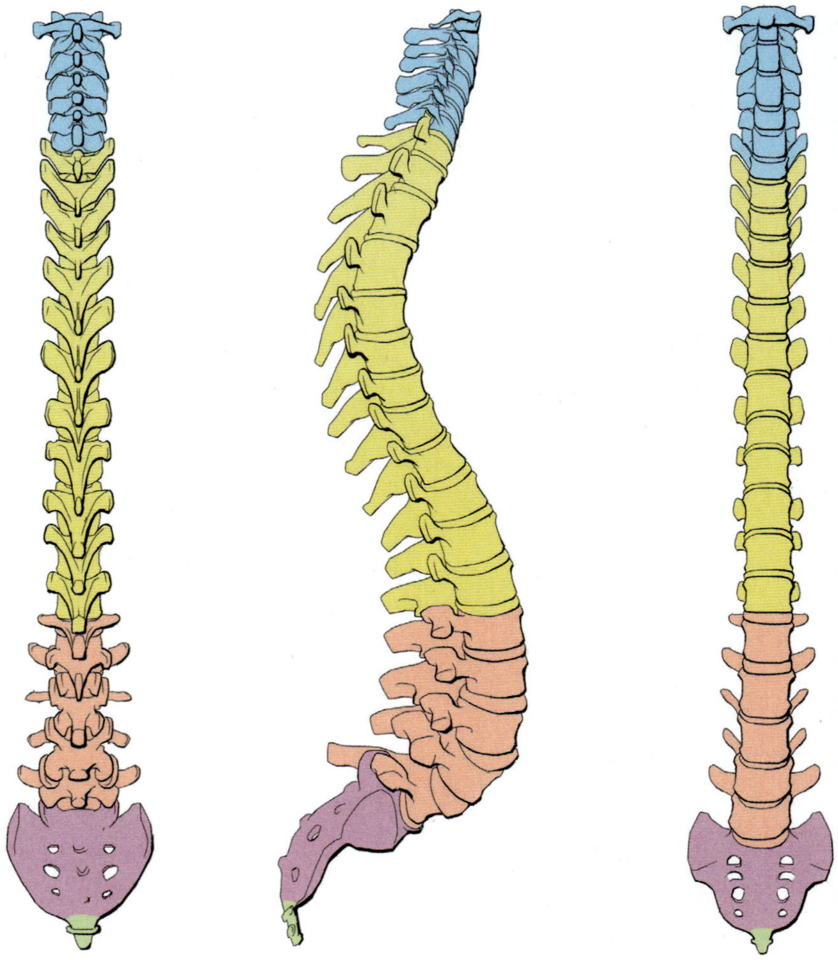

The **cervical region** is responsible for the movement of the neck and head. A key landmark here is the **seventh cervical vertebra**. If you lower your chin to your neck and place your hand at the back of your neck, you will feel this bone protruding. It is the most prominent of the spinal column and is easily identified.

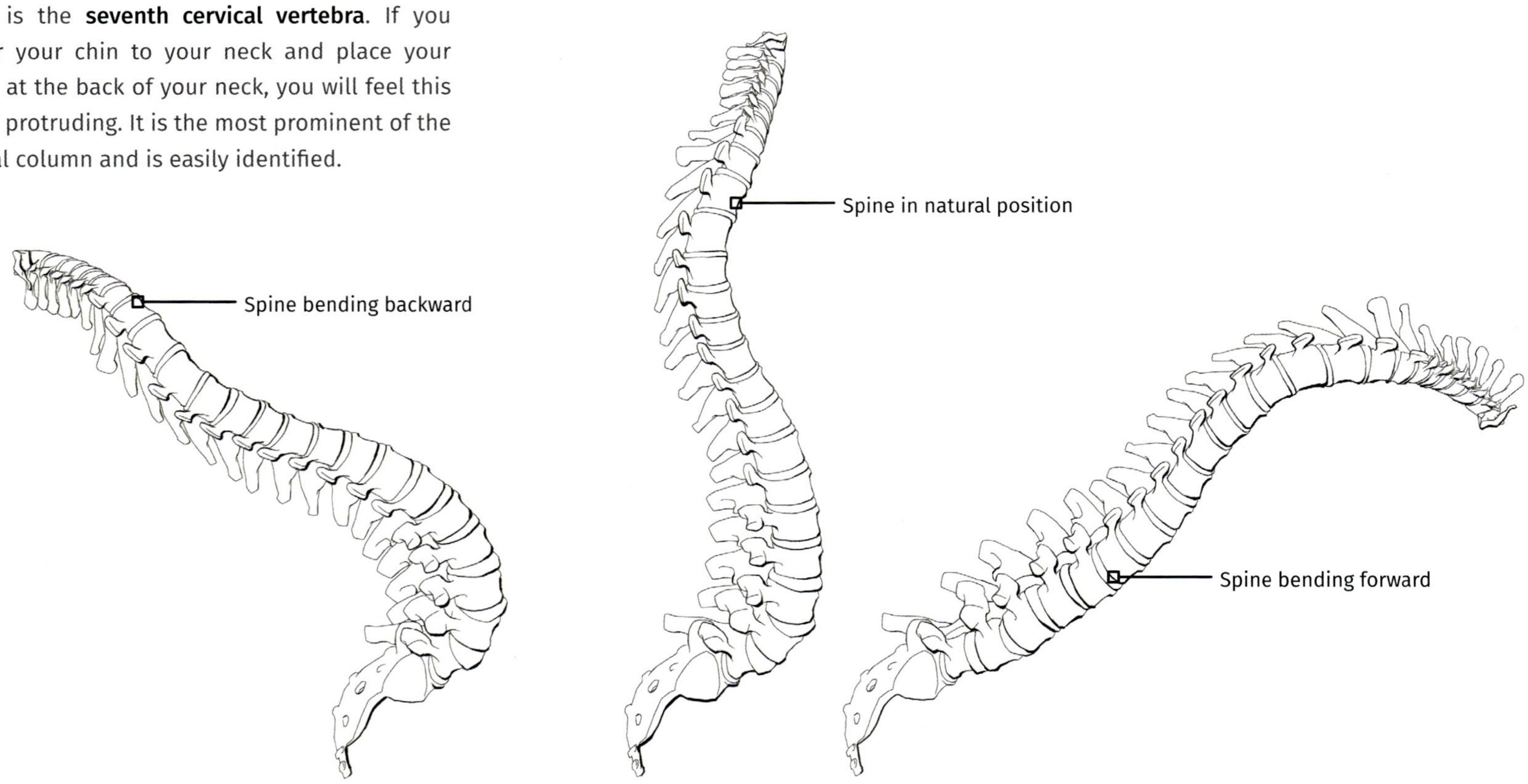

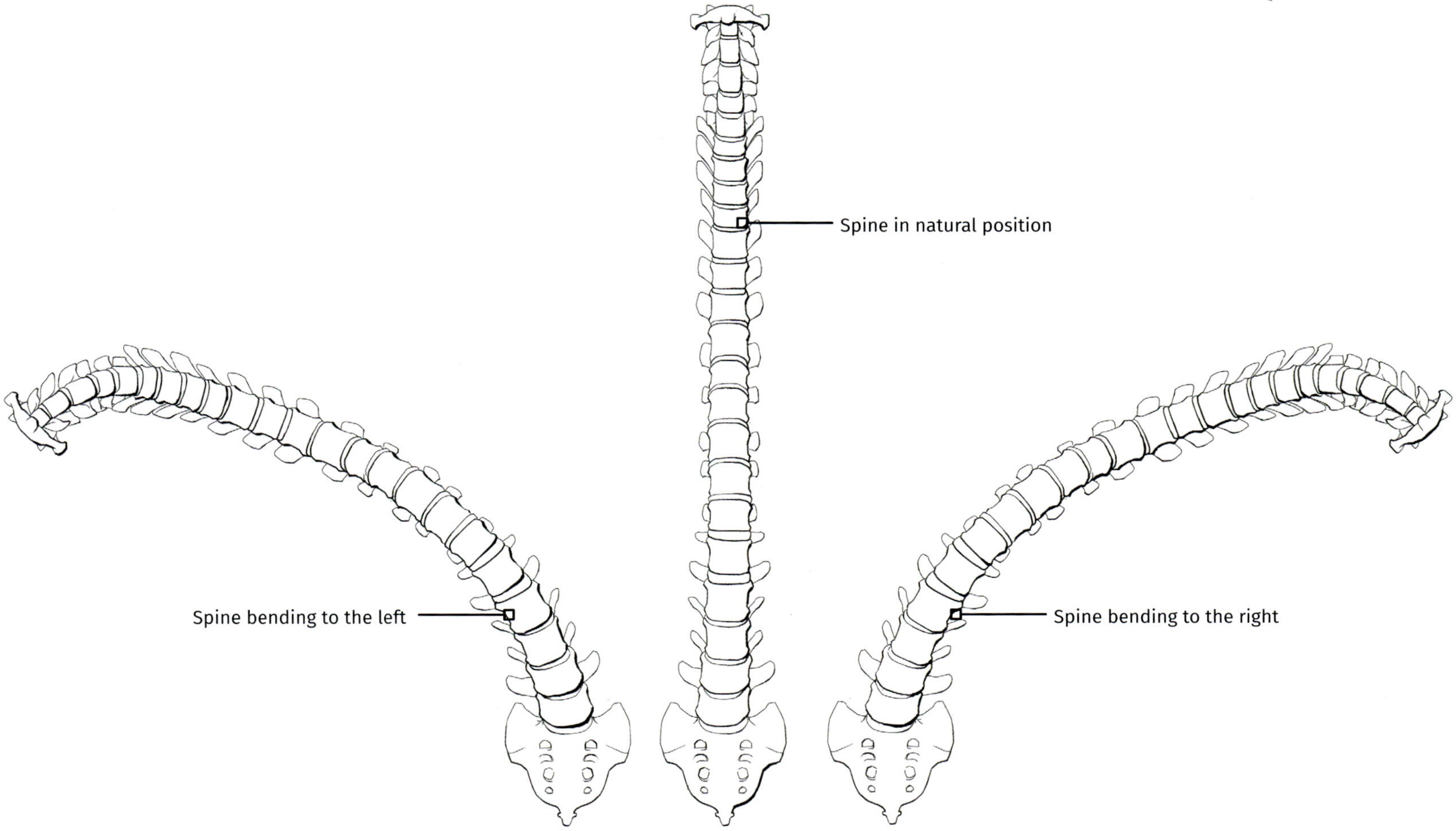

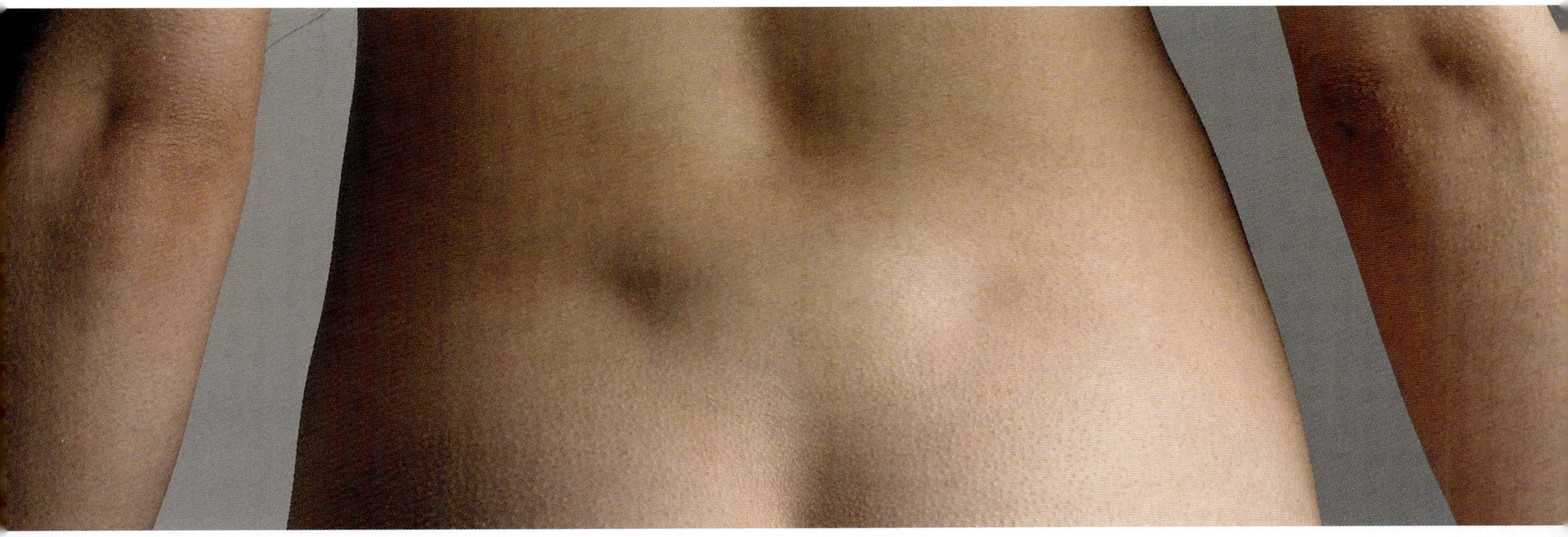

The remainder of the spinal bones are less visible when in the anatomical position. They can be seen more easily when the back is in an extreme position, the superficial muscles becoming thinner to reveal them. The **lumbar region** is partly responsible for flexion, extension, and lateral flexion, as well as bearing the weight of the upper body. As the **thoracic vertebrae** each have a rib bone attached, it creates more of a rigid volume, but allows for the thoracic rotation to the left and right.

The **sacrum**, shaped like a triangle and wedged between the two bones of the pelvis, may not have much flexibility, but it does create the sacral triangle, also known as the dimples of Venus. These are two indentions lateral to the median (midsagittal) plane and slightly superior to the gluteal cleft (the groove between the buttocks).

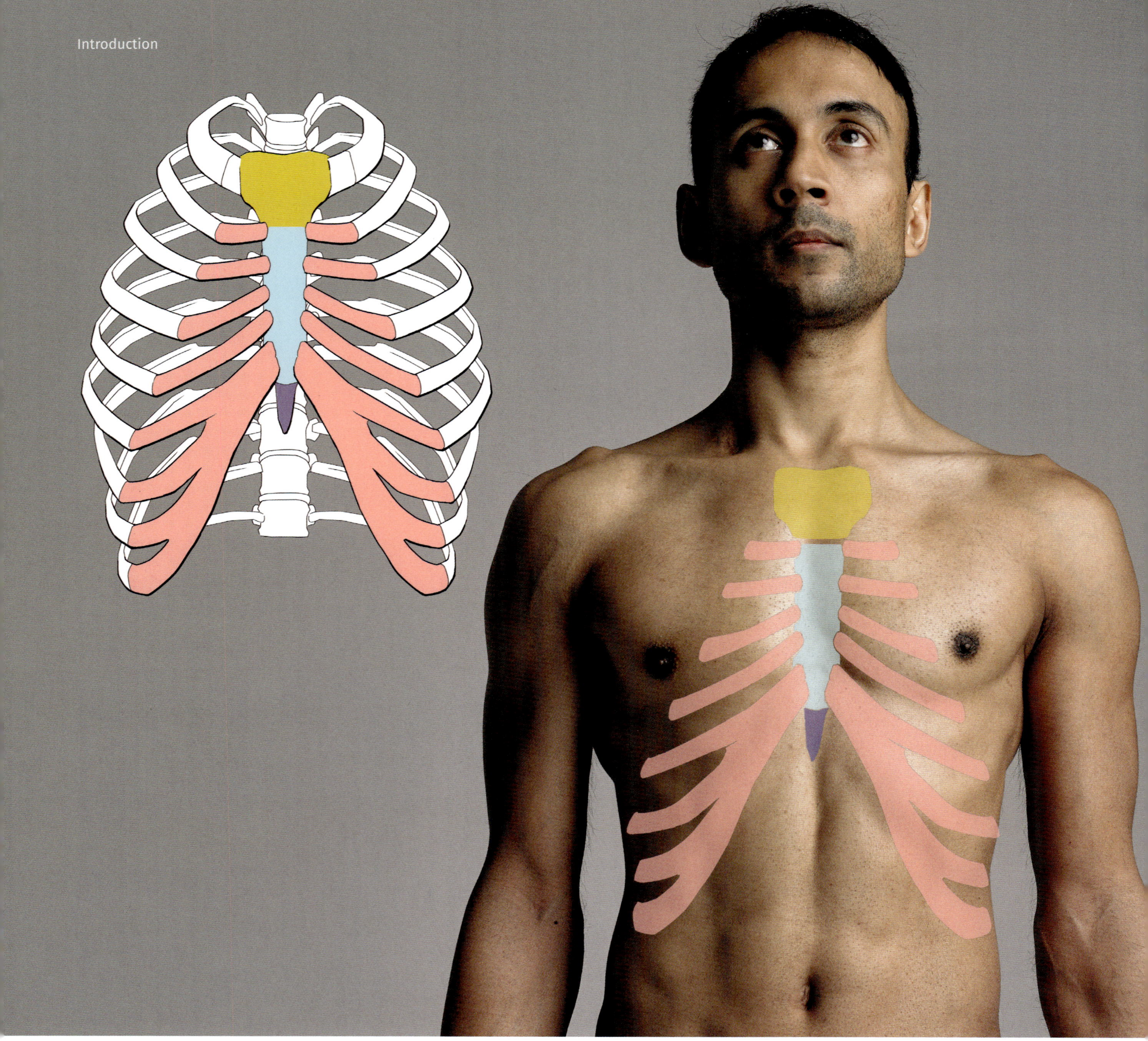

The sternum and the rib cage

Next on the axial skeleton are the sternum and the rib cage.

The **sternum**, fused together by three bones, creates a noticeable plane change to the surface of the skin where the **manubrium** and the **gladiolus** bones meet. The costal cartilage of the rib cage, made from a hyaline substance, adds elasticity to the thorax. The ribs that are of most interest here are the **false ribs**, eight to ten, which do not directly attach to the sternum. These form the **costal arch**, an area that is superficial depending on the articulation of the subject. These ribs can also be seen from the posterior view when the body is in an extreme pose.

- Costal cartilage
- Manubrium
- Gladiolus
- Xiphoid process

The appendicular skeleton

Next we look at the appendicular skeleton, which is comprised of the shoulder girdle, the pelvic girdle, the upper extremity, and the lower extremity. An adult appendicular skeleton is comprised of 126 bones.

Acromioclavicular joint

Sternoclavicular joint

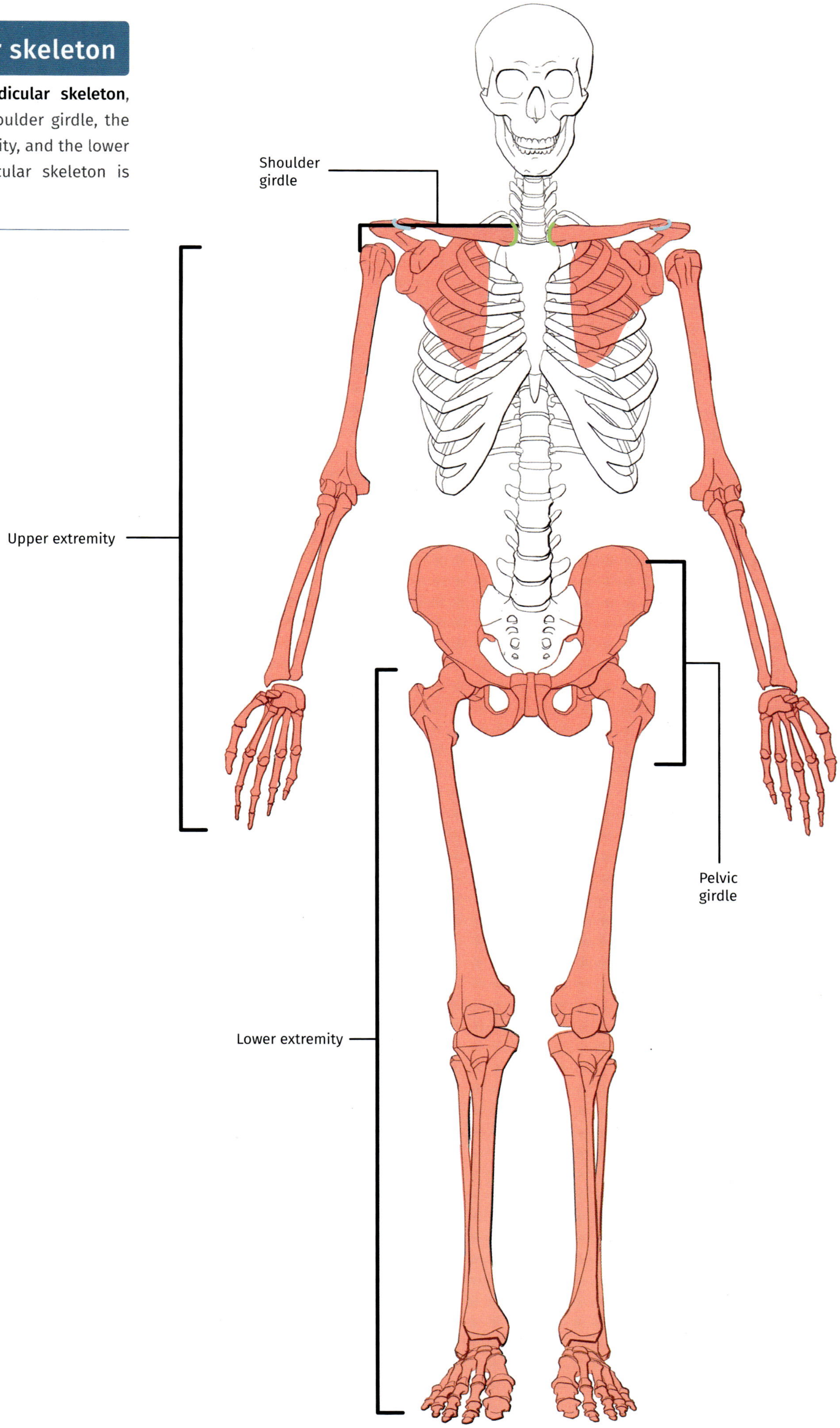

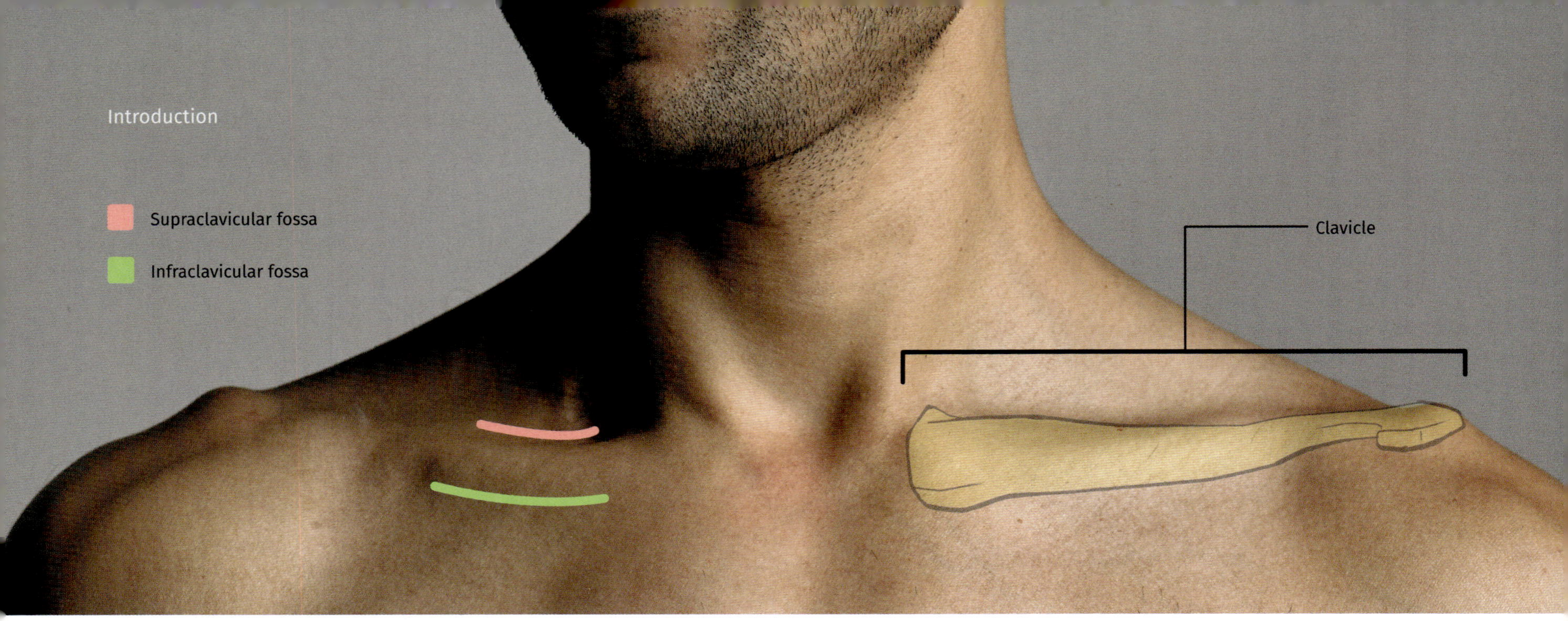

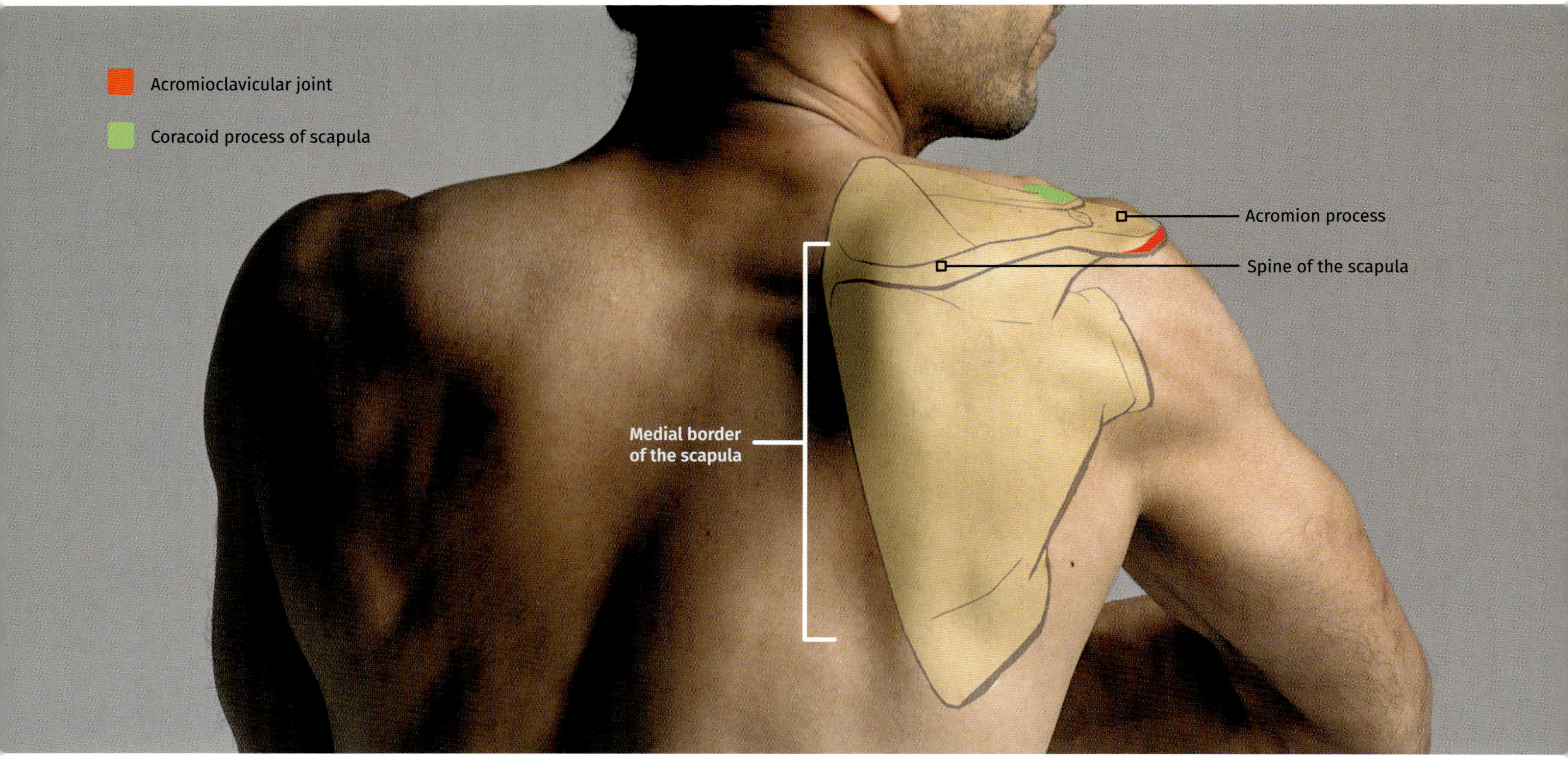

The shoulder girdle

Starting with the **shoulder girdle**, also known as the **pectoral girdle**, this is made up of the **clavicles** and the **scapulae.** The gently s-shaped bone of the clavicle is clearly visible, especially on those with less fat, and connects the trunk to the upper extremities. It is connected to the sternum through the **sternoclavicular joint** and meets the **acromion process** of the scapula by the **acromioclavicular joint**. The acromion process is a key landmark to consider as the arm articulates. It is a small, flat bony process that creates a depression as the arm is raised.

You should also notice that a small pocket is visible between the clavicular region of the pectoralis major muscle and the anterior portion of the deltoid. This is known as the **infraclavicular fossa**. Where there is an "infra" there is almost always an opposite, in this case, the **supraclavicular fossa:** a small depression above the clavicle.

Moving round to the **scapula**, this flat triangular bone is held in place by the surrounding muscles, allowing it to float over the rib cage. The two landmarks for consideration are the **spine of the scapula** and the **medial border of the scapula**, both of which are superficial. As the arm is raised to a horizontal level, it is also worth noting the manner in which the scapula begins to pivot, allowing for the **trapezius** (see page 58) and **pectoralis** muscles (see page 54) to continue pulling the arm up.

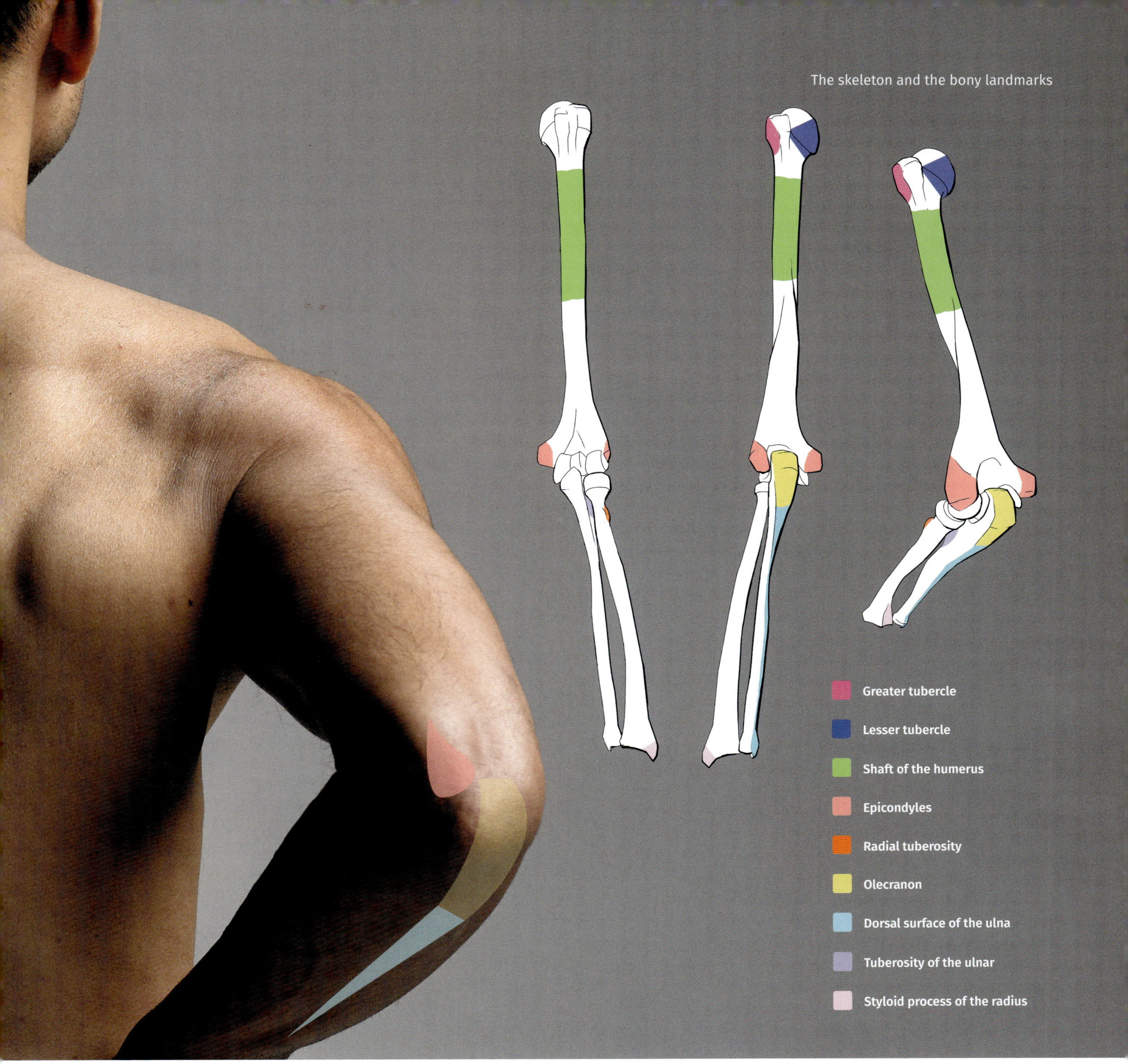

The upper extremity

Studying the **upper extremity**, there is the **humerus**, which connects to the **scapula** through the **glenohumeral joint**. At the distal end of the humerus there are two key landmarks that form the elbow: the **lateral** and **medial epicondyles**. The **ulnar nerve** travels along here and causes the funny bone effect; its name a play on words between "humerus" and "humorous." As the elbow bends, the lateral and medial epicondyles, along with the **olecranon** (a large, curved eminence situated at the upper and back part of the ulna bone), create a triangular landmark that you also need to look out for. On a straight arm, the lateral epicondyle will also create distinct dimples.

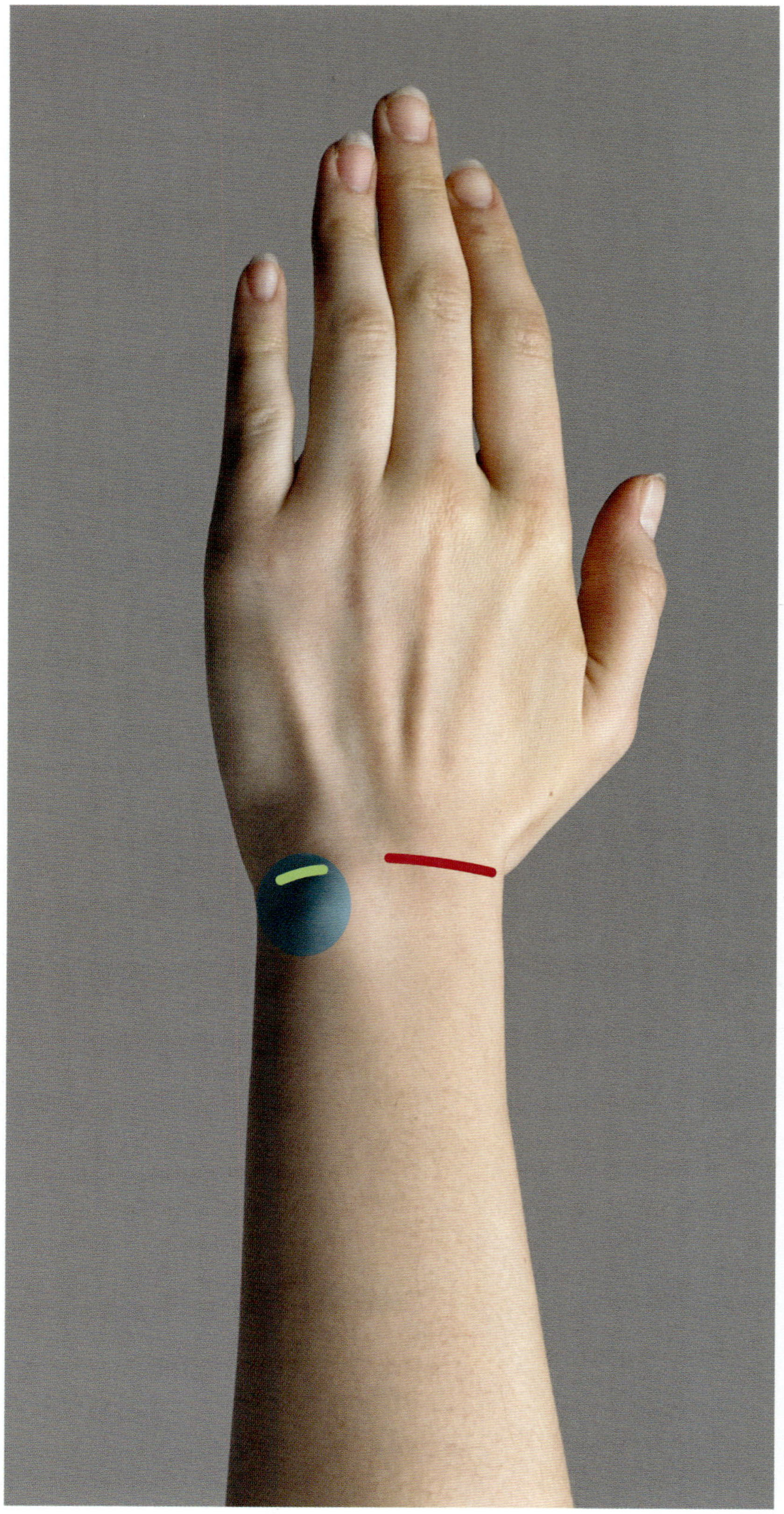

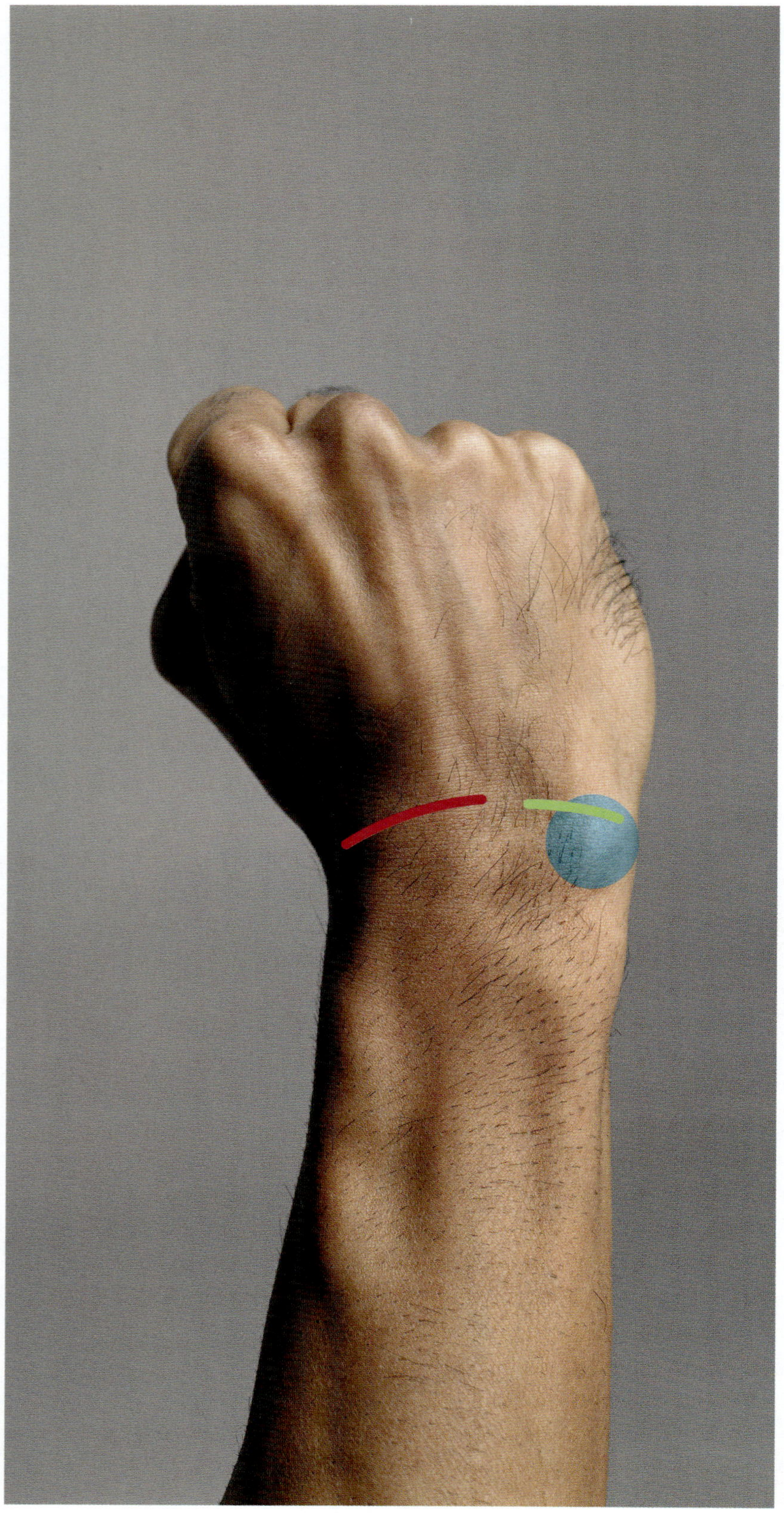

Moving down the forearm, you come to the **styloid process** of the ulna, which can be seen affecting the surface of the skin as a rounded protrusion. You could also take into consideration the head of the ulna and the head of the radius, but these are generally dependent on the articulation of the wrist and the weight of the character.

- Styloid process of the ulna
- Head of the ulna
- Head of the radius

At the distal end of the upper extremity, there are the **hands** and **fingers**. Considered the second most expressive part of the body after the face, they comprise of the **carpals, metacarpals**, and the **phalanges**, and create an intricate amount of surface change.

The carpals form two rows of slightly irregular-shaped bones. The distal row consists of the **trapezium**, **trapezoidium**, **capitate**, and **hamate**. The proximal row consists of the **scaphoid**, the **lunate**, the **triquetral** and the **pisiform**. The two bones that can be prominent during extension of the wrist are the trapezium (found below the thumb) and the pisiform (found below the pinky/little finger).

The metacarpals add curvature to the hand from the index finger to the pinky finger (metacarpals two through to five) and the distal ends are exposed as spherical knuckles. The phalanges are also very superficial on the dorsal surface of each finger, and if you were to bend any of your fingers, you can again feel and see the knuckles on the surface. The bones sit on the top third of each finger and have a layer of fat beneath, acting as a padded cushion. The thumb, unlike the four fingers, has a saddle joint (the **carpometacarpal joint**). This allows for flexion and extension, abduction and adduction, as can be achieved with the fingers, but also opposition (bringing the thumb to the fingers) and circumduction (moving a limb around in a circle).

DORSAL SIDE VIEW

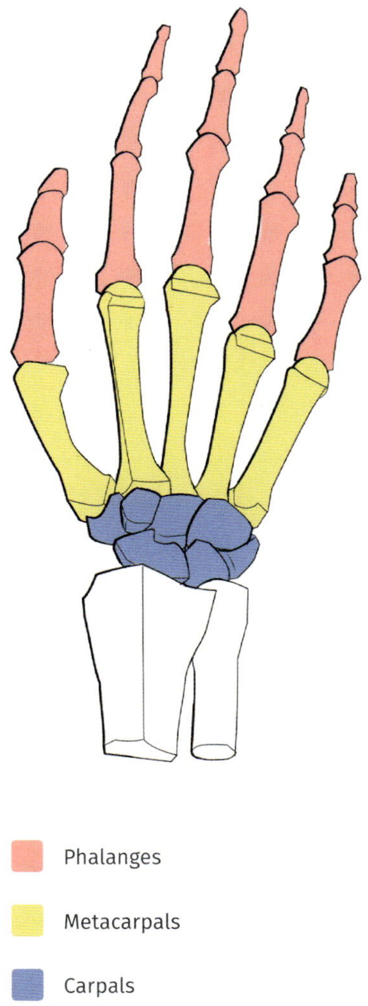

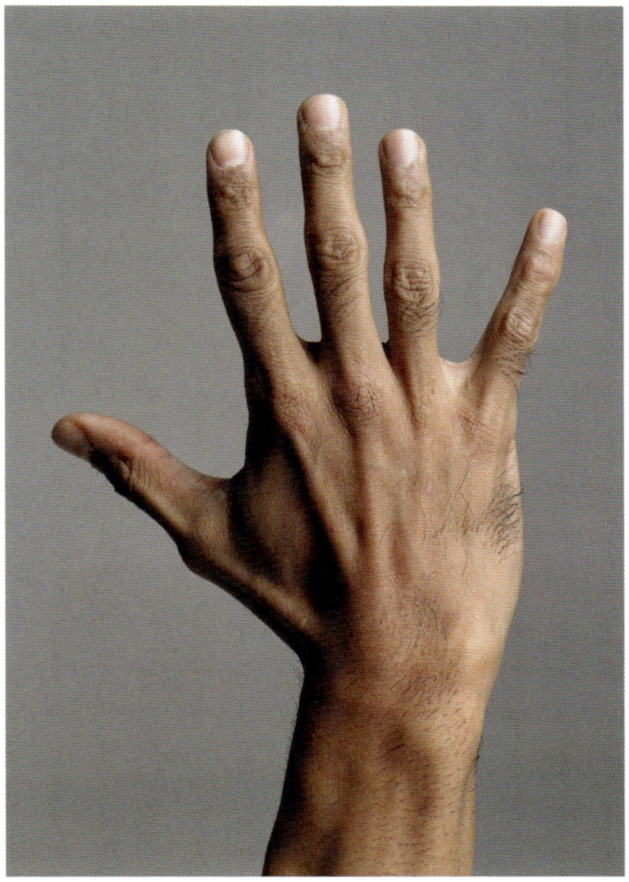

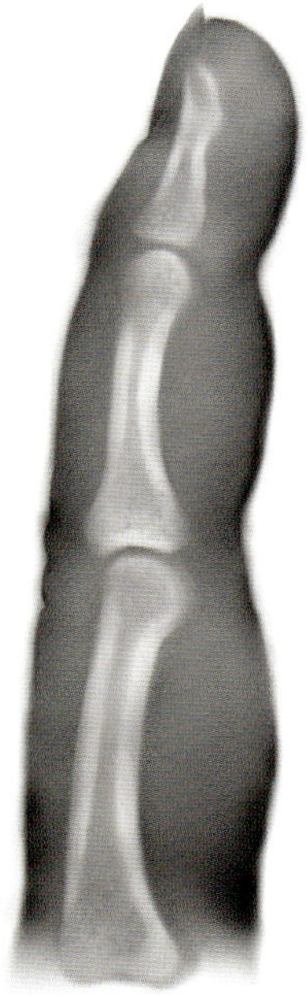

DORSAL SIDE VIEW

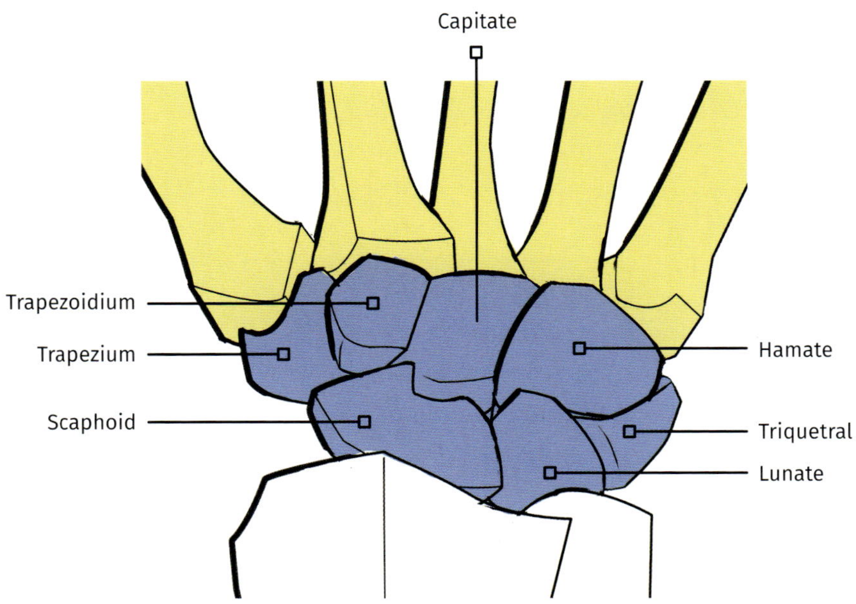

PALMAR SIDE VIEW

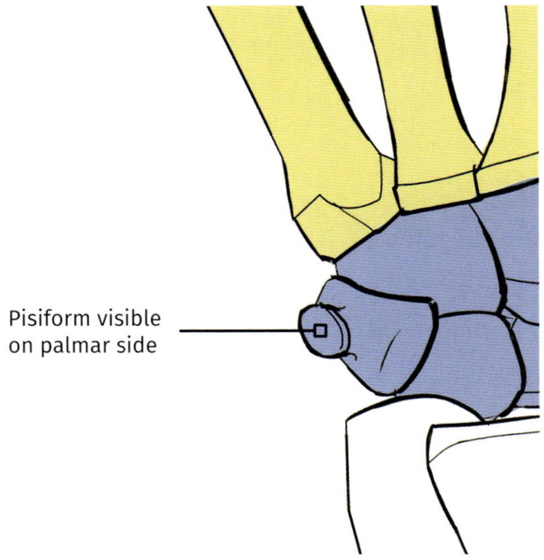

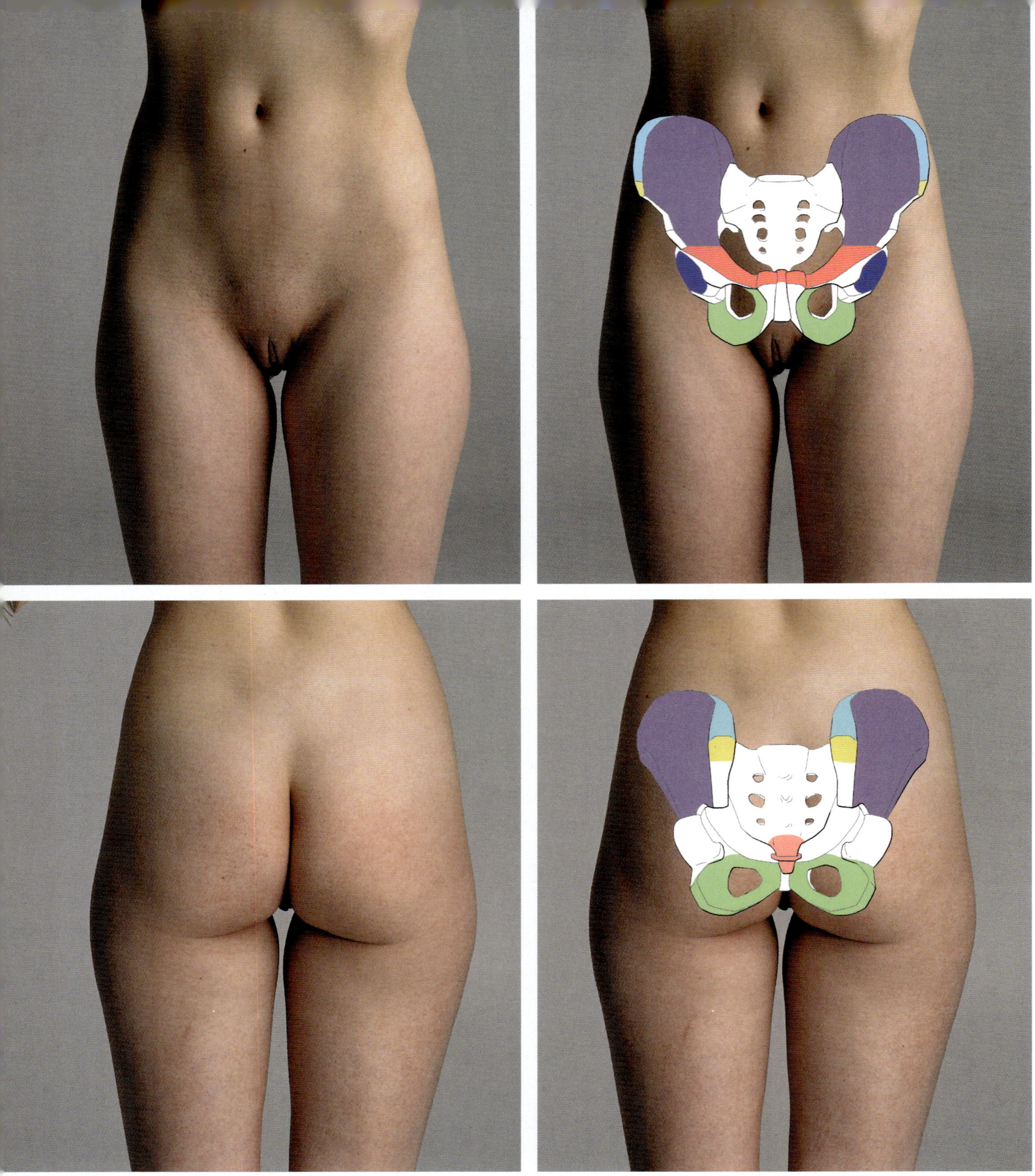

ANTERIOR VIEW

- Pubis
- Anterior superior iliac spine (ASIS)
- Iliac crest
- Ilium
- Ischium
- Acetabulum

POSTERIOR VIEW

- Tip of sacrum
- Posterior superior iliac spine (PSIS)
- Iliac Crest
- Ilium
- Ischium

The pelvic girdle

The **pelvic girdle** consists of two mirrored bones attached on the anterior side of the body, with the **sacrum** wedged between them on the posterior side. Each of the two **hip bones** is made up of three bones: the **ilium**, the **ischium**, and the **pubis**. Areas of interest are the **anterior superior iliac spine**, the **posterior superior iliac spine**, and the **iliac crest** (also known as the crest of ilium). They form landmarks that protrude into the skin and together create a bony ring dividing the upper and lower body. The posterior superior iliac spine with the sacrum creates the dimples of Venus. By keeping these forms in mind as the hip articulates, you can ensure your character maintains volume around the pelvis.

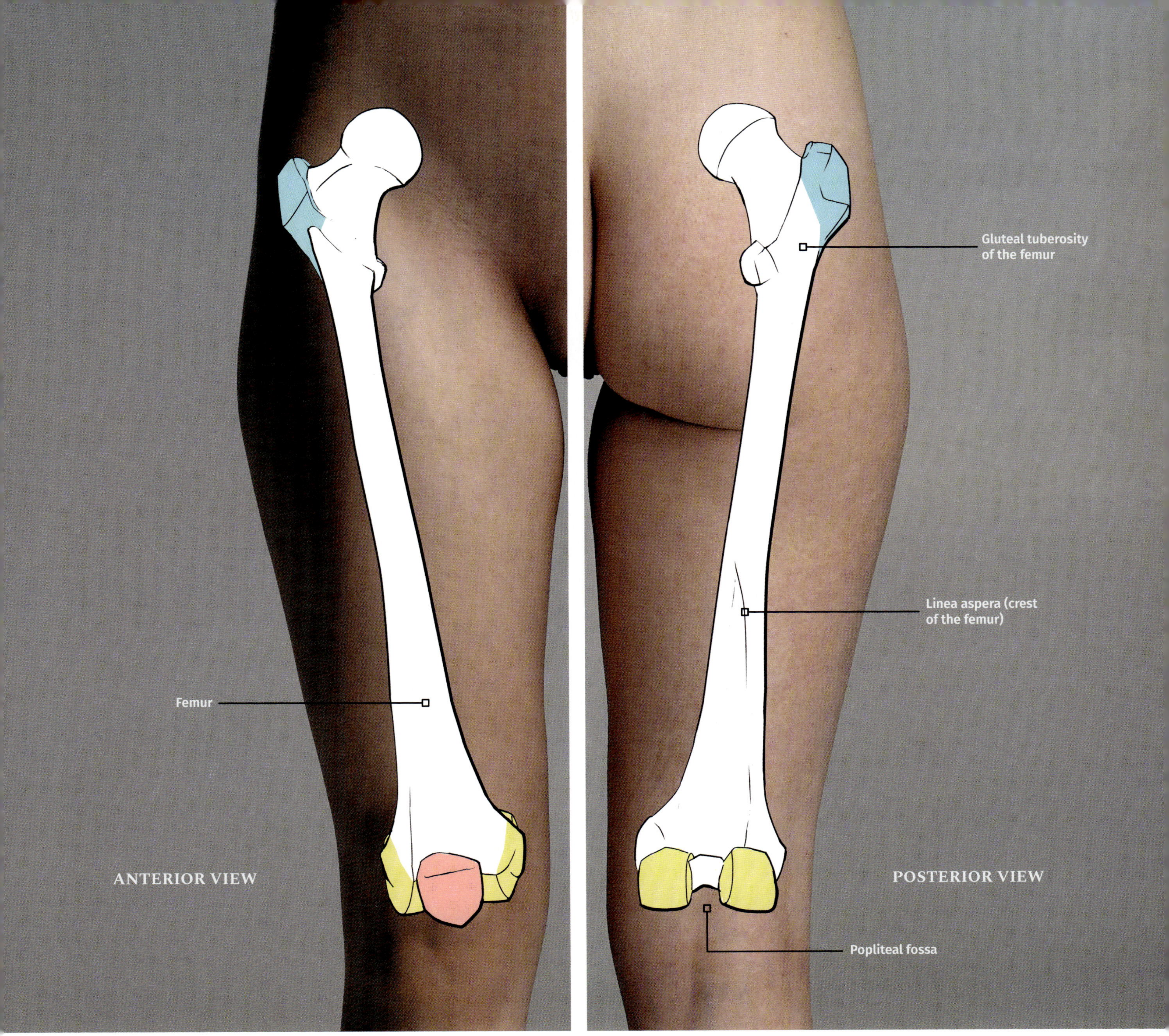

The lower extremity

Slotting into the **acetabulum** of the pelvis to create the ball and socket joint of the hip is the **femur**. This is the longest bone in the human body. The femur has a big bony protrusion, the **greater trochanter**, which sits between the head and the neck of the bone. Using your fingers, you should be able to feel the bone protruding through just below the hip. Like the humerus bone, two **condyles, medial** and **lateral**, are also present at the distal end, creating surface changes along with the **patella** during articulation. The patella, being triangular in shape, also creates two prominent dimples on the straightened leg. At the back of the leg, between the femur and the tibia, there is also a diamond-shaped depression, known as the **popliteal fossa**. This is to allow for nerves and veins to pass from the upper portion of the leg to the lower.

- Greater trochanter
- Patella
- Condyles

The bones of the lower leg, the tibia and fibula, articulate at the knee and ankle. Although they may appear similar to the radius and ulna of the forearm, they have less freedom in movement.

The **tibia**, also known as the **shin bone**, sits on the inside of the leg and is the larger of the two bones, bearing the majority of the weight. It has a sharp anterior surface that is easily visible when the leg is flexed. On the proximal end, two condyles (the medial and the lateral) meet the distal condyles of the femur, allowing the lower leg to hinge at the knee. A key landmark is the **medial malleolus** on the distal end of the bone, also known as the **inner ankle bone**.

The **fibula**, or **calf bone**, lies parallel to the tibia and slightly behind. It is the thinner of the two, with both its proximal and distal ends attached to the tibia. It helps to maintain stability in the lower leg as well as presenting a key landmark, the **lateral malleolus** (outer ankle bone), that sits slightly lower than the inner ankle bone.

- Malleolus (medial and lateral)
- Tibial tuberosity
- Dorsal surface of tibia
- Head of the fibula
- Patella

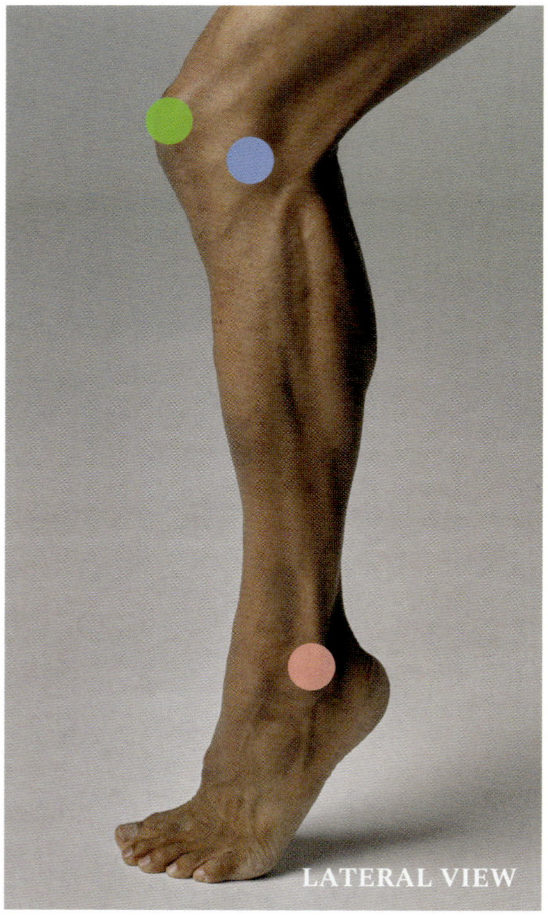

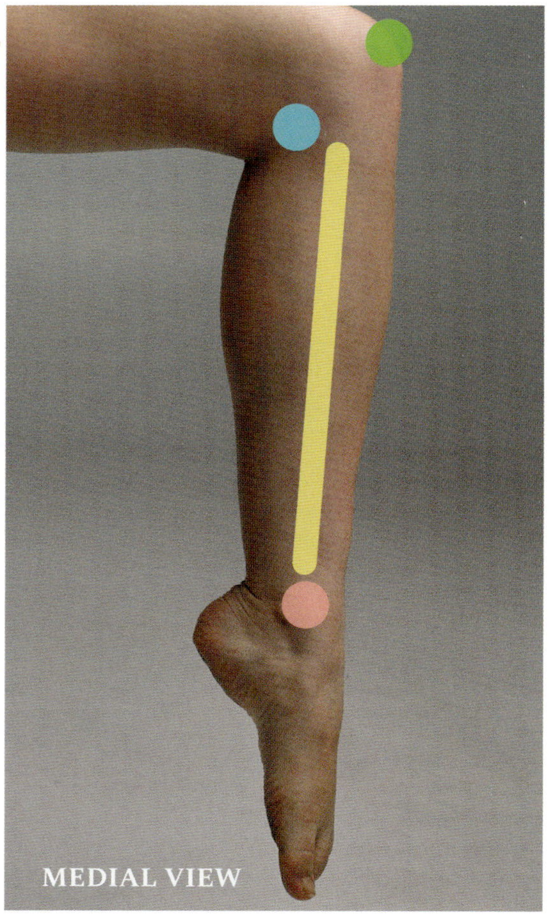

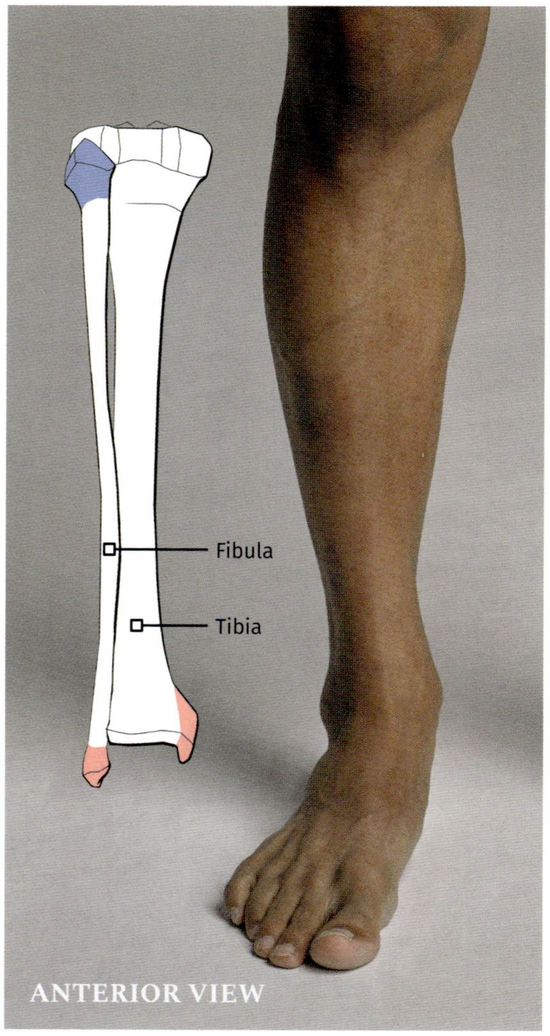

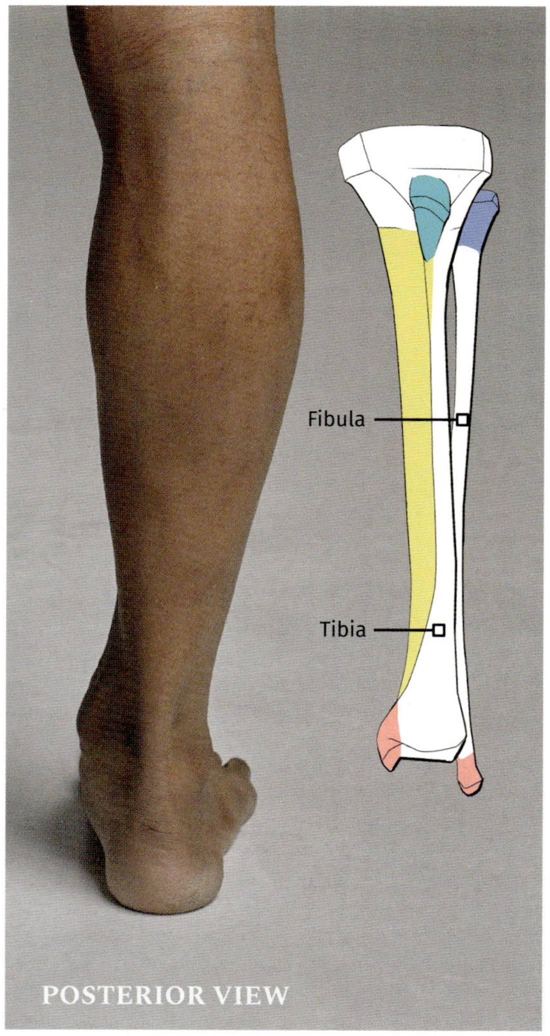

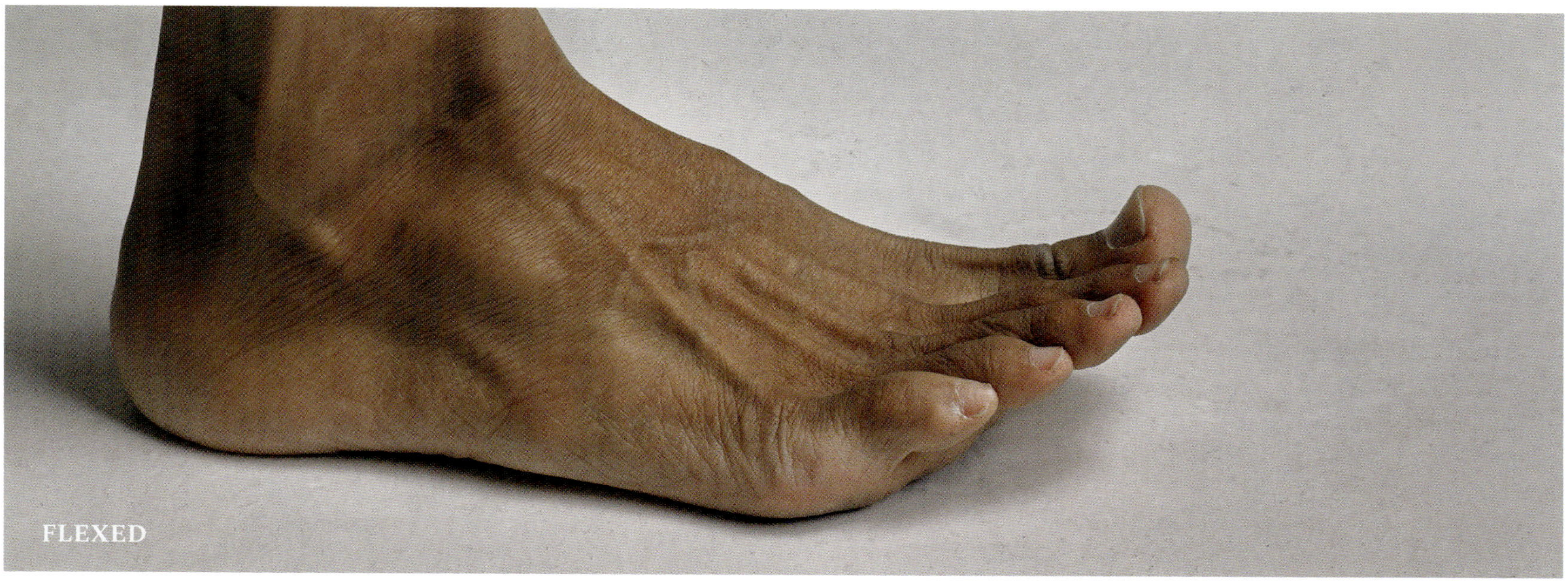

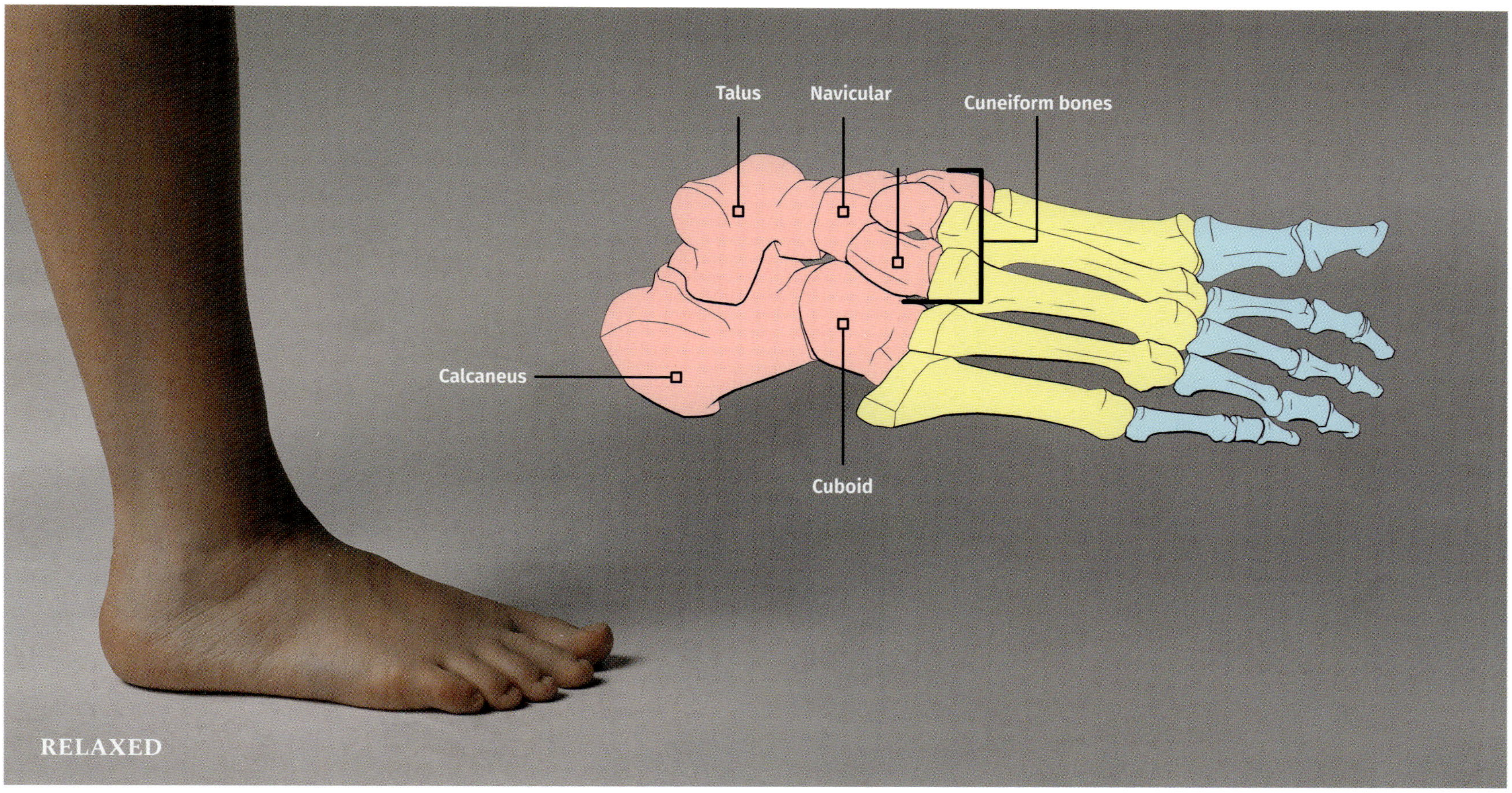

The foot, like the hand, has an arrangement of three sets of bones; the tarsus, the metatarsus (made up of the metatarsals), and the phalanges.

The **tarsus** consists of seven bones: **calcaneus**, **talus**, **cuboid**, **navicular**, and three **cuneiform bones**. The calcaneus, the largest of the bones, is also known as the heel bone and can be seen and felt against the skin. The **medial and lateral malleoli**, as well as the base of the tibia, sit on top of the talus bone. The foot is able to support the weight by the arched arrangement of the bones, distributing the load over the padded areas of the sole of the foot. Along with the calcaneus, the **metatarsals** and **phalanges** sit close to the surface of the dorsal side, creating the majority of surface change through the bony spherical knuckles. Also, note that the large toe only has two phalanges, whereas the rest have three.

Tarsal bones

Metatarsals

Phalanges

MUSCLES AND TENDONS

Everything we do, from kickboxing to flower arranging, is driven by muscular motion. Our muscles, like the engine of a car, are used to propel our bodies by turning energy into movement.

Muscles can be broken into three distinct types: **skeletal (striated) muscles, cardiac muscles**, and **smooth muscles**. This chapter will primarily focus on the skeletal muscles, as cardiac muscles and smooth muscles, which are found in the walls of organs, do not generally affect the body visibly.

The muscles and tendons detailed in this chapter will provide you with a solid foundation when drawing the human form or designing characters. There are some additional factors to consider, however, including proportions, fat, wrinkles, age, and sex, which will be covered in the next chapters.

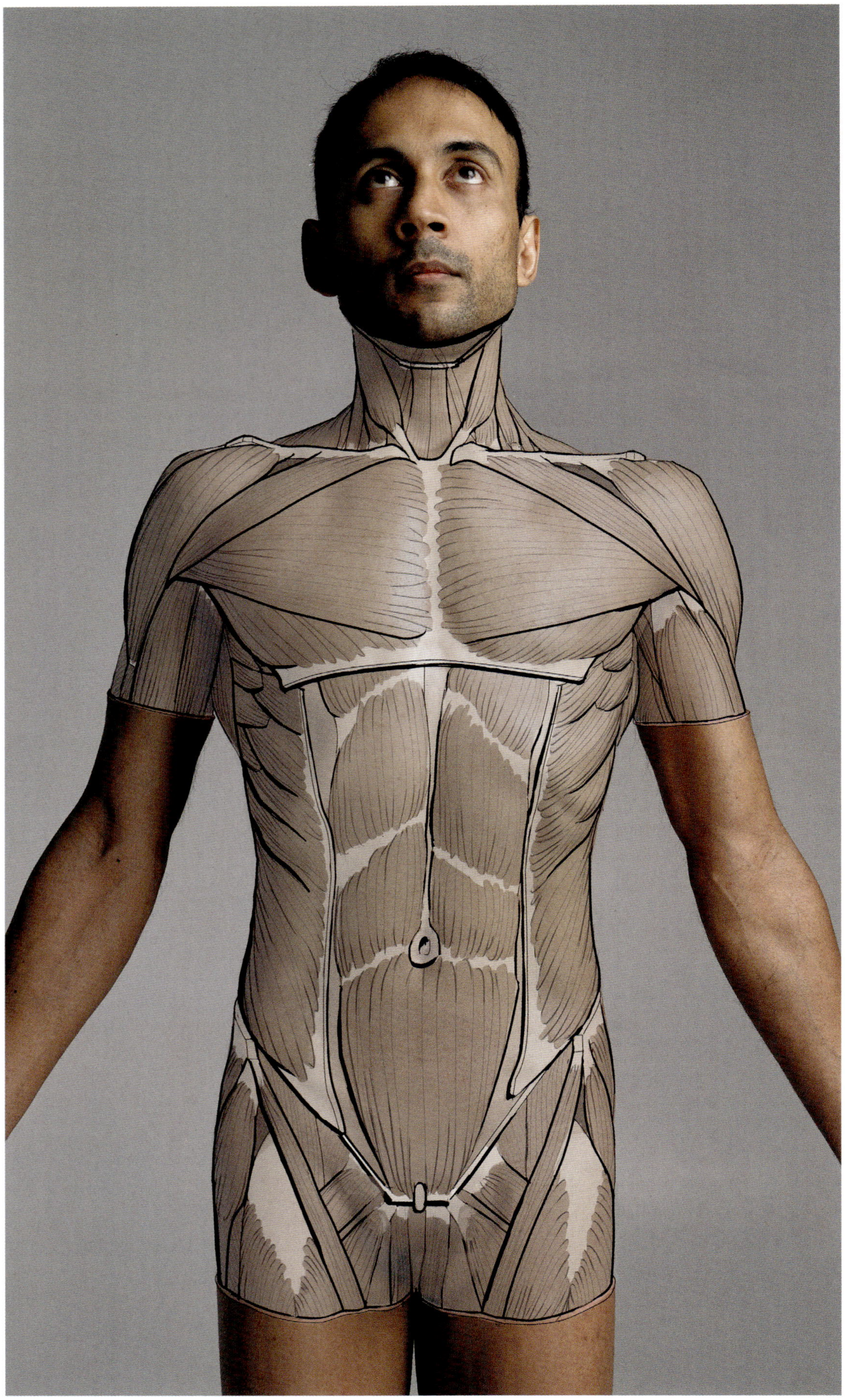

The skeletal muscles, of which there are between 639 and 850 (sources vary), will be of most interest to artists drawing the body, as these are the muscles that affect the surface forms. These are muscles that are within our conscious control and receive their signals through the peripheral nervous system. This chapter will focus on what the core muscles do to create the surface change that you will want to mimic when drawing. It will therefore be muscles such as the pectorals, biceps, triceps, deltoids, and the muscles of the face that will require the most attention.

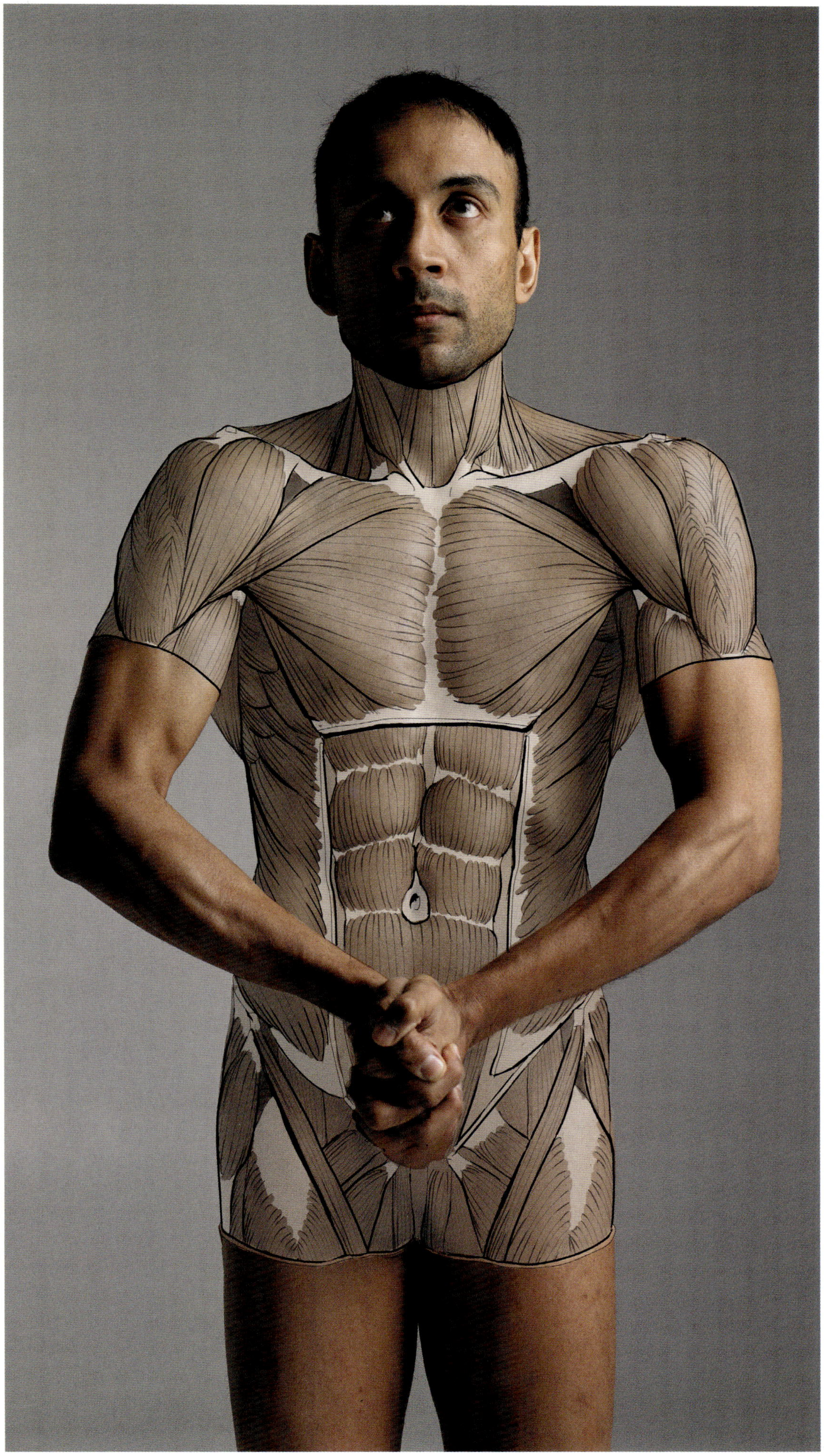

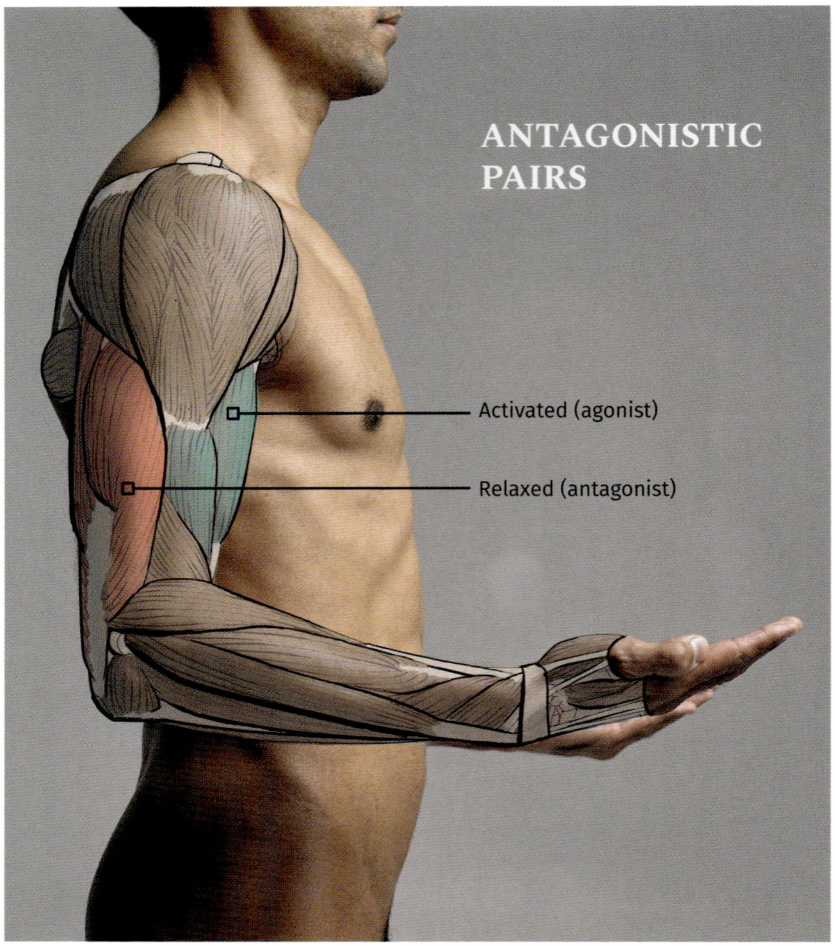

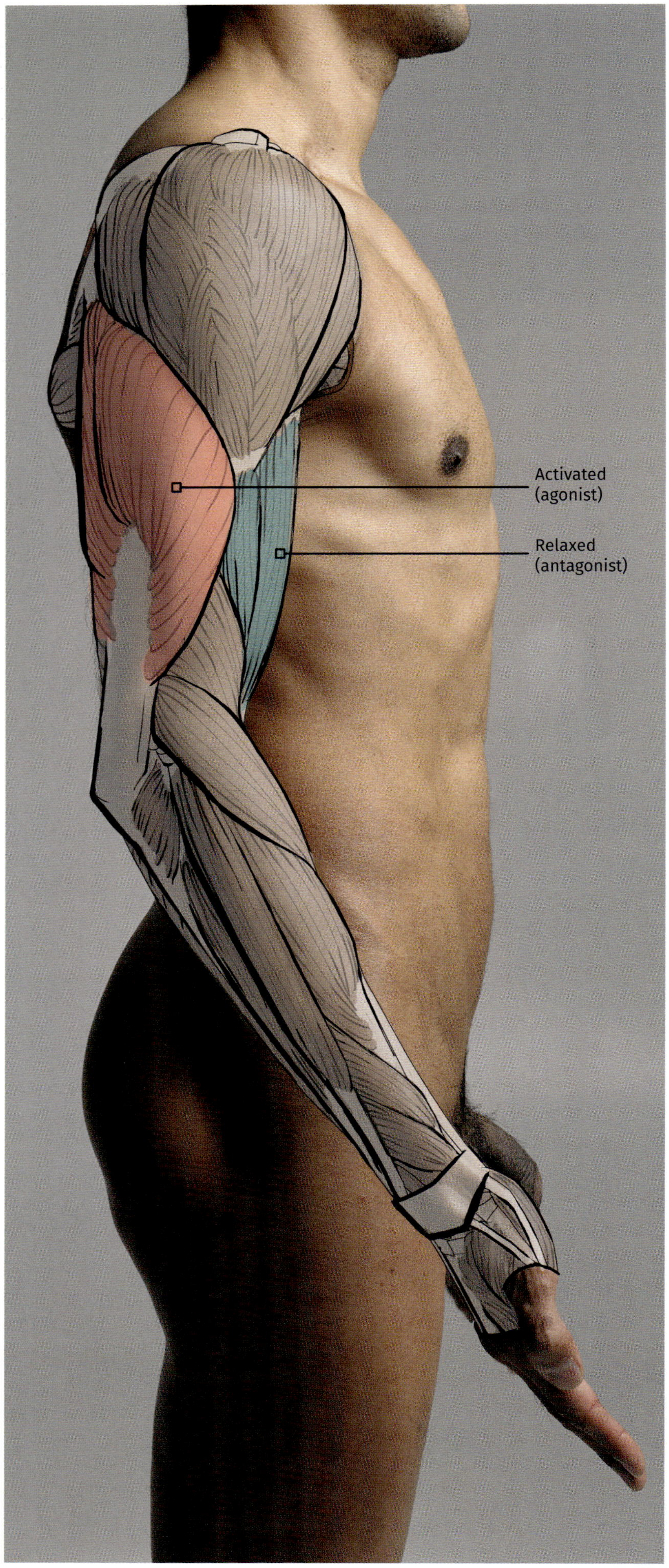

Before looking at the relevant muscles, it is first important to understand what a muscle is and how it works. Essentially, a **muscle** is a band of fibrous tissue found in a human or animal body. There are two key points on a muscle: an **origin** and an **insertion**. These two points are attached to the bones through **tendons** and allow the muscle to contract.

The contractions are caused by electrical impulses (action potentials) which are sent from your brain and travel down to the muscle through nerve fibers. The contractions pull the muscle fibers together, making the muscle shorter and thicker. They do not push – they only pull. Muscles can only pull in one direction and work in pairs to stop your body from locking up. The muscle pairs are known as **agonists** (activated muscle) and **antagonists** (relaxed muscle). An example would be the relationship between the biceps and the triceps. When the biceps (a flexor muscle) pulls the lower arm in, it is activated (agonist), and the triceps is relaxed (antagonist). Then when the triceps (an extensor muscle) pulls the lower arm out straight, it becomes activated (agonist) and the biceps becomes relaxed (antagonist).

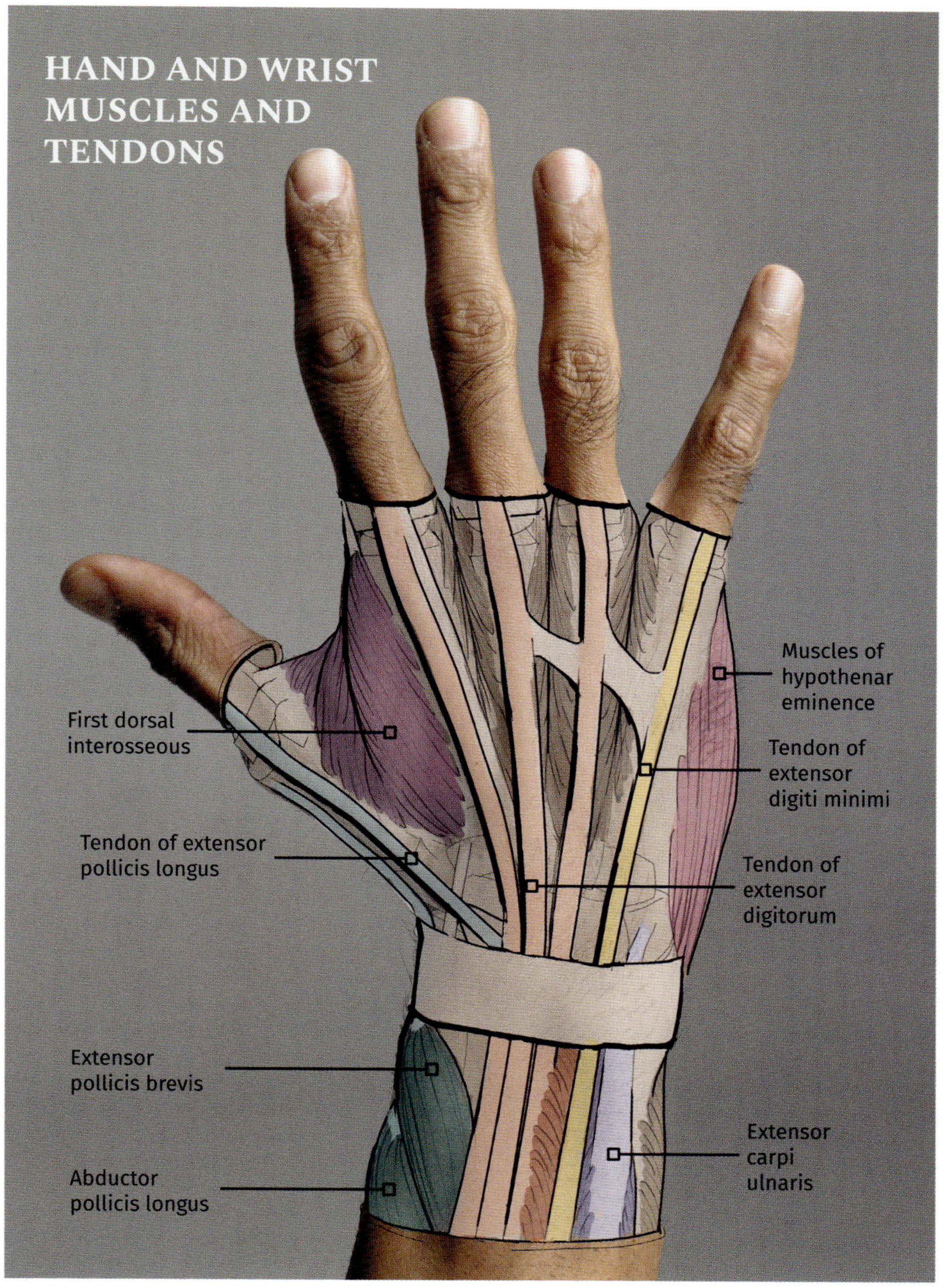

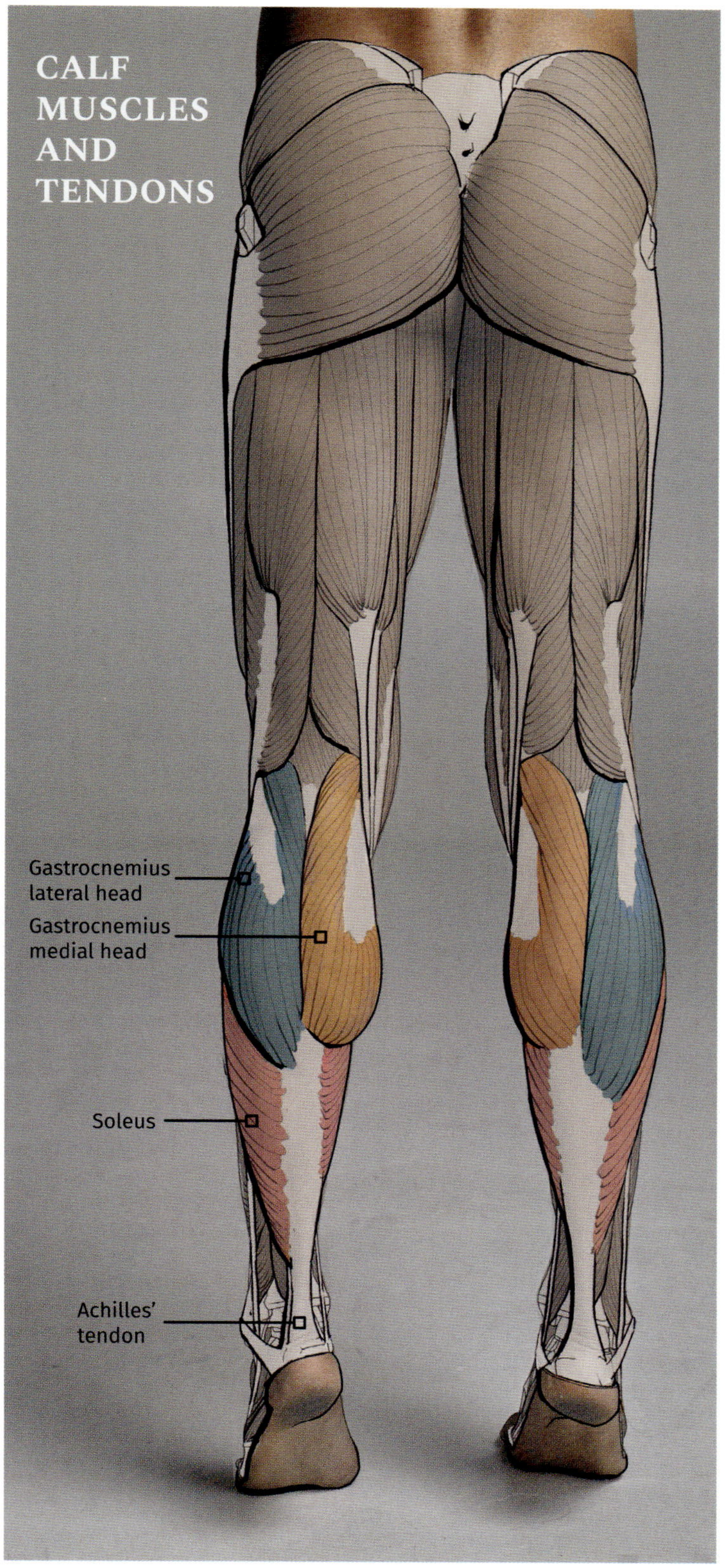

As muscles are connected to bone through tendons, this chapter will look at them together, where applicable. Tendons are tough but flexible fibrous tissues made from collagen and can vary in size from muscle to muscle and person to person. The largest tendon in the body is the Achilles' tendon, which can be seen as the heel of the foot lifts off the ground. Tendons in the hands and feet are also very visible beneath the skin and should therefore be considered. Unlike muscles, tendons do not change shape from exercise and can cause depressions on highly muscular forms. They do not have much stretch to them, but are able to withstand tension as well as store and release (but not produce) energy like a spring.

Muscles of the head and neck

The human face is usually made up of forty-three muscles. Facial muscles are flat and intertwined, which can create confusion as to how to label them and what to class as muscle rather than tendons or fascia (a band or sheet of connective tissue beneath the skin that attaches, stabilizes, encloses, and separates muscles and organs). The core muscles are universal; the forehead, eyes, cheeks, mouth, and chin region allow for facial expressions to be a language which transcends words. Interestingly, some research shows that the face is the only part of the body that has a varying number of muscles from person to person. Some people only have sixty percent of the core set of facial muscles, while two thirds of the population are missing the key muscle for expressing fear: the risorius.

Forehead and brow

Let's begin with the **frontalis**, located on the anterior side of the head. The muscle originates at the galea aponeurotica (the tissues of the scalp) and the fibers of its insertion points blend with the procerus, corrugator supercilii, and orbicularis oculi muscles (the muscles of the eye and brows). The function of the frontalis is to raise the brows up, and in doing so, it creates horizontal forehead wrinkles. Place your fingers over the bridge of your nose or on your upper eyelids and raise your brows and you should feel a slight tug of the skin in those regions. The frontalis can be broken into two regions: the **medial** and **lateral**. These two inner and outer parts allow for independent motion along the brow.

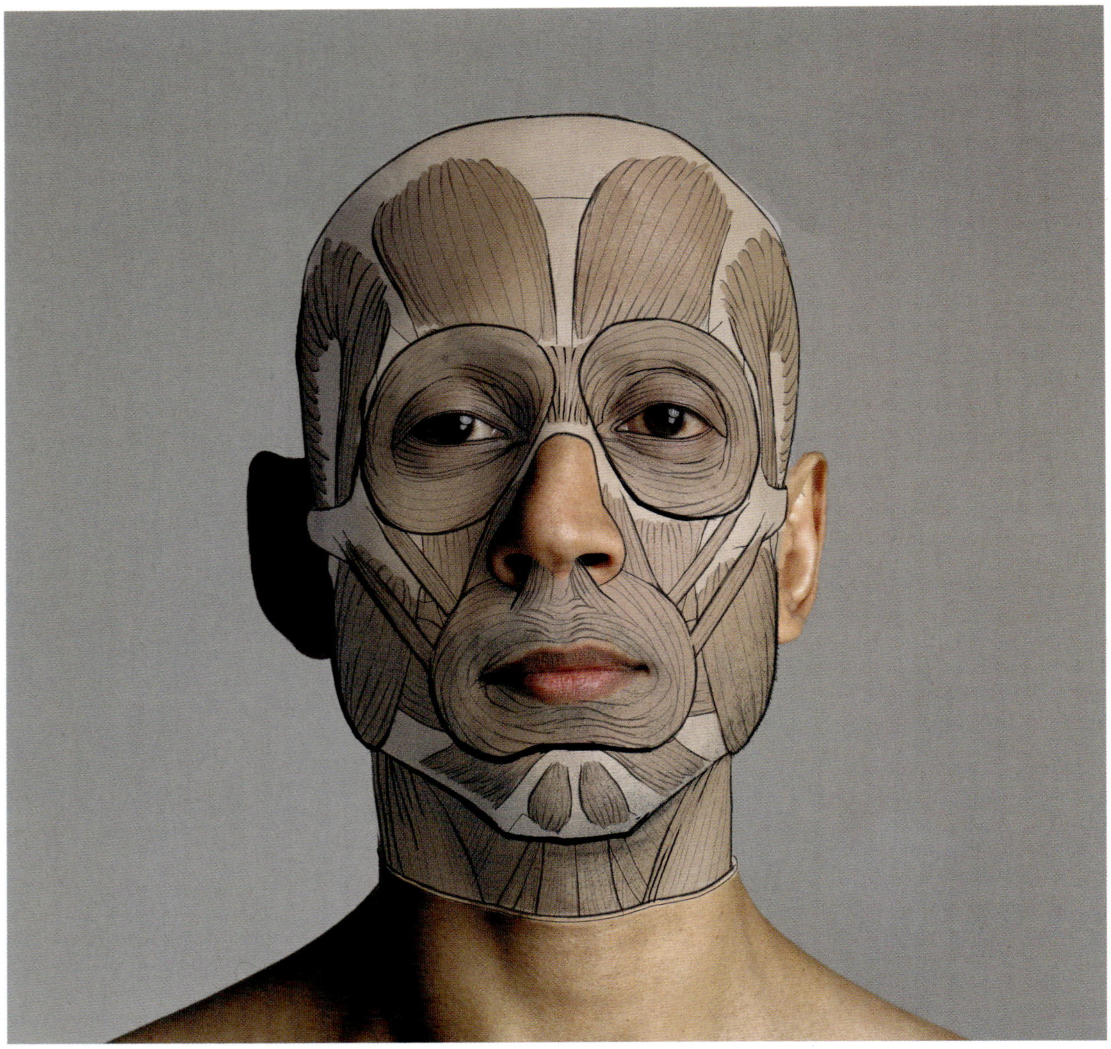

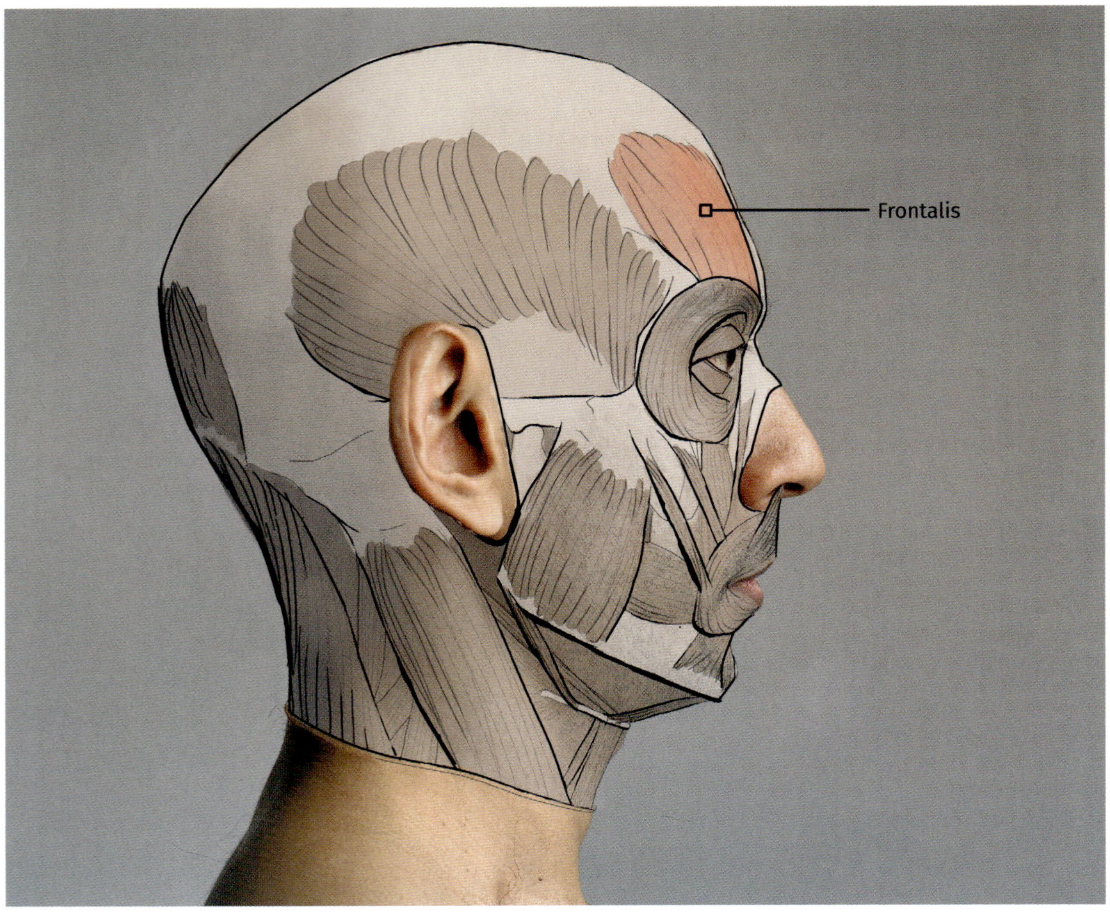

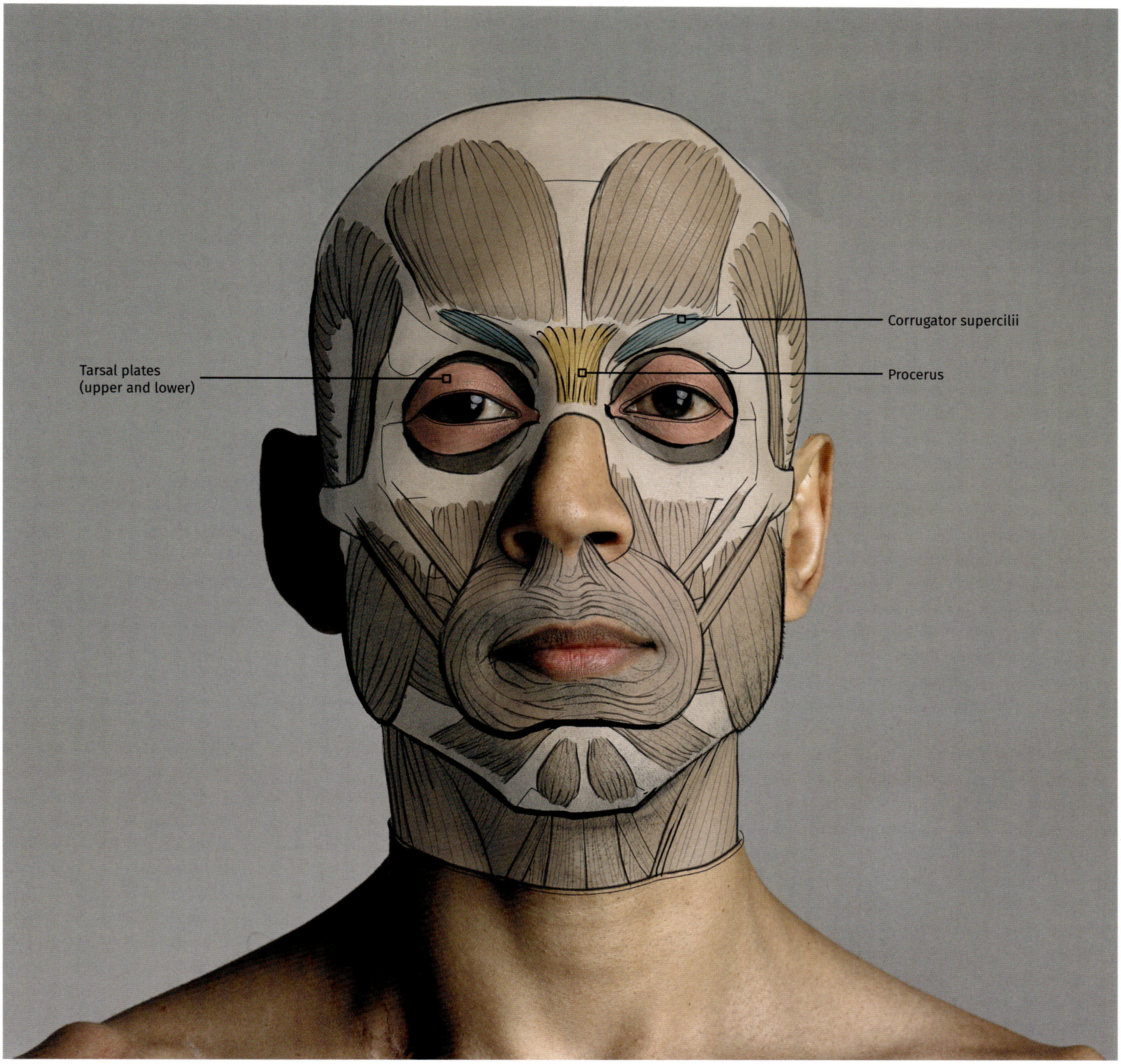

Staying with the brows, there is another important muscle: the **corrugator supercilii**. This is a small muscle that sits beneath the frontalis and slightly above the orbicularis oculi. It pulls downward on the brow, resulting in wrinkle lines around the bridge of the nose as the muscles come together and have nowhere else to go. The relationship between this muscle and the orbicularis oris (the mouth) is important, as they are connected through other muscles. Pulling the brows down will automatically lift the upper lip up. Try it yourself. The **procerus** also helps to pull the brows down and is one of the key muscles used to express anger. It originates at the lower part of the nasal bone, its fibers merging with the frontalis muscle.

Eyes

Next are the eyes and the ring-like sphincter muscle (a circular muscle which normally maintains constriction): the **orbicularis oculi**. This muscle is comprised of three parts: the **palpebral**, **orbital**, and **lacrimal**. The function of this muscle that is of interest to us is its ability to close the eyelid. It originates at the frontal and maxilla bones (upper jaw) and surrounds the orbit of the eye, as well as the temple and part of the cheek. In addition to closing the eyelids, the muscle pulls on the forehead, cheek, and temple when in action.

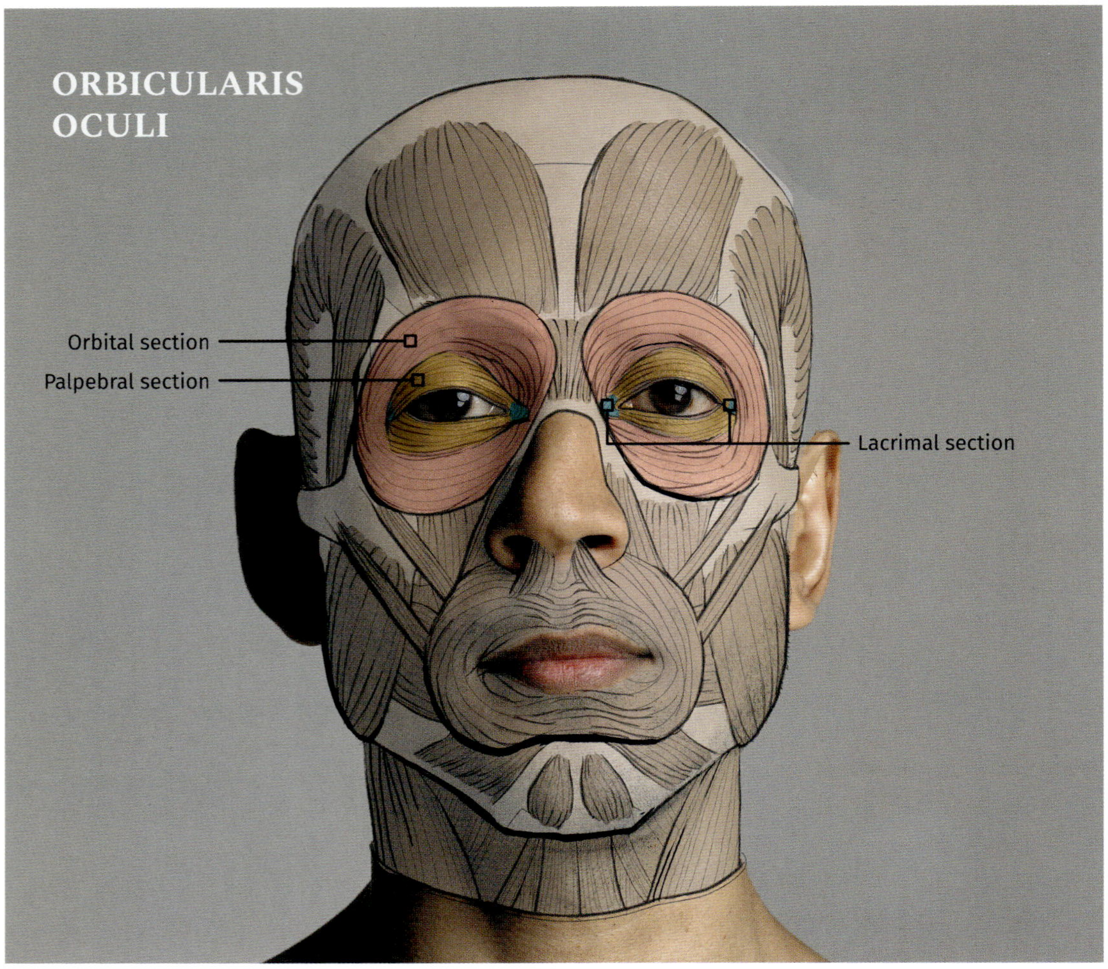

Mouth and lips

Moving downward, you come to the **orbicularis oris** muscle. Although this muscle is treated like a sphincter muscle, much like the orbicularis oculi, new studies reveal that it is actually comprised of four separate muscles that interlace to create the look of a sphincter.

The muscle can be divided up into two portions: the upper and lower. Those parts can then be divided into two more portions into the marginal (red lip) and peripheral (outer) portions. In total, there are four elongated muscular bands covering an area that reaches up to the base of the nose and down to the tip of the chin. The fibers of the muscle originate from the surrounding muscles, as shown in the images to the right, and the corners of the lips, called **nodes**, and insert into the mucous membrane of the lips.

The orbicularis oris plays a huge role in the expressions created by the mouth. There are four main types of movement that are created with this muscle:

- The pressing together of the lips
- The tightening and thinning of the lips
- Being able to roll the lips inward and beneath the teeth
- Thrusting the lips forward

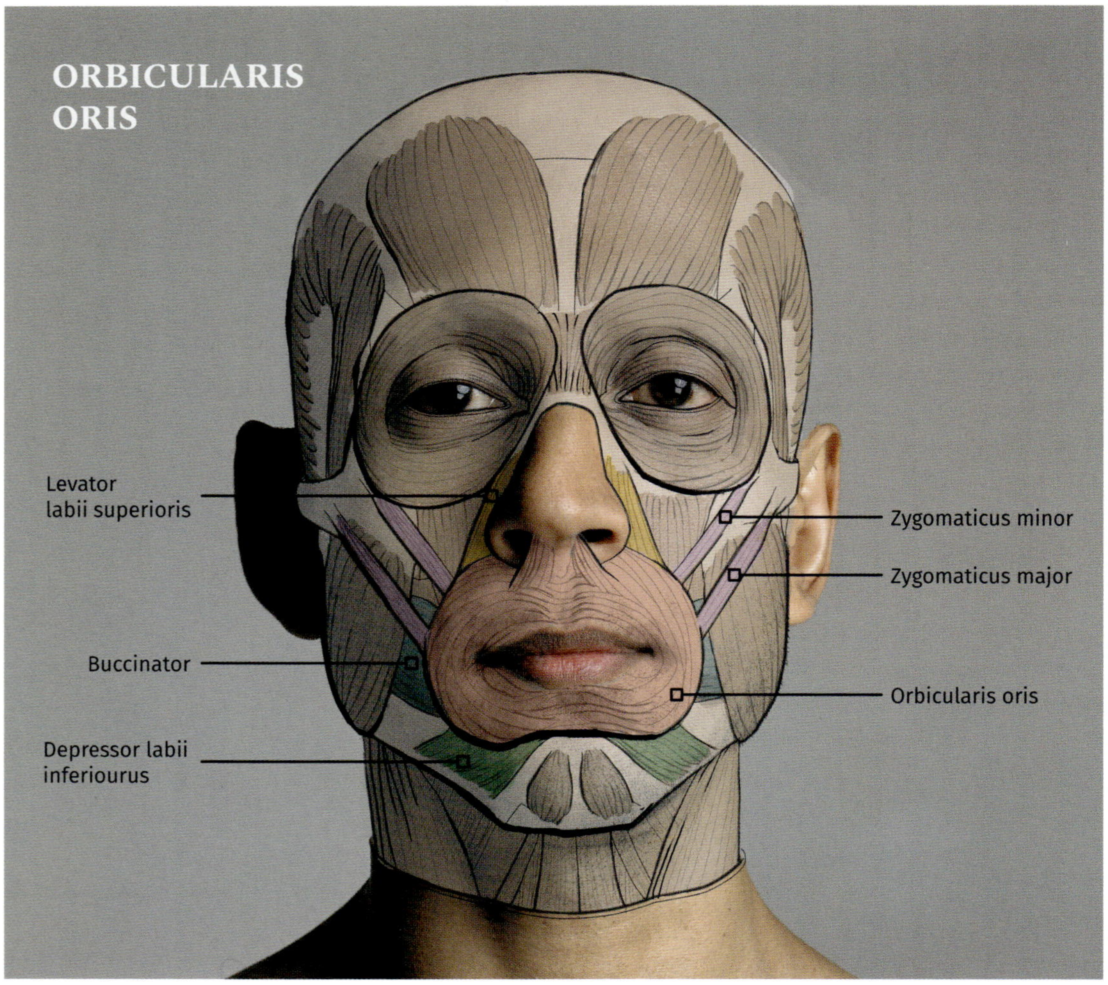

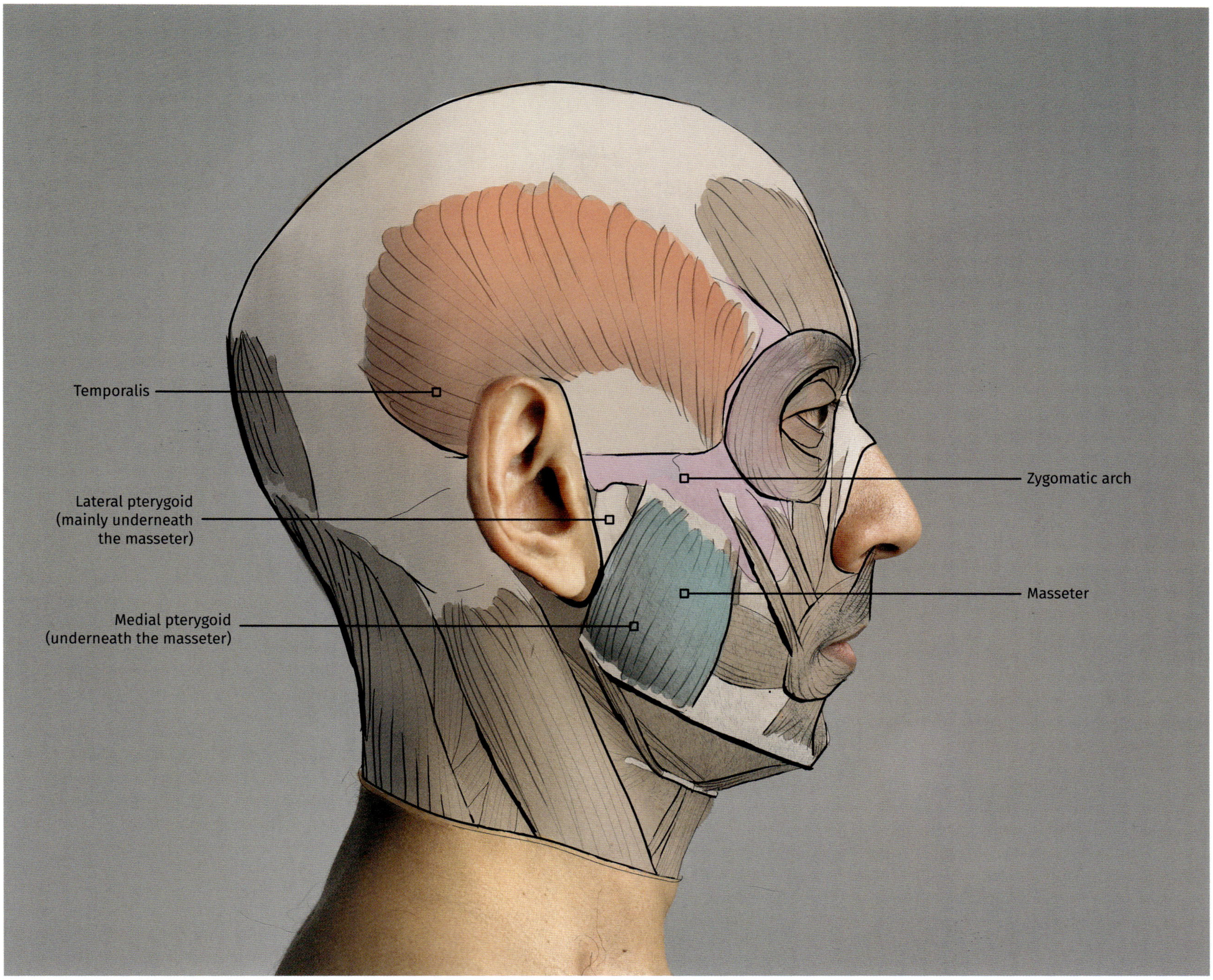

There are also the muscles of mastication: the **masseter**, the **temporalis**, and the **medial** and **lateral pterygoid**. These muscles provide movement to the **mandible** (jawbone), as well as being the core muscles responsible for chewing and clenching the jaw. The pterygoid muscles provide the side-to-side movement of the jaw and the lateral pterygoid is the only muscle out of the four that helps in the lowering of the jaw.

The two of most interest when drawing the human form are the temporalis and the masseter, which create the majority of the surface change (the lateral and medial pterygoids sit deeper, away from the surface). The **temporalis** covers the temporal bone, originating at the temporal fascia, and travels through the **zygomatic arch** (commonly referred to as the cheekbone), inserting into the coronoid process of the mandible. Place your fingers against your temple and you should feel the temporalis in action when you clench your jaw or chew your food. The **masseter** is a major muscle in the aid of chewing and, again, you can feel this muscle with your fingers pressed against the side of your jaw. This muscle originates at the zygomatic process (a triangular process projecting from the lower part of the zygomatic arch) of the maxilla (upper jaw) and inserts into the mandible. The temporalis and masseter, along with the medial pterygoid, aid in closing the jaw, and the digastic, geniohyoid, and mylohyoid (muscles of the neck) help in lowering the jaw.

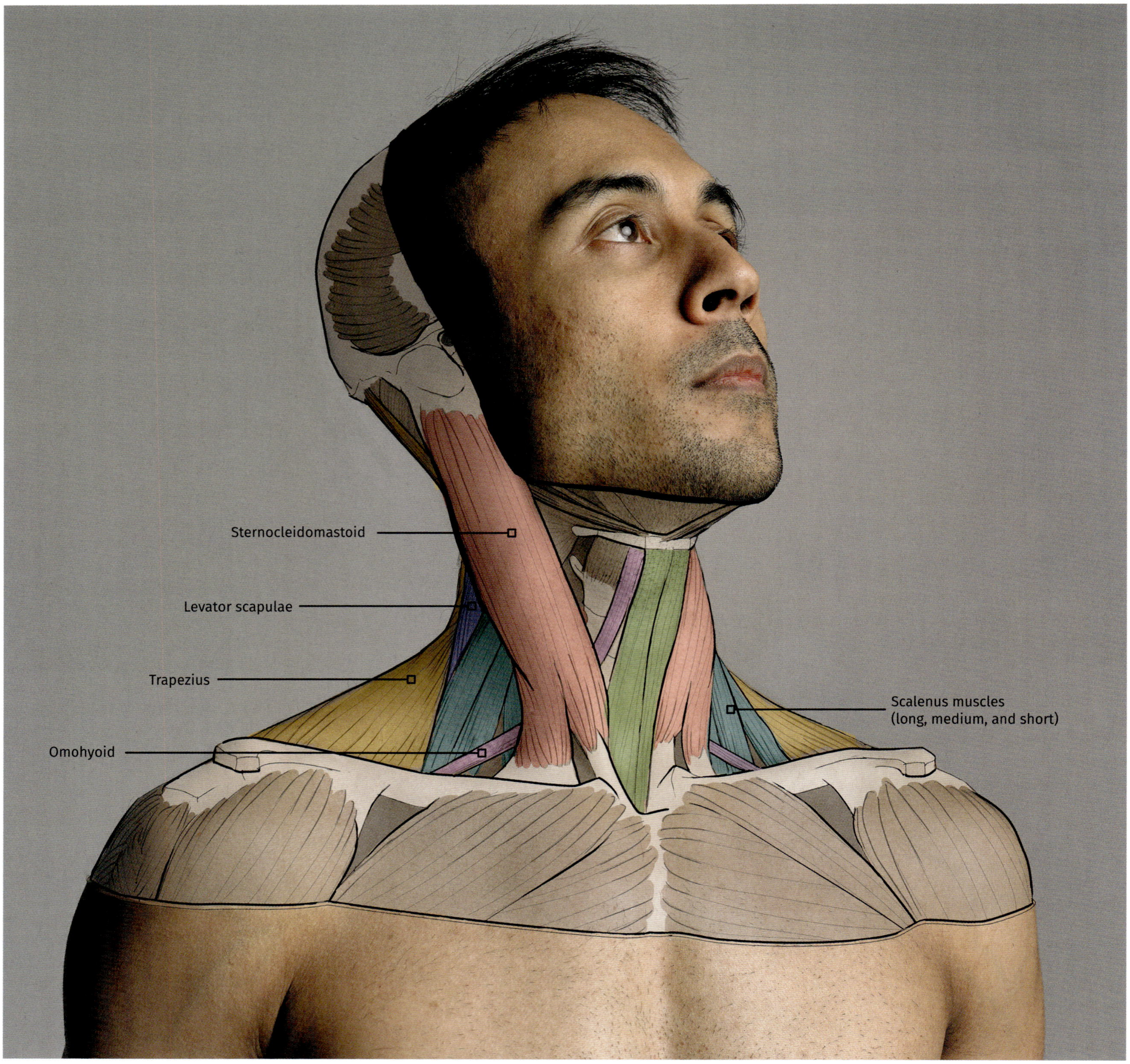

Neck

Moving on to the neck, there is a major muscle that sits on the lateral side and creates very evident surface change: the **sternocleidomastoid**. This muscle gets its name from its two origin points (the sternum and the clavicle) and its insertion point: the mastoid process (a pyramidal bony projection from the posterior section of the temporal bone). The sternal head (medial) attaches to the superior anterior surface of the manubrium of the sternum, and the clavicular head (lateral) attaches to the superior anterior third of the clavicle. This muscle is responsible for tilting and turning the neck from side to side and pulling the head forward.

The **platysma** is a broad, thin sheet of striated muscle that originates from the fascia of the deltoid (see page 60) and the pectoralis (see page 54) and inserts into the mandible and the lower face. During tension, this superficial muscle lifts the neck outward, producing wrinkling on the surface as well as lowering the jaw slightly. The platysma is a key muscle for expressing sadness, horror, and fright, as it also pulls the corners of the mouth down.

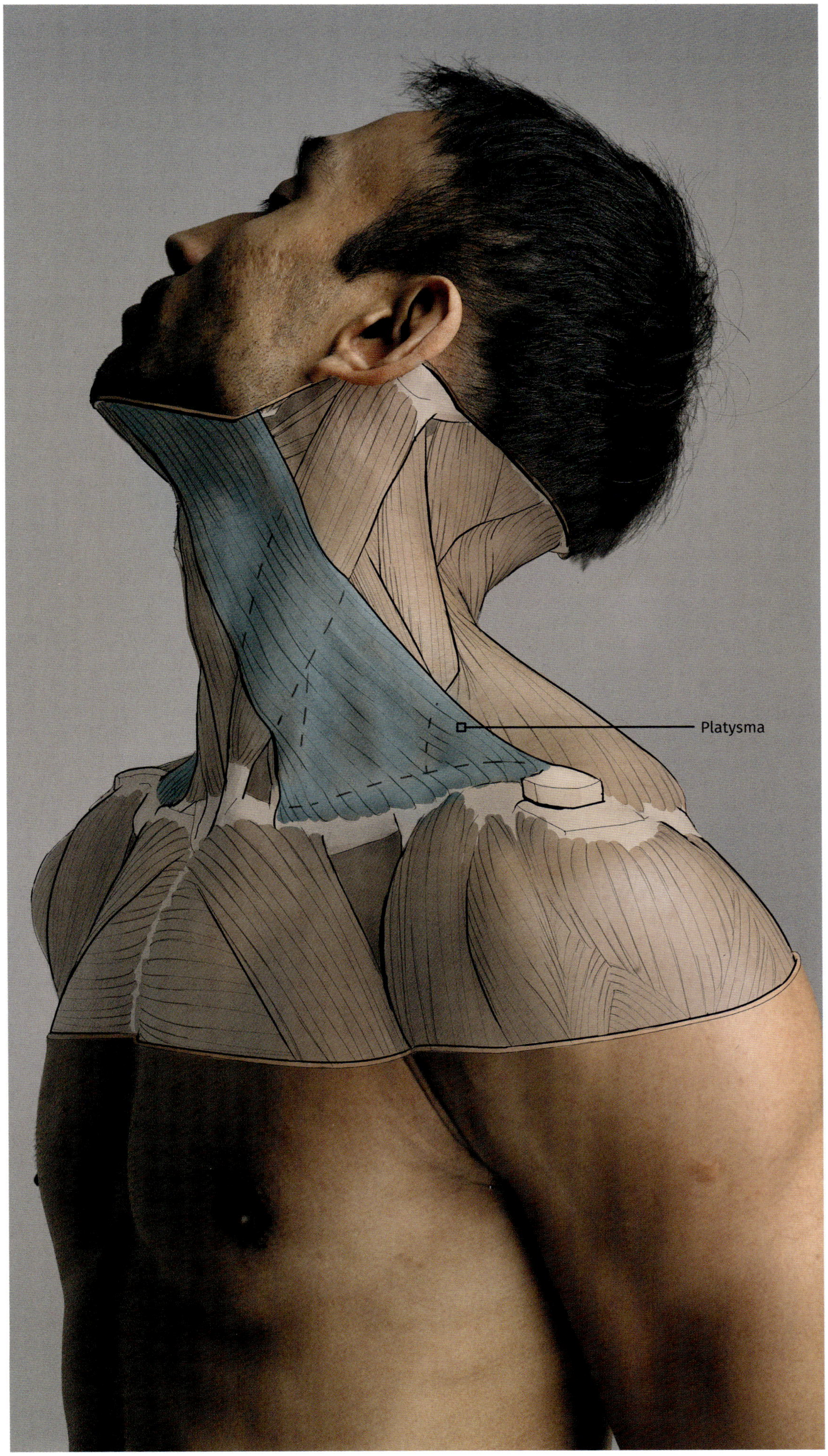

Muscles of the trunk

The **trunk** houses the muscles that move the vertebral column and naturally affects, and is affected by, the movement of the upper and lower extremities. The muscles of interest here will be the pectoralis major, latissimus dorsi, trapezius, teres major, serratus anterior, external obliques, and the rectus abdominis.

Pectorals

Starting with the **pectorals** (the chest region), there are two muscles here: the pectoralis major and pectoralis minor.

The **pectoralis major** creates the majority of surface change around the area and is comprised of three distinct sections originating at the sternum, the clavicle, and the abdominals, each of which insert into different points of the humerus bone.

The **pectoralis minor** is a thin muscle that sits behind the major, originating at ribs three, four, and five, and inserting into the coracoid process (a small hook-like structure on the anterior superior portion of the scapula). Though it is not visible, it can have an effect by creating some extra volume underneath the major muscle, depending on the articulation of the humerus.

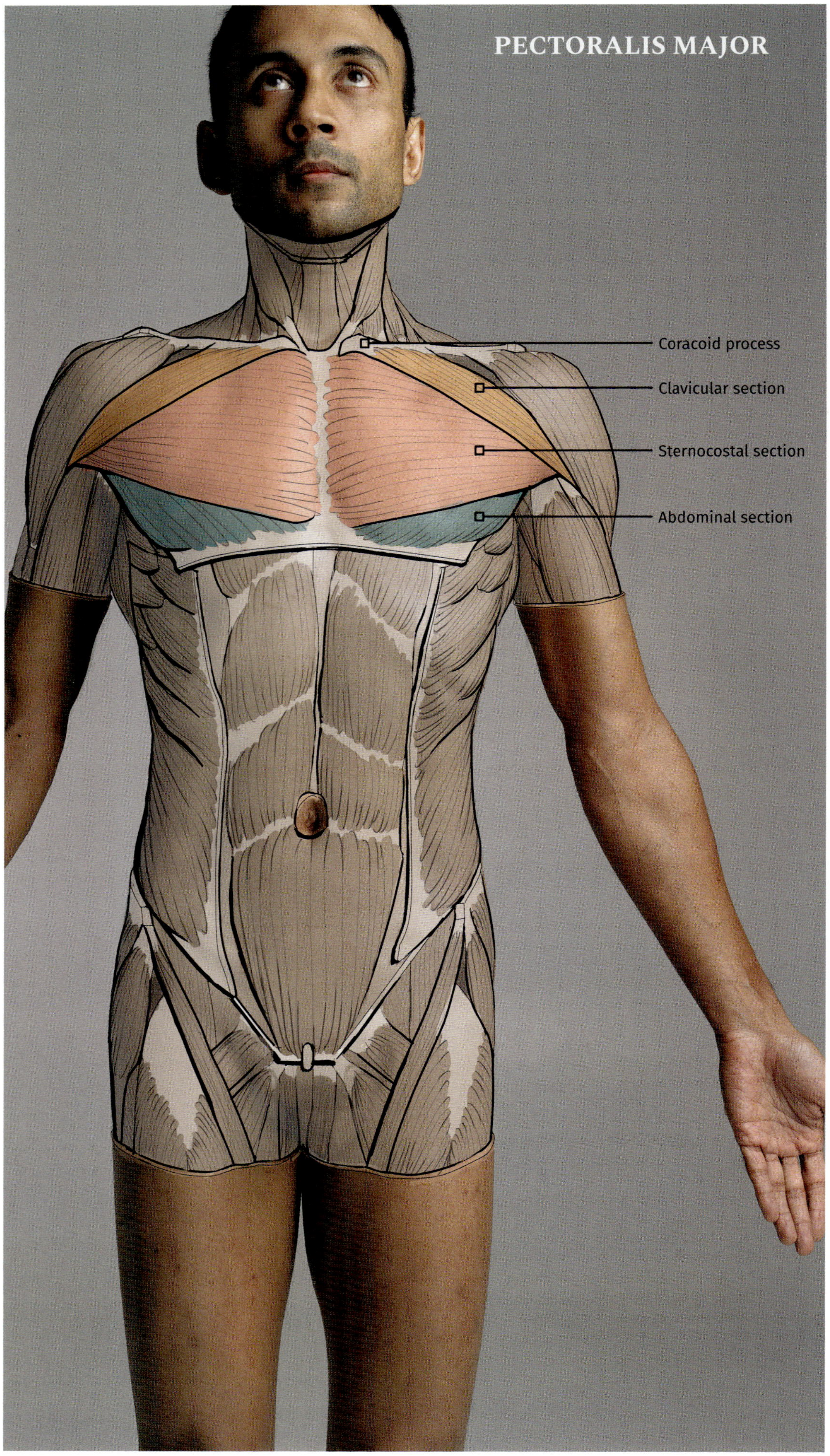

The **clavicular section** originates at the anterior medial half of the clavicle and inserts into the crest of the greater tubercle of the humerus bone.

The **sternal section** originates along the length of the sternum (excluding the xiphoid process, the cartilaginous section at the lower end of the sternum) and inserts slightly above the insertion of the clavicular section of the humerus.

The **abdominal section** originates at the base of the fifth rib and the aponeurosis (flat tendinous tissue which runs down the center of the abdomen, starting at the bottom of the ribs and ending at the pubis) of the external oblique, and inserts above the sternal insertion of the humerus.

As the fibers of the three sections of the pectoralis major overlap, they create the creasing and dimples under the arm. This muscle combined connects the arm to the torso and is responsible for four types of movement:

- The clavicular section contributes to flexion.
- The sternal section contributes to extension.
- Both sections contribute to adduction and medial rotation.

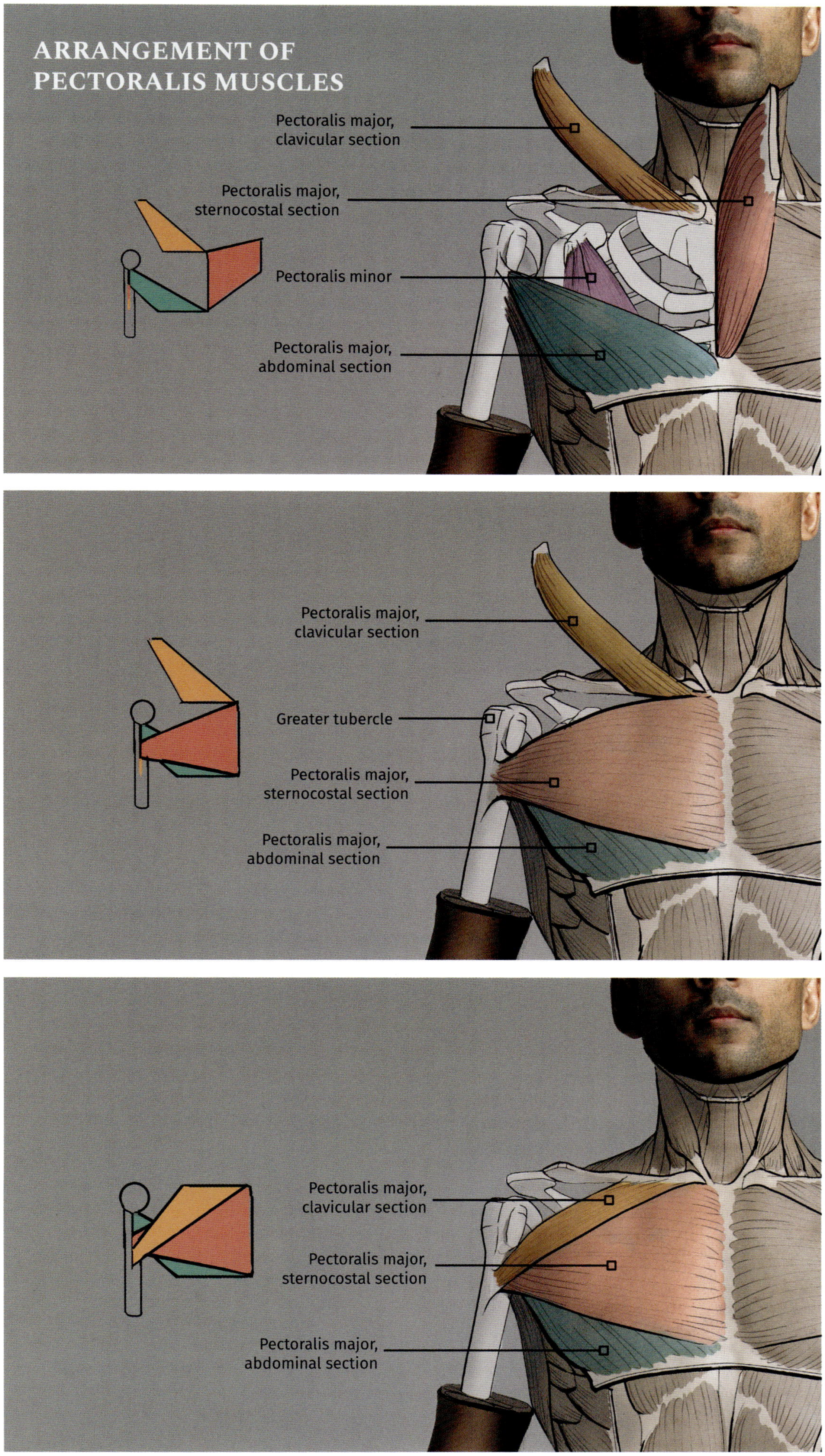

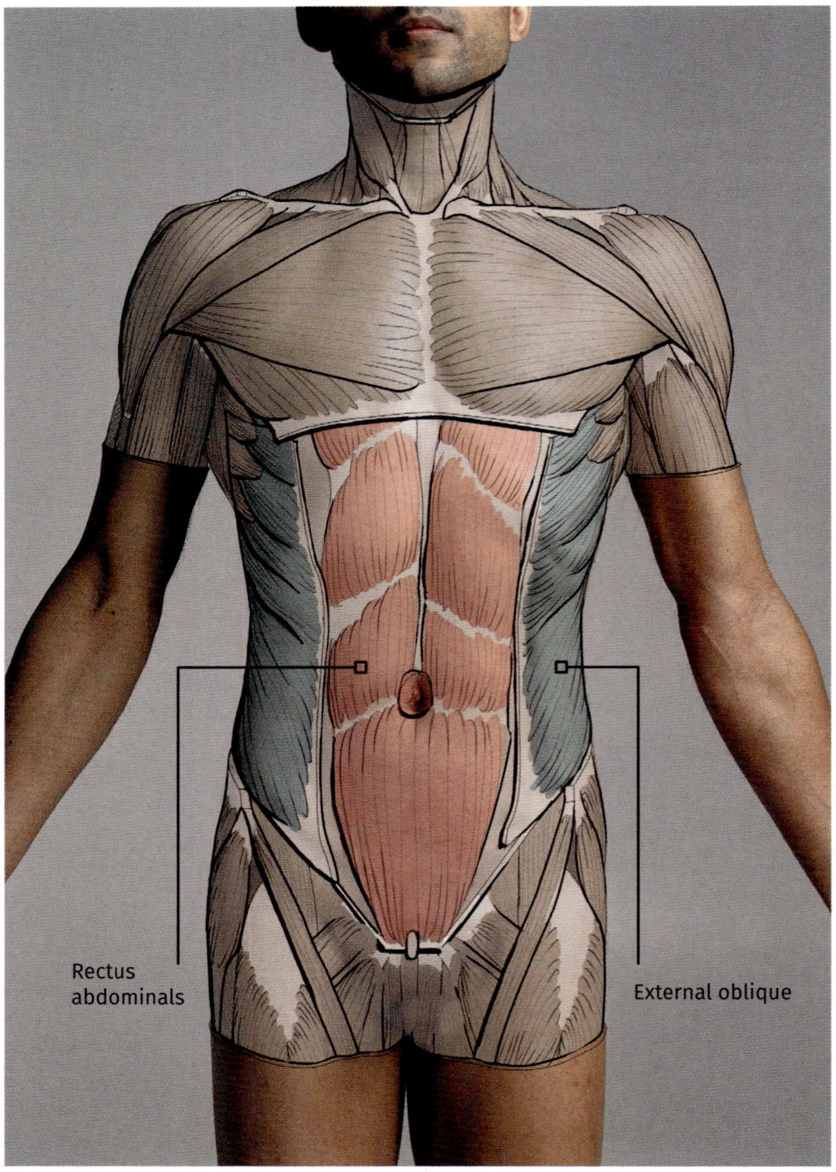

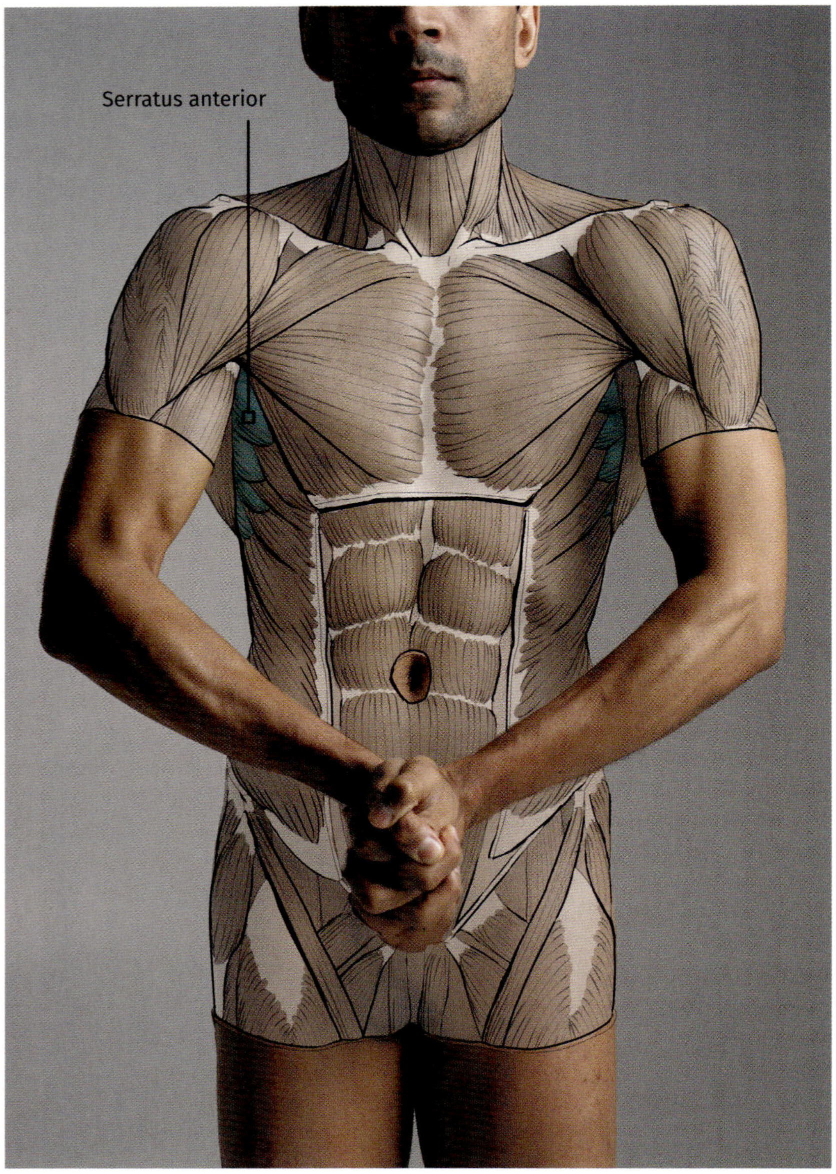

Rectus abdominals

Staying with the anterior portion of the torso, there are the rectus abdominals and the external obliques.

The **rectus abdominals** form a long vertical muscle that runs parallel to the anterior wall of the abdomen. They have two sides that are not truly symmetrical, are separated in the middle through connective tissue called linea alba, and are covered by aponeurosis called the rectus sheath. The muscle originates at the pubic symphysis, the pubic crest, and the pubic tubercle, and inserts into the anterior of the xiphoid process and the costal cartilage of the fifth, sixth, and seventh ribs. The muscle is responsible for the flexion of the lumbar spine, narrowing the distance between the rib cage and the pelvis, and adding stability to the trunk.

External obliques

Sitting on the anterior and lateral side of the abdomen, either side of the rectus abdominals, are the **external obliques**. These broad and quadrilateral-like muscles originate at the underside of ribs five to twelve and interdigitate with the fibers of the serratus anterior. They run down at around a 45-degree angle and insert into the anterior portion of the iliac crest, the inguinal ligament, and the aponeurosis of the abdomen. The muscles are responsible for flexion of the spine, compressing the abdomen, rotating the torso, and lateral flexion (side to side).

Serratus anterior

The sausage-shaped digits of the **serratus anterior** originate from ribs two to nine (sometimes also the tenth rib), and insert into the bottom edge of the scapula and part of the medial border, creating surface change from under the scapula. From above, the muscle is covered by the pectoralis major, which ends around the line of the fifth rib, and from the posterior lateral side, the latissimus dorsi also covers the ninth digit. This leaves about three digits at ribs six, seven, and eight that are exposed. Depending on the articulation of the torso and the muscle-to-fat ratio of the subject, sometimes the ninth digit can be seen as the latissimus dorsi muscle is thinned out. The function of the serratus anterior is to pull the scapula toward the ribs, with the rhomboid muscle acting as the other half of the antagonistic pair, pulling the scapula back toward the vertebral column.

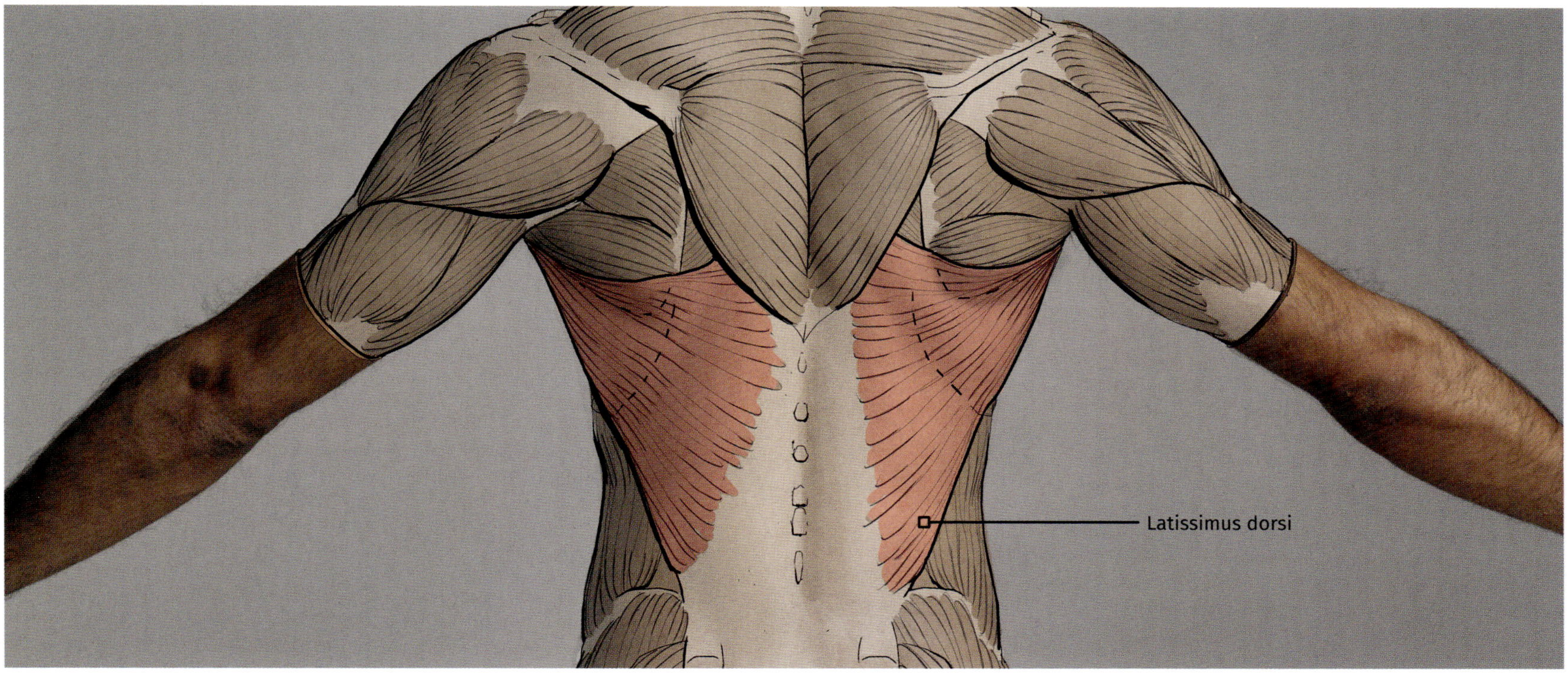

Latissimus dorsi

The **latissimus dorsi** is the largest muscle in the back. This muscle originates at the vertebral column (from T7 to T12 and L1 to L5), at the posterior side of the crest of ilium, and at the sacrum, as well as at the lowest three to four ribs, and is connected by the posterior aponeurosis (tendon-like material). It inserts into the intertubercular groove at the front of the humerus and is responsible for a lot of movement in the shoulder. The muscle performs the actions of pulling the arm downward, allowing for adduction and extension of the shoulder, internal rotation (turning the upper arm inward), and transverse extension (moving the upper arm away from the midline of the body with the elbows out). The pectoralis aids the latissimus dorsi by acting as a synergist muscle. (Synergist muscles assist agonist muscles, often acting to reduce excessive force generated by agonist muscles and are often referred to as neutralizers.)

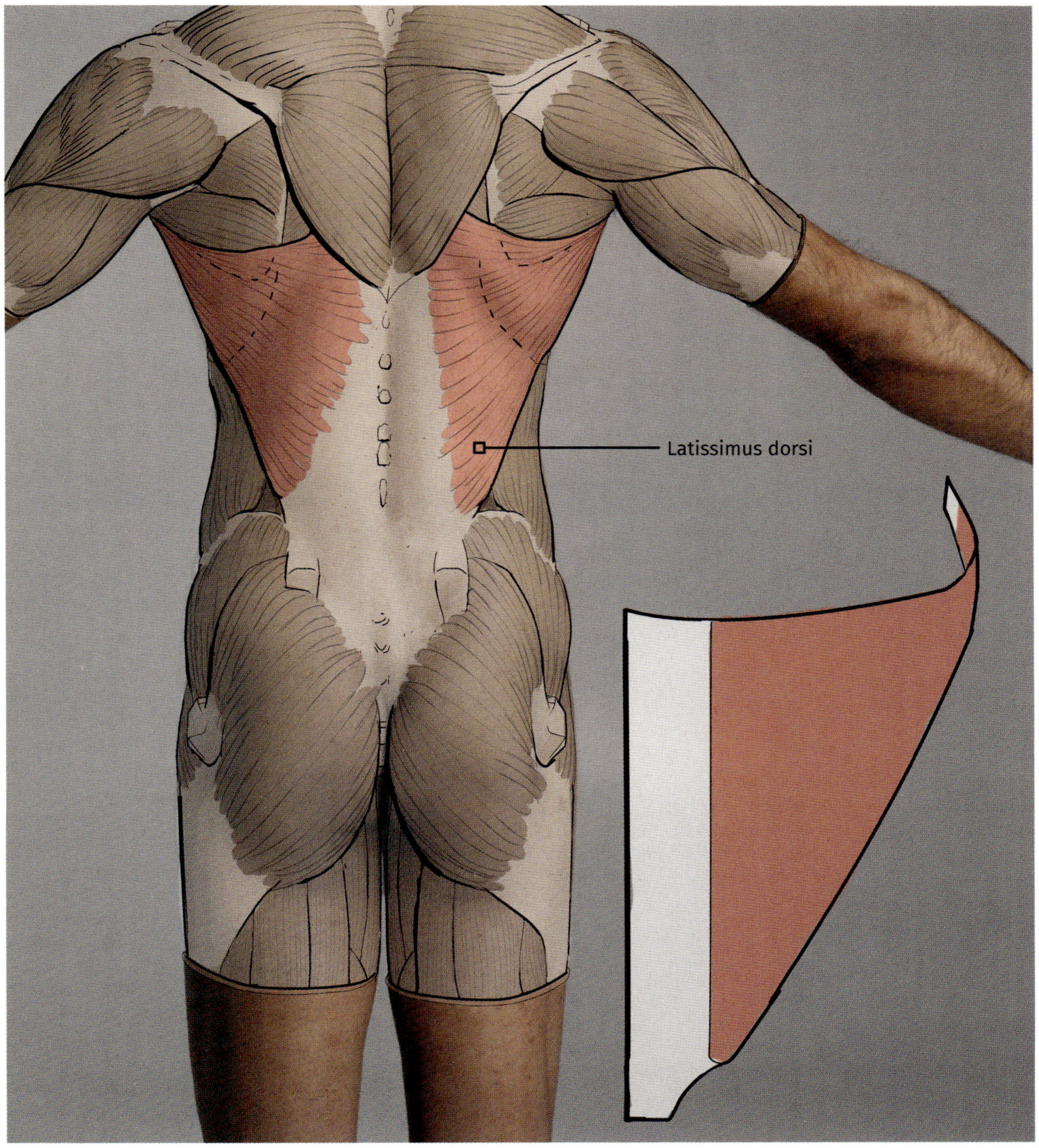

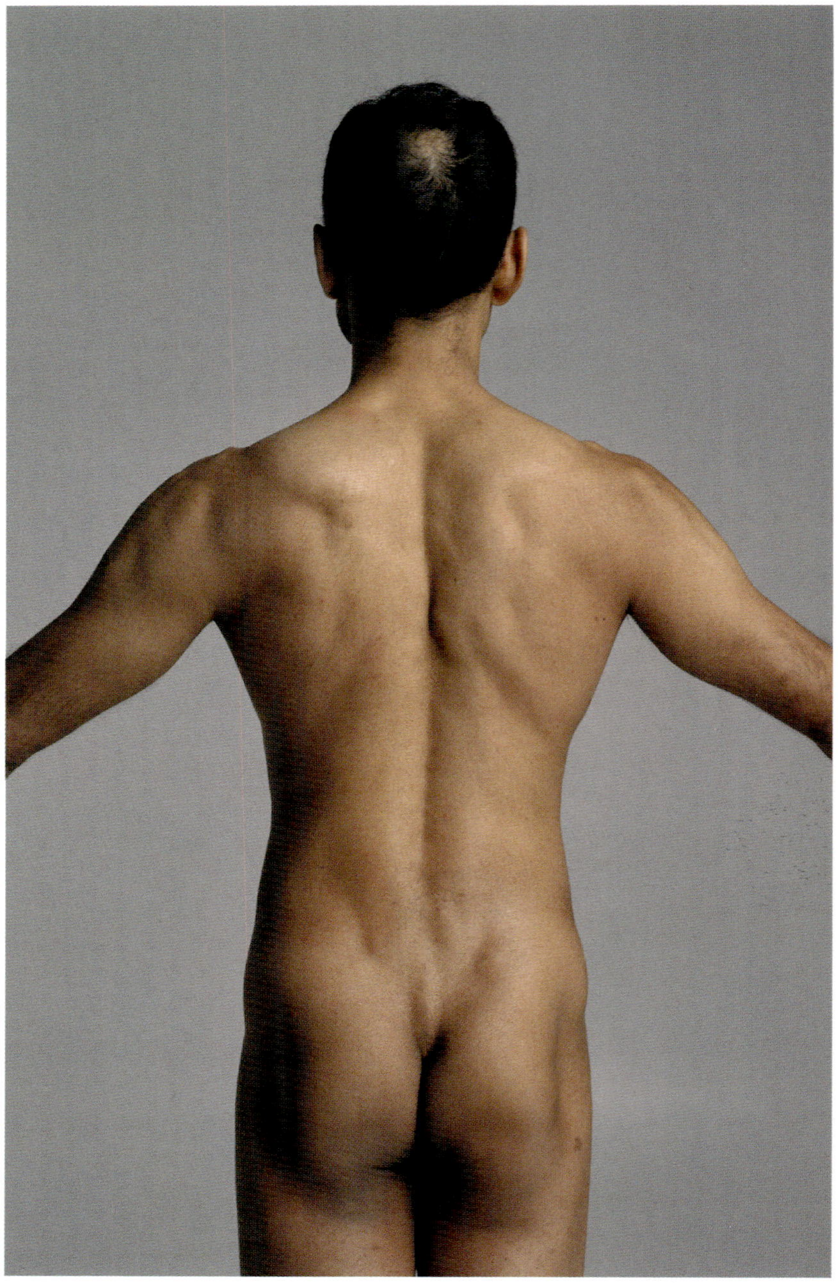

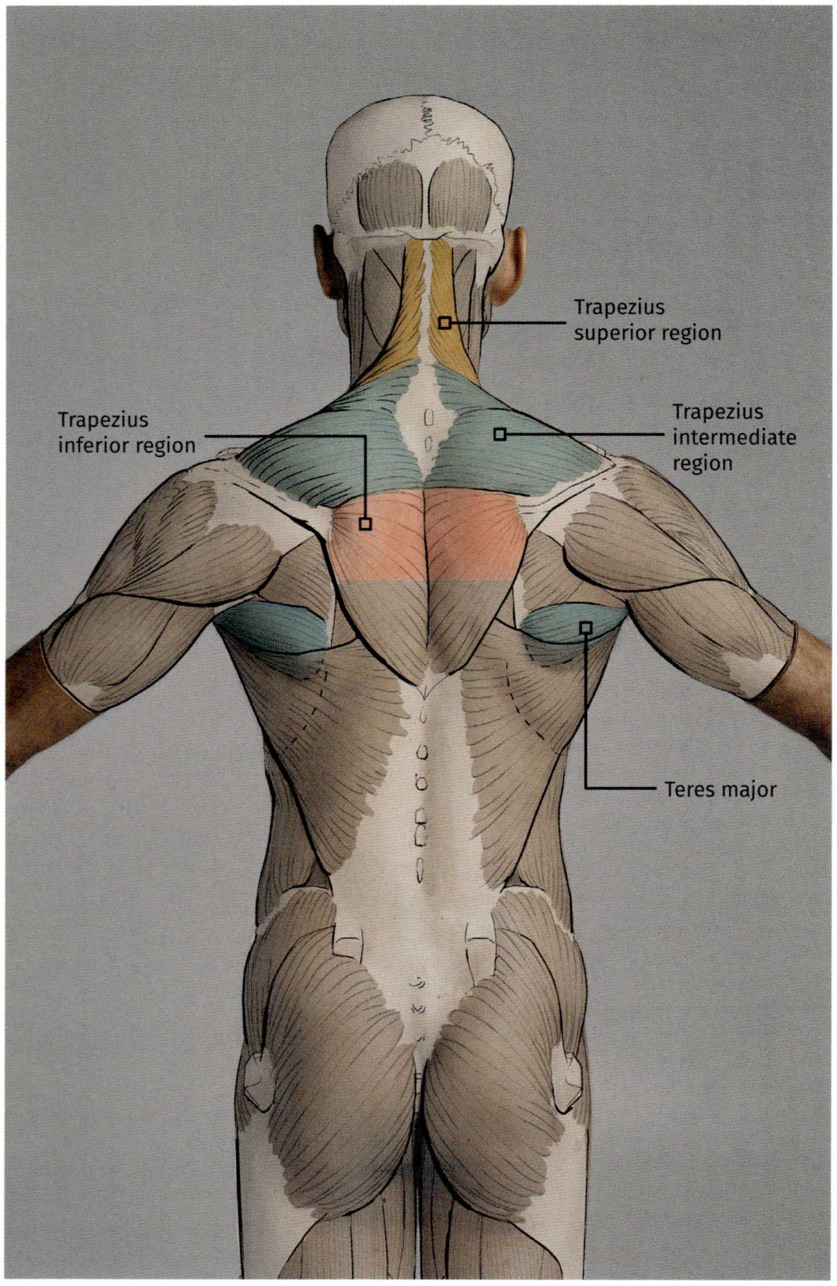

Teres major

The latissimus leads us nicely onto the next muscle: the **teres major**. This muscle works with the latissimus dorsi in internal rotation, and extension and adduction of the humerus. It originates from the inferior angle of the scapula and inserts into the intertubercular sulcus of the humerus. During articulation of the upper arm, it can be seen to affect the surface of the skin, especially in well-developed people.

Trapezius

Next is the diamond-shaped **trapezius**. This superficial muscle is composed of three sets of fibers: the superior, intermediate, and inferior regions.

The **superior (upper) region** originates at the occipital bone (the lower back of the skull) and inserts into the lateral third of the clavicle. Its functions are to elevate the scapula, allow for extension in the cervical region of the spine, and extension, lateral flexion (moving the head toward the shoulder), and rotation of the head.

The **intermediate fibers** originate at the spinous process of the seventh cervical vertebrae and between the first and third thoracic vertebrae. They insert into the acromion process and the superior border of the scapula. These fibers are responsible for elevation, adduction, and upward rotation of the scapula.

The final third set of fibers, the **inferior region**, originates at the spinous processes of the thoracic vertebrae, between T4 and T12, and inserts into the inferior medial border of the scapula and the triangular surface at the medial end of the spine of the scapula. The main function of this region is to allow adduction, depression, and upper rotation of the scapula.

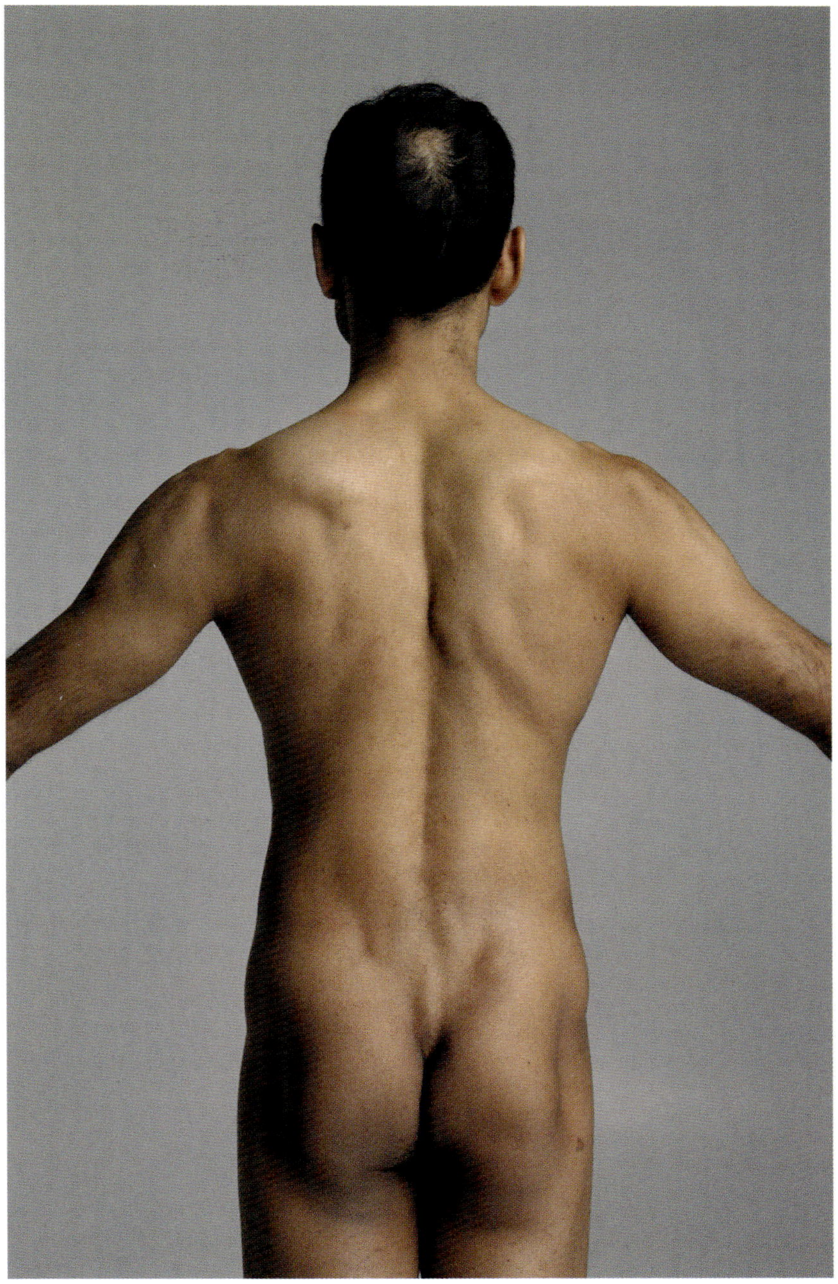

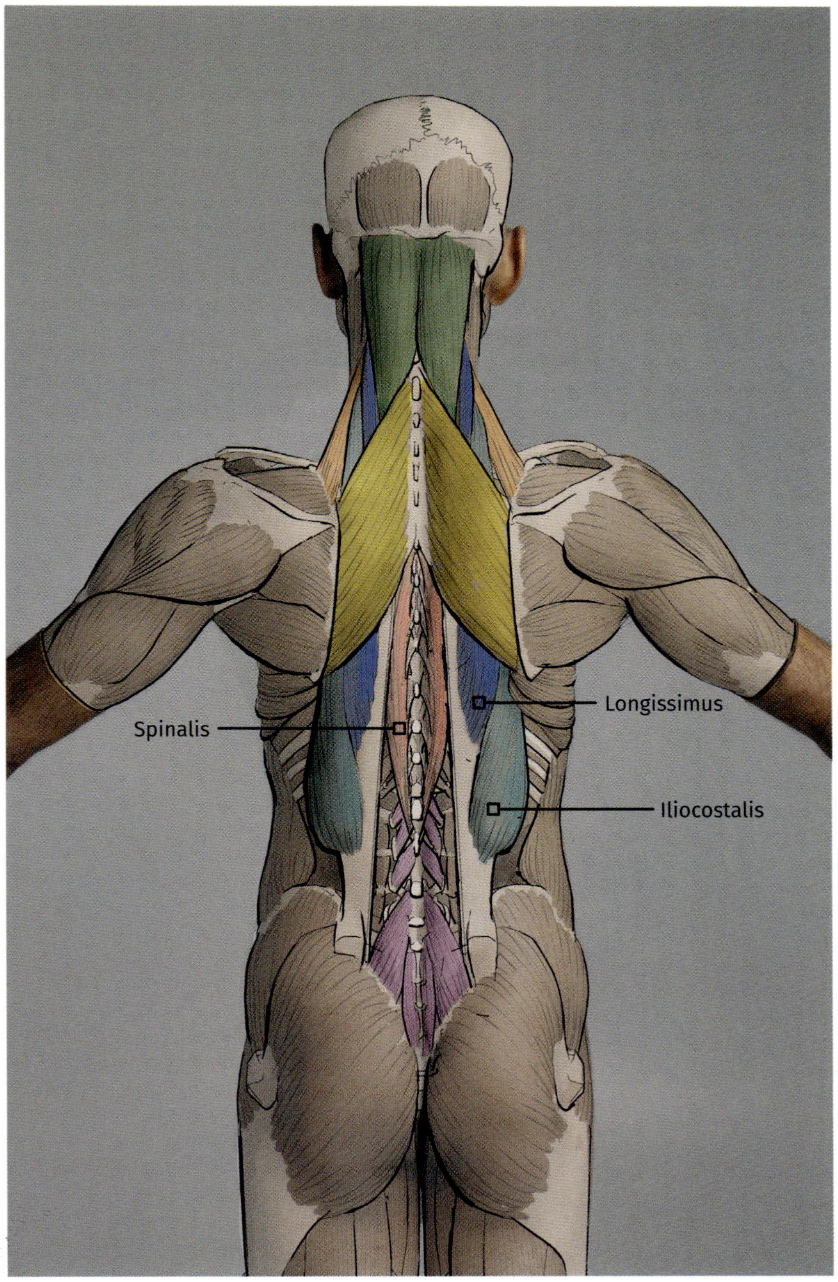

Erector spinae

The final set of trunk muscles to examine is the **erector spinae**. This is a set of three muscles: the iliocostalis, longissimus, and the spinalis. Each of the three can then be broken into a further three regions.

- The **iliocostalis** has the lumborum, thoracis, and cervicis.
- The **longissimus** has the thoracis, cervicis, and capitis.
- And the **spinalis** has the thoracis, cervicis, capitis.

Together the muscles extend the entire length of the vertebral column, originating at many points along the way, as well as originating from the ribs and sacrum. The insertion points also occur along the vertebral column, the ribs, the mastoid process (the portion of the temporal bone behind the ear), and the occipital bone. The function of the muscle is to allow extension, lateral flexion, and rotation of the spine and neck.

The muscle is most visible on the surface at the lumbar region. Here it creates two pillars of fleshy mass running up the along the spine.

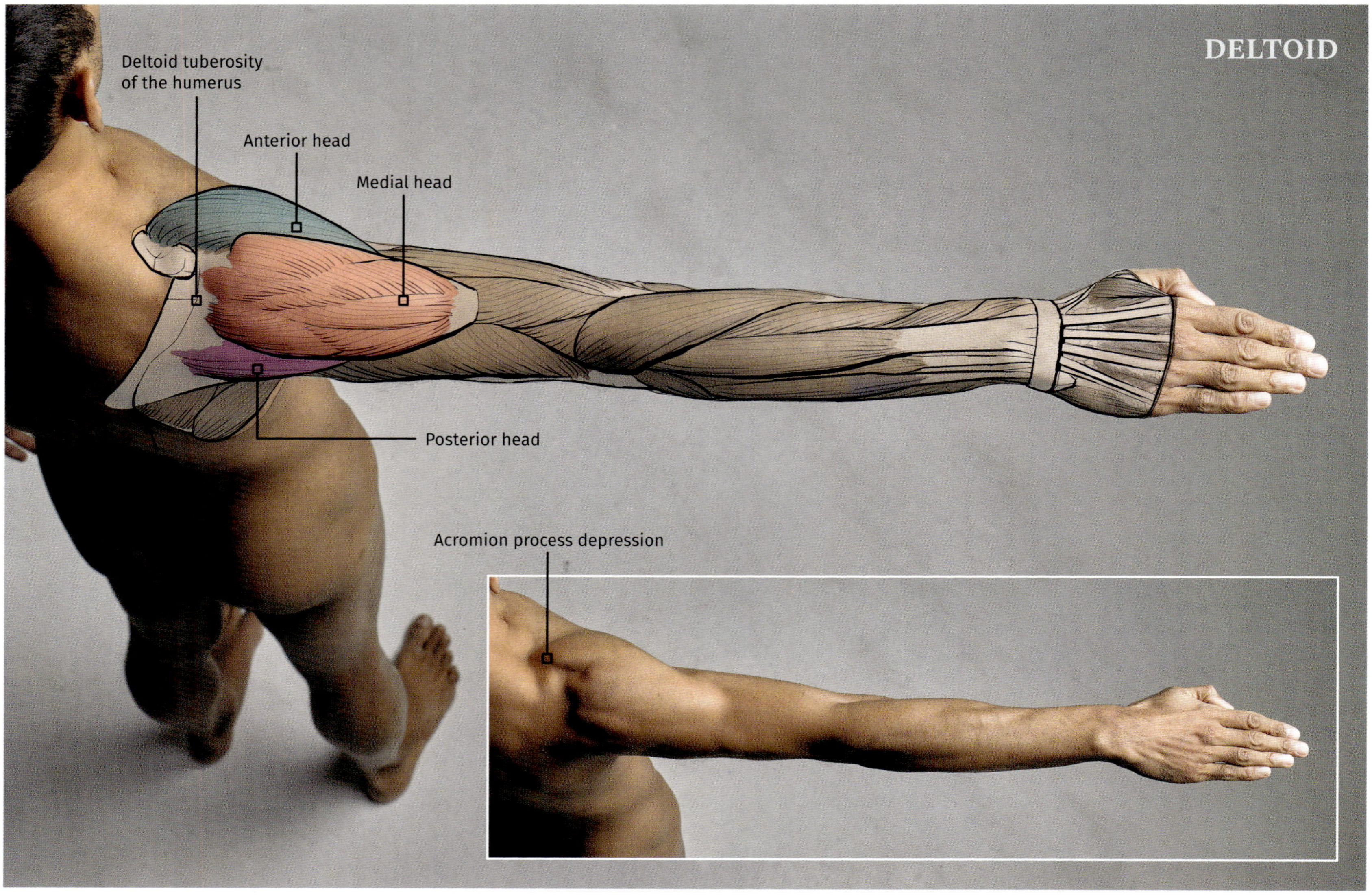

Muscles of the arms and hands

Deltoid

The **deltoid** is a three-headed muscle, each head being responsible for a different type of movement. All three heads – namely the anterior, lateral, and posterior – originate from different points between the clavicle and the scapula, but insert into a common point at the deltoid tuberosity of the humerus.

The **anterior head** originates at the anterior lateral third of the clavicle and is responsible for pulling the arm forward (flexion).

The **medial head** comes from the acromion process and creates the majority of the volume of the deltoid. Its main function is to pull the arm out to the side (abduction). As mentioned when looking at the shoulder girdle (see page 36), notice the depression on the acromion as the arm is raised.

The **posterior head** originates at the spine of the scapula through a larger amount of tendon and is responsible for pulling the arm backward (extension).

Biceps

The **biceps** muscle (biceps brachii) is a flexor muscle used to pull the lower arm up. As its name suggests, this is a two-headed muscle with both heads (a long head and a short head) originating at the coracoid process of the scapula. The long head goes through the intertubercular groove (between the lesser and greater tubercle) of the humerus and helps to stabilize the arm, while the shorter head circumnavigates around the lesser tubercle. The long head inserts into the radial tuberosity of the radius and the shorter head inserts into the fascia of the forearm around the elbow. By inserting into the fascia, it helps to strap down the flexor muscles of the forearm that originate at the medial epicondyle of the humerus. It also creates some surface change in the form of a small egg-shaped bulge.

Now to the behavior of the biceps and how it affects the surface of the skin. As its main insertion is at the radius, it is the pronation and supination of the forearm that gives it its shape. When the palm is down (prone), the muscle fibers are longer, causing the muscle bulge to appear flatter. With the palm up (supine), the muscle is compressed and creates the bulge that we associate with the biceps. The brachialis muscle is also slightly exposed on the lateral side of the arm when in the supine pose.

The **brachialis** muscle is the base muscle that the biceps sits on. It can be seen on the lateral side as mentioned, with its shape staying constant during pronation and supination. Its insertion point is around the lower third of the humerus and it inserts into the tuberosity of the ulna. Its function is to help flex the arm.

The **coracobrachialis** helps to stabilize the humerus in its socket. Its origin is the coracoid process and it inserts into the shaft of the humerus. This muscle is most visible when the arm is raised and can be seen tucking into the armpit.

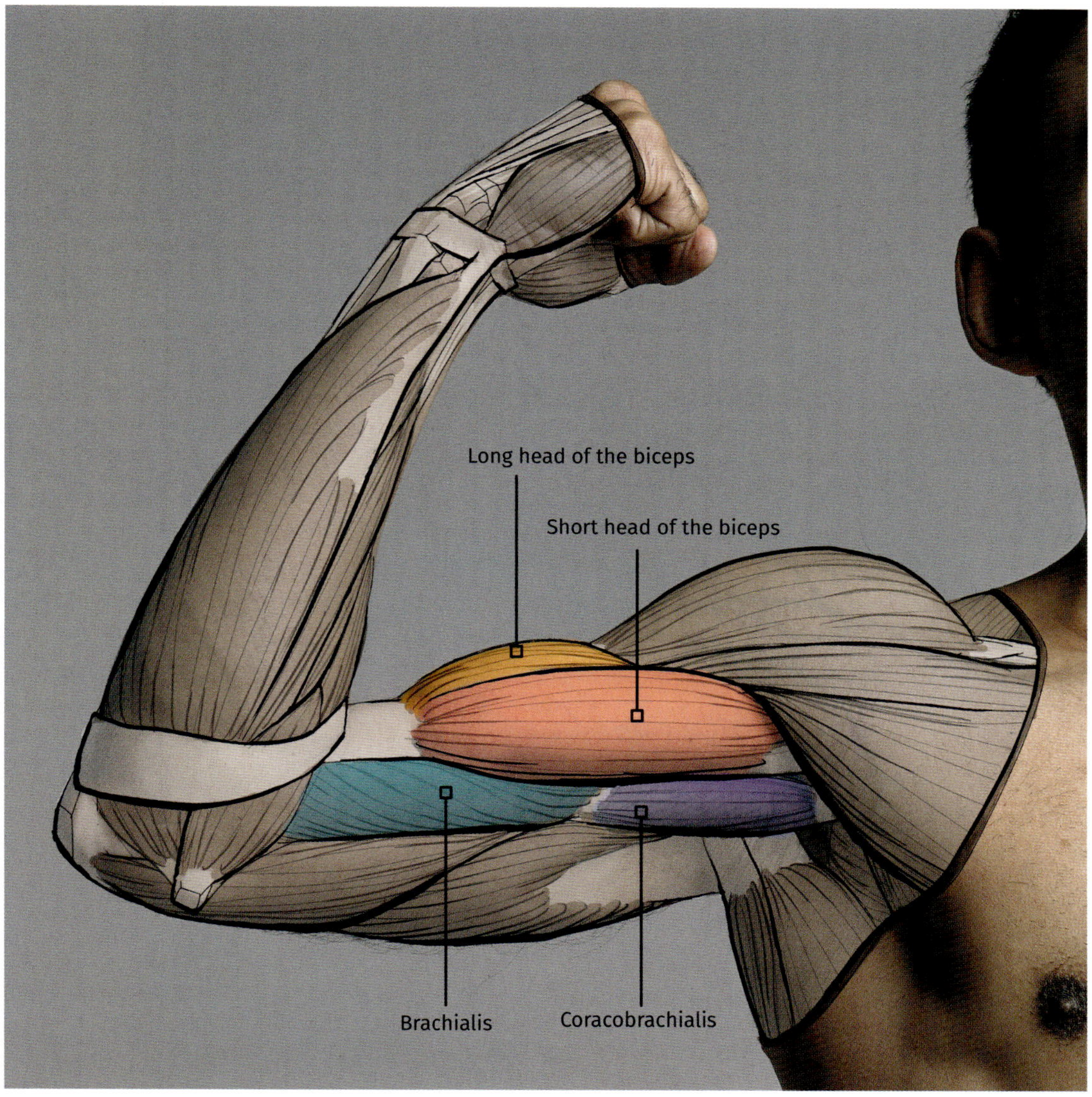

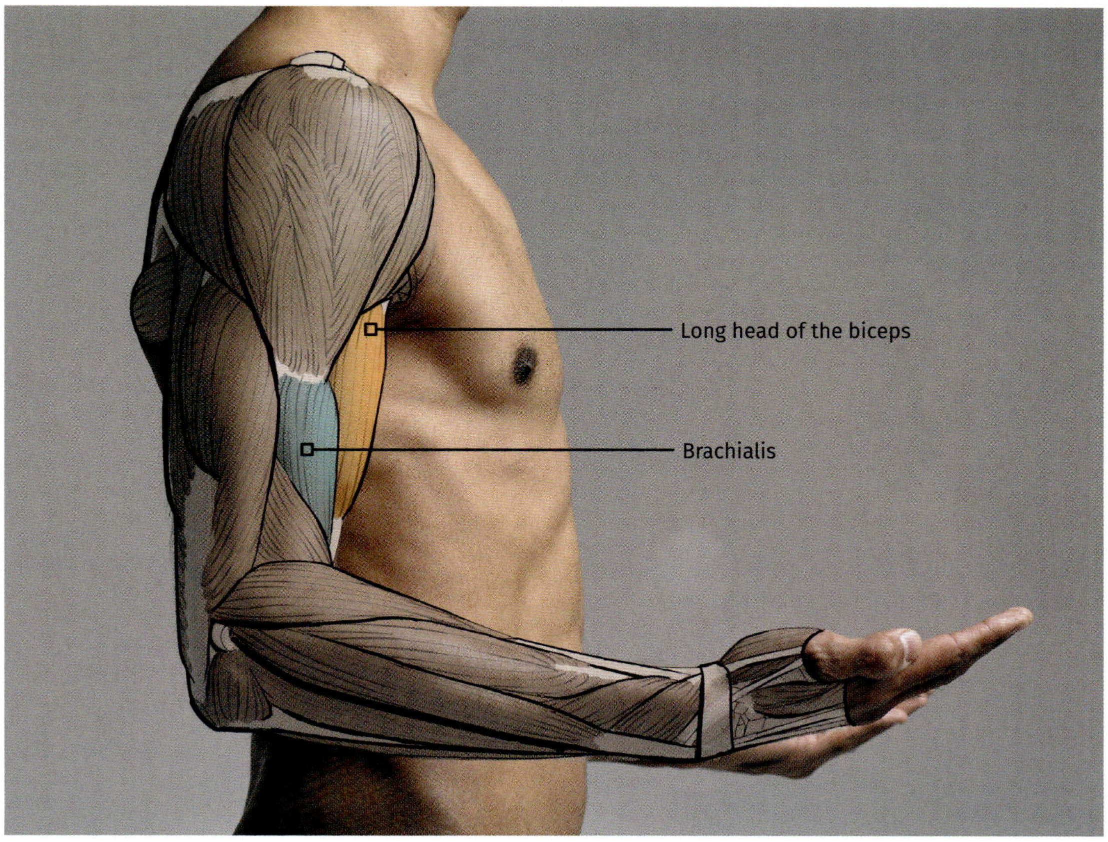

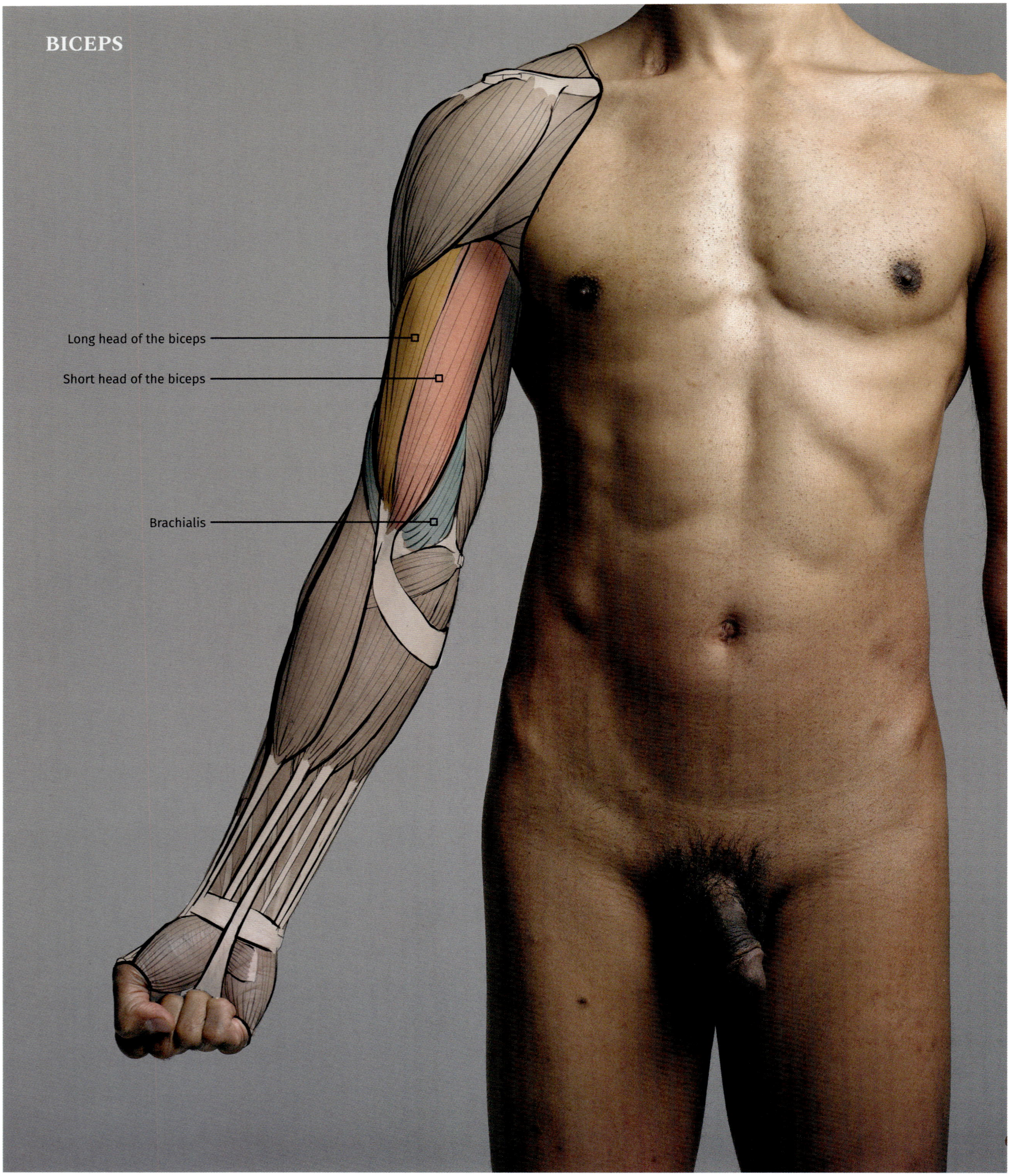
BICEPS
Long head of the biceps
Short head of the biceps
Brachialis

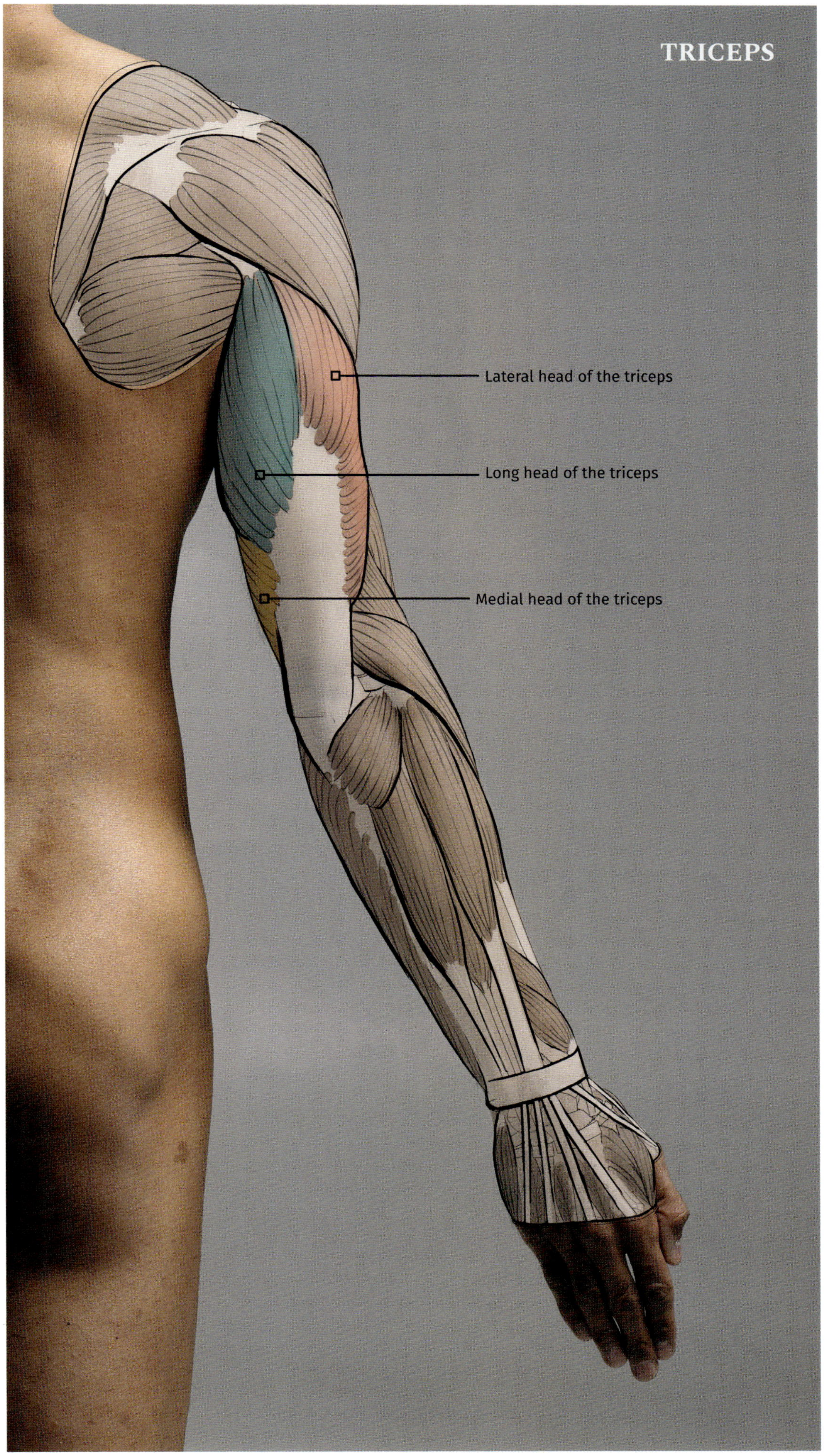

Triceps

The **triceps** muscle (triceps brachii) forms an antagonistic pair with the biceps. It is a three-headed muscle that pulls the forearm down. All three heads of the triceps (lateral, long, and medial) originate at different points, but come together at a common tendon that connects to the olecranon of the ulna, creating the distinct u-shape in the posterior of the arm. The **lateral head** originates on the upper third of the humerus, the **long head** from the inferior of the scapula, and the **medial head** from the lower third of the humerus. As well as extension of the elbow, the muscle aids the extension and adduction of the shoulder.

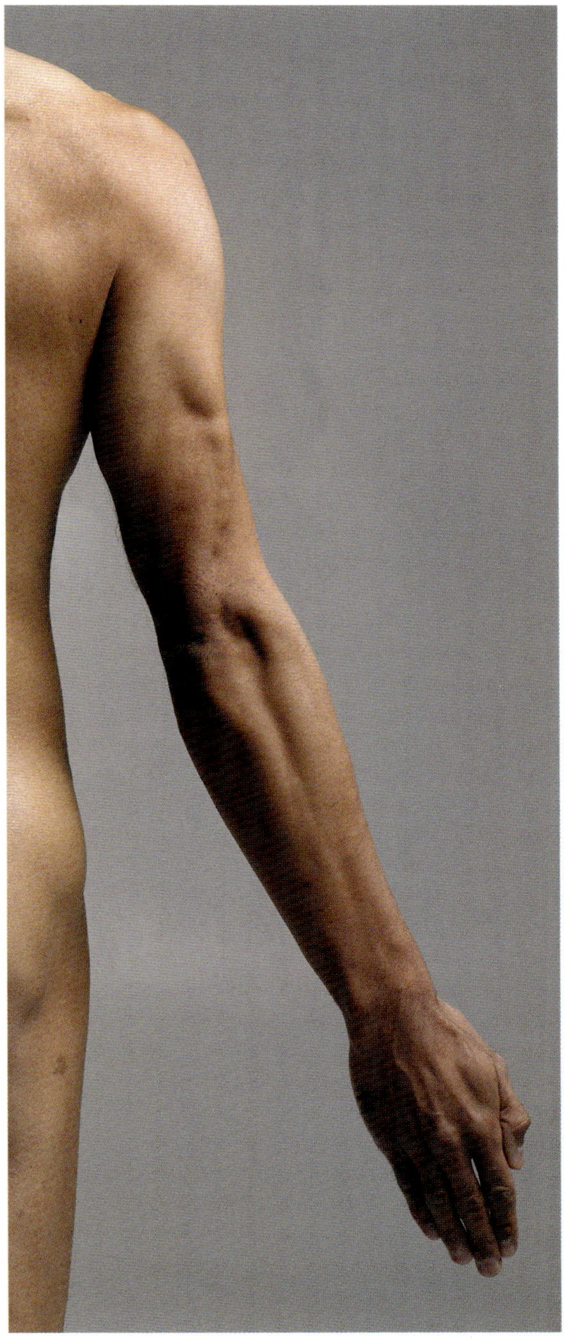

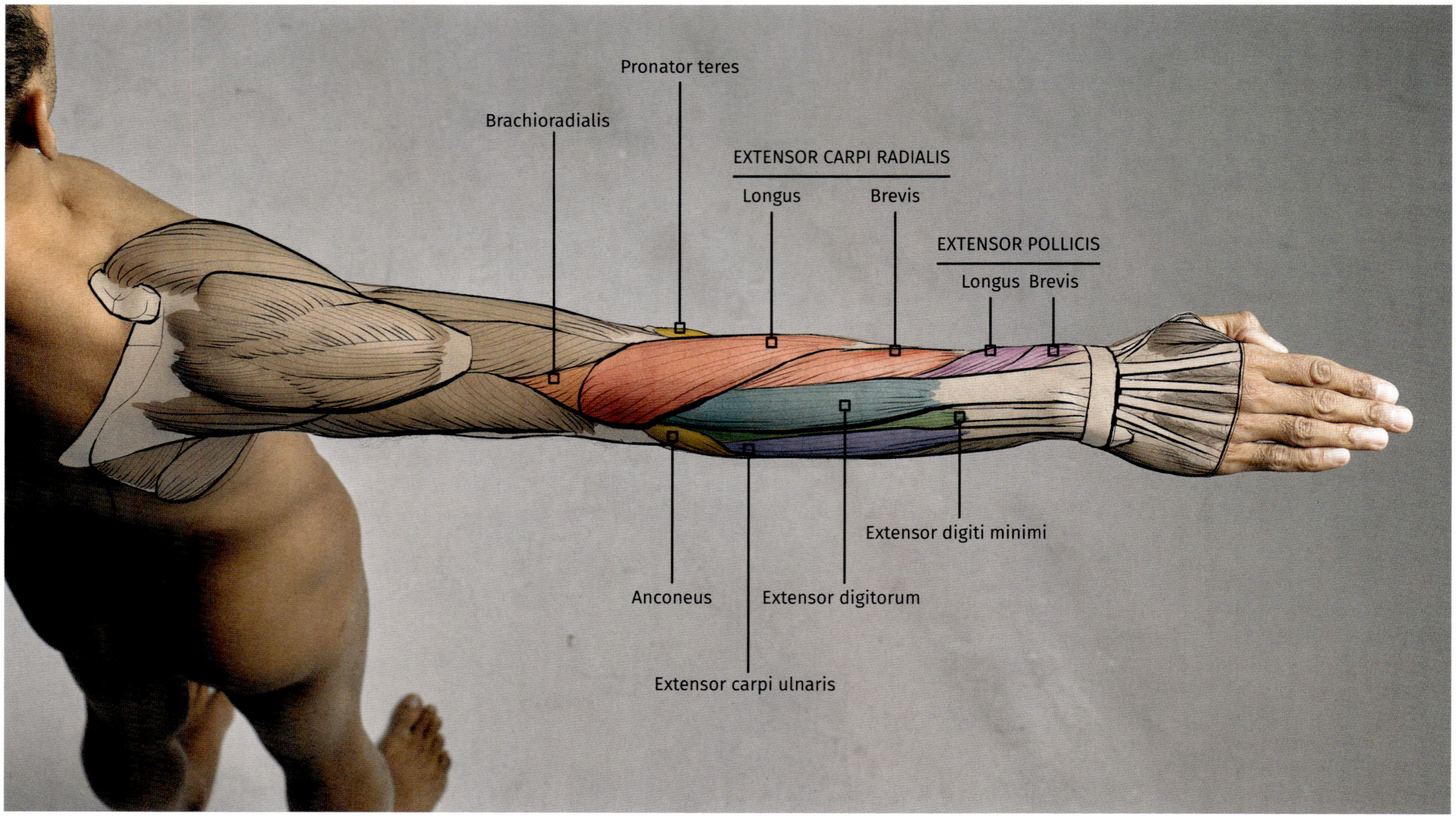

Forearms

The forearms are comprised of two sets of muscles of interest when drawing the body: the **flexor/pronator** and **extensor/supinator** groups. The two groups can be divided into two regions on the forearm: the **anterior region** (flexor) and the **posterior region** (extensor). There are over twenty muscles within the forearm and the twisting nature of the muscles serves to make the region even more complex, as does the fact that the two groups slightly spill into one another.

On the posterior side, the two main muscles that create surface change are the extensor carpi ulnaris and the extensor digitorum. Both originate from a common tendon from the lateral epicondyle of the humerus.

The **extensor carpi ulnaris** lies closest to the crest of the ulna and inserts into the base of the fifth metacarpal (pinky finger), while the **extensor digitorum**, which is slightly larger, divides and then inserts into the second, third, and fourth metacarpals. Between these two sits a smaller muscle, the **extensor digiti minimi**, which can be seen in a more muscular figure. The function of all three muscles is to extend the wrist and forearm.

On the posterior side there are three muscles that are of importance to surface change: the brachioradialis, the extensor carpi radialis longus, and the extensor carpi radialis brevis.

The **brachioradialis** originates at the distal end of the humerus and inserts into the styloid process of the radius. This muscle is mostly visible on the inside of the arm and is responsible for helping to flex the arm.

Between the brachioradialis and the extensor digitorum sits the **extensor carpi radialis longus** and the **extensor carpi radialis brevis**. The brevis is the shorter of the two, with its muscle belly laying in between the longus and the extensor digitorum. The longus creates a noticeable bulge just above the olecranon of the elbow. The two muscles help to extend and abduct the wrist.

On the anterior region of the forearm you will mainly see the tendons of the wrist. Depending on the individual, the number of visible tendons will vary. There are two tendons that can be very prominent: those of the **palmaris longus** and **flexor carpi radialis** muscles. Both originate from a common tendon of the medial epicondyle of the humerus, with the palmaris longus inserting into the palmar aponeurosis, and the flexor carpi radialis inserting into the base of the second and third metacarpal.

You may notice that the tendons on the dorsal side of the hand are most visible past the wrist. The reason for this is that there is a sheet covering them to strap them down and allow for safe passage between the forearm and the hand. This sheet of fascia is called the **extensor retinaculum**. On the anterior portion of the forearm, the extensor retinaculum keeps the flexor muscles in place, though the palmaris longus runs over it, thus making it easier to spot.

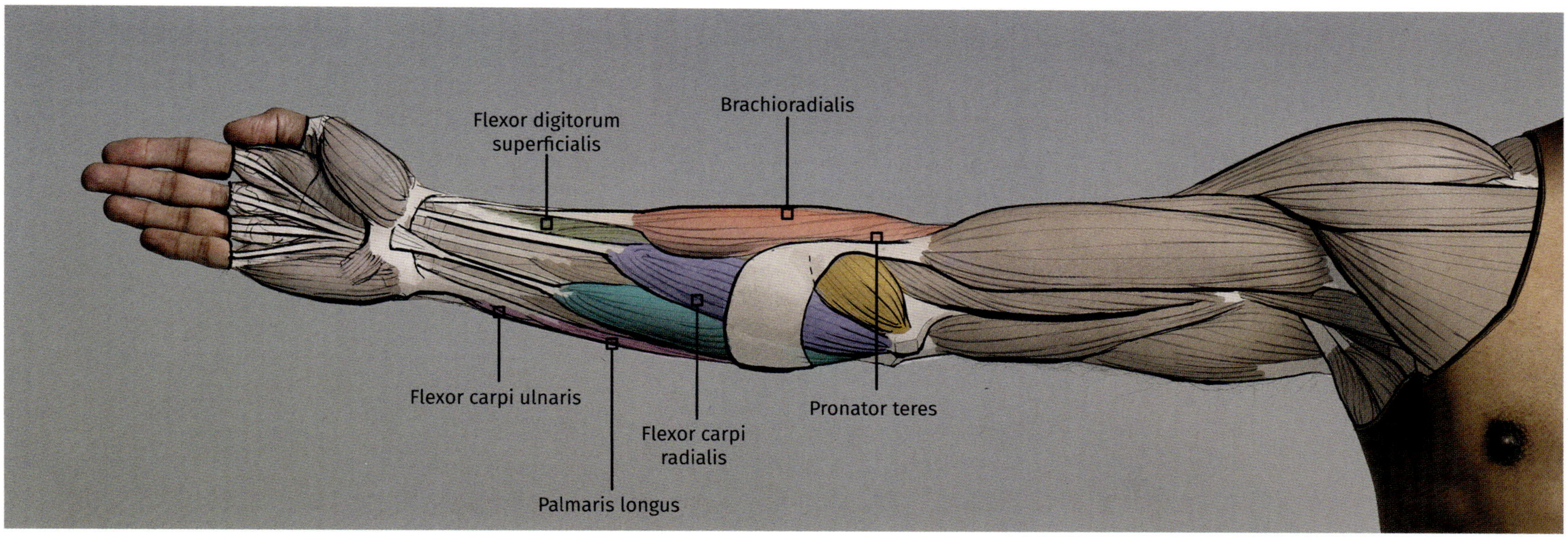

The hands

The hands consist mostly of fat, tendon, and bone, with the fat mainly on the palmar (anterior) side, and the tendon and bone on the back (posterior) of the hand.

The tendons that cross over the **extensor retinaculum** and **annular ligaments** (also known as the retinaculum, this is a strong band of fibers which functions to keep the extensor tendons in alignment), are the main source of surface change on the hand. You may be surprised to hear that there are no muscles within the fingers or the thumb for flexion and extension; it is the tendons that grab onto the side of the bones and are pulled by the muscles of the forearm. The tendons of the **extensor carpi ulnaris** and the **extensor digitorum** take care of the four fingers, while the thumb has the **abductor pollicis longus**, the **extensor pollicis brevis**, and the **extensor pollicis longus** inserting into its metacarpal and the first knuckle. The muscles of the thenar eminence are three short muscles at the base of the thumb (producing a bulge) which are responsible for the fine movements of the thumb.

Between each finger and the thumb sit the **interosseous** muscles. These sit between the metacarpal bones on the anterior and posterior side and are used to abduct and adduct the fingers. Between the thumb and the index finger, the first interosseous muscles create an egg-shaped mass through the adduction of the thumb.

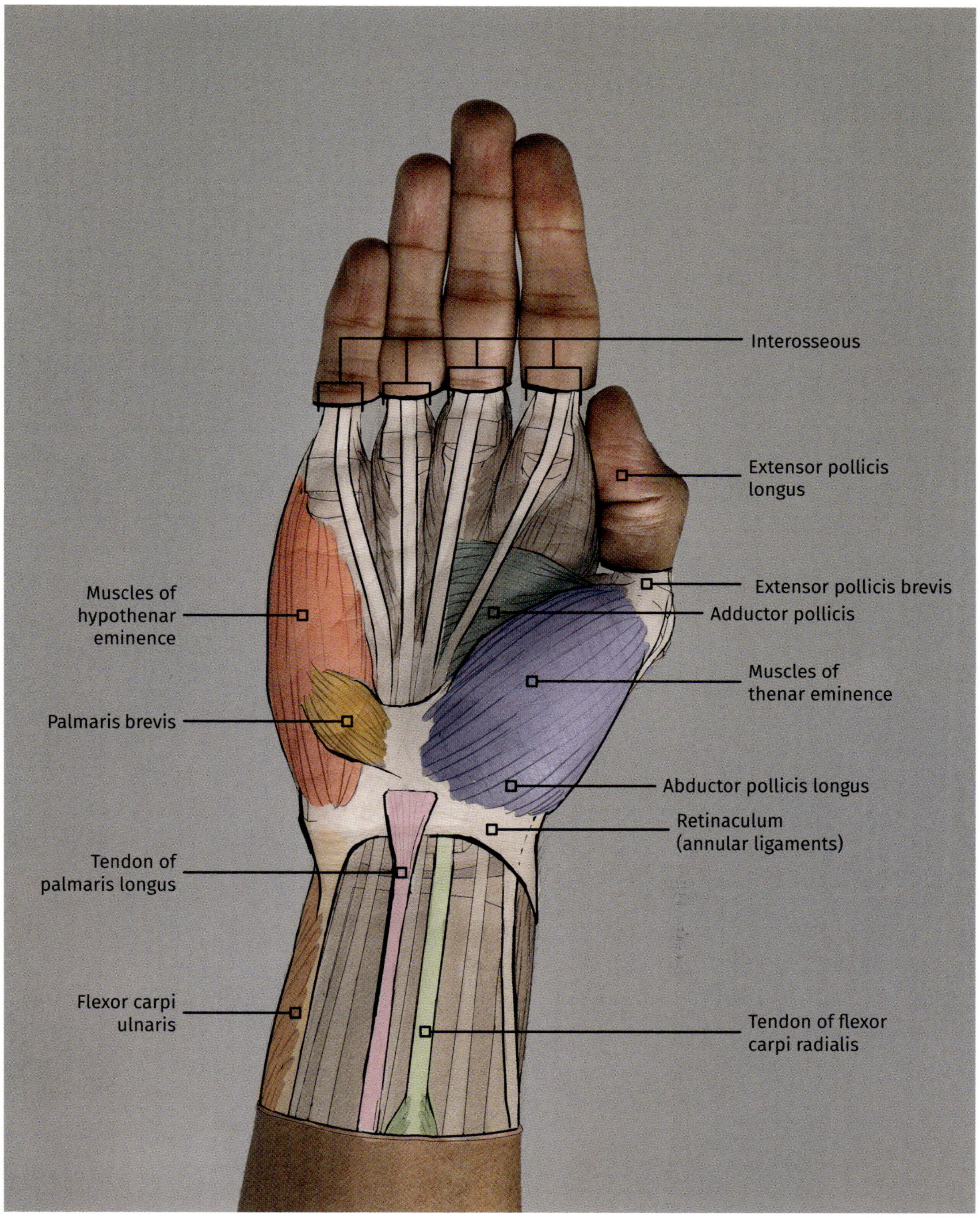

Muscles of the pelvis

Of the pelvis, the gluteal muscles, the sartorius, and the tensor fasciae latae will be of greatest importance when drawing the human form.

Gluteal muscles

The **gluteal muscles** are comprised of three muscles: the gluteus maximus, medius, and minimus.

The **gluteus minimus**, as the name suggests, is the smallest of the three and sits beneath the gluteus medius. As this muscle does not affect the surface forms, detail is not needed here.

The **gluteus medius** and **gluteus maximus** muscles both originate at the posterior portion of the iliac crest, with the maximus also arising from the sacrum. They travel downward and laterally, with the medius muscle inserting into the greater trochanter of the femur and the maximus muscle grabbing on to the gluteal tuberosity of the femur, and, more importantly here, the iliotibial band.

The **iliotibial band** is a long, thick fibrous tendon running from the tensor fasciae latae (see next page) to the outside of the tibia bone. Together the muscles create a butterfly-like shape at the posterior portion of the pelvis, functioning to abduct the leg as well as performing medial and lateral rotation.

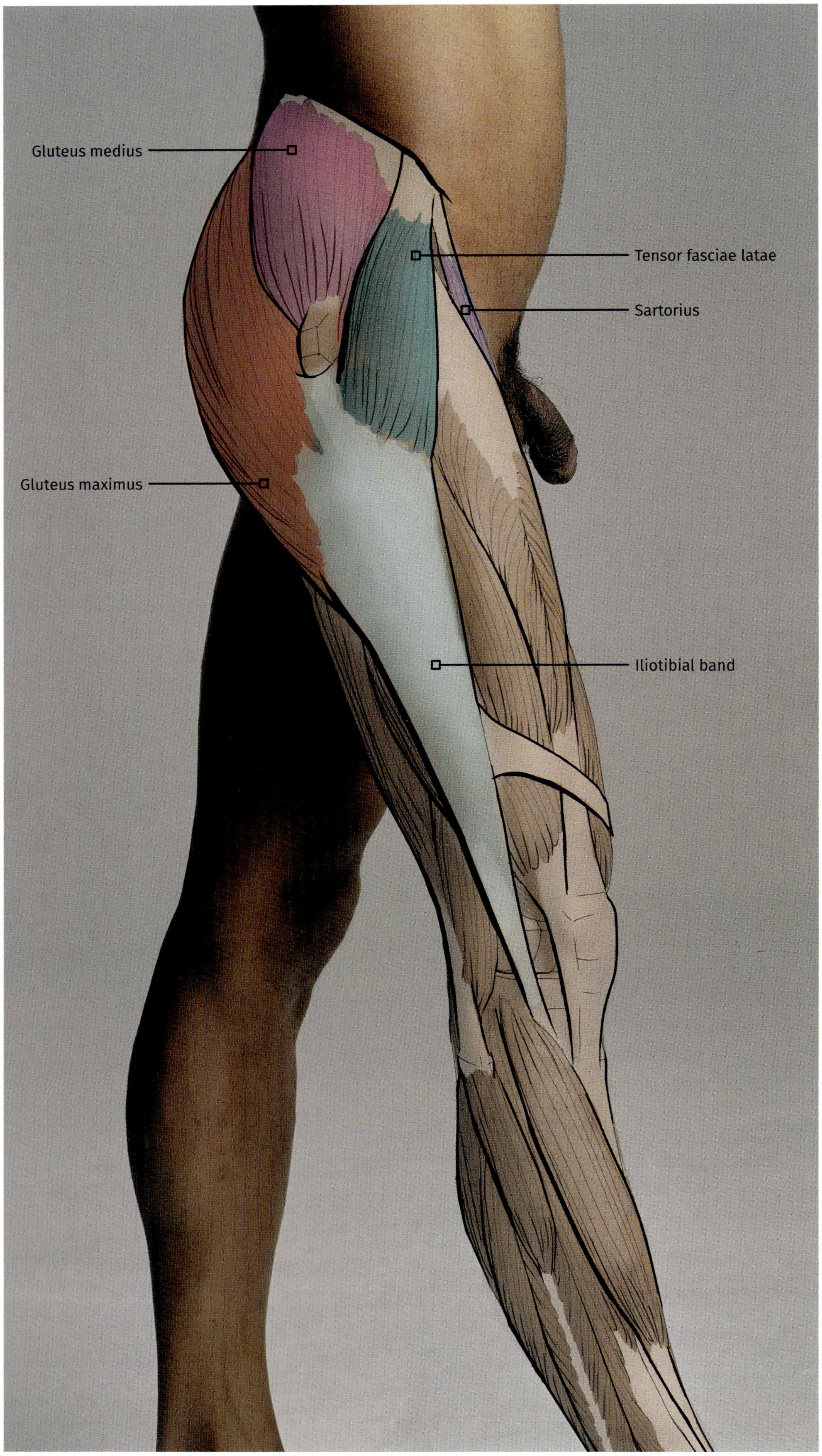

Tensor fasciae latae and sartorius

Next is the tensor fasciae latae and the sartorius, the latter being the longest muscle in the human body.

The **sartorius** originates at the anterior superior iliac spine and creates a ribbon-like shape running downward, inserting into a tendon connected to the proximal part of the tibia. As the leg is bent, the muscle shortens and appears thicker and rounder closer to its origin. This muscle, along with the tensor fasciae latae, creates a visible v-shape from the anterior superior iliac spine on a muscular form, with the quadriceps (see next page) being contained in-between.

The **tensor fasciae latae**, also originating from the anterior superior iliac spine, is a small muscle that is encased in thick fascia and inserts into the iliotibial band.

Both perform flexion and abduction of the hip. The sartorius is responsible for medial rotation and the tensor fasciae latae takes care of lateral rotation. The sartorius also helps to flex the knee.

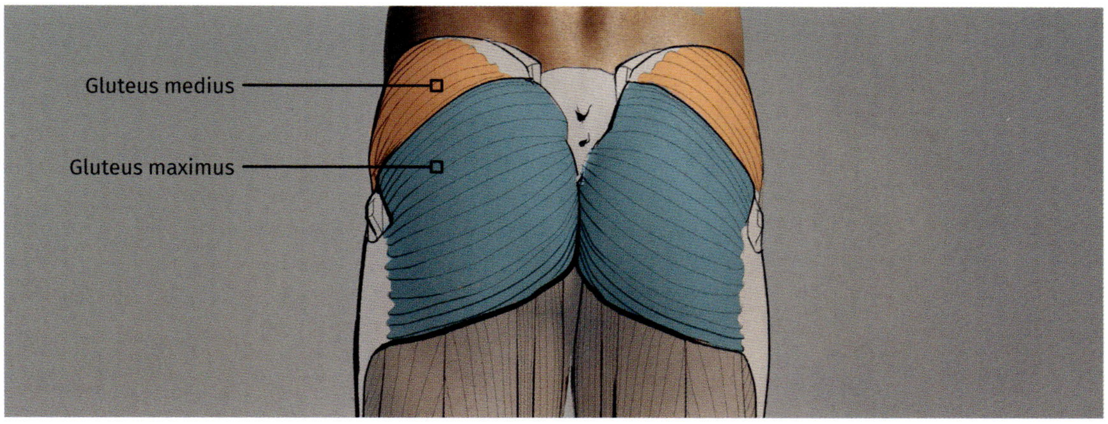

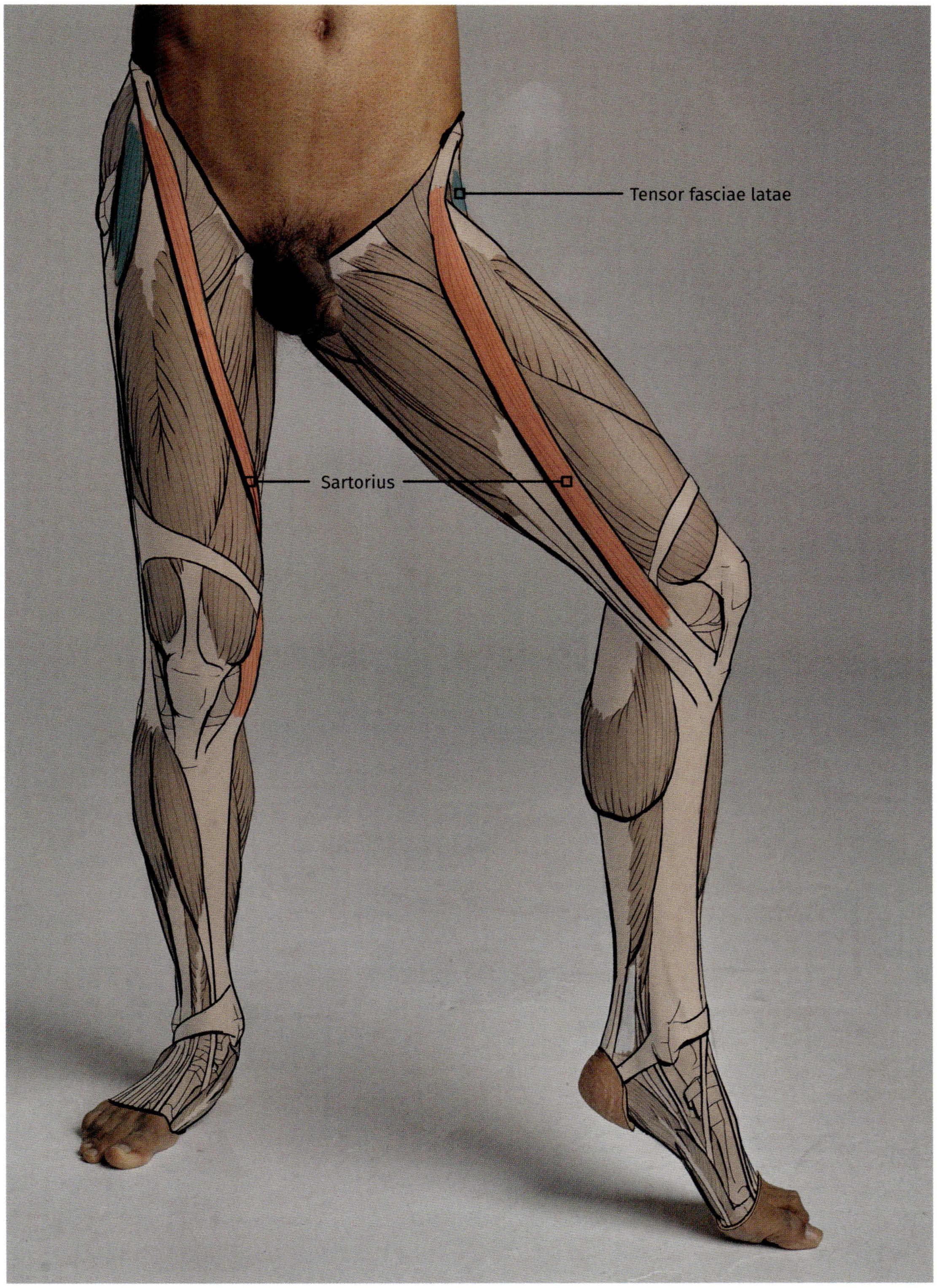

Muscles of the thigh

Quadriceps

As mentioned earlier, in between the sartorius and the tensor fasciae latae lies a group of muscles known as the **quadriceps**. From the name you can derive that four muscles are present: the **rectus femoris**, **vastus medialis**, **vastus intermedius**, and **vastus lateralis**. Of the four, three are clearly visible, while the vastus intermedius, sitting along the axis of the femur, is hidden behind the rectus femoris.

The **rectus femoris** originates at the anterior inferior iliac spine, with the remaining heads originating from the medial, anterior, and lateral surface of the femur. All four share a common tendon that encases the patella, becomes a ligament, and then terminates at the tibial tuberosity (the point of kneeling).

The **vastus medialis** is a teardrop shaped muscle whose fibers are closest to the patella. The rectus femoris grabs the tendon at the highest point and its fibers radiate either side, as this is a bipennate muscle. (Bipennate muscles have two rows of muscle fibers, facing in opposite diagonal directions with a central tendon.)

The **vastus lateralis** may seem small when viewed from the front, but from the lateral view, this muscle mass takes up almost two thirds of the leg with the biceps femoris muscle of the hamstrings (see next page) filling in the remainder. Together they allow for extension of the knee, while the rectus femoris allows for flexion of the hip.

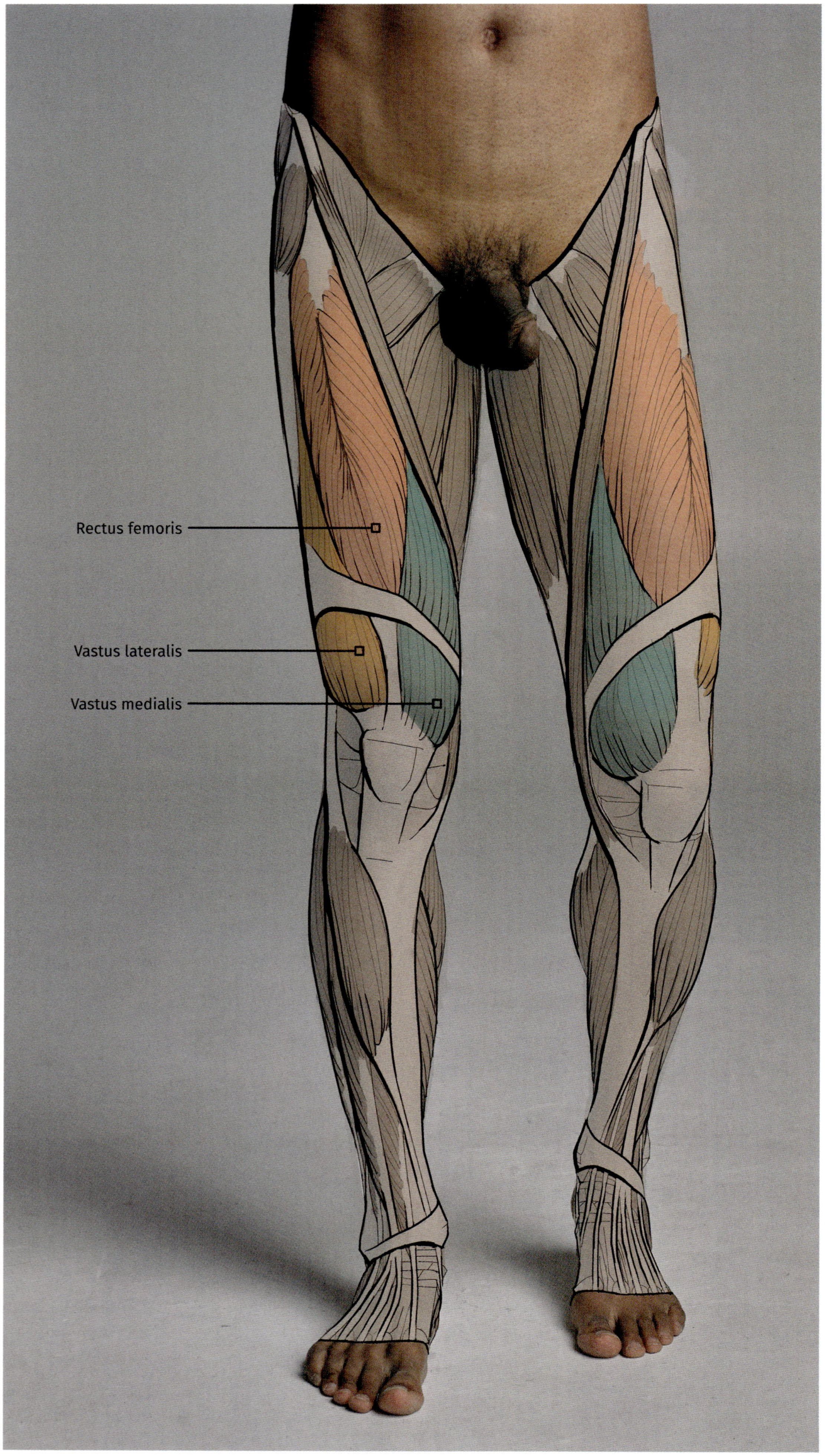

Adductor muscles

Situated superior and medial to the quadriceps are the adductor muscles: **adductor longus**, **adductor brevis**, and **adductor magnus**. These muscles originate at the pubic bone, insert into the crest of the femur (the linea aspera), and together they pull the leg into the medial plane. Visually they create a common mass, but are more defined on the muscular form.

Just lateral to the adductor muscles is the **femoral triangle**, which creates a deep hollow in the leg. This region also allows the passing of important veins and arteries.

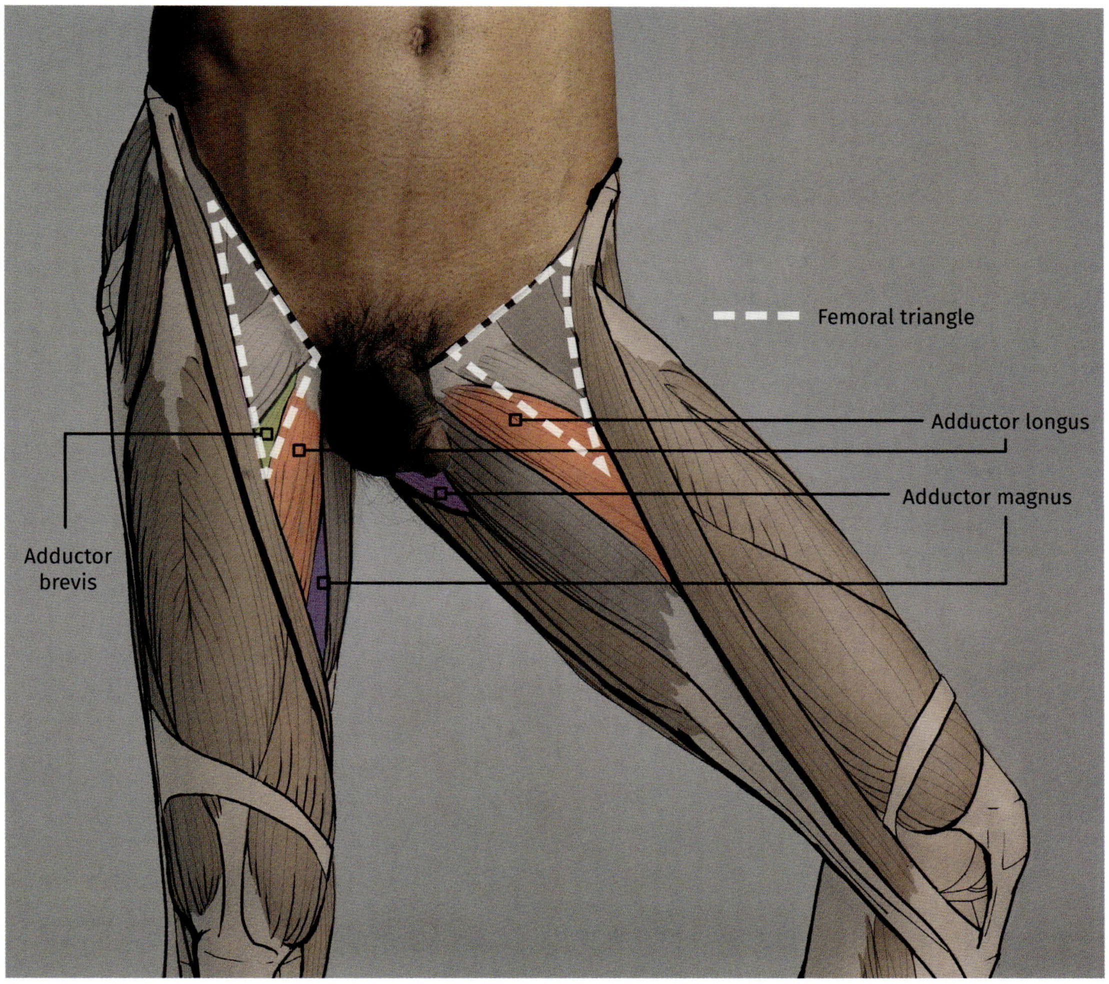

Hamstrings

The final muscle set of the upper leg that is useful to know when drawing the body is the **hamstrings**, situated on the posterior side of the leg. This is a set of three muscles that, on the average person, creates a common surface mass in the shape of a loose oval. On the more muscular form, some separation between the individual heads can be seen. The heads are the biceps femoris, the semitendinosus, and the semimembranosus.

The **biceps femoris** is a two-headed muscle running down the lateral side of the leg. Its long head originates at the ischium of the pelvis, and the short head (hidden behind the long head) originates at the linea aspera of the femur. Both insert into the head of the fibula and deal with flexion and medial rotation of the knee, with the long head also contributing to extension of the hip.

Next to those, the **semitendinosus** sits upon the **semimembranosus**, both originating at the ischium of the pelvis and running inferiorly down the medial side of the leg. The muscles insert into the medial condyle of the tibia, allowing medial rotation of the leg as well as extension of the hip. You will also notice that the muscles insert either side of the back of the knee, revealing the **popliteal fossa**.

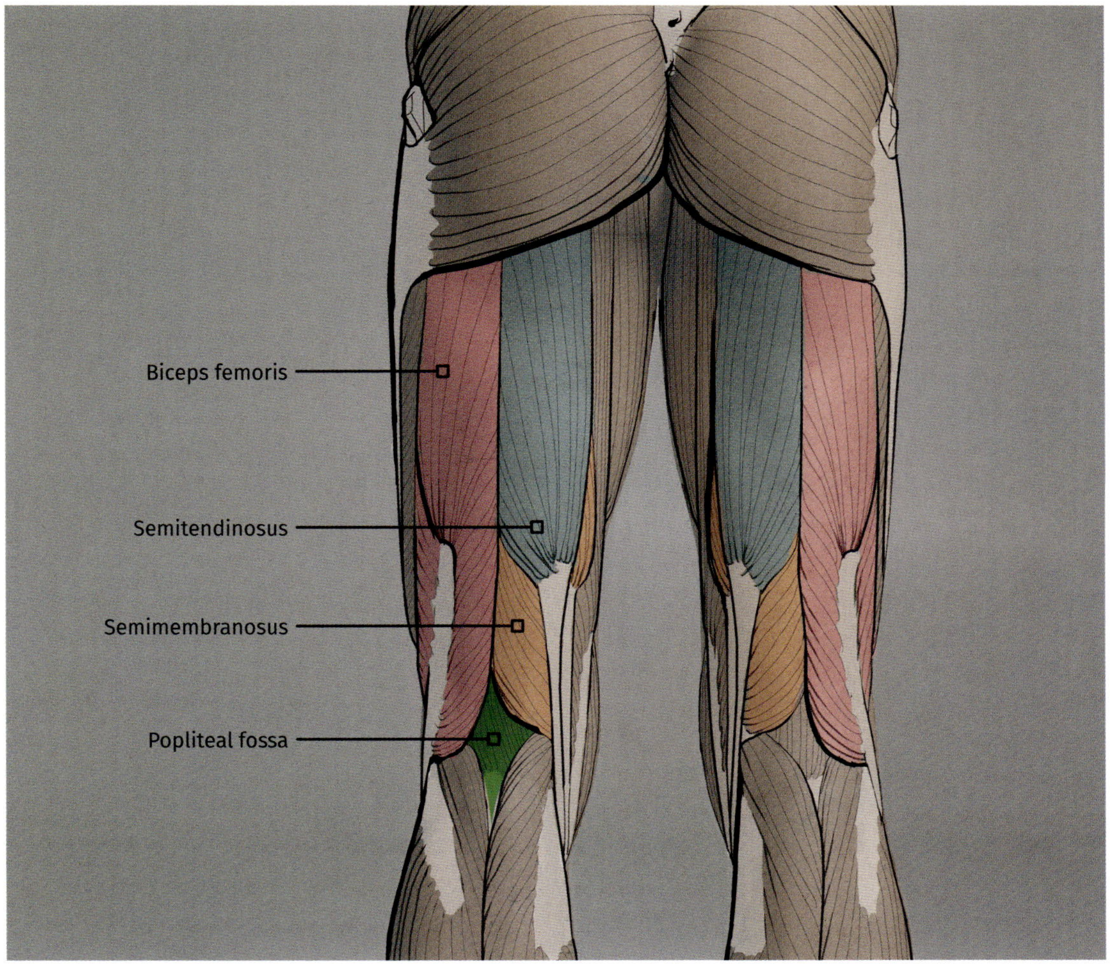

Muscles of the lower leg

Calf muscles

The muscles of note in the lower leg are the muscles of the calf, the gastrocnemius and the soleus, and then the muscles of the shin, the tibialis anterior and the peroneus longus. Other muscles in the region will also be briefly mentioned, as they have relevance to the workings of the feet and therefore also cause some surface change.

The **gastrocnemius** is a large superficial muscle that sits at the posterior side of the lower leg. It is a two-headed muscle with a **medial head** (originating at the posterior medial condyle of the femur) and a **lateral head** (originating at the posterior lateral condyle of the femur). As the origins are on either side of the femur, this reveals the lower half of the popliteal fossa. The gastrocnemius, along with the soleus, inserts into a common tendon called the calcaneal tendon (also known as the Achilles' tendon). As the muscle originates on the femur, this allows it to flex the knee, as well as aid plantarflexion of the ankle.

The **soleus** muscle sits beneath the gastrocnemius muscle, with its fibers viewable on the medial and lateral side of the gastrocnemius. This muscle originates at the middle third of the posterior of the tibia and the superior posterior of the fibula, and also aids plantarflexion of the ankle.

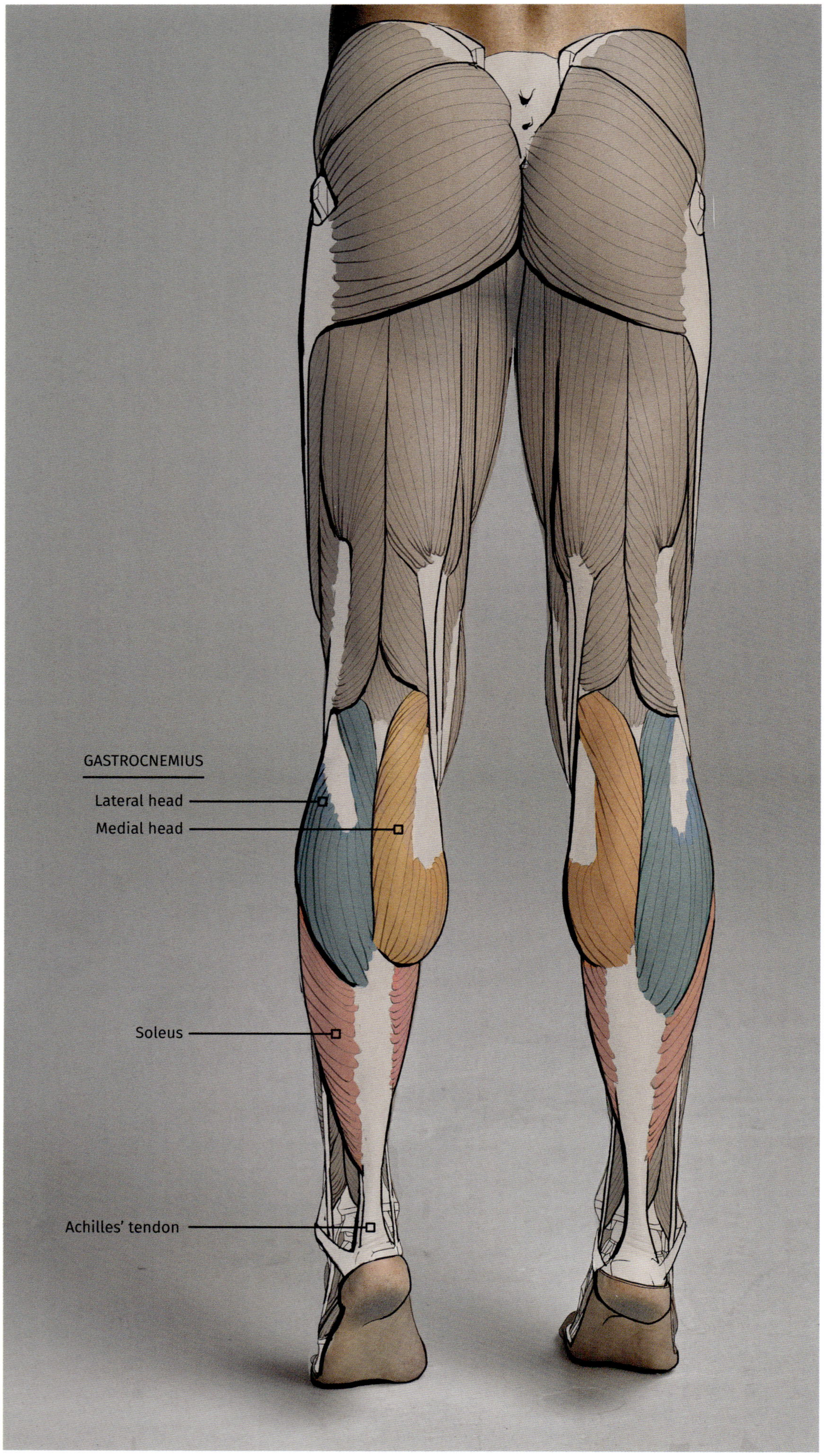

Shin muscles

On the anterior side of the lower leg, the **tibialis anterior** muscle creates the majority of the surface forms, originating at the lateral border of the tibia and traveling medially and inferiorly to insert into the first metatarsal bone (big toe) and medial cuneiform bone.

Sitting between the tibialis anterior and the soleus on the lateral side of the leg is the **peroneus longus**. This muscle originates at the head of the fibula and travels around the lateral malleolus, crossing the sole of the foot before inserting into the base of the first metatarsal bone and the lateral side of the medial cuneiform bone.

Between the peroneus longus and the tibialis anterior are three smaller muscles whose tendons lead into the foot: the **peroneus brevis**, the **extensor digitorum longus**, and the **extensor hallucis longus**. Like the wrist, these tendons are held in place by a sheet of fascia: the **extensor retinaculum**.

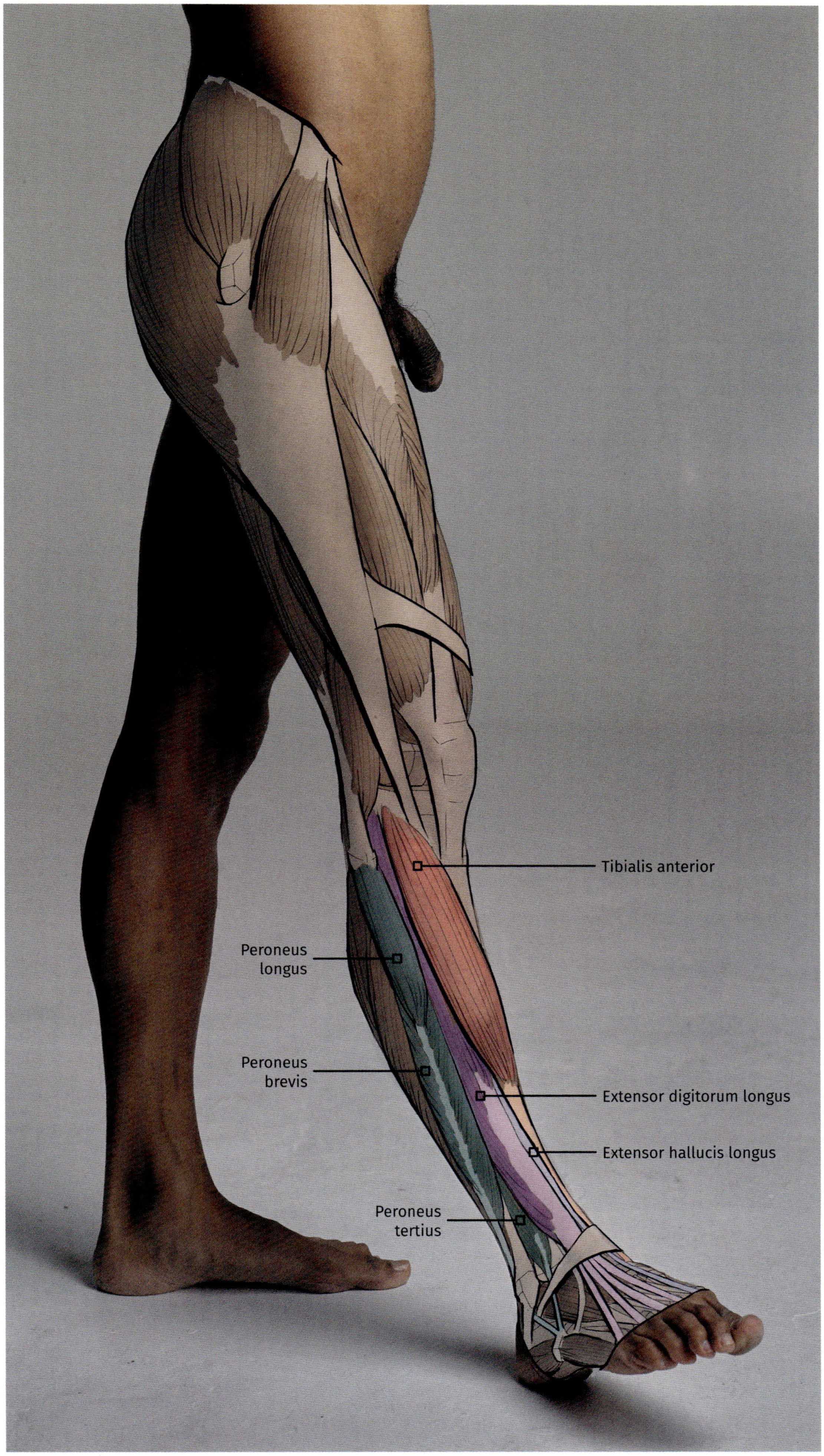

Muscles of the foot

Similar to the hand, the dorsal (top) side of the foot consists mainly of tendons and bones, while the plantar (bottom) side is fleshier, allowing for the distribution of force.

The tendons of the **peroneus brevis** (originating at the lateral surface of the fibula) insert into the base of the fifth metatarsal (little toe), functioning to aid eversion (tilting of the foot so that the sole faces away from the midline) and plantarflexion.

The **extensor digitorum longus** (originating on the upper third of the shaft of the fibula), has the most noticeable effect on the dorsal side of the foot, as the tendon divides into four and inserts into the middle and distal phalanges of toes two to five.

The tendon of the **extensor hallucis longus** muscle (originating on the middle anterior surface of the fibula) inserts into the distal phalanx of the big toe. Together the tendons help to extend the toes, while the flexor digitorum brevis and the flexor hallucis brevis will flex the toes. As they have less influence on the surface, this chapter will not go into detail on these muscles.

Finally, there are two abductor muscles that help to spread the toes: the abductor hallucis and the abductor digiti minimi. The **abductor hallucis** originates at the border of the calcaneus on the medial side and inserts into the first metatarsal. The **abductor digiti minimi** originates at the front of the calcaneus on the lateral side and first passes the head of the fifth metatarsal, then into the first phalanx of the little toe. If you press your fingers against your foot, you will be able to feel both muscles when in action, though their effect on the surface is quite minimal.

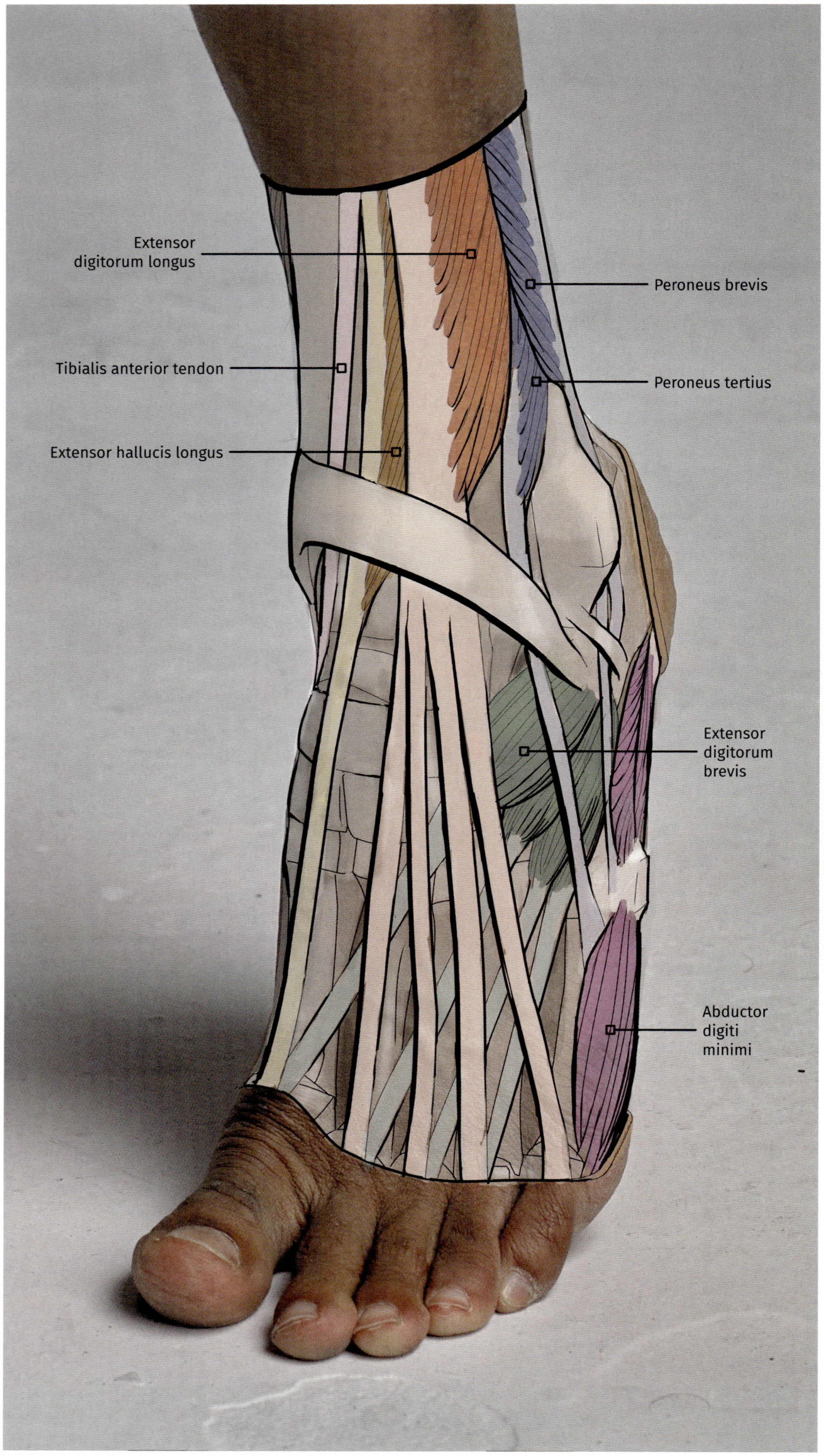

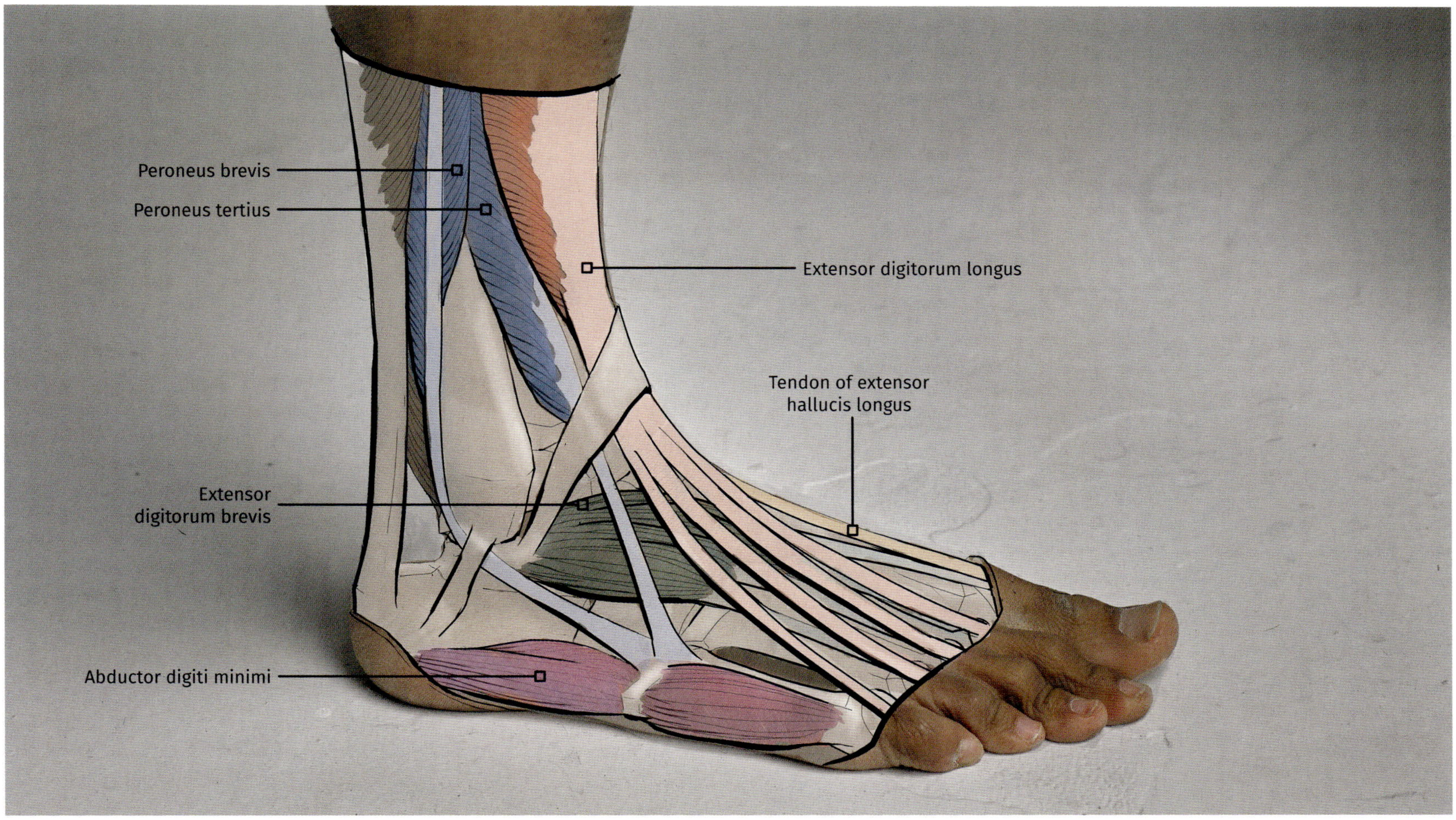
Peroneus brevis
Peroneus tertius
Extensor digitorum longus
Tendon of extensor hallucis longus
Extensor digitorum brevis
Abductor digiti minimi

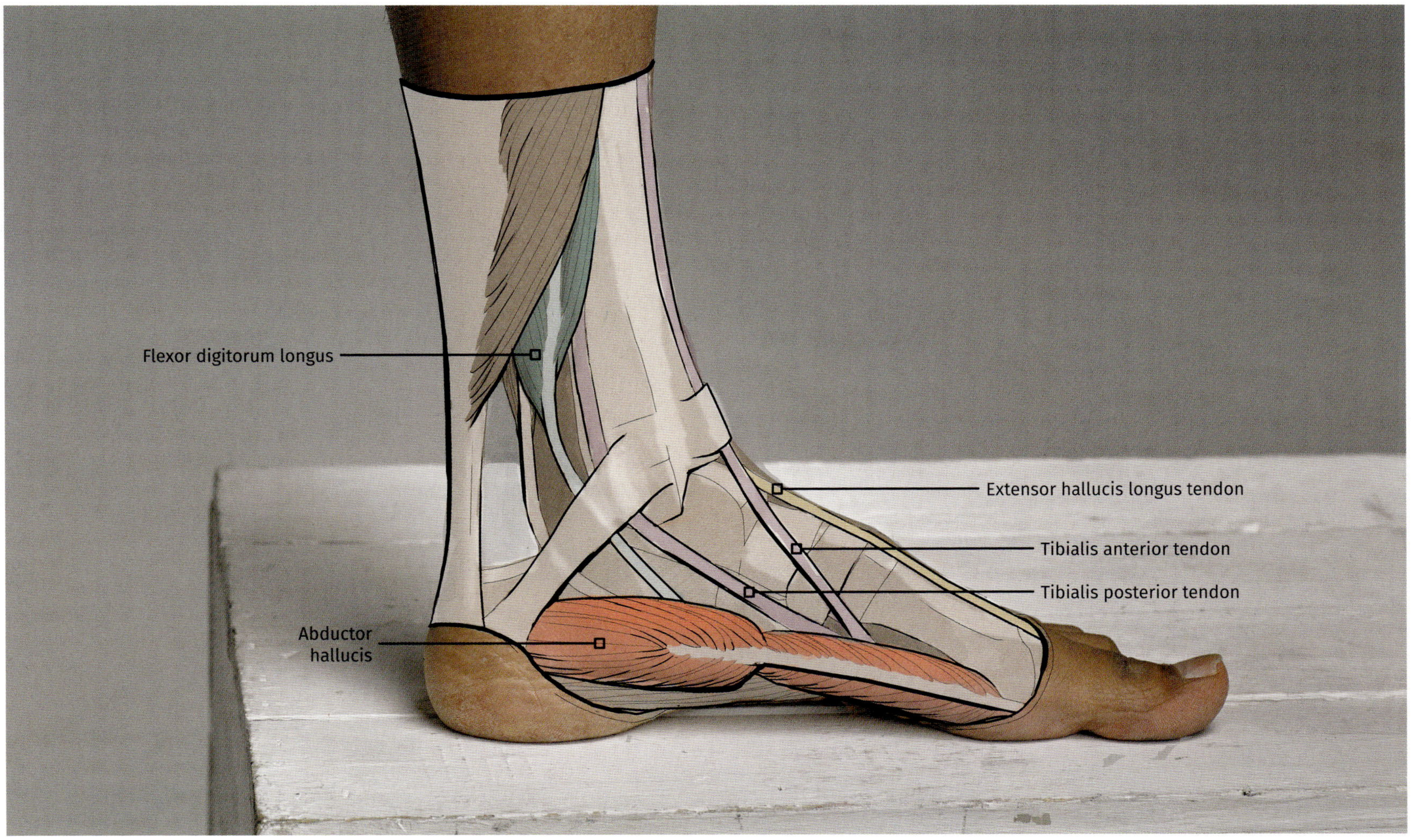
Flexor digitorum longus
Extensor hallucis longus tendon
Tibialis anterior tendon
Tibialis posterior tendon
Abductor hallucis

BODY TYPES

Whether you are in a life-drawing session, designing a character in 2D, or rigging or animating a 3D character, it can be helpful to consider the body type of your subject in the process. Human bodies come in all shapes and sizes, so it is important to be able to portray them accurately.

According to the somatotypes idea (popular in the bodybuilding world), there are three generalized body types: ectomorph, mesomorph, and endomorph. Although this chapter will discuss each type separately, you should be aware that in most cases, people will have a combination of body types. For example, a person could be primarily an endomorph but have a dash of mesomorph, or they could be an endomorph with a hint of ectomorph. Therefore, when examining real-life reference or designing well-rounded characters, try to put a little time into understanding how you can mix the body types fluidly.

It is also worth noting that somatotypes are theoretical, rather than scientific. However, they can be helpful in thinking about the different components that shape how a body looks: the amount of fat and where it sits on the body, the size of the muscles, and the size and proportions of the skeleton.

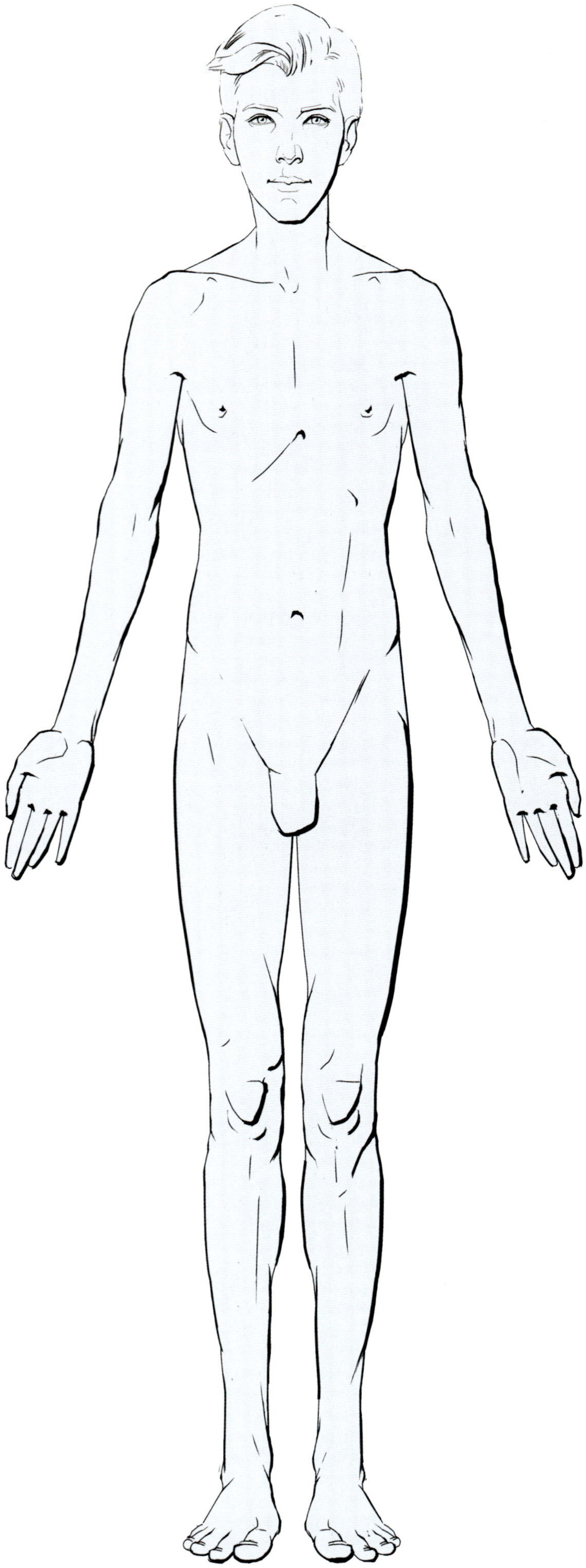

Ectomorph

Ectomorphs are thin, even skinny, and can find it difficult to put on weight. They have lean muscle mass and are small-jointed, with narrow shoulders and long limbs. It is hard for people with this body type to build muscle and they are consequently known as "hard-gainers."

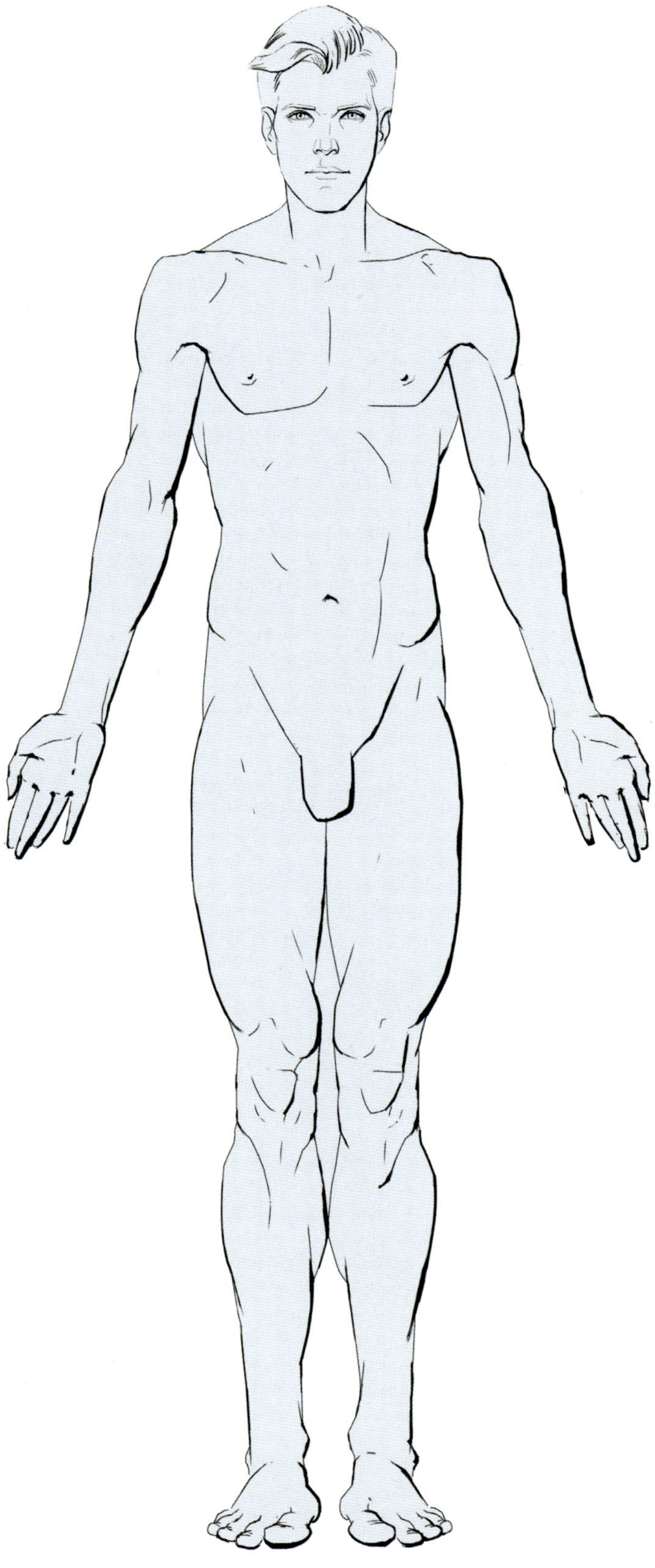

Mesomorph

Mesomorphs have a large bone structure and are naturally strong and athletic. They can gain muscle quickly, and can just as quickly gain fat, though the fat can be lost very easily. Whereas the ectomorph is long and lean, the mesomorph is rectangular in shape and well-built, with clearly defined muscle mass.

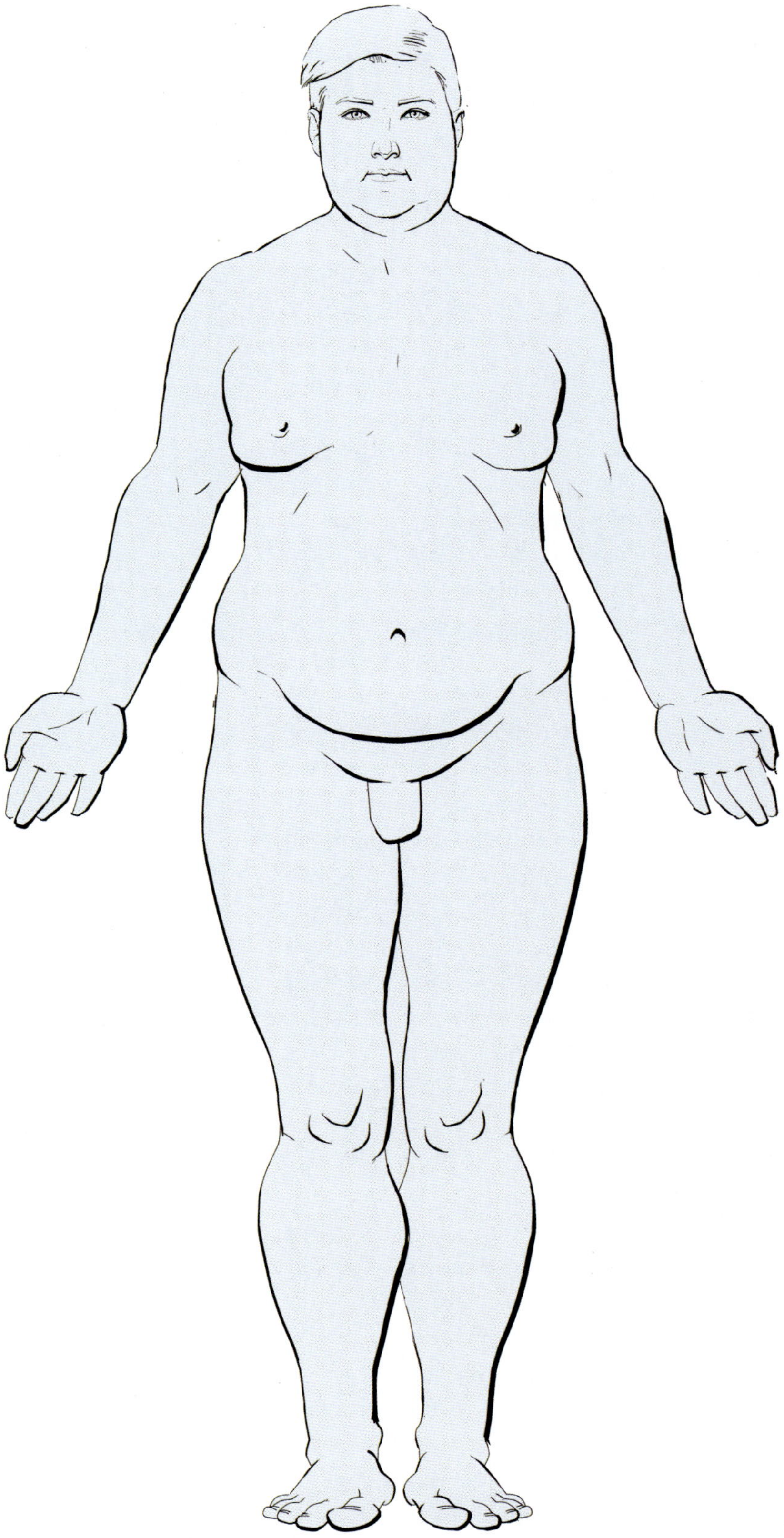

Endomorph

An endomorph's body frame is rounded and soft-looking. Both muscle and fat can be gained easily, though the muscle is not well-defined and the weight cannot be lost easily. People with this body type are often stocky or pear-shaped, short in stature, and have short limbs.

PROPORTION AND SYMMETRY

Proportion

When it comes to proportion, it is likely you will have come across the method of using the head (from the top of the head to the bottom of the chin) as a unit of measurement. For example, you may construct an average human as seven and a half to eight heads tall, or a child may be five heads tall. Then you could use the unit of head measurement to figure out where the nipple line should be, or where the belly button should go, for example. (See page 92 for example growth of the human body, from baby to adult, measured in heads.)

That may well work for the average human, with body parts lining up nicely, however you will likely find that as you design characters with different heights, weights, ages, and so on, the unit of head ceases to be so reliable. There are a number of reasons for this. Gravity gradually pulls the features down over time and so the nipple line will follow, for example. Similarly, the placement of the belly button will vary in accordance with any gains or losses in weight. This diagram shows that while it can be used as a basic guideline, the reality is that it doesn't always exactly work out.

One feature that does stay consistent, however, is the skeleton. The skeleton can therefore be used as a reliable source for laying out the proportions of a character. The unit of measurement based on the skeleton is referred to as a **cranial unit**, which uses the **cranium** (typically a box the width of five eyes) as a unit of measure. Using this method makes it easy to strike upon the skeletal landmarks, enabling you to quickly map out the underlying skeletal structure to which you can then attach muscles, tendons, and fat.

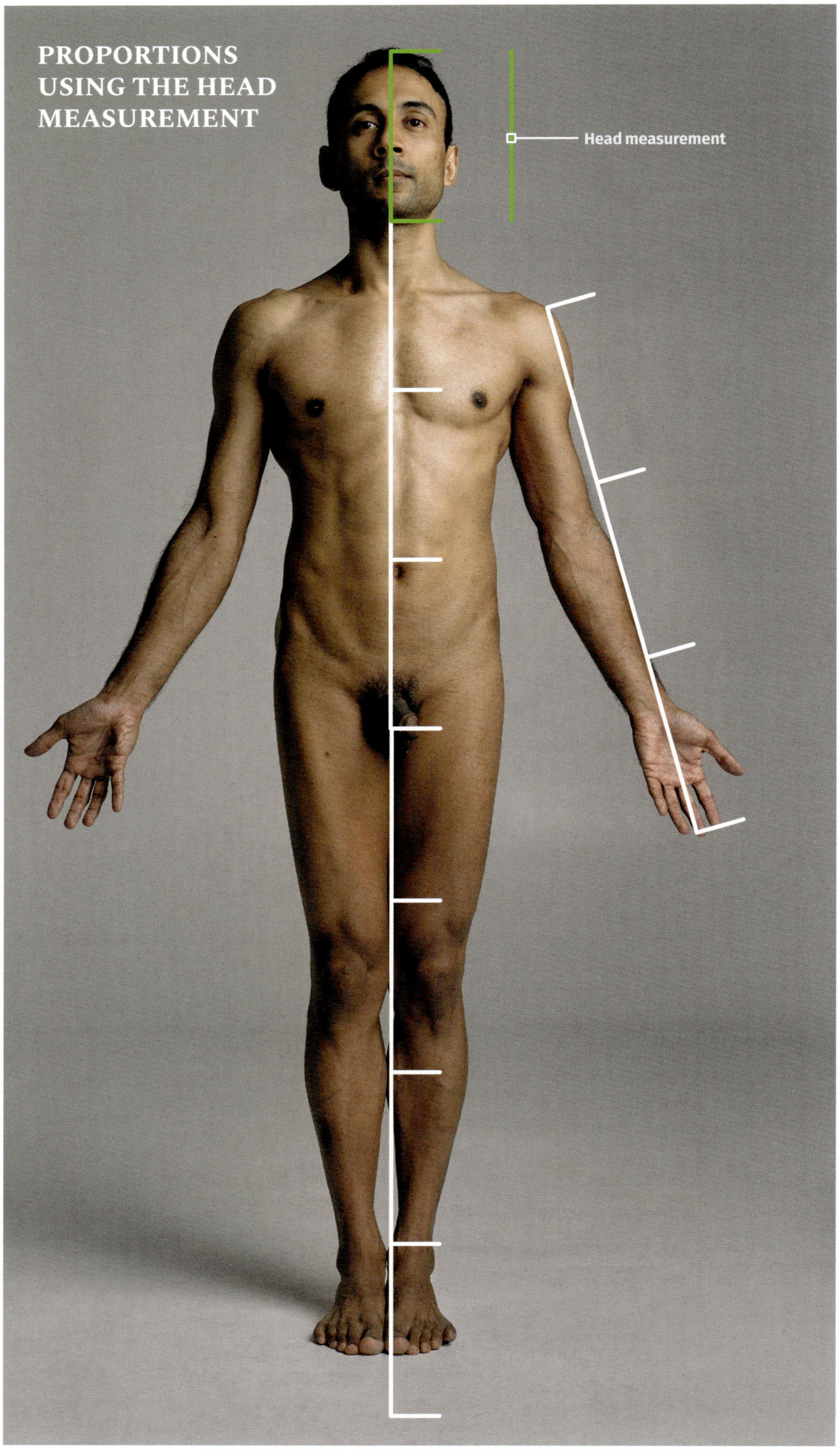

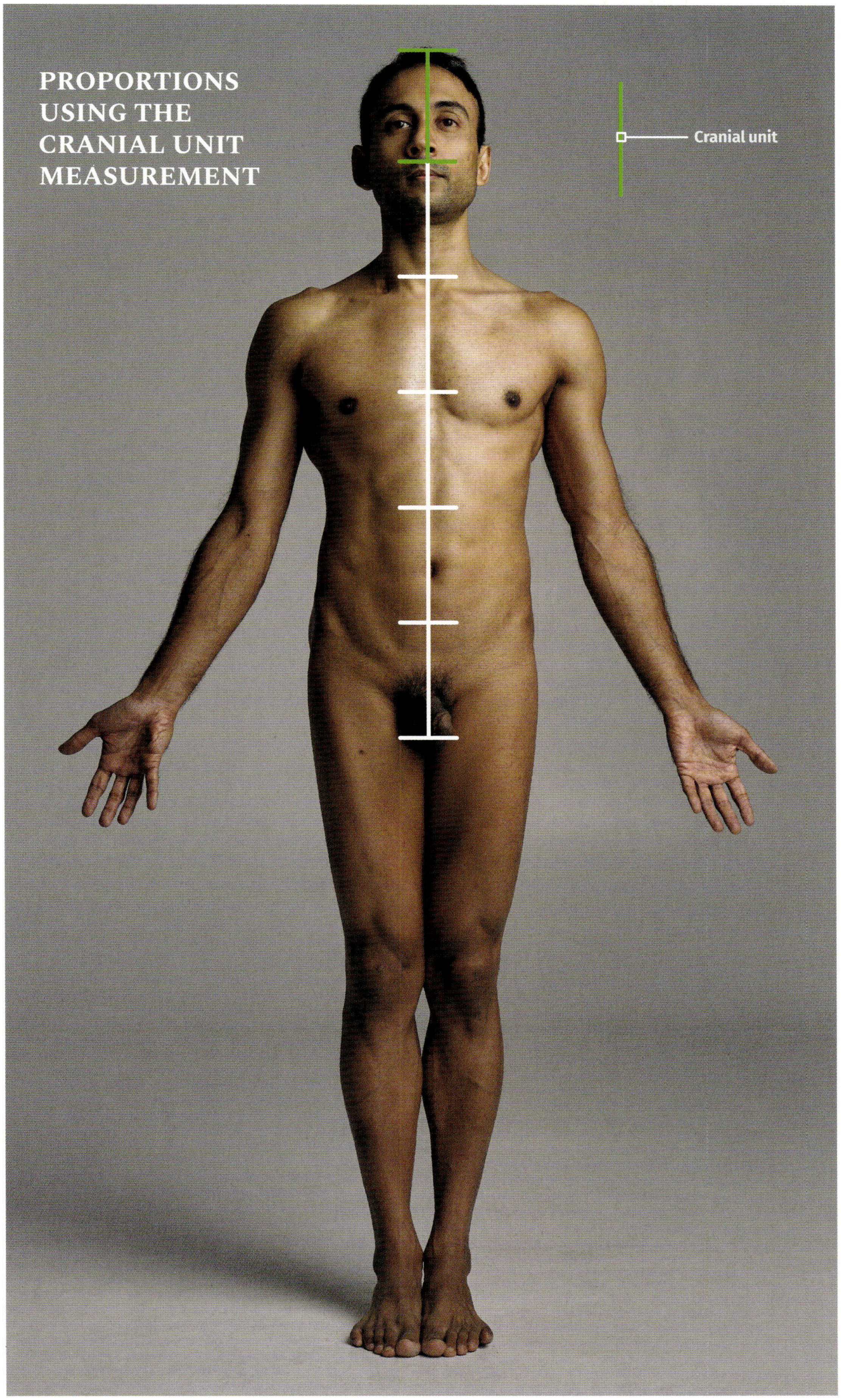

Here are some examples of using the cranium as a unit of measurement. Start by taking the cranium (from the top of the head to the base of the nose), then drop another unit of measure down, which will take you to the pit of the neck where you hit the clavicles. Another cranial unit down and you have the length of the sternum (excluding the xiphoid process), and a further unit down, you hit the tenth rib. One more unit down, and you hit the anterior superior iliac spine. Down again, you hit the pubic symphysis.

Interestingly, the length of the clavicles is typically a cranial unit, as is the length of the sternum (as mentioned previously), so is the length of the spine of the scapula, and the length of the medial border of the scapula. The femur is around three cranial units, and a further three units down will take you to the heel. The length of the humerus is two cranial units.

You will find that anatomy and skeletal structure will differ slightly from person to person. Everyone is different. Some people will conform nicely to having a standard idealized set of proportions that follows the mold of seven and a half to eight heads tall, or having everything line up to fit into a series of five-eyes-wide boxes. However, know that for the most part, the majority of people won't fit into this mold. This isn't a bad thing; it gives you the opportunity to experiment and play with proportions to create new and interesting characters. Regardless of how far you want to push the anatomy, keep things functional and always have a sense of purpose in mind so the audience can believe the design they're looking at on the page or screen is one that could exist in reality.

RIGHT LATERAL VIEW

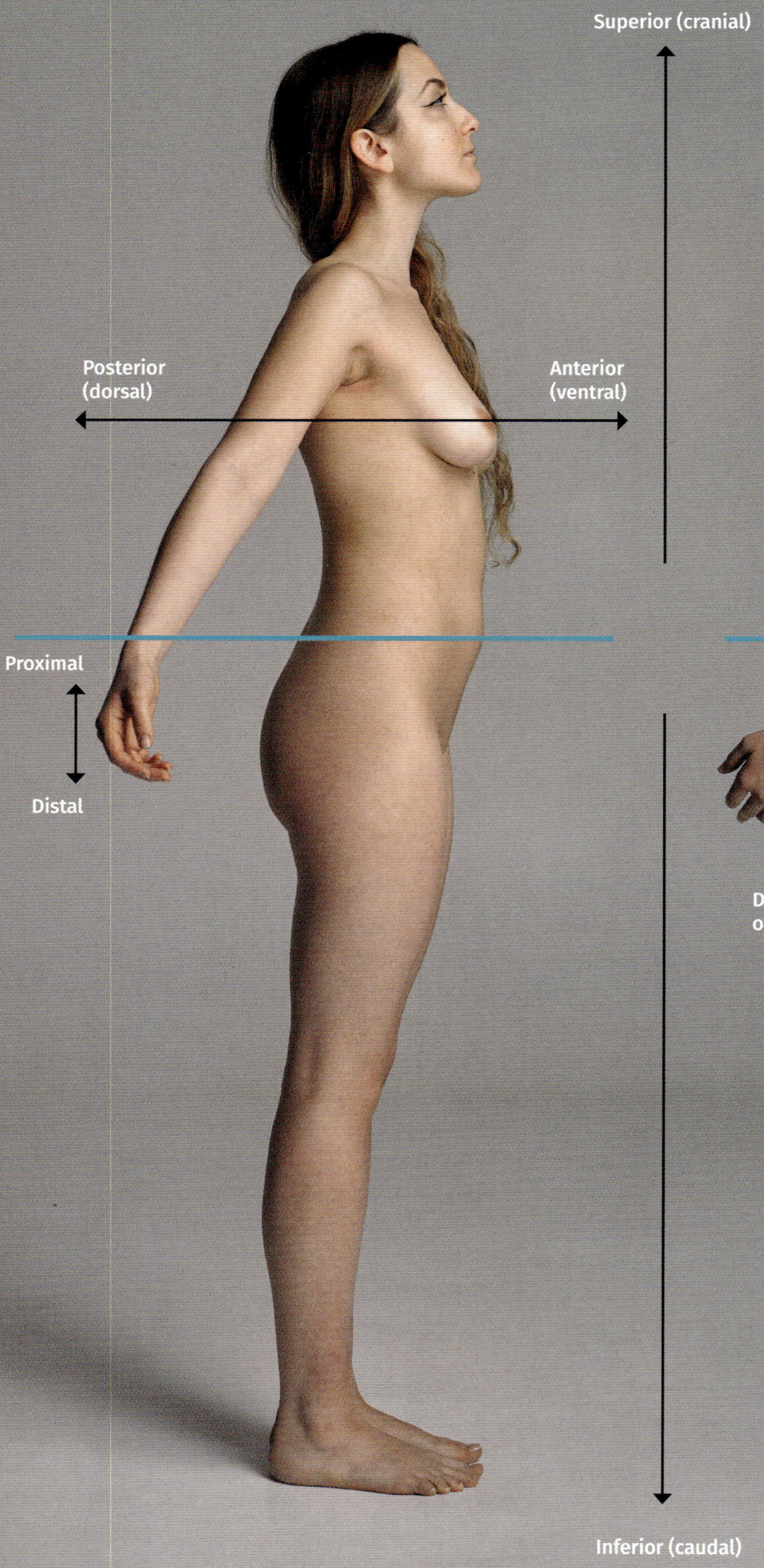

POSTERIOR VIEW

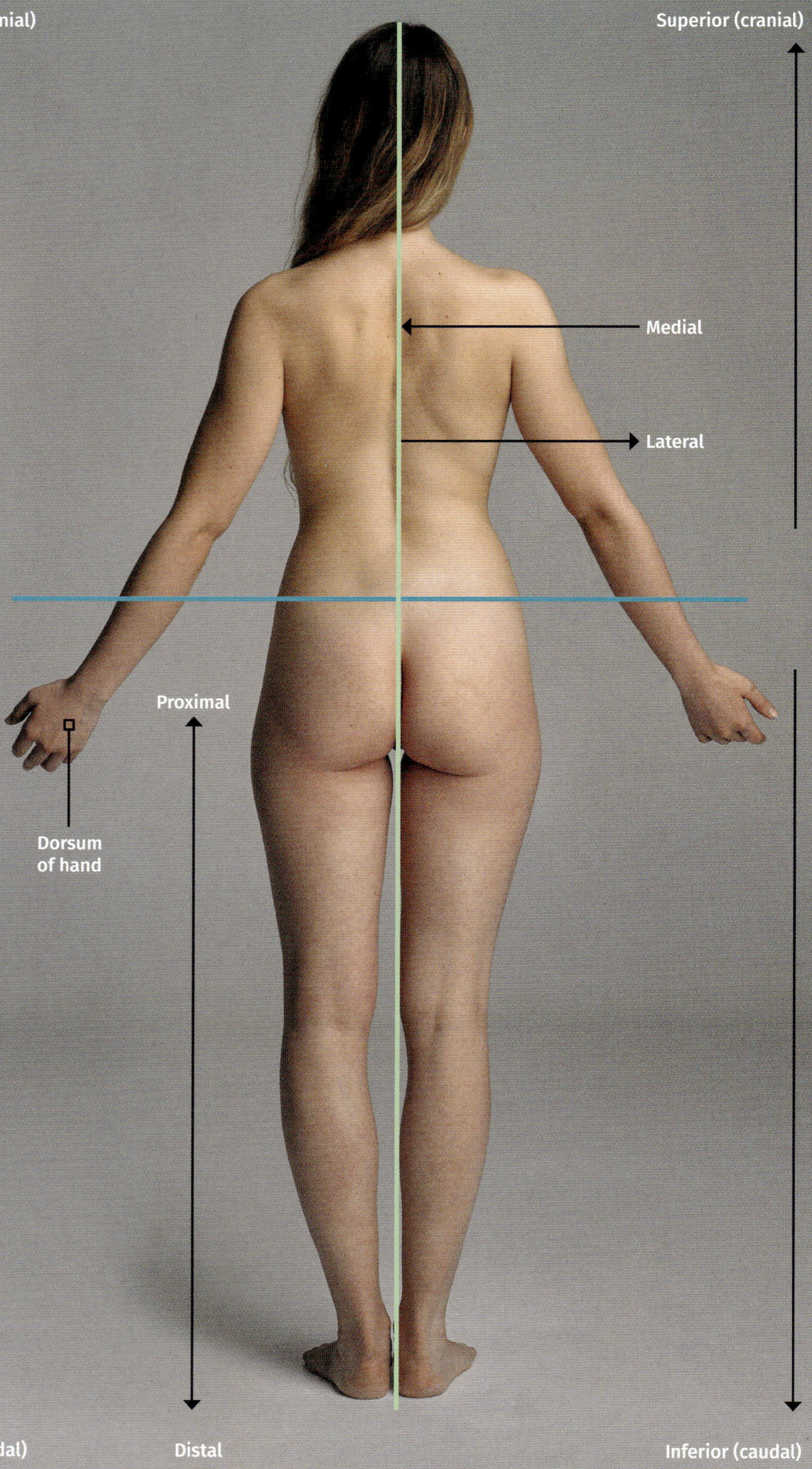

Symmetry

When it comes to creating and designing characters and creatures, whether 2D or 3D, you may be tempted to work symmetrically, especially when it comes to faces. Doing so certainly speeds things up, especially when working digitally. However, while symmetry does exist in nature, when considering faces in particular, it is the slight asymmetries which create believability and interest.

To test this, take a photo of your head and then load the picture into photo-editing software such as Adobe Photoshop. Use the software to mirror the left side of your head over to the right, and then take a look at the results. Next, flip the right side of your head over to the left and, again, analyze the results. You will probably find one side is thinner, while the other side is wider. Interestingly, in right-handed people, the right side of the face (and body) is often slightly larger, and the same in reverse for those who are left-handed. Asymmetry will also be evident in the body, but less noticeably than in the face.

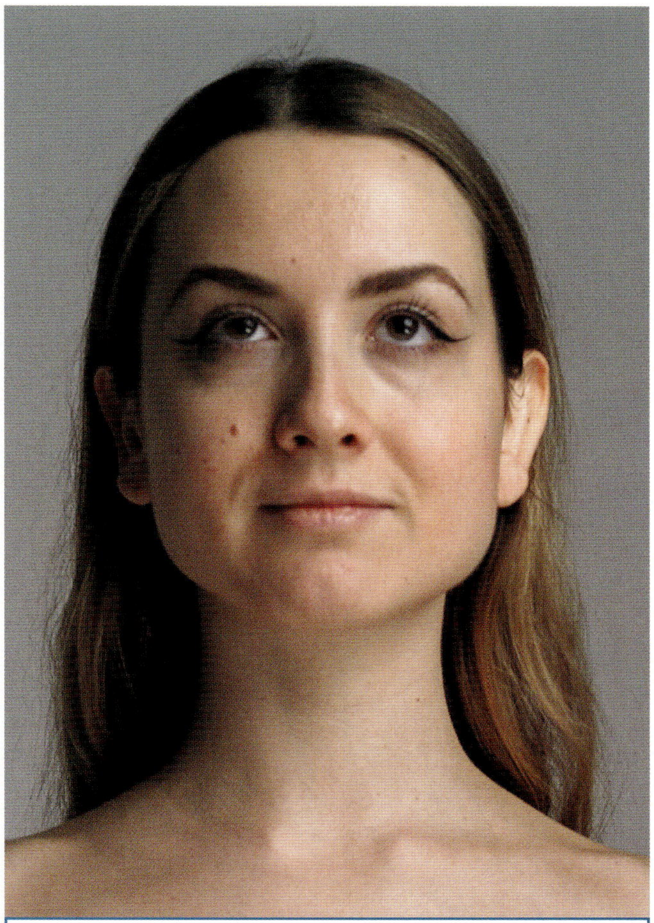

Original photo

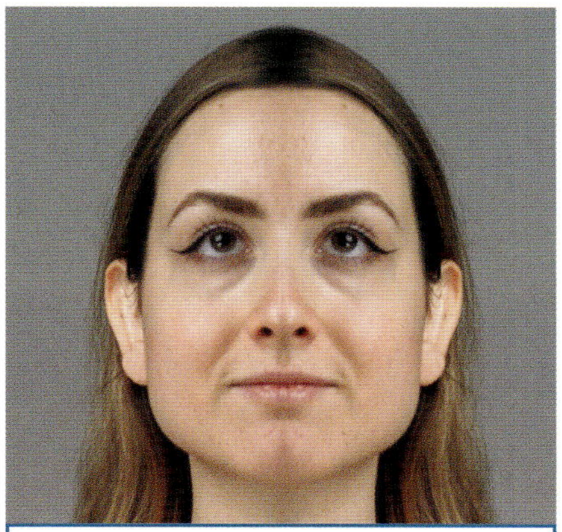

Right-side flipped

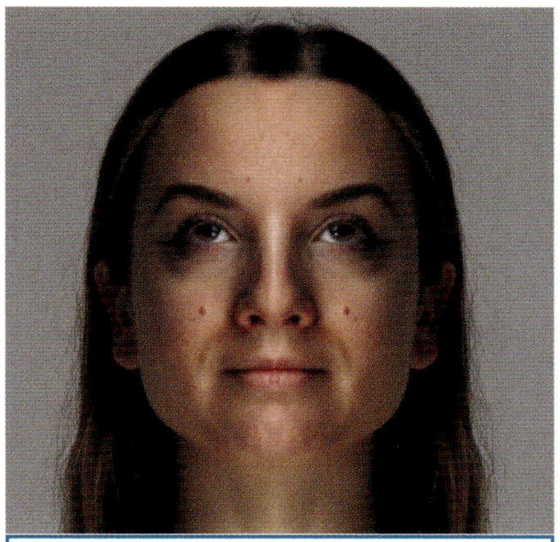

Left-side flipped

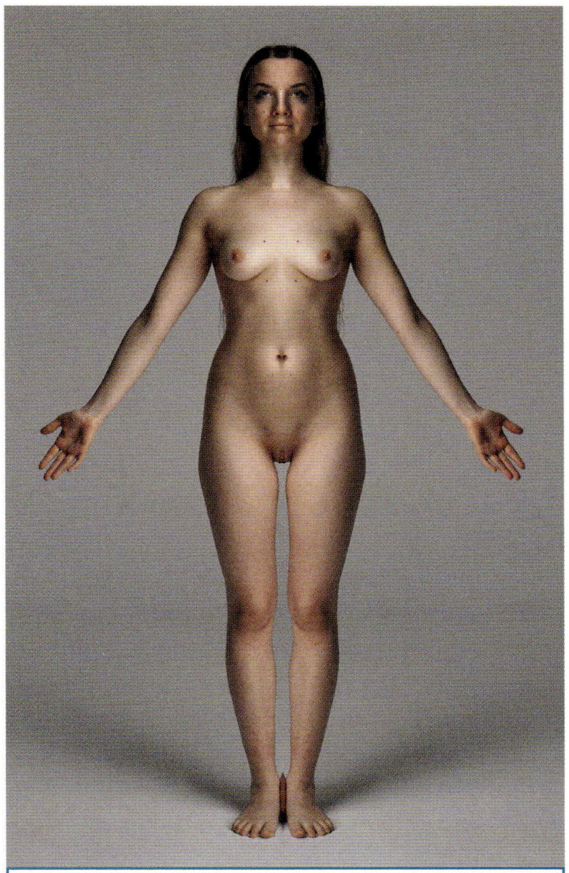

Left-side flipped

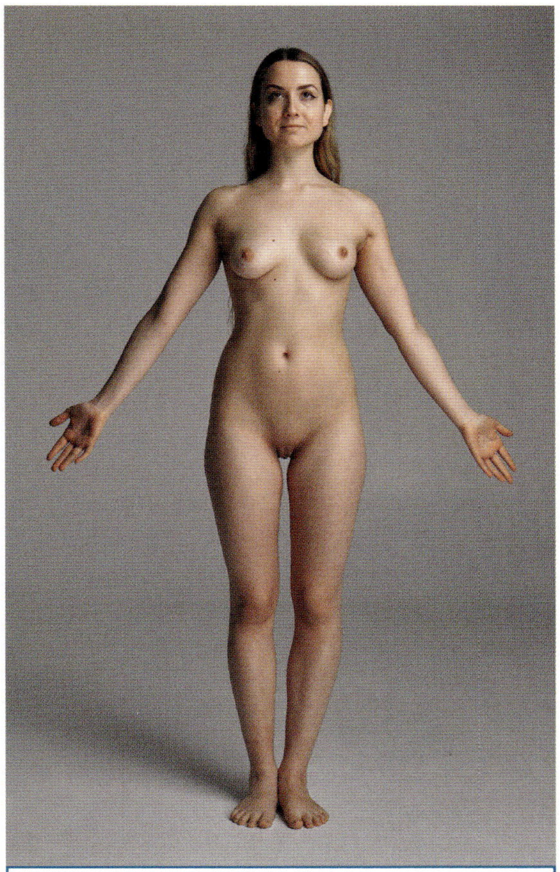

Original photo

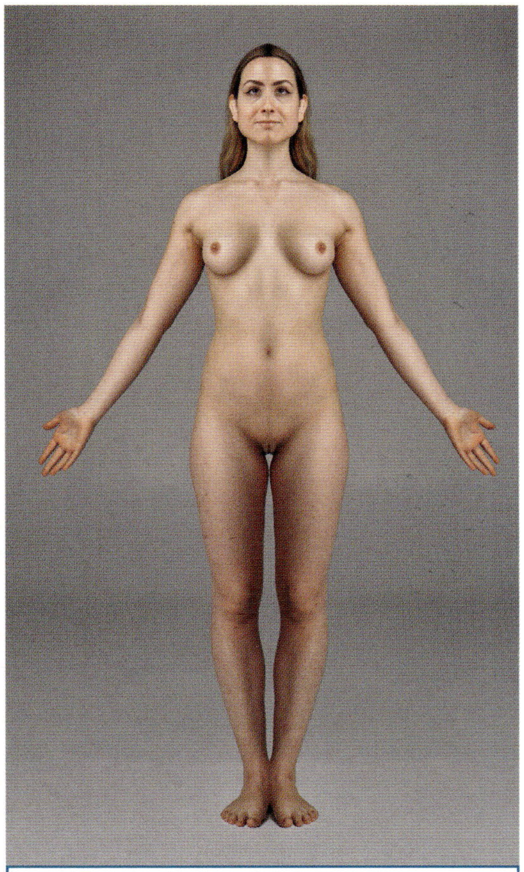

Right-side flipped

■ THE SKIN: FAT AND WRINKLES

Although these introductory chapters have primarily studied the skeleton, muscles, and tendons of the human body, it is important to remember that sitting on top of all of this like a draped cloth is the largest organ of all: the skin. And with skin comes fat and wrinkles.

Fat

Fatty deposits can be found throughout the body, even on the leanest of individuals. As well as fatty deposits on the face, hips, hands, and feet, you should also take into consideration areas such as the back of the knees as well as gluteal fat. The back of the knee is an interesting area, as a depression, known as the popliteal fossa, is present where the muscles of the hamstrings interlock with the calf muscles. Therefore, if you were to purely focus on the muscles and ignore the fat, your model may look slightly less believable. Adding fat is a good thing and will ultimately add further life to your design.

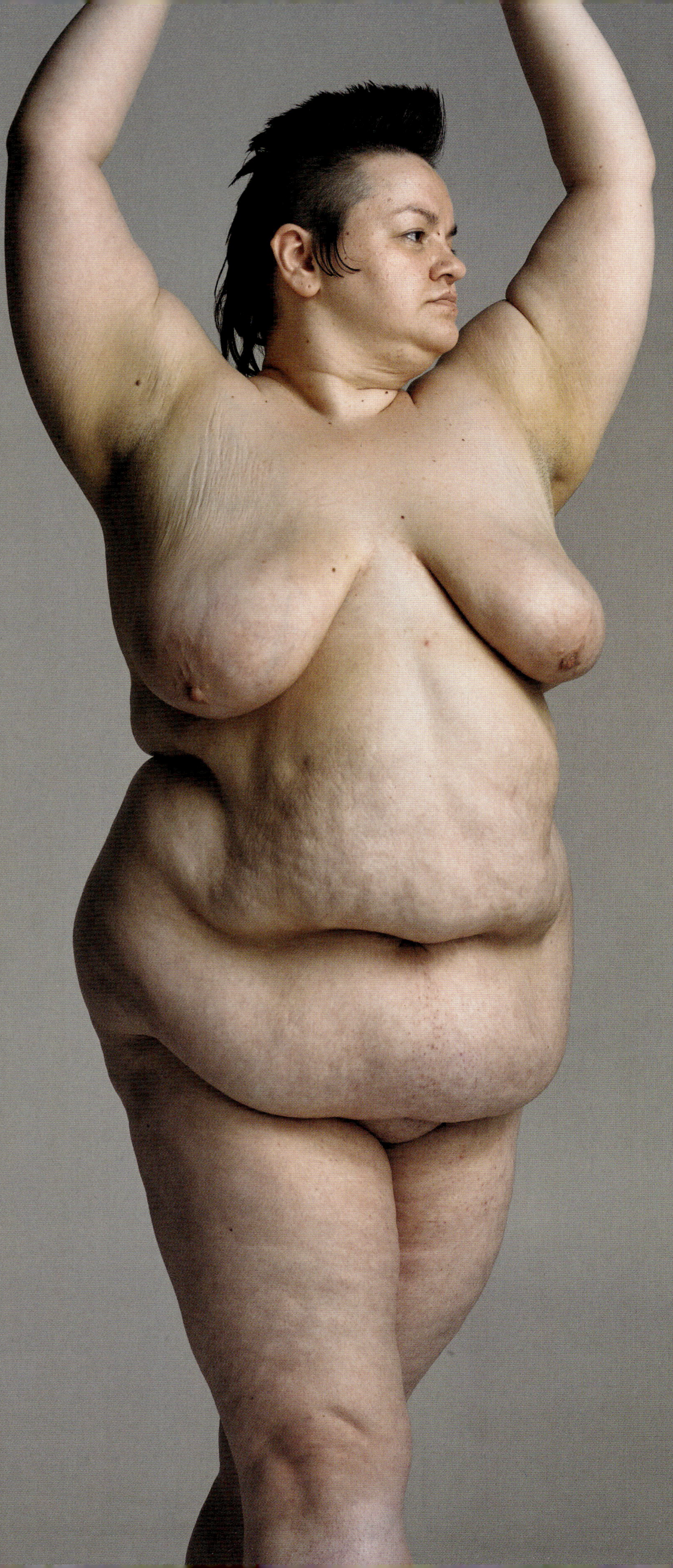

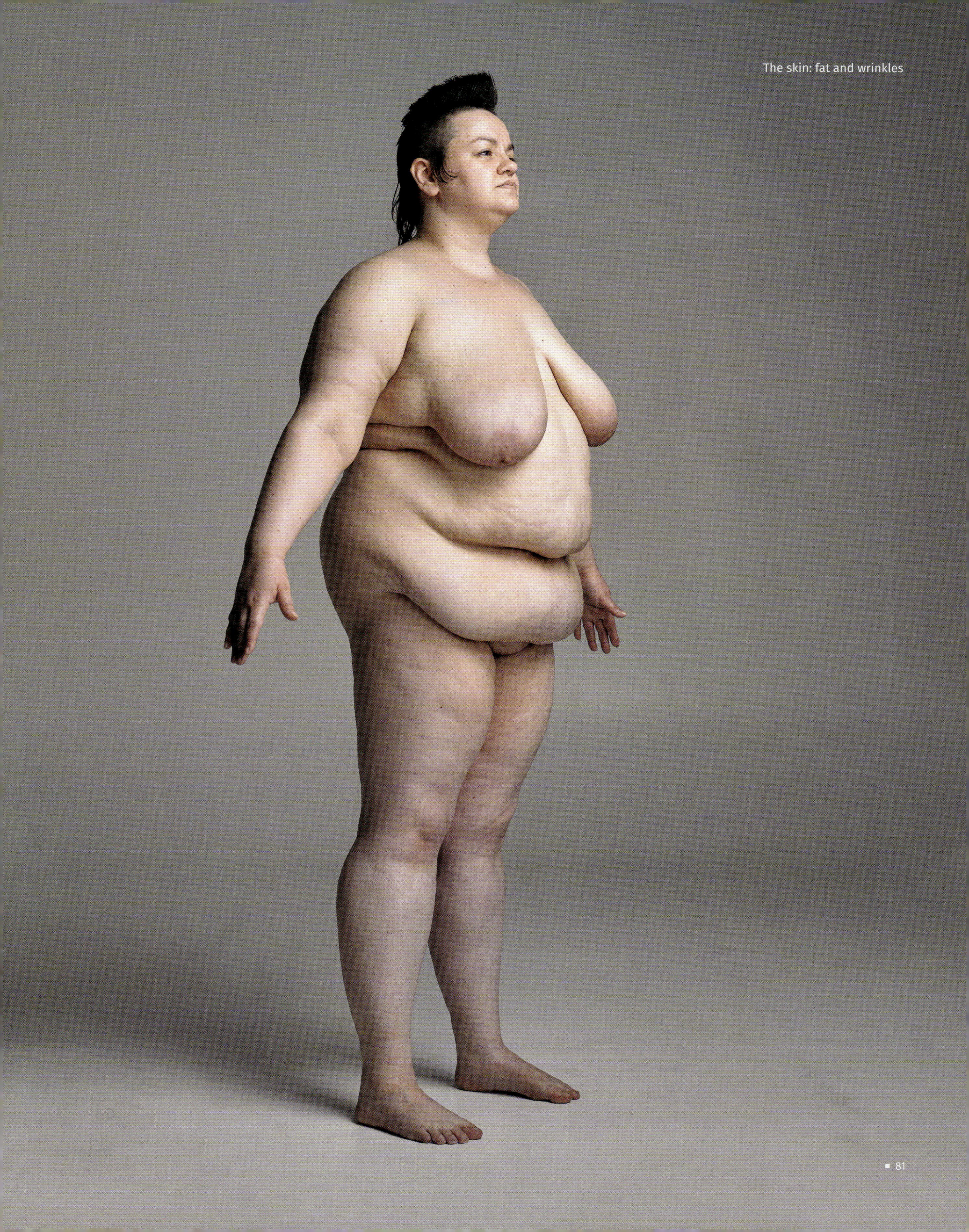

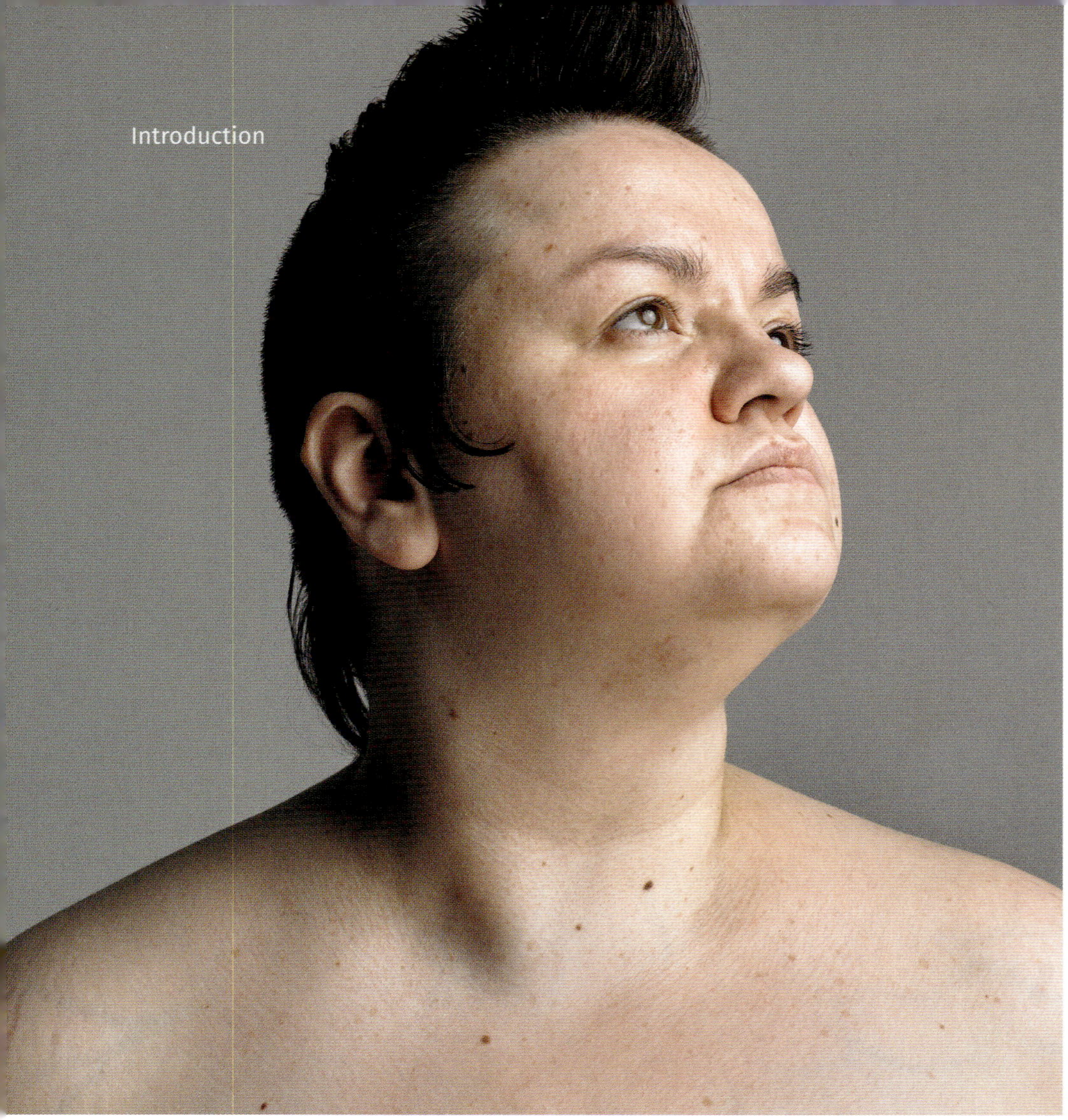

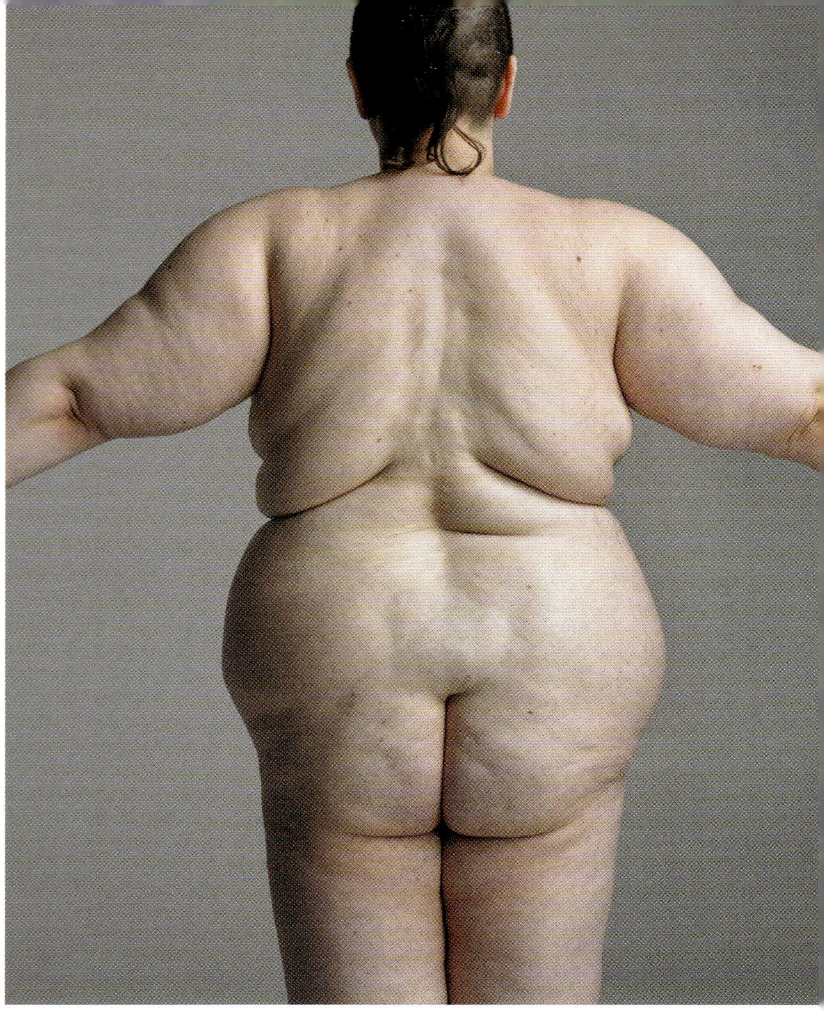

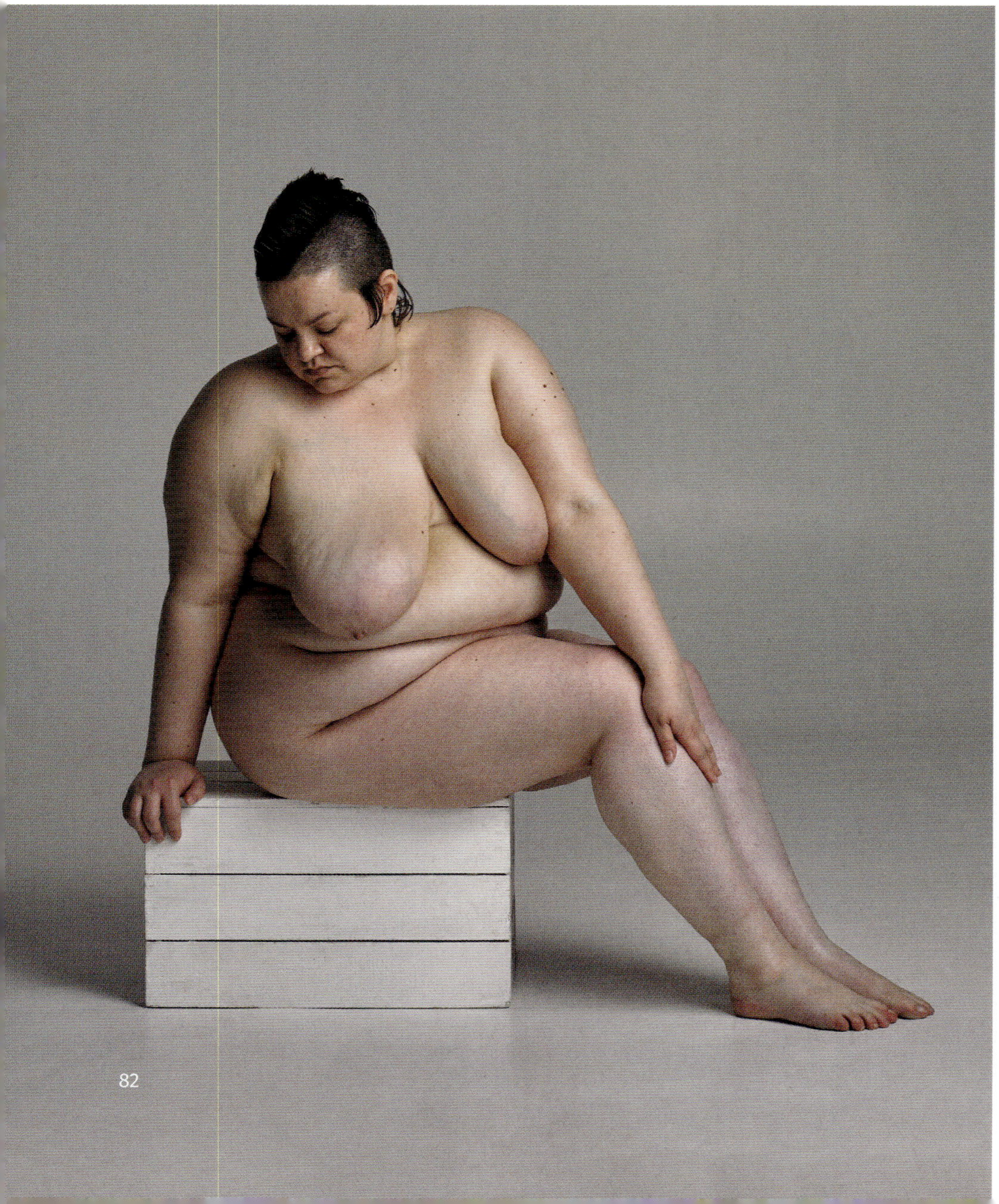

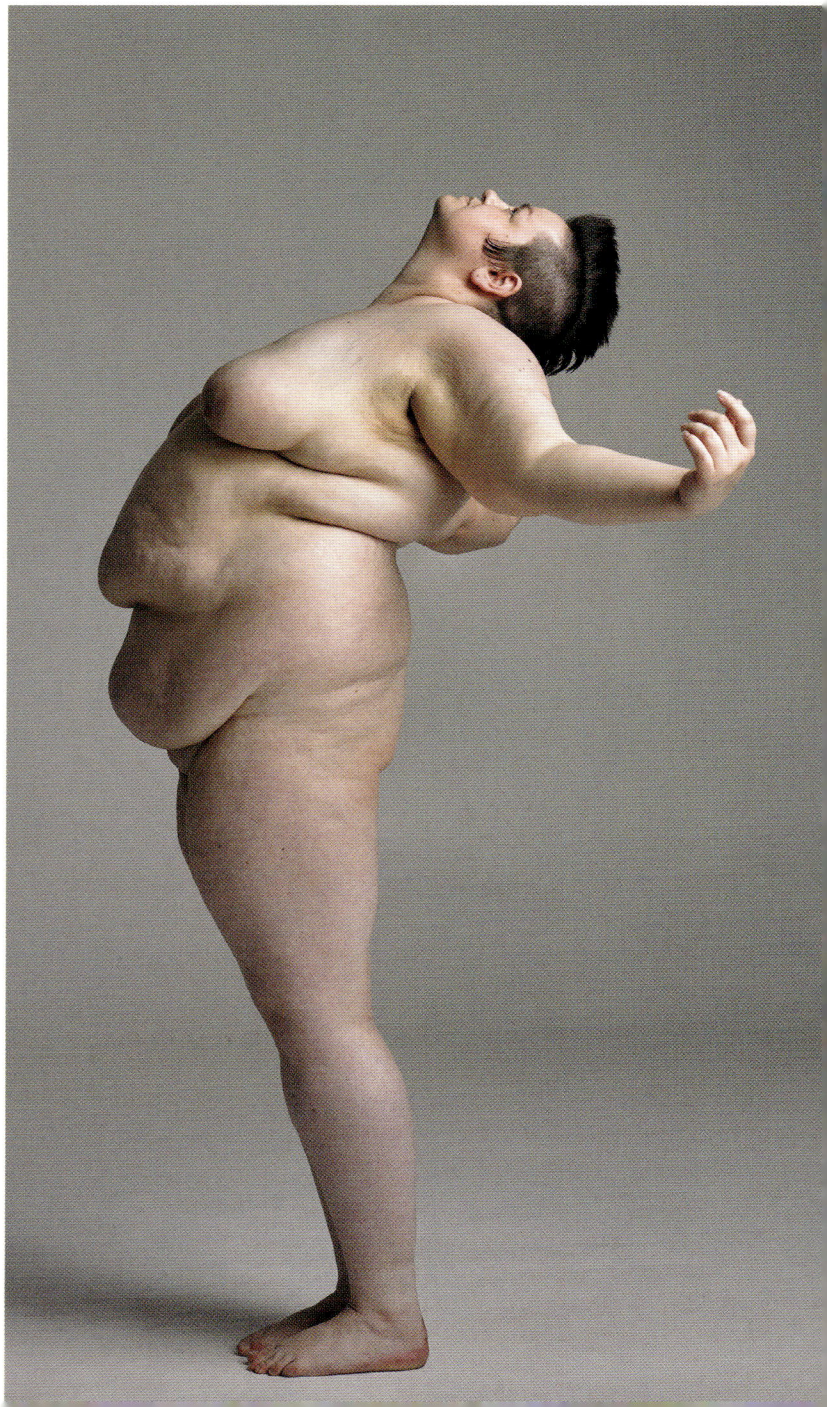

Wrinkles

It is also important to pay attention to wrinkles and to the direction of wrinkle lines in particular. You will notice that throughout the body, wrinkles tend to flow perpendicular to the muscles. Flexing your wrist will demonstrate this.

Look at the wrinkles and folds created by your clothing as you move around. You should notice that the position of the wrinkles tends to be in the same place as on your skin.

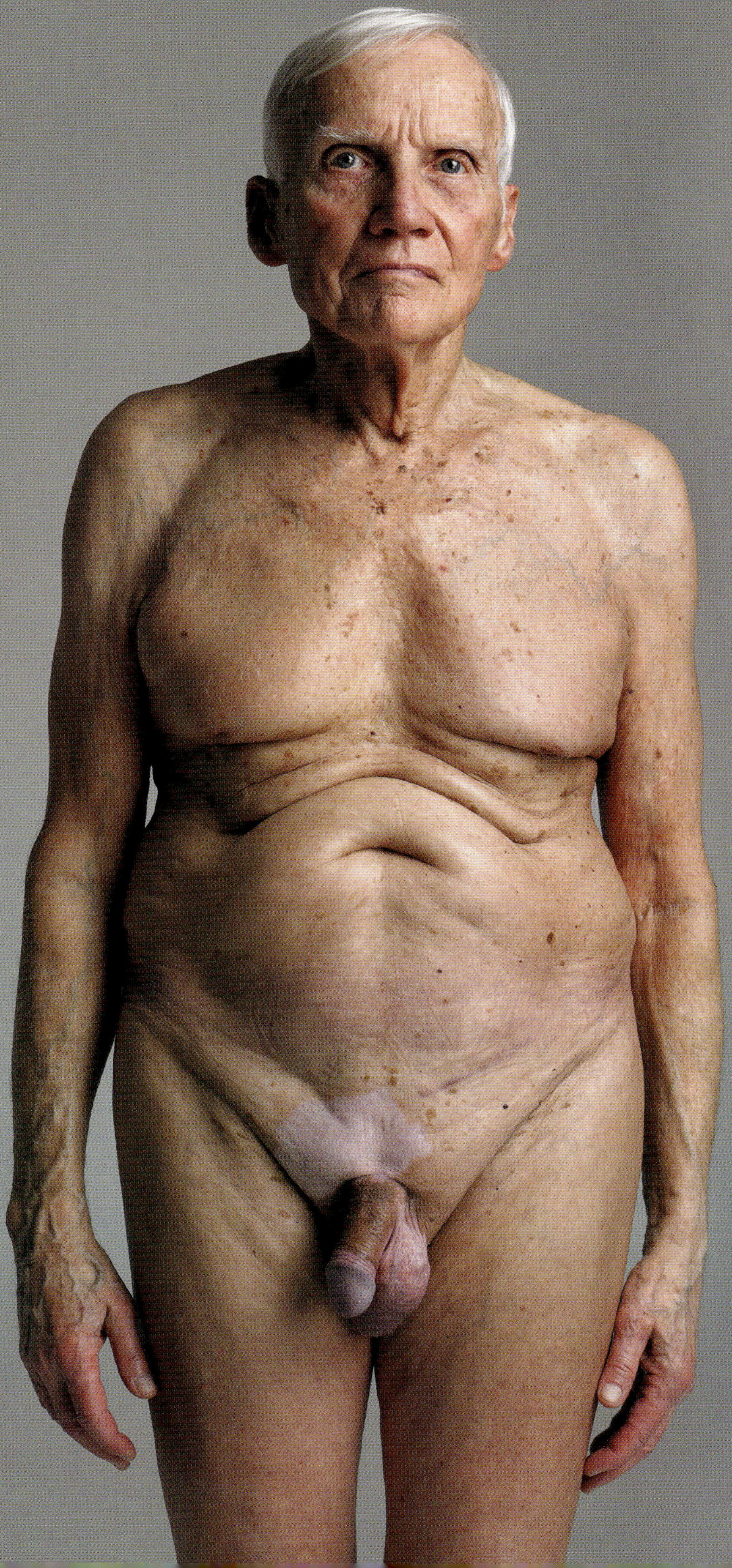

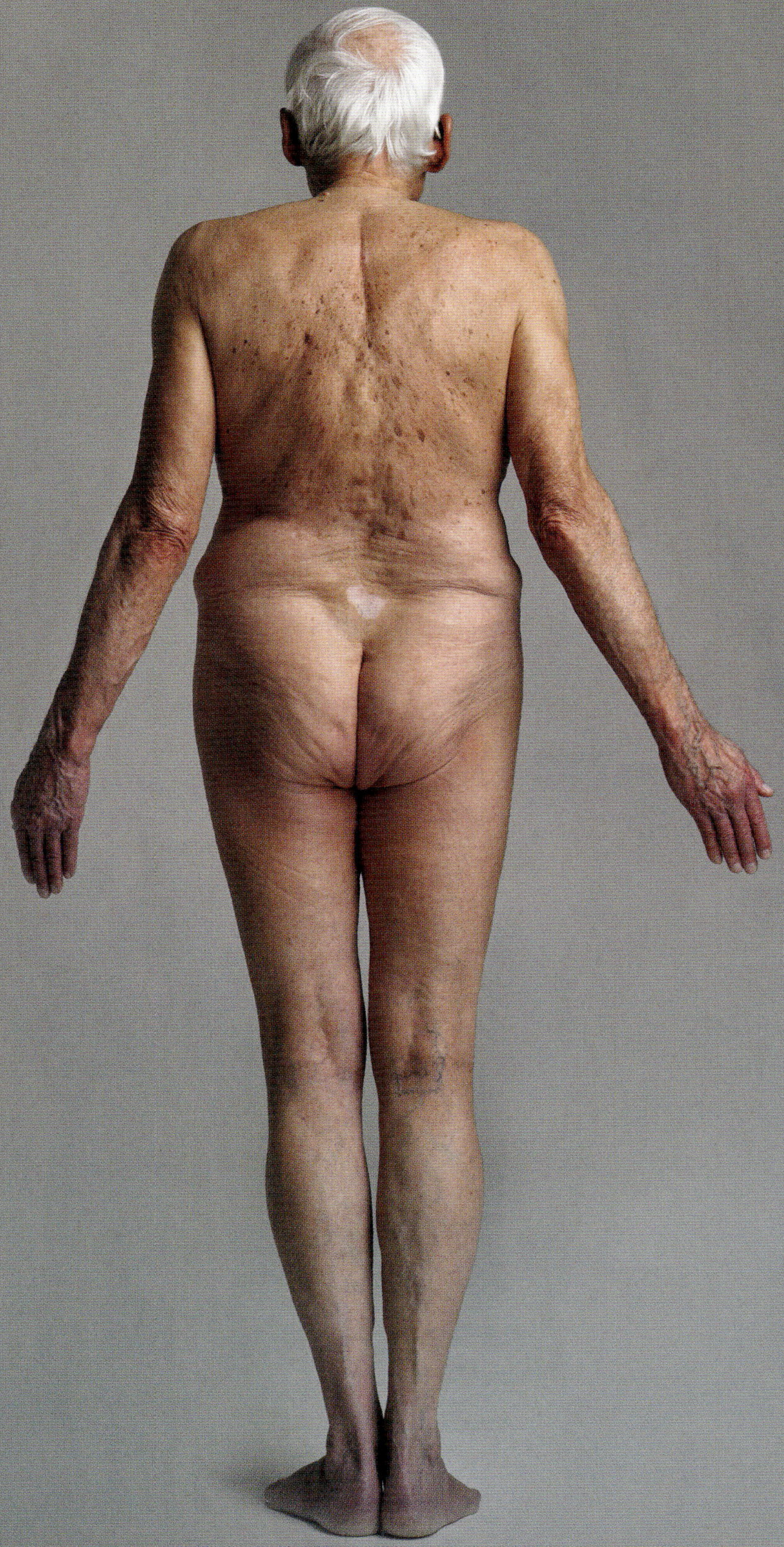

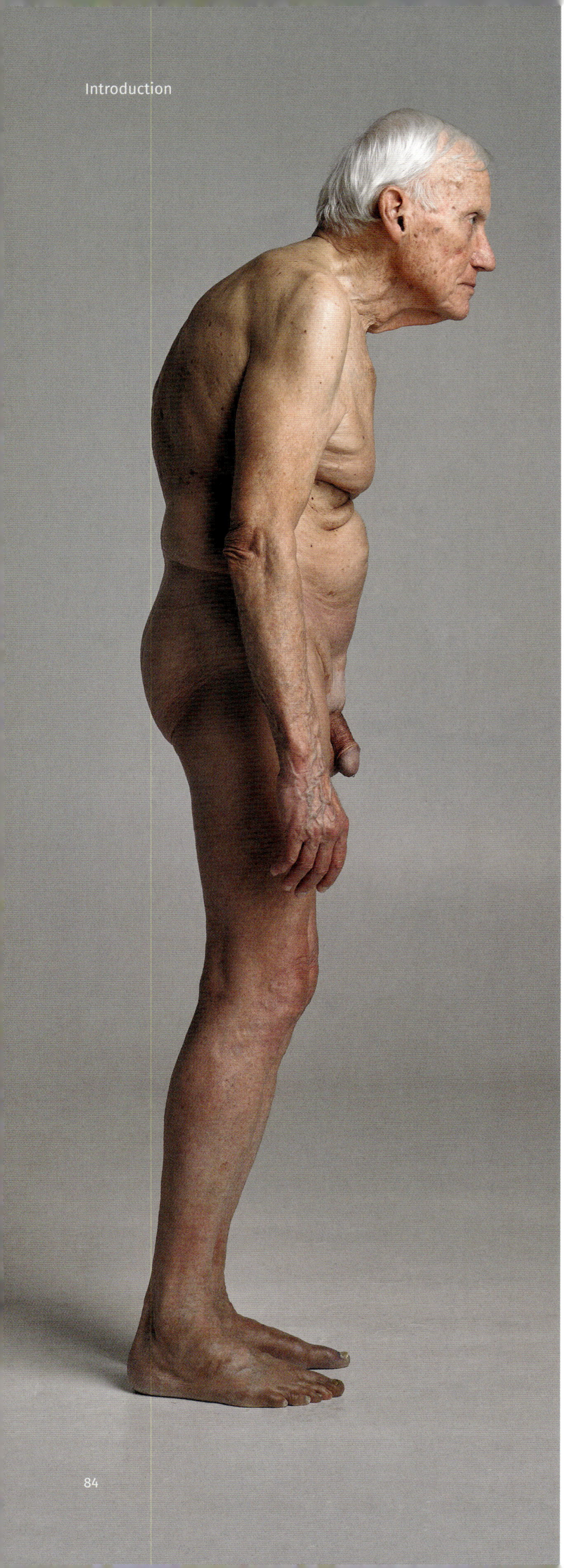

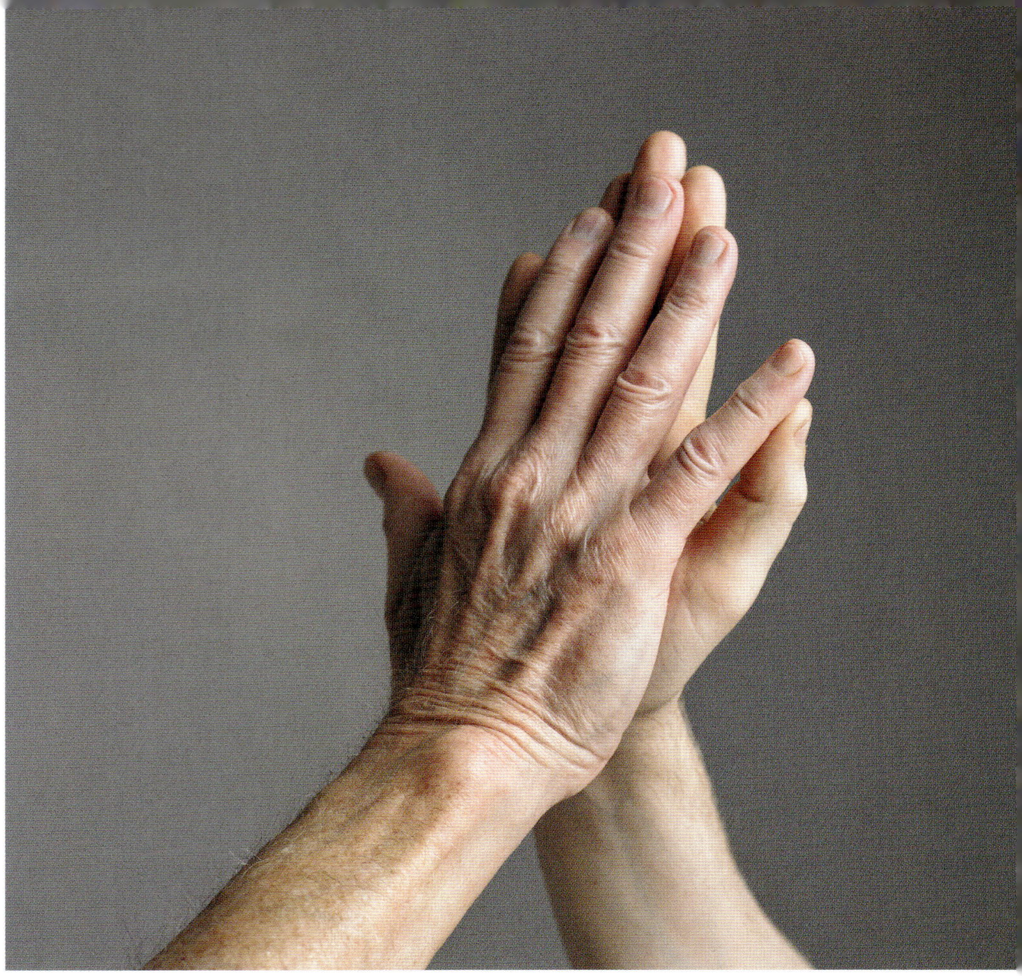

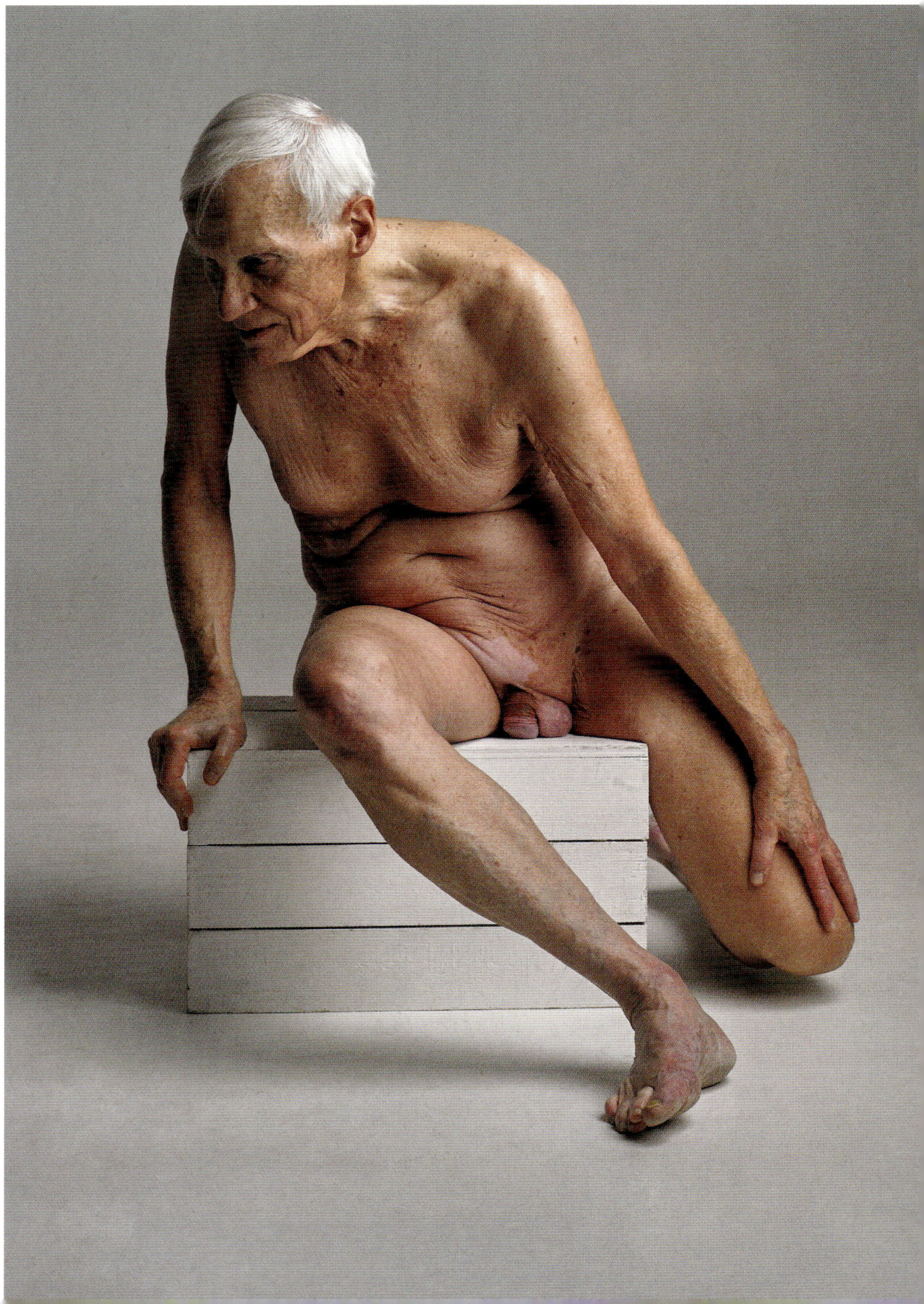

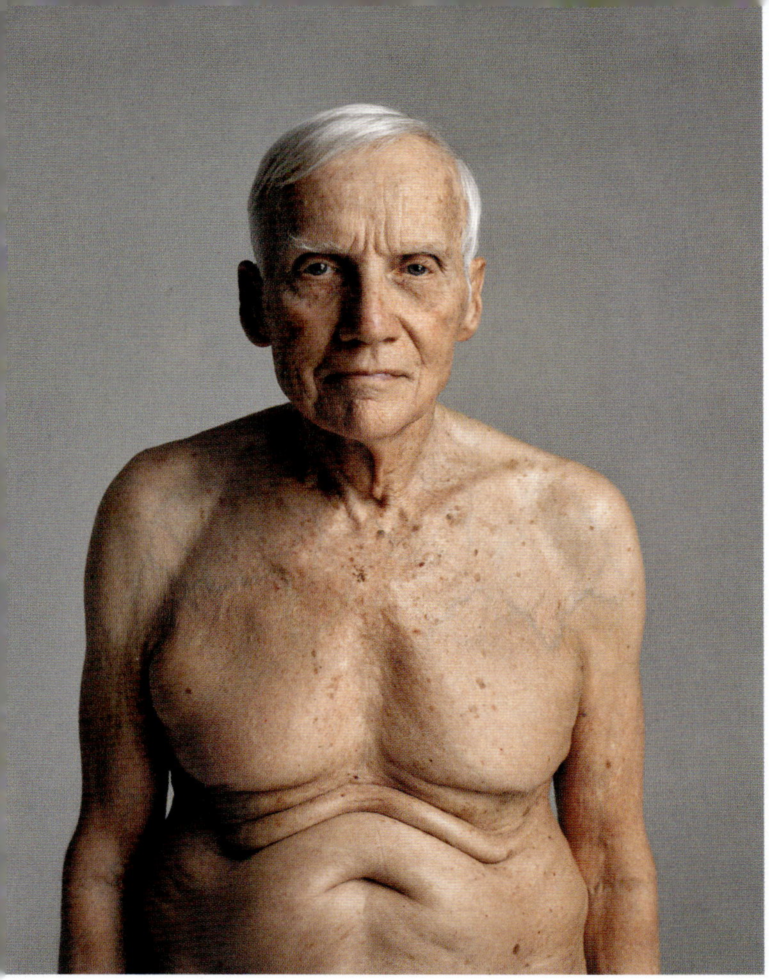

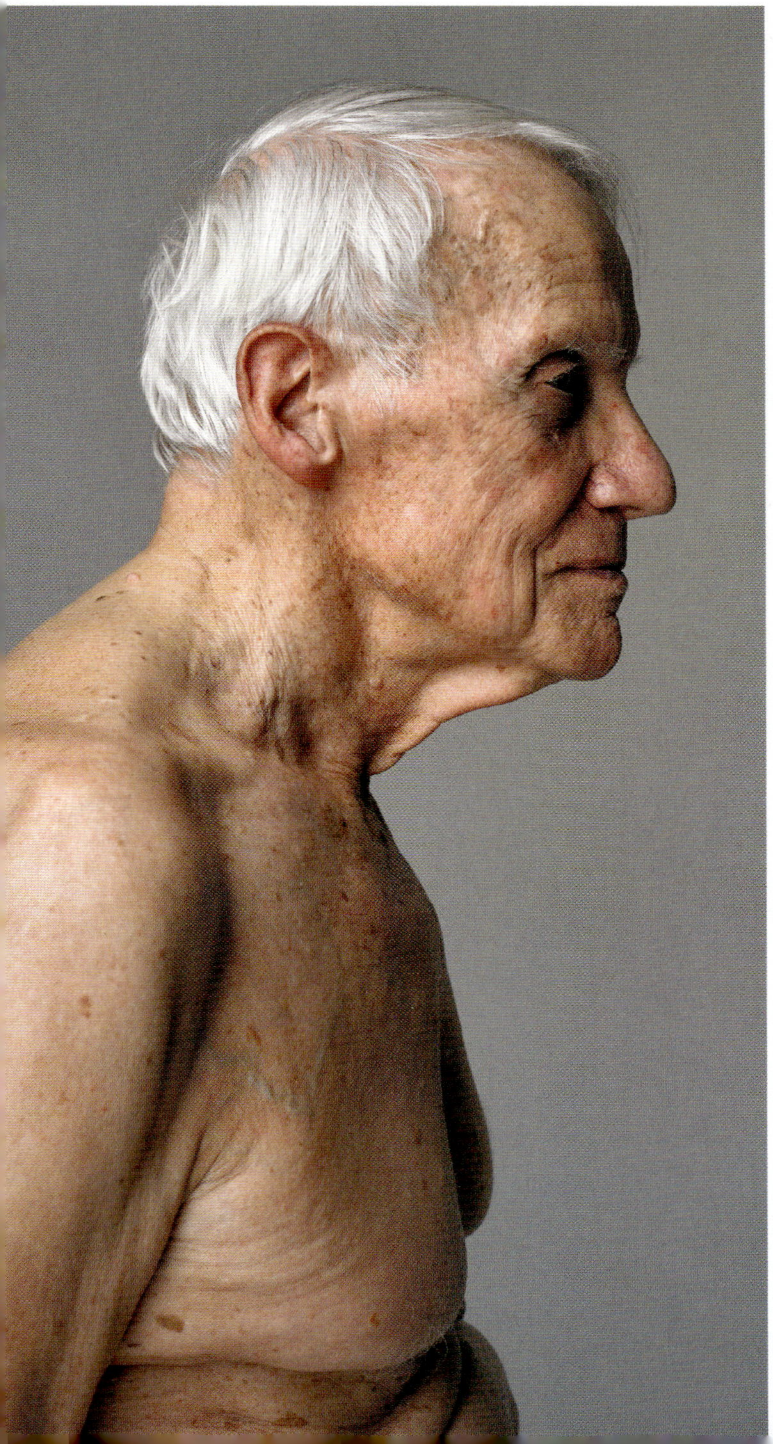

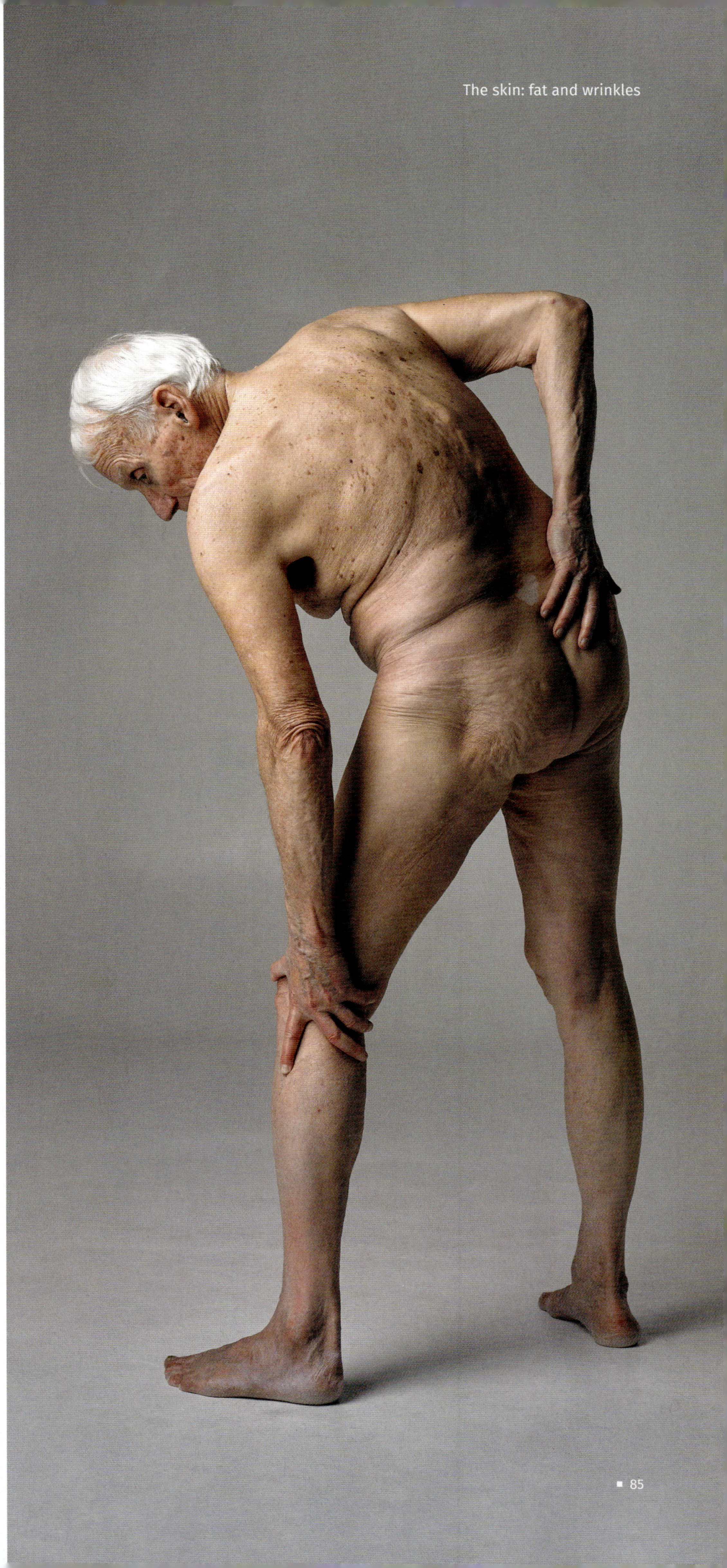

SEX AND AGE

Sex: the male and female forms

Structurally, the male and female forms are the same. Differences occur with shape, mass, skeletal form, and fatty deposits. The vertical midpoint of the male form is at the pubic arch, while on the female it is above the pubic symphysis.

The female form is generally smaller, both proportionately and overall. The head is smaller and the forehead is smoother and more rounded, while the male forehead has a strong brow ridge. Female features are generally smaller, with fuller lips, and the neck is more slender, the shoulders narrower. The male form has a noticeable Adam's apple, while the female thyroid cartilage is more rounded.

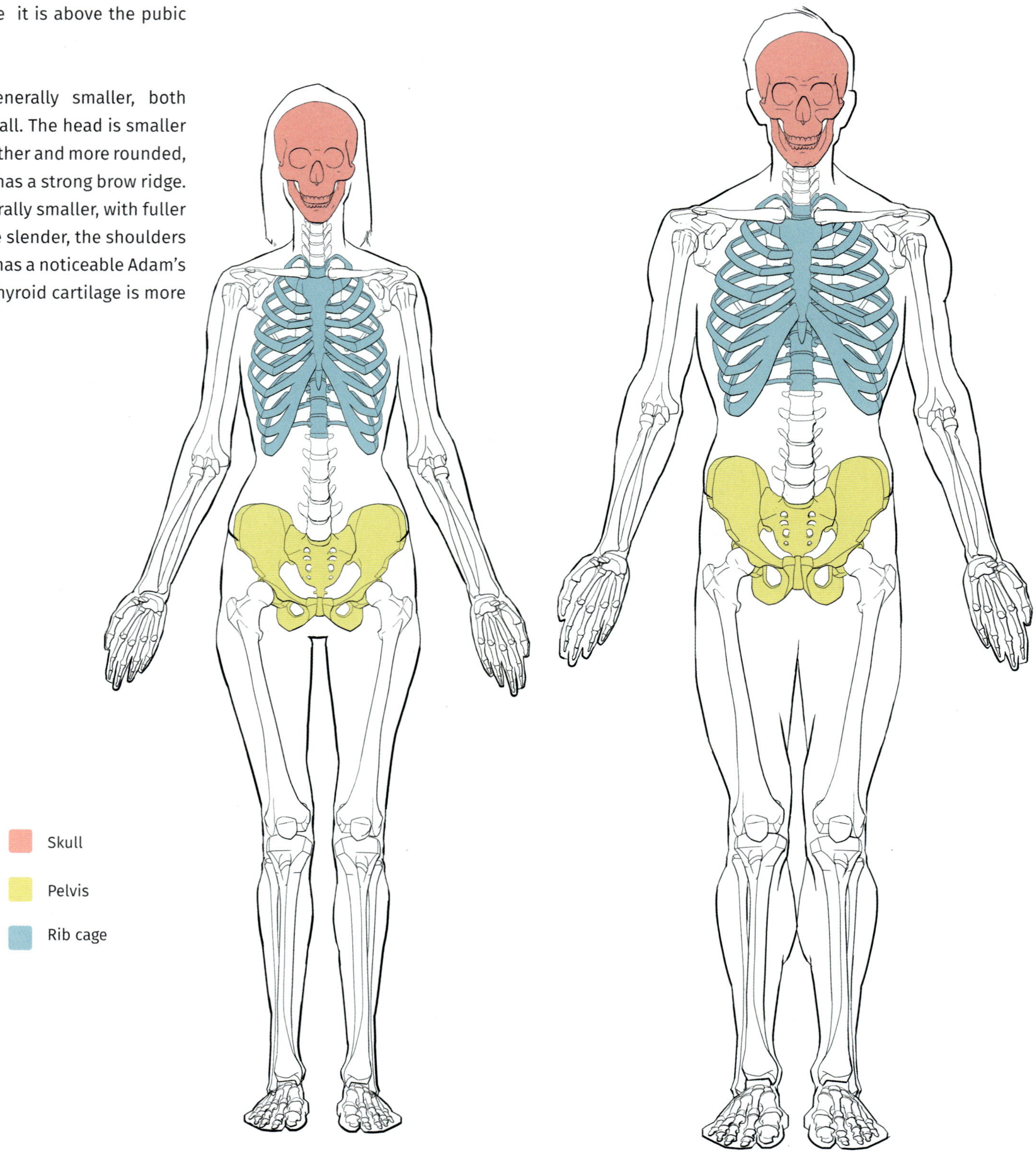

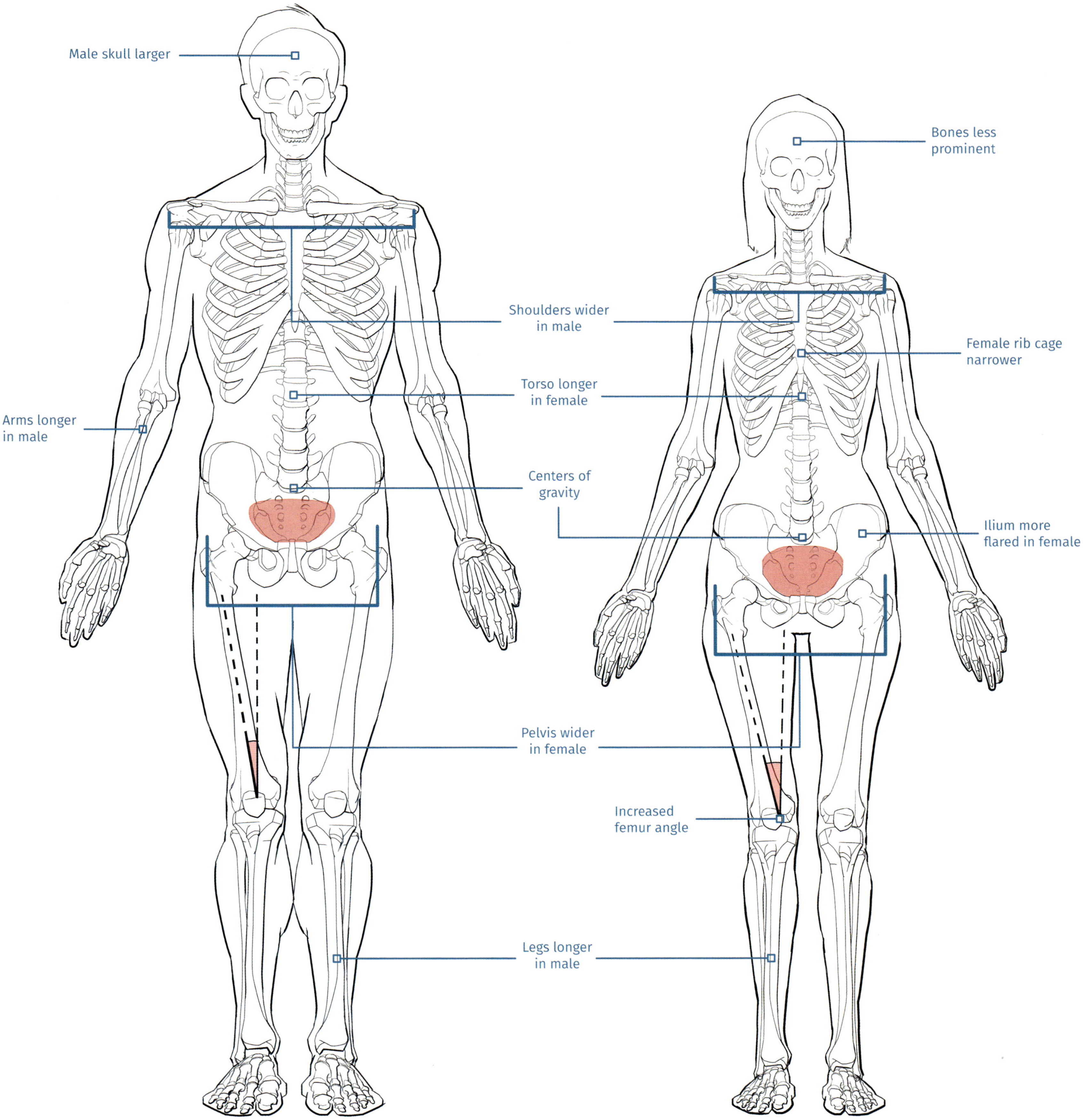
Male skull larger
Bones less prominent
Shoulders wider in male
Female rib cage narrower
Torso longer in female
Arms longer in male
Centers of gravity
Ilium more flared in female
Pelvis wider in female
Increased femur angle
Legs longer in male

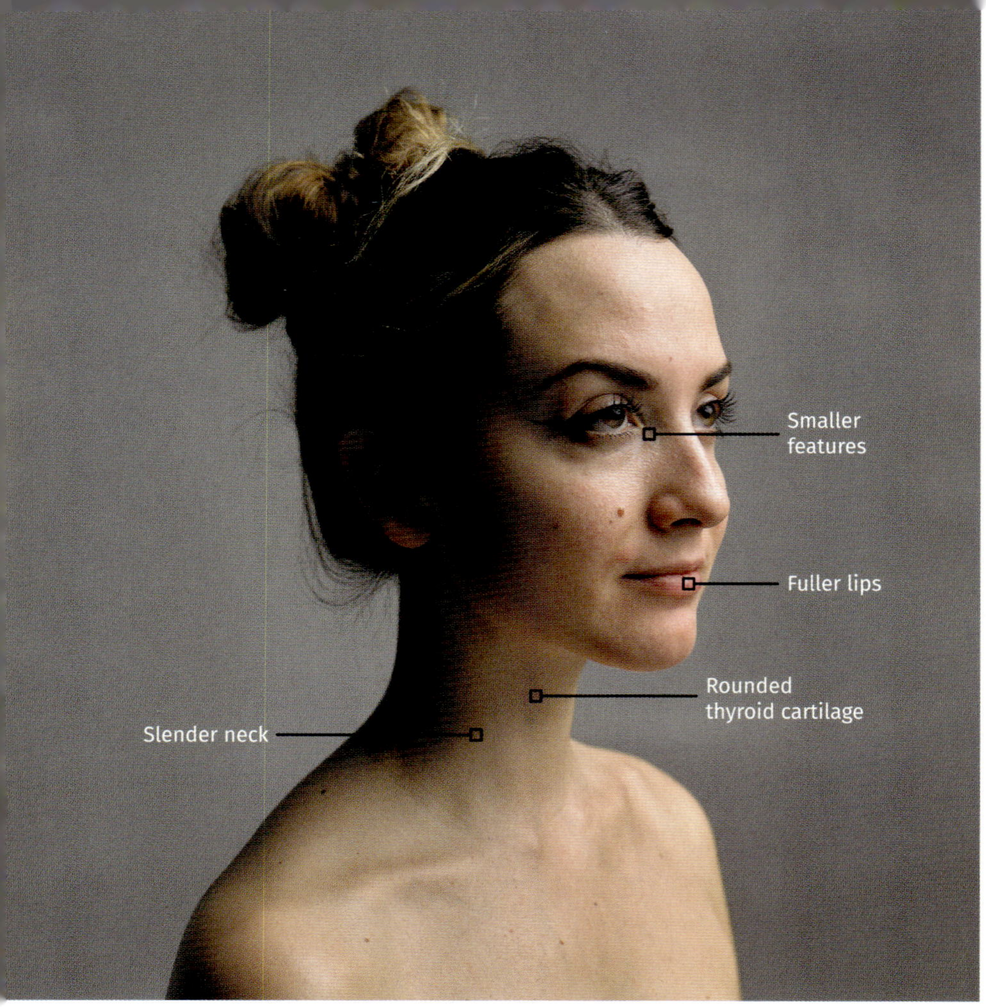
Smaller
features
Fuller lips
Rounded
thyroid cartilage
Slender neck

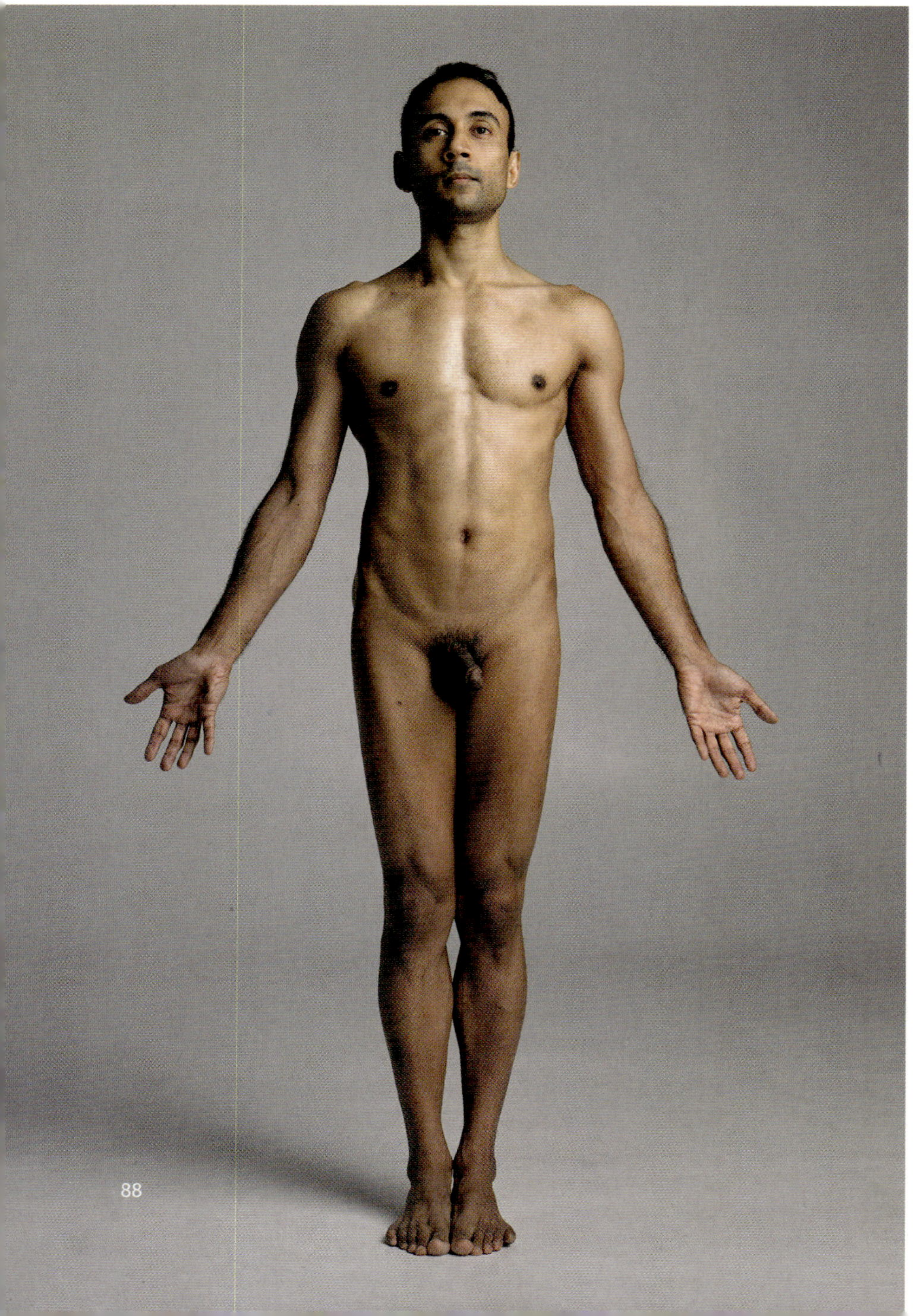

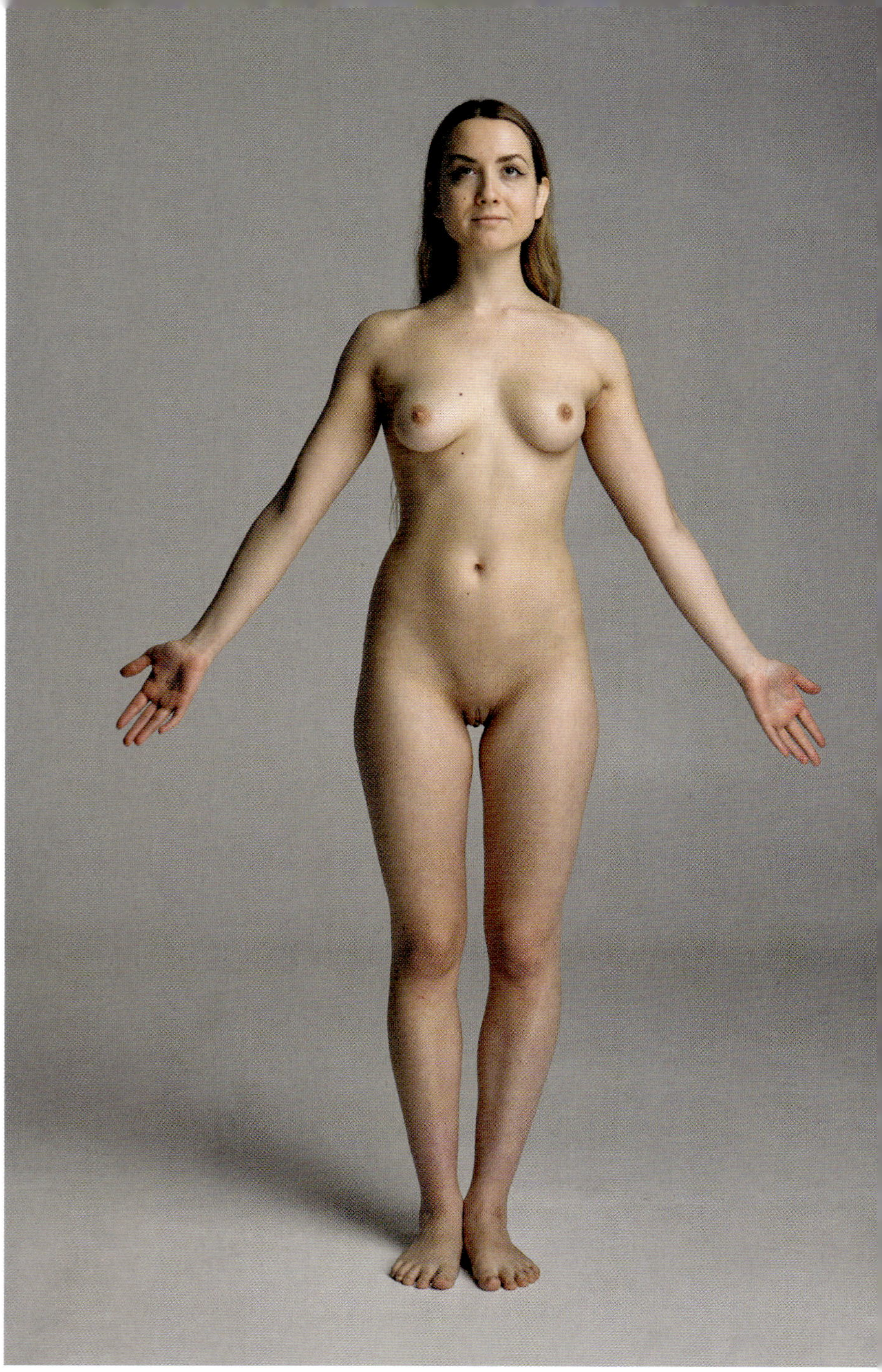

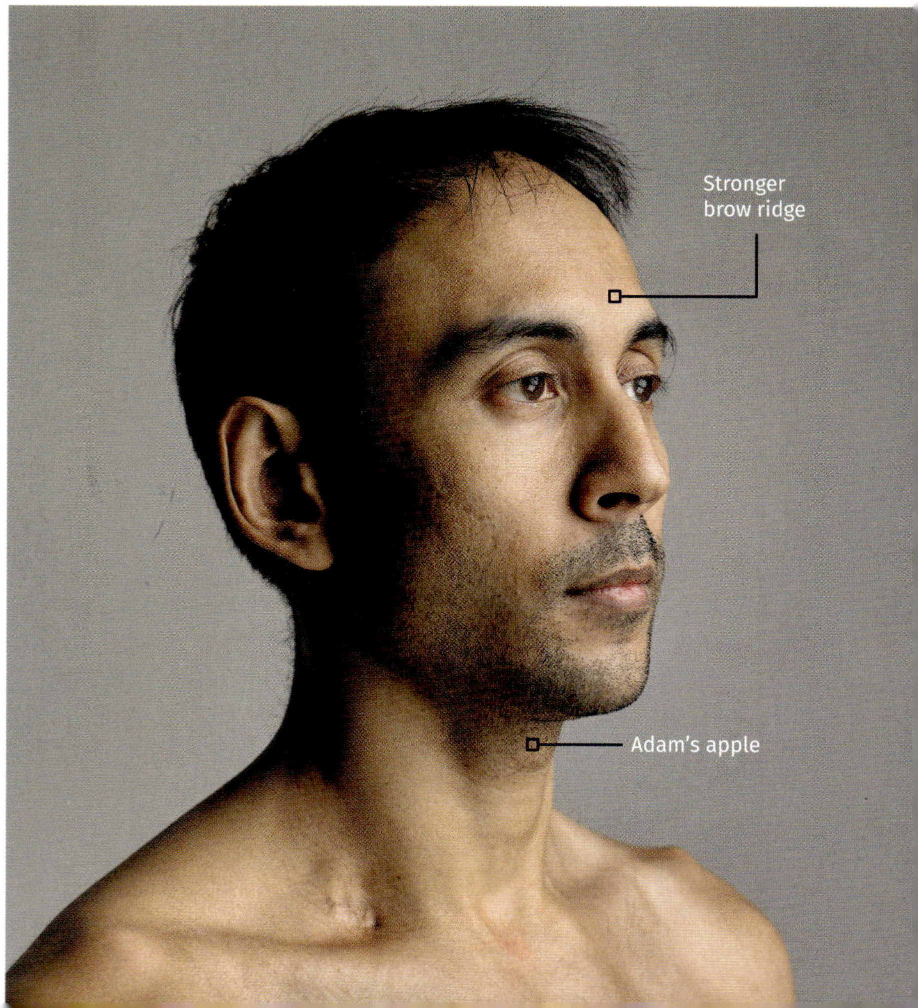
Stronger
brow ridge
Adam's apple

A major area of difference to note is the pelvis. The female pelvis is shorter, but wider and deeper, and is angled further forward. The hip joints are also further apart in the female, making the hips wider.

MALE PELVIS

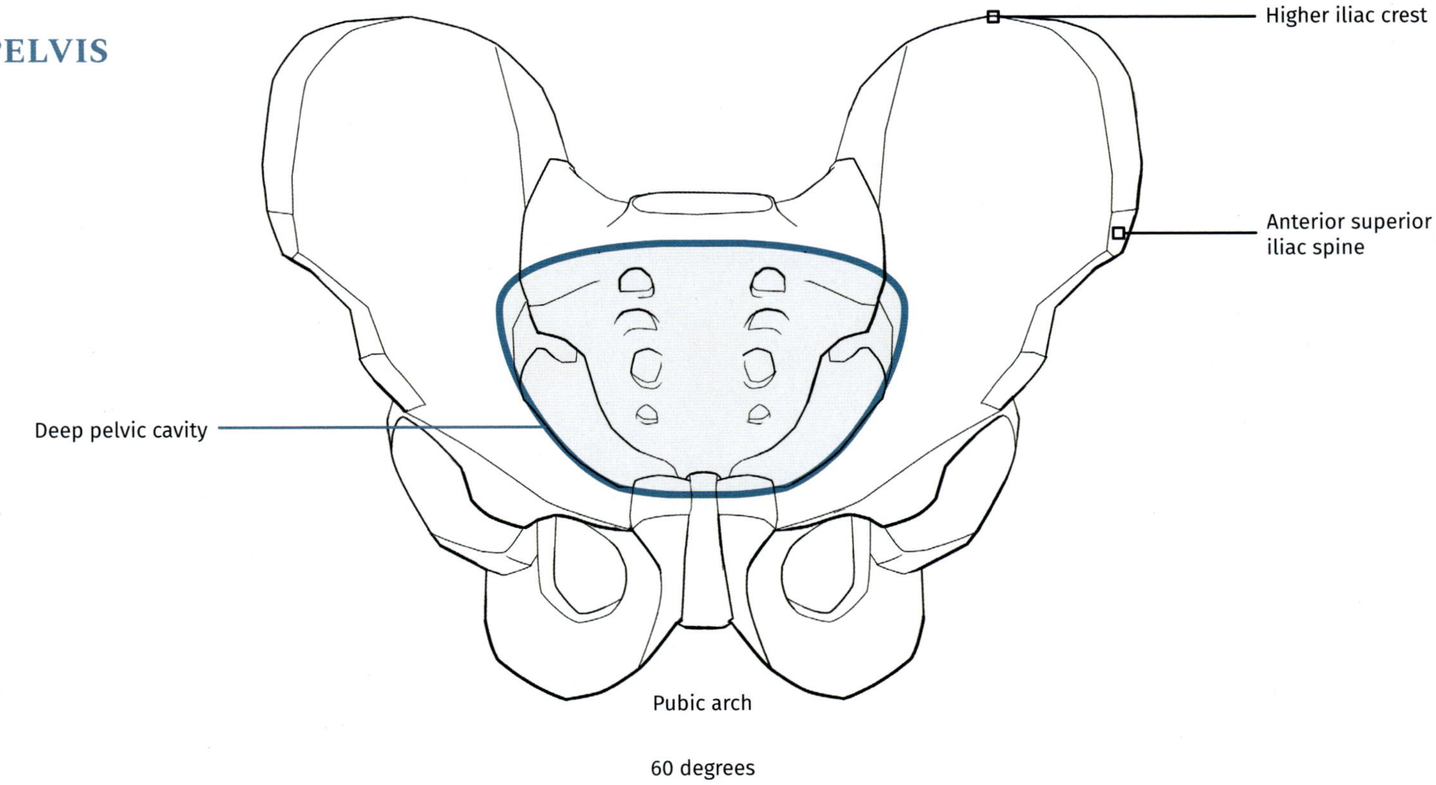

FEMALE PELVIS

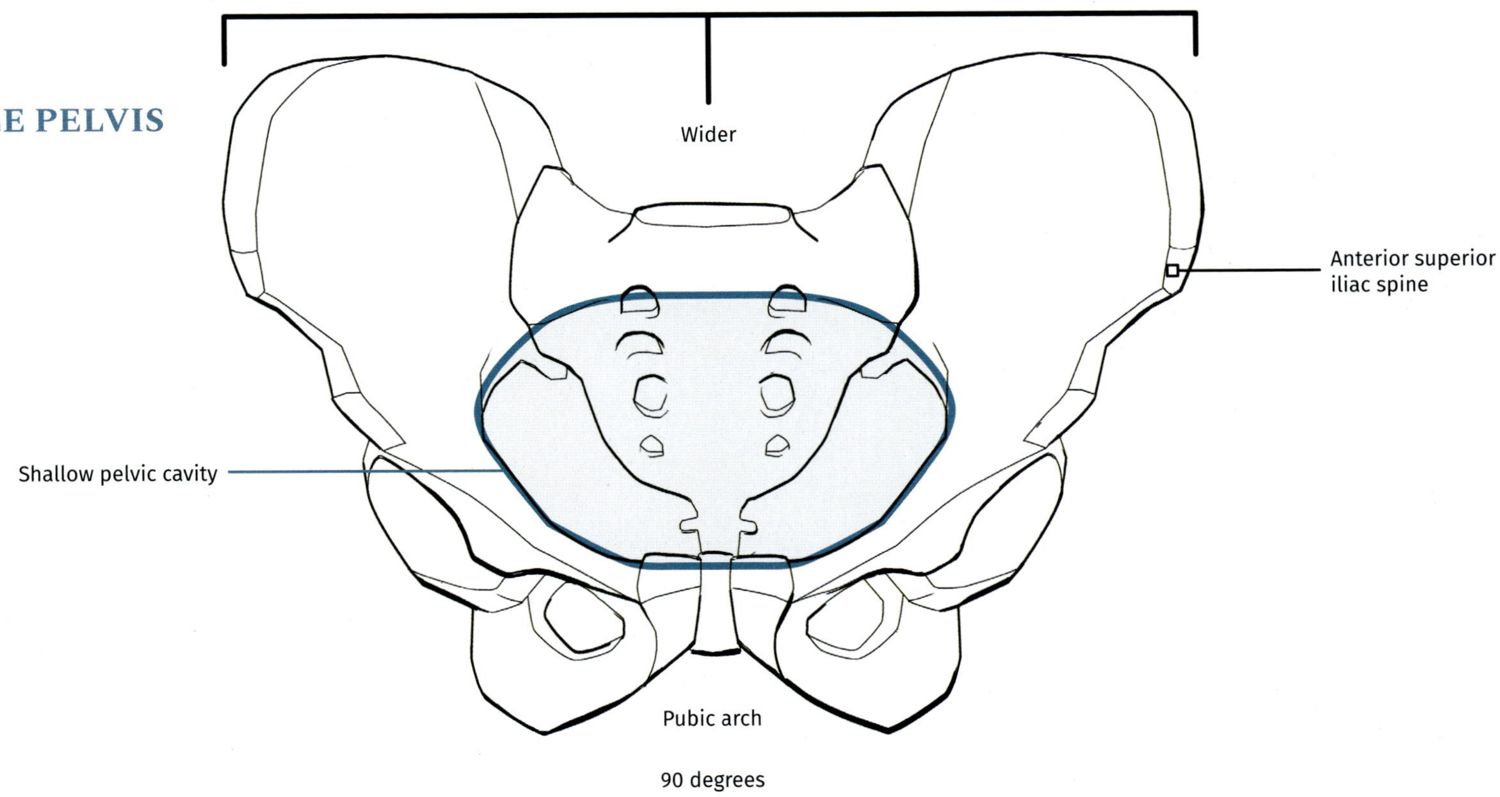

The male form generally has longer arms, as the humerus is longer, and the torso itself is longer too. Similarly, the wrists and hands are proportionately larger, and the thighs and legs are longer also. However, the knees on the female are rounder.

Nearly all fatty deposits are larger in the female. The principal fatty deposits are those of the breasts, abdomen, buttocks, and thighs. For males, it is primarily the abdomen and buttocks.

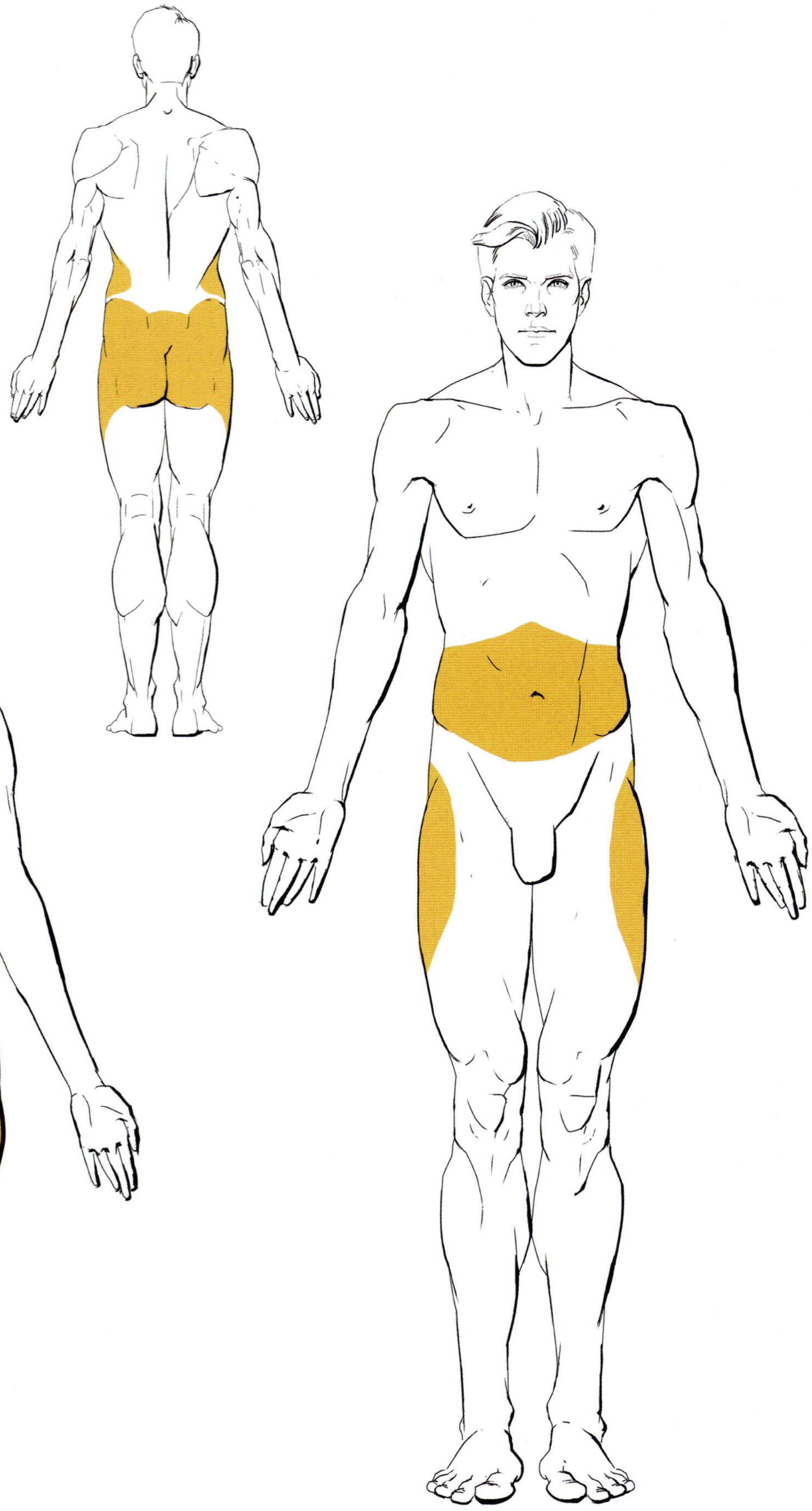

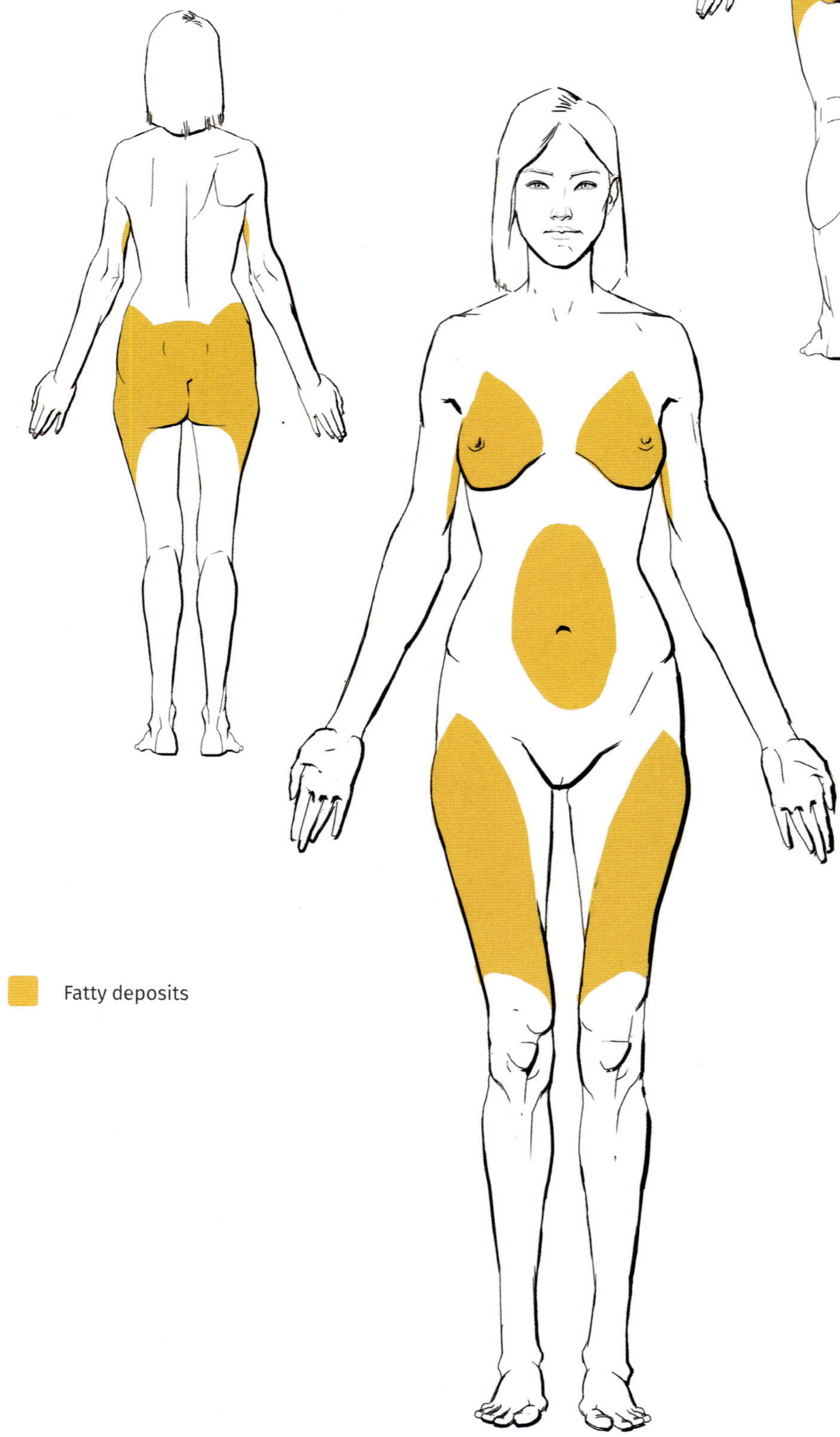

Age

The human body grows and changes gradually from birth until death, but development is concentrated at certain stages. This chapter will look at each stage in chronological order.

Birth

The center of a baby's body is the navel. The head is generally fifty percent larger proportionately than the adult head and is mainly cranium. All four limbs are rounded and are more or less the same length.

Infancy and childhood

The areas above and between the nipples go through a period of considerable growth, as do the forearms and thighs, which lengthen significantly. The spine, which has only one backward convex curve at birth, starts to develop a four-arch curve.

Puberty

This period of change shows both adult and child figures in varying proportions as time progresses. Sexual distinctions become increasingly apparent: the male form being angular, the female generally curvaceous. Breasts and other fatty deposits develop on the female, and the lumbar curve of the spine is fully formed in both sexes.

Young adulthood

At this stage the male musculature becomes visible, while the female develops fuller breasts, hips, and thighs.

Maturity

Full maturity comes at approximately twenty-one for females and twenty-five for males. During later maturity or middle age, there is weight gain and reduced pigment.

Old age

At this stage elasticity of muscle and ligament reduces and wrinkles form. The flesh wastes away and therefore the veins below the skin become increasingly apparent. Due to the wasting of flesh, the joints, hands, feet, and head seem proportionately large. The spine loses its strength and begins to slouch forward, so the overall height of the human form is reduced. Adding to this development is the shrinkage of the vertebral disks. The ears and nose, being mainly cartilage, appear relatively large.

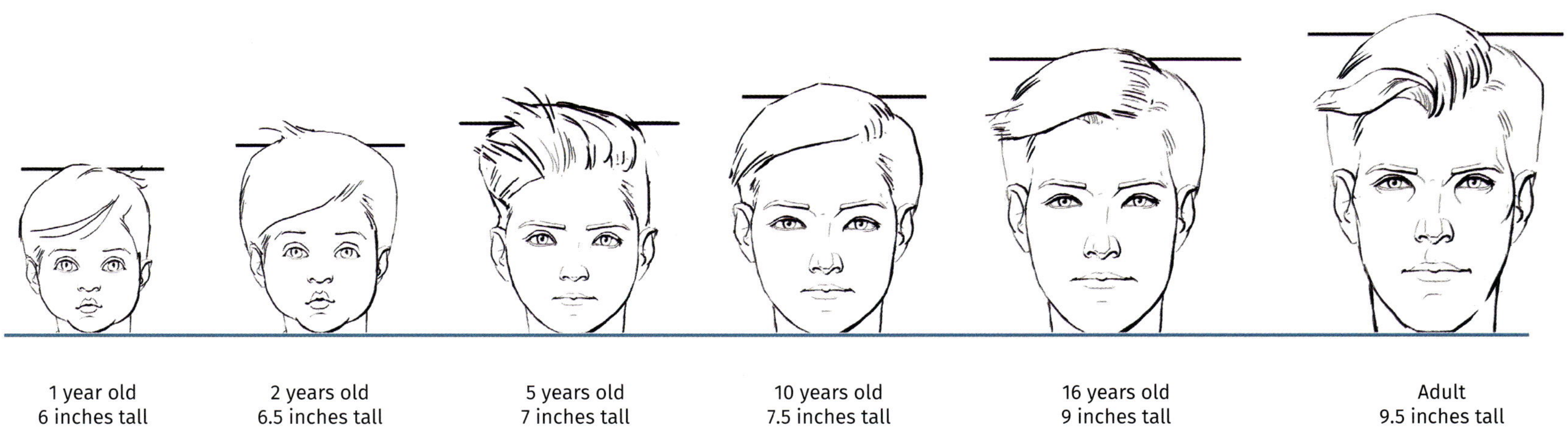

Example head growth from baby through to adult, measured in inches. This is an approximate guide only.

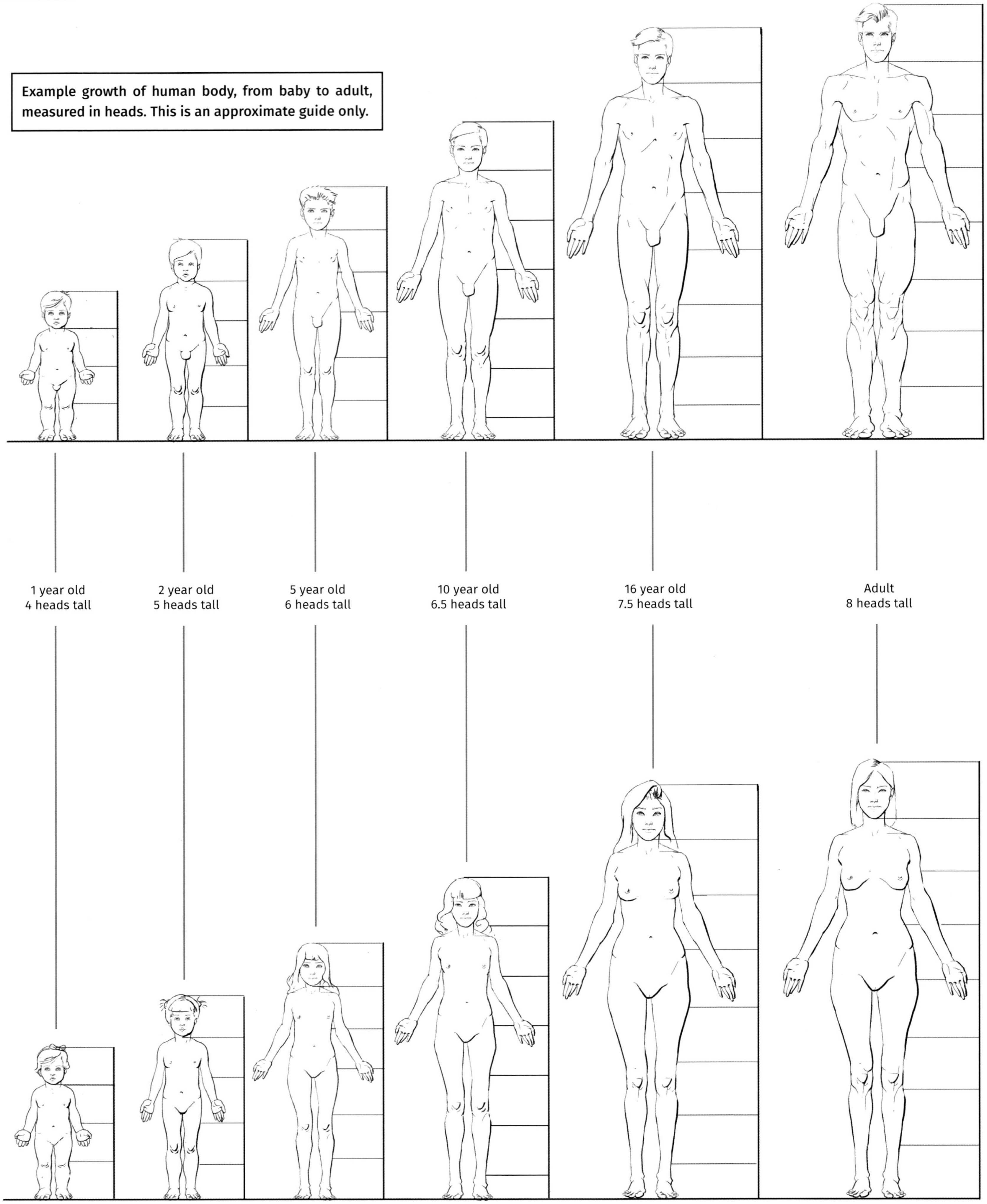
Example growth of human body, from baby to adult, measured in heads. This is an approximate guide only.
1 year old
4 heads tall
2 year old
5 heads tall
5 year old
6 heads tall
10 year old
6.5 heads tall
16 year old
7.5 heads tall
Adult
8 heads tall

WRINKLES OF OLD AGE

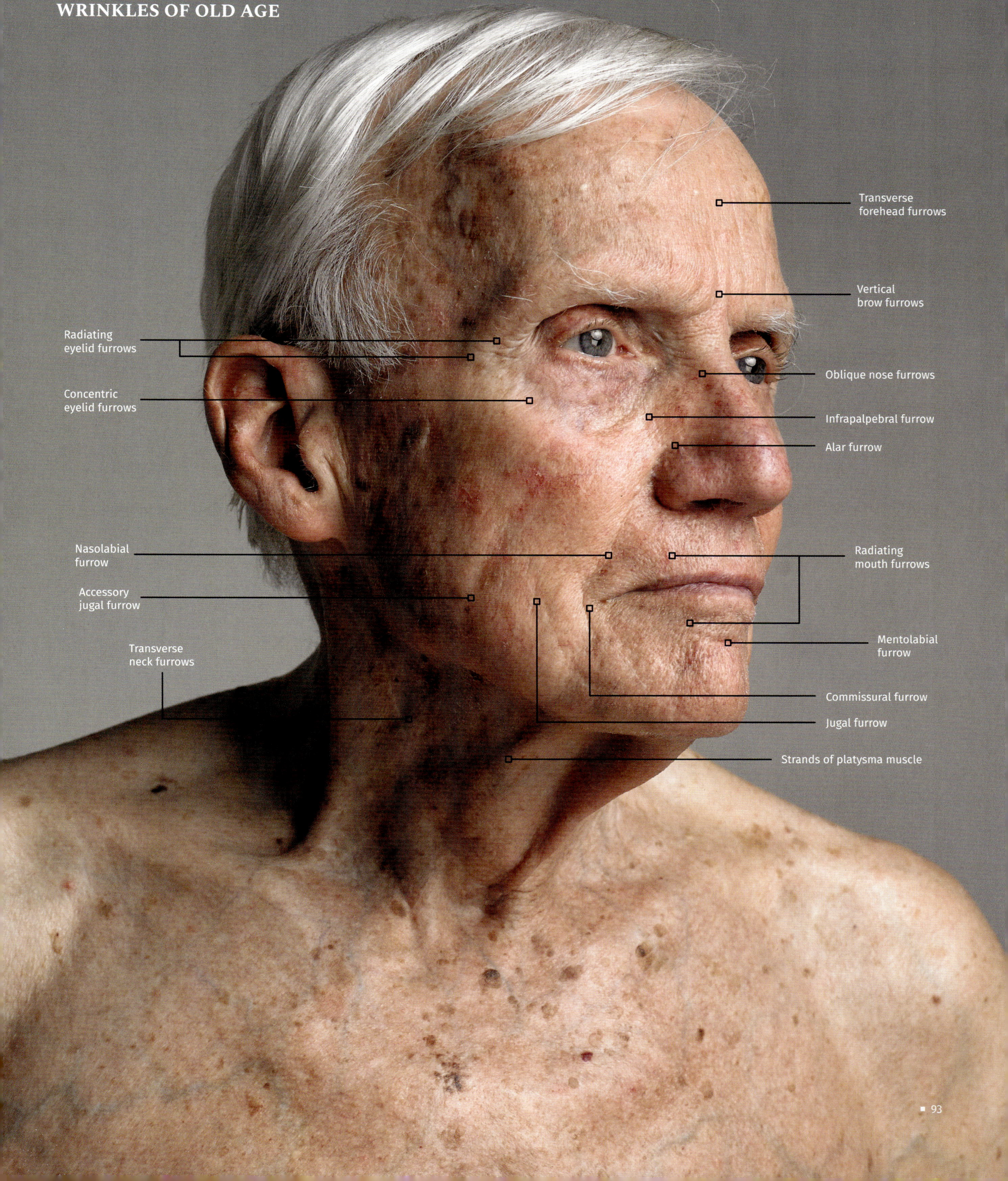

Visual reference library

Artwork by Charlie Pickard

TORSO

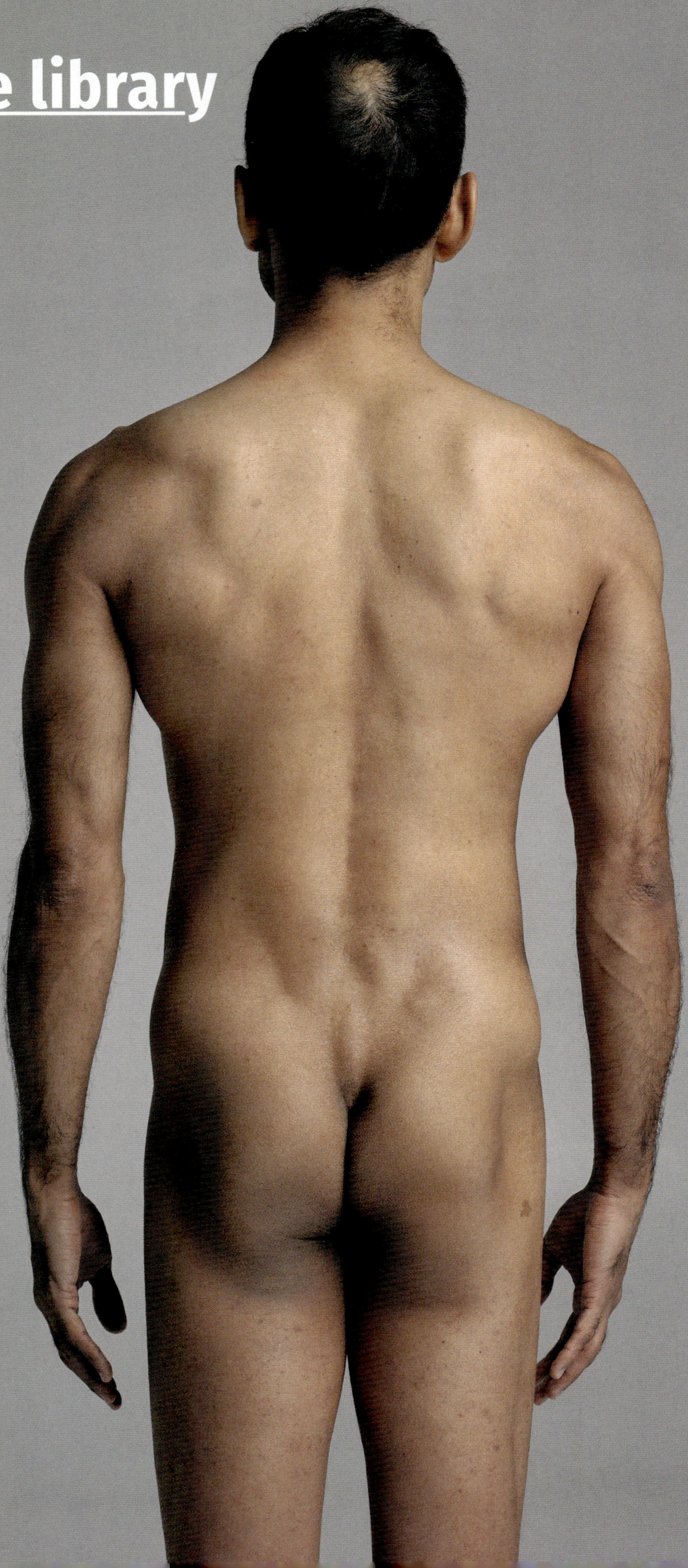

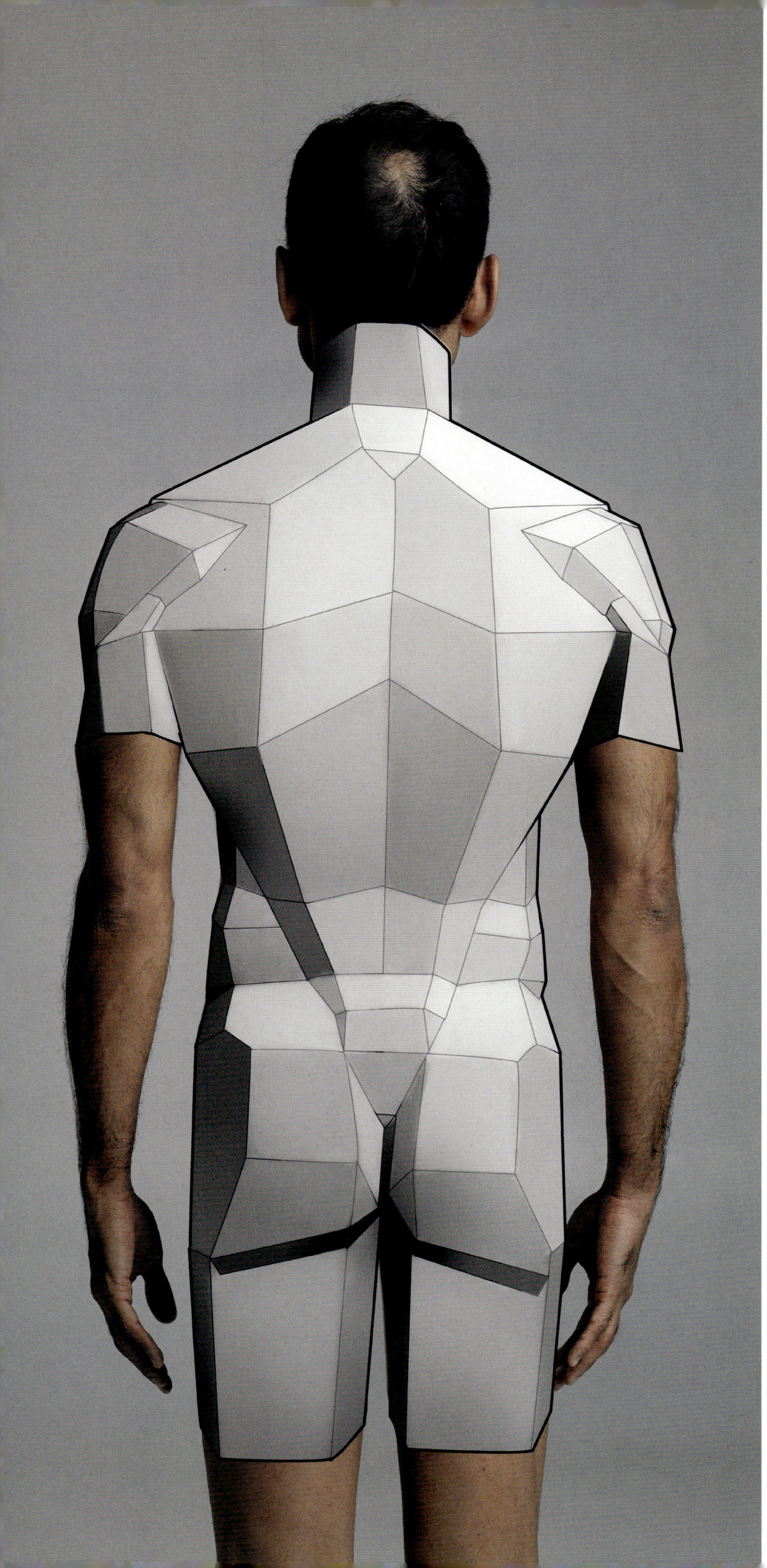
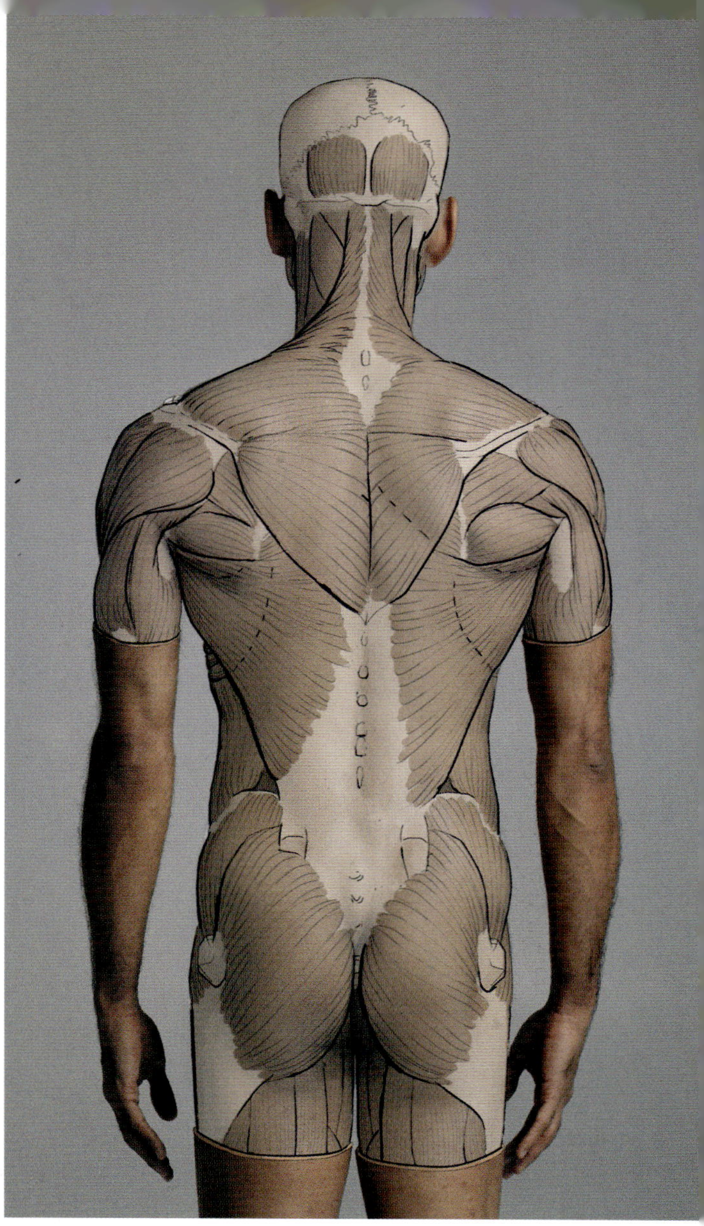
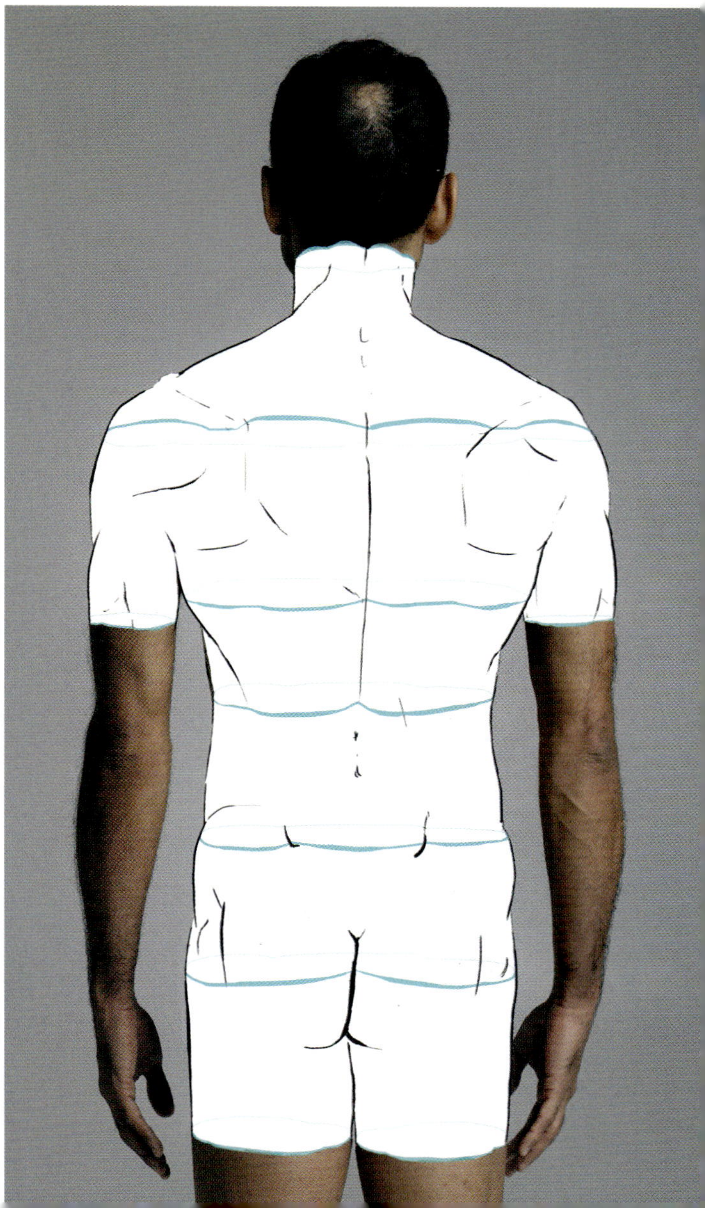

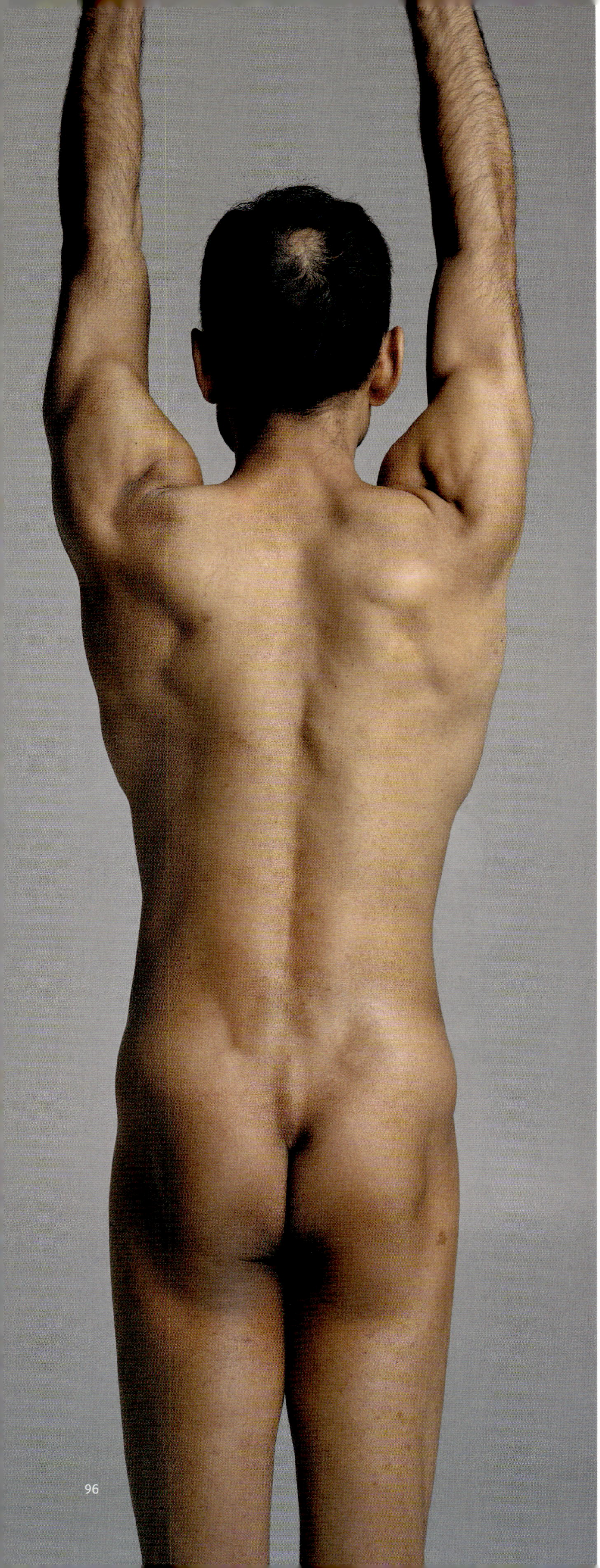

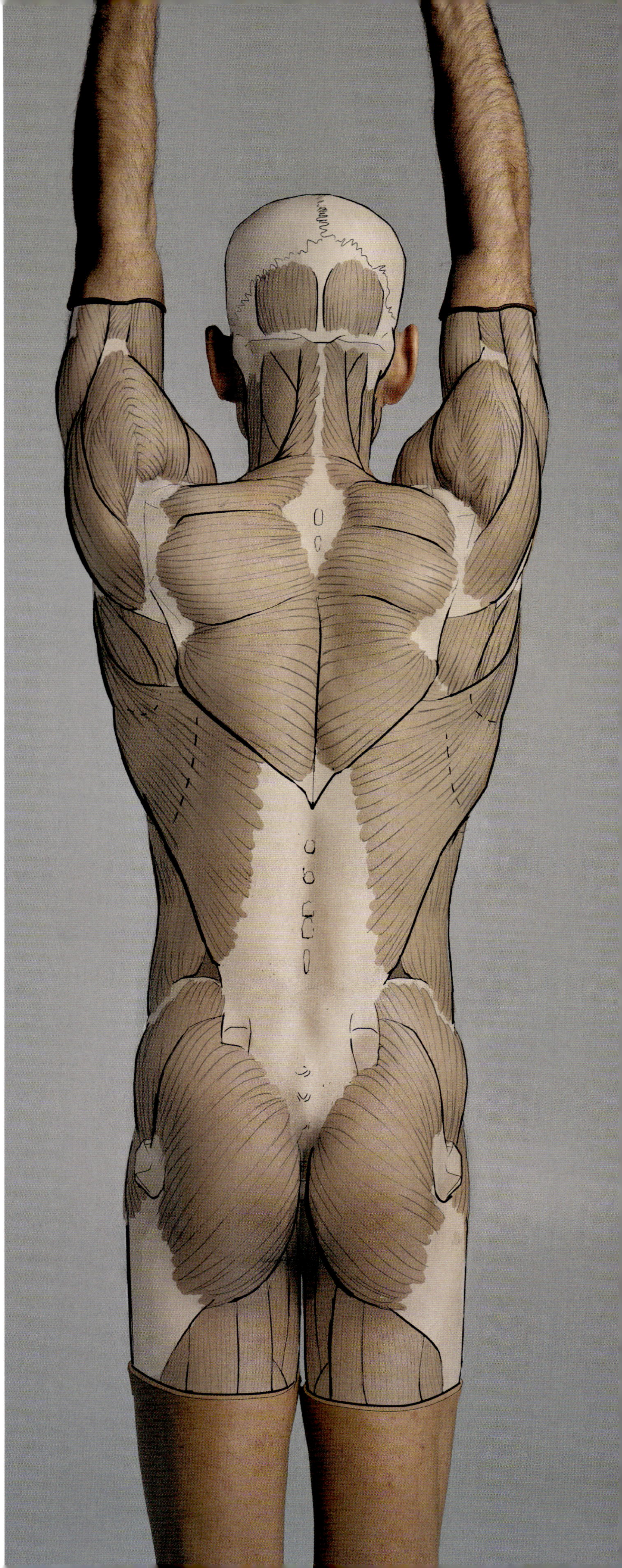

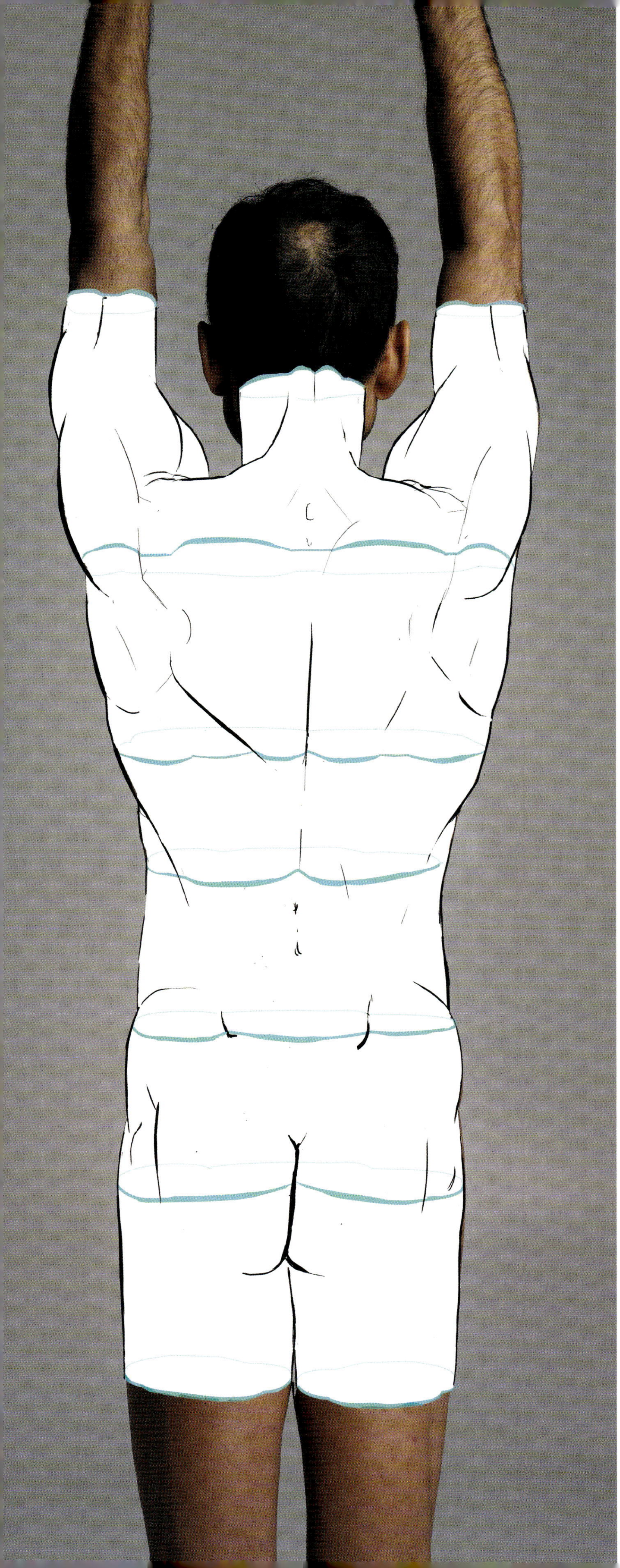

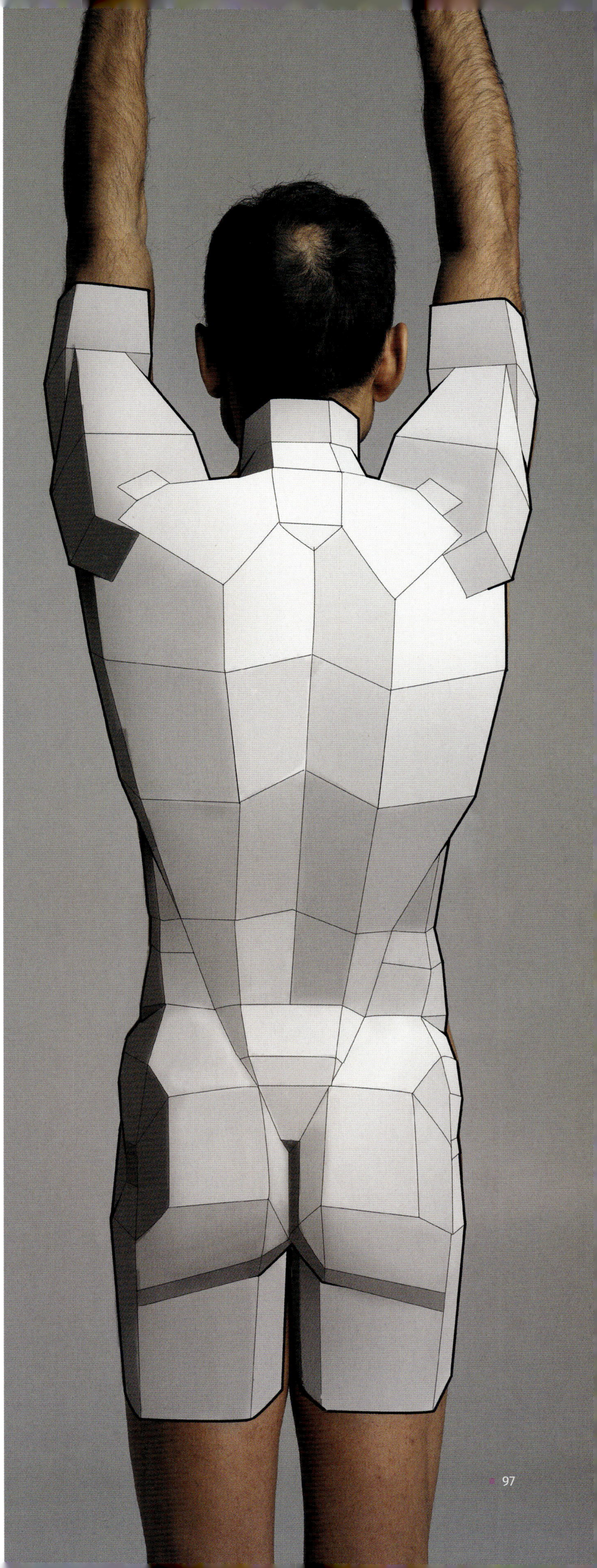

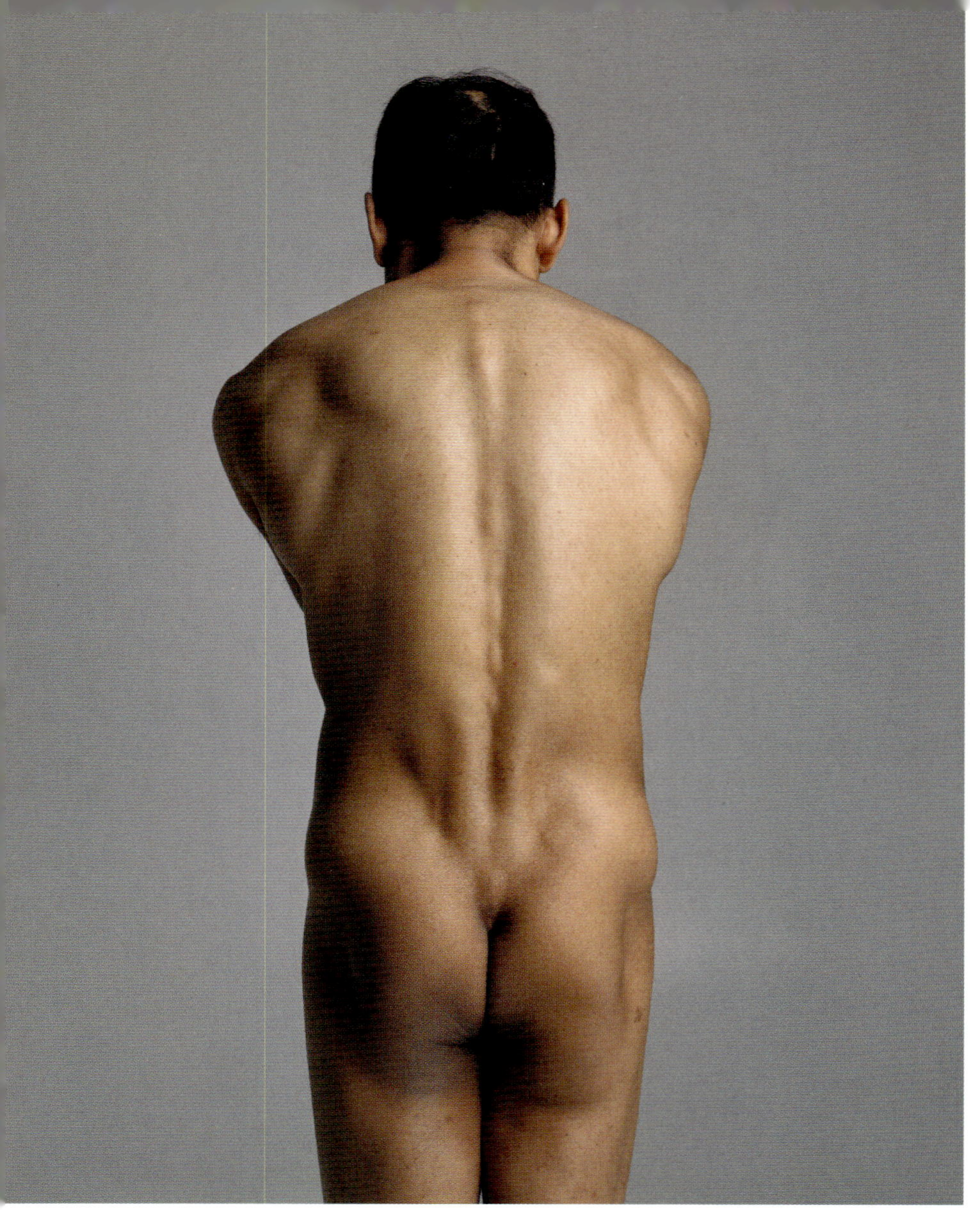
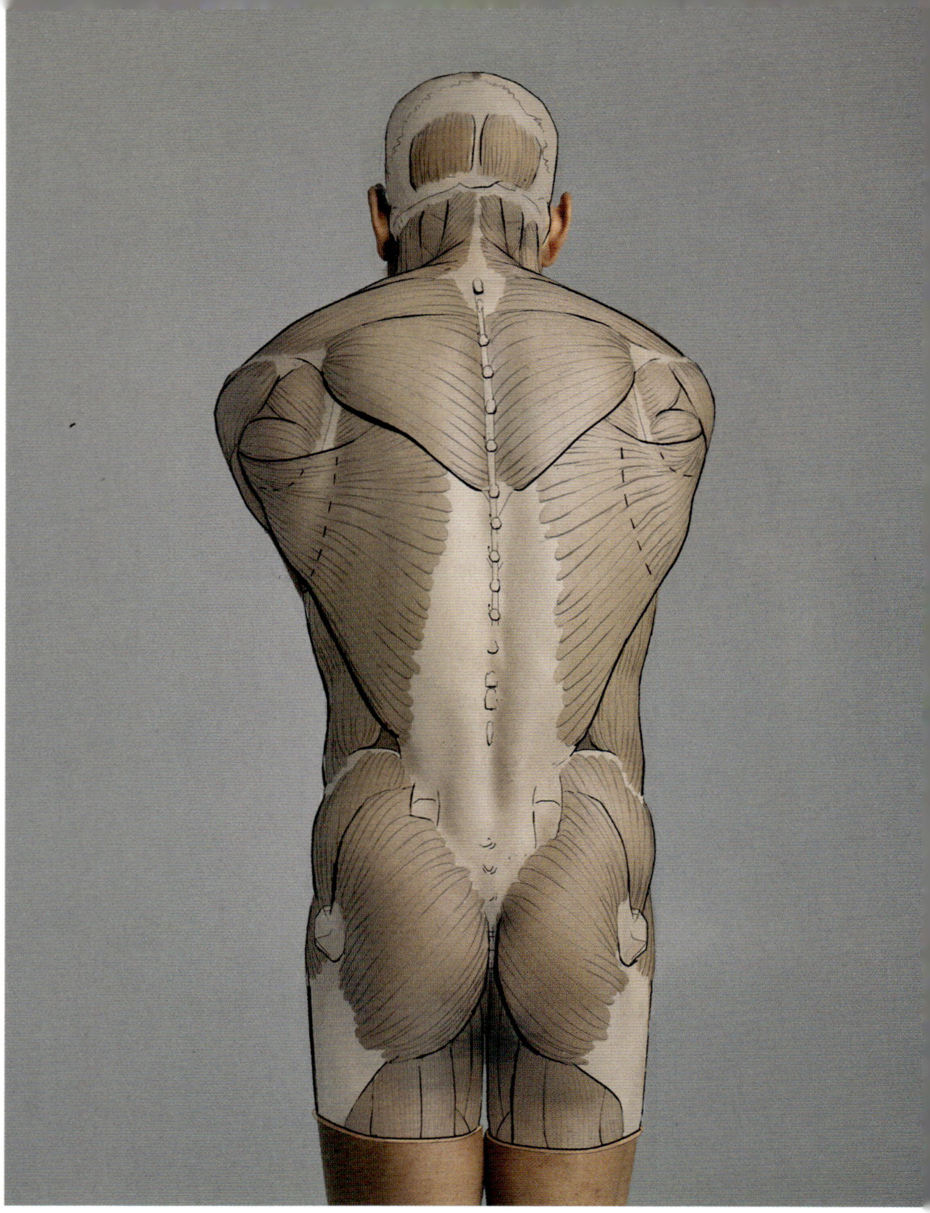
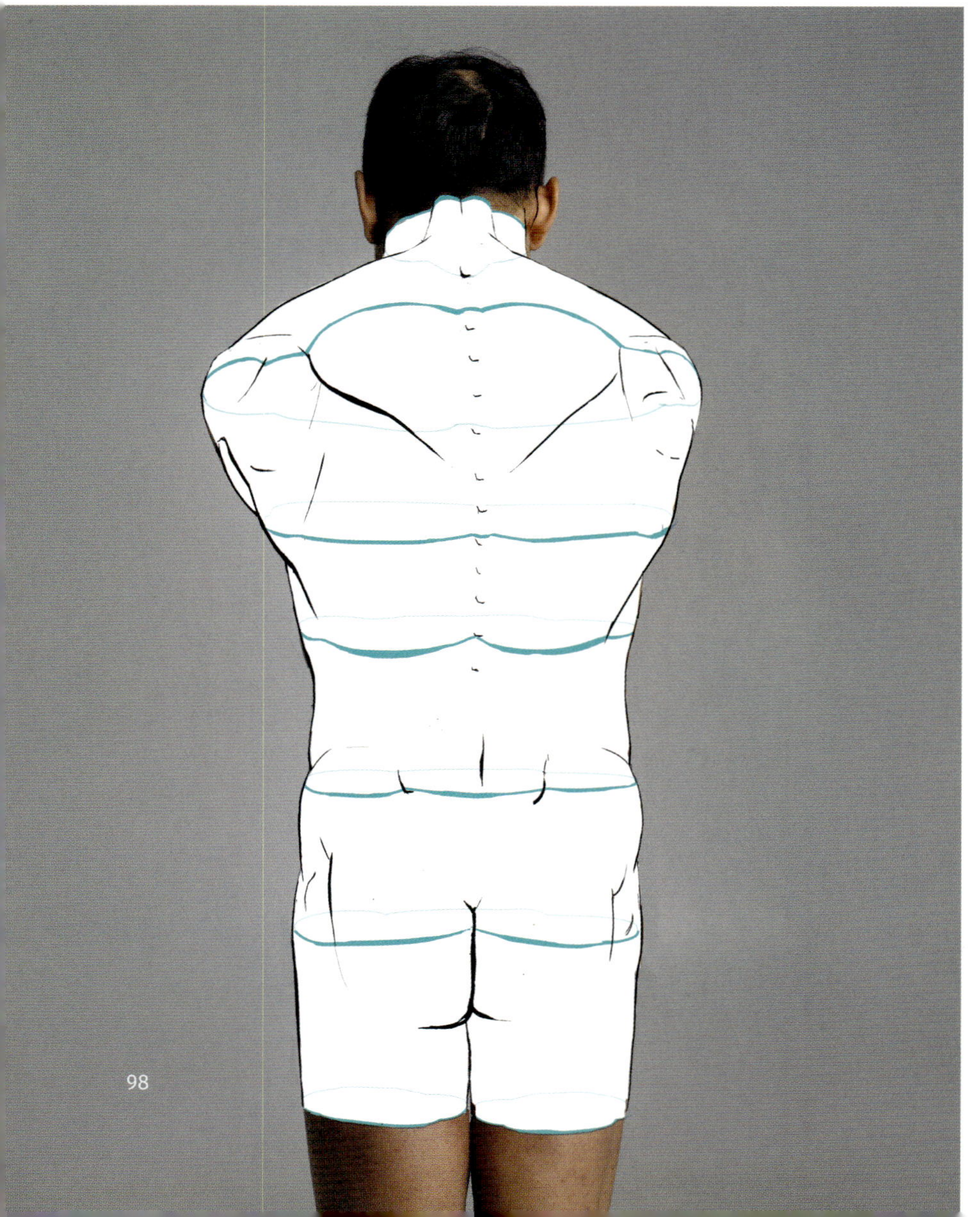
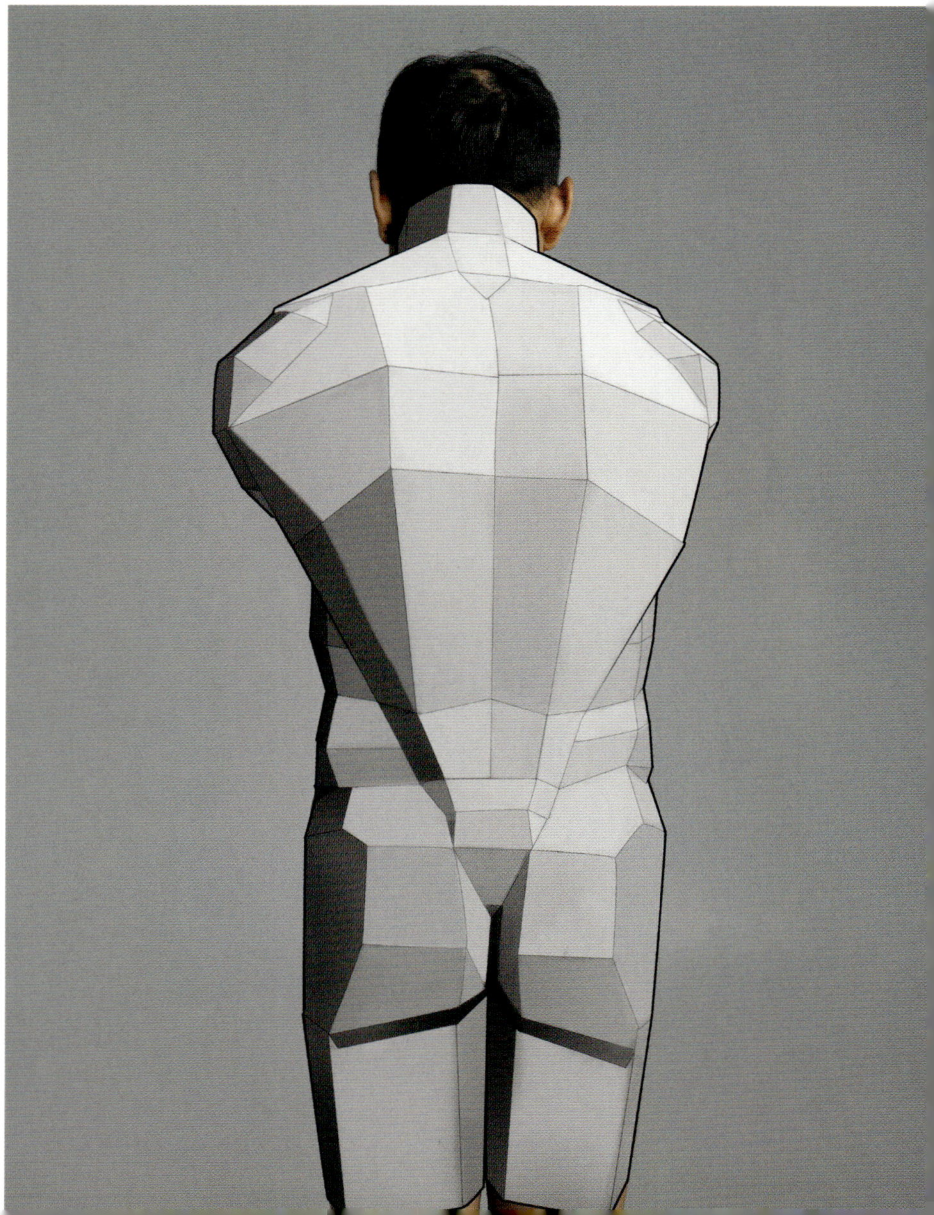

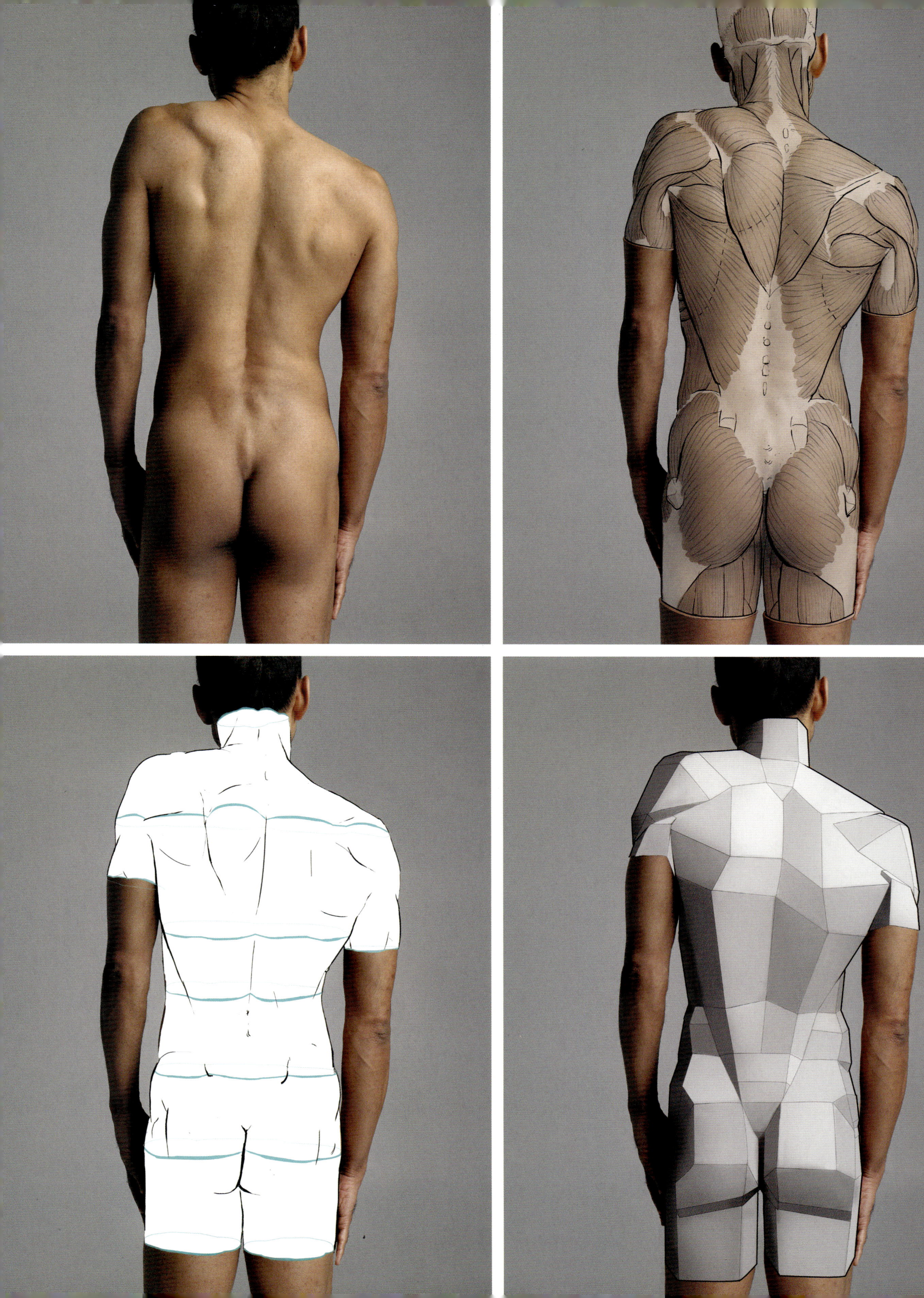

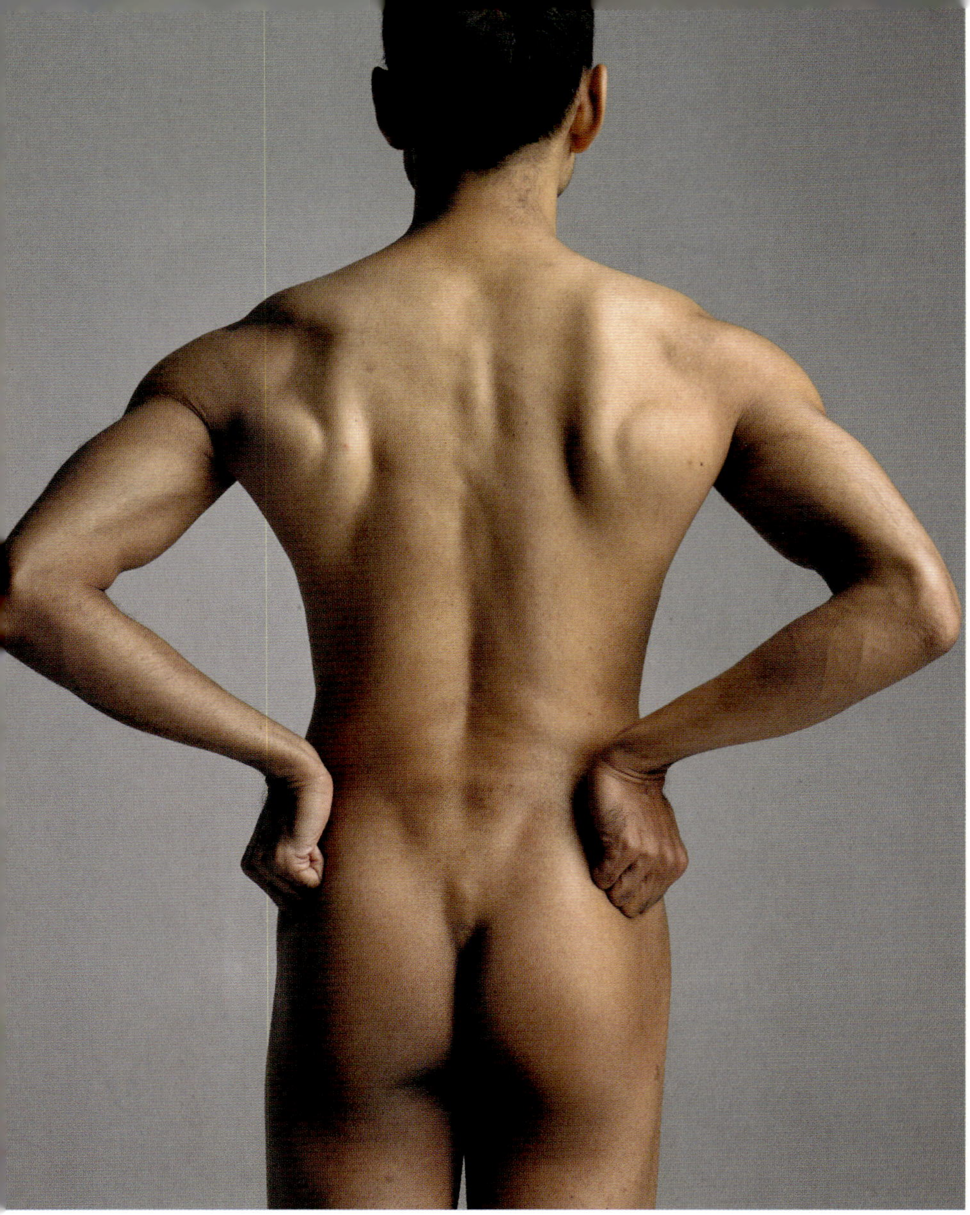
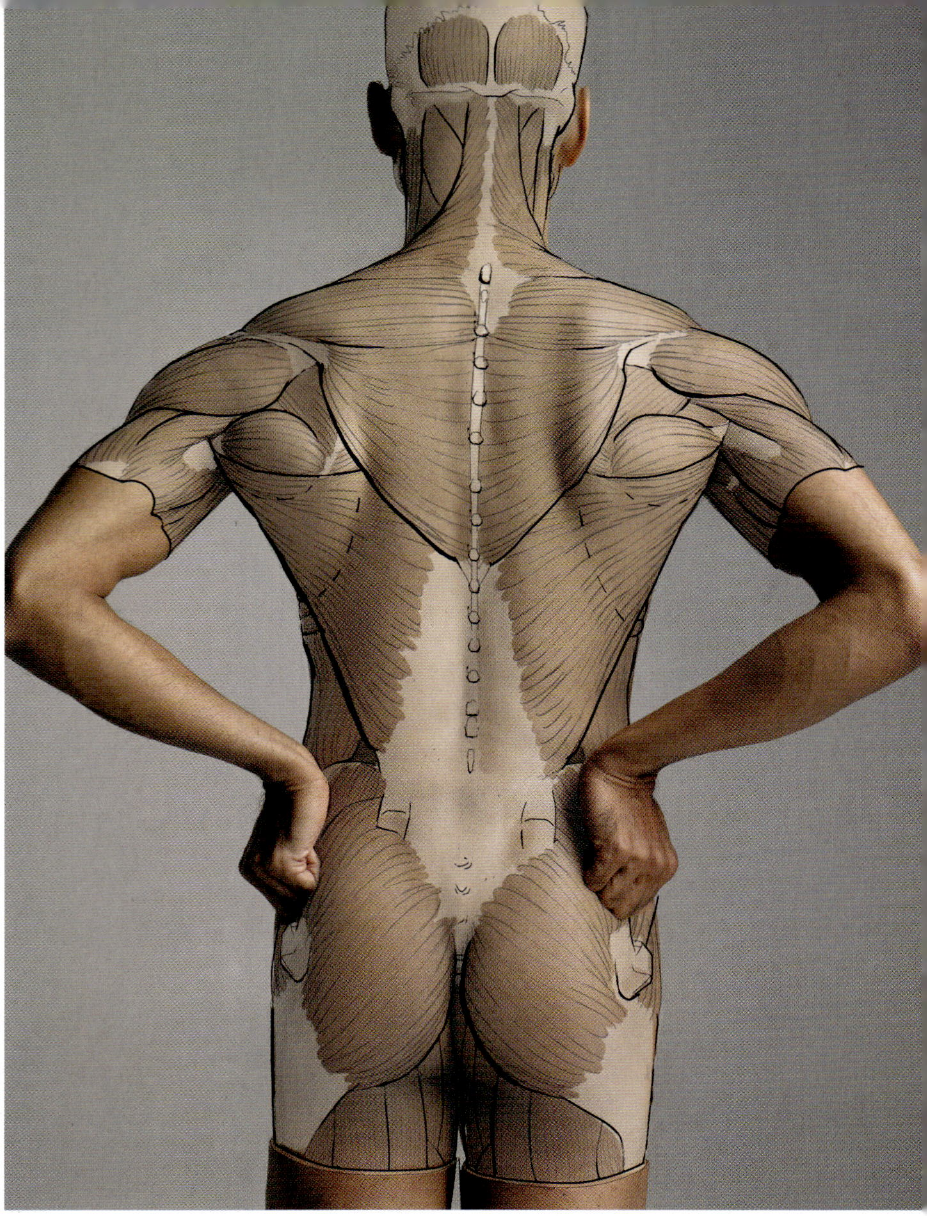
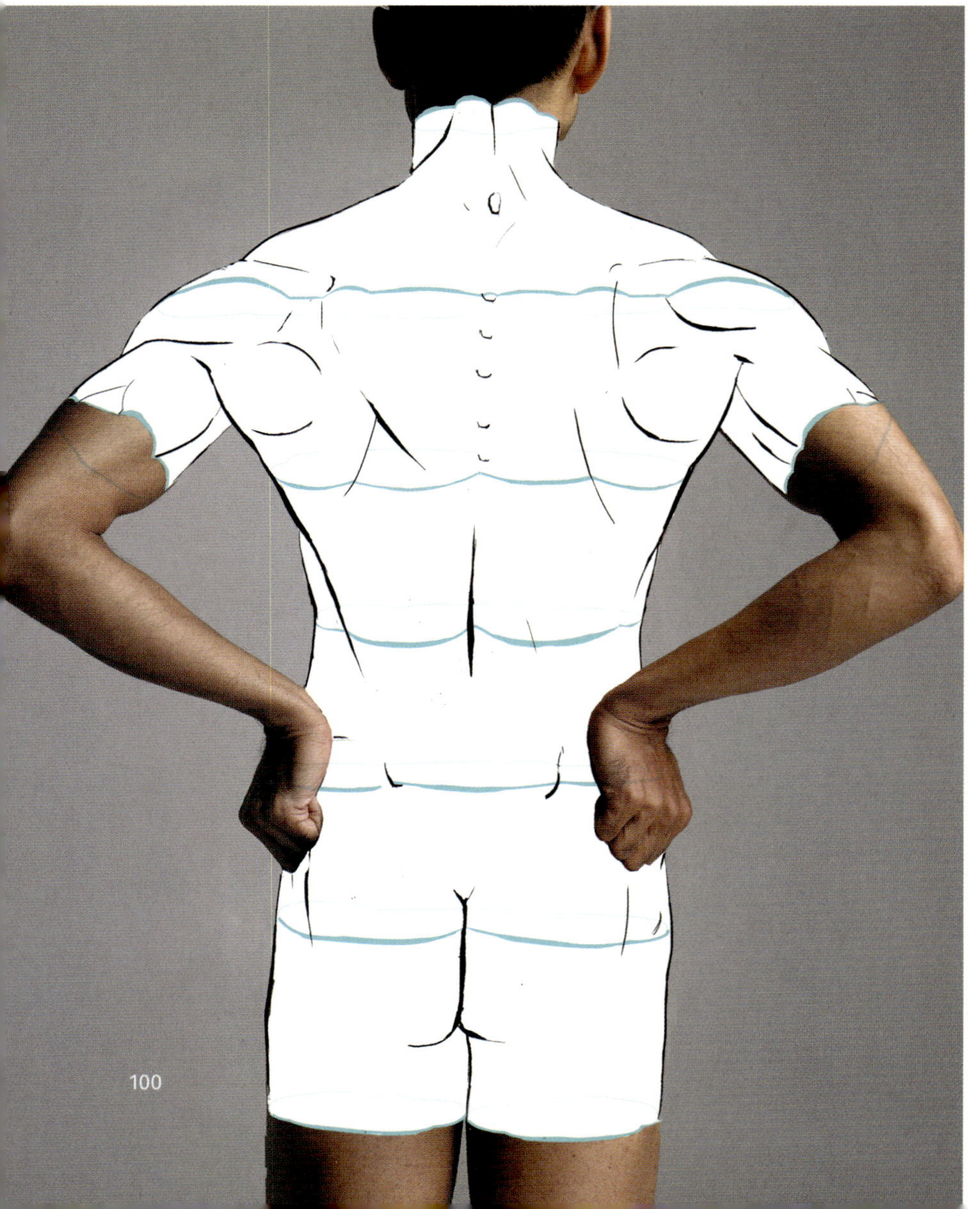
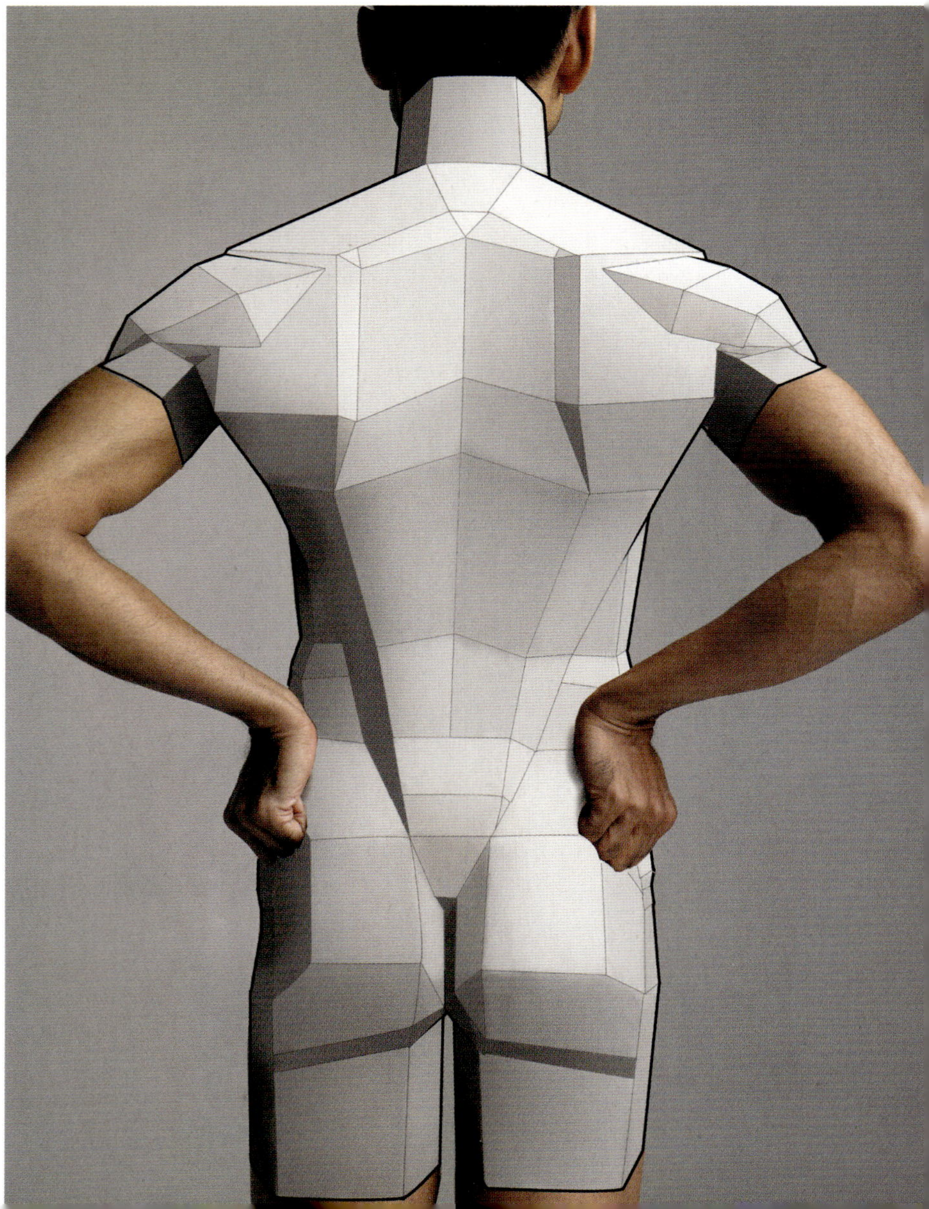

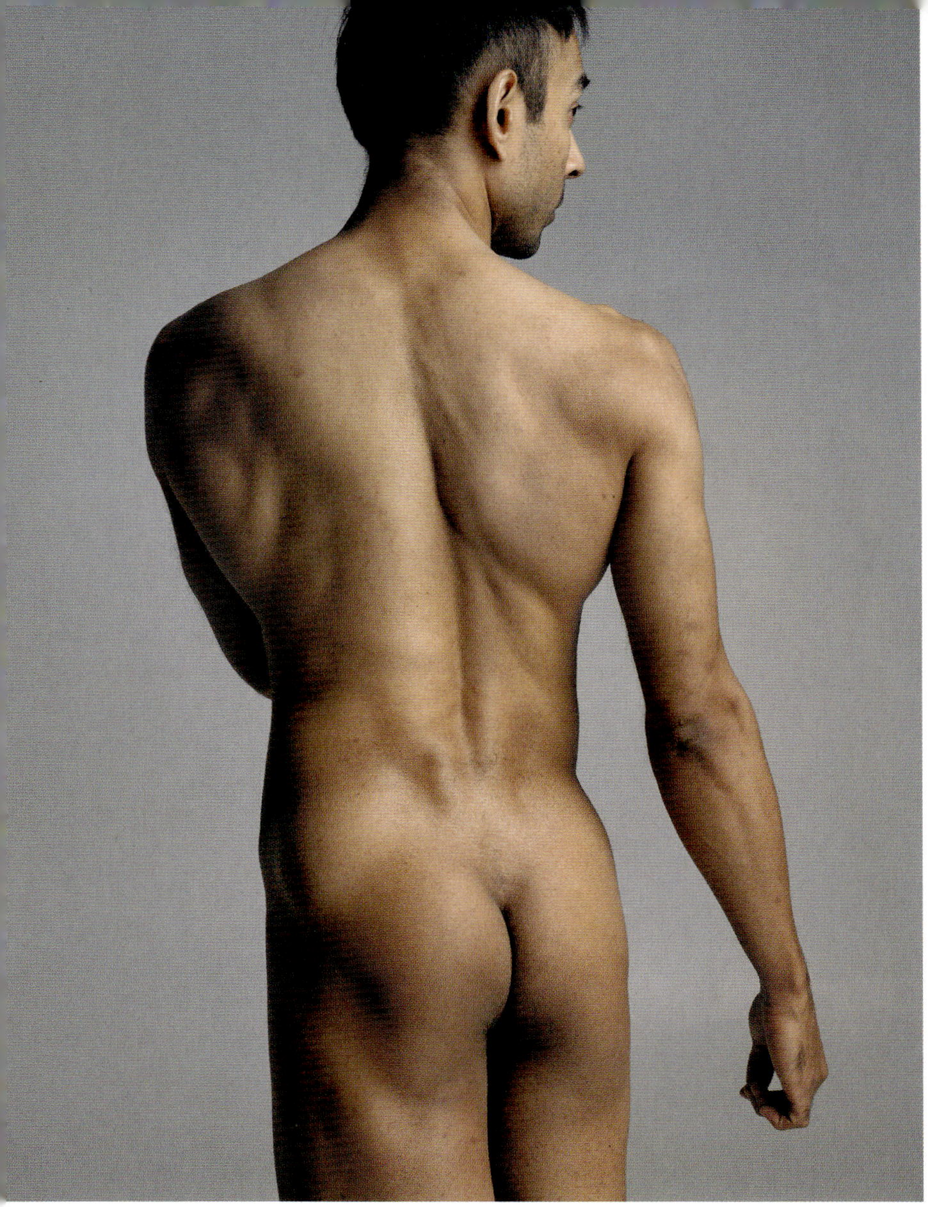
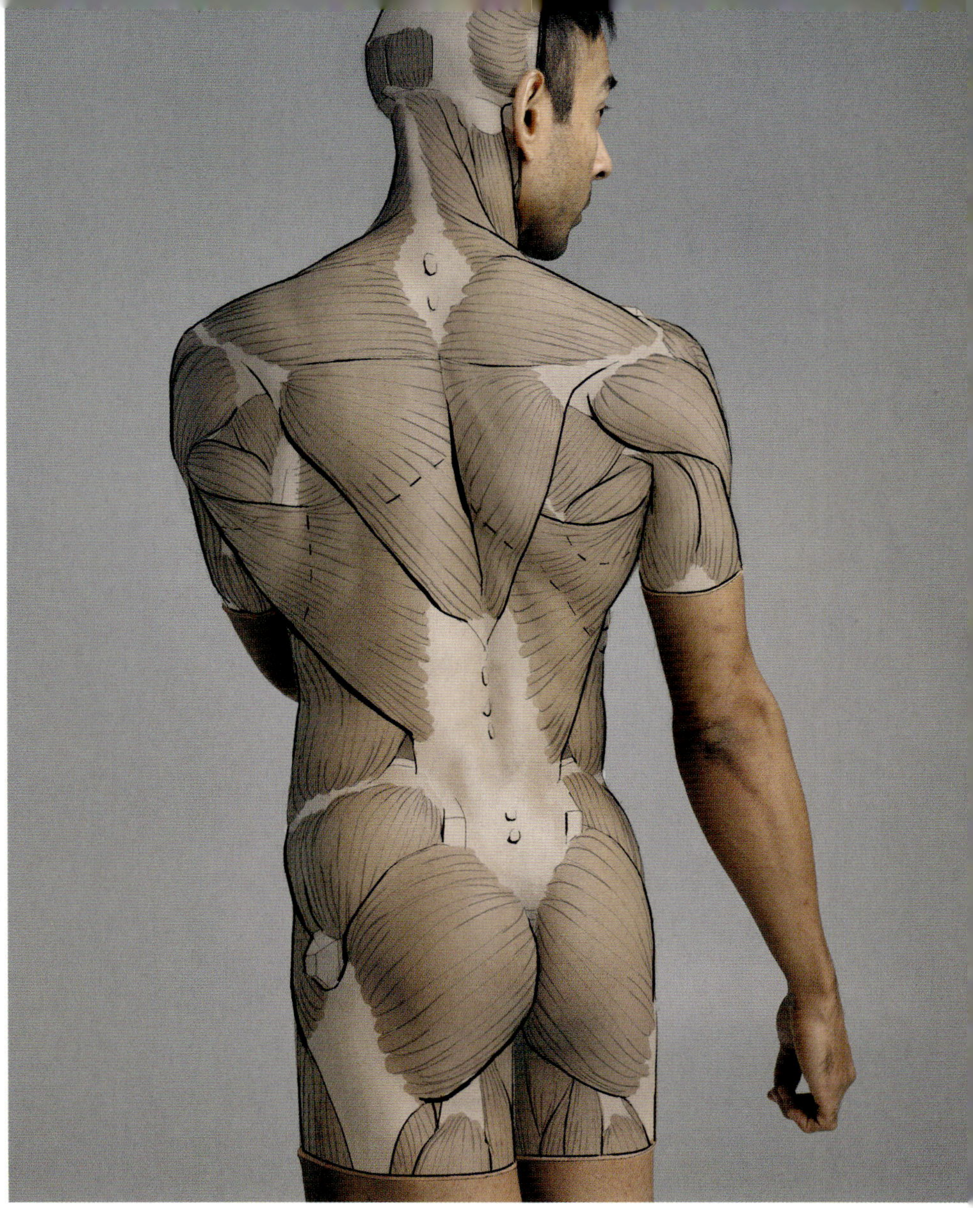
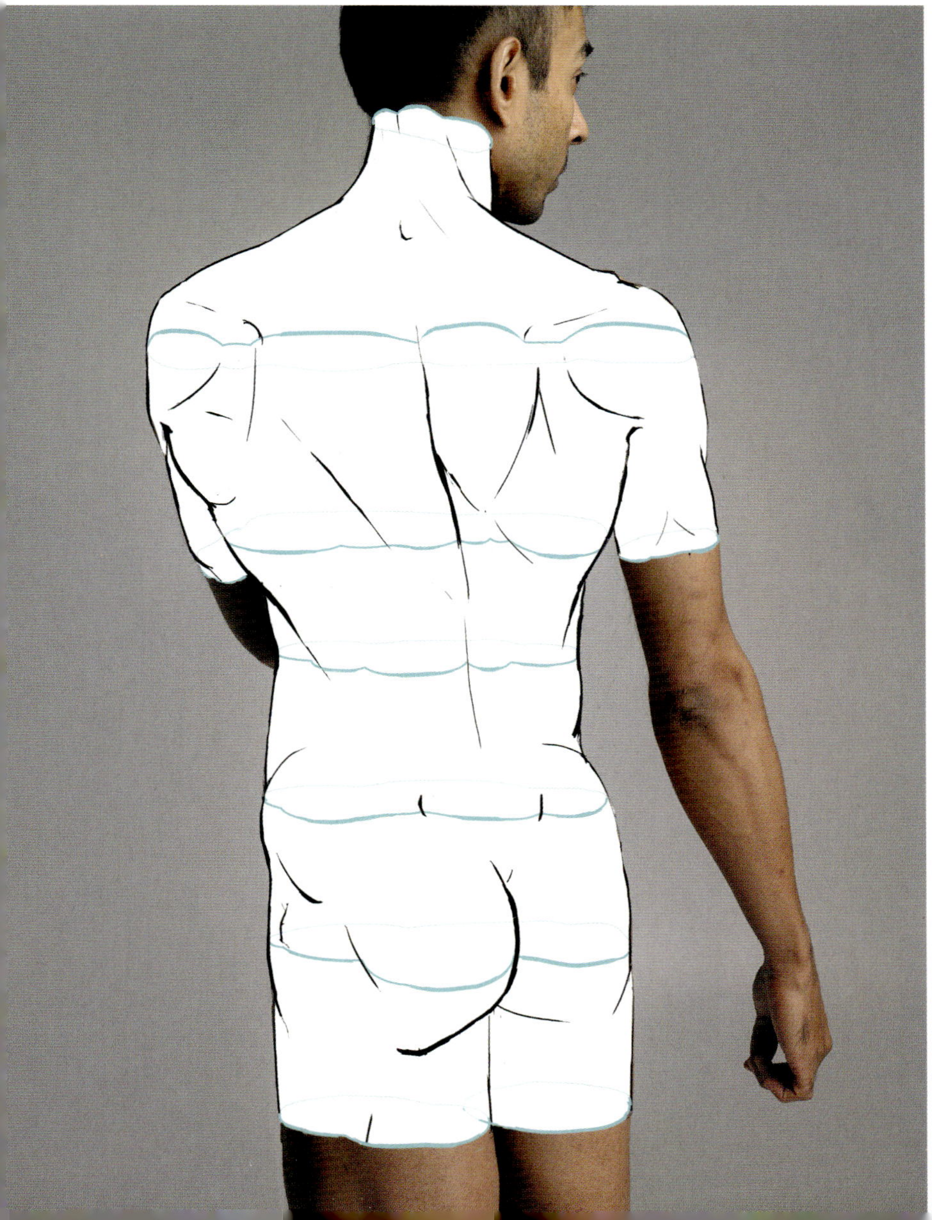
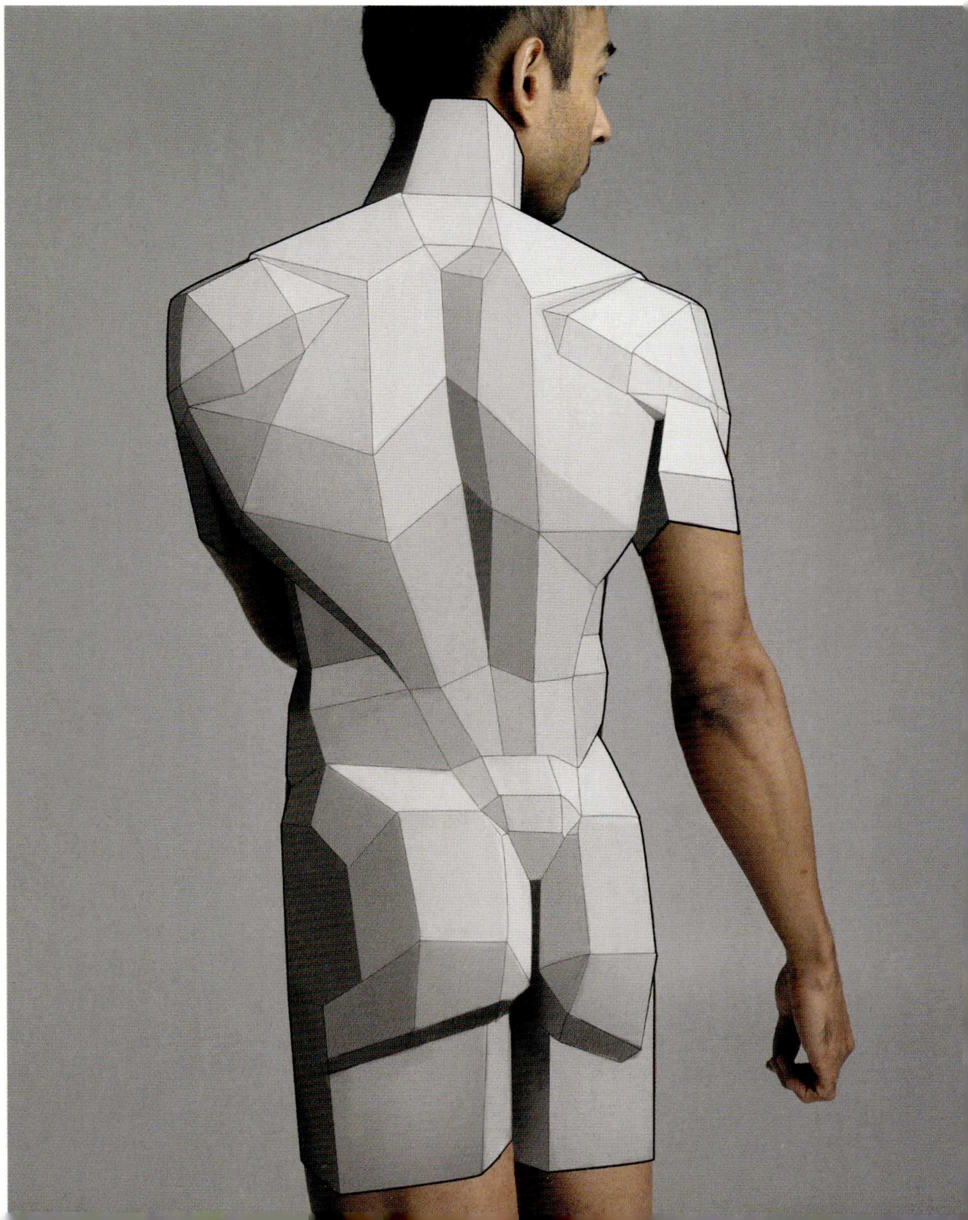

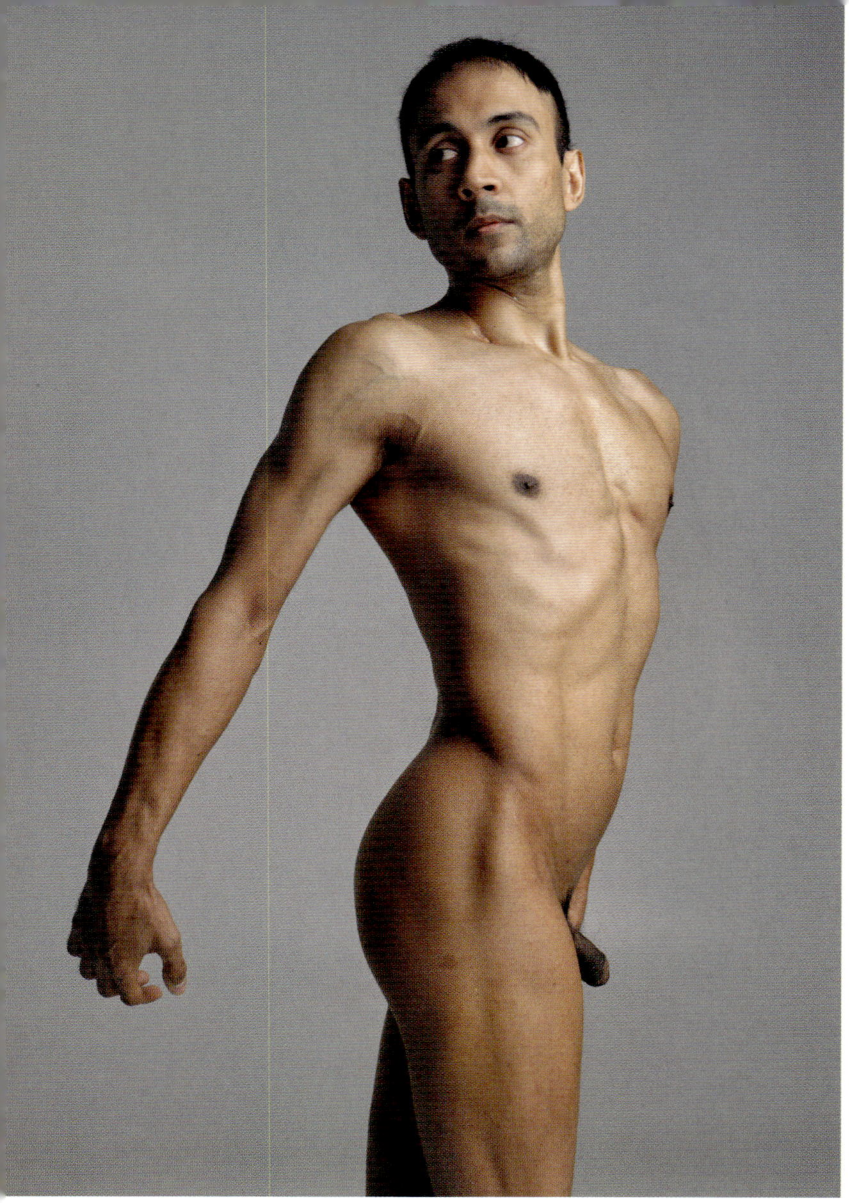

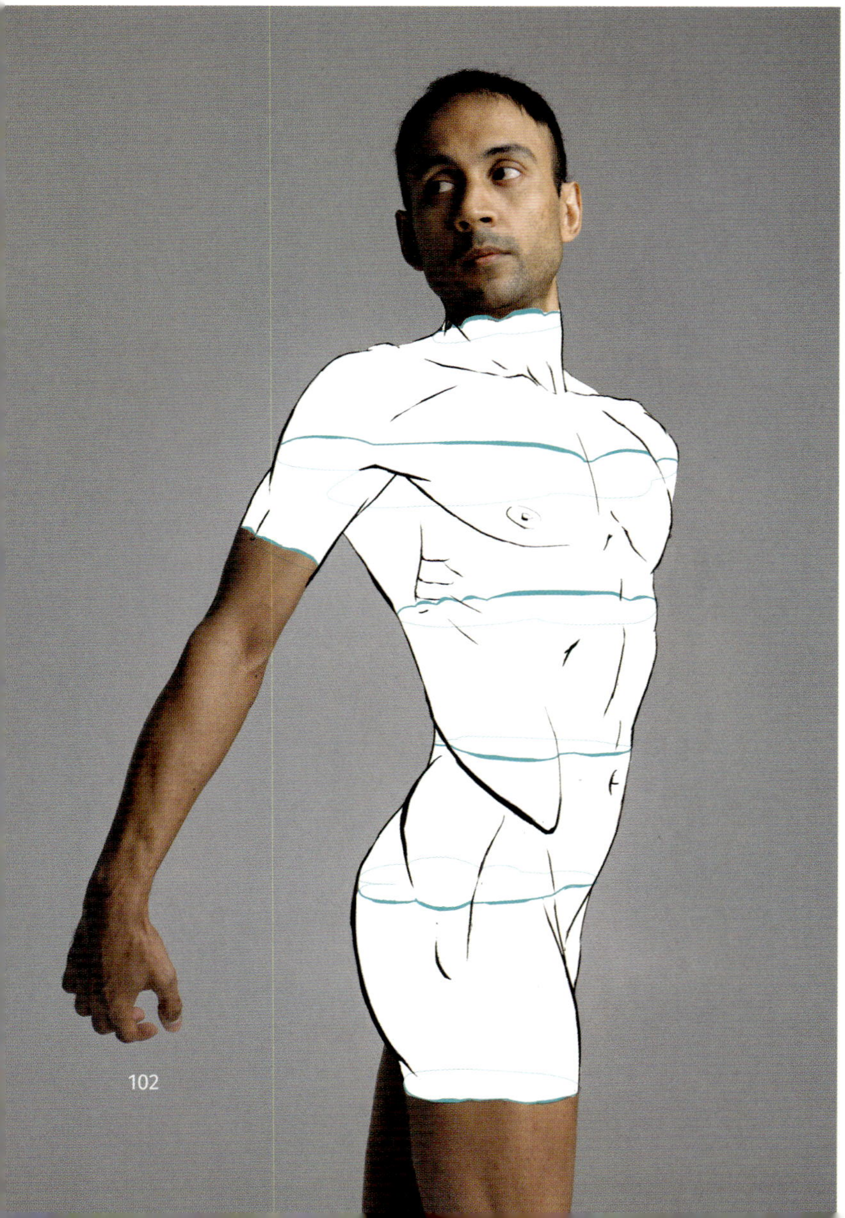

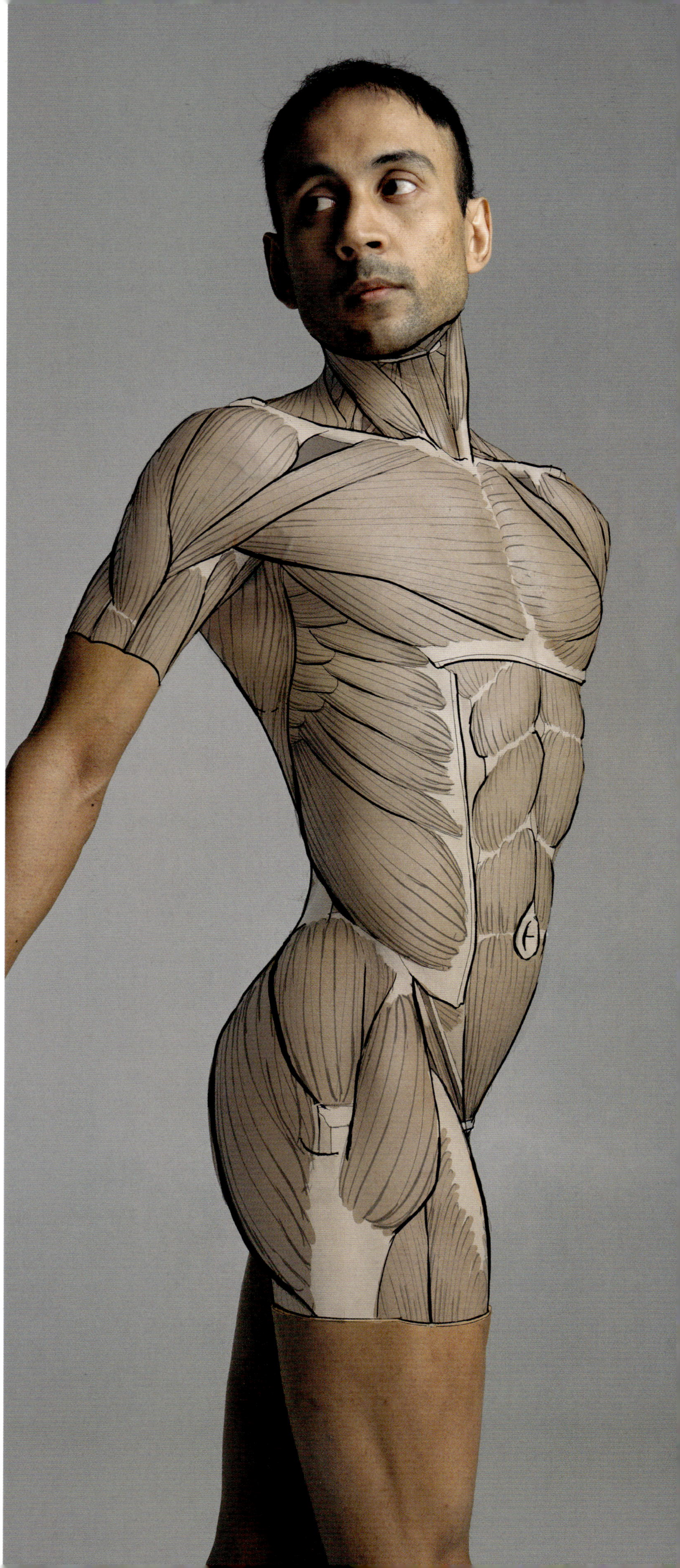

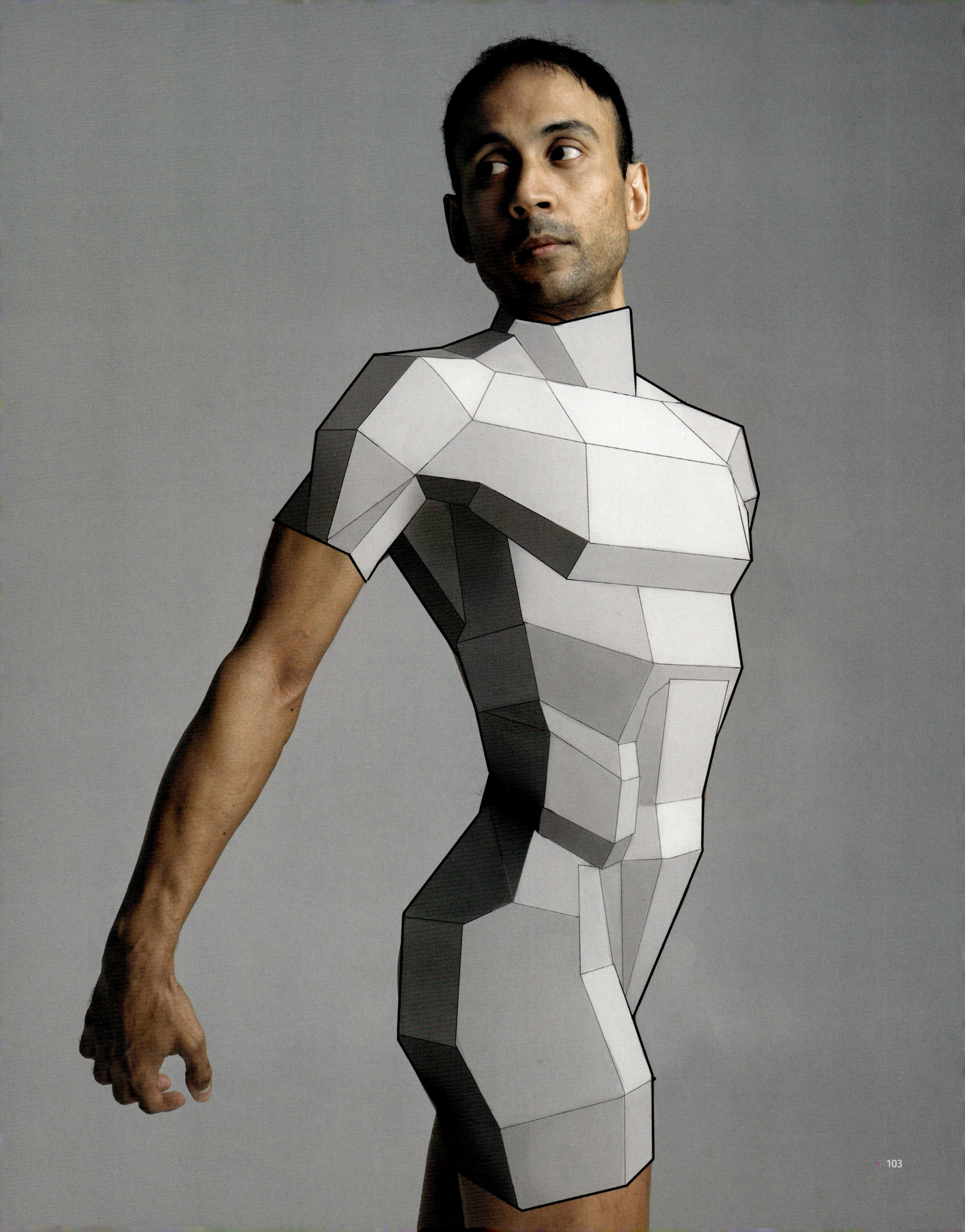

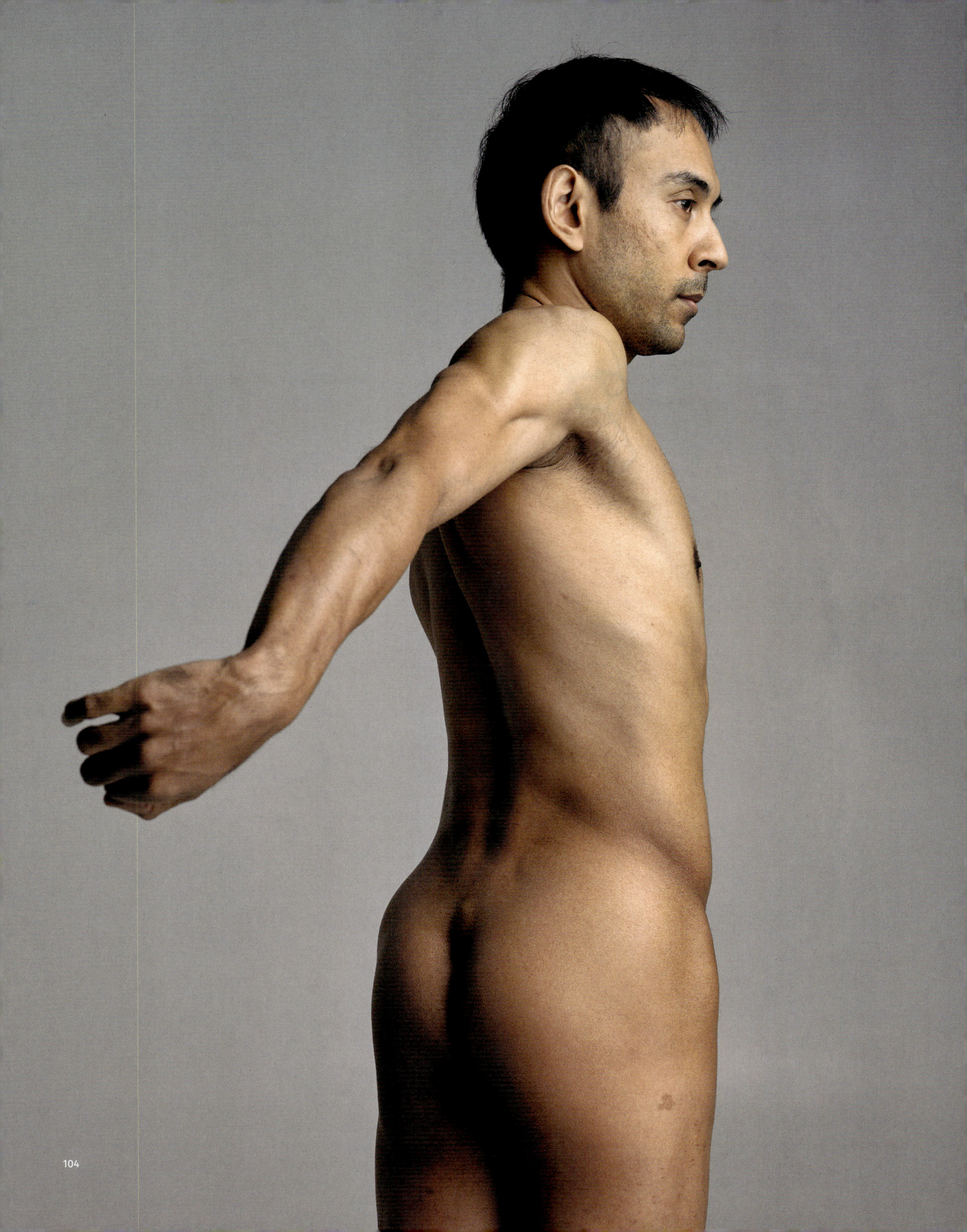

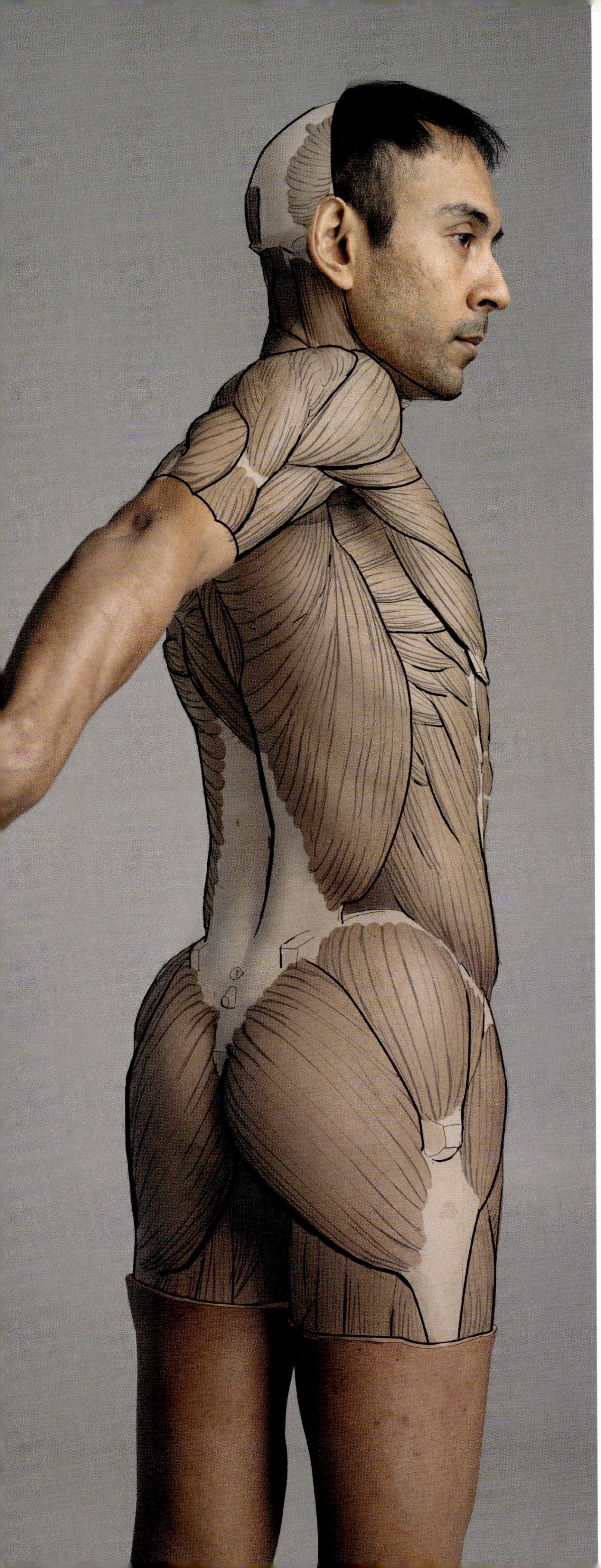

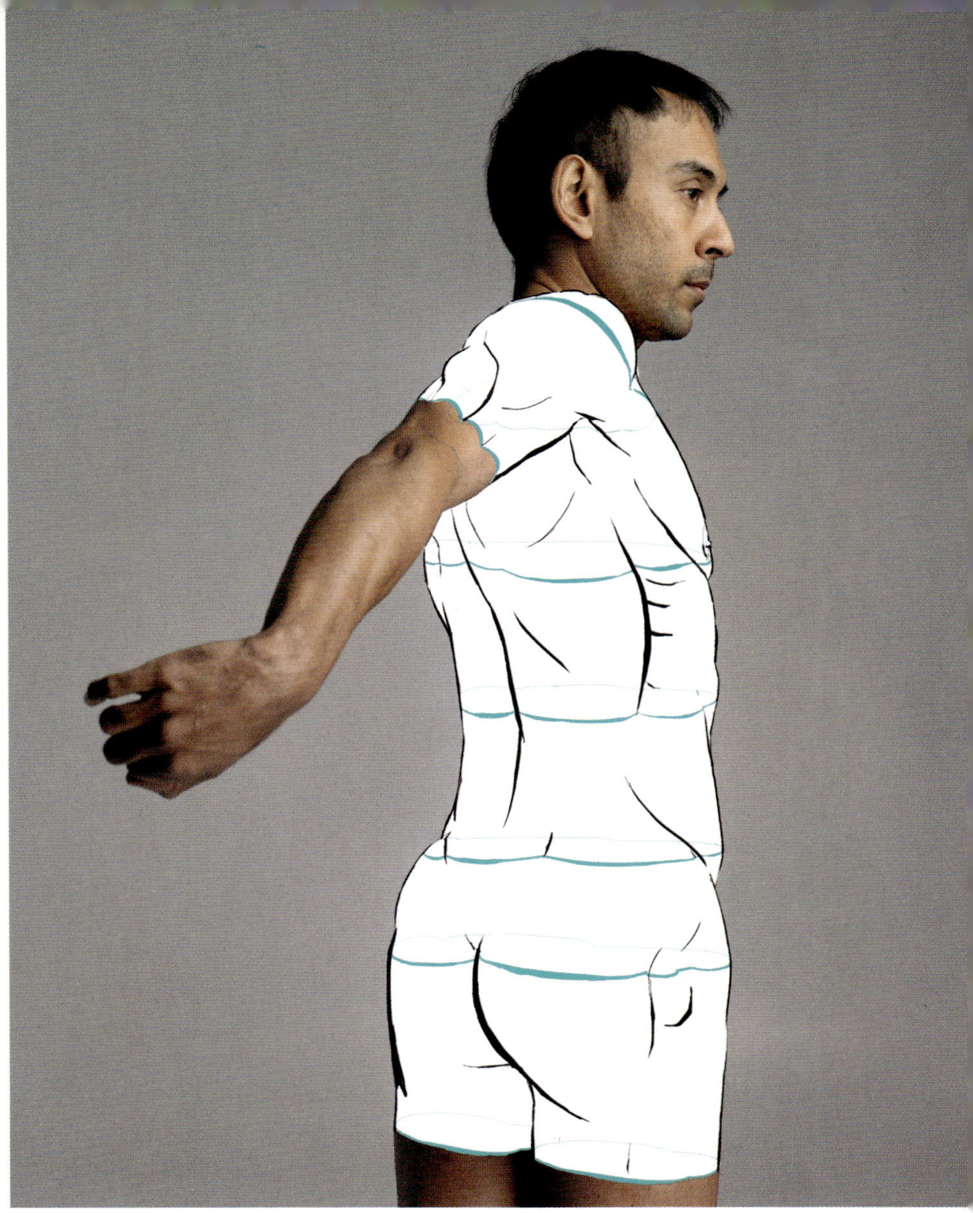

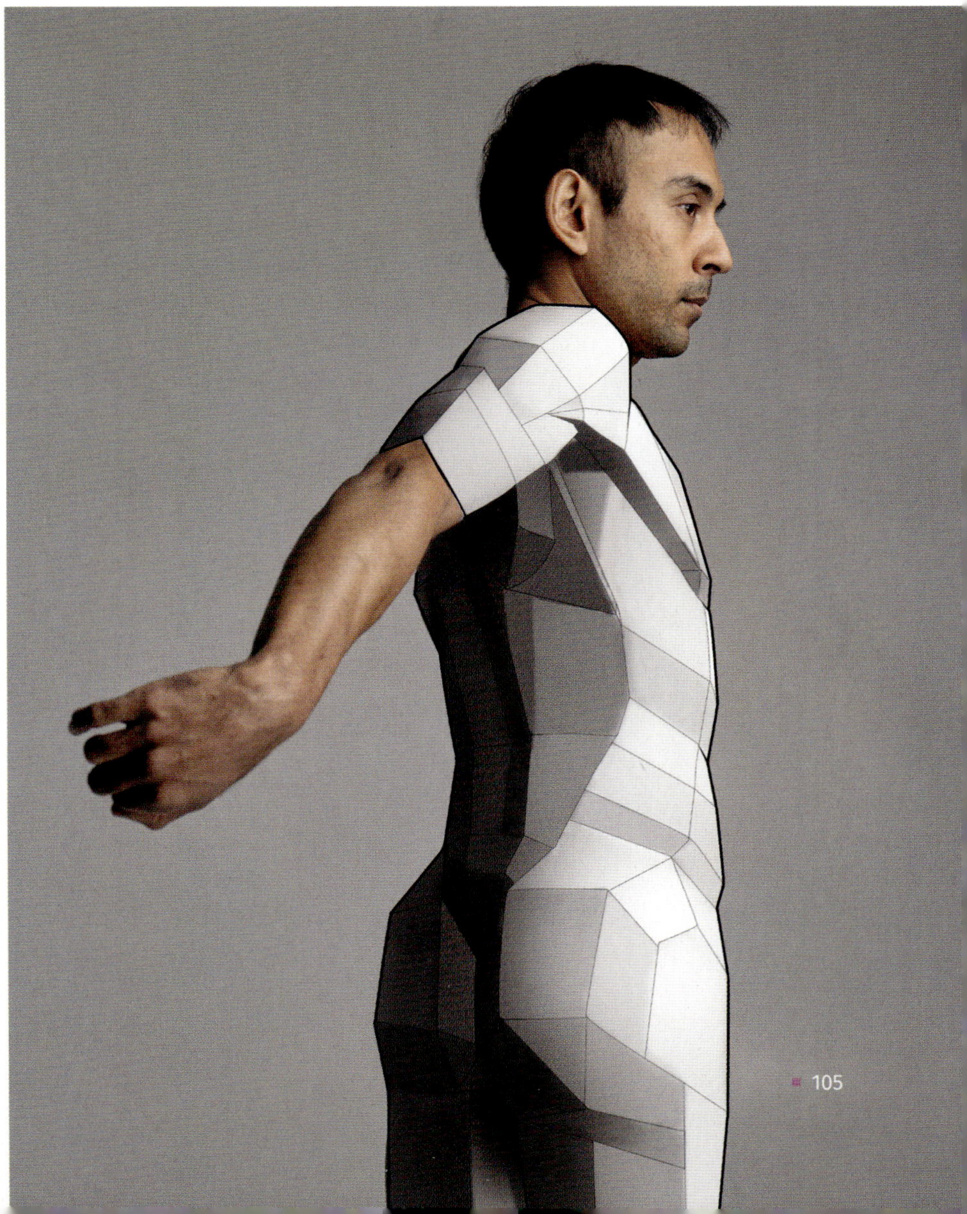

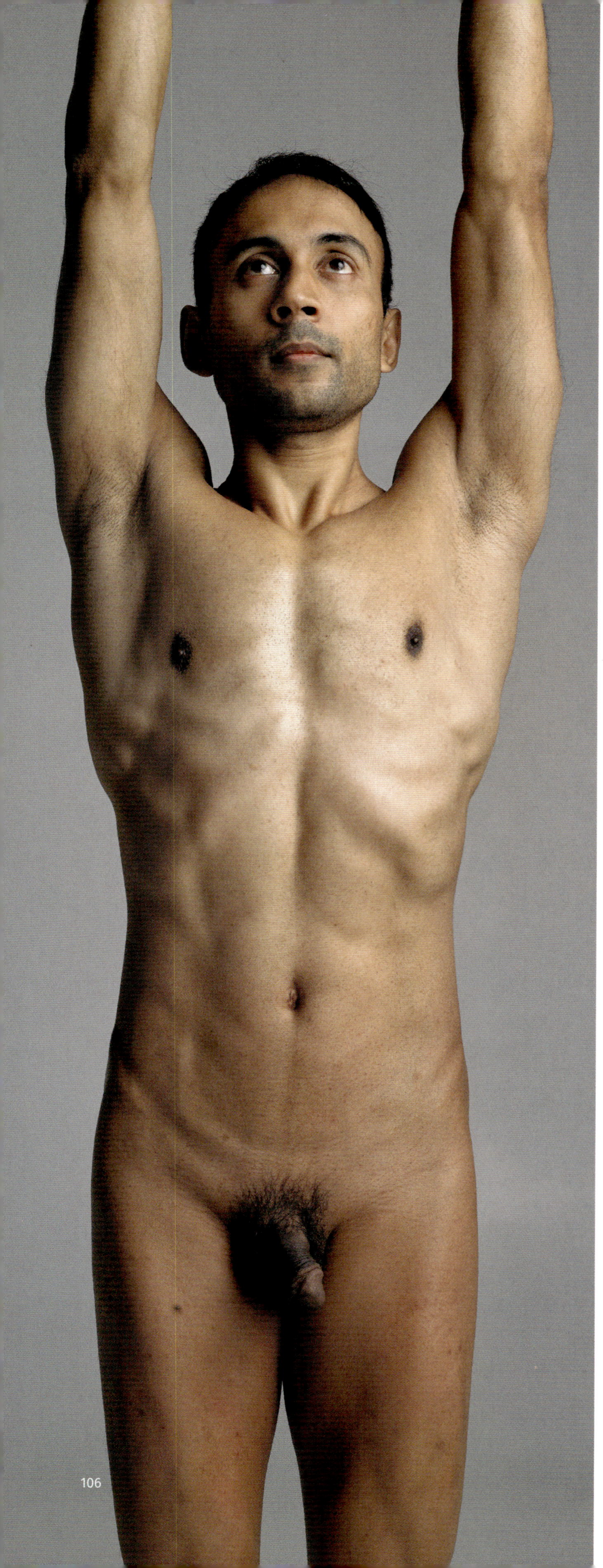

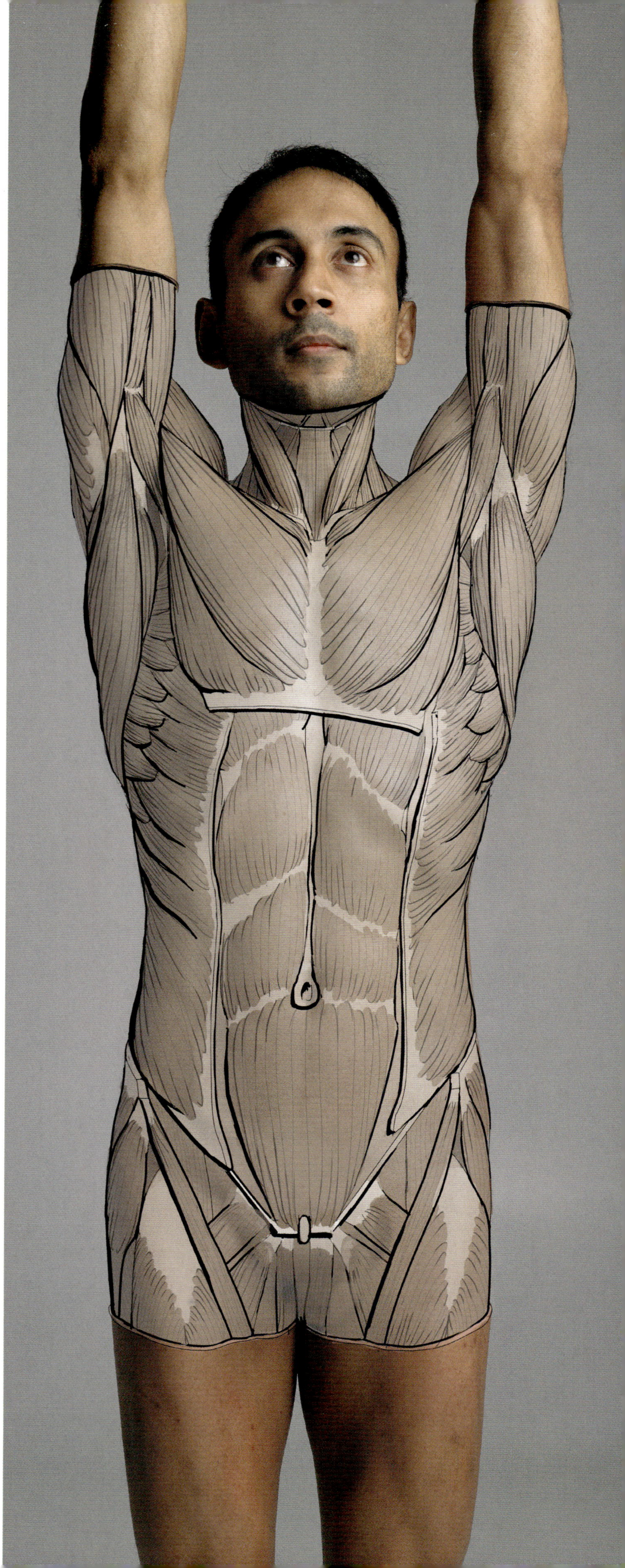

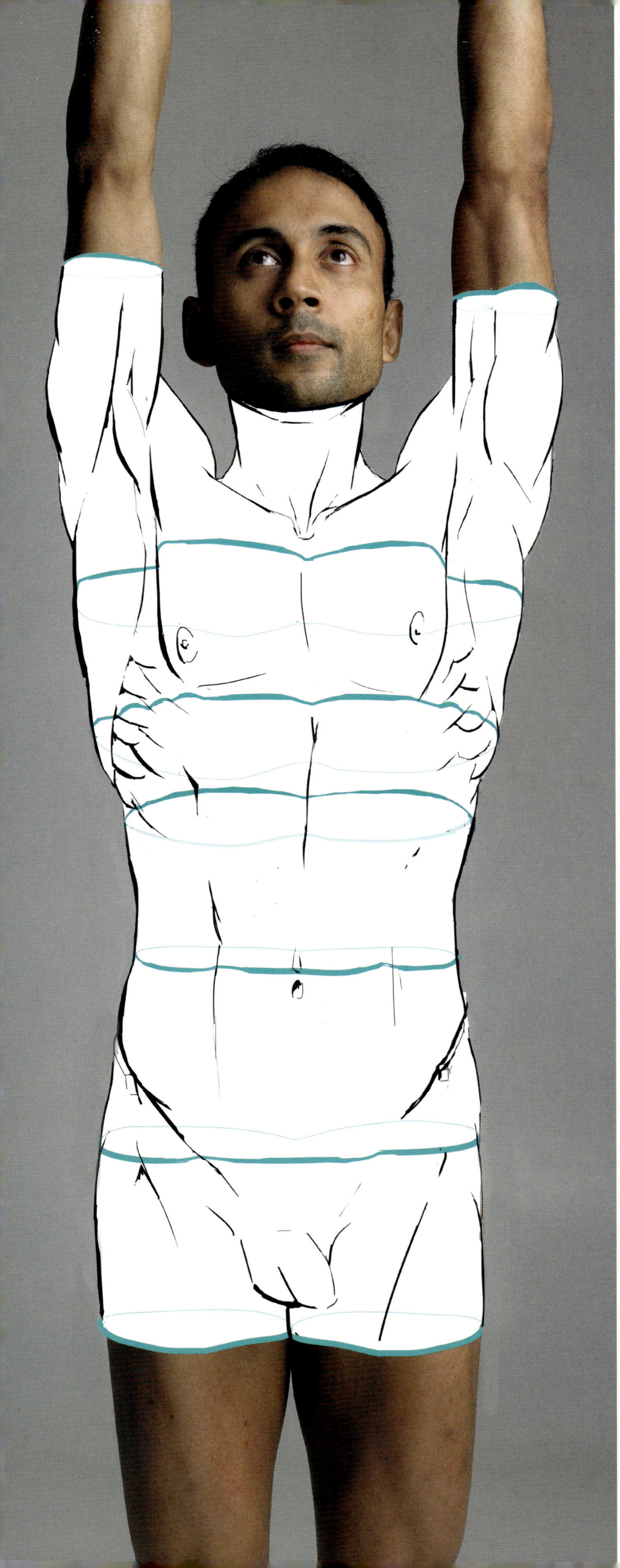

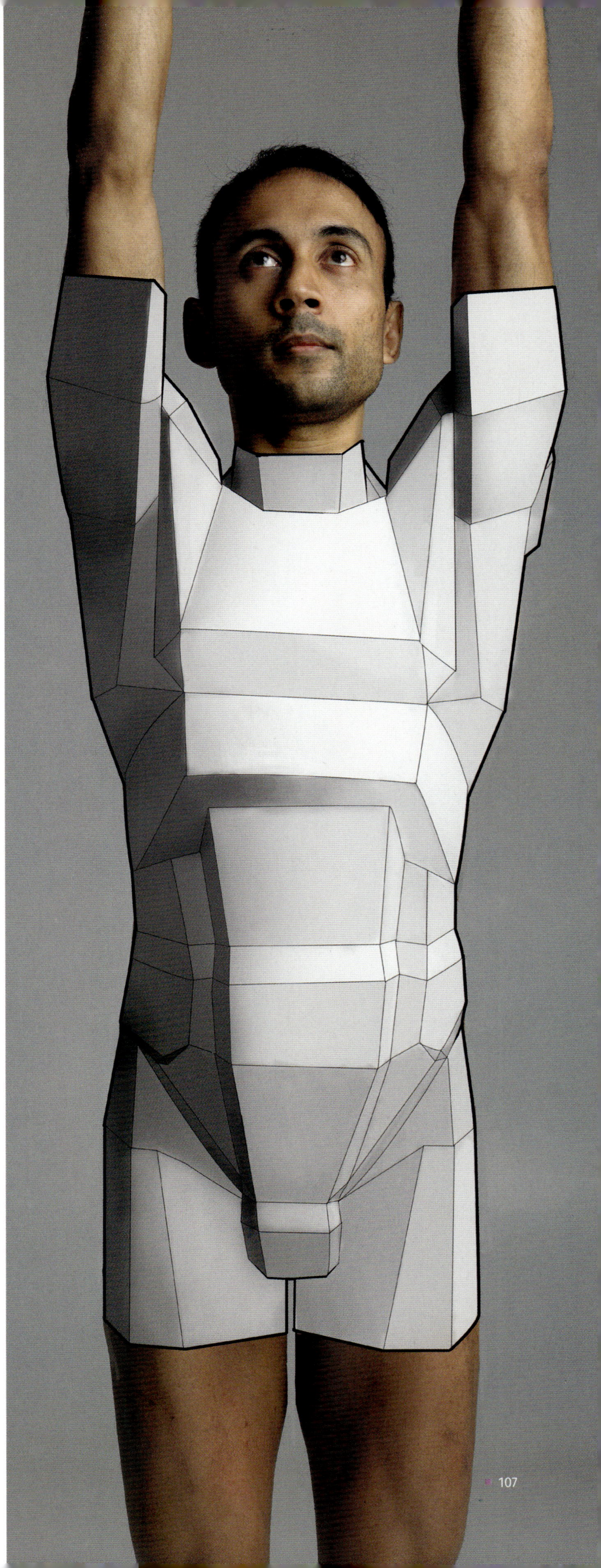

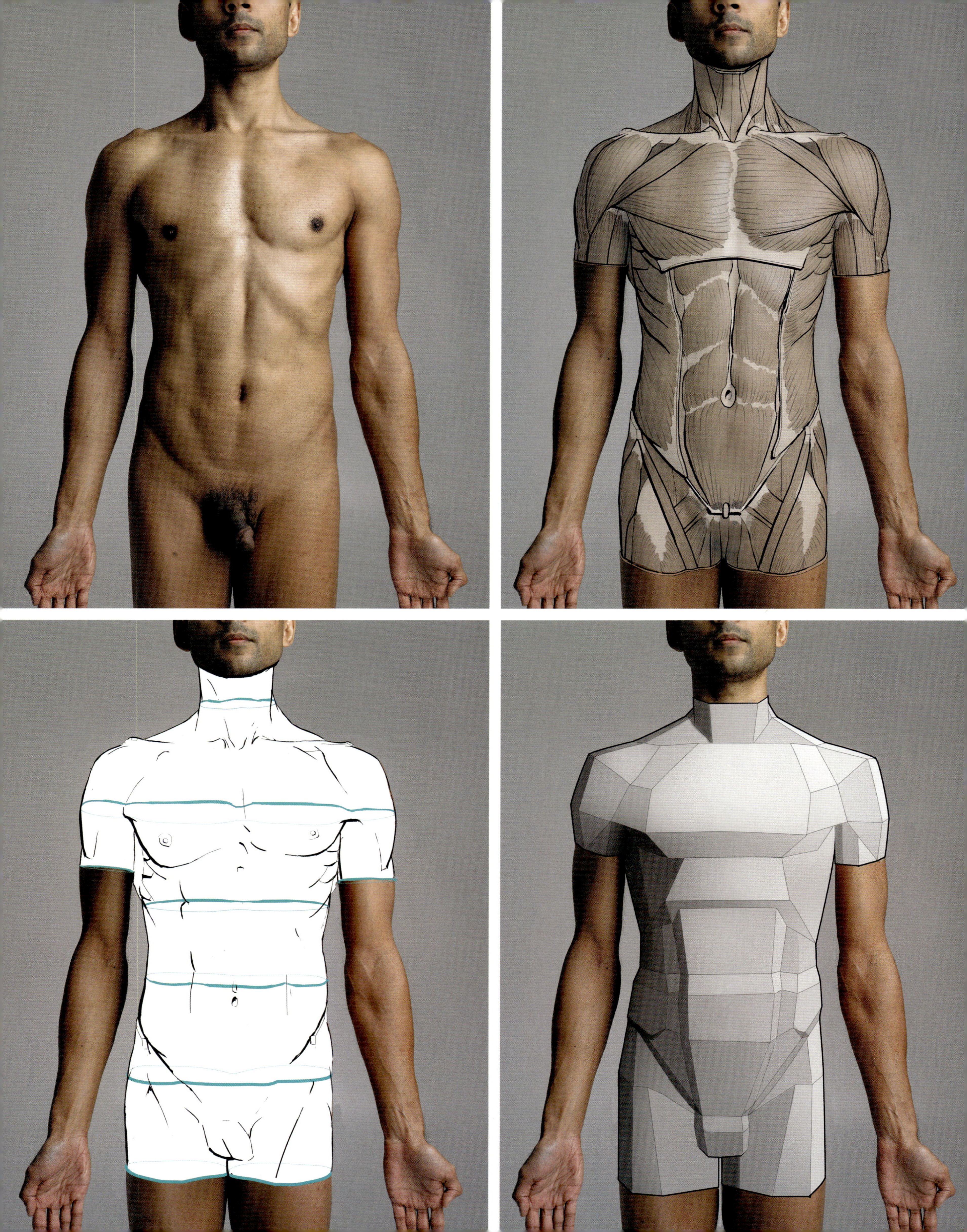

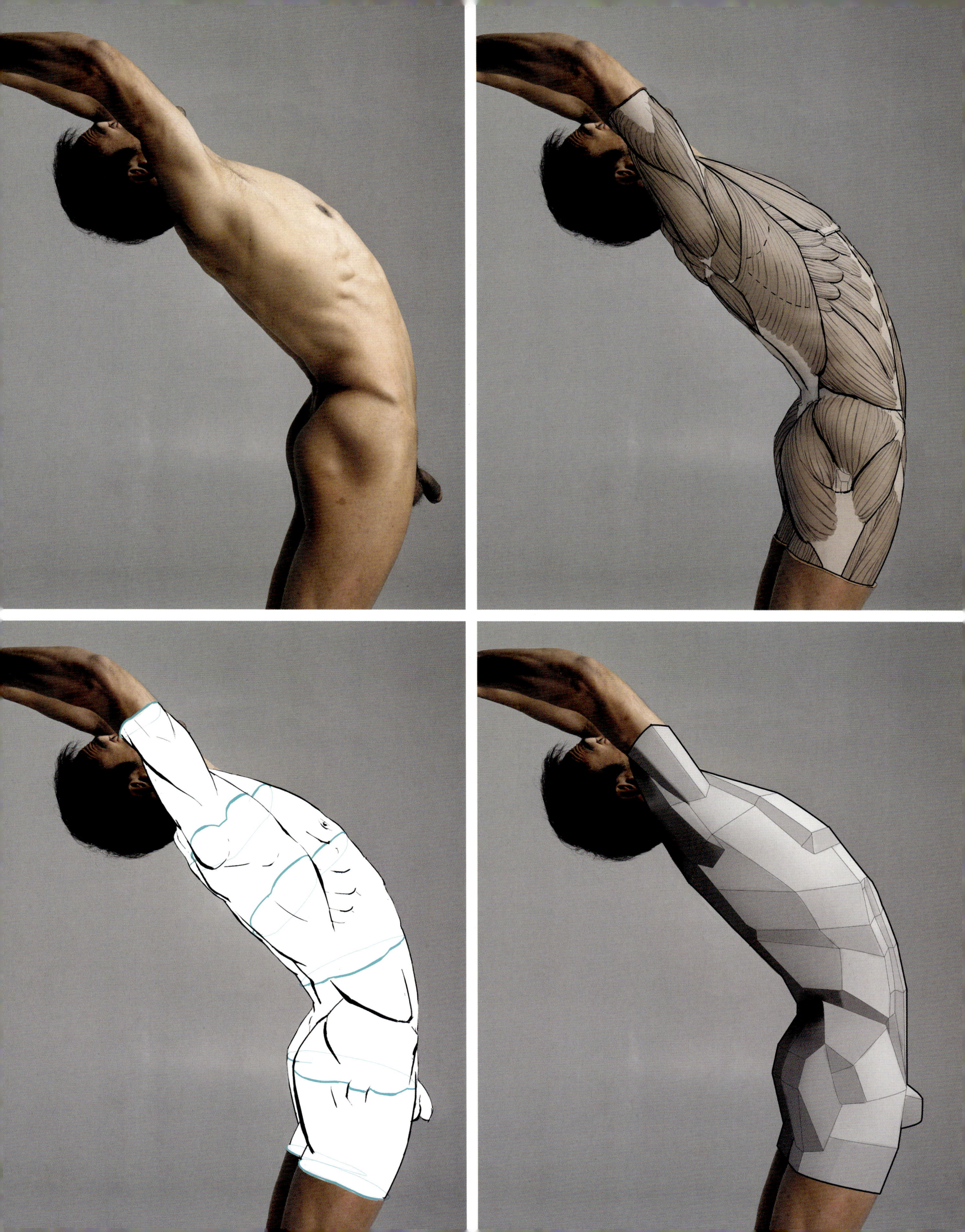

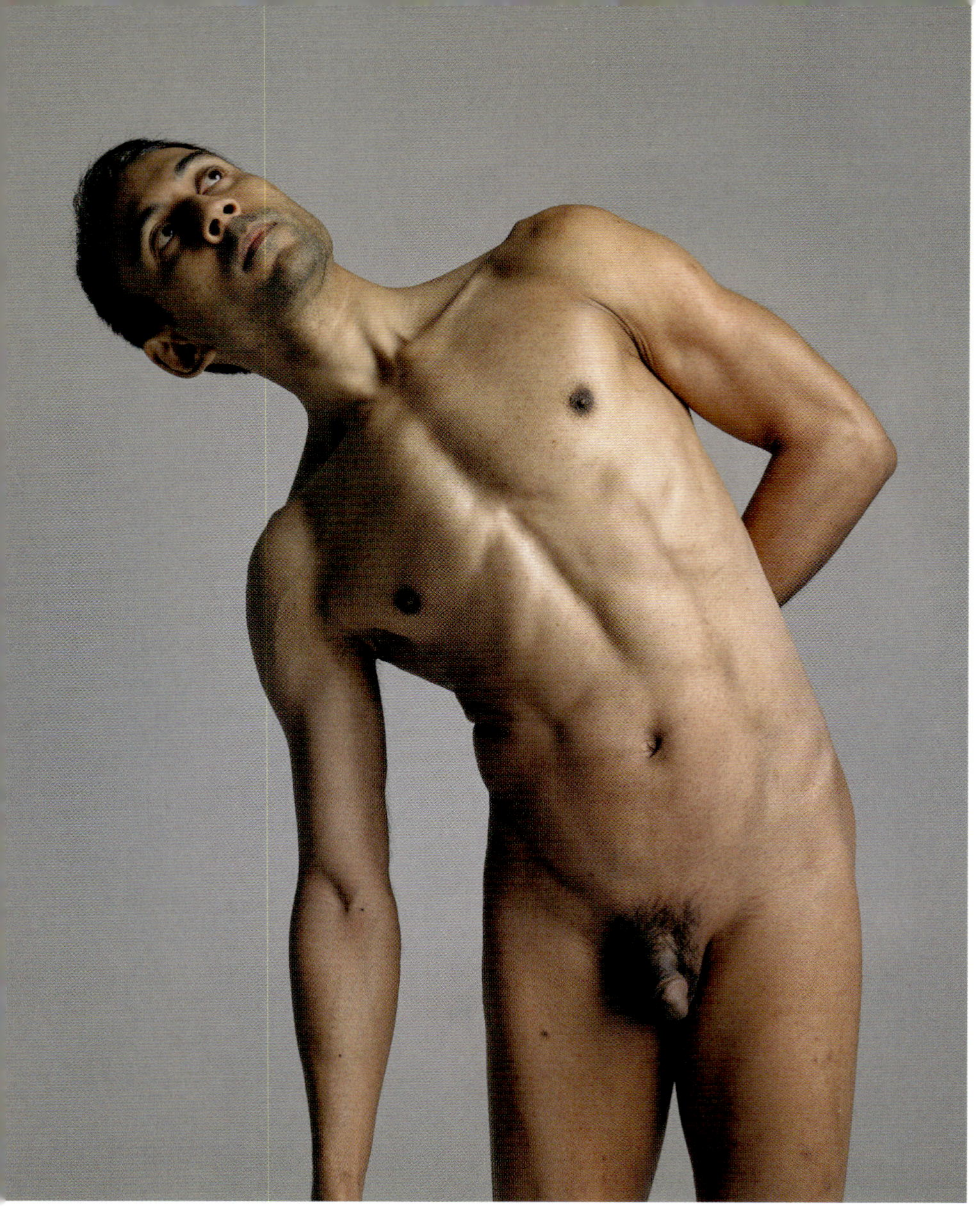
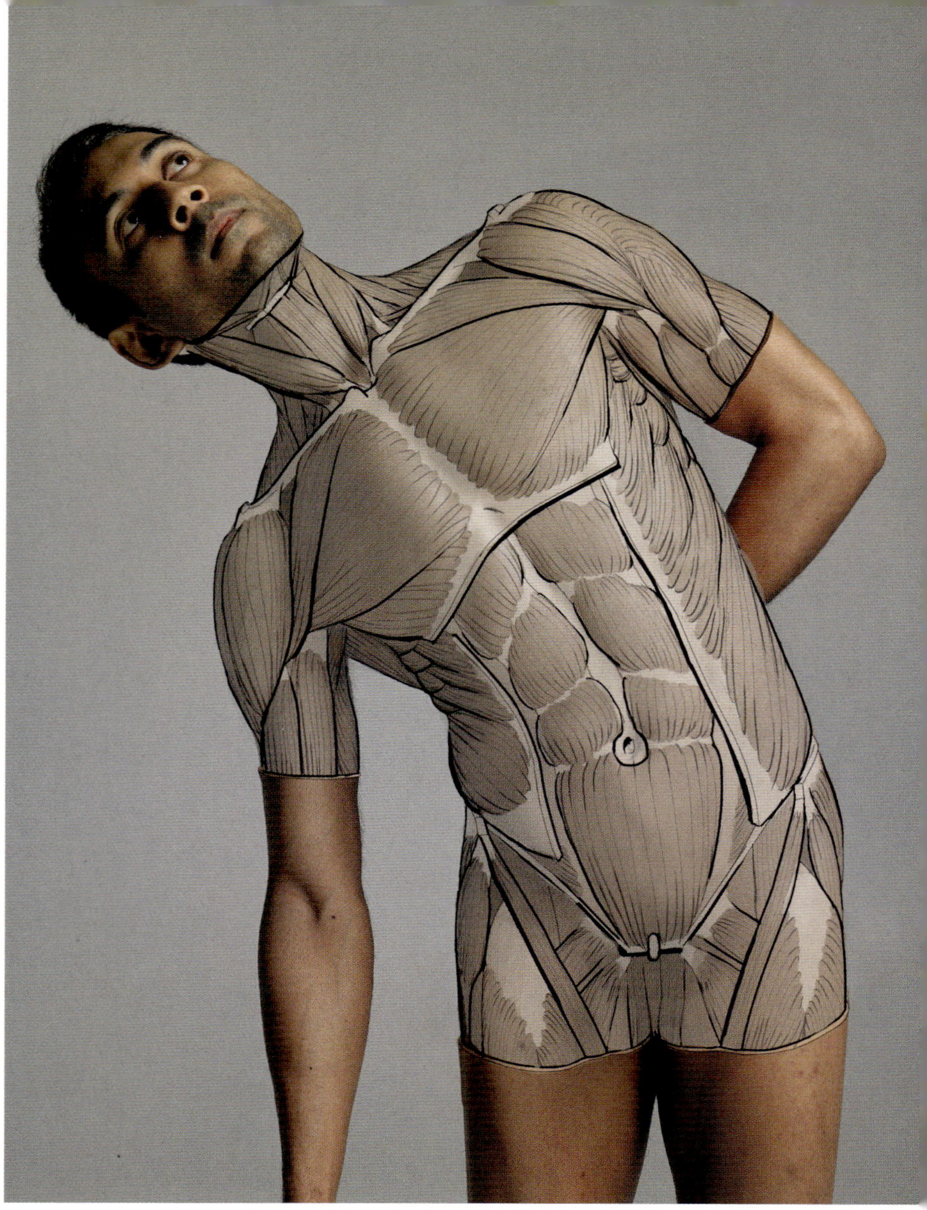
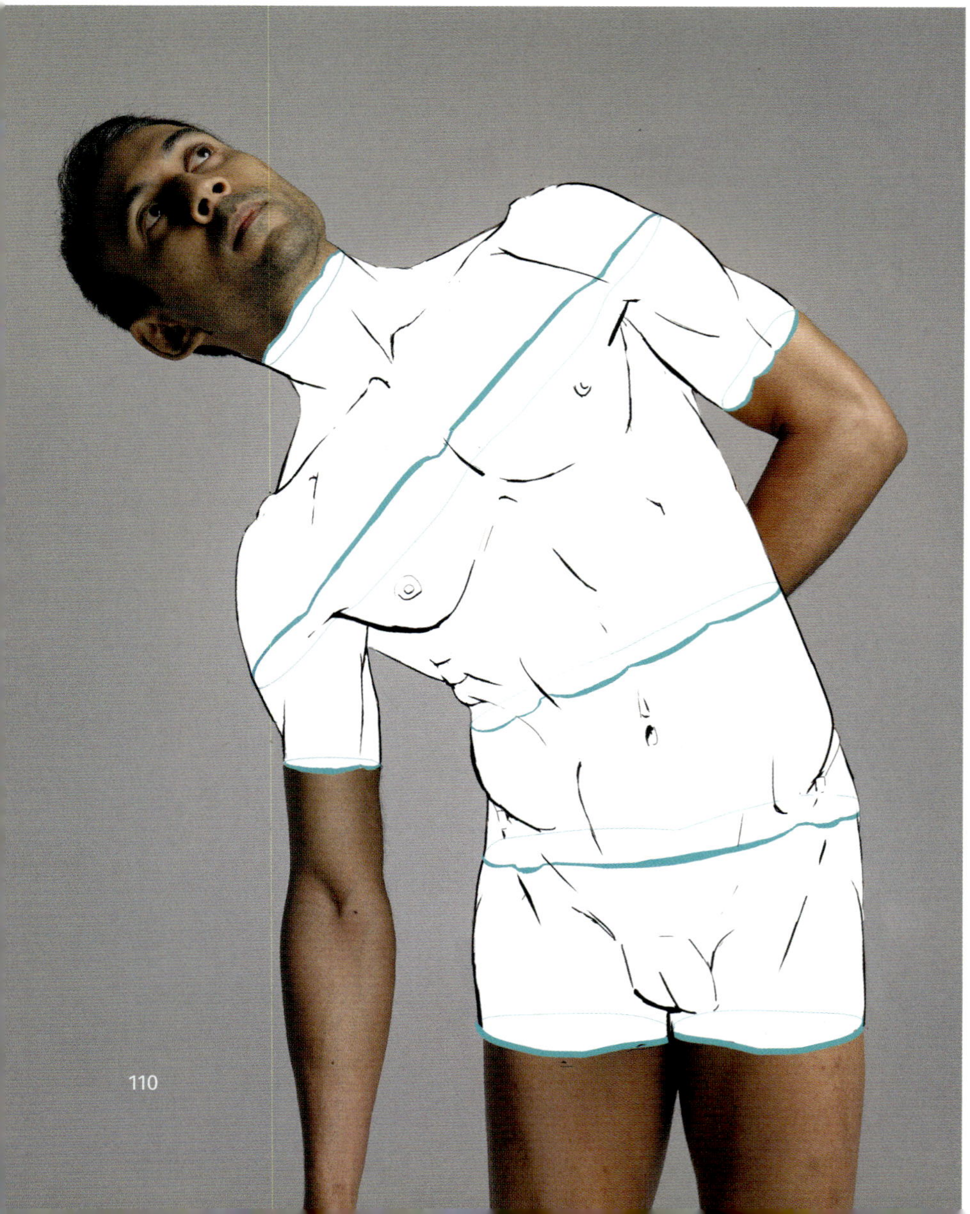
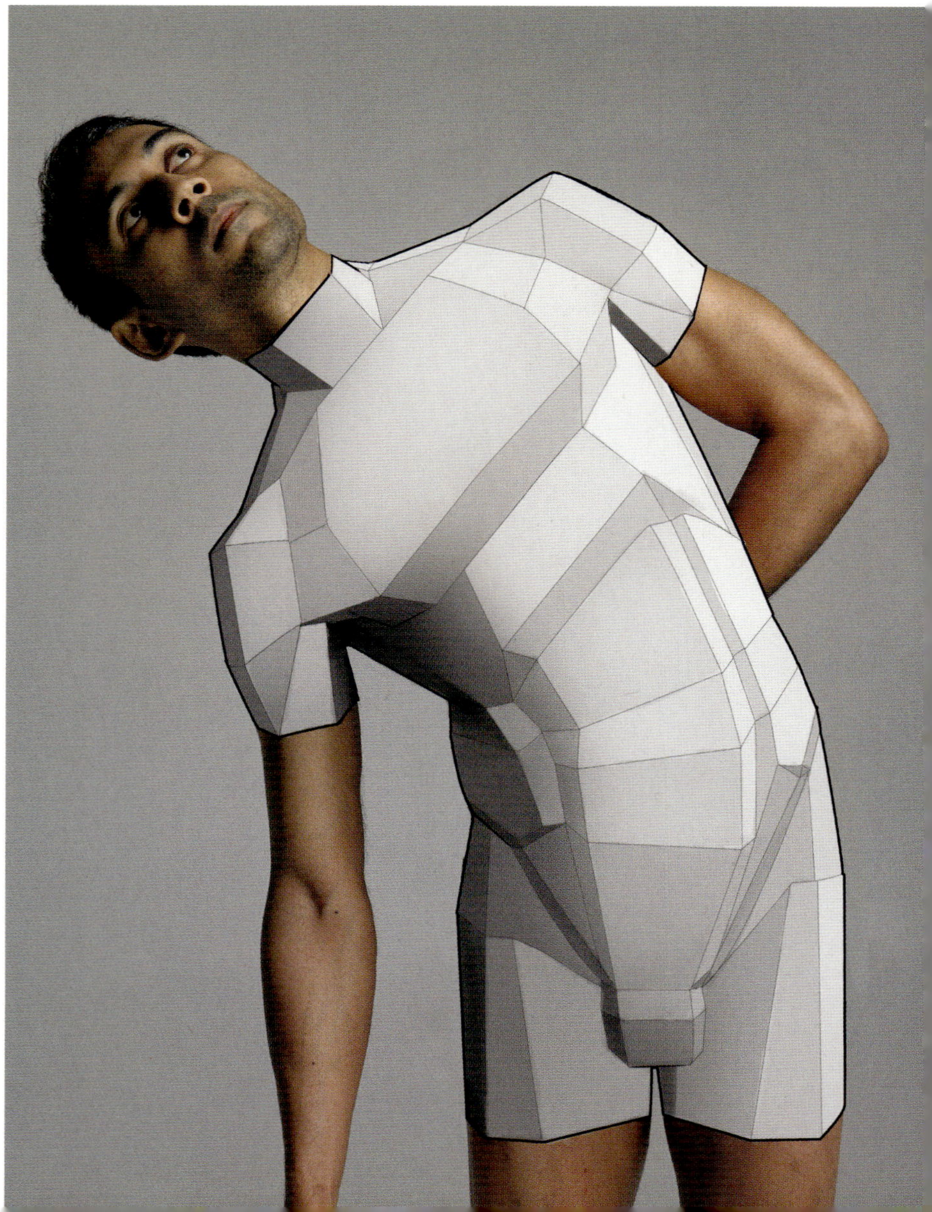

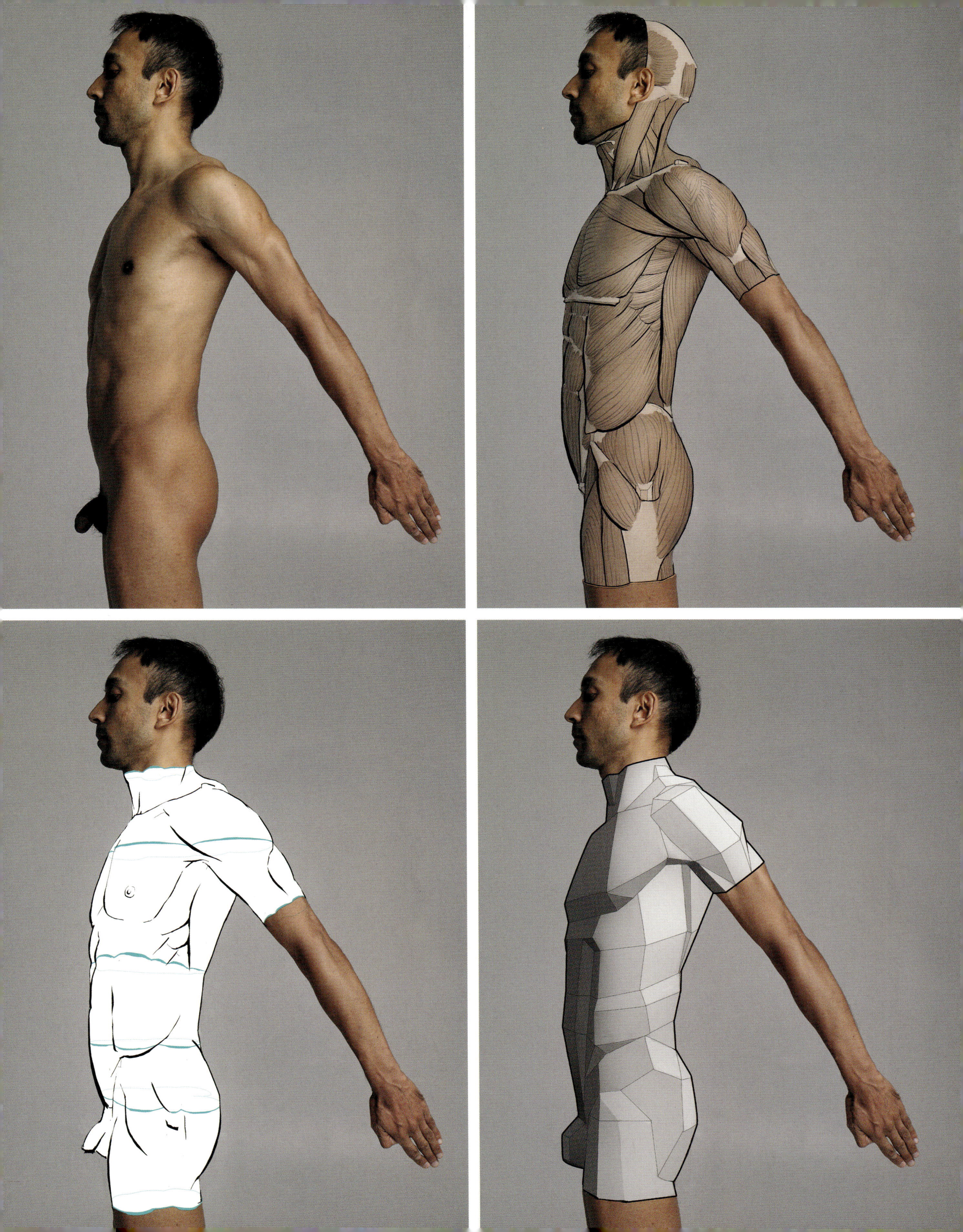

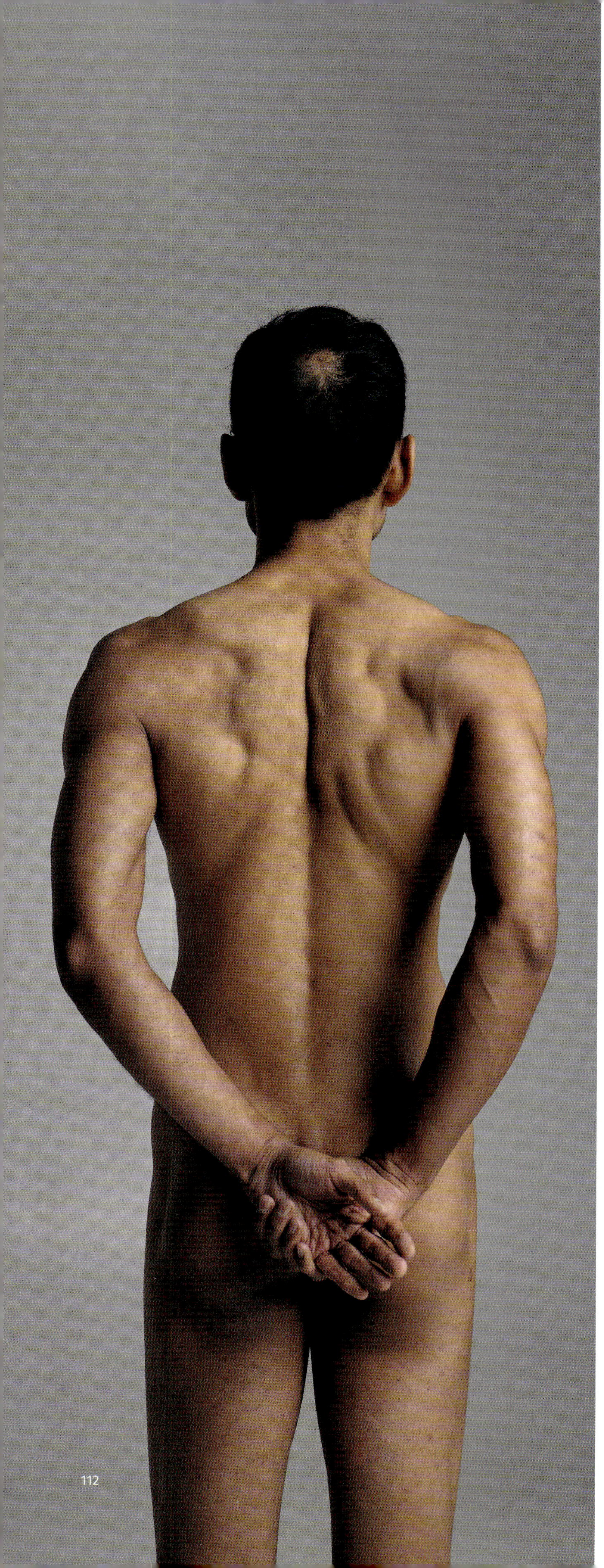

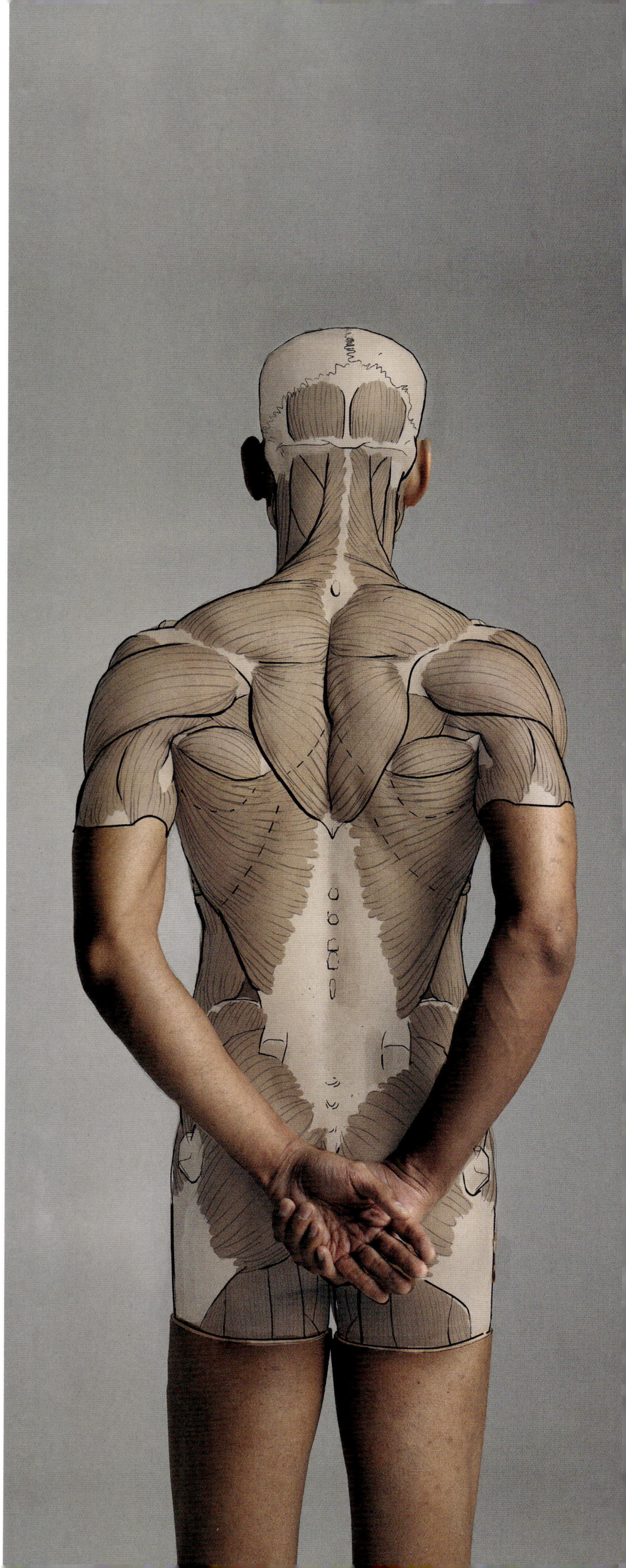

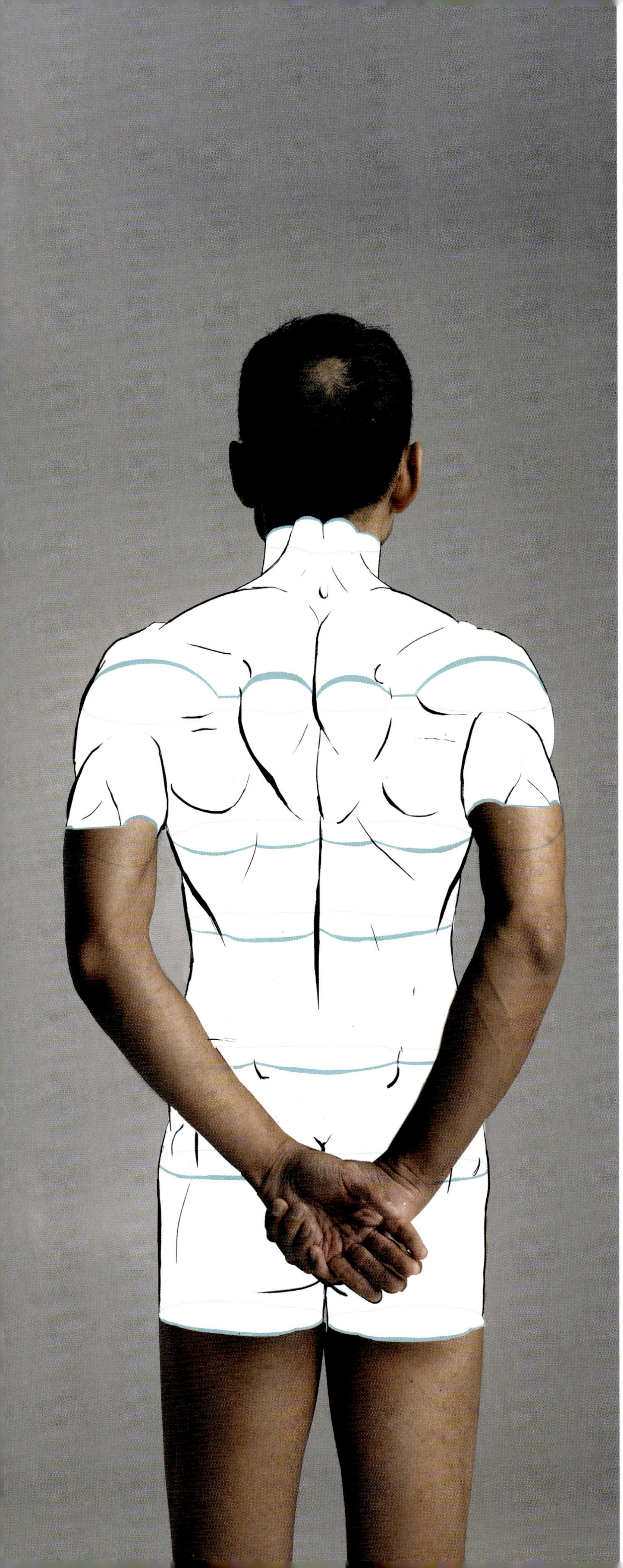

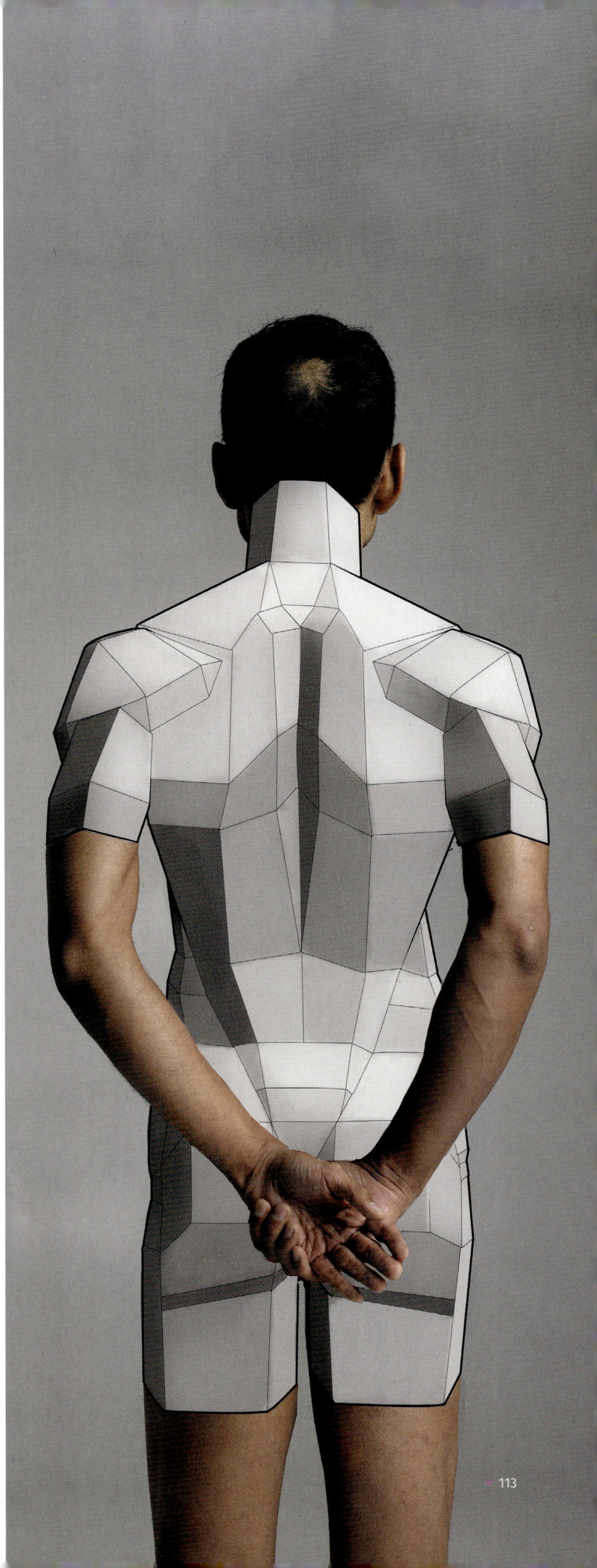

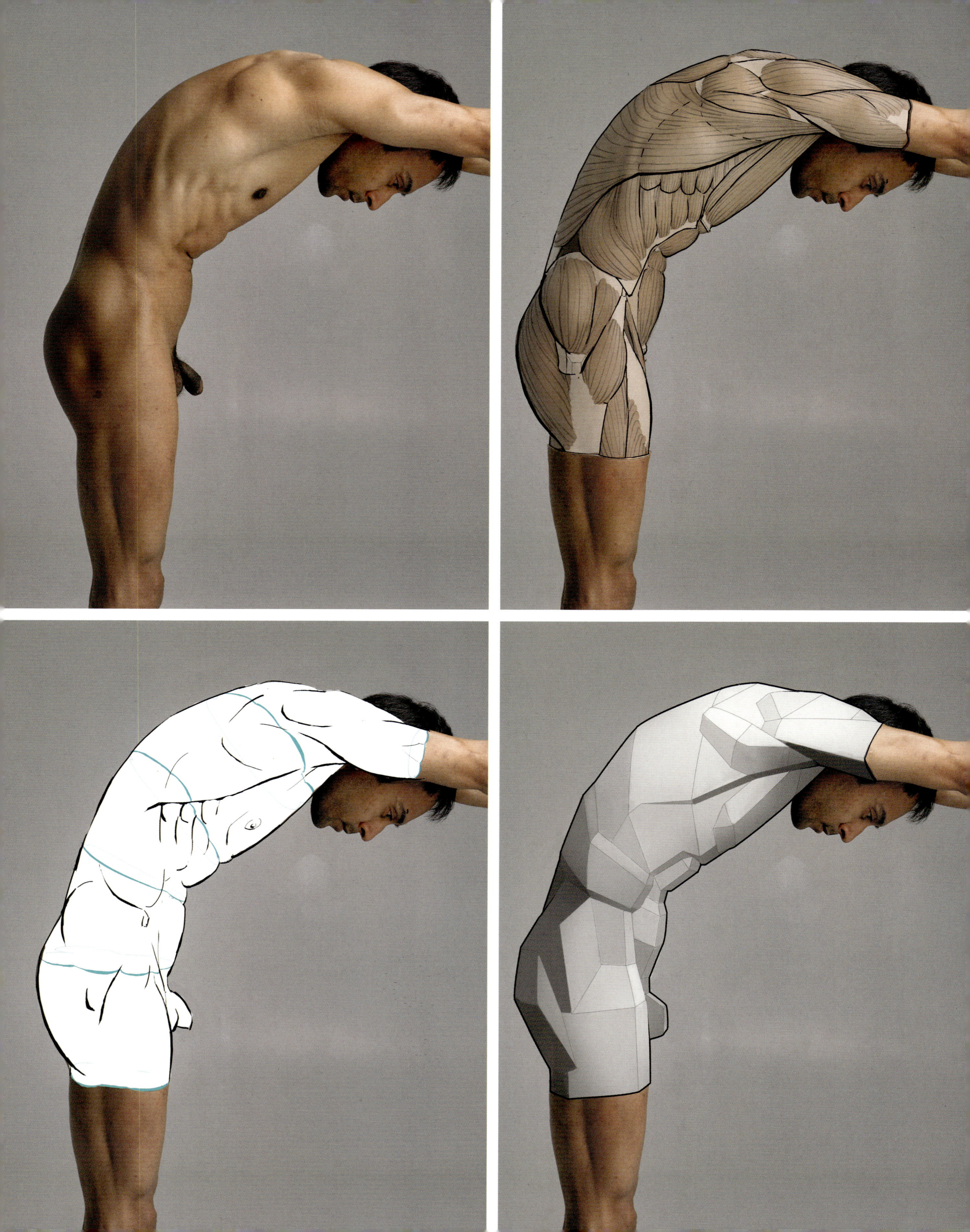

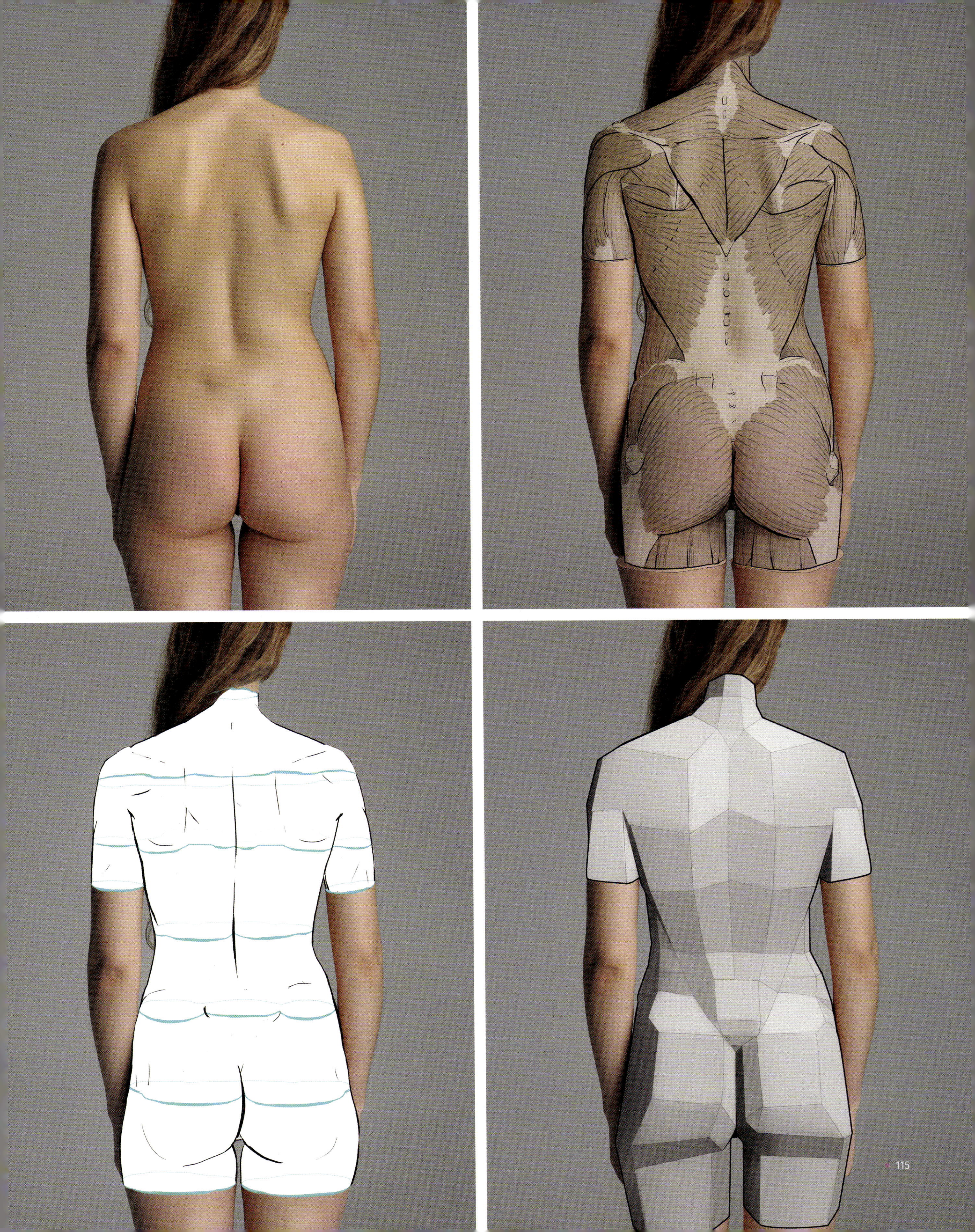

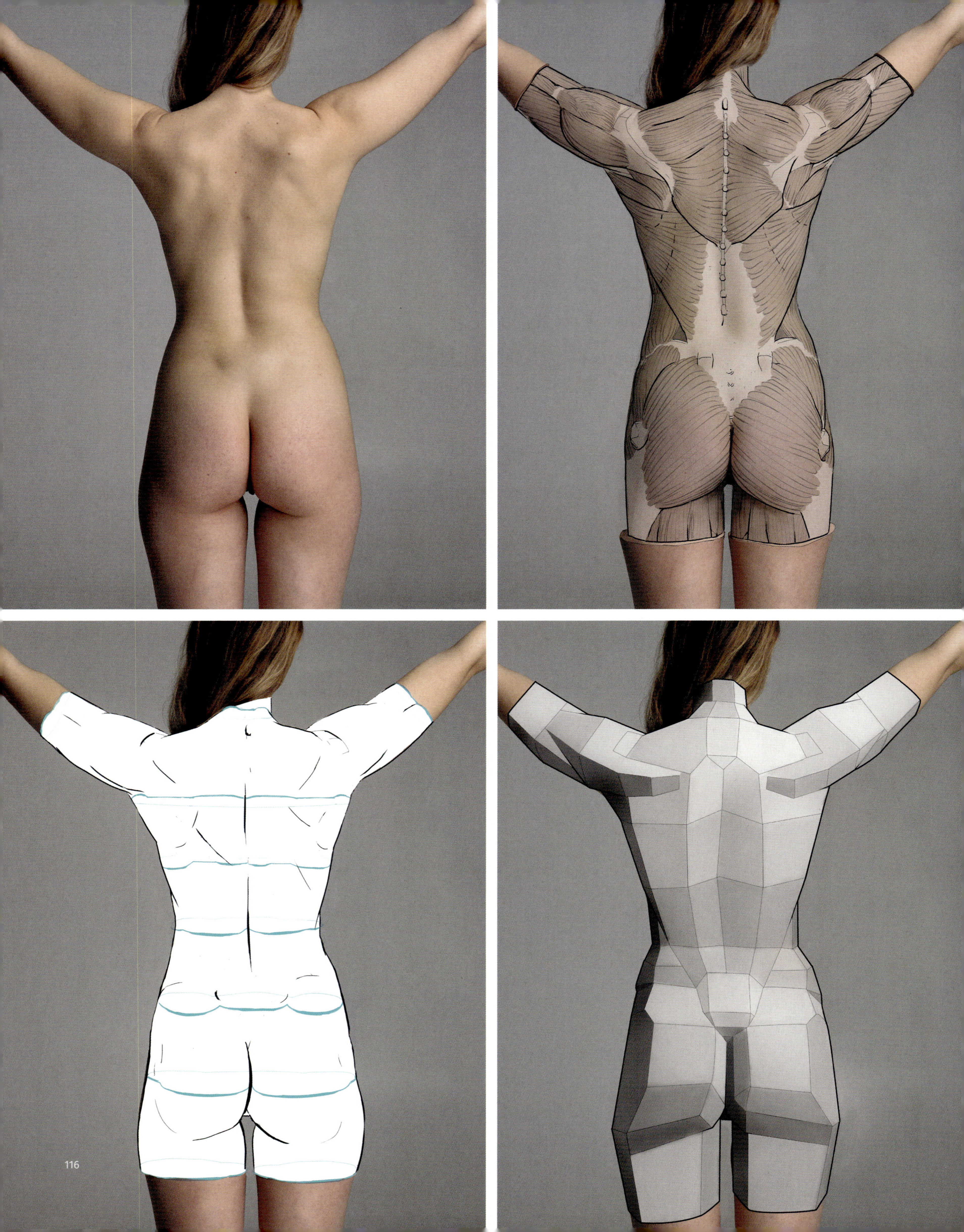

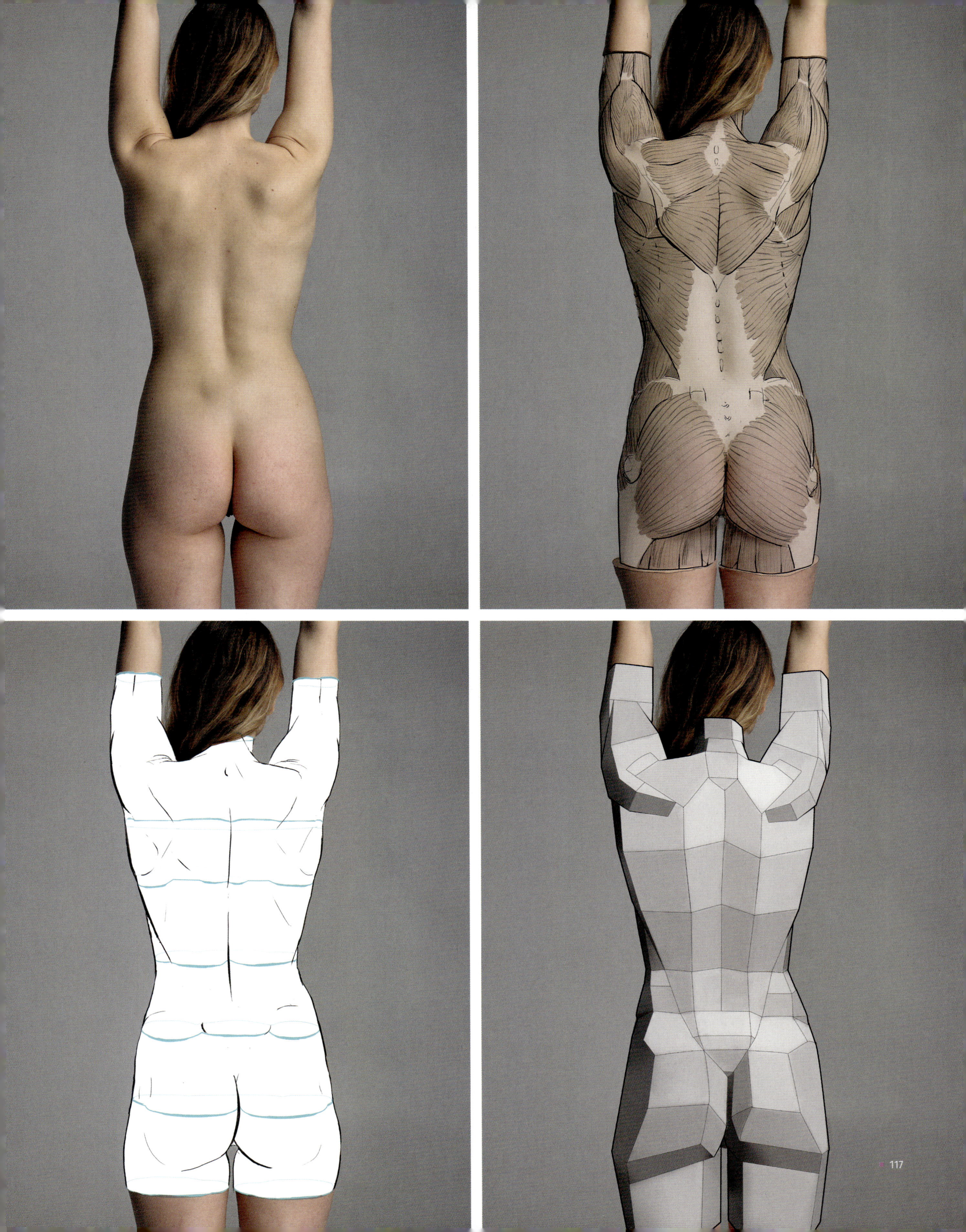

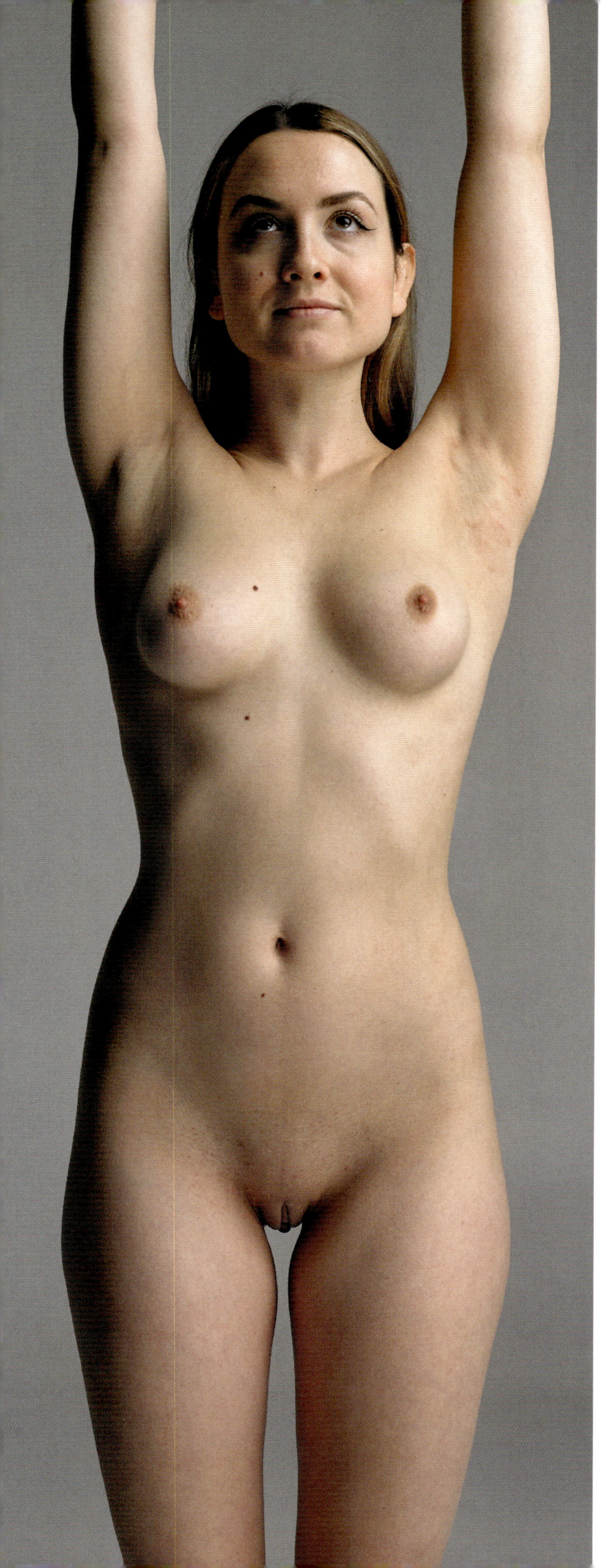
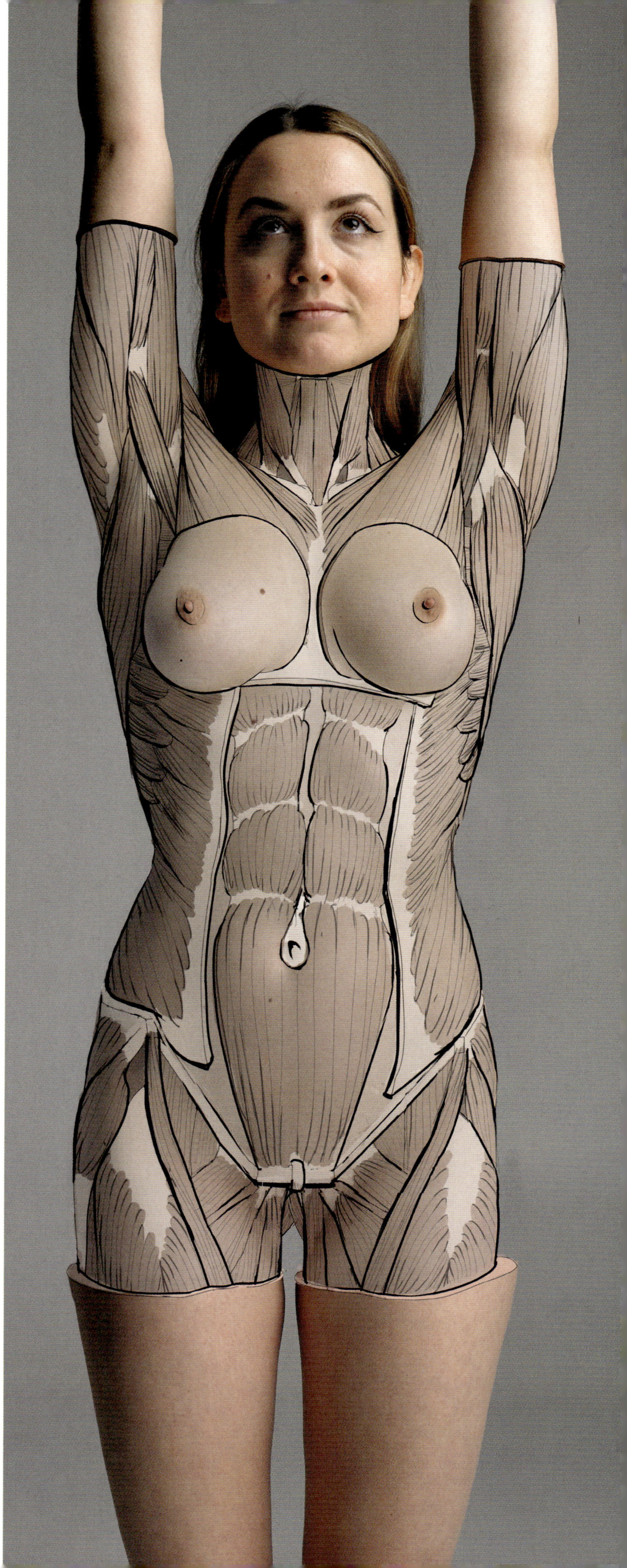

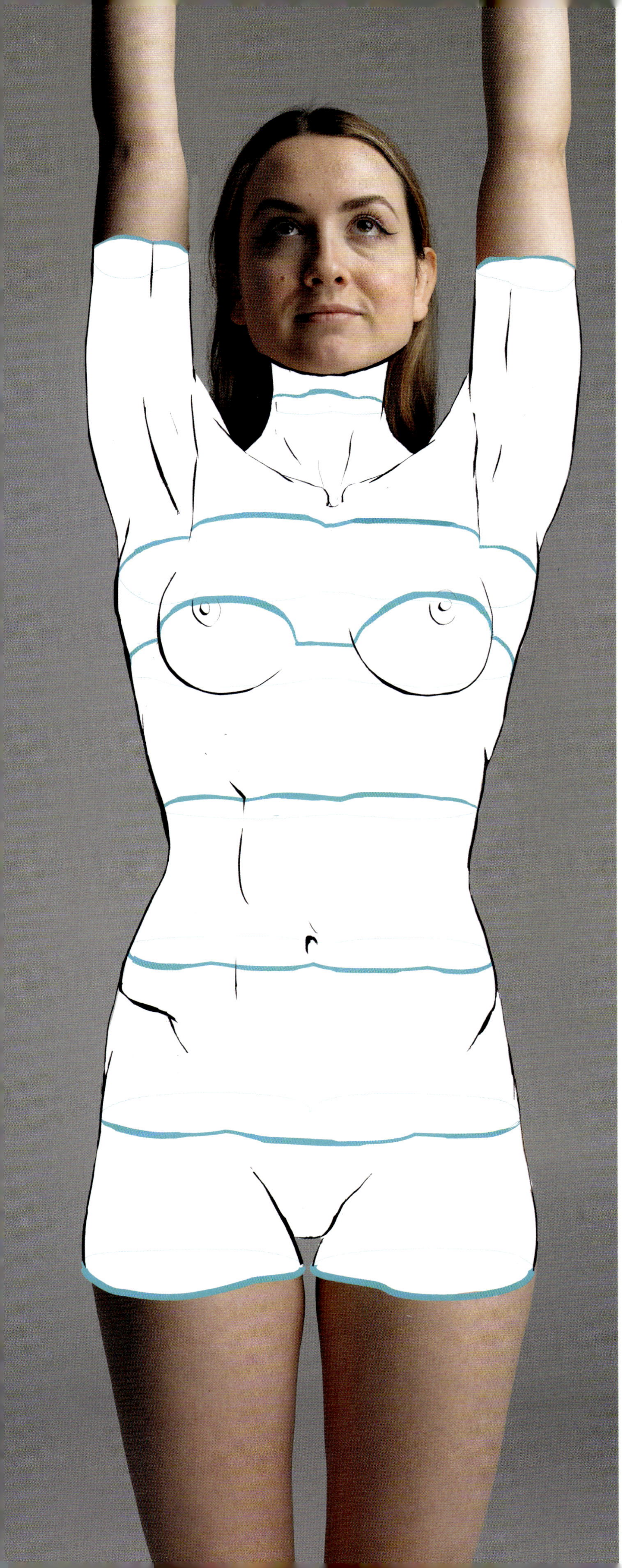

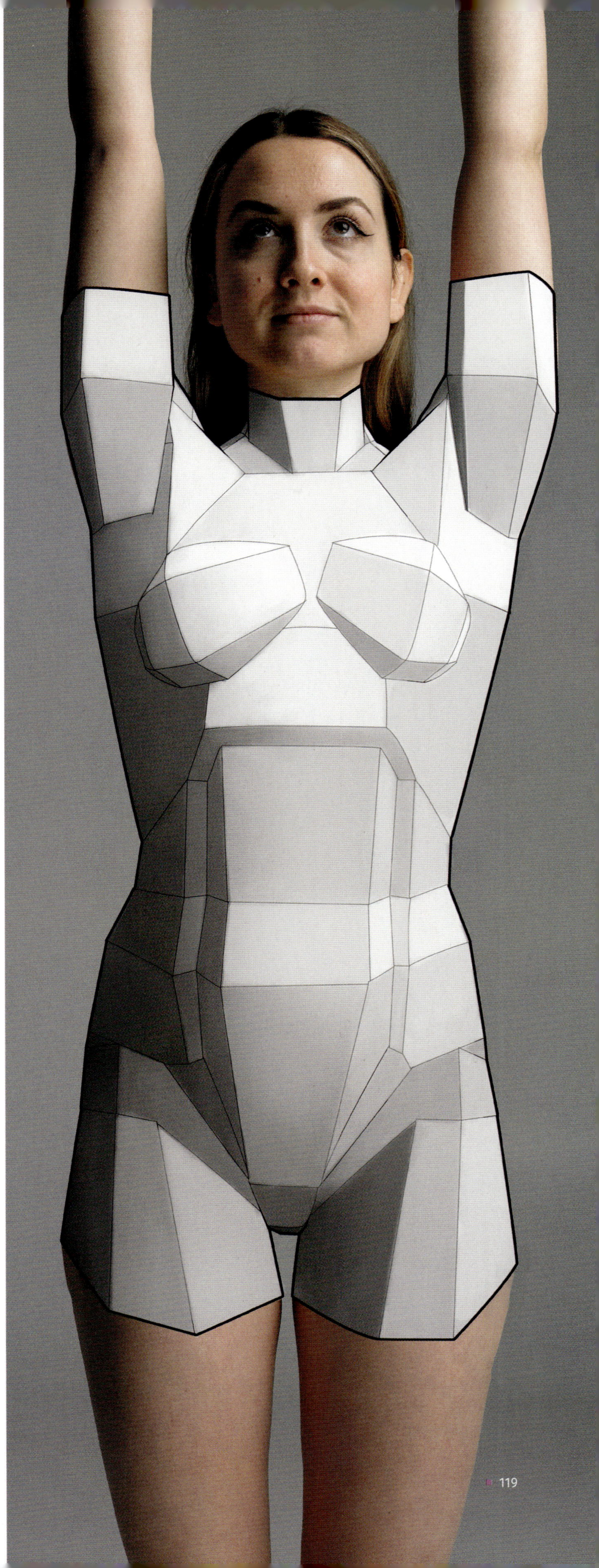

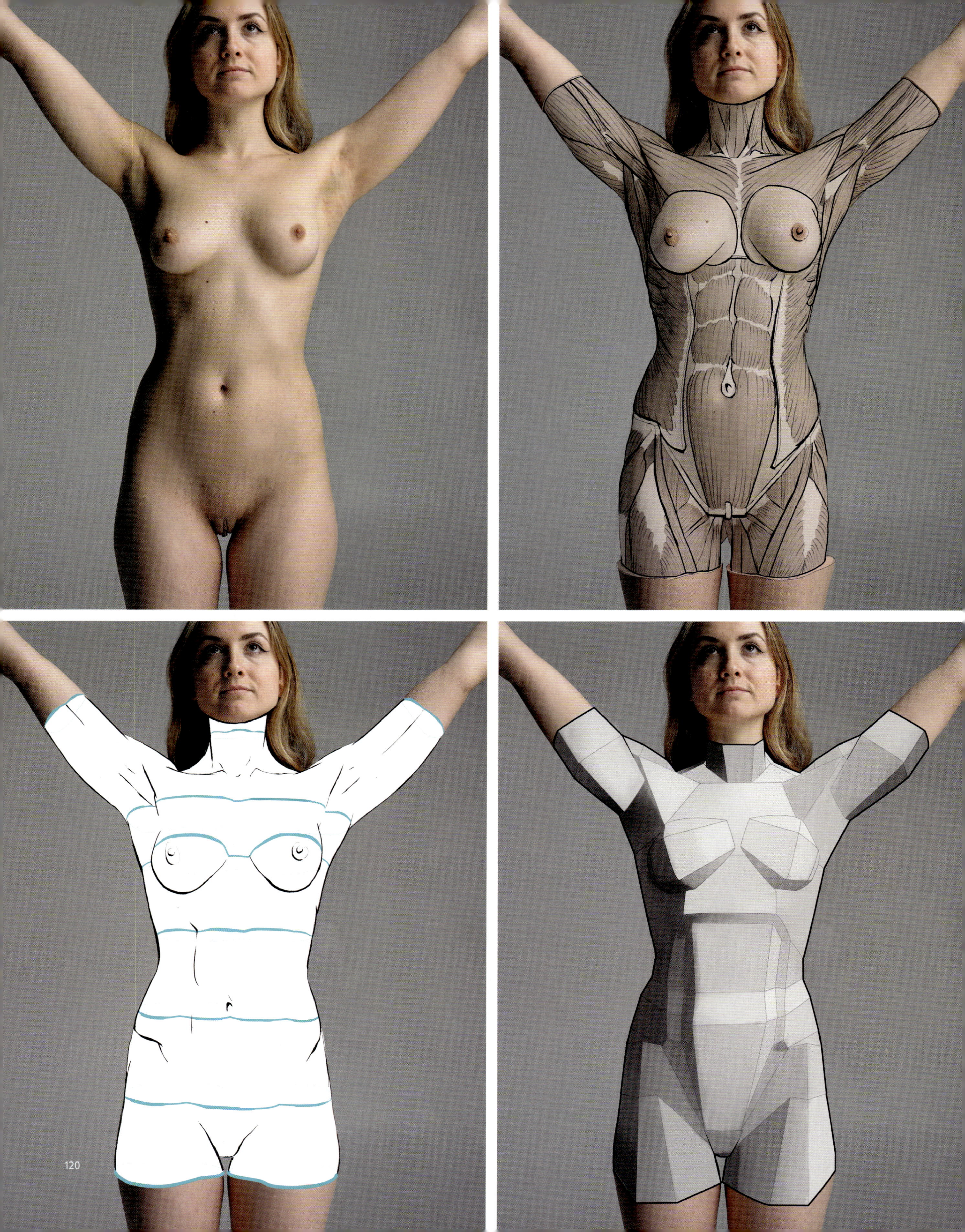

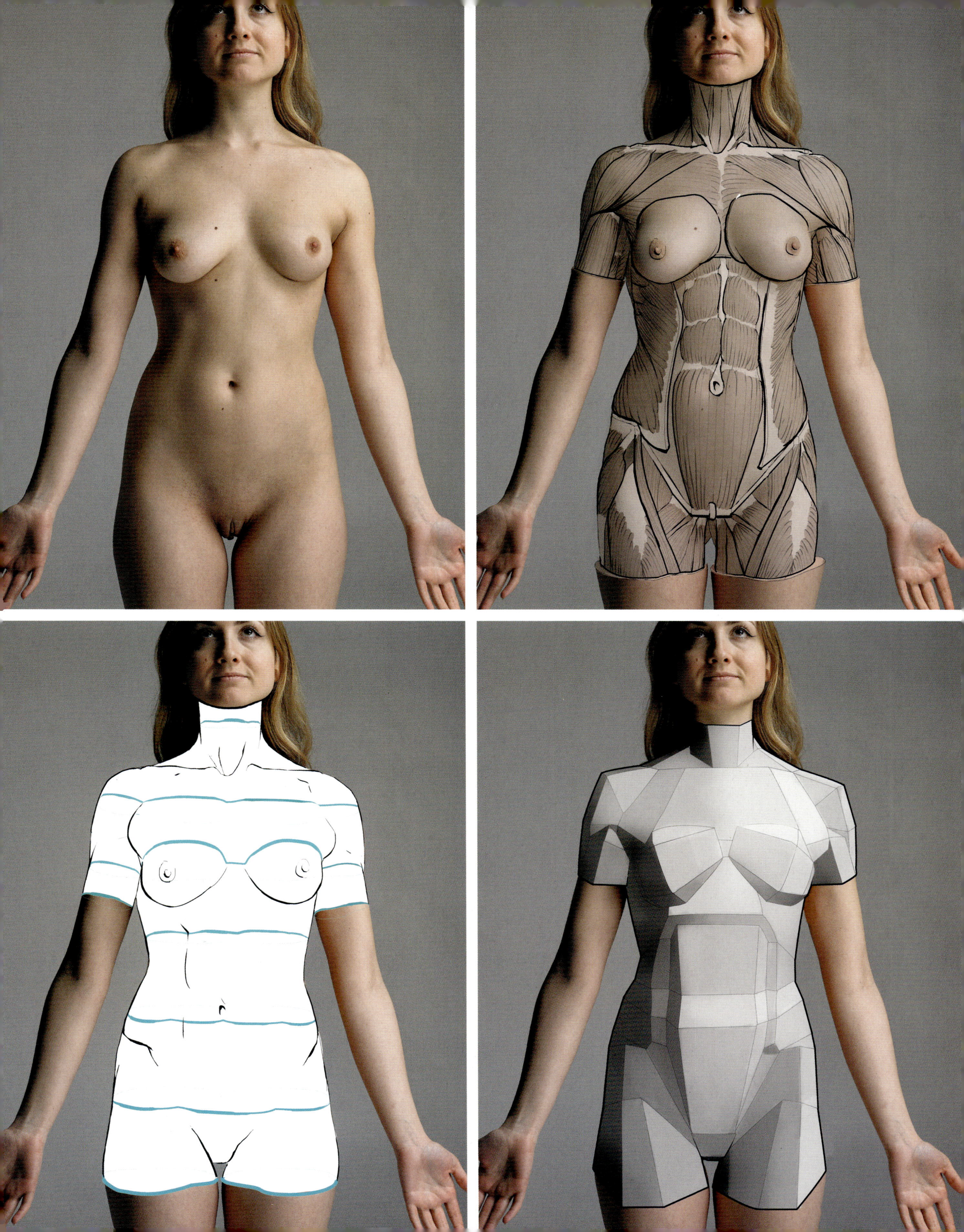

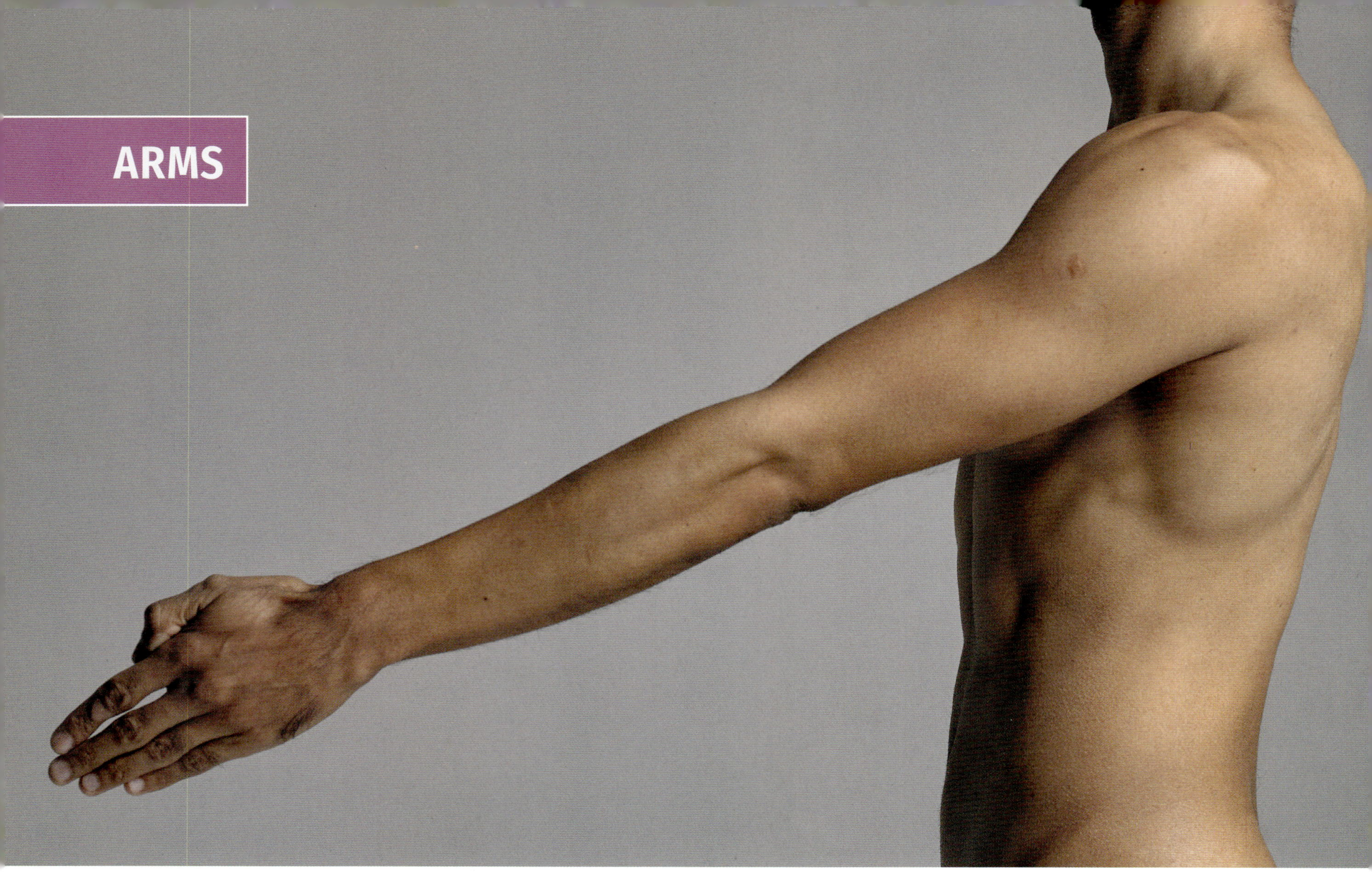

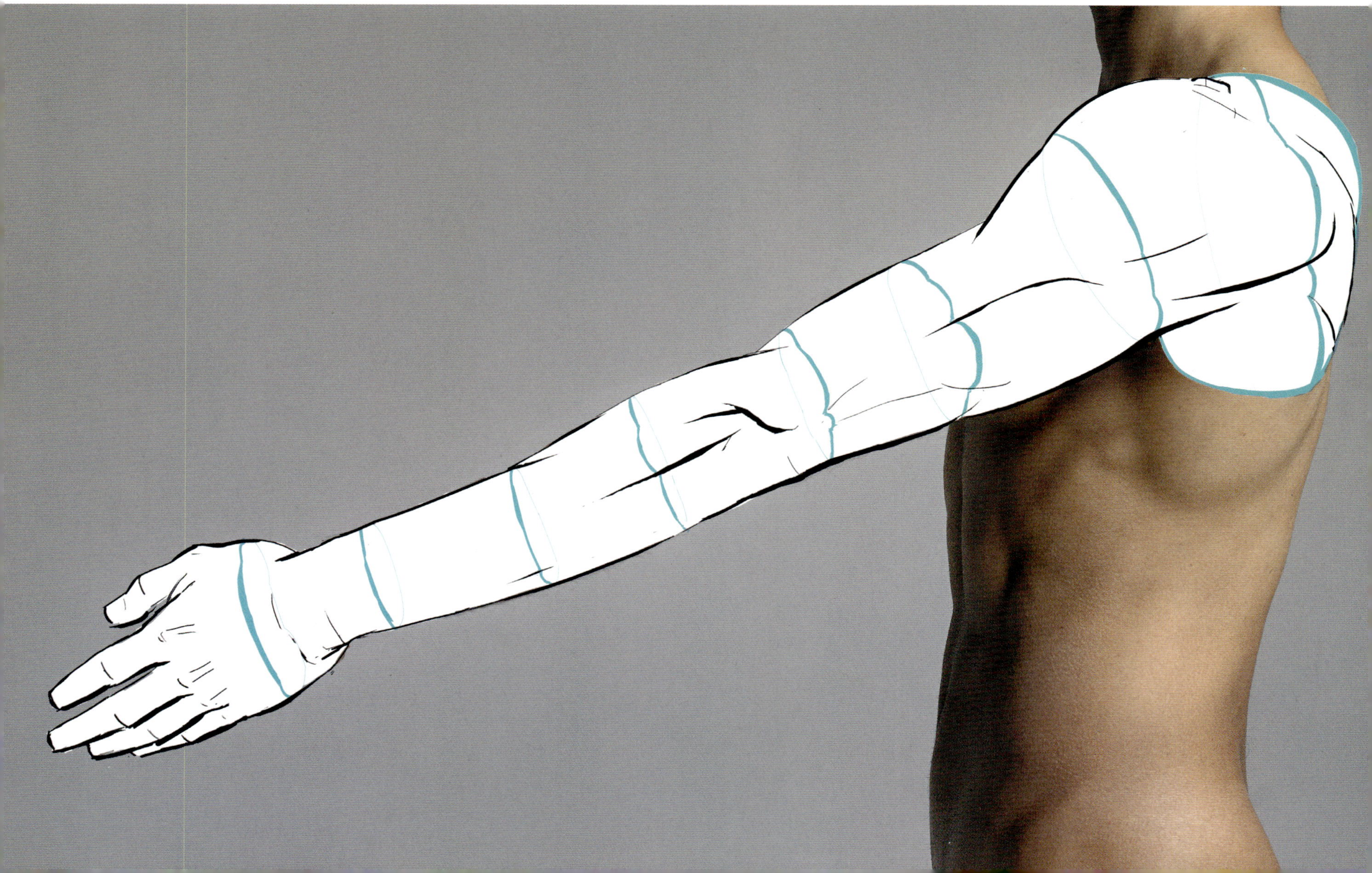

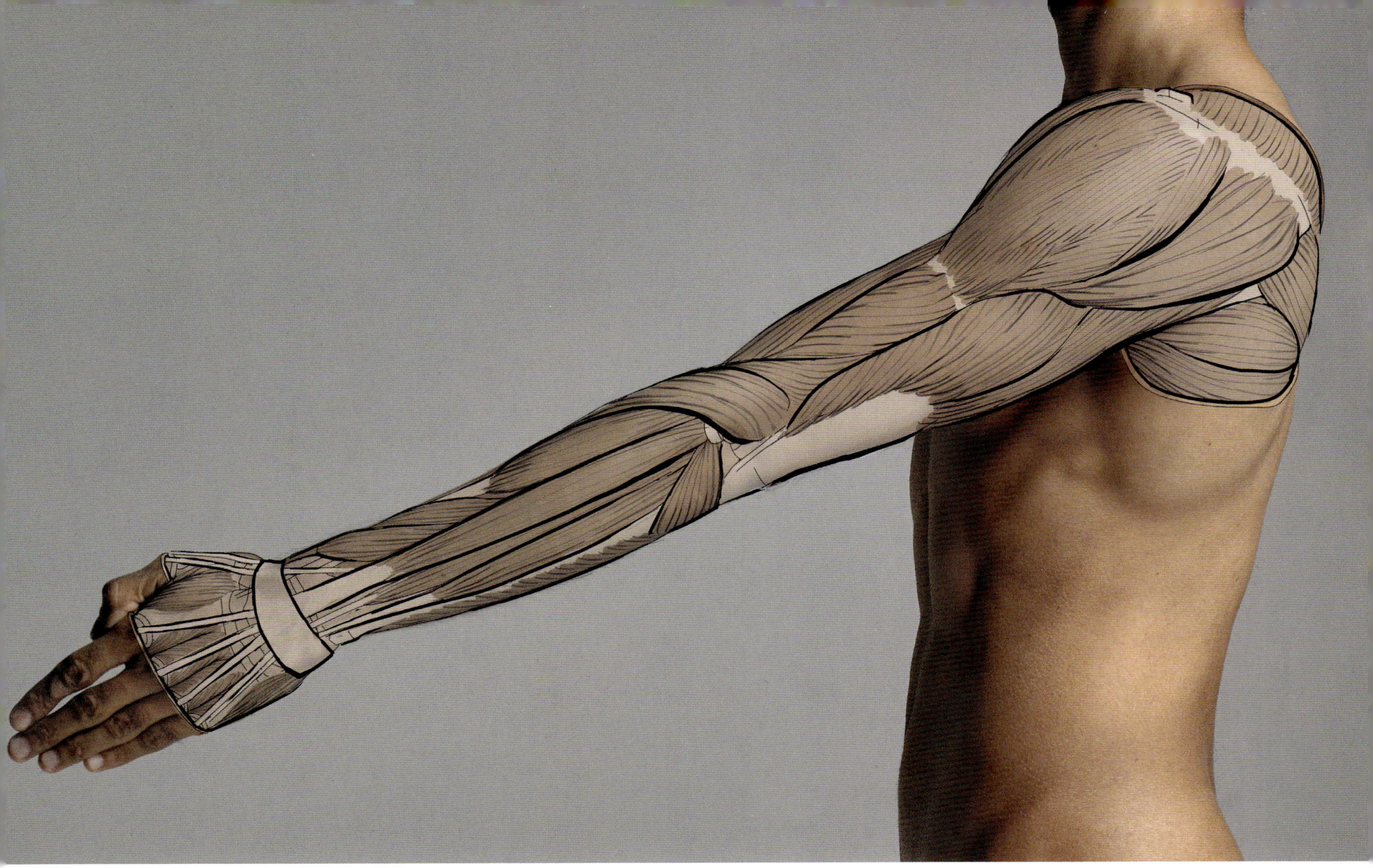

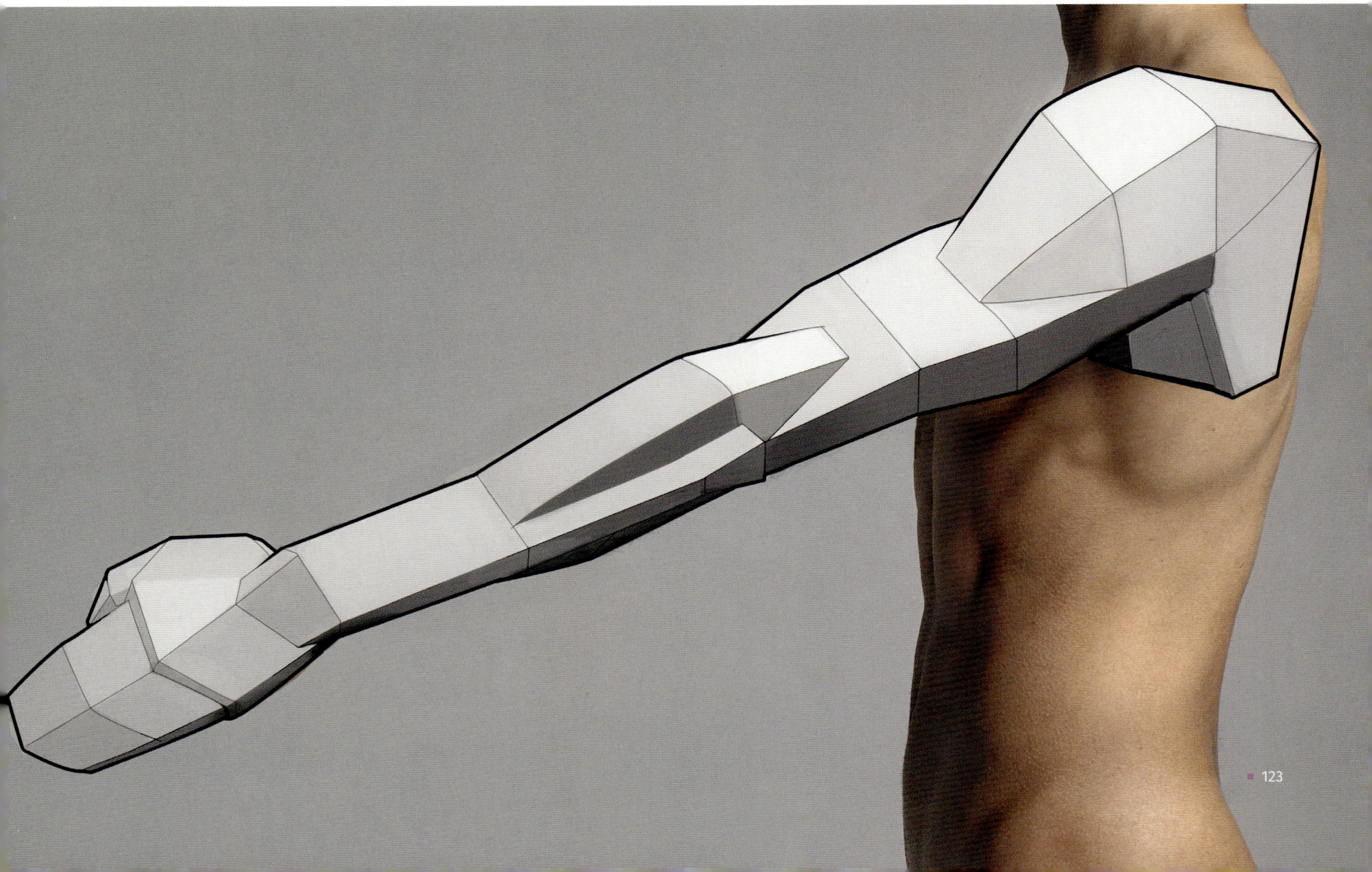

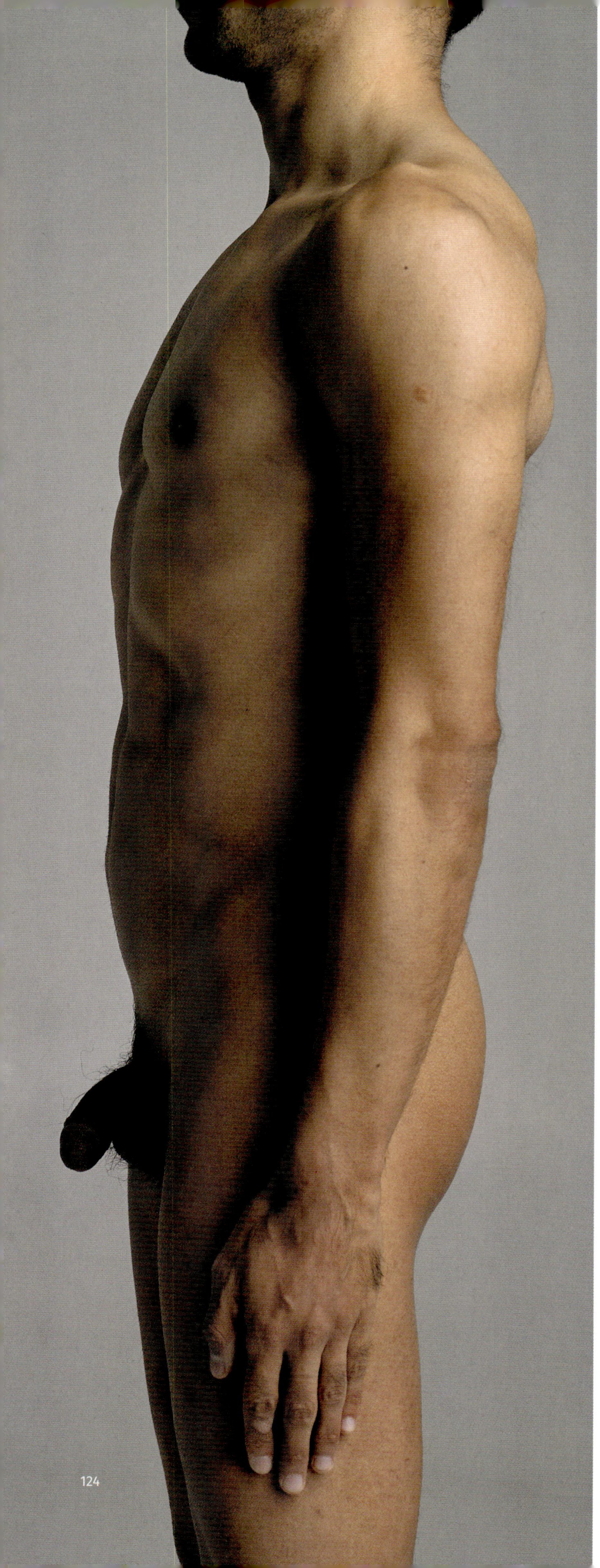
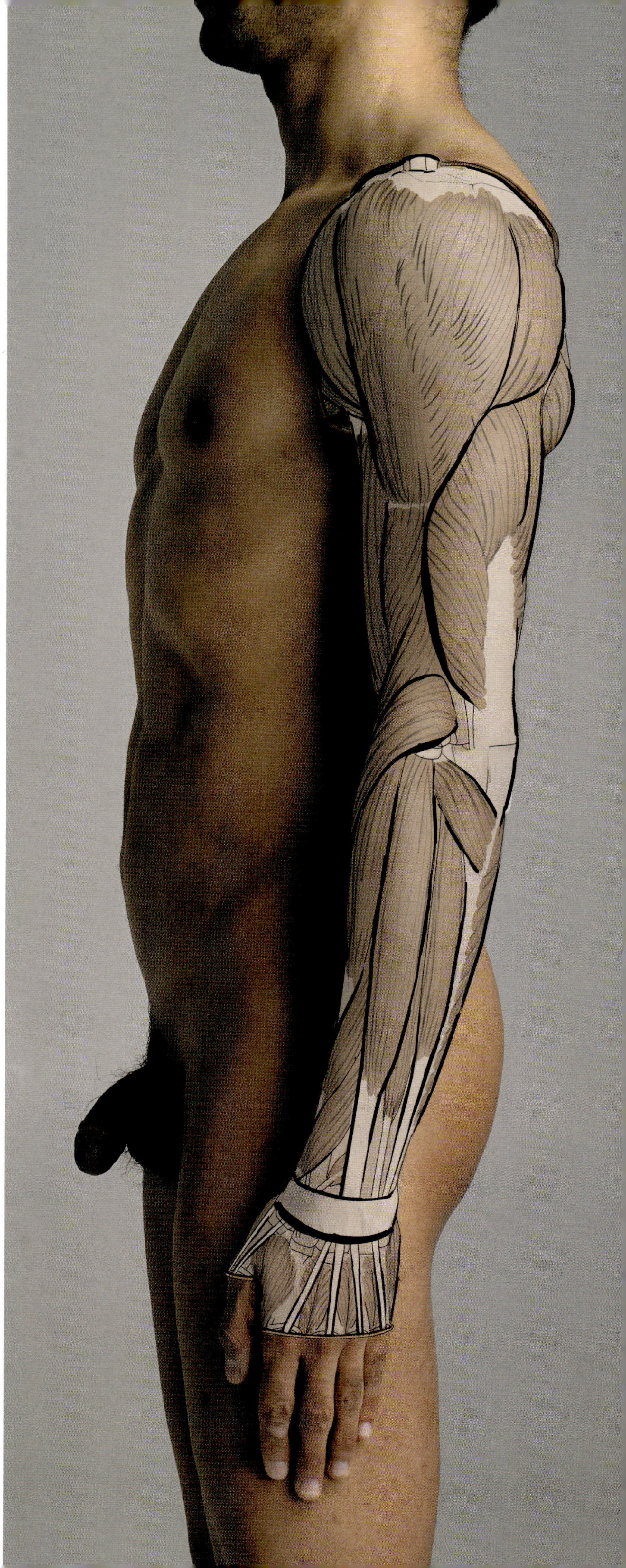

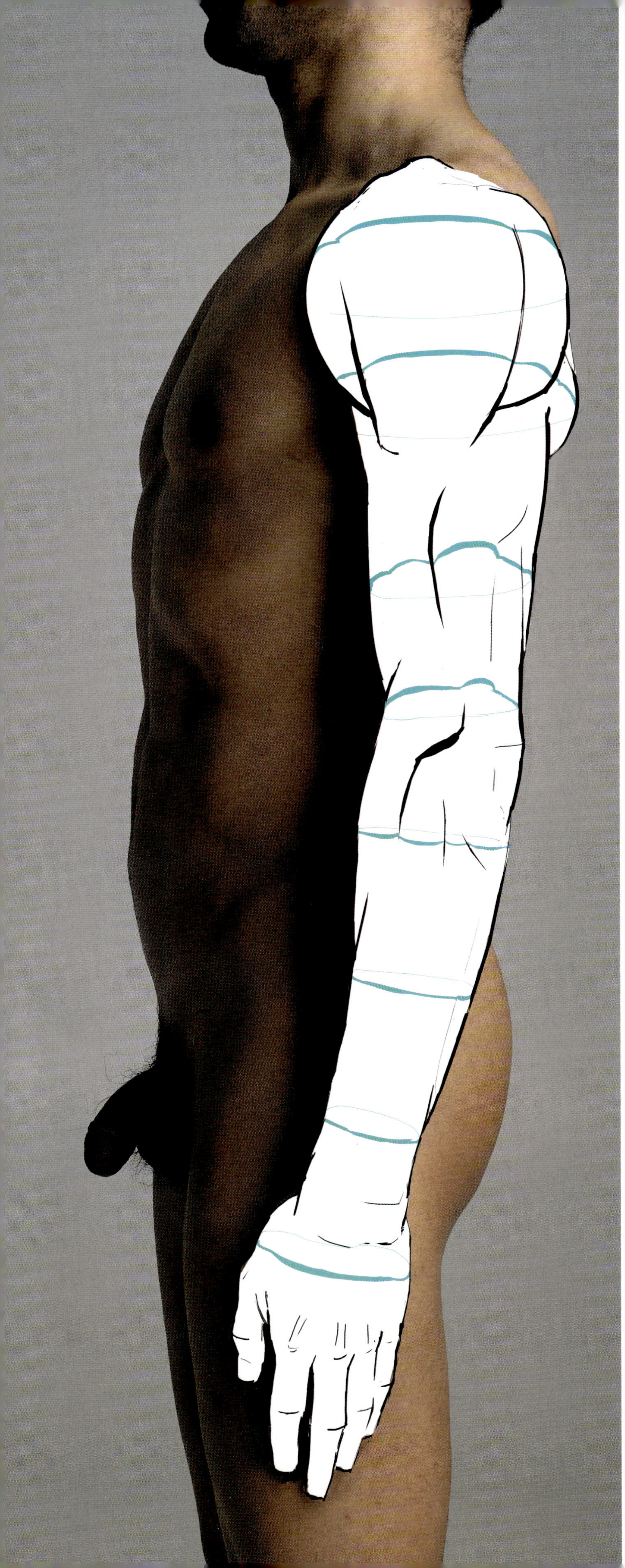

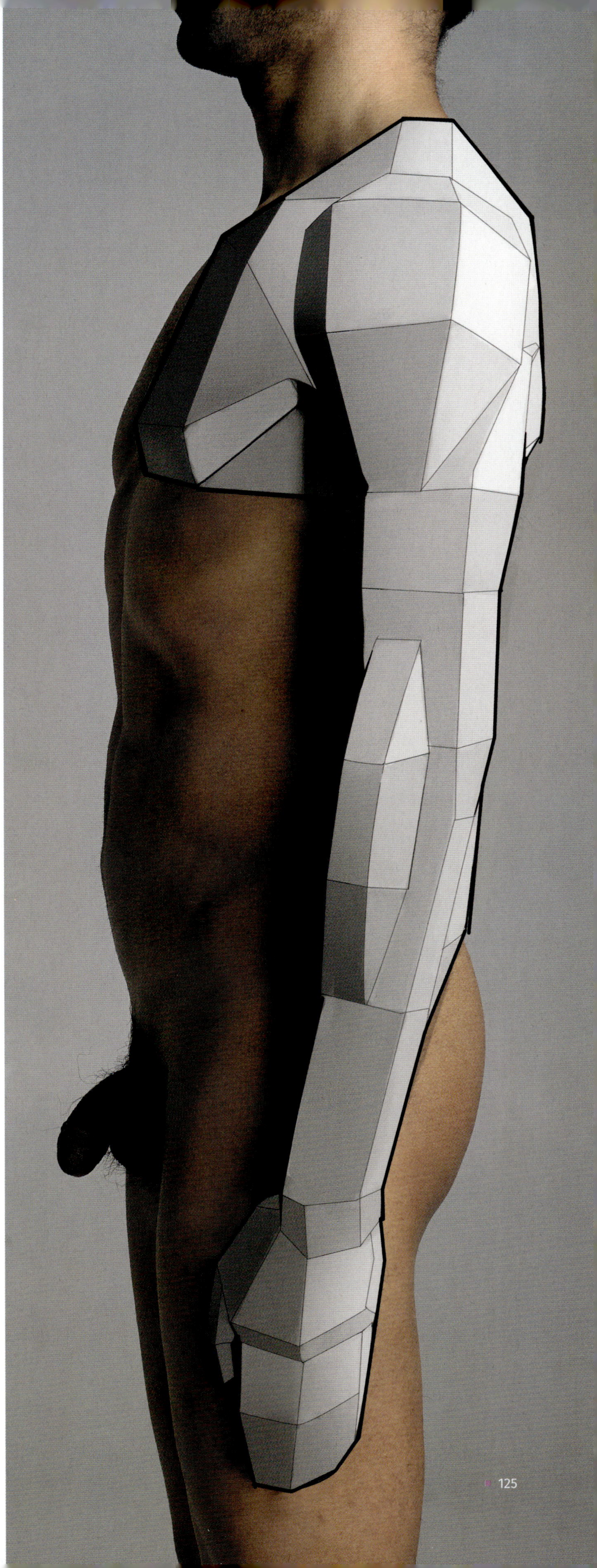

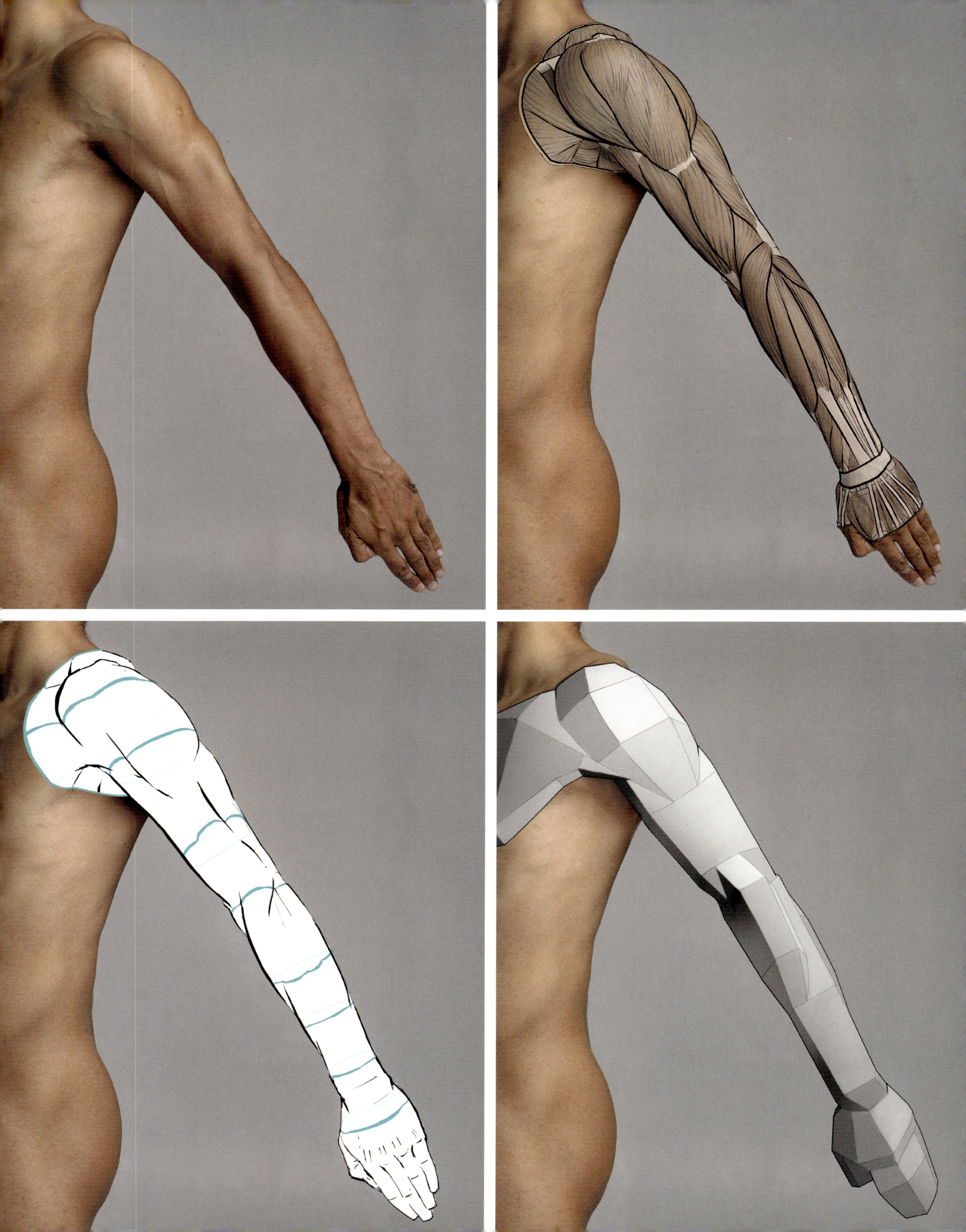

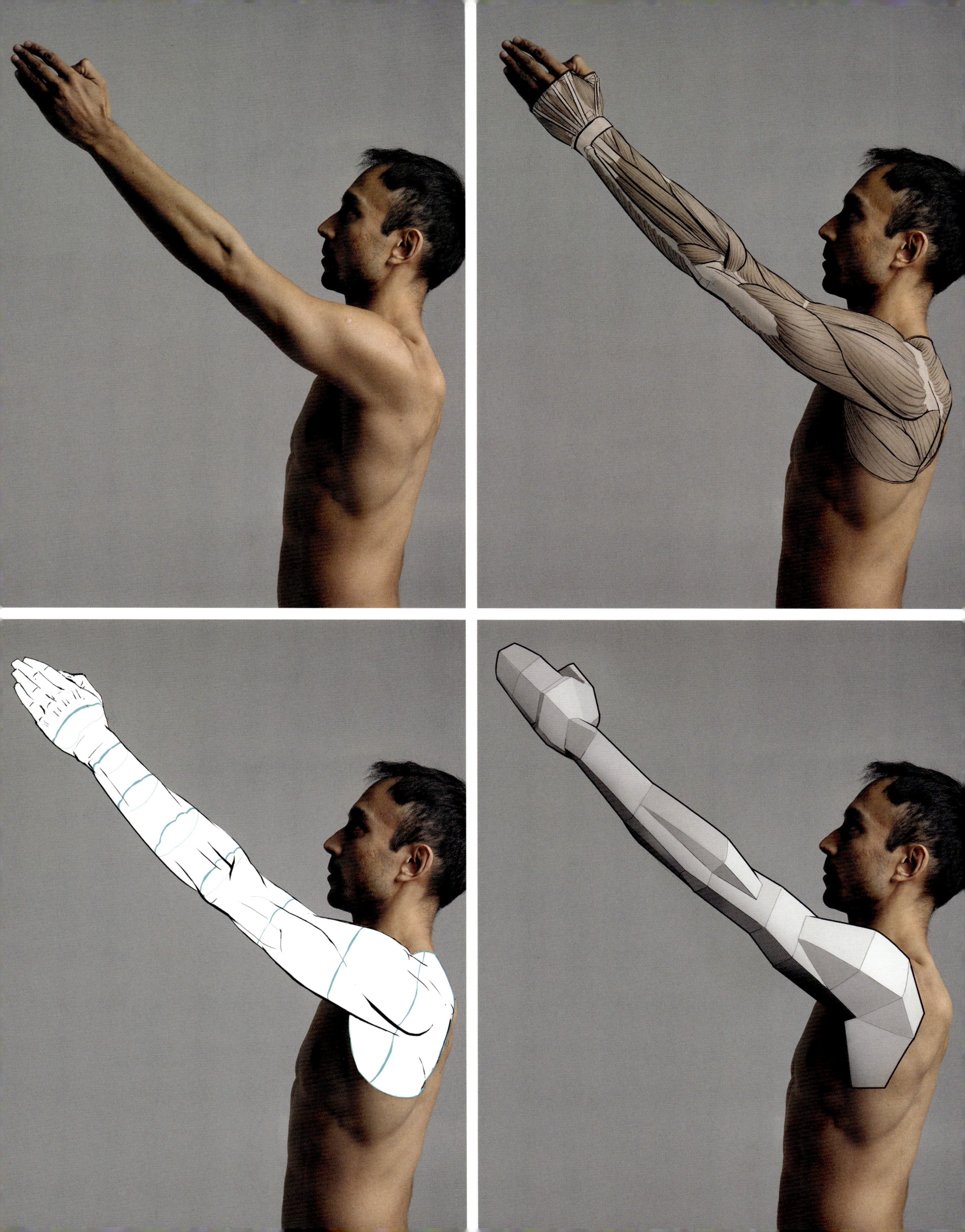

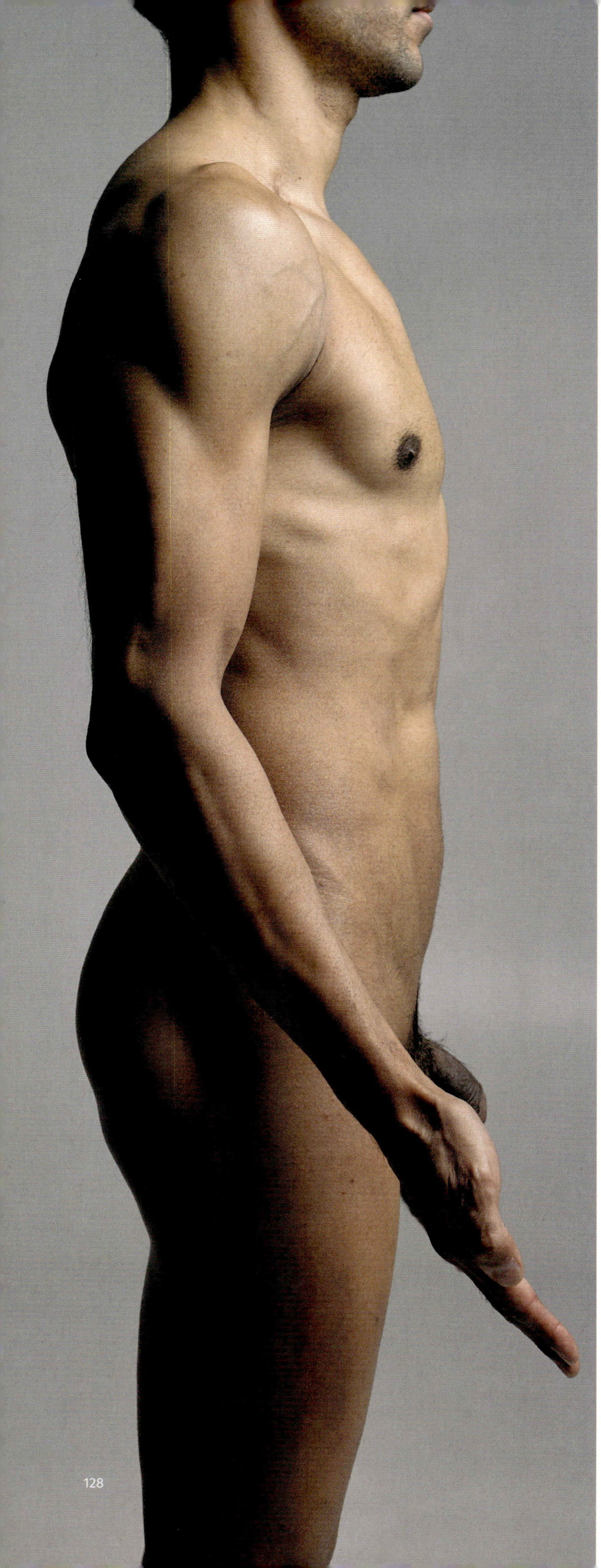
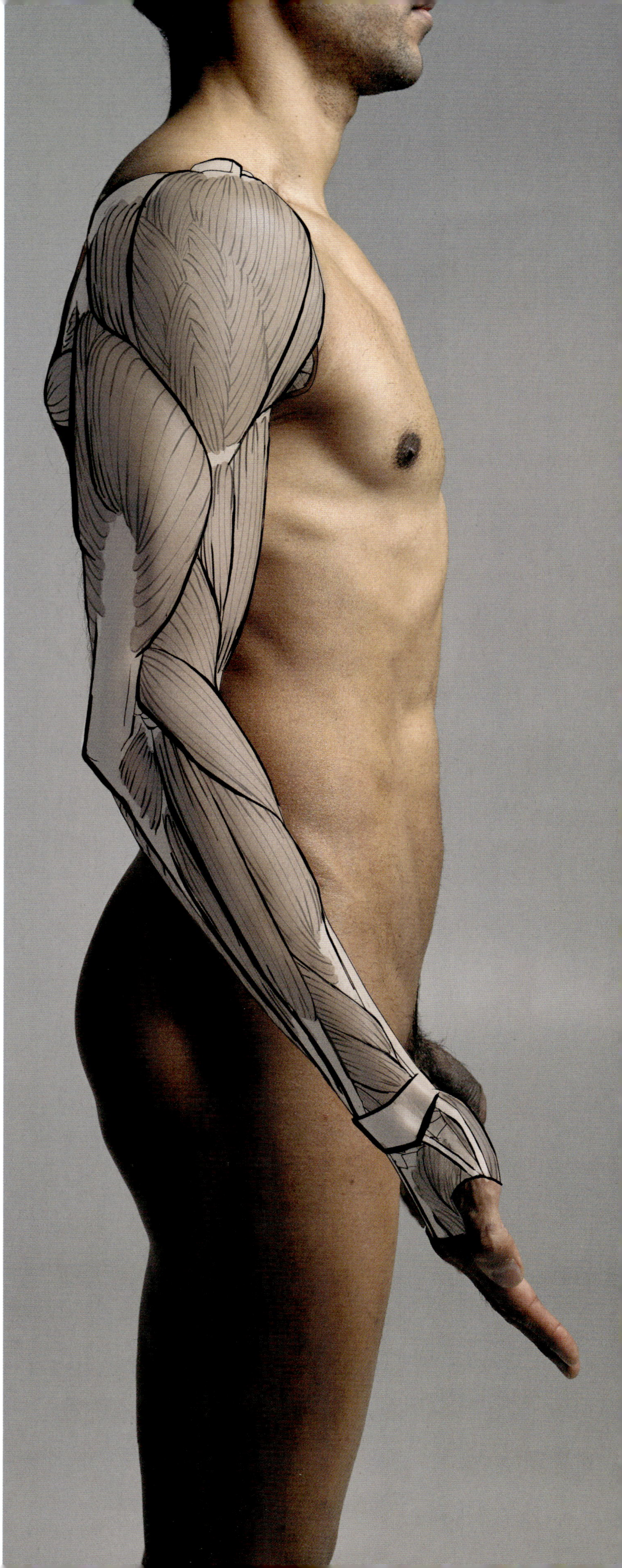

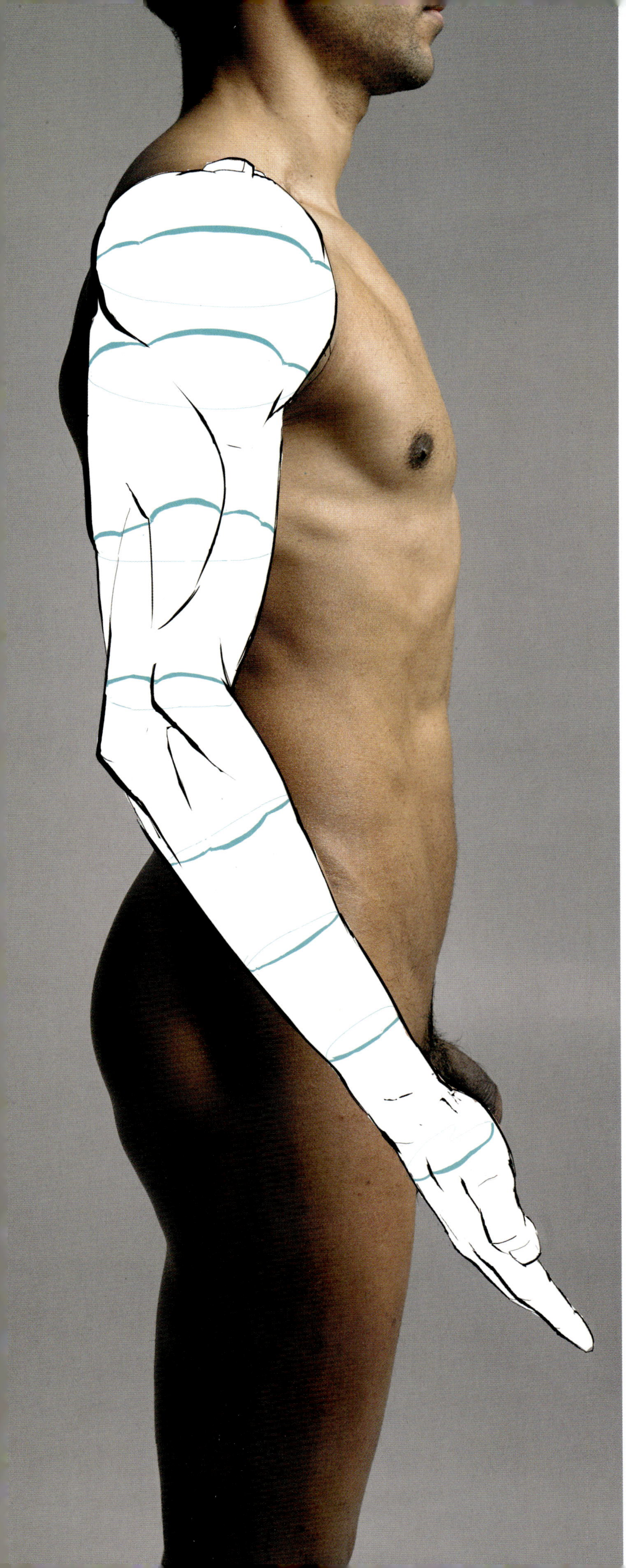

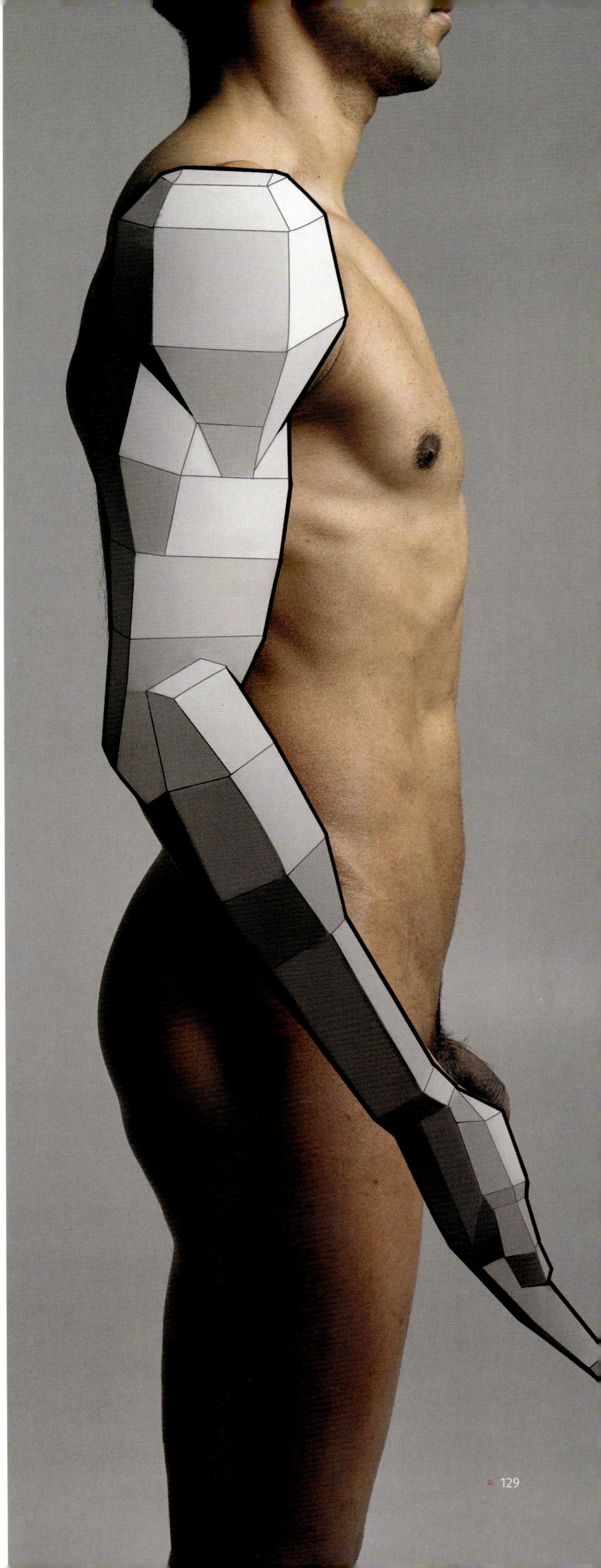

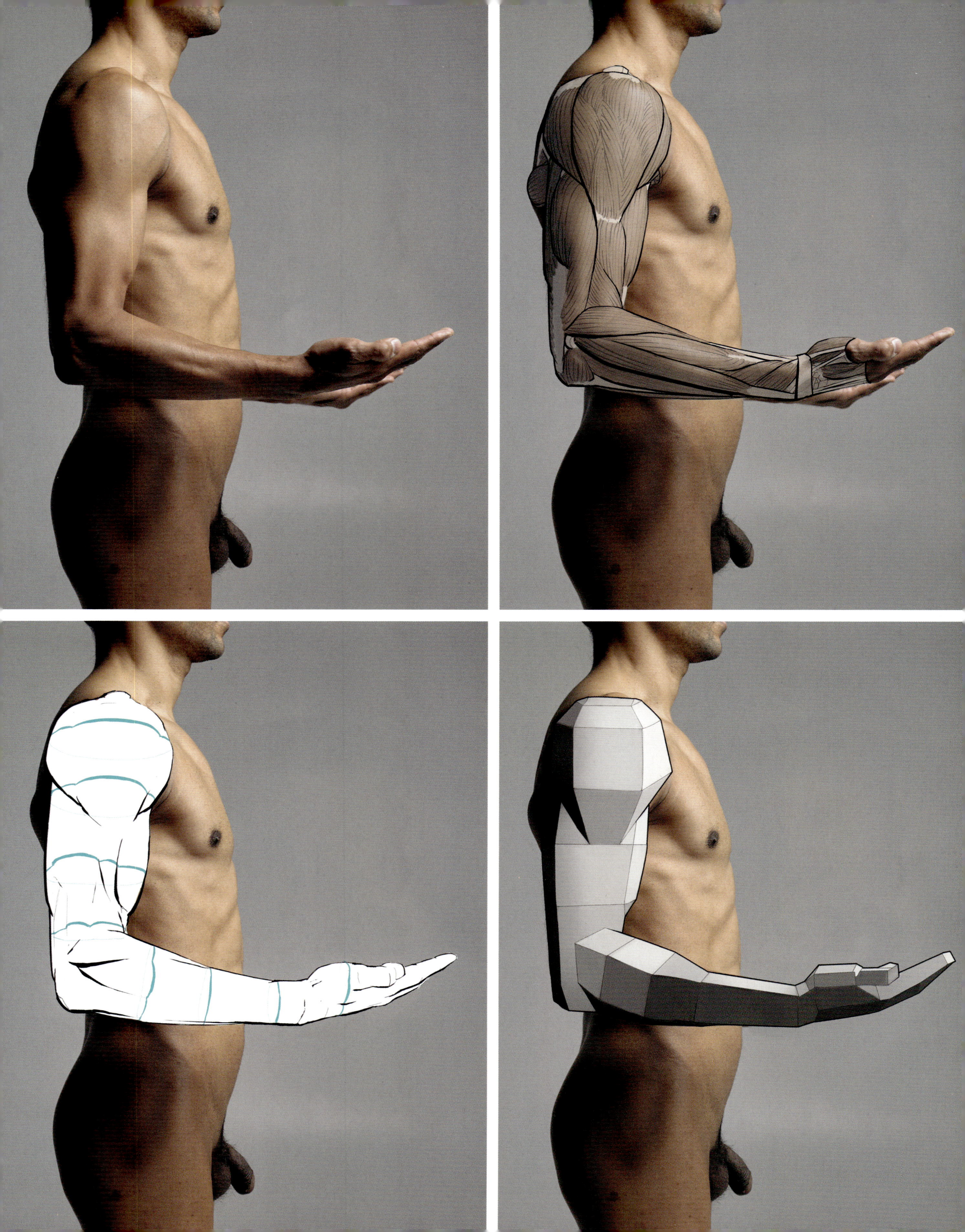

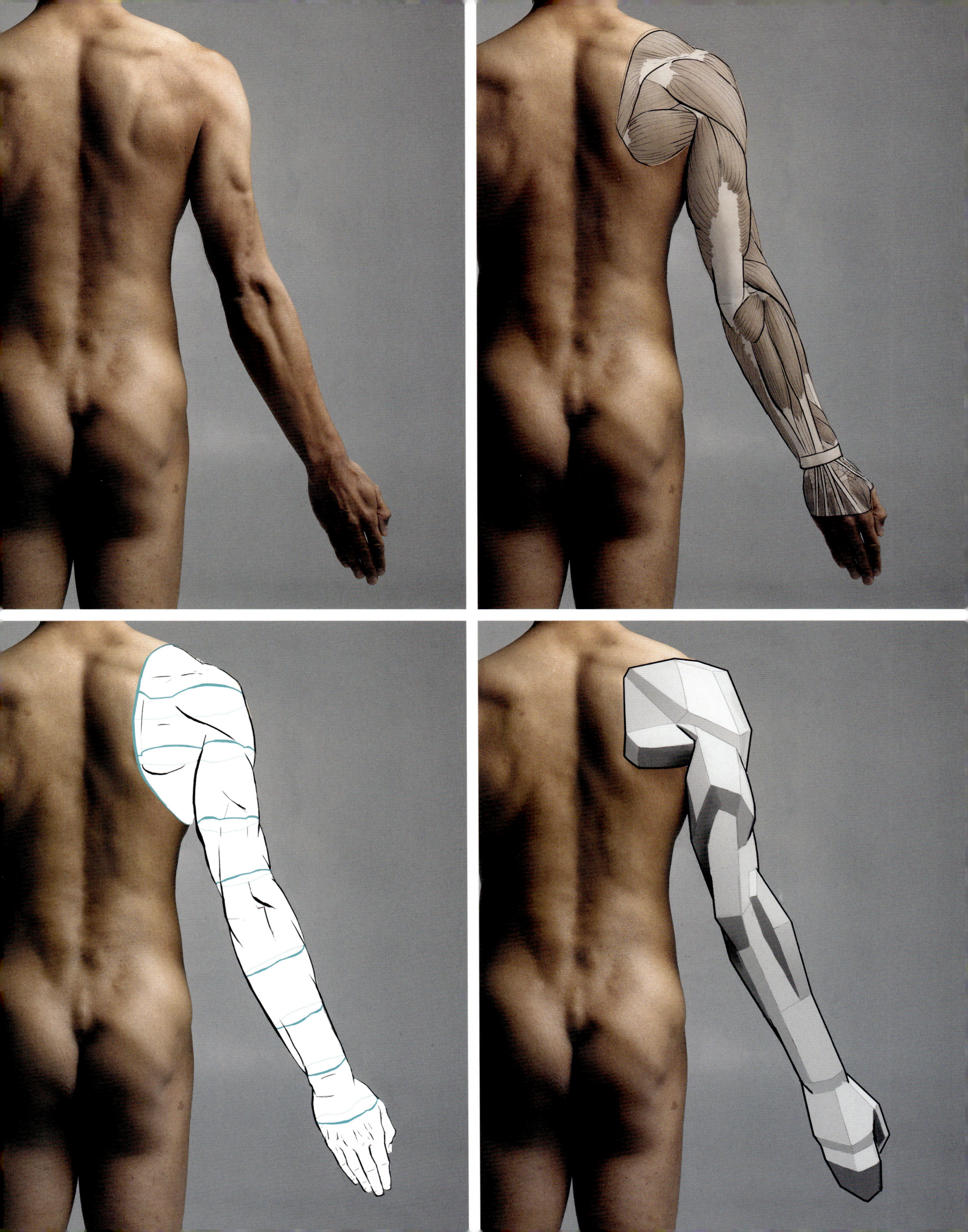

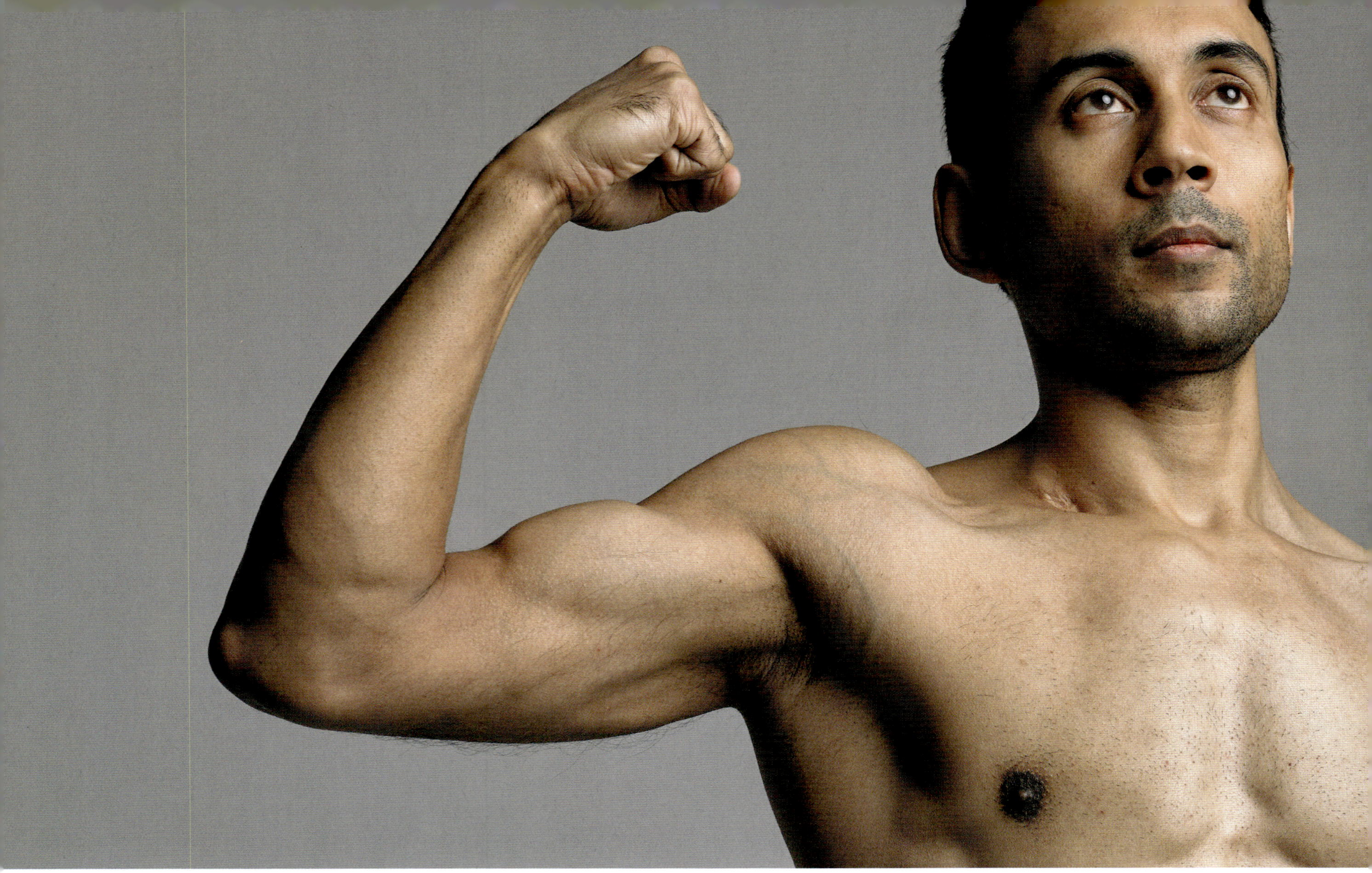

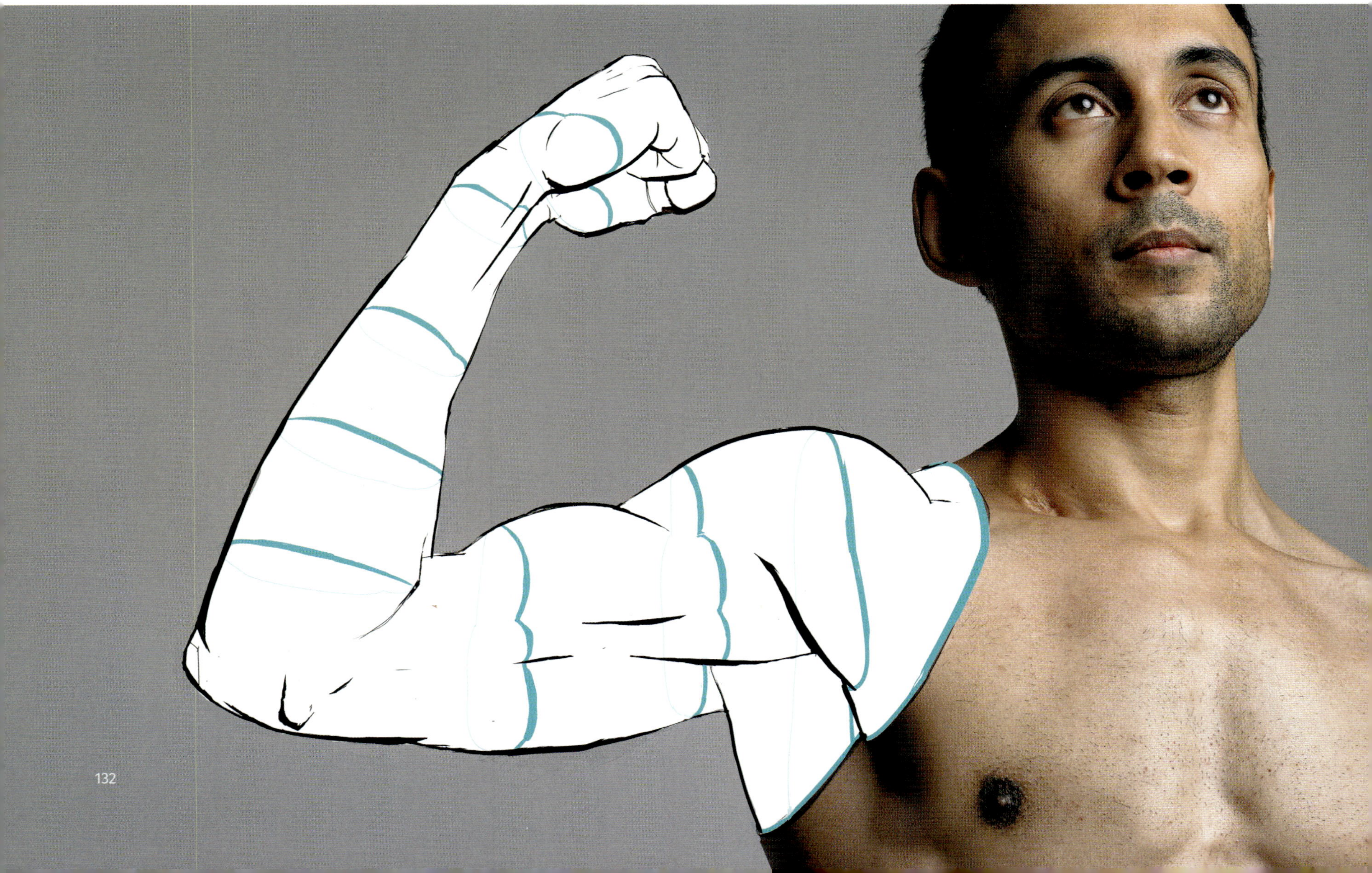

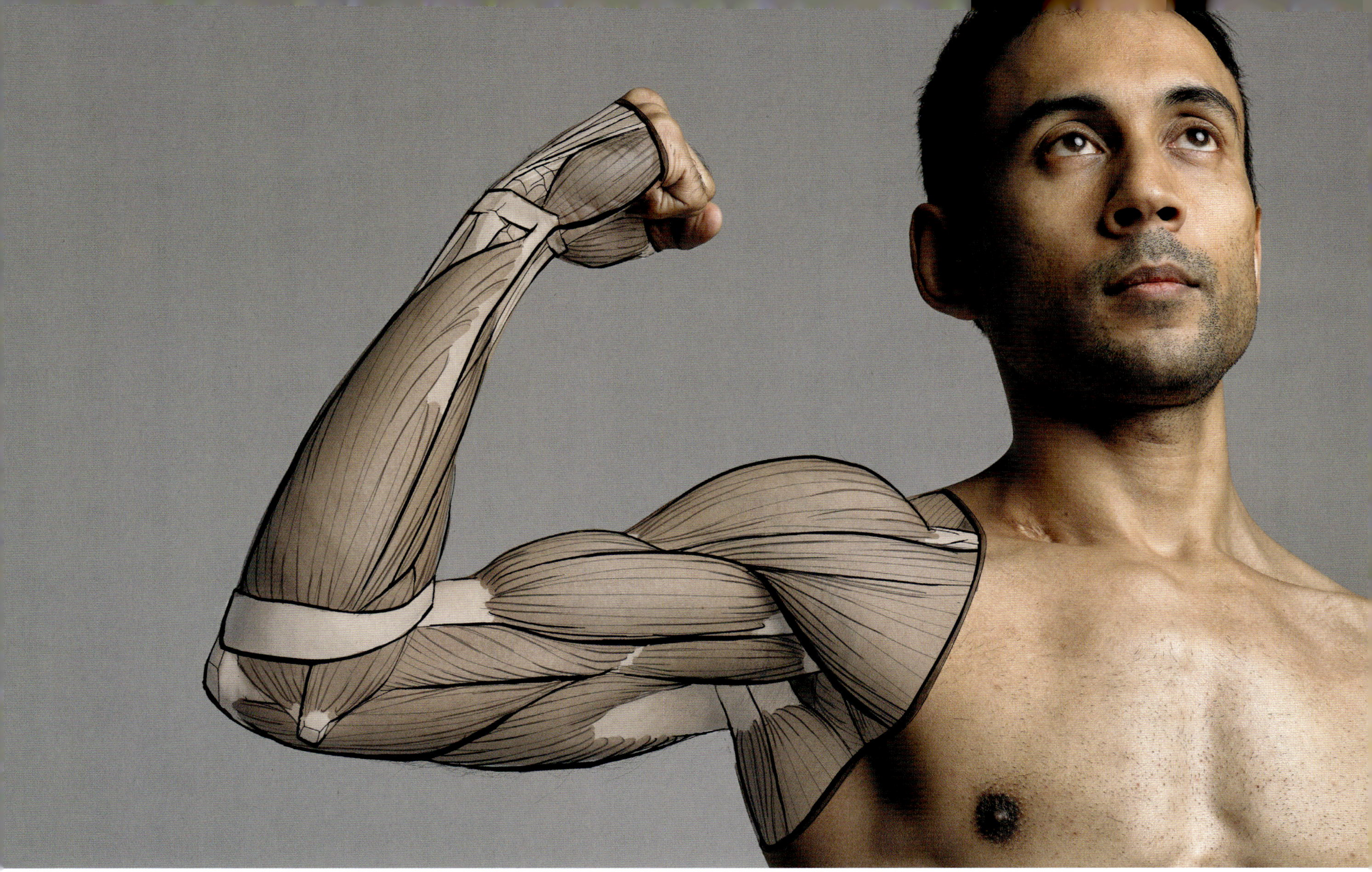

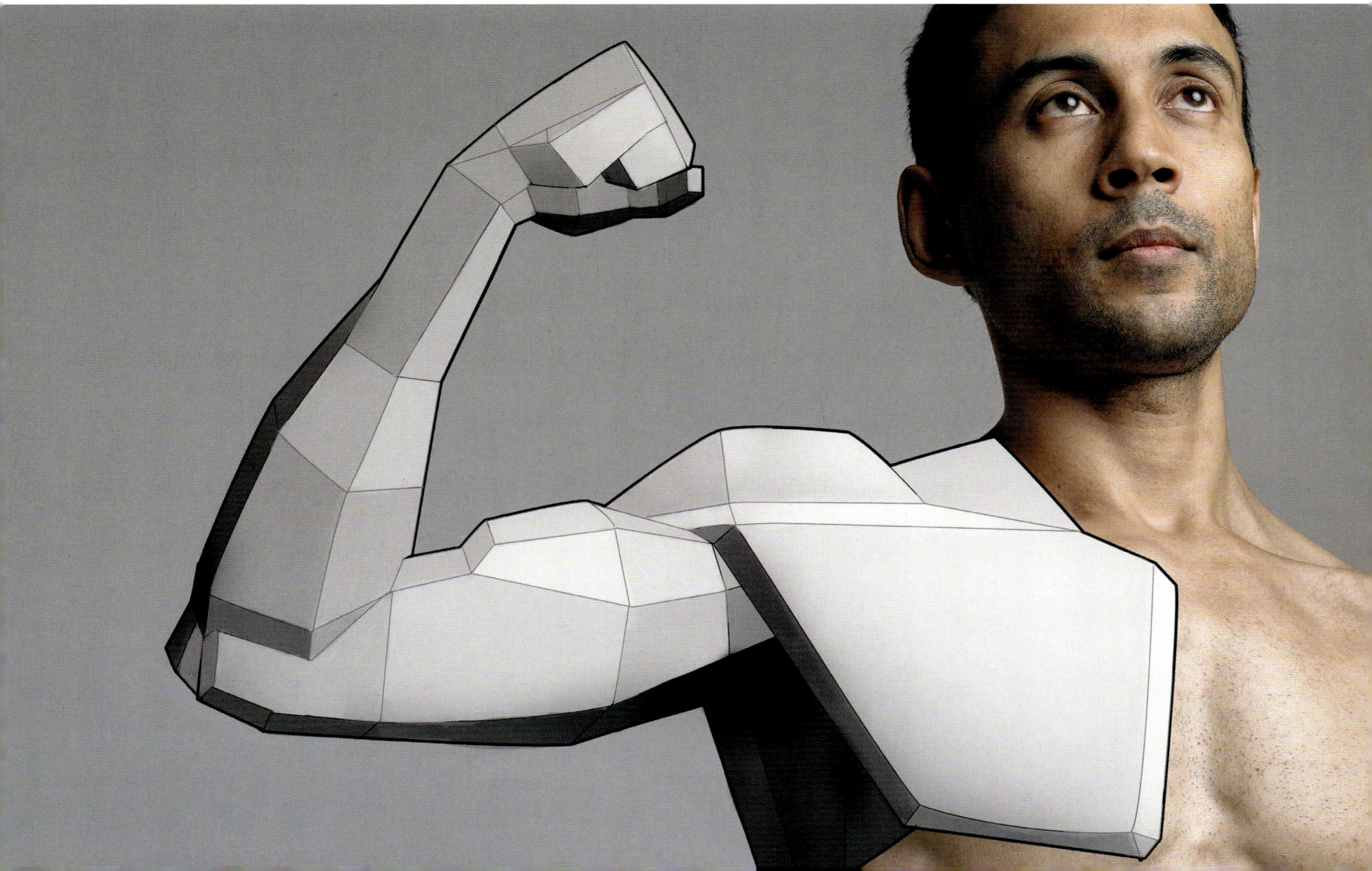

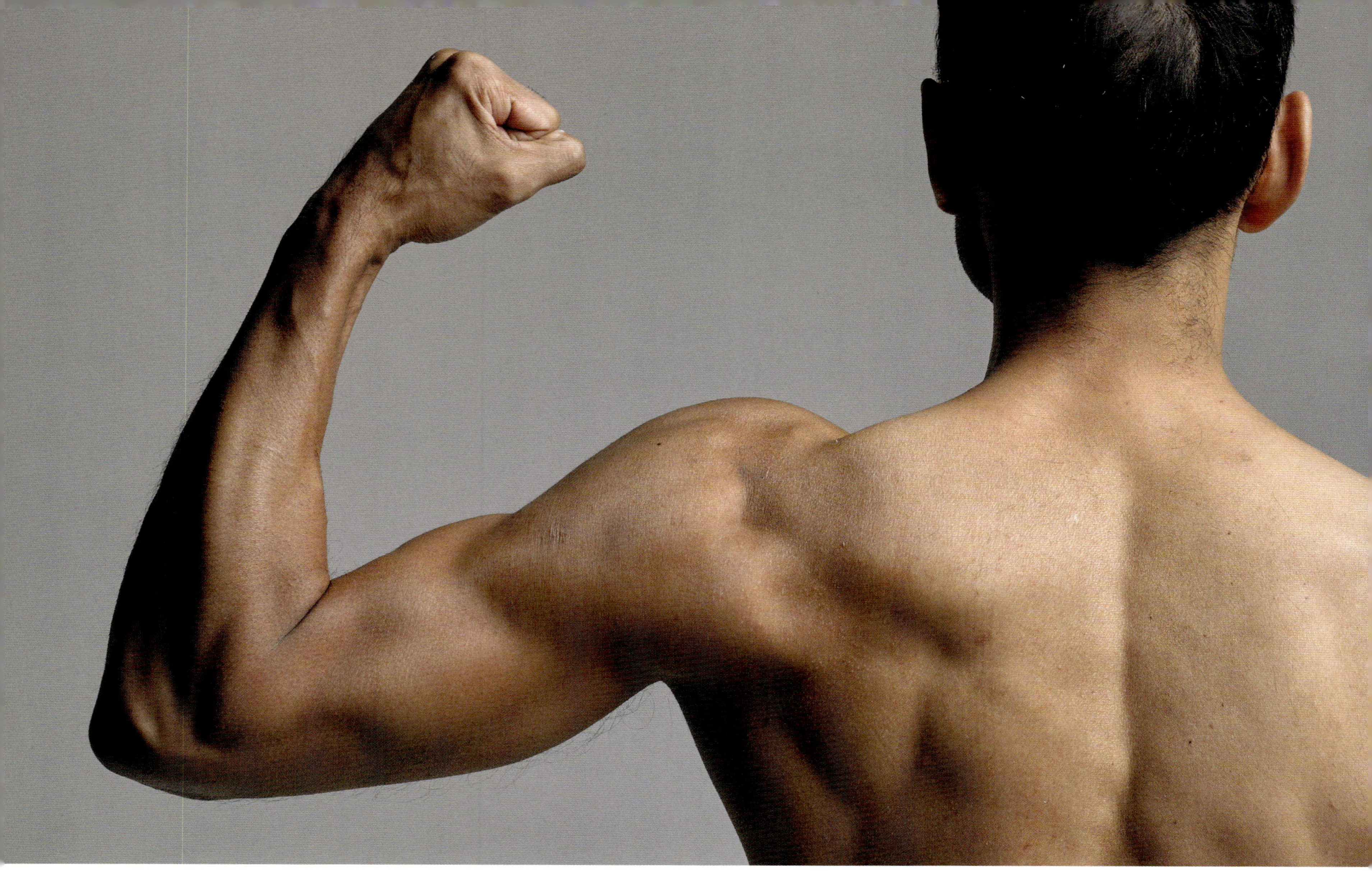

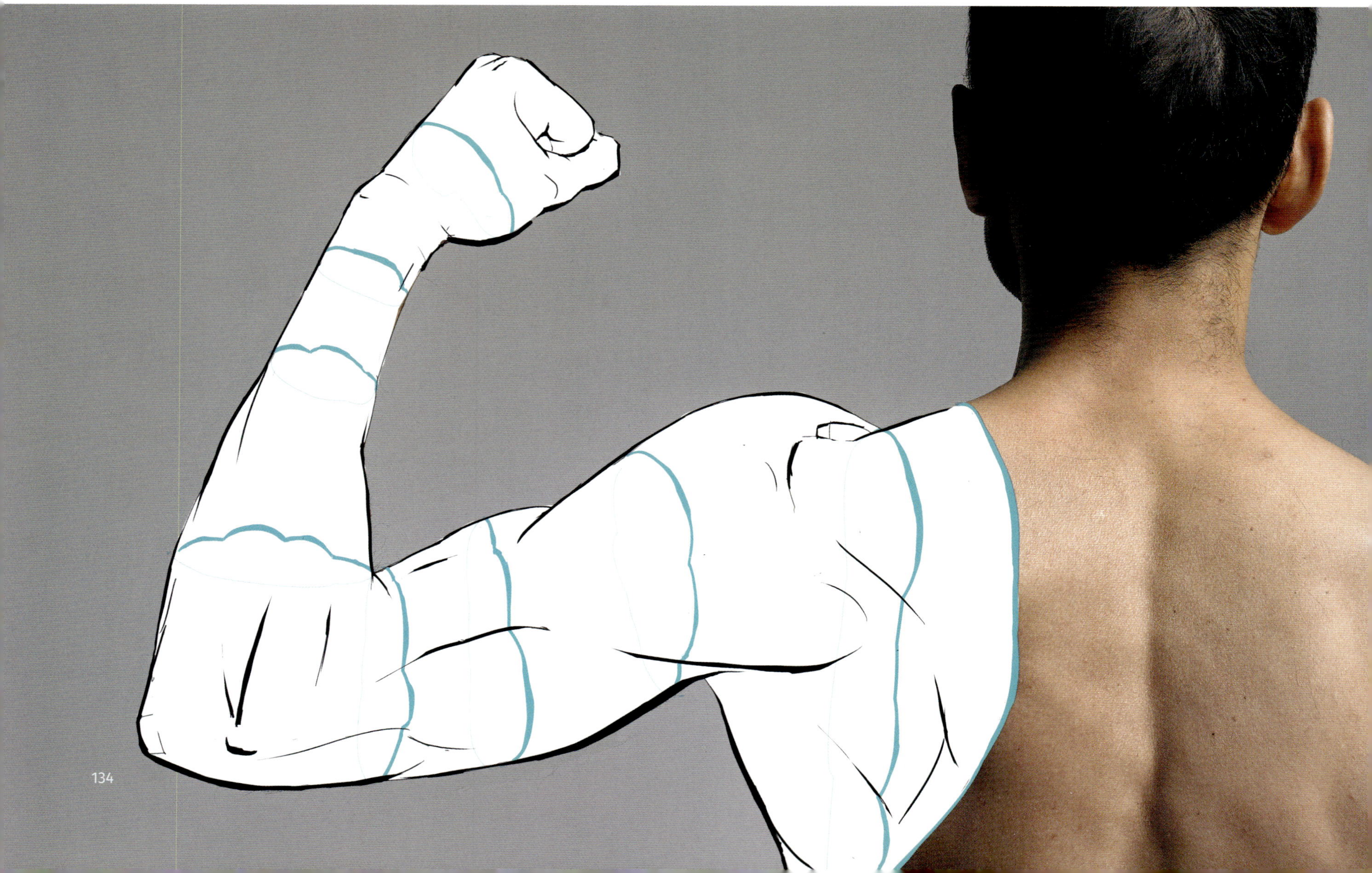

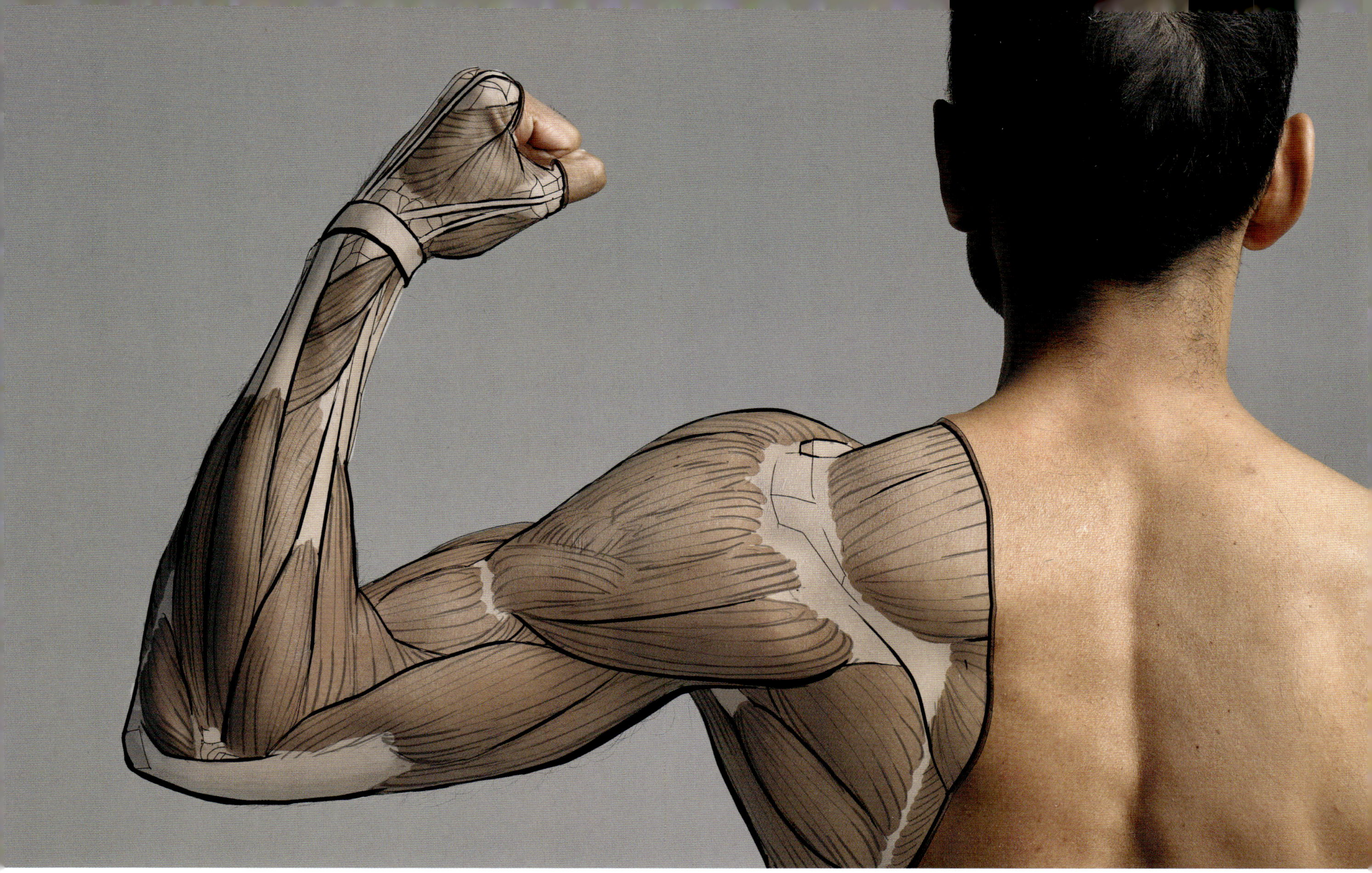

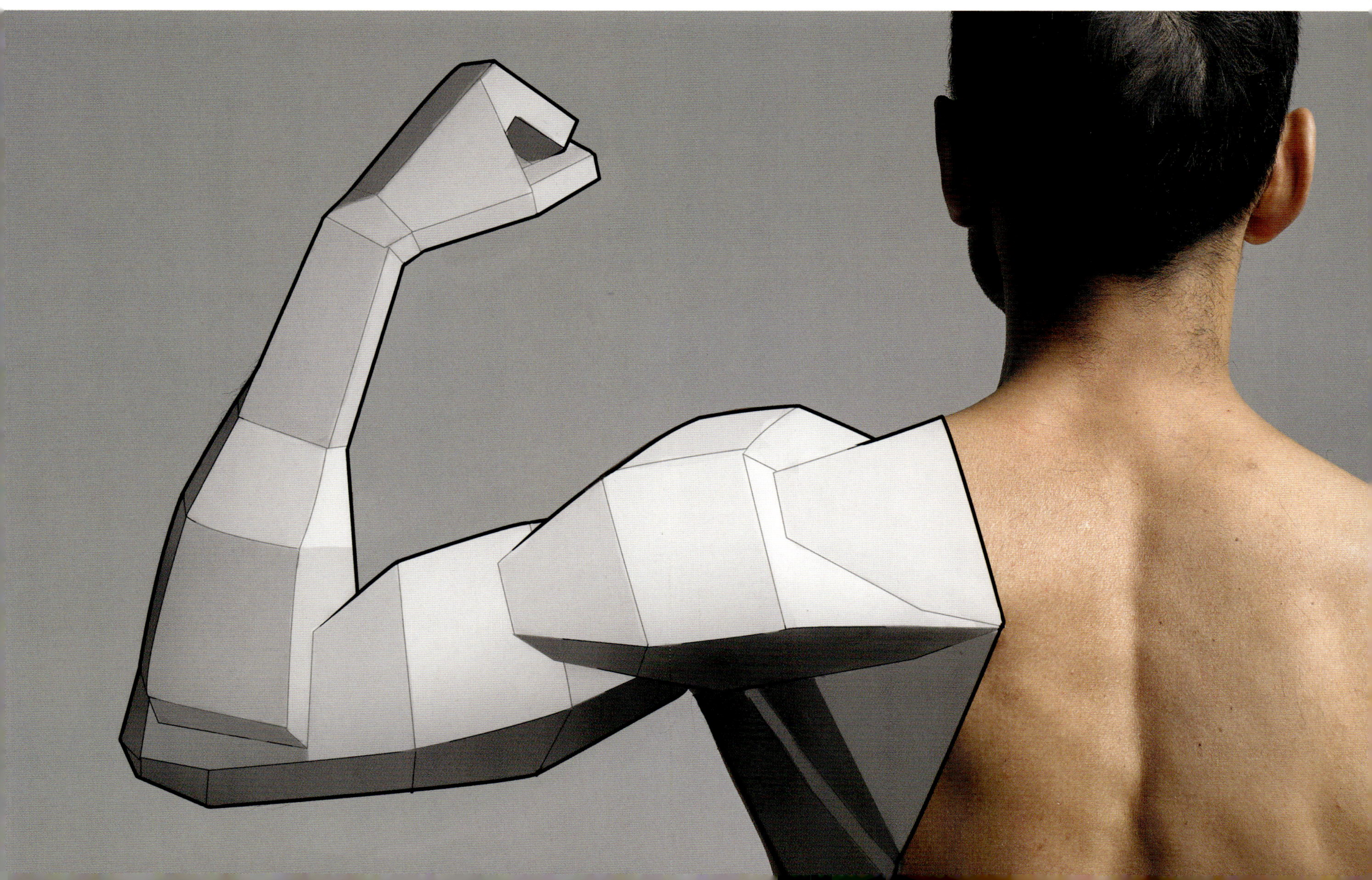

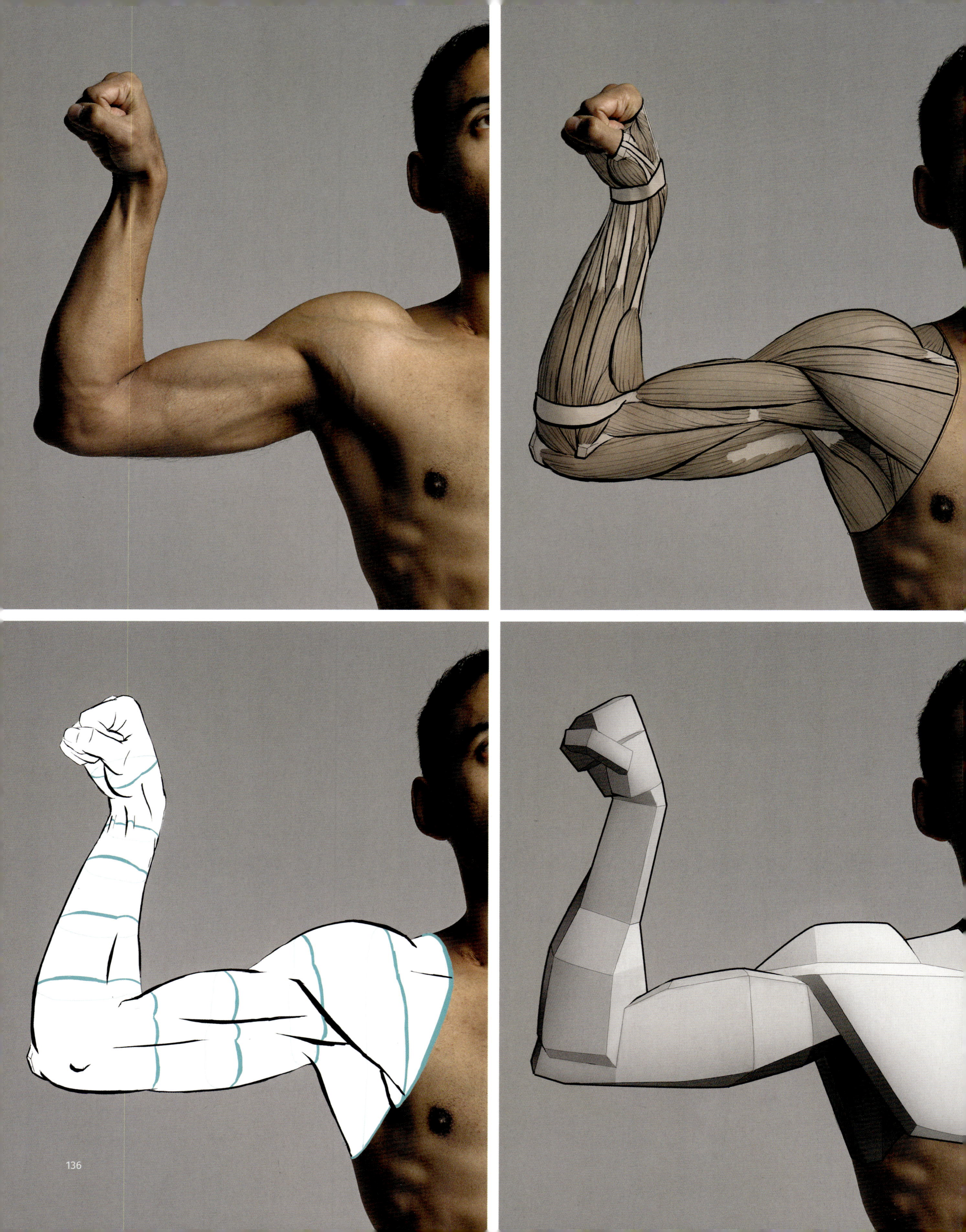

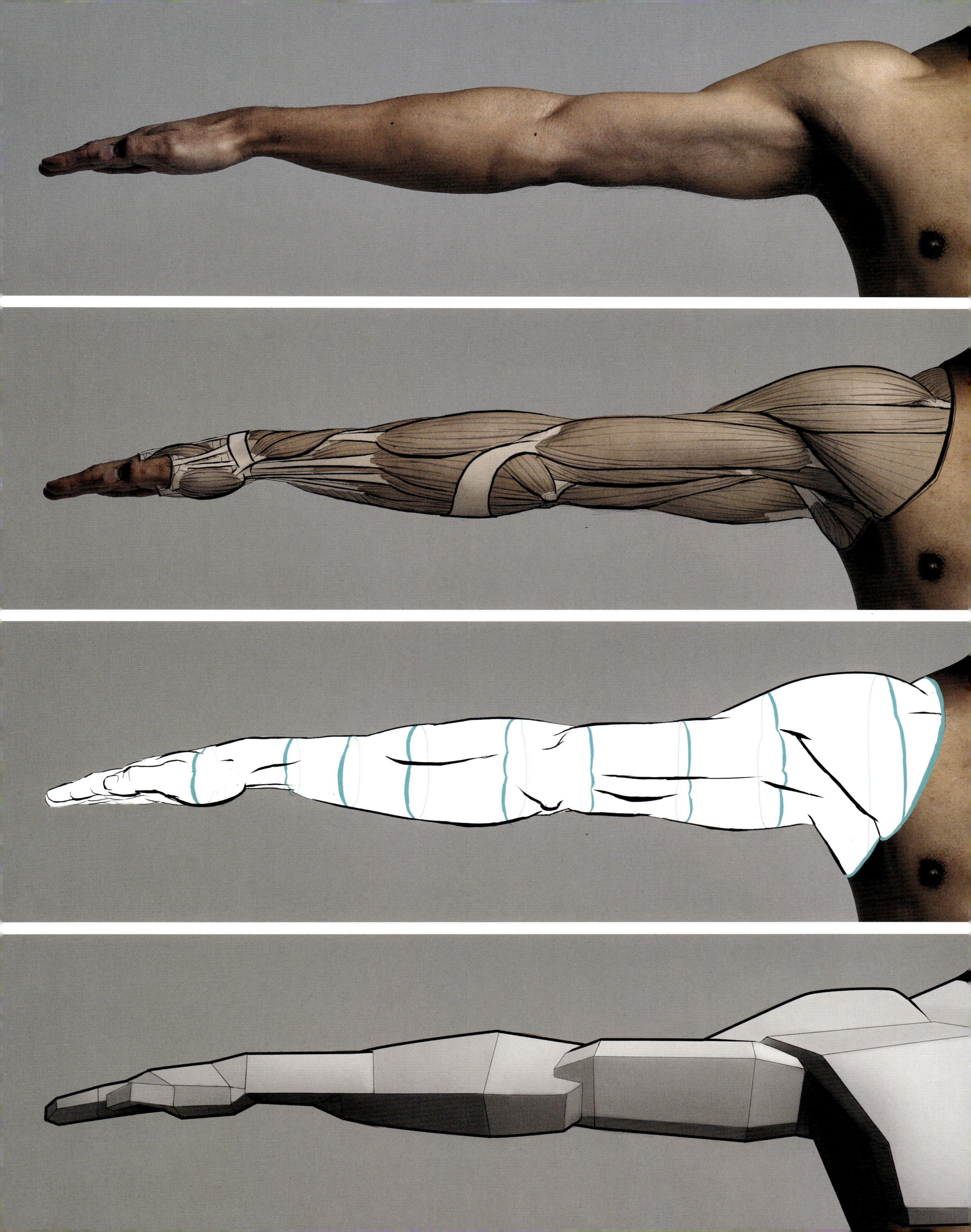

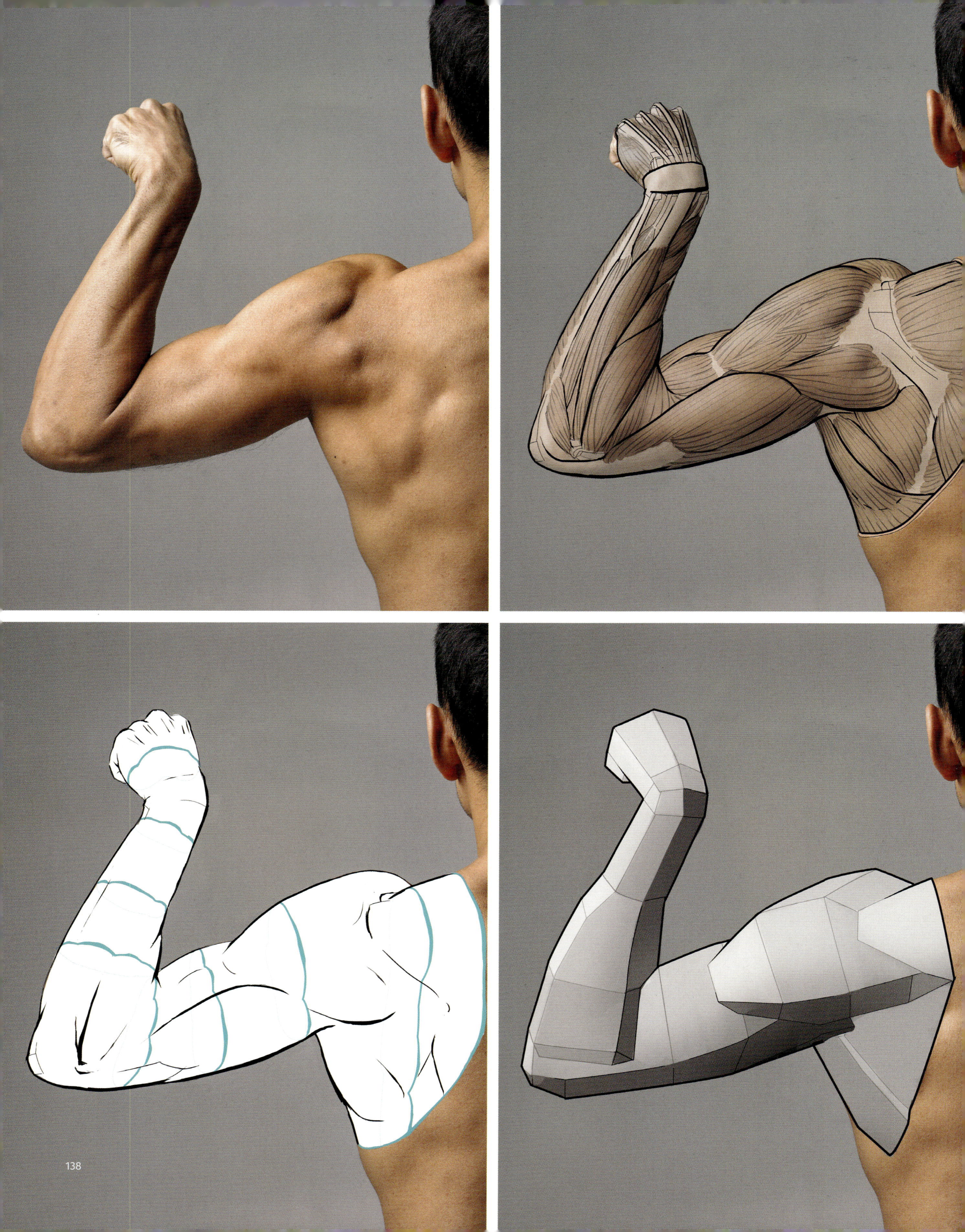

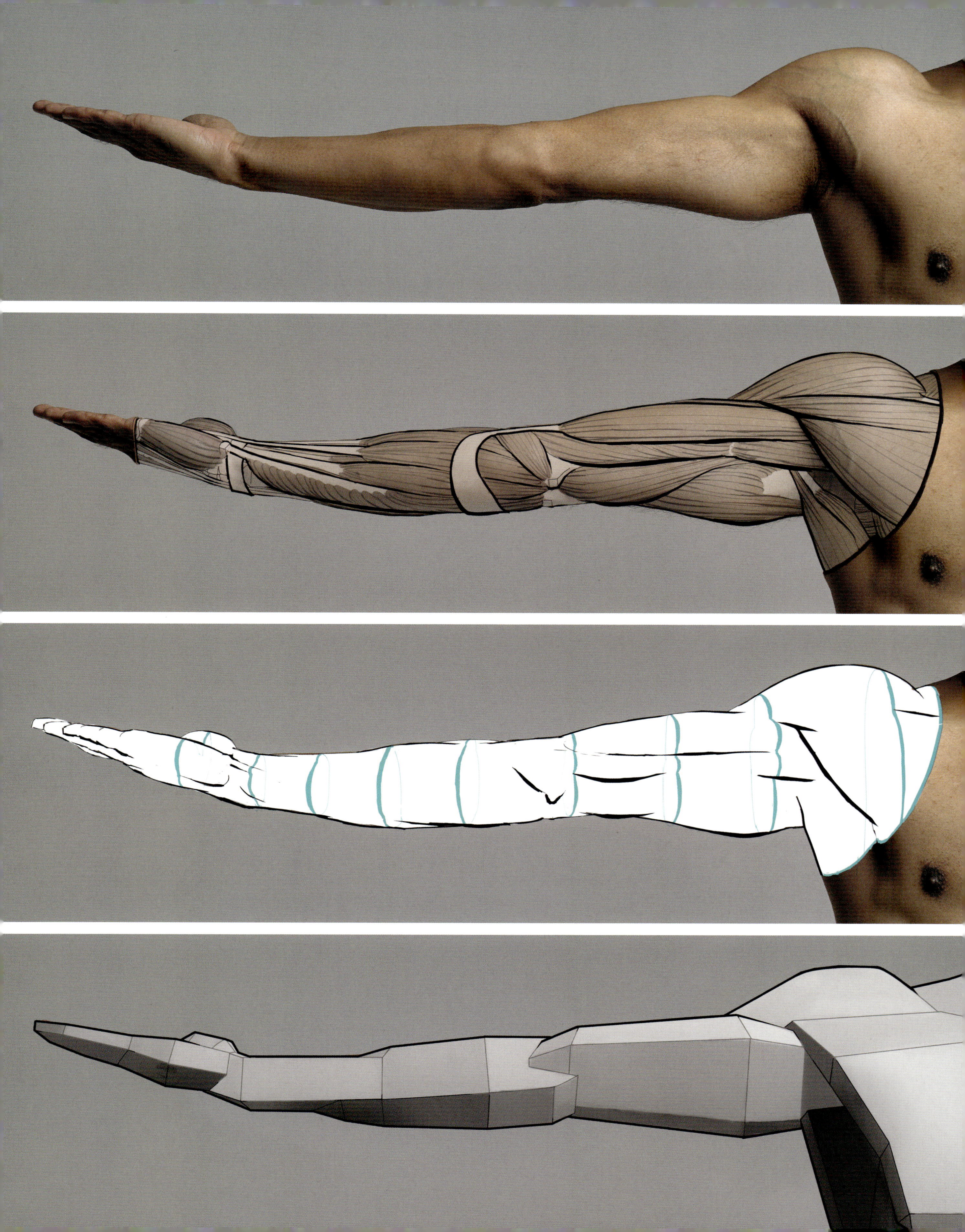

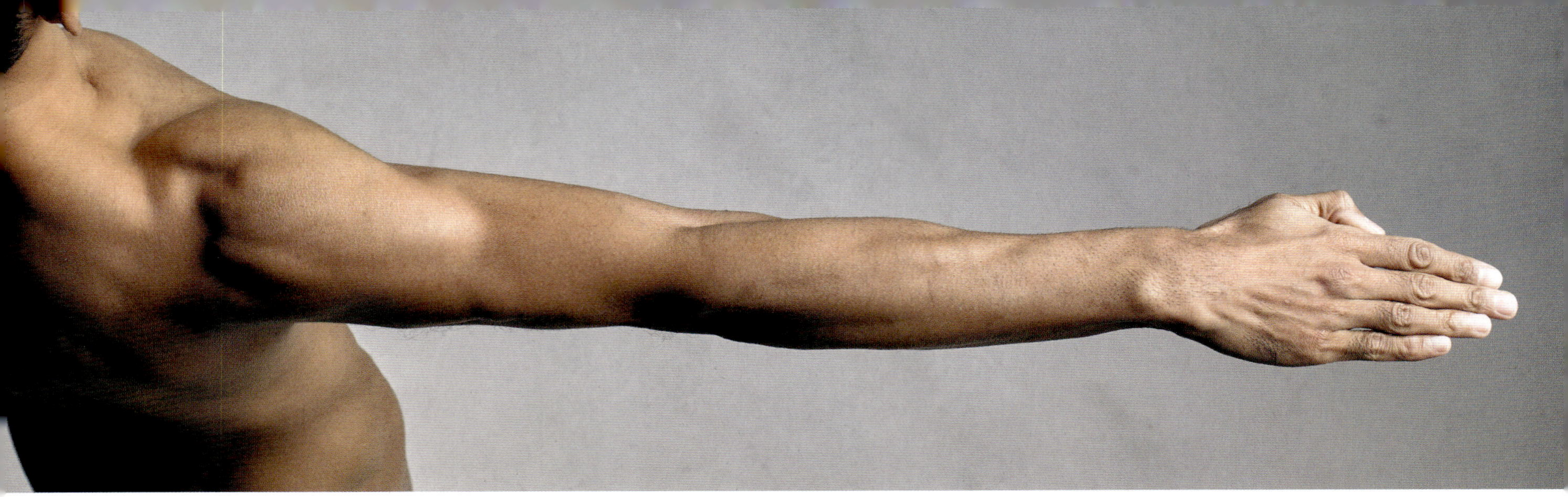

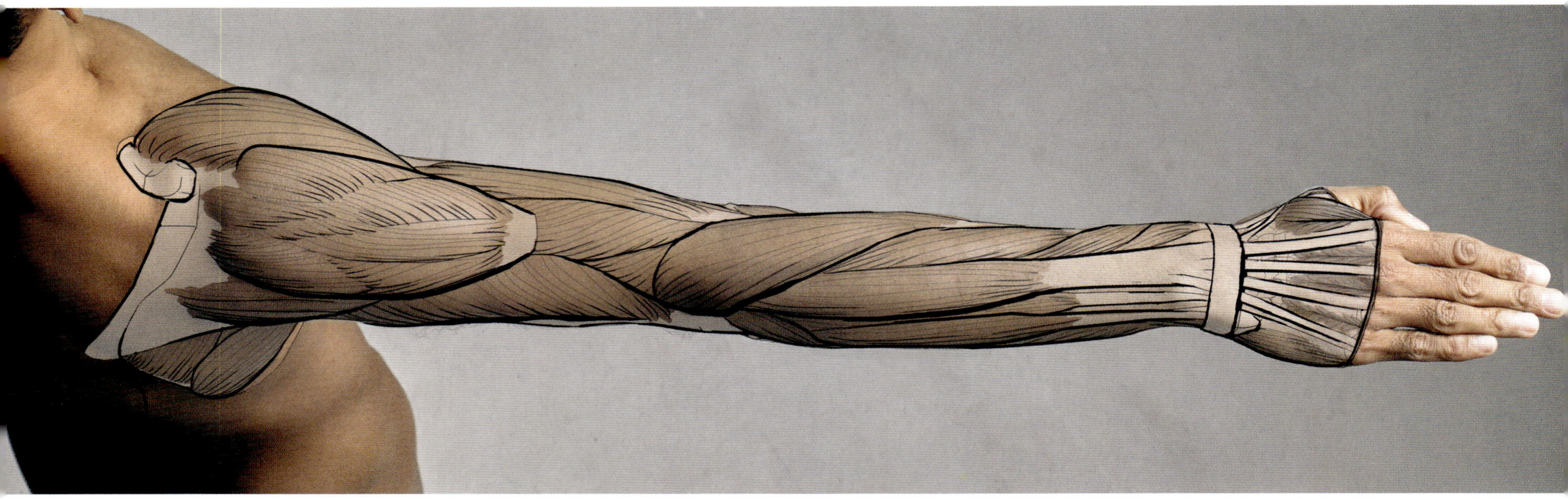

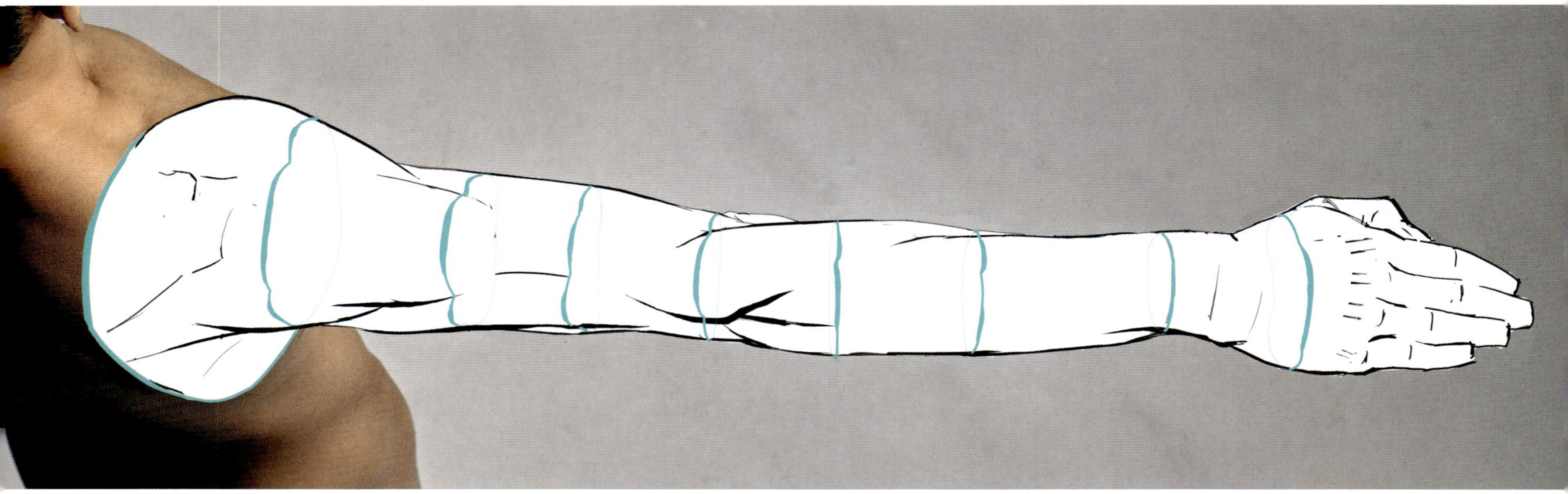

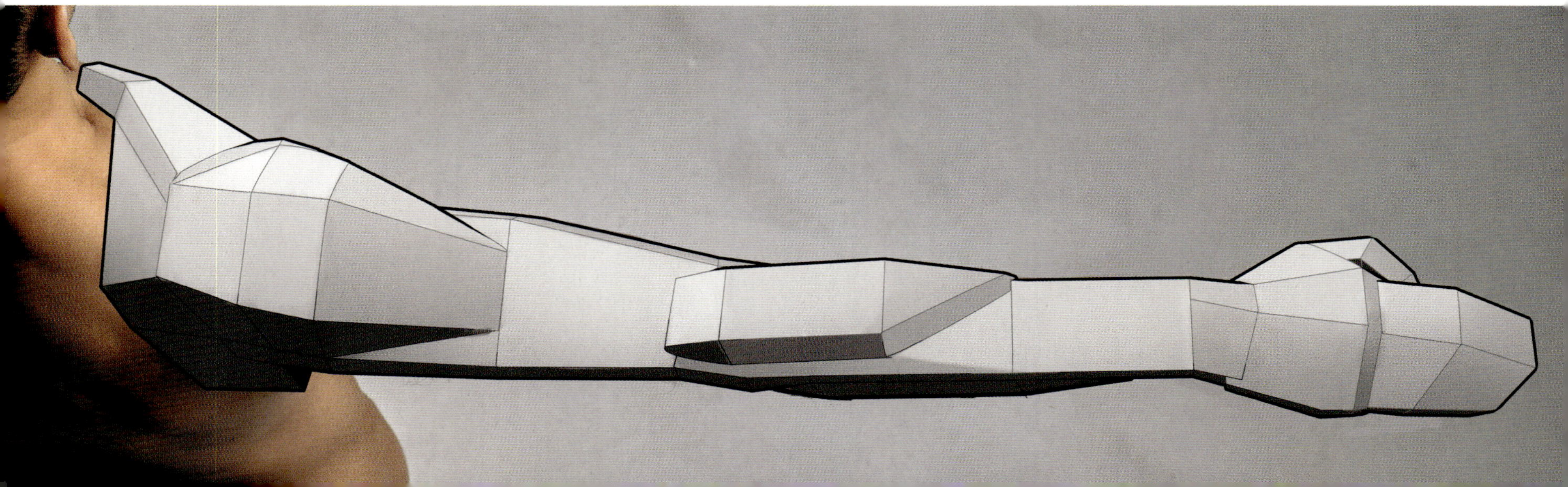

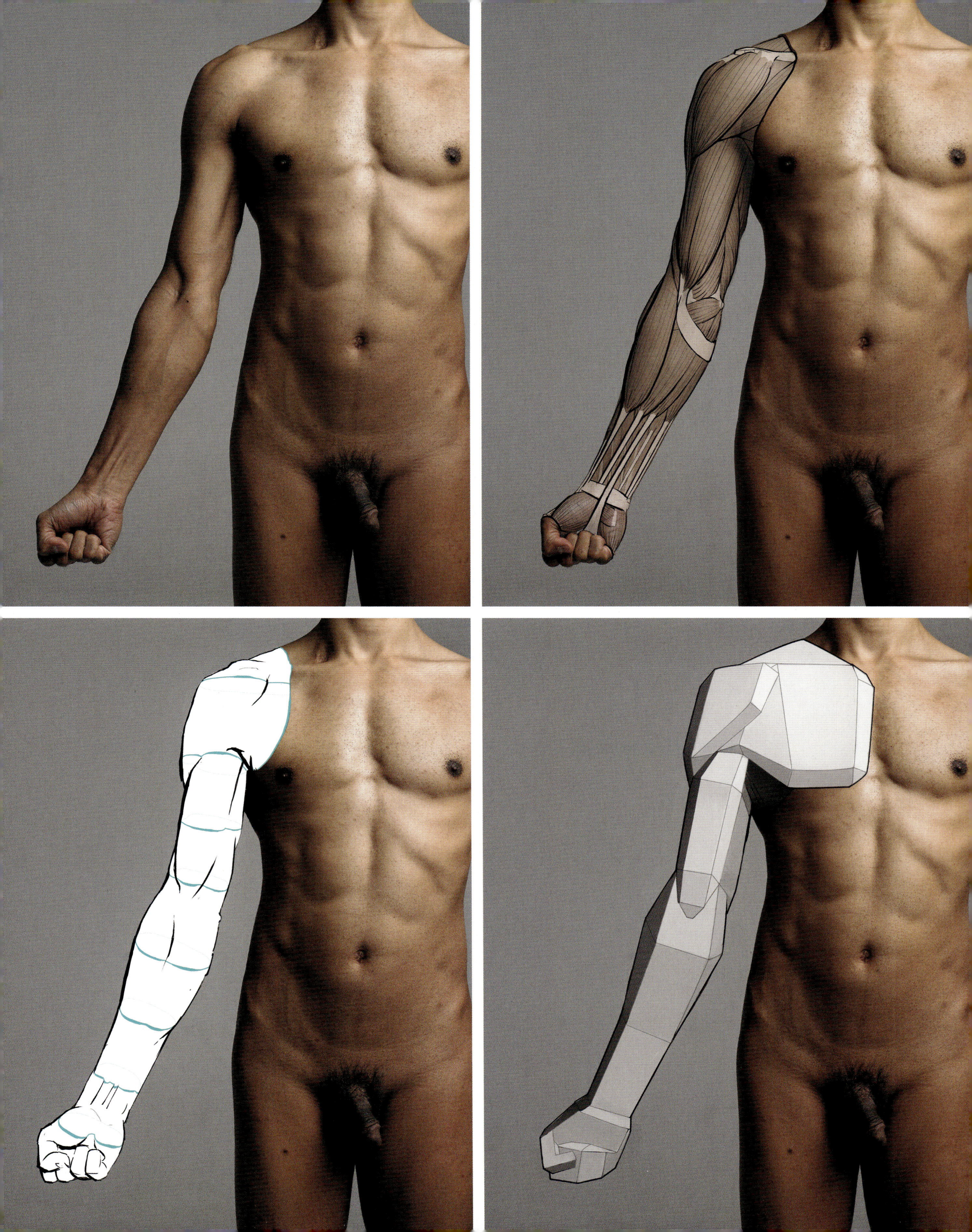

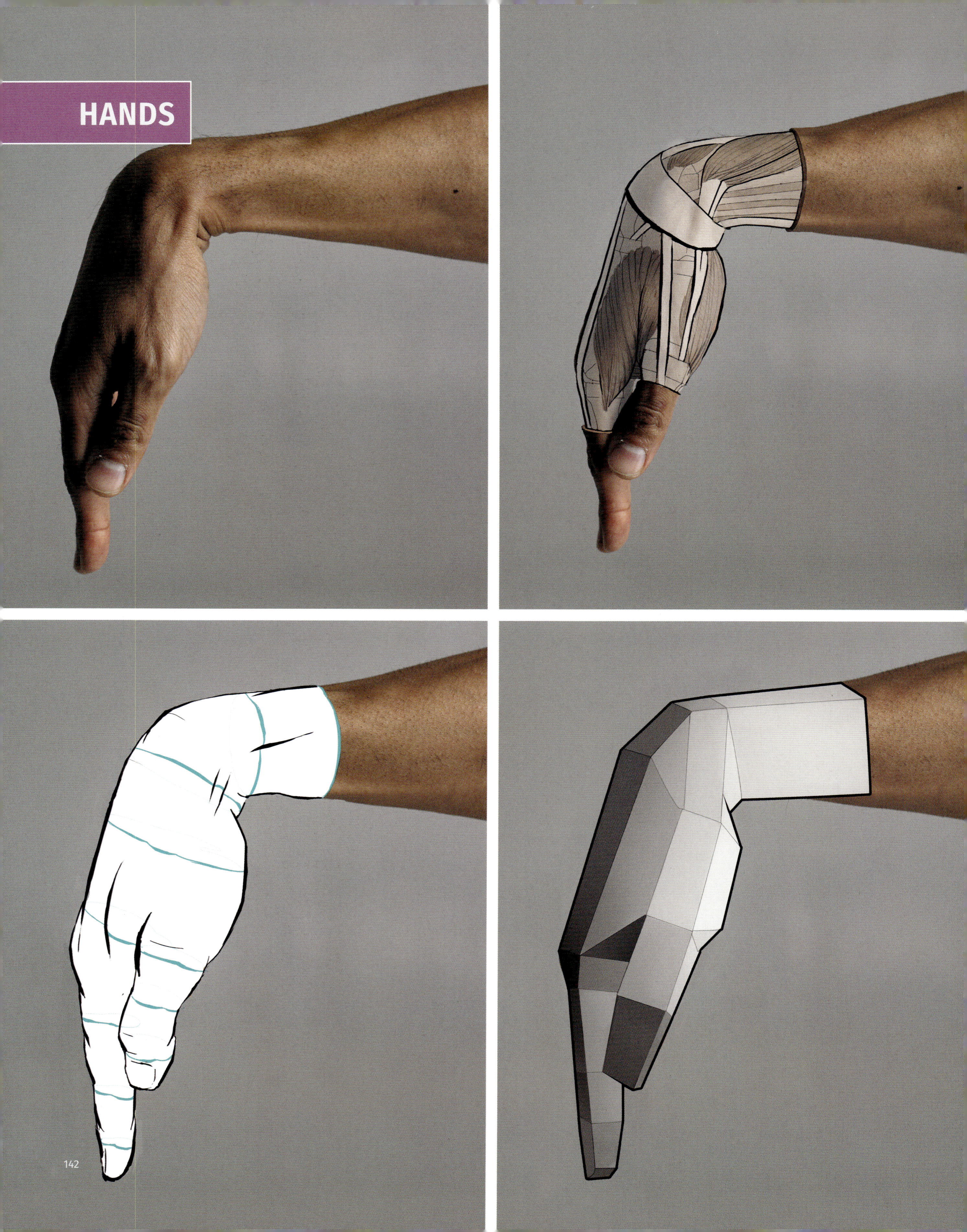

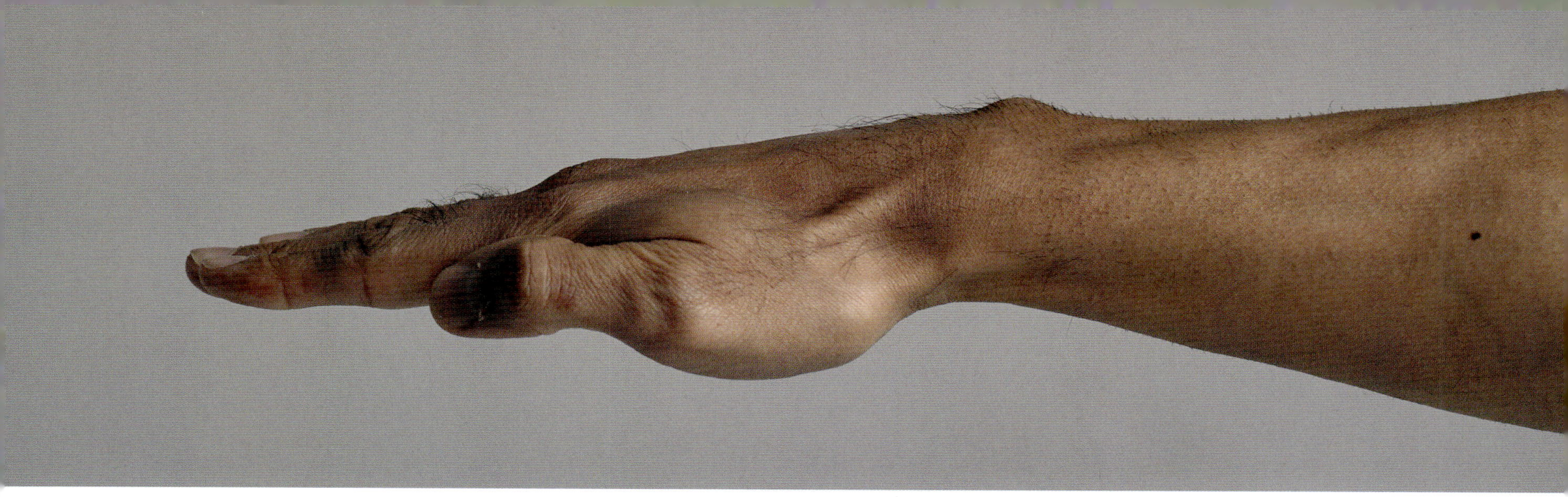
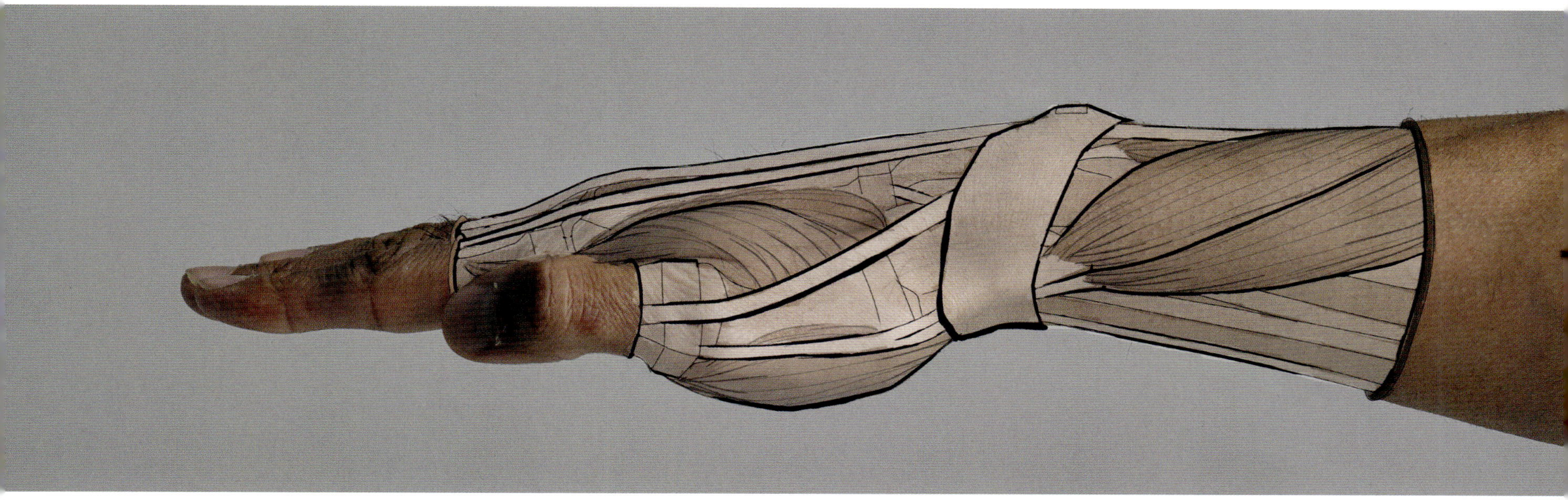
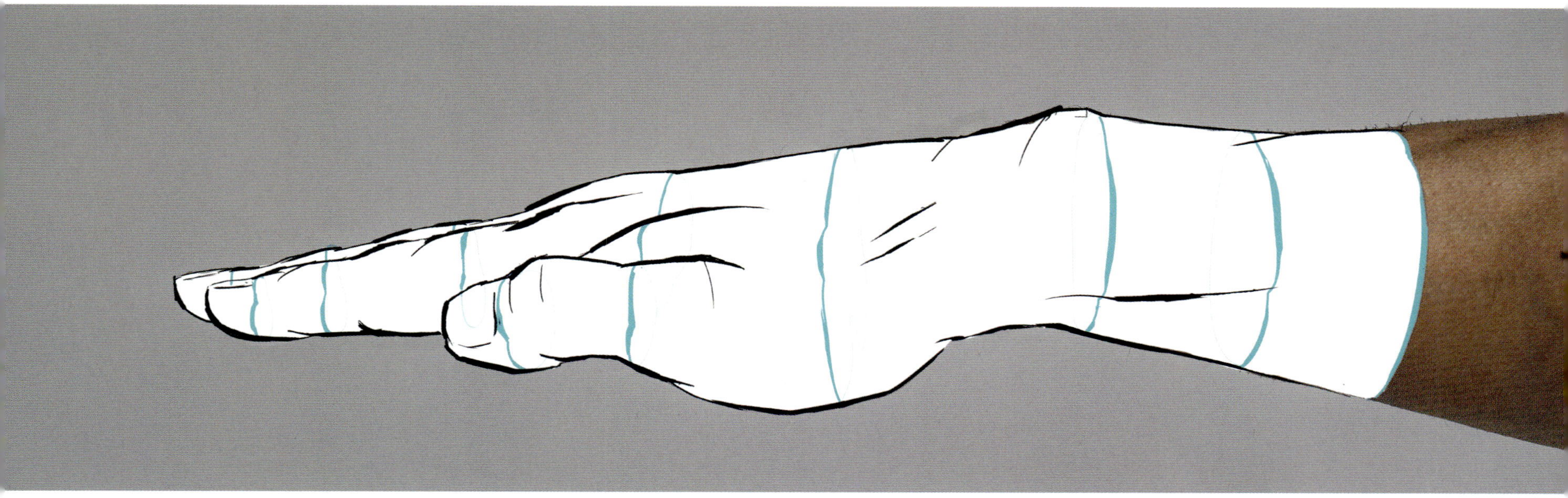
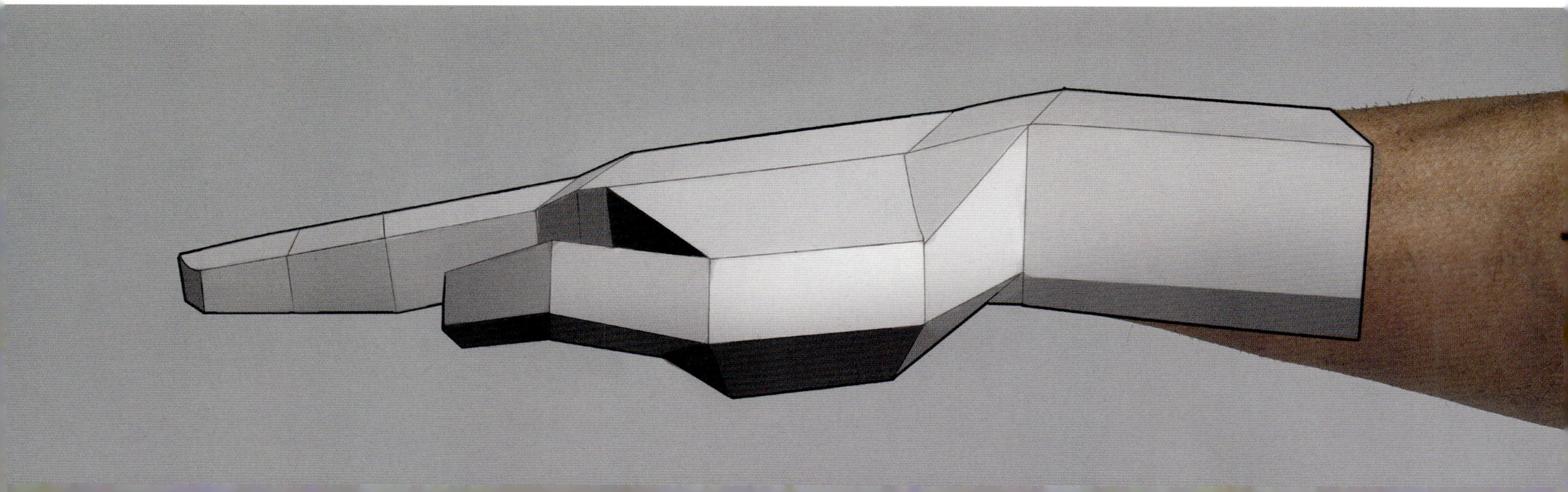

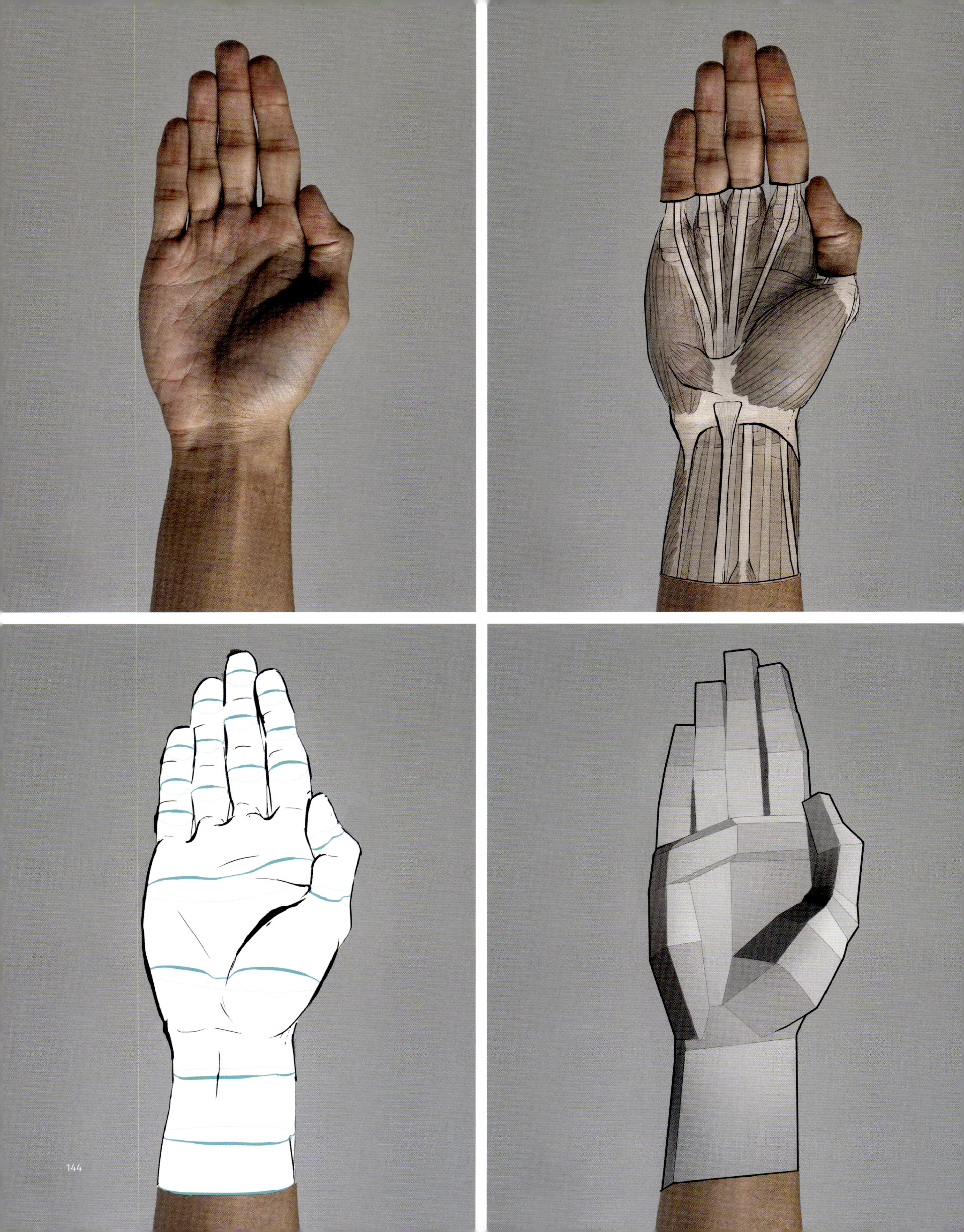

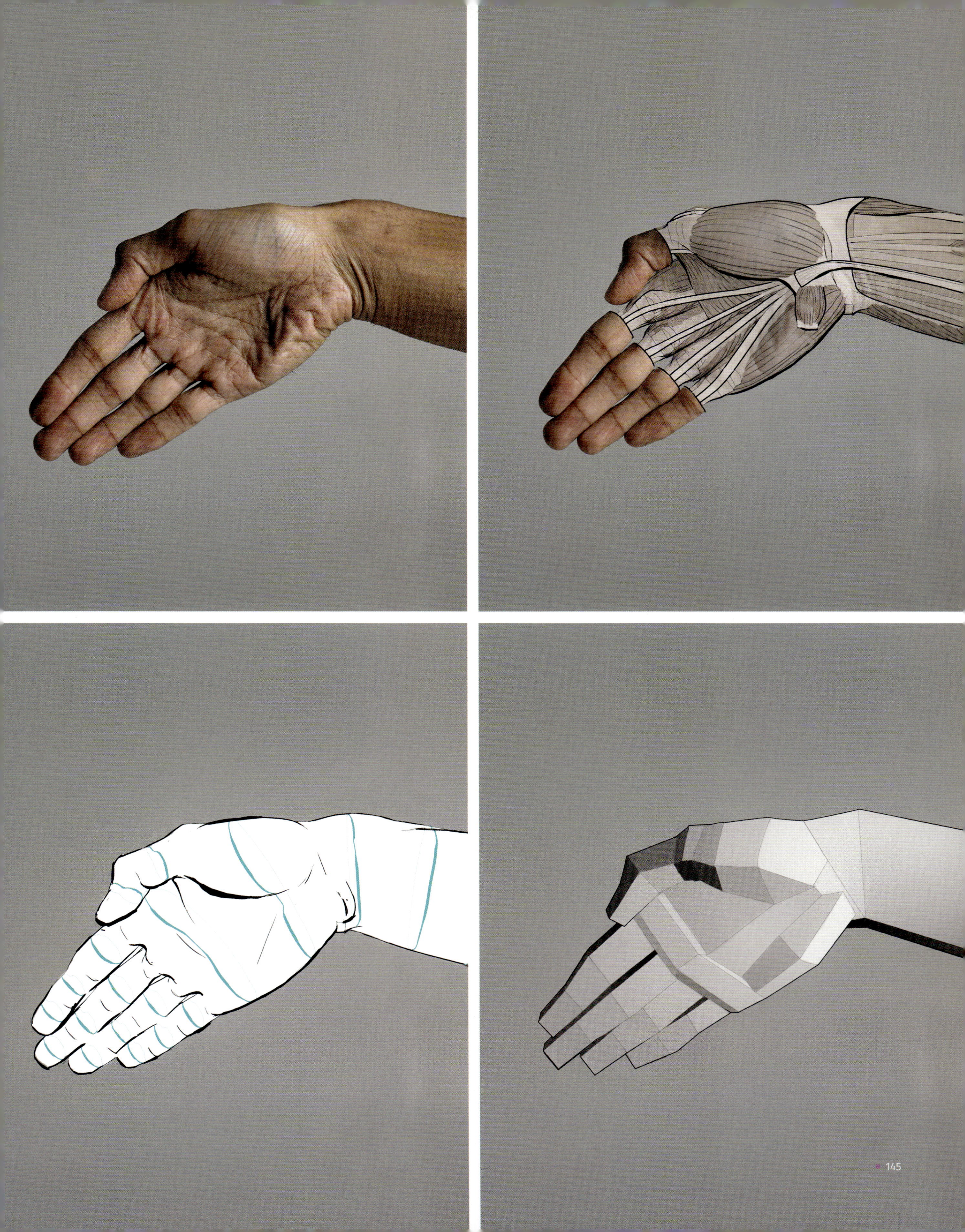

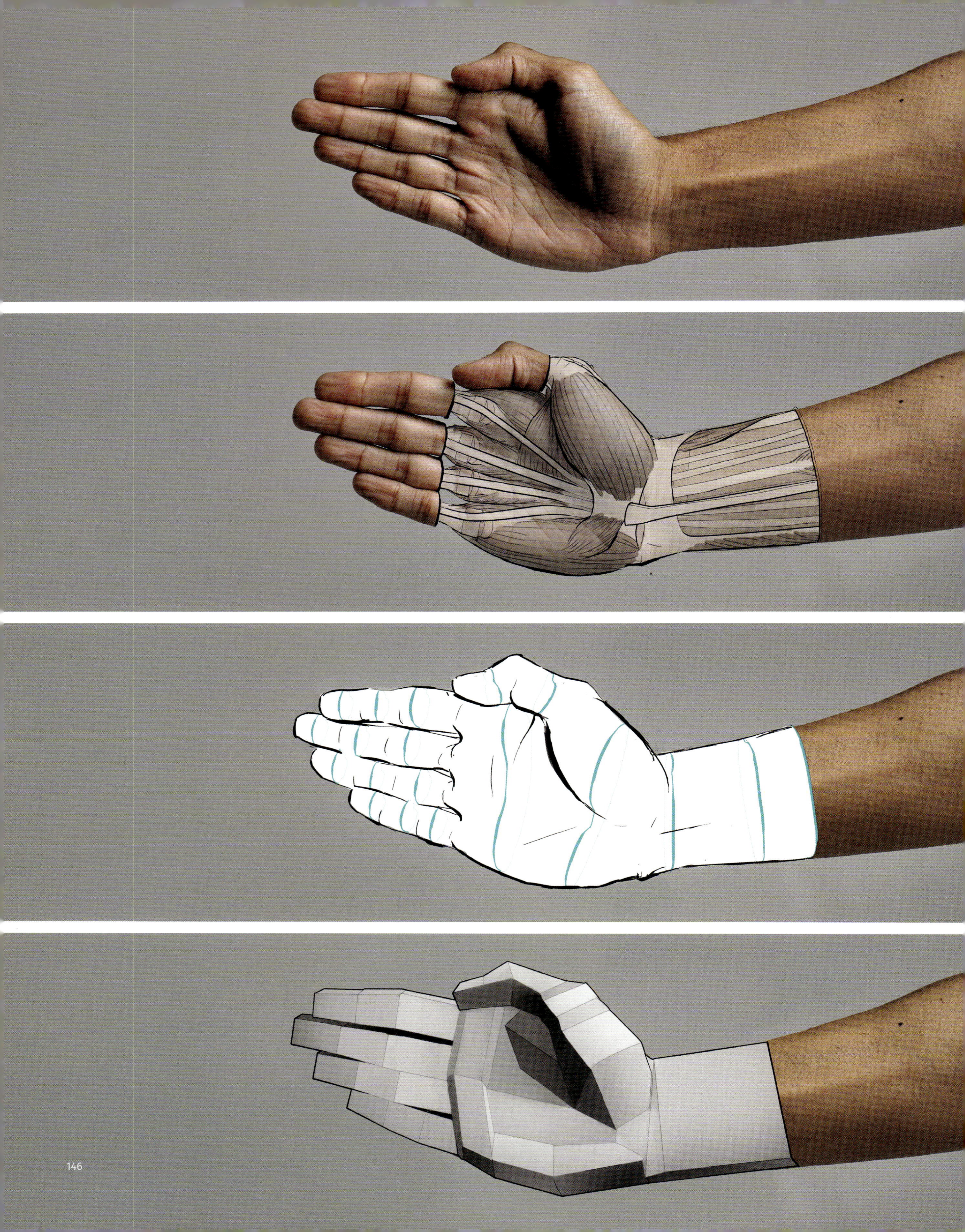

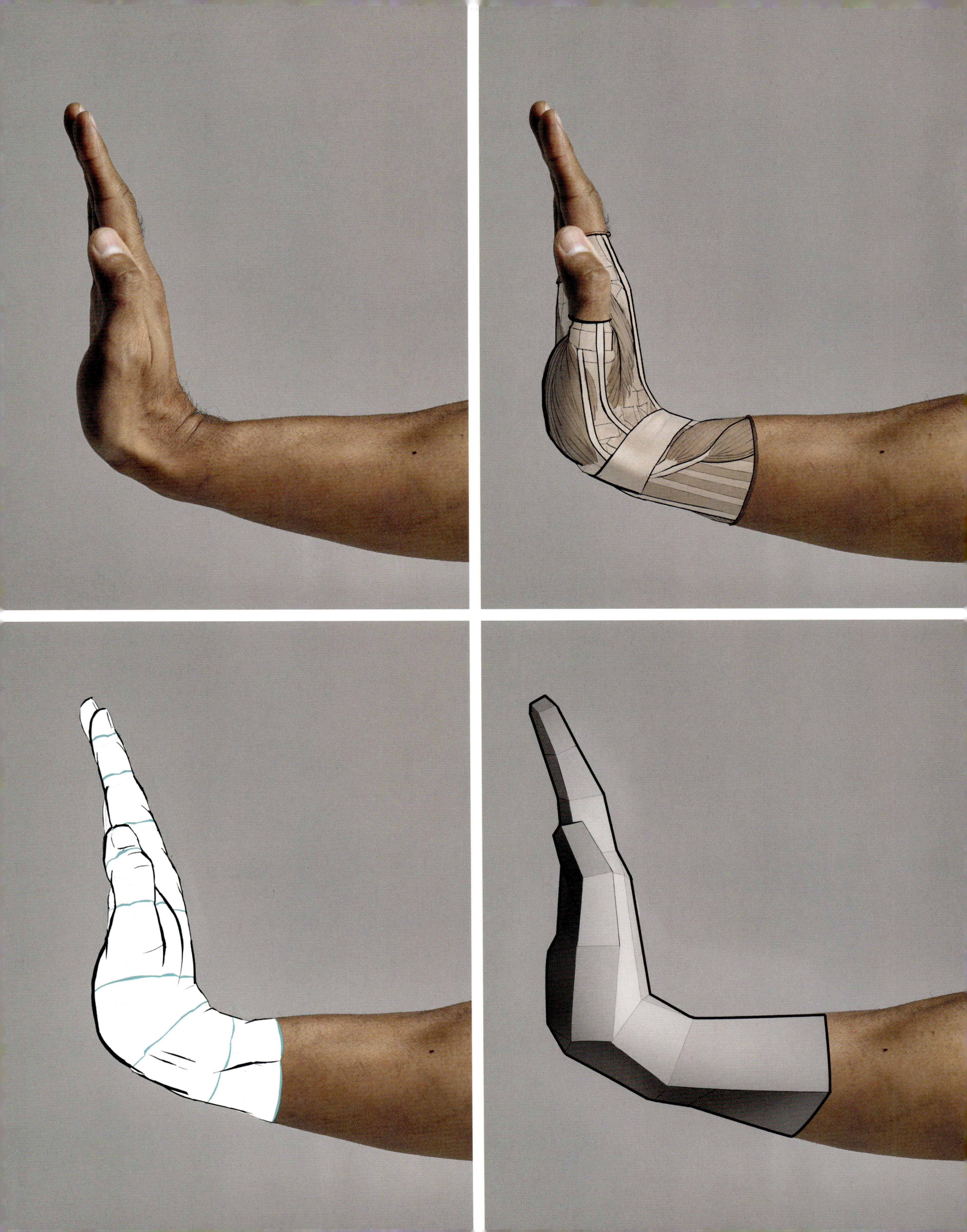

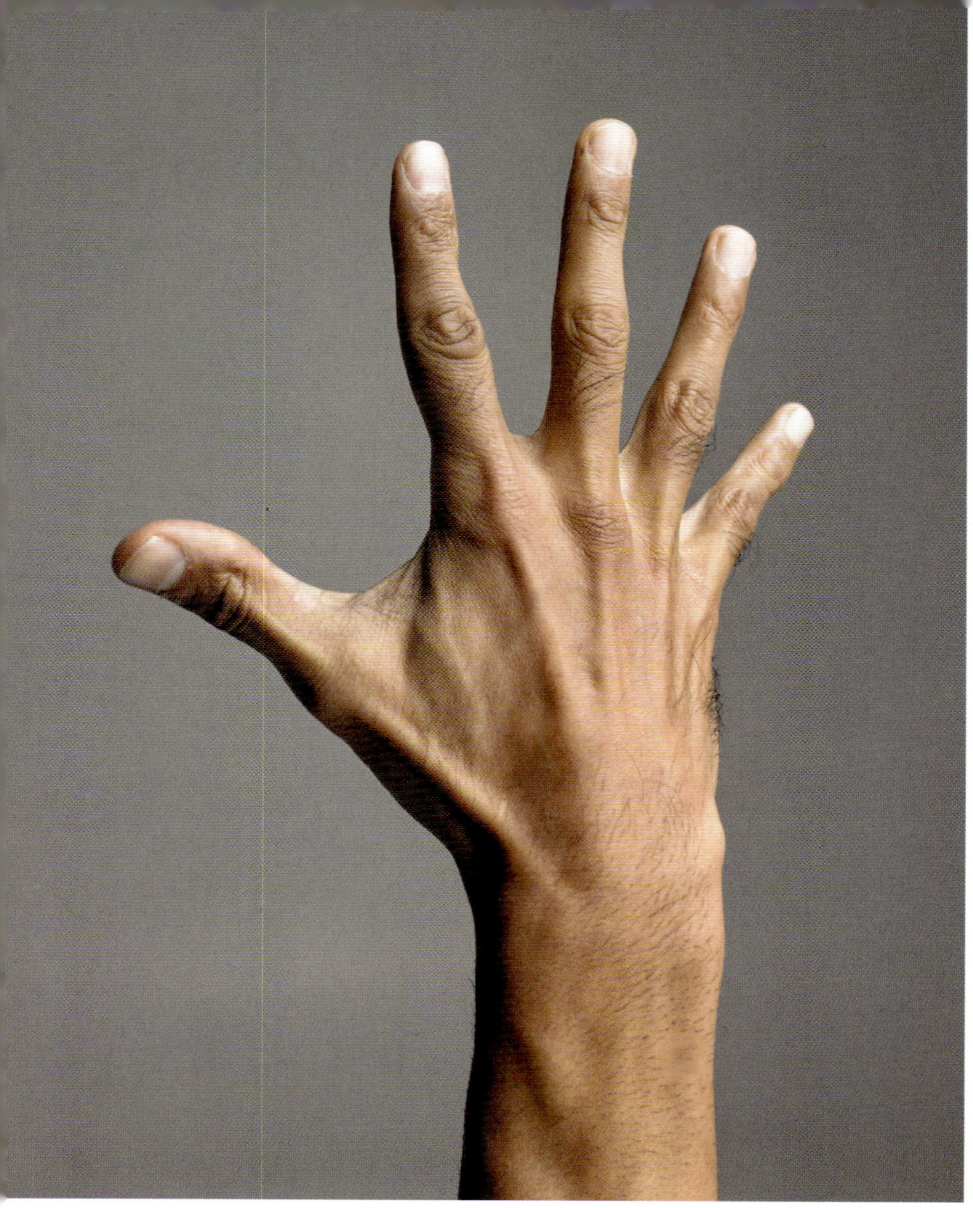

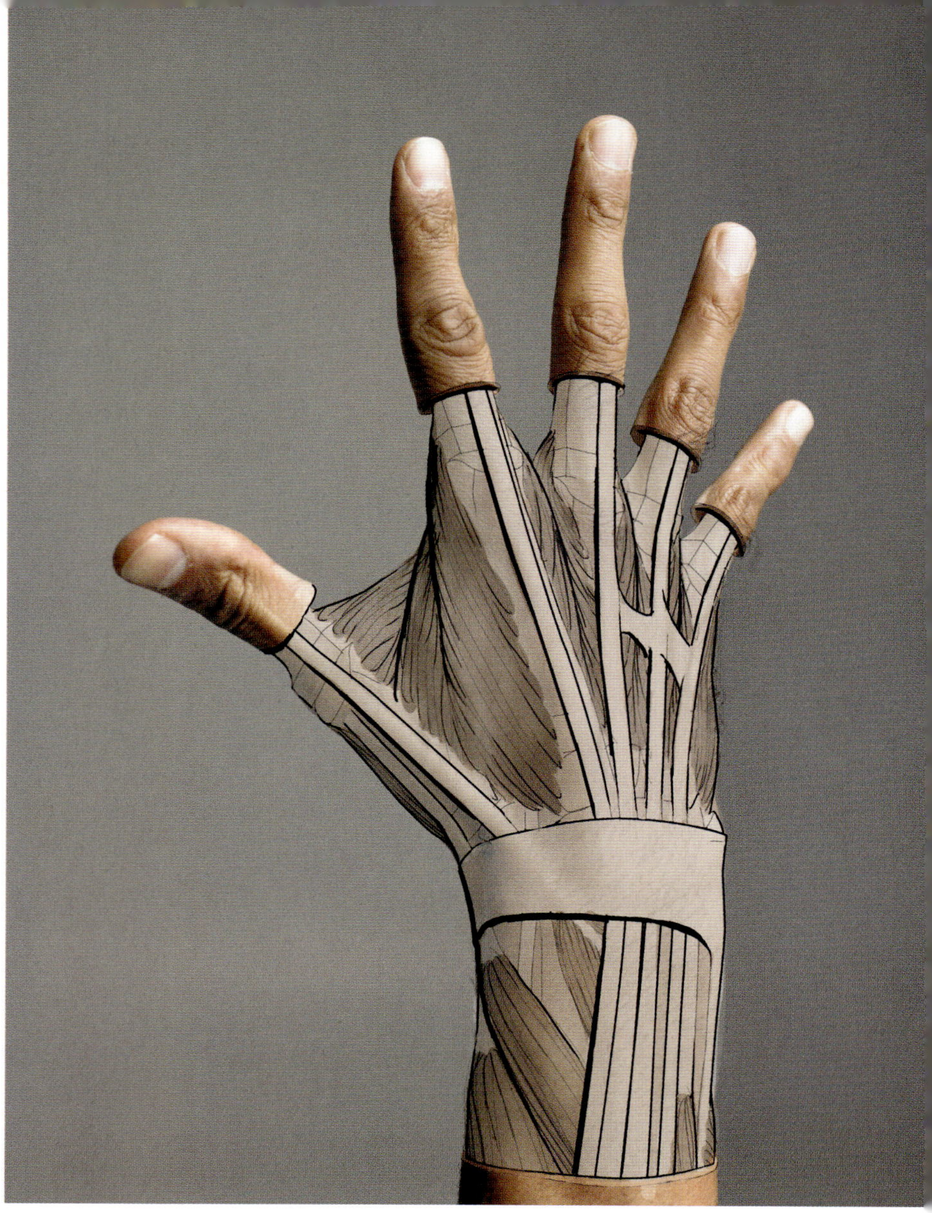

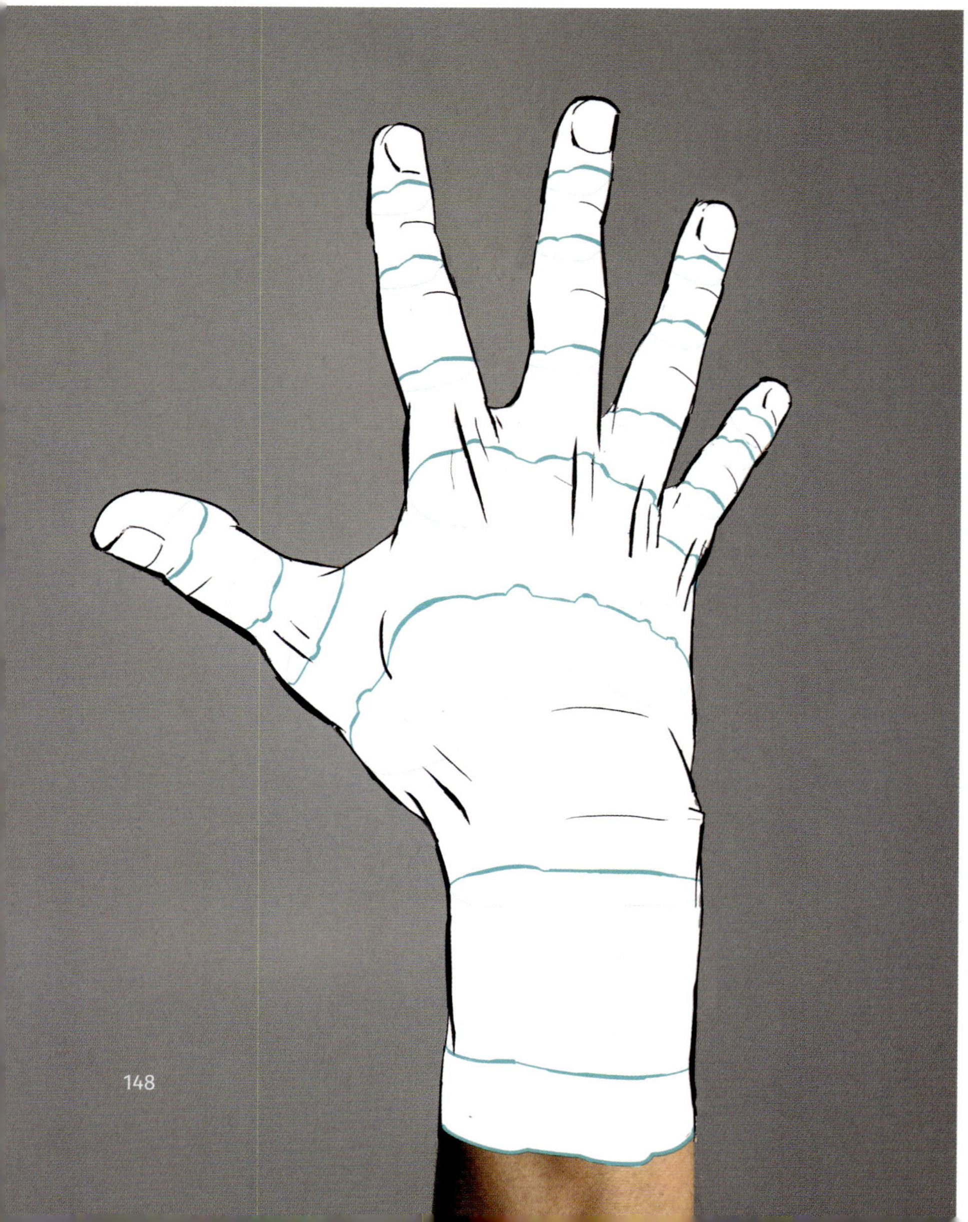

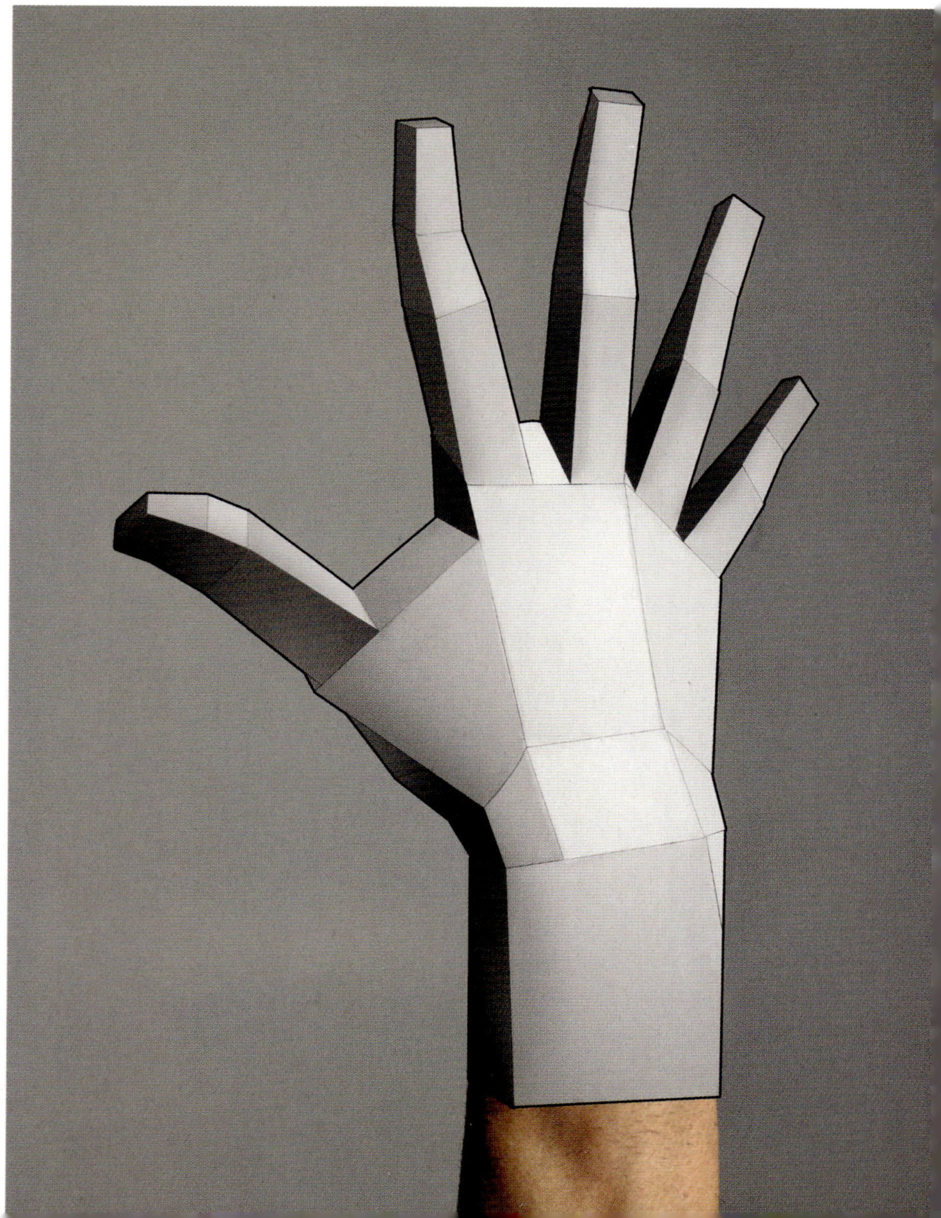

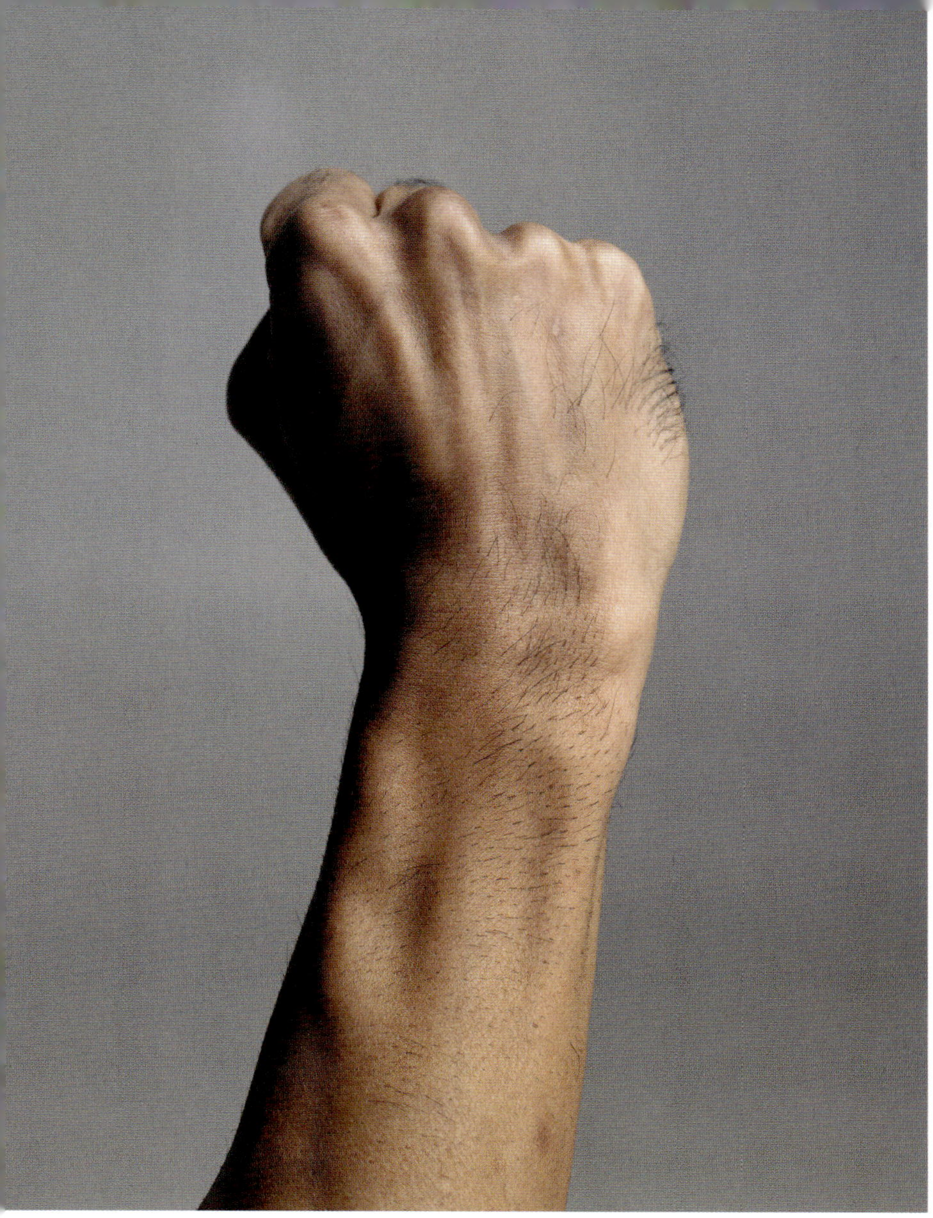

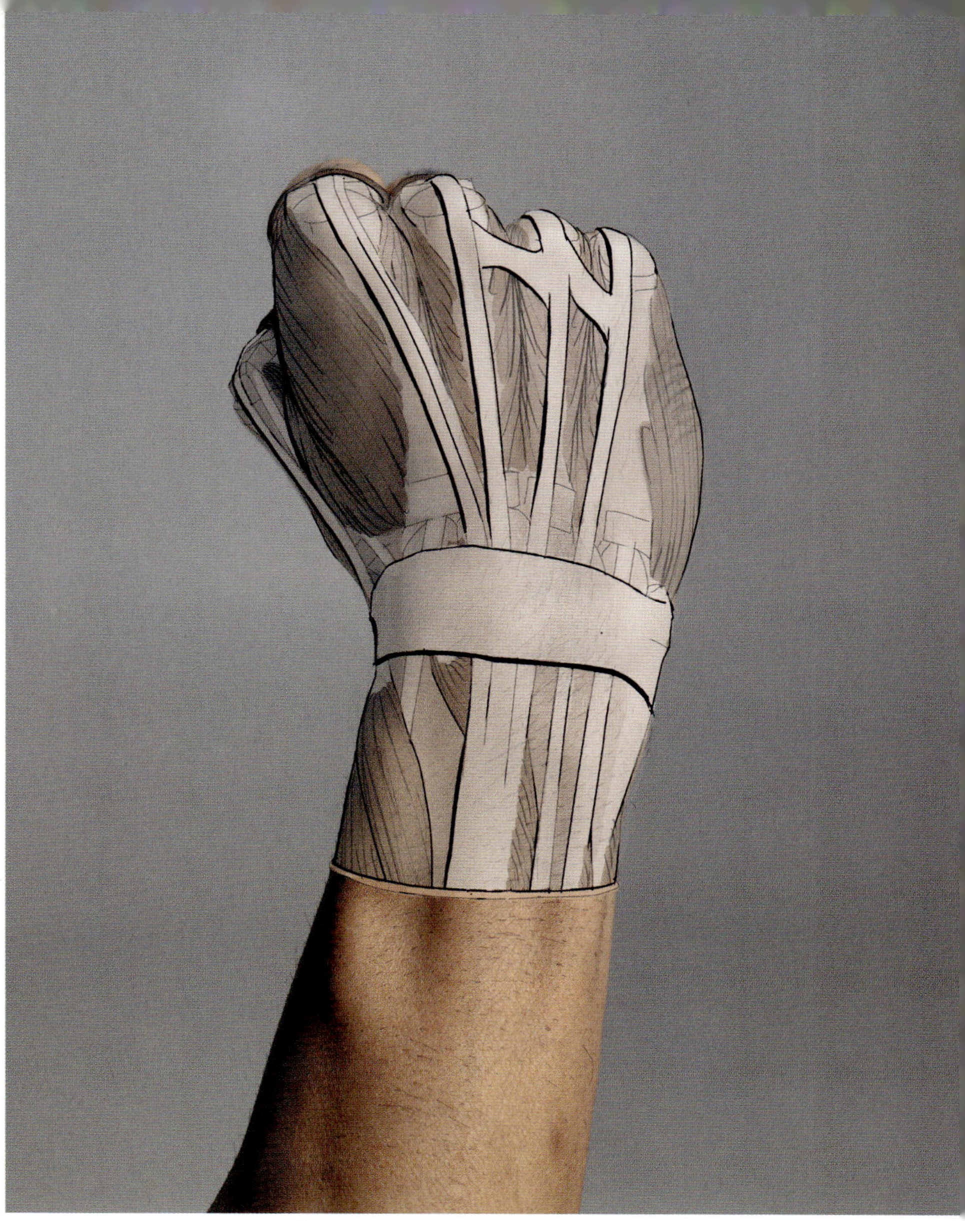

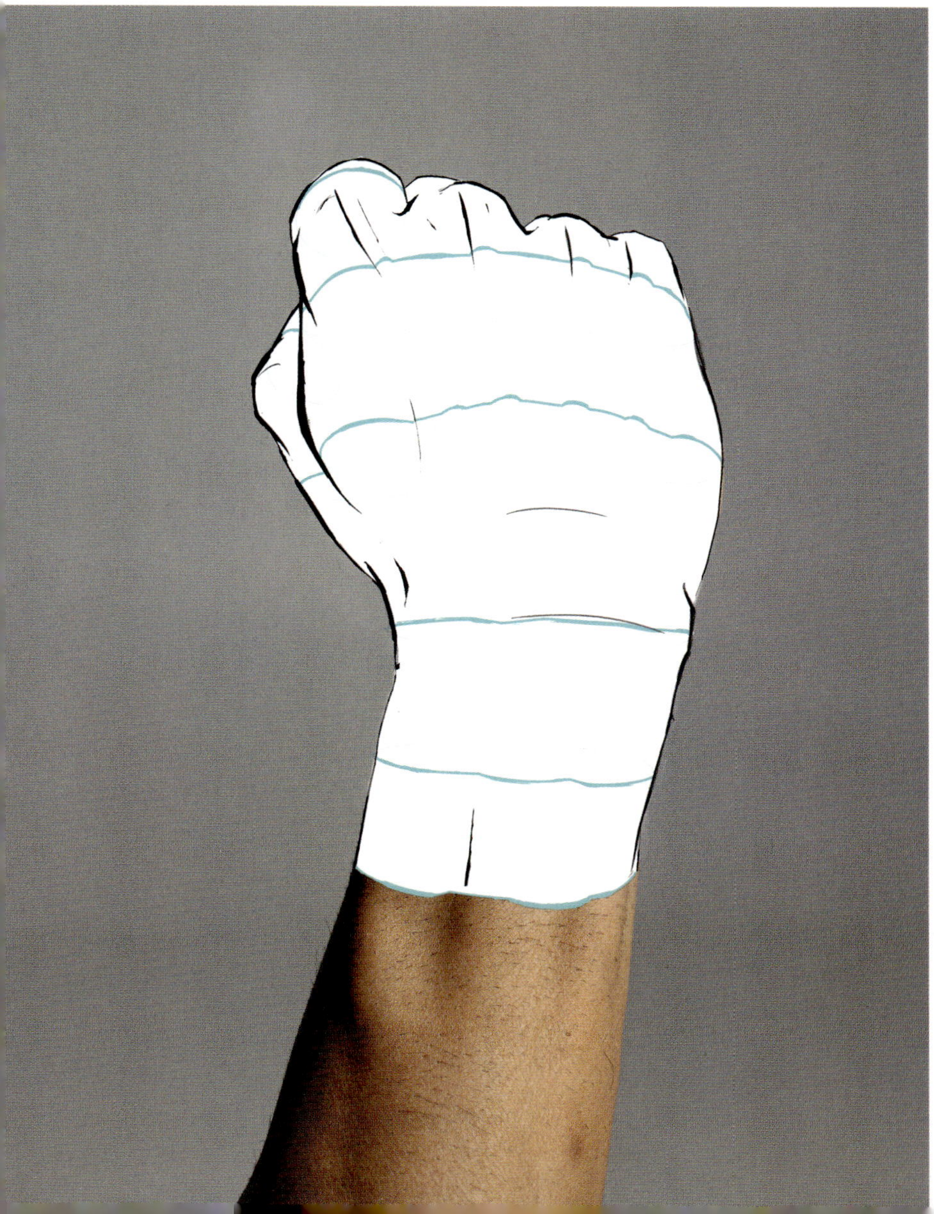

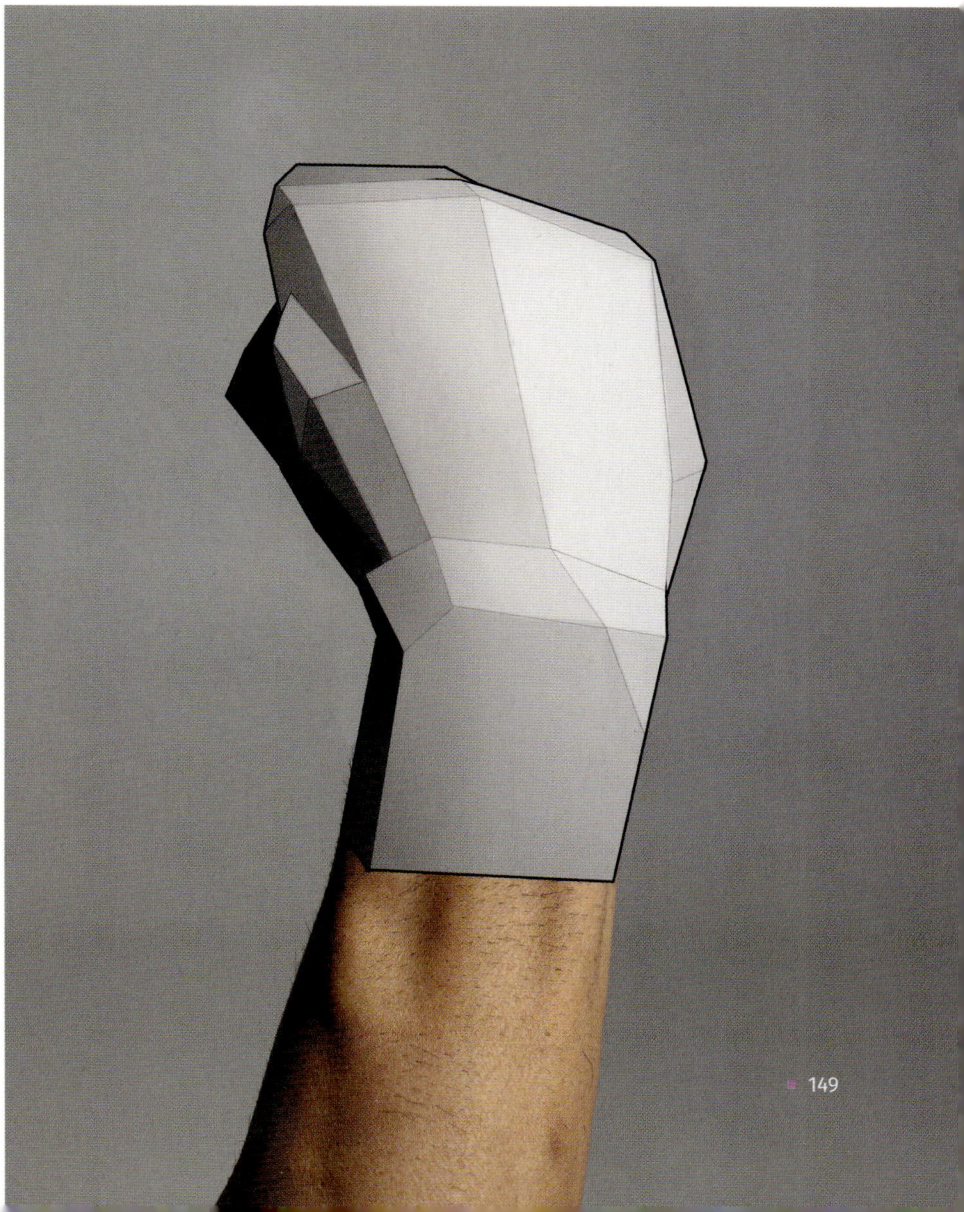

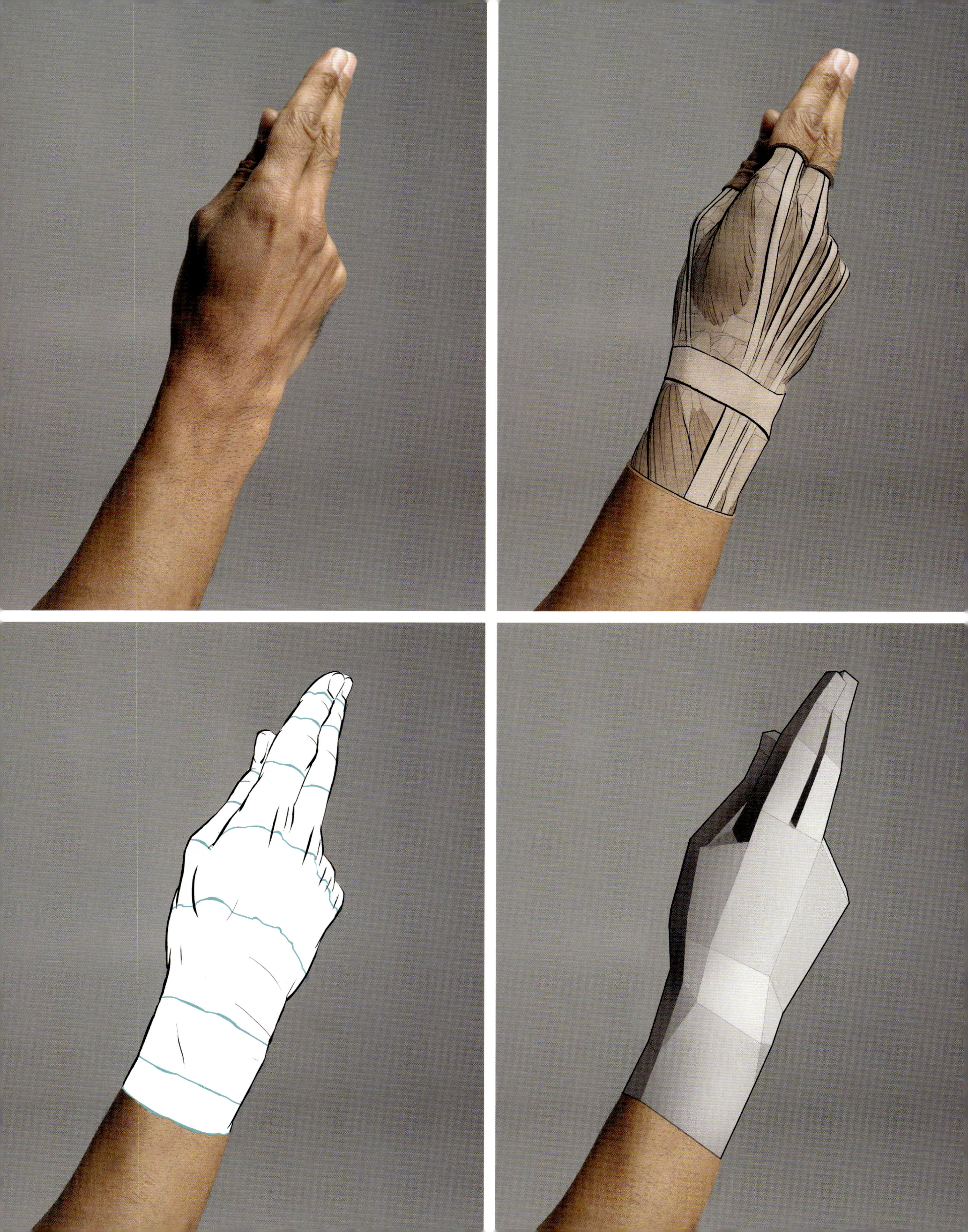

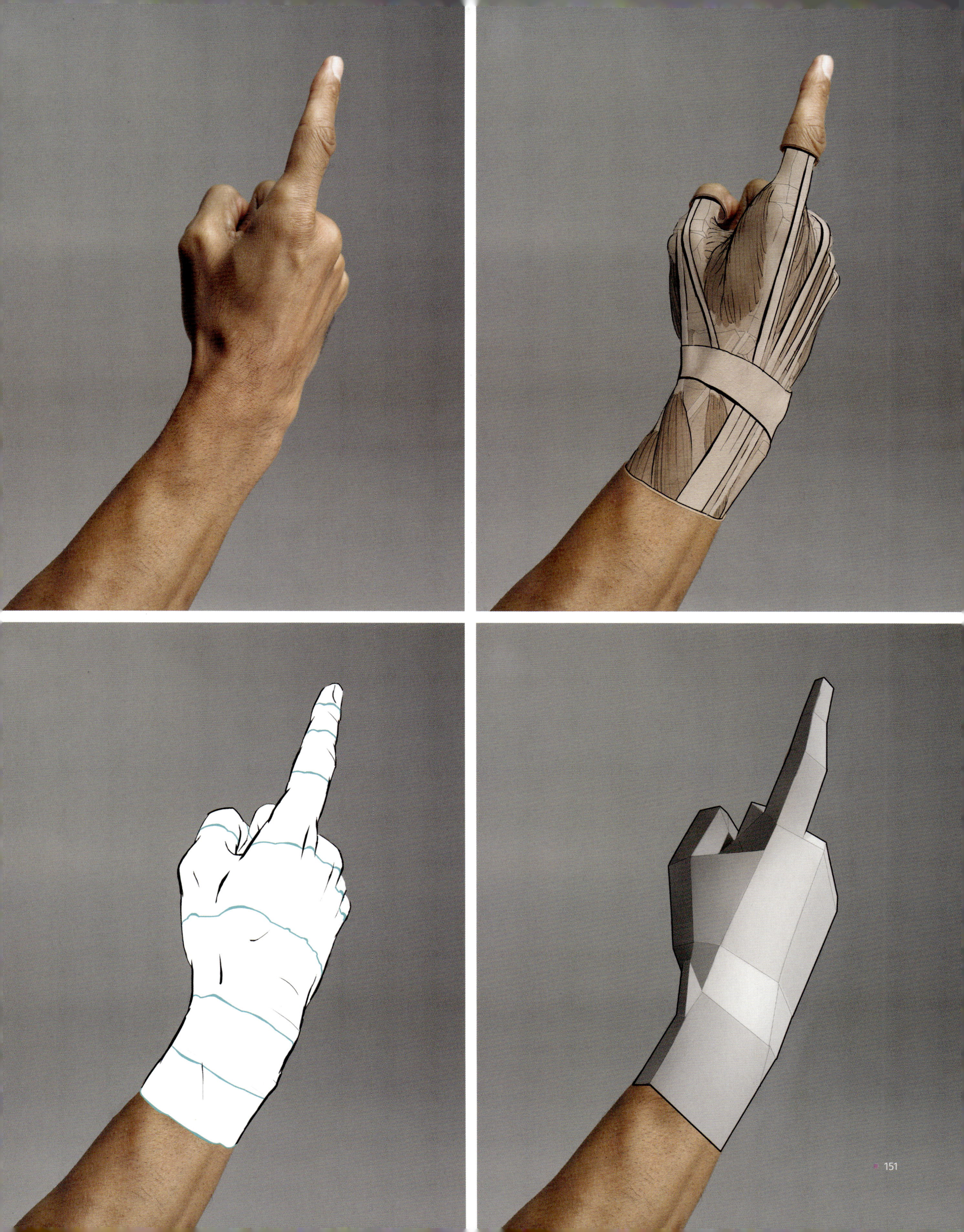

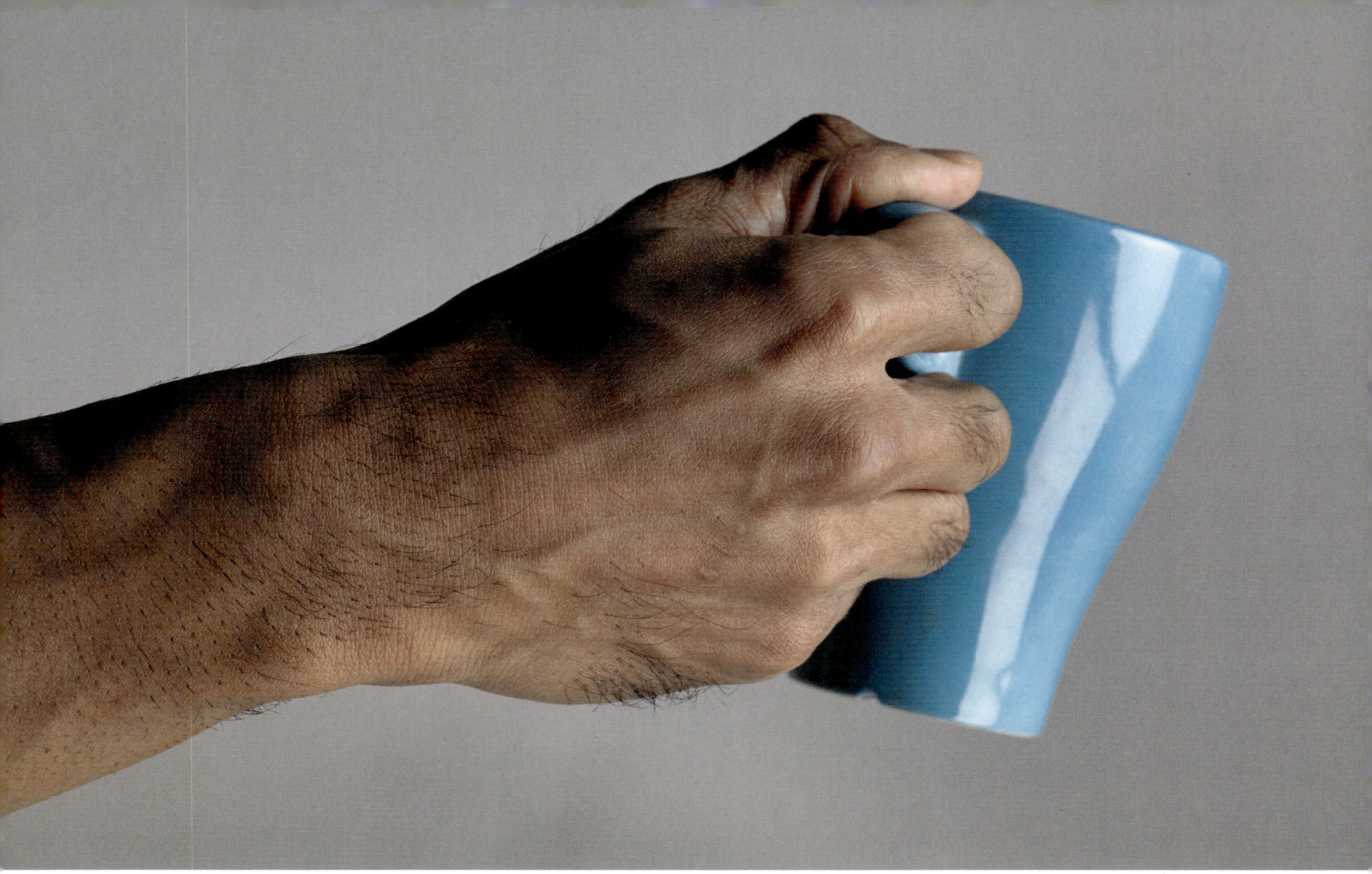

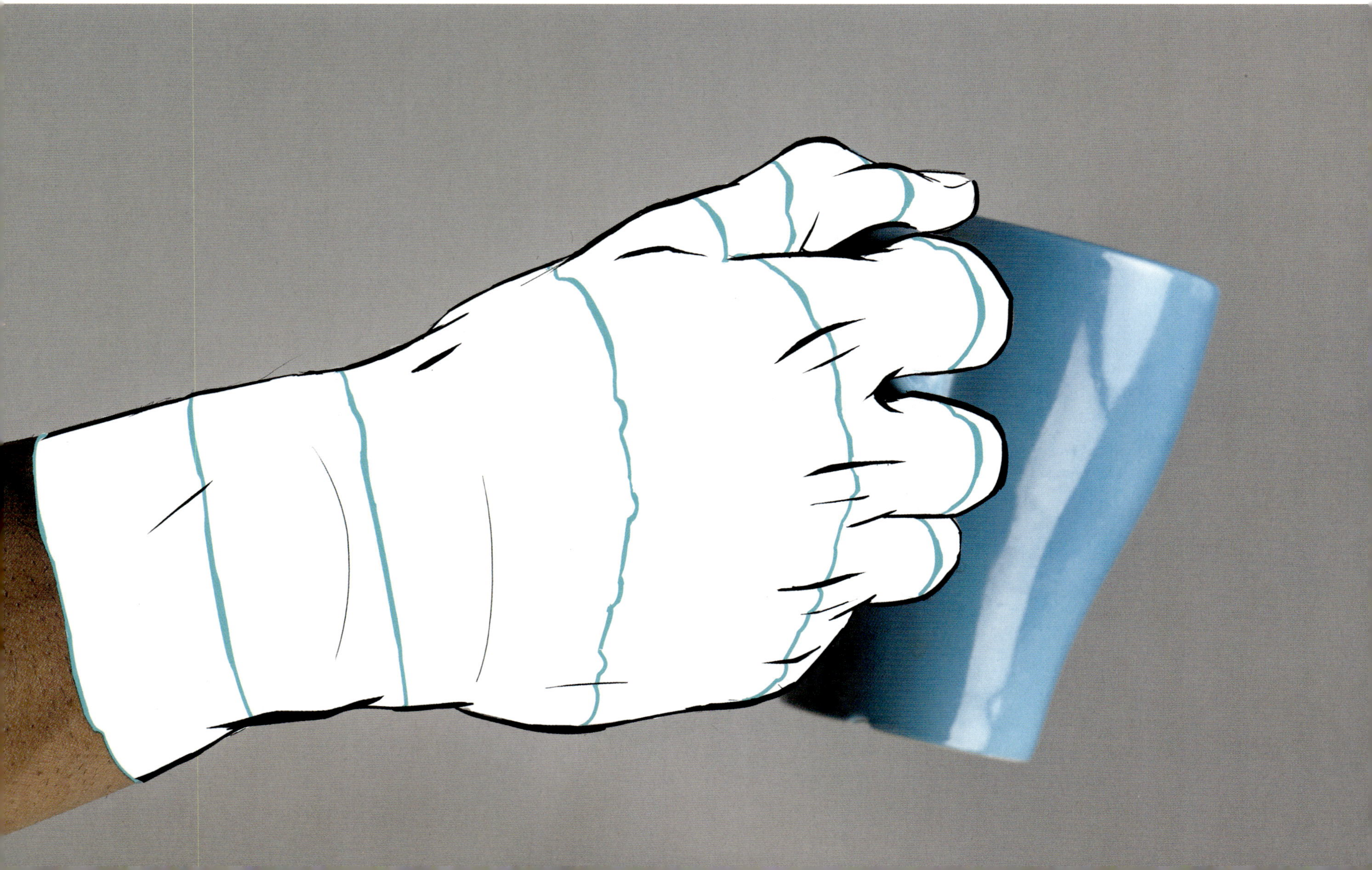

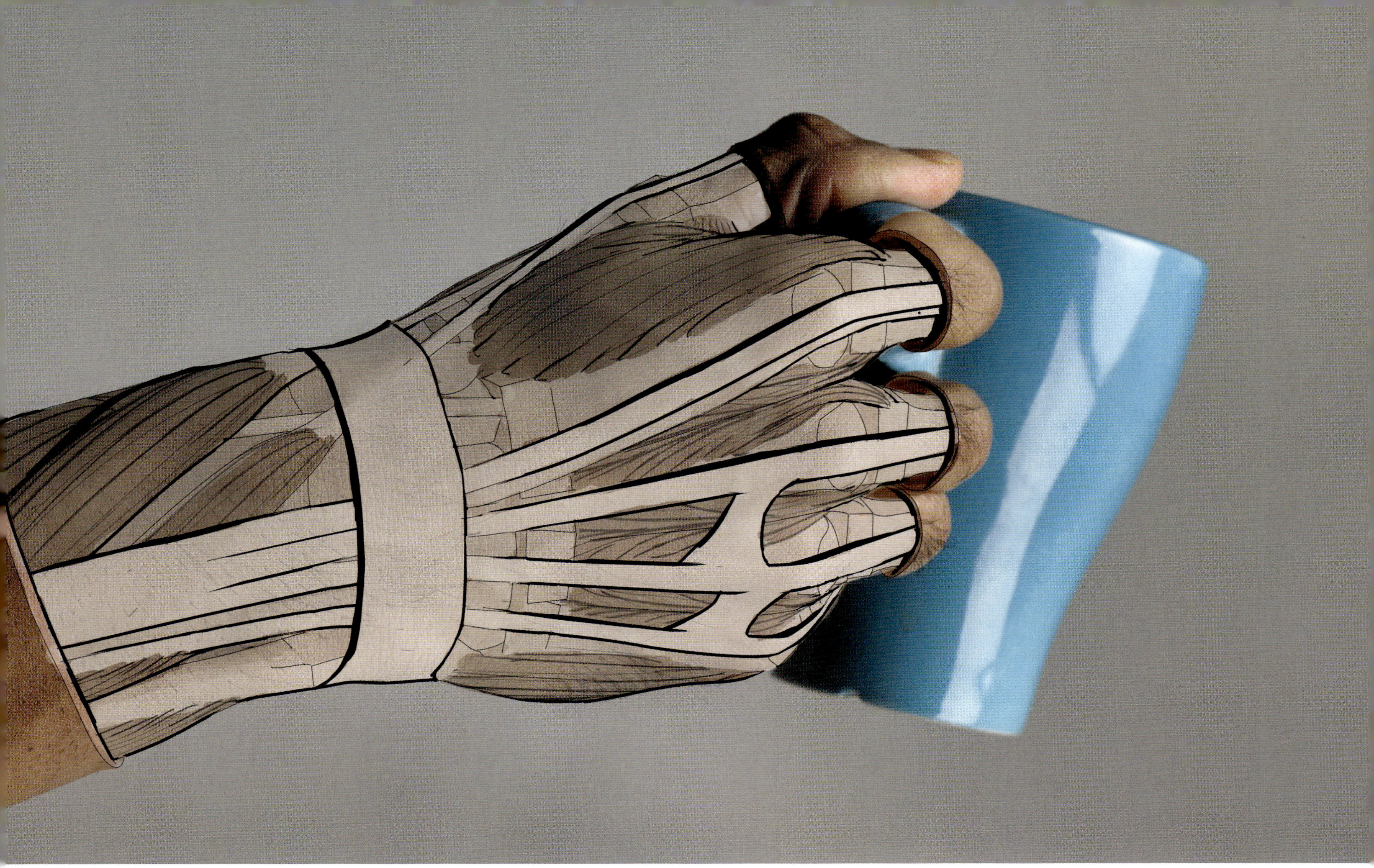

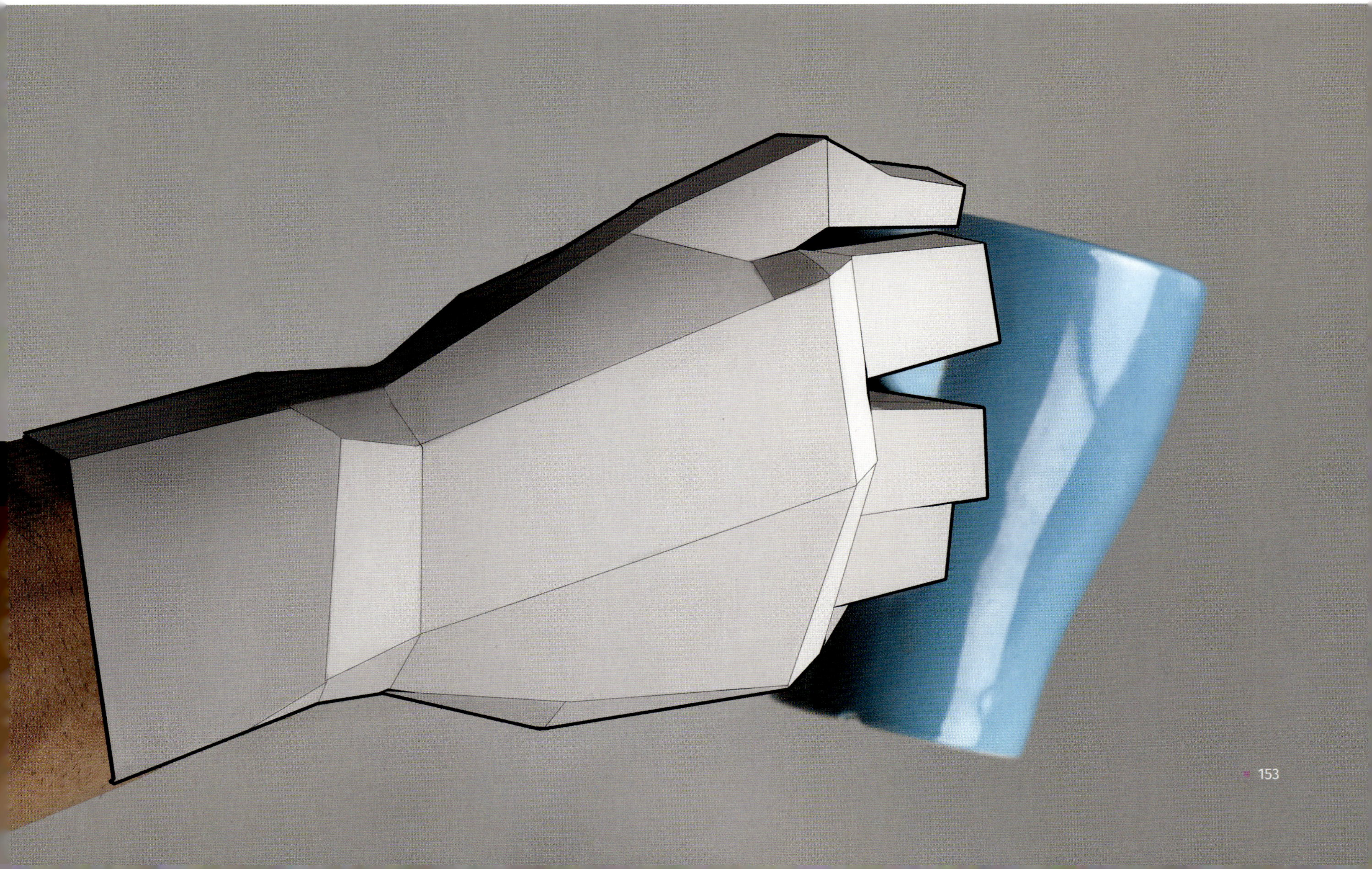

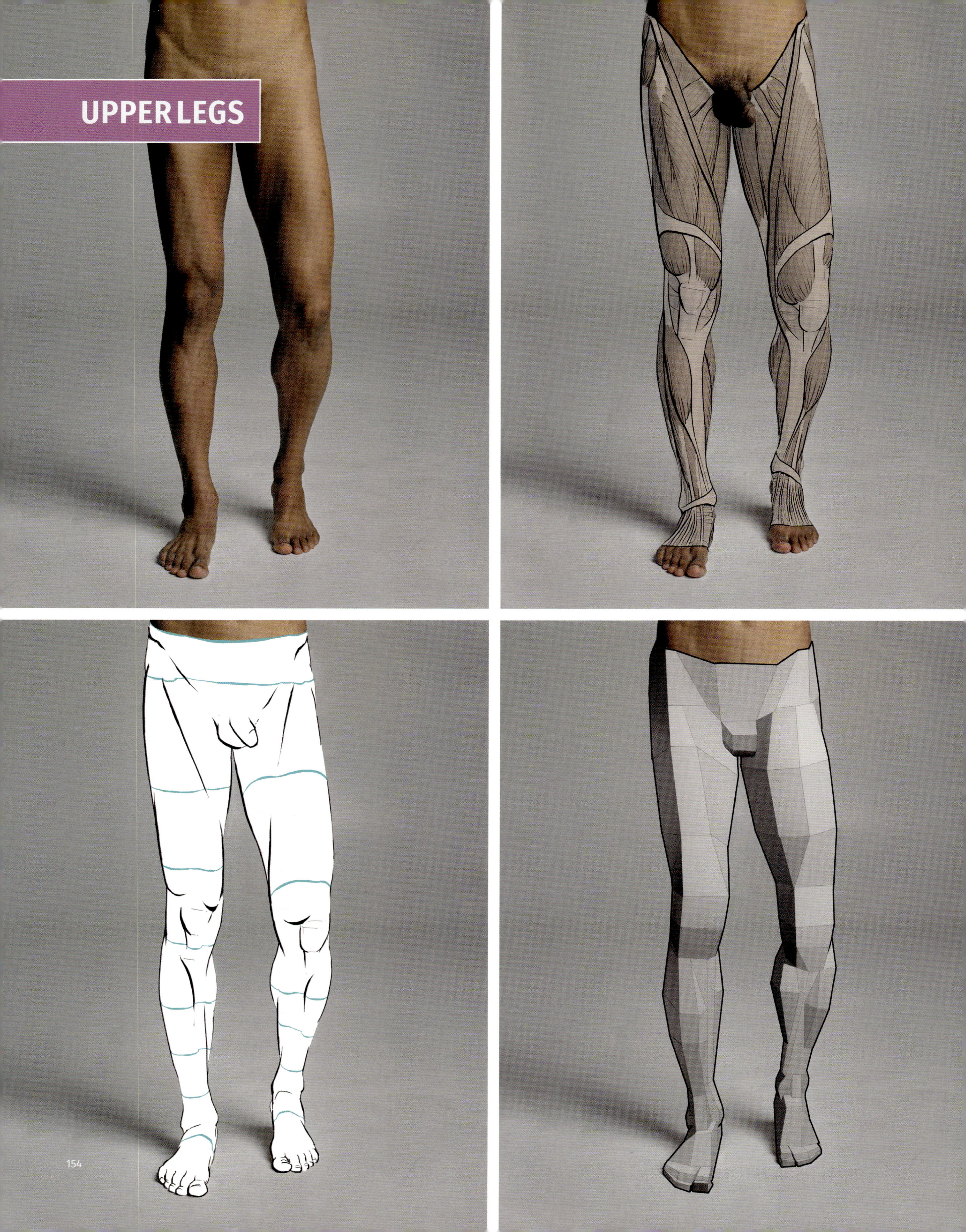

UPPER LEGS

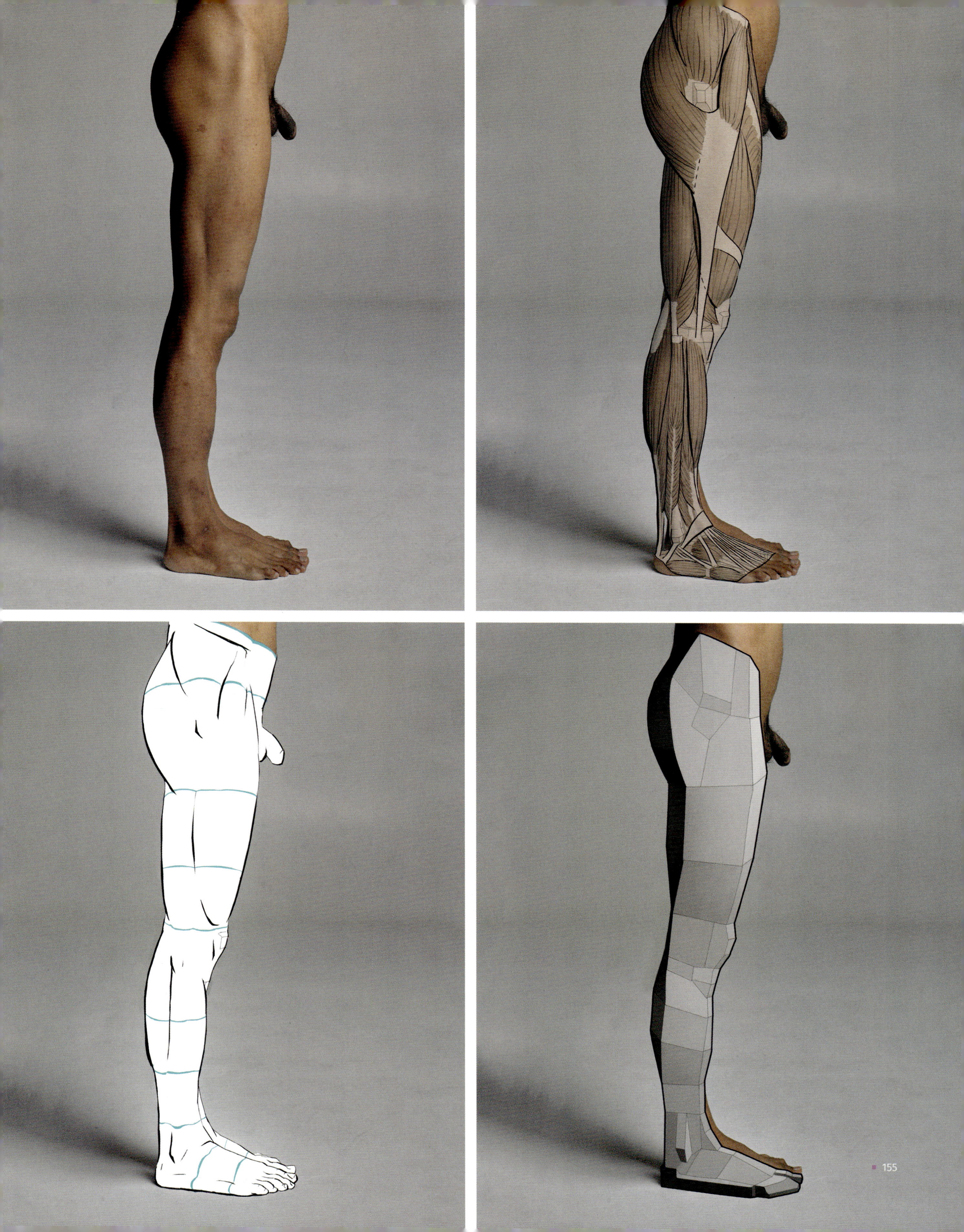

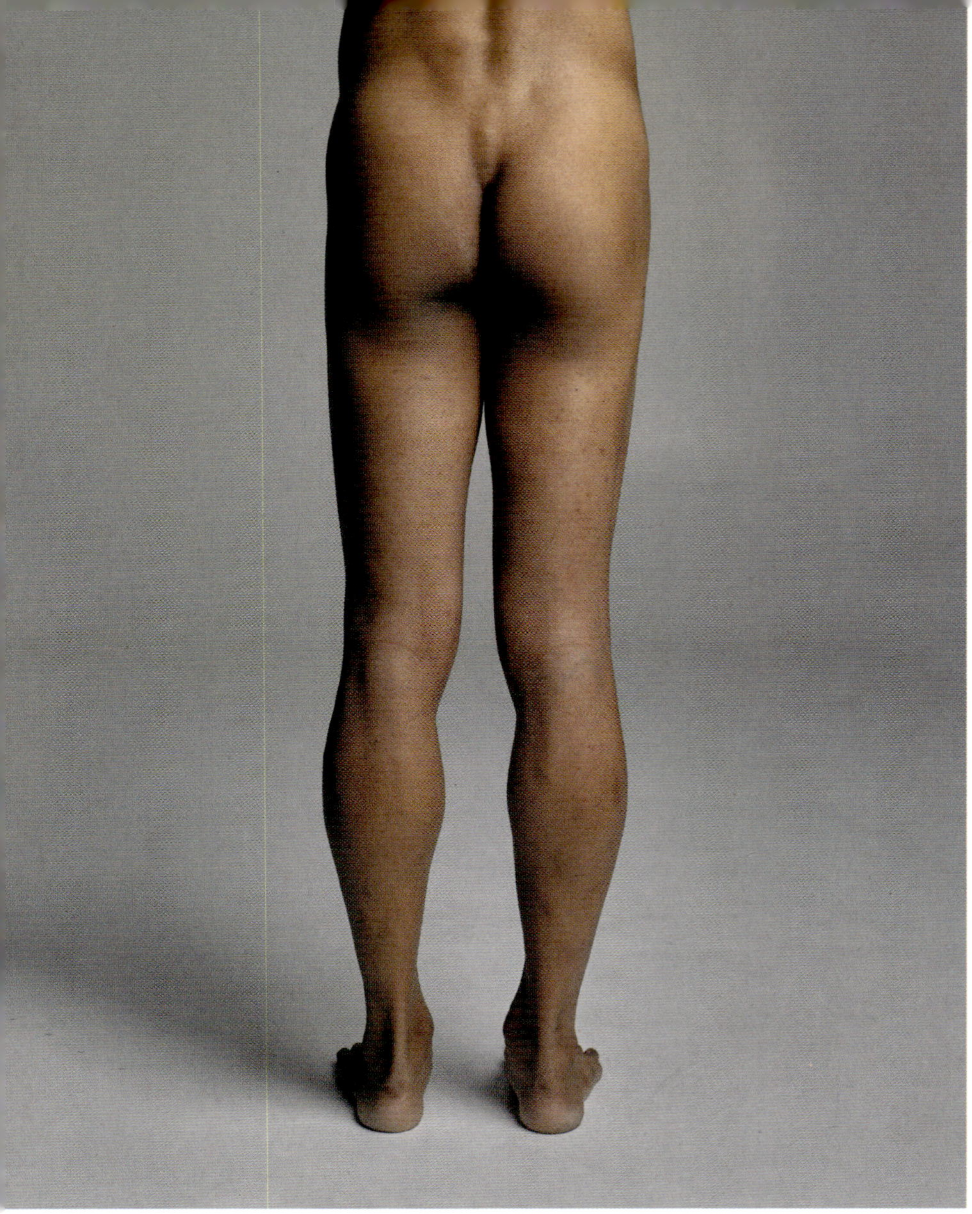
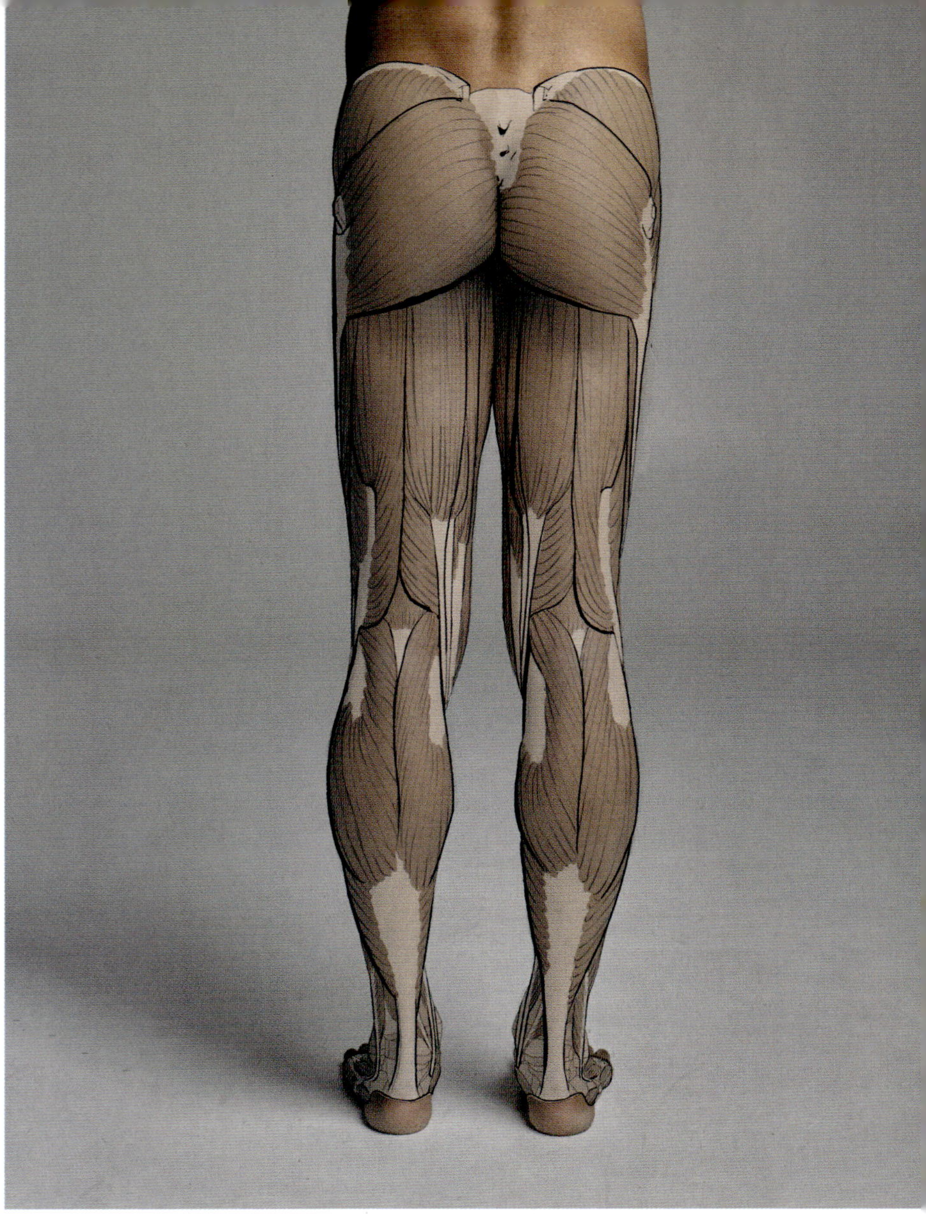
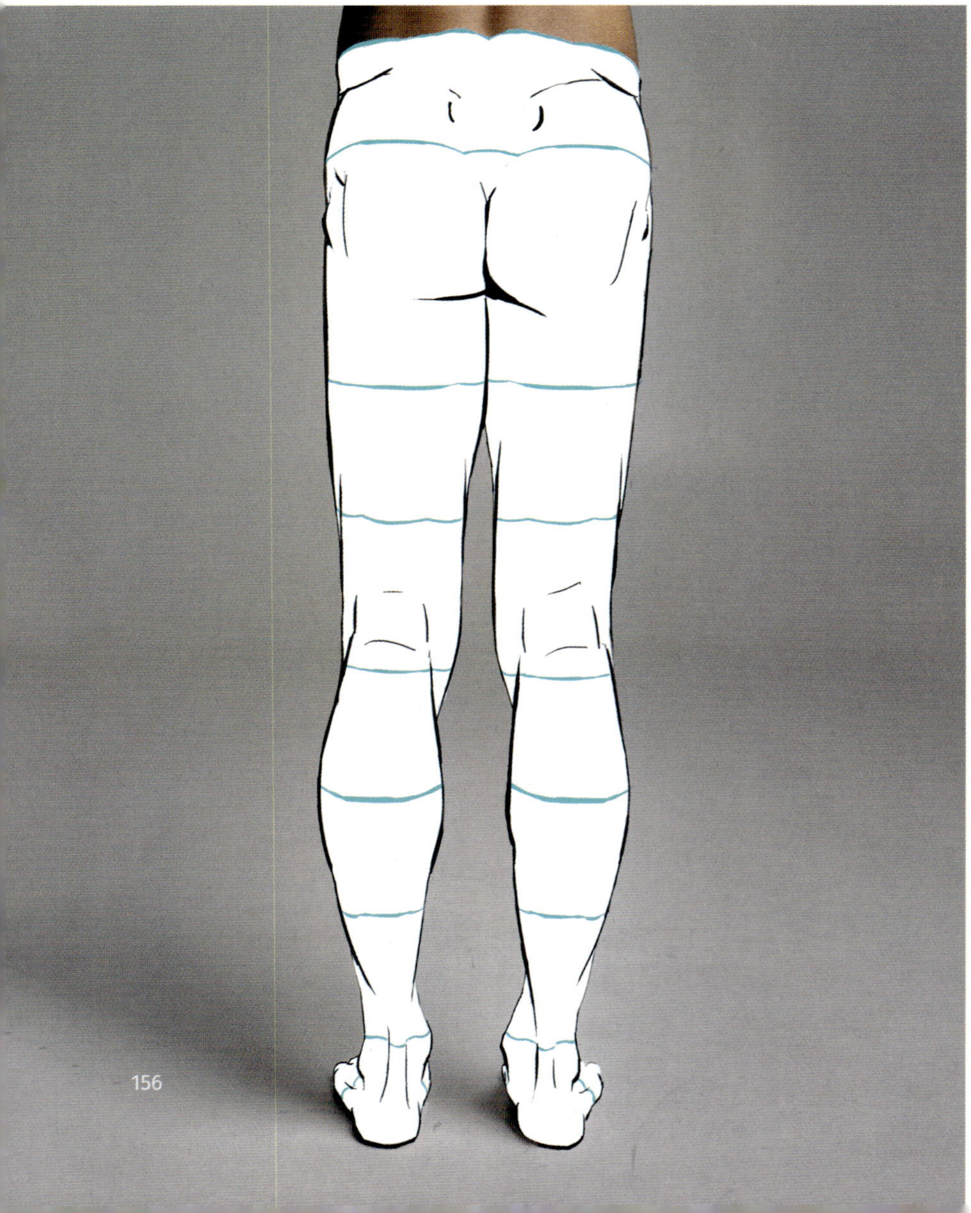
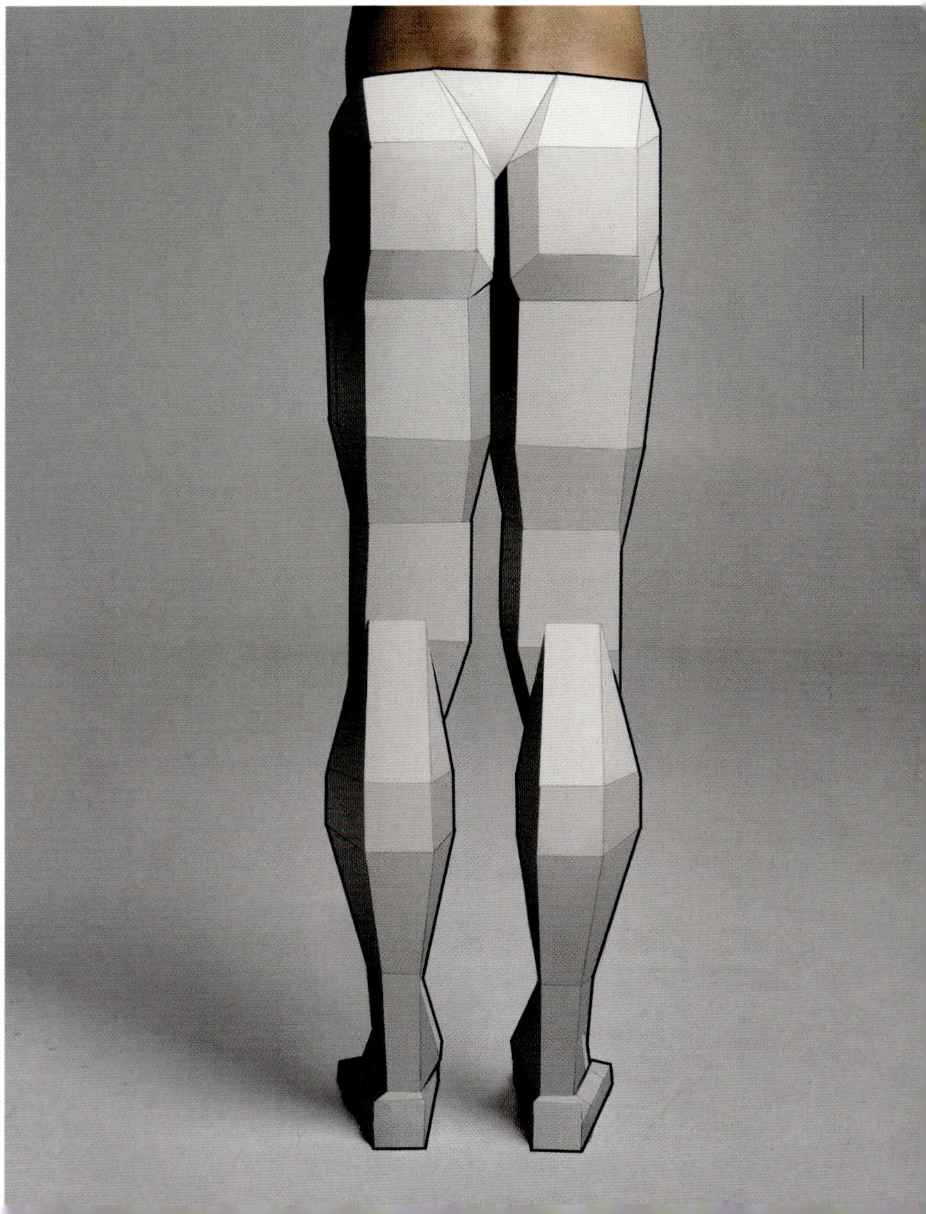

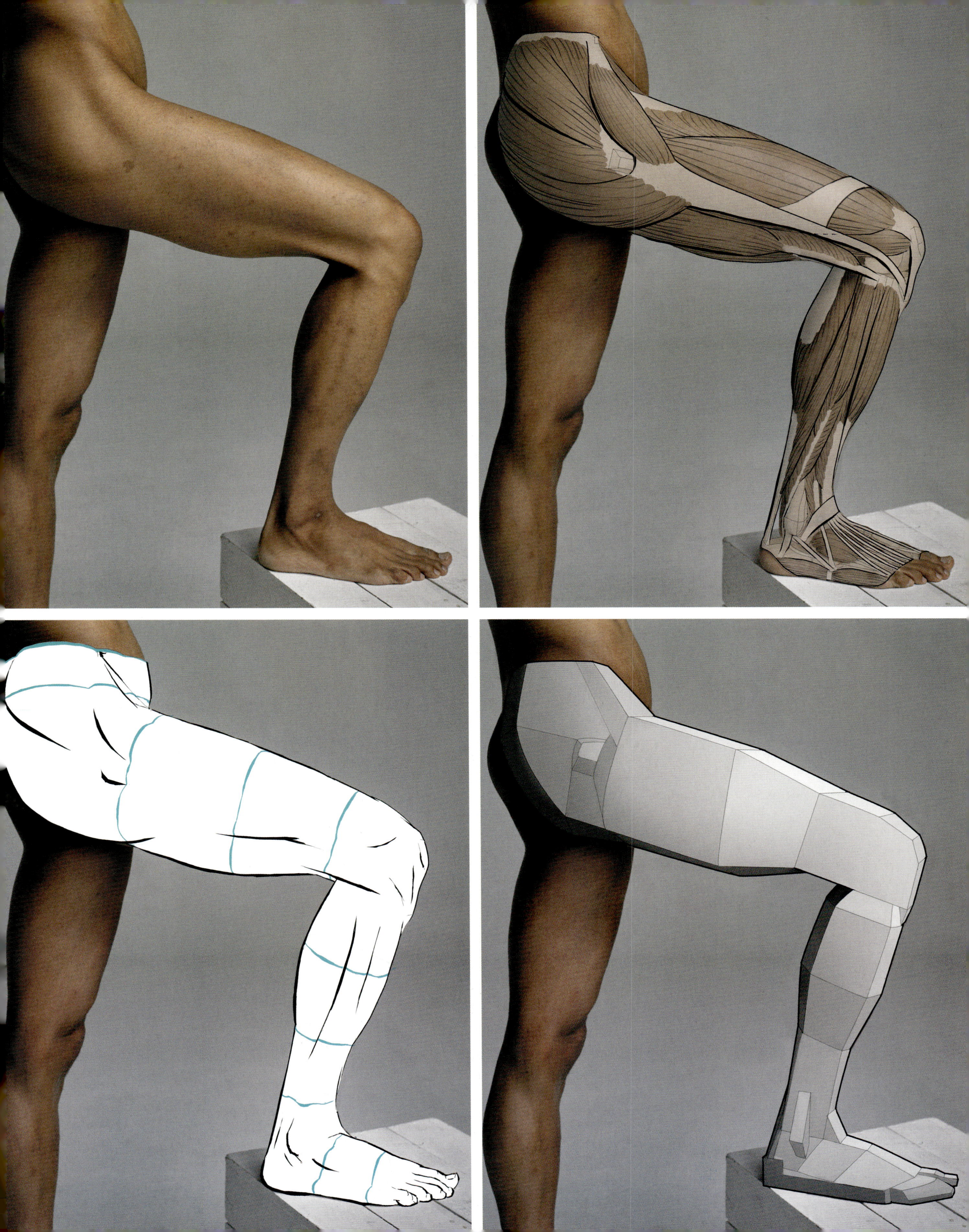

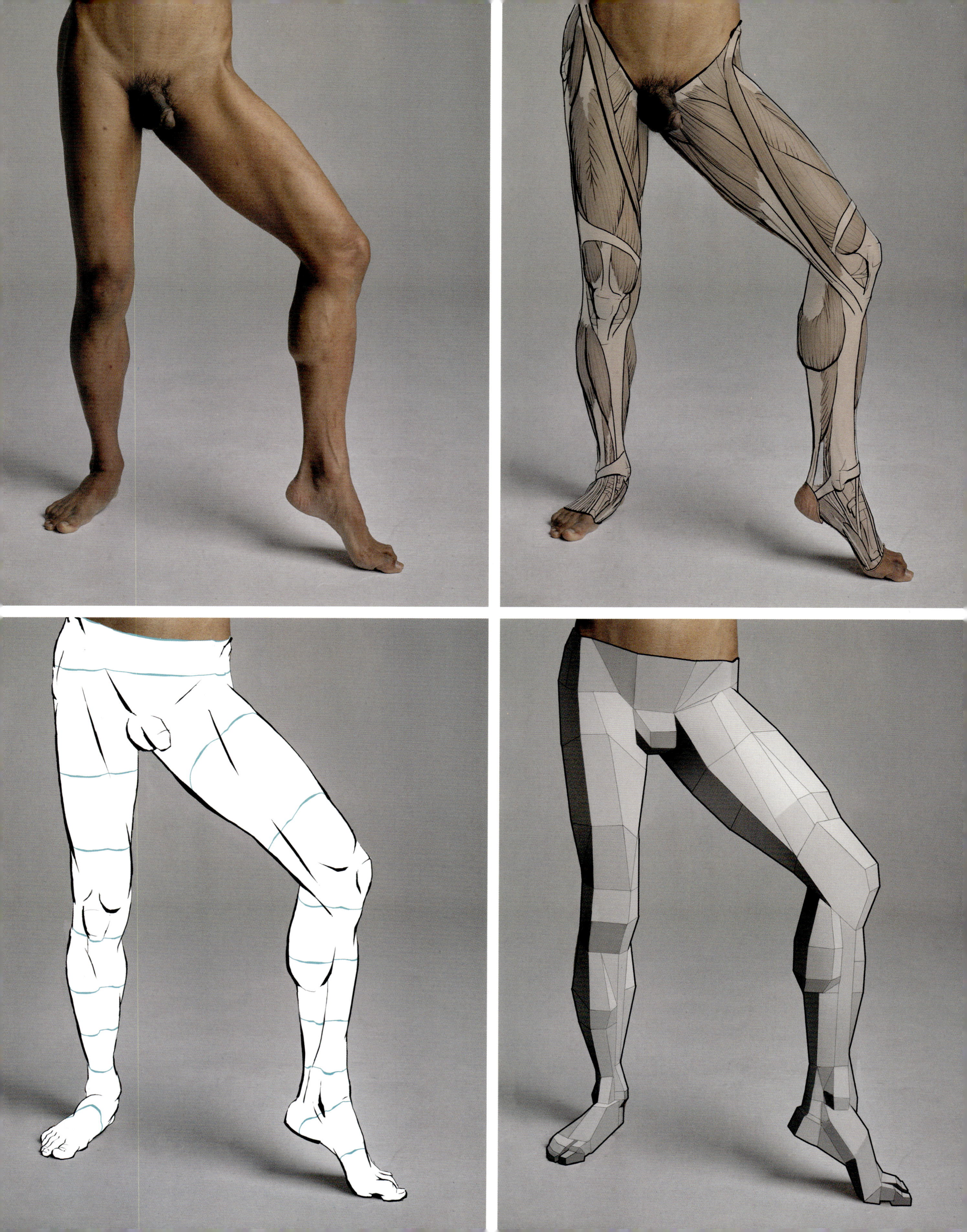

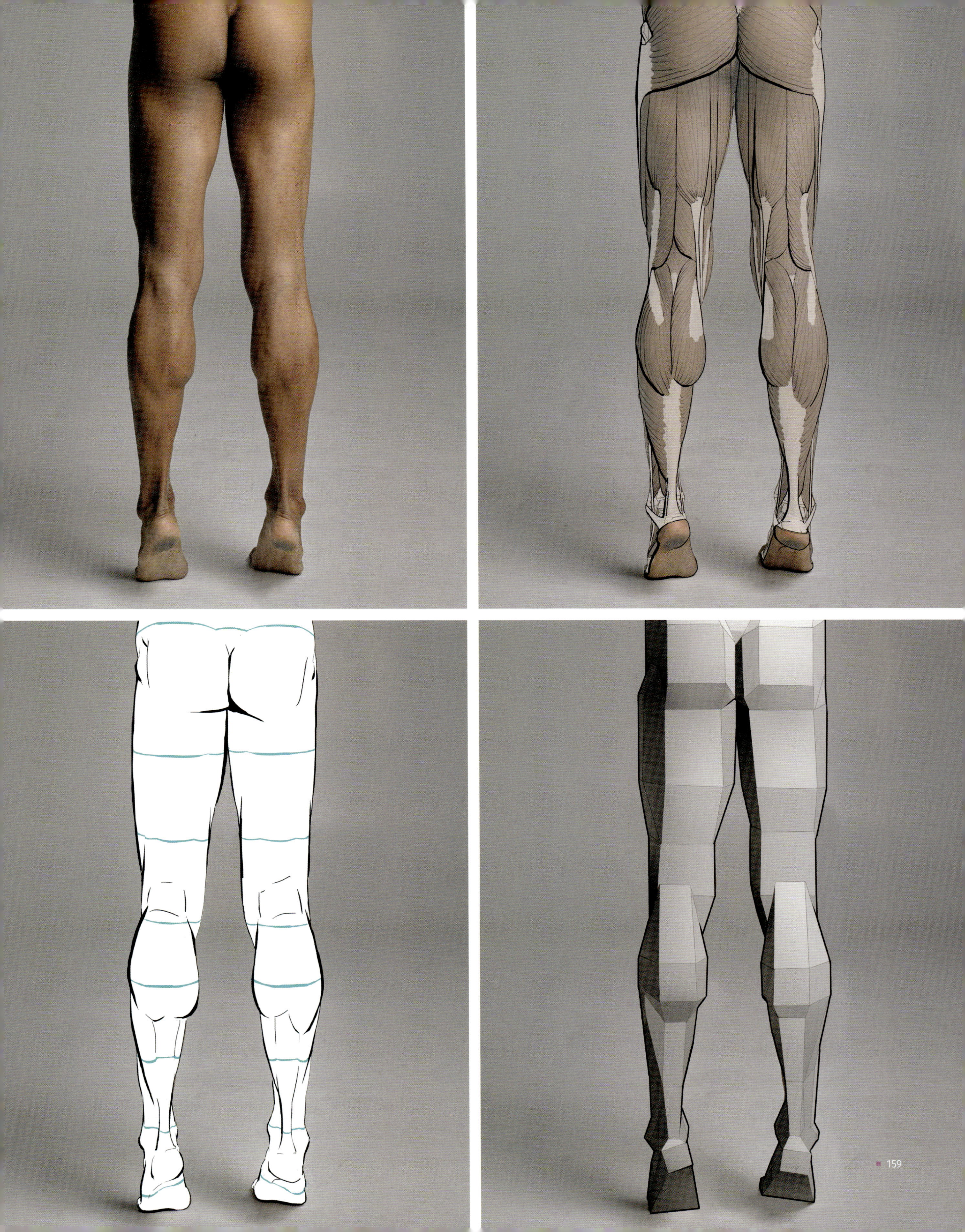

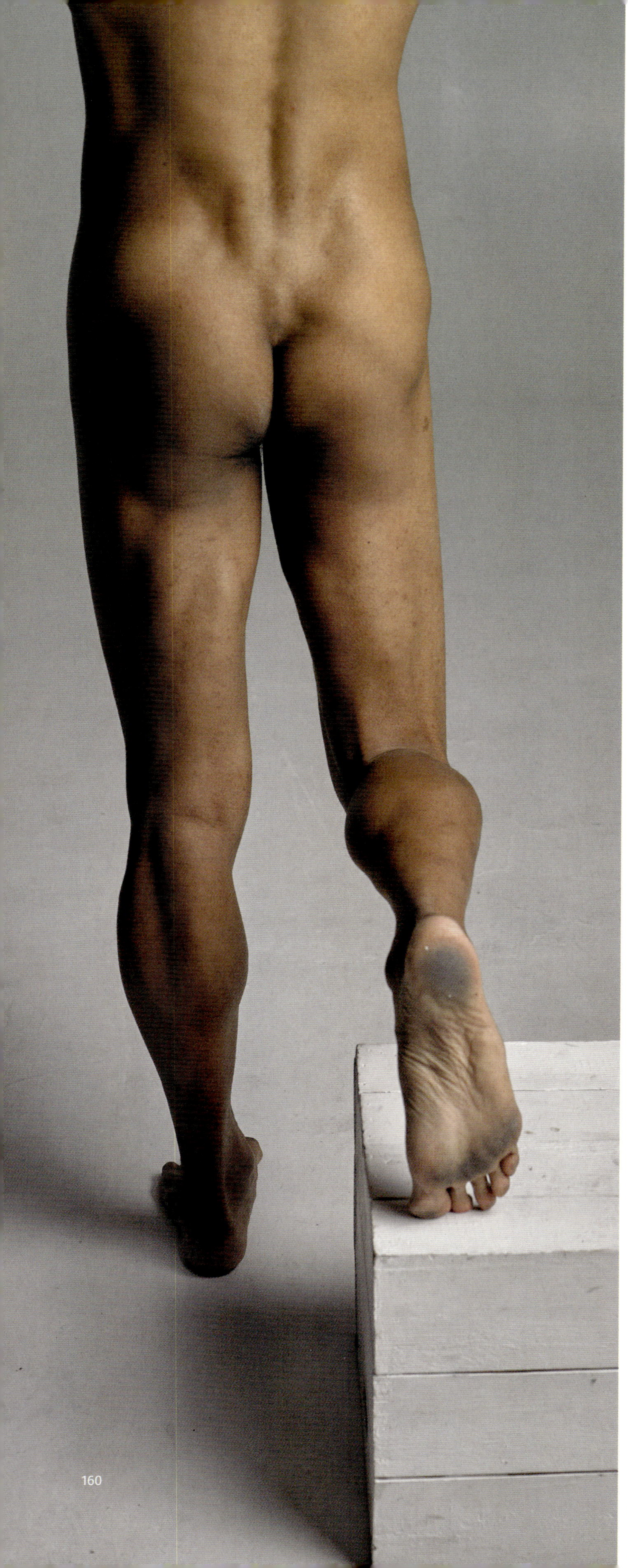

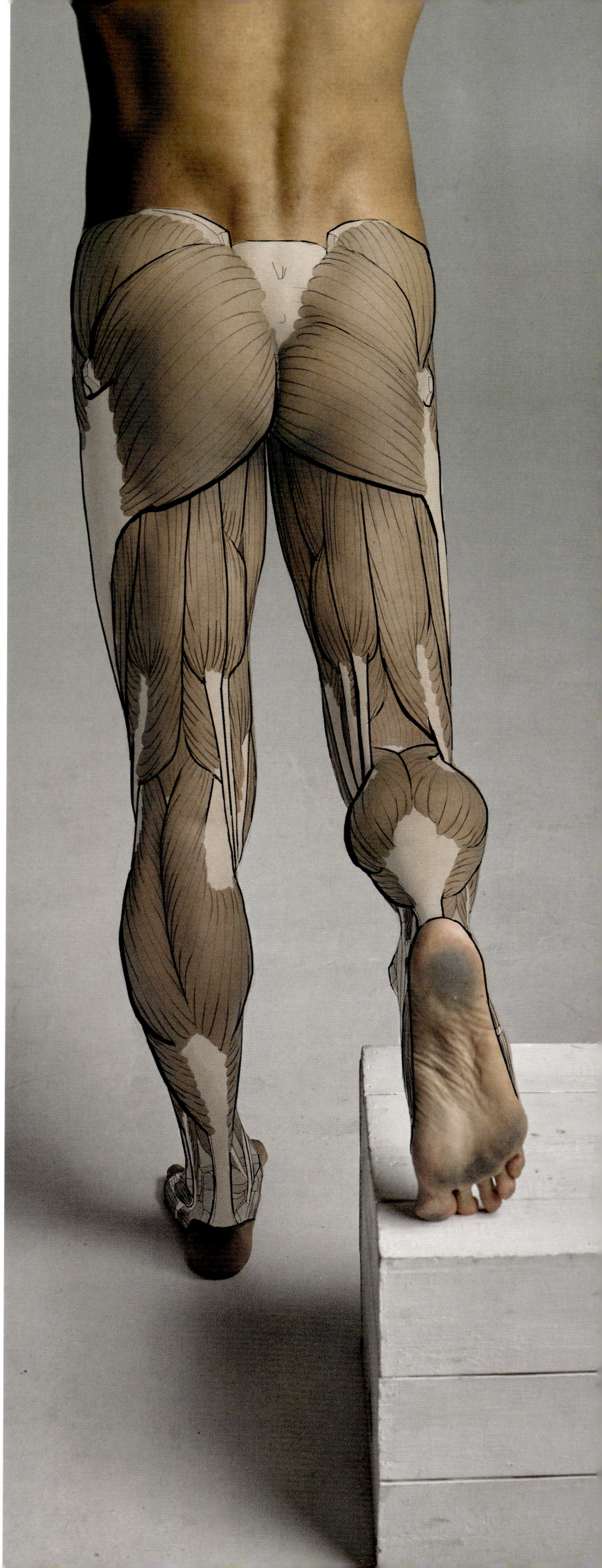

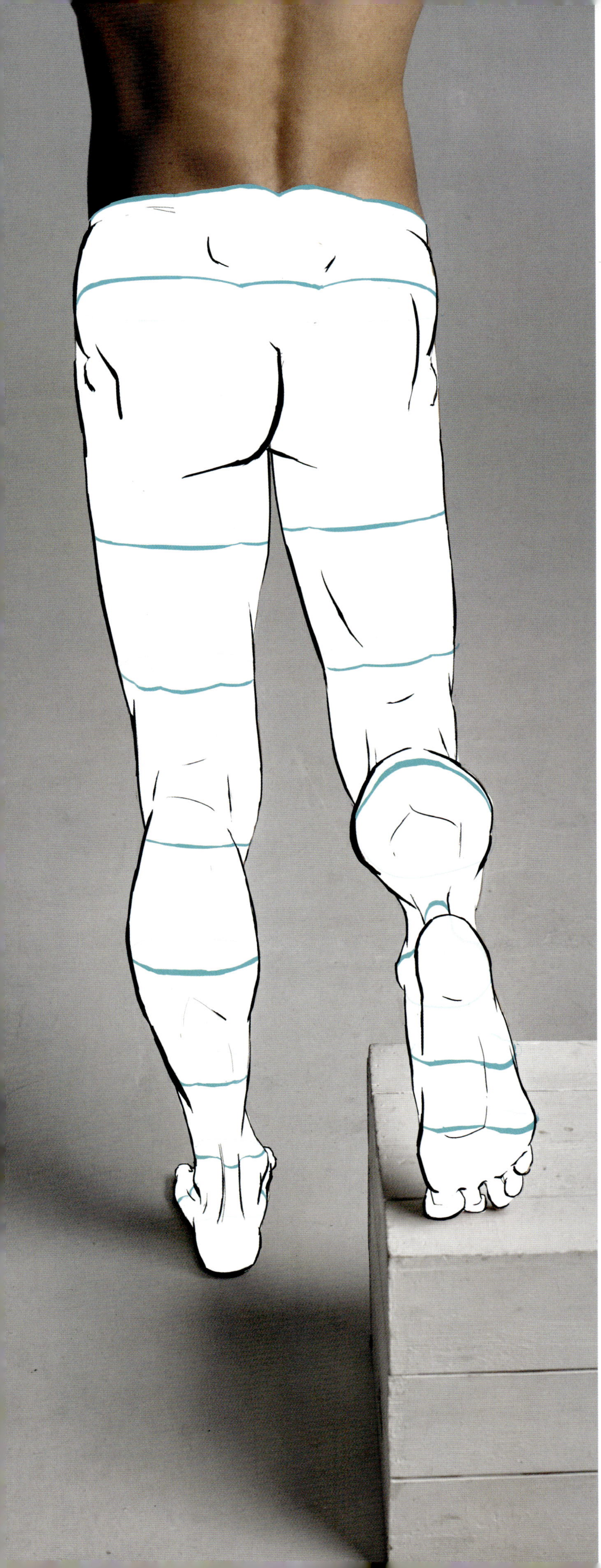
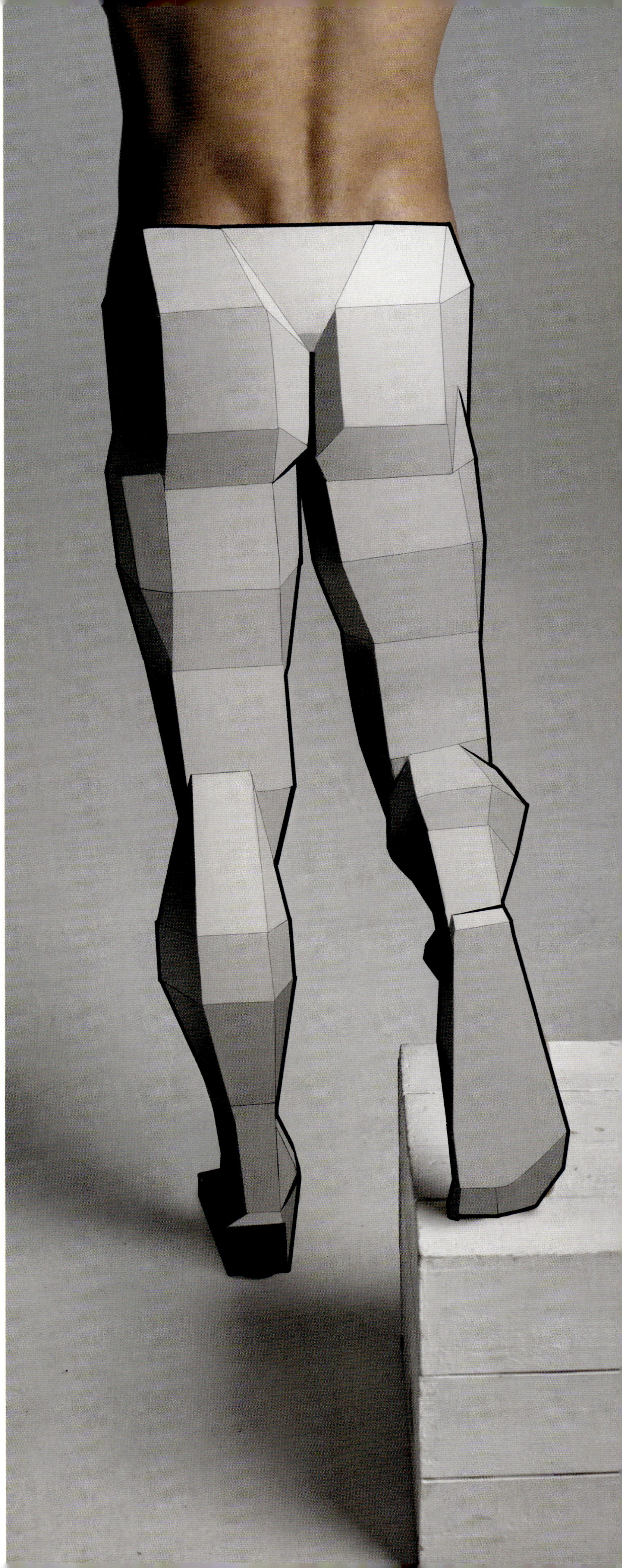

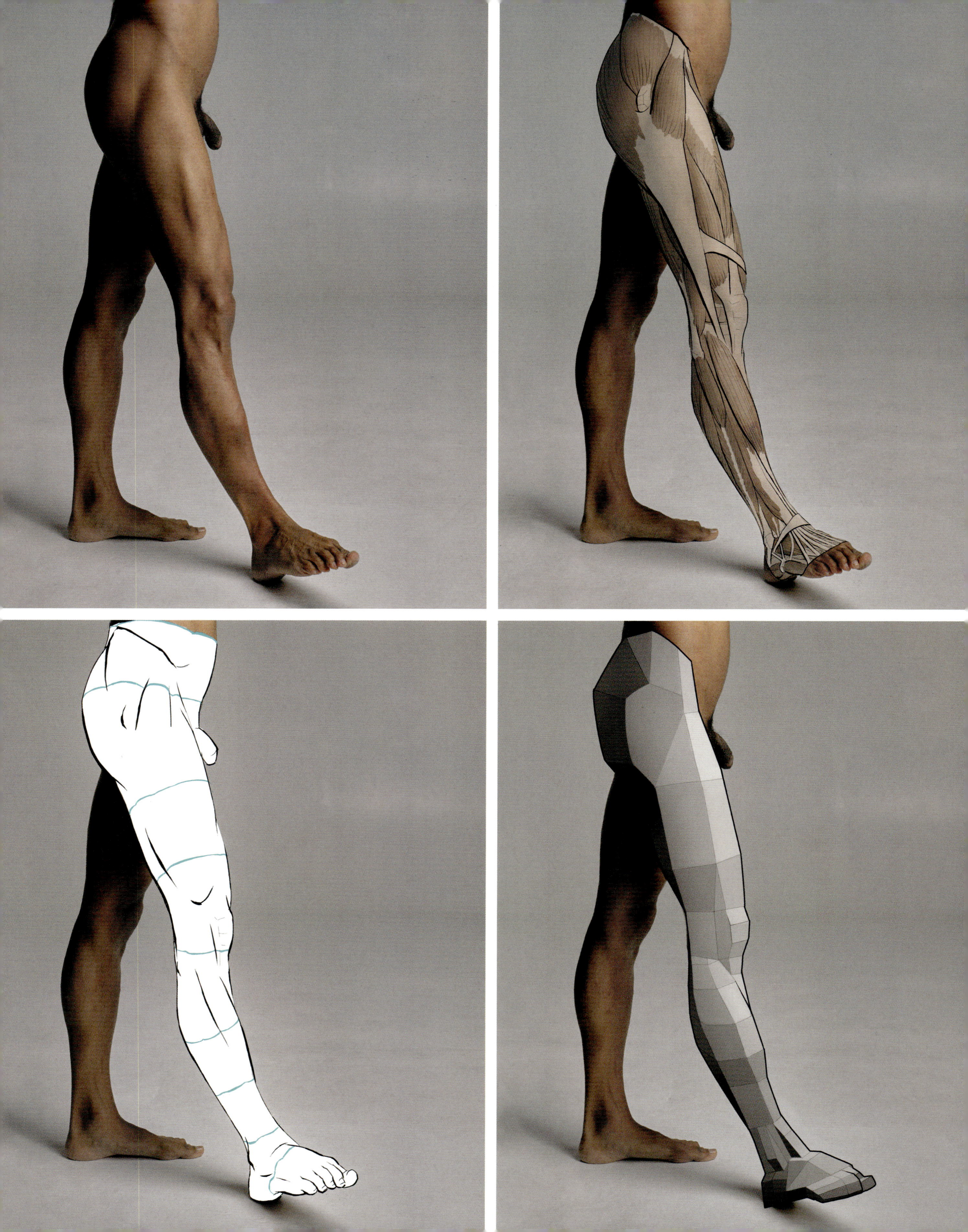

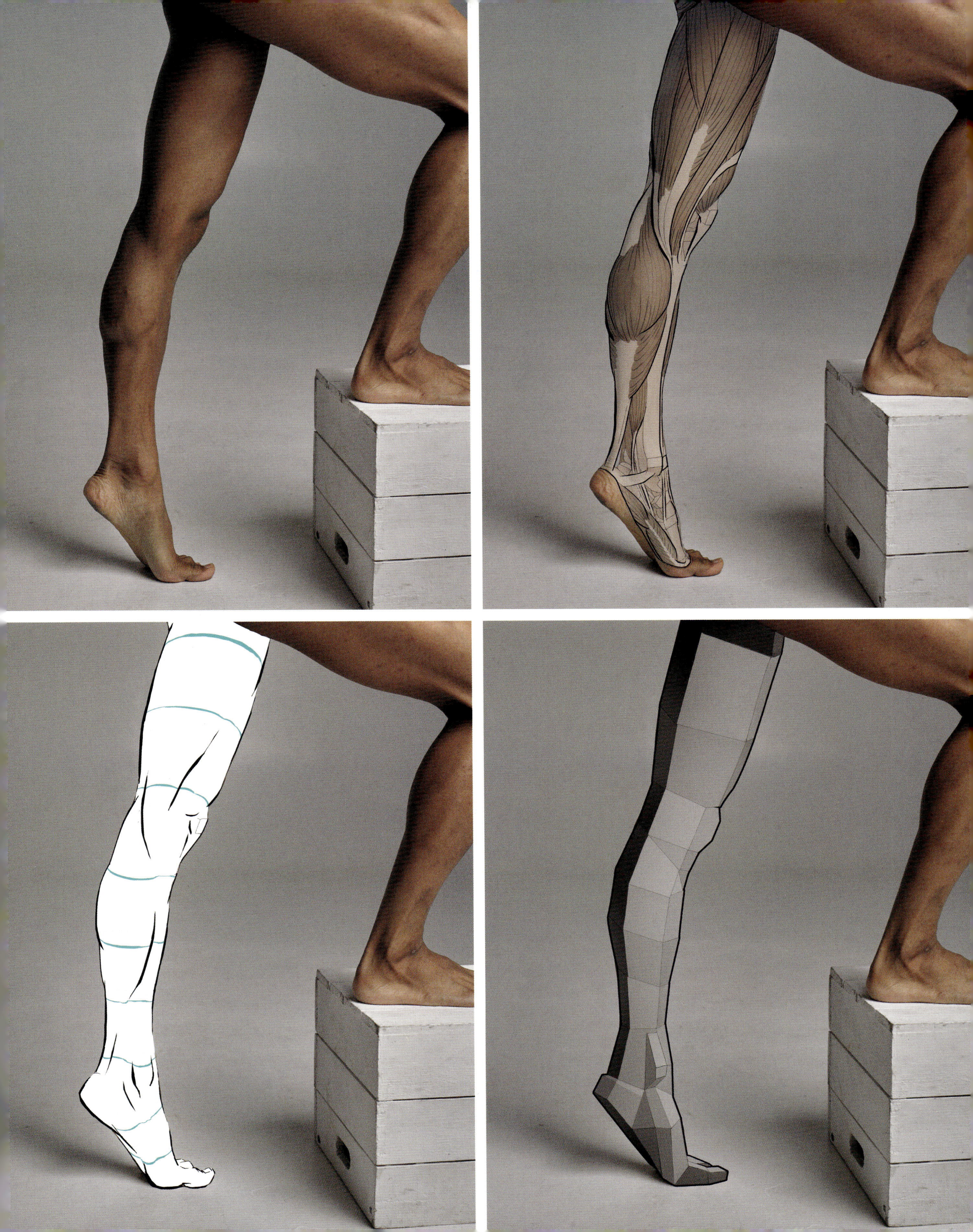

LOWER LEGS

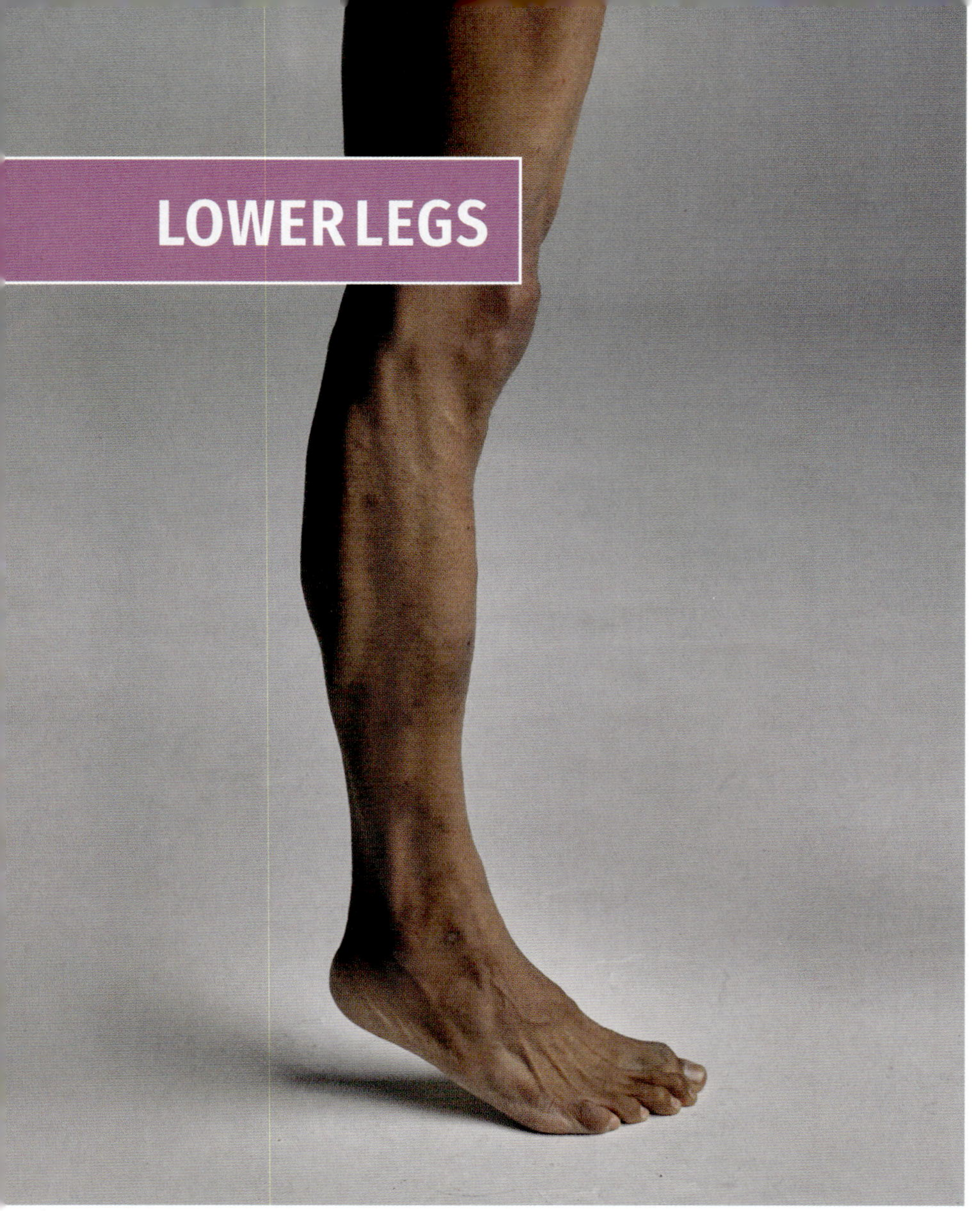

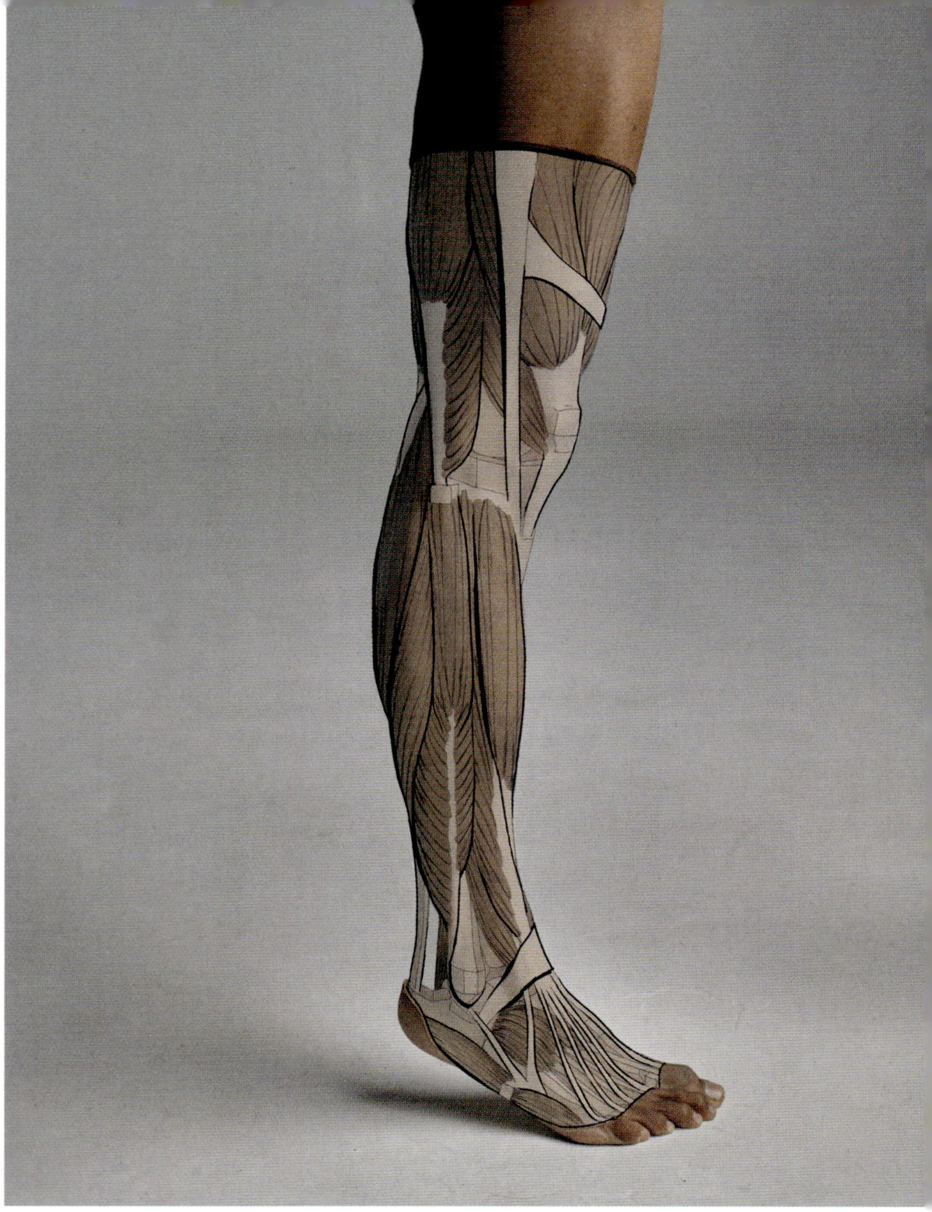

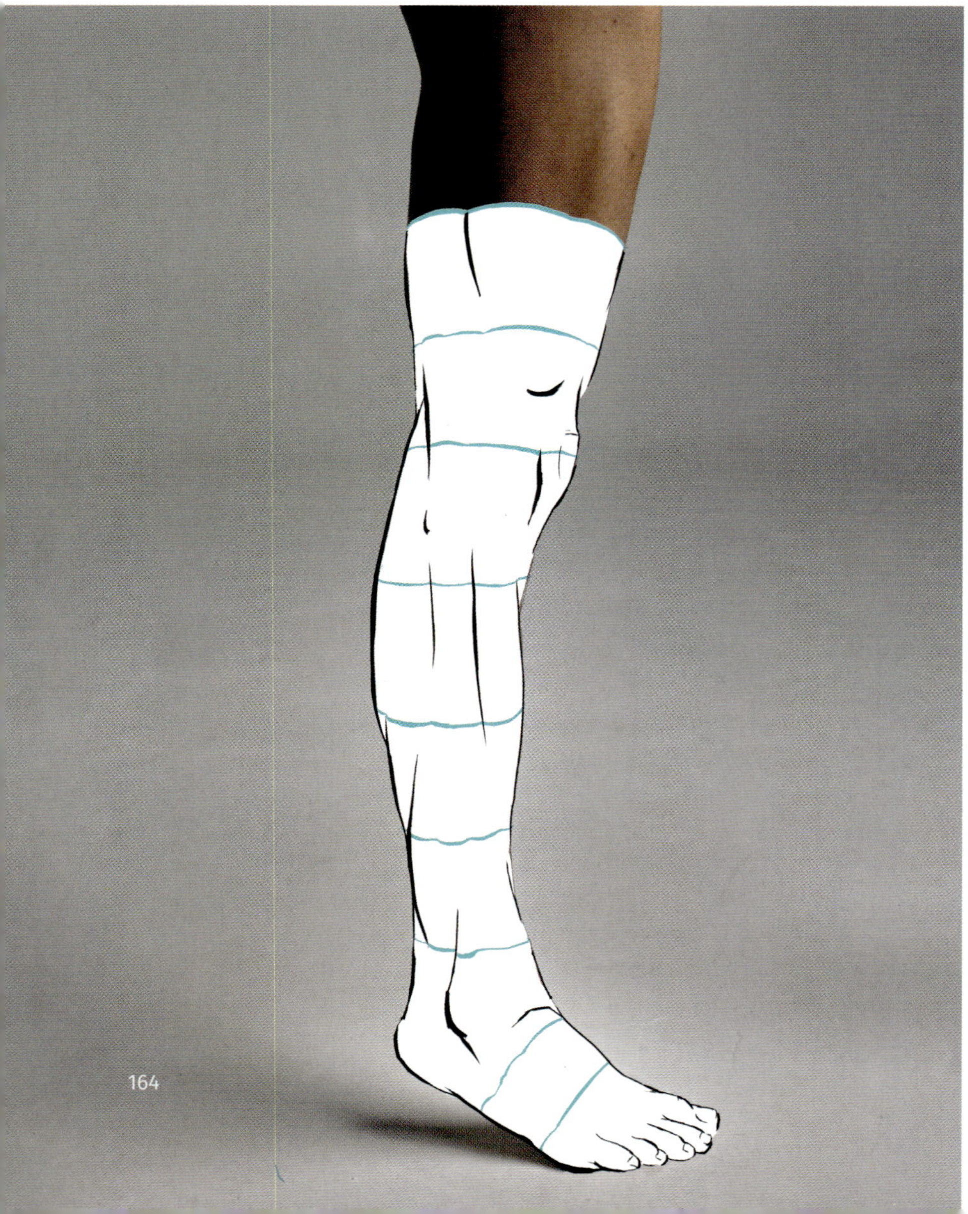

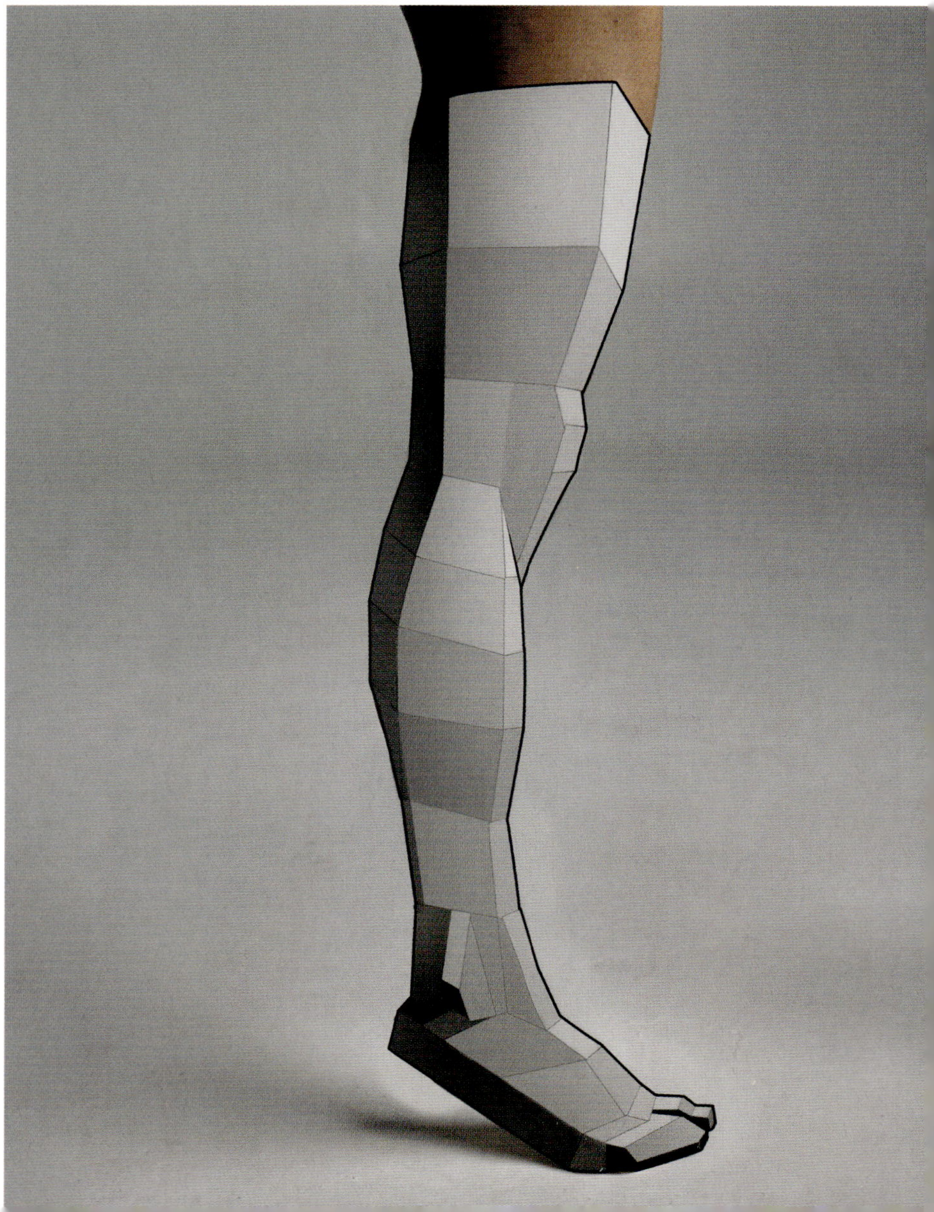

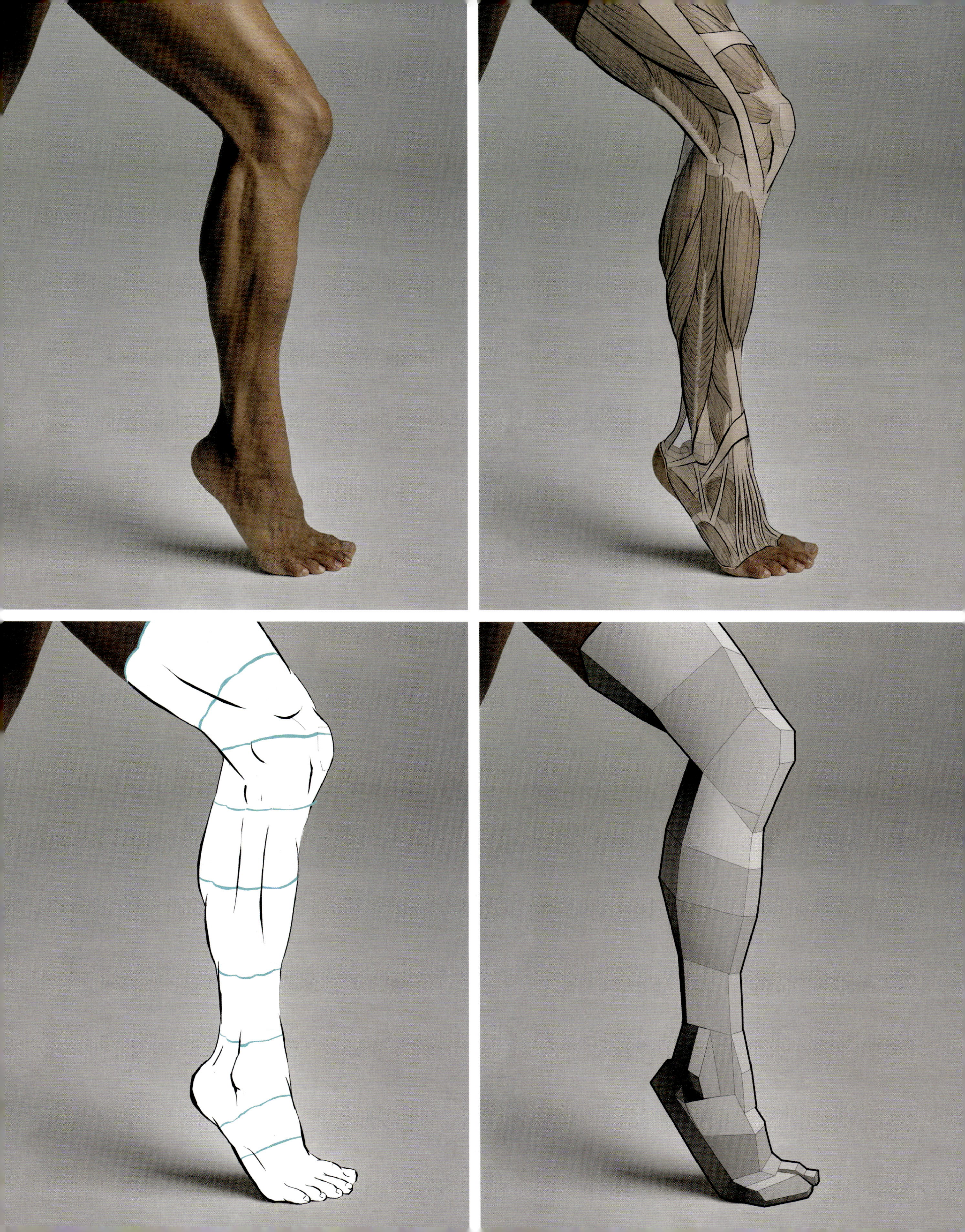

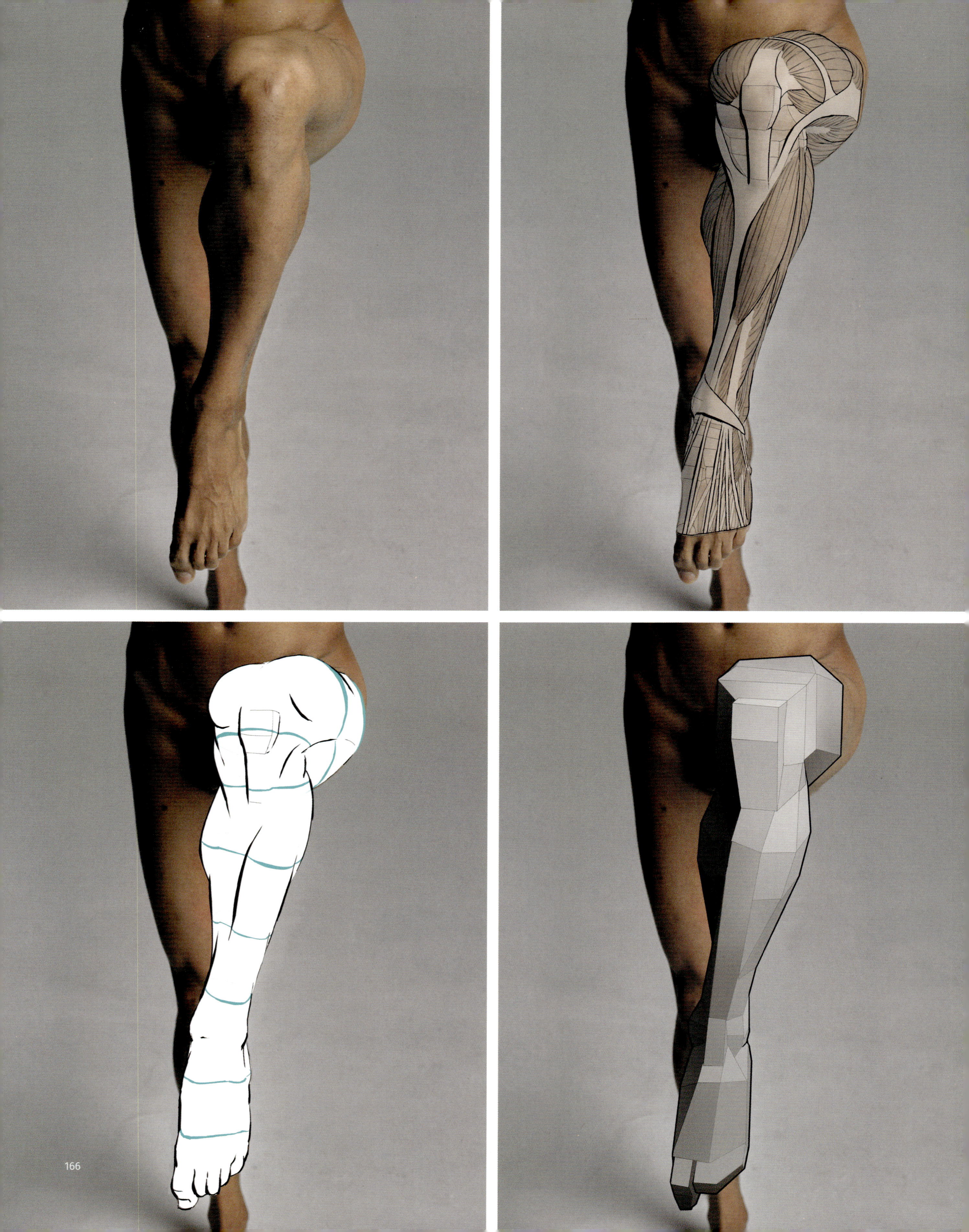

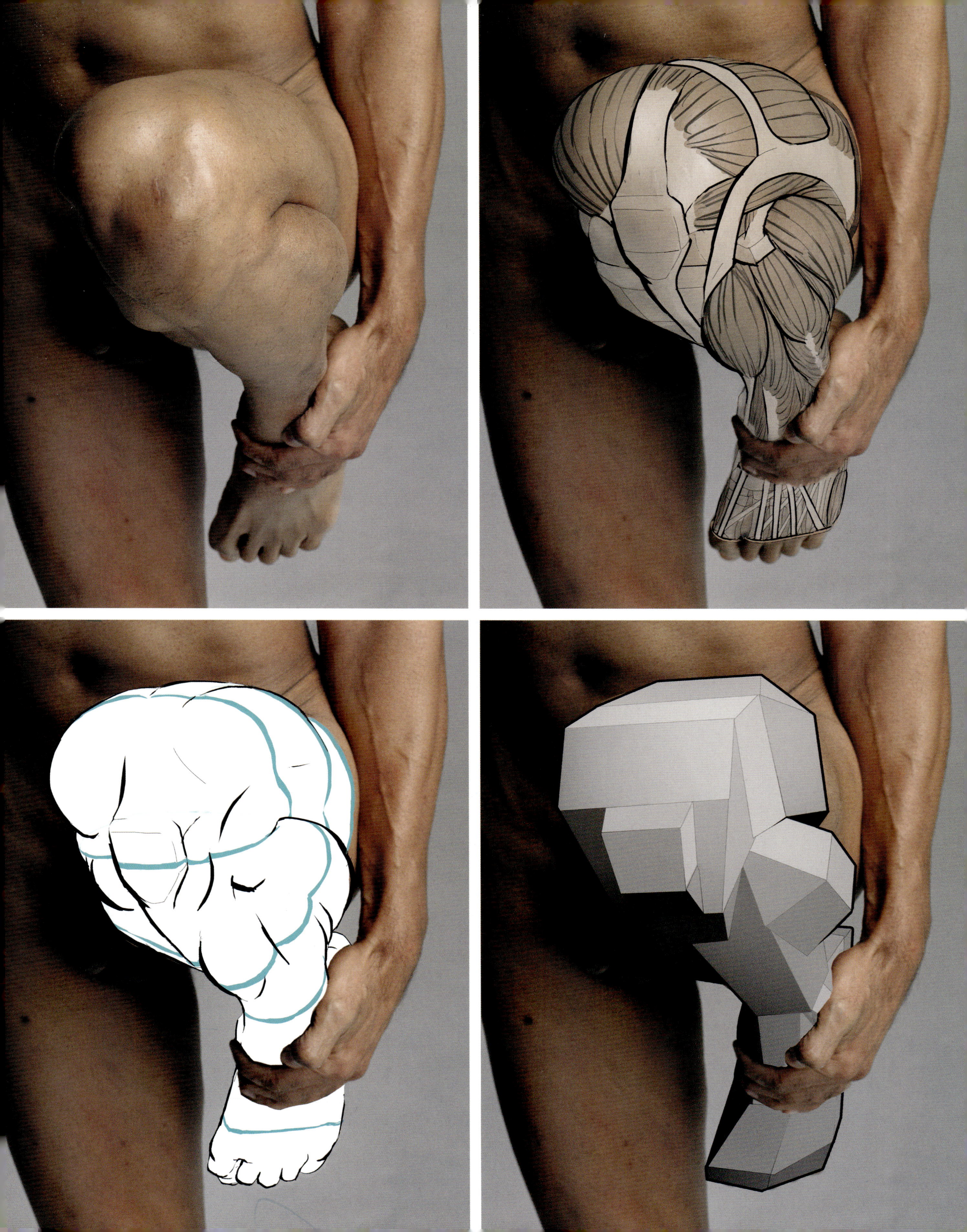

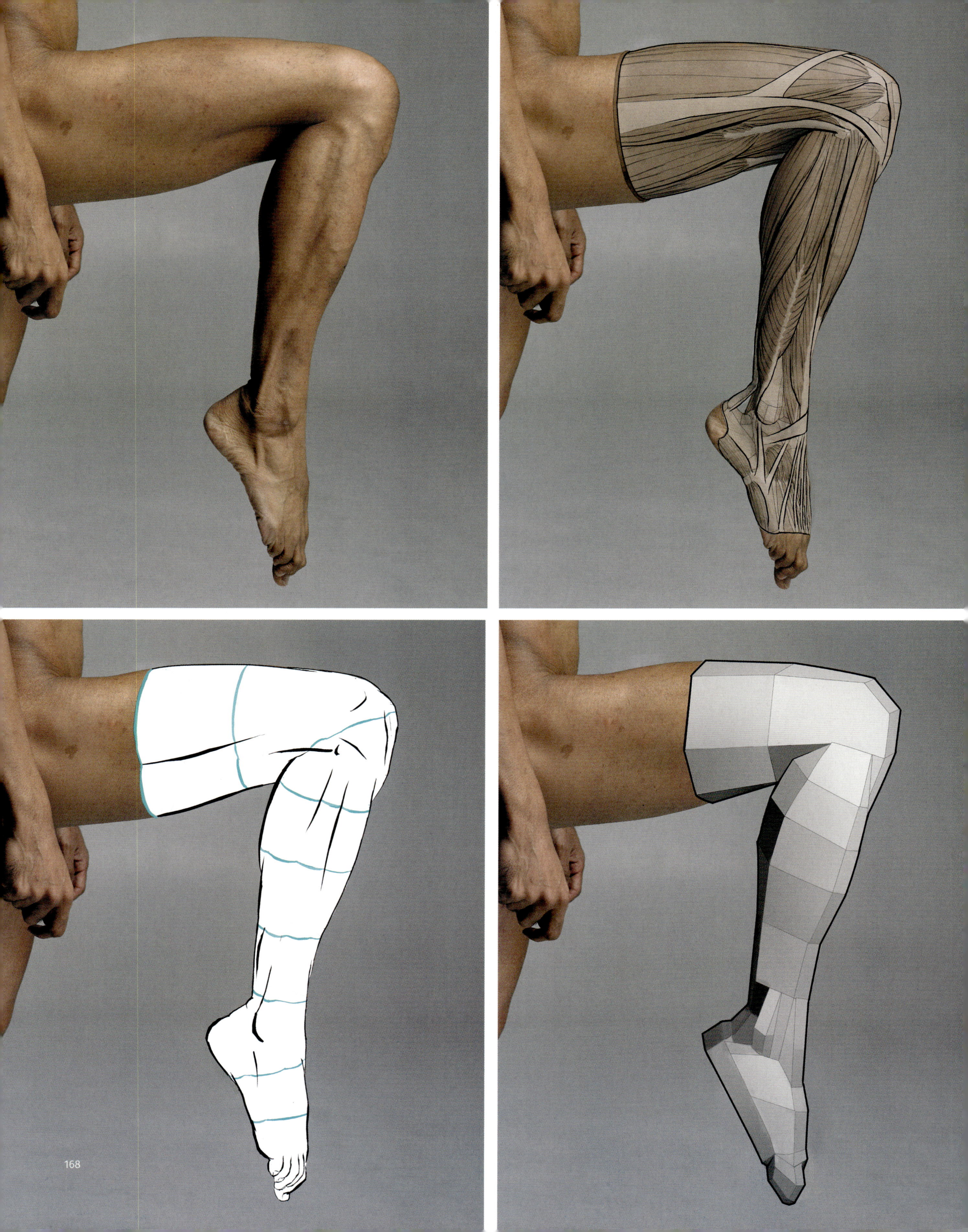

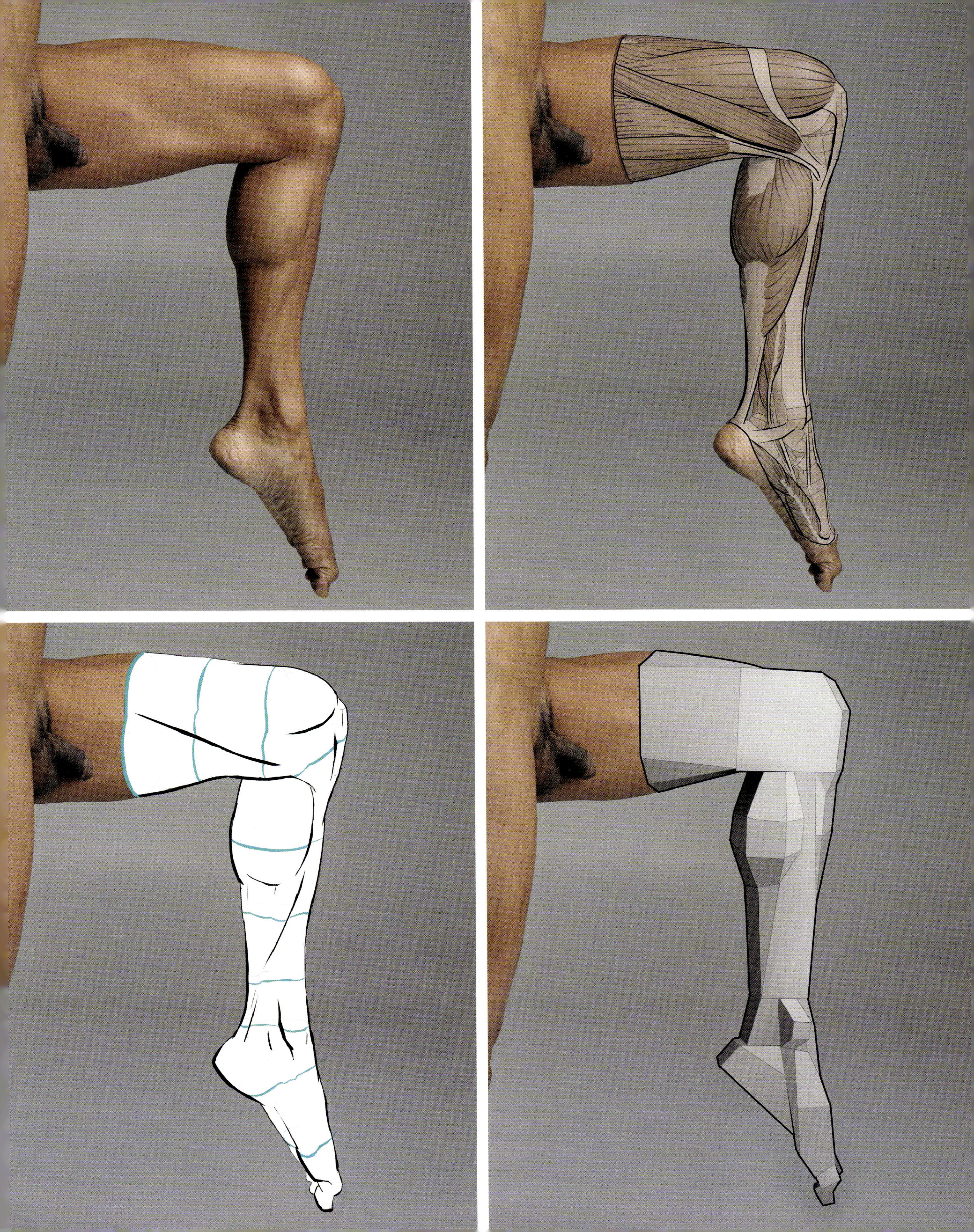

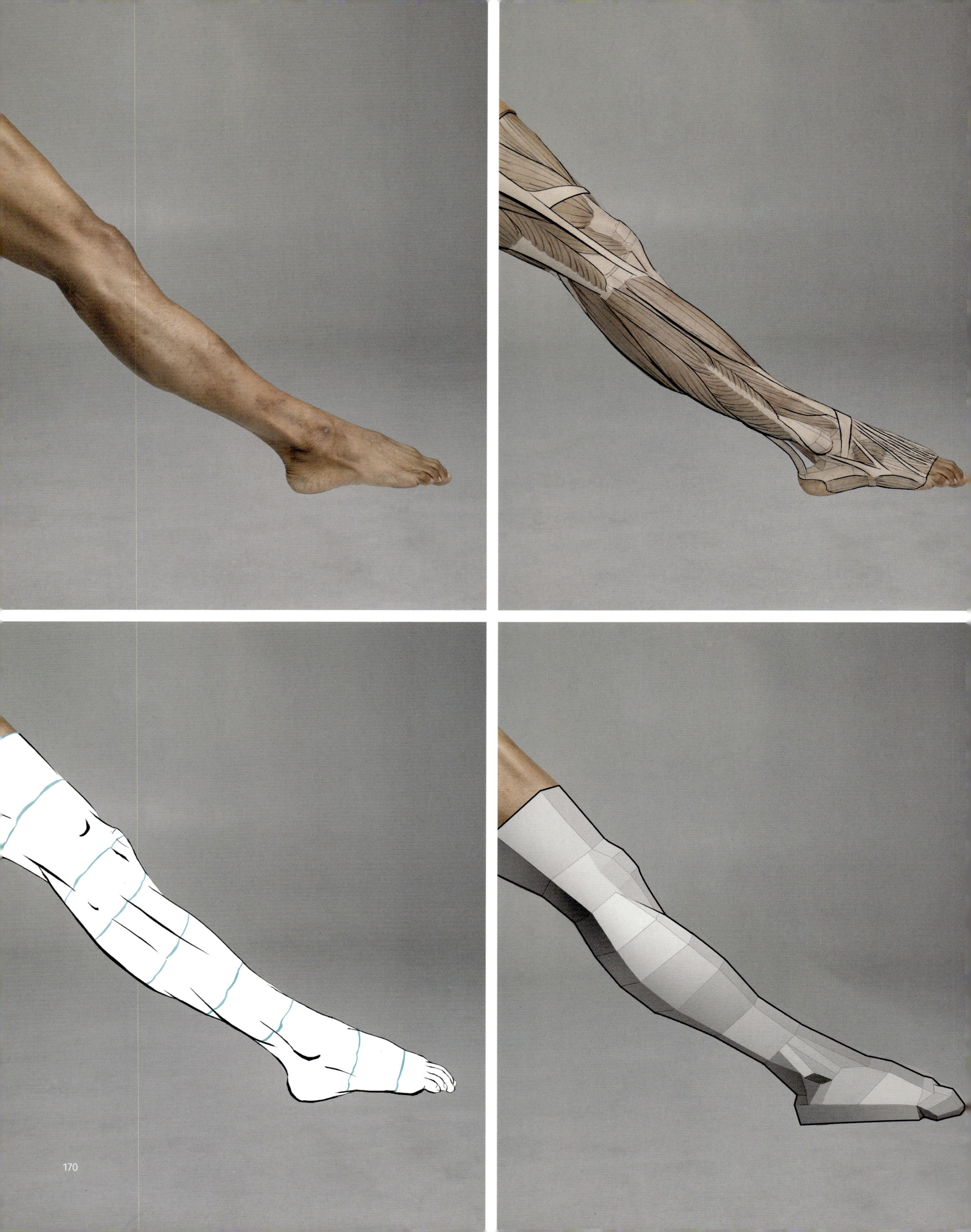

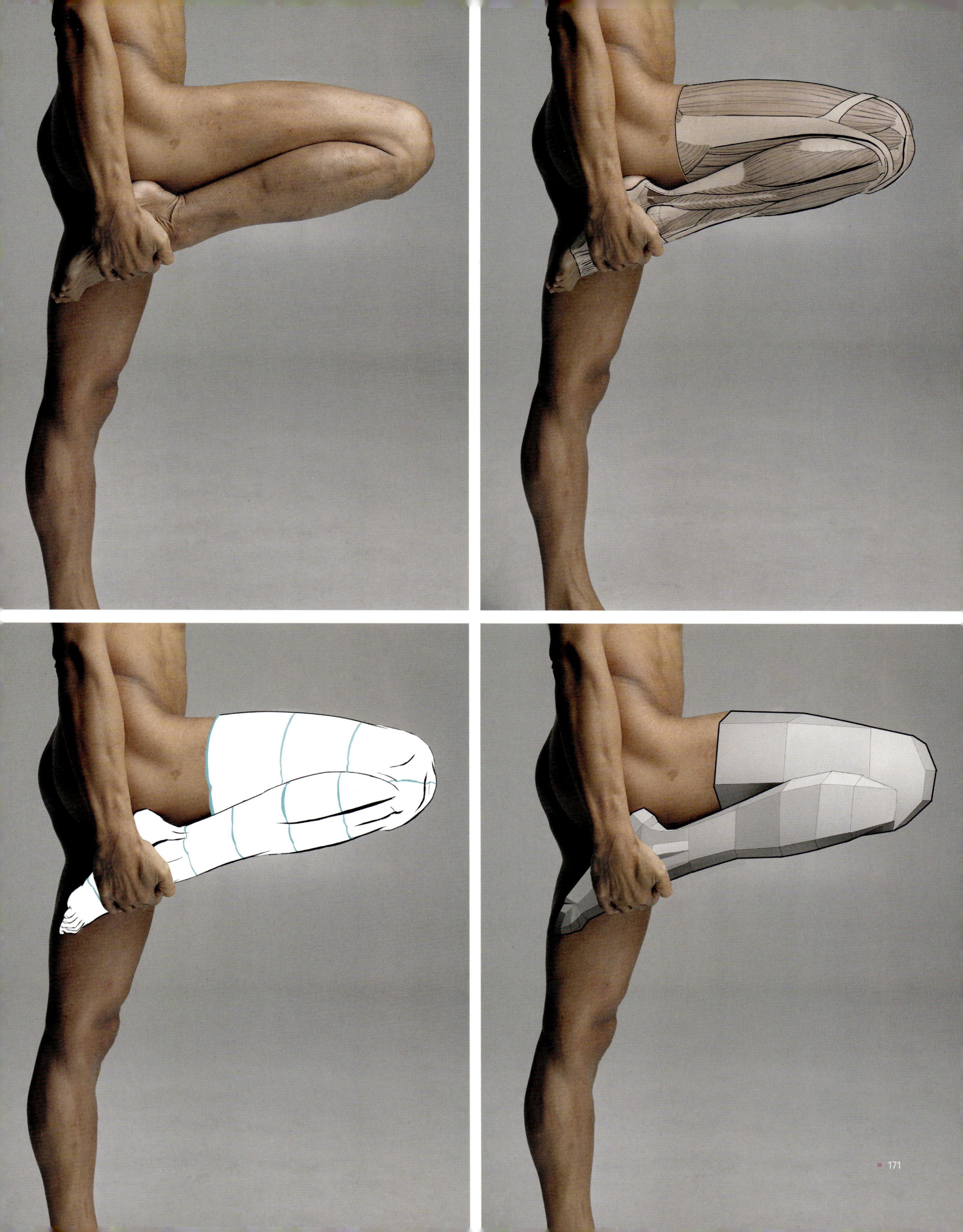

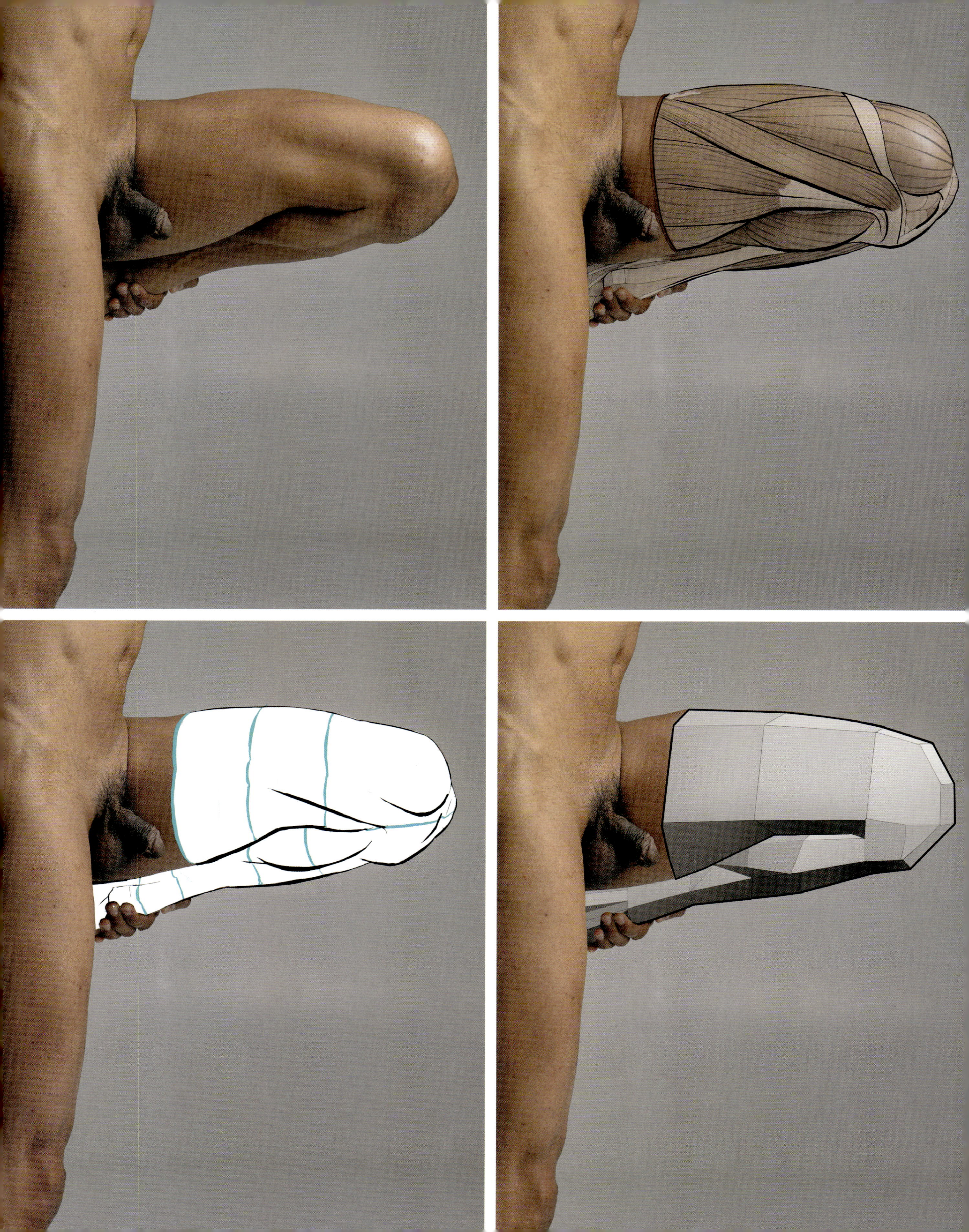

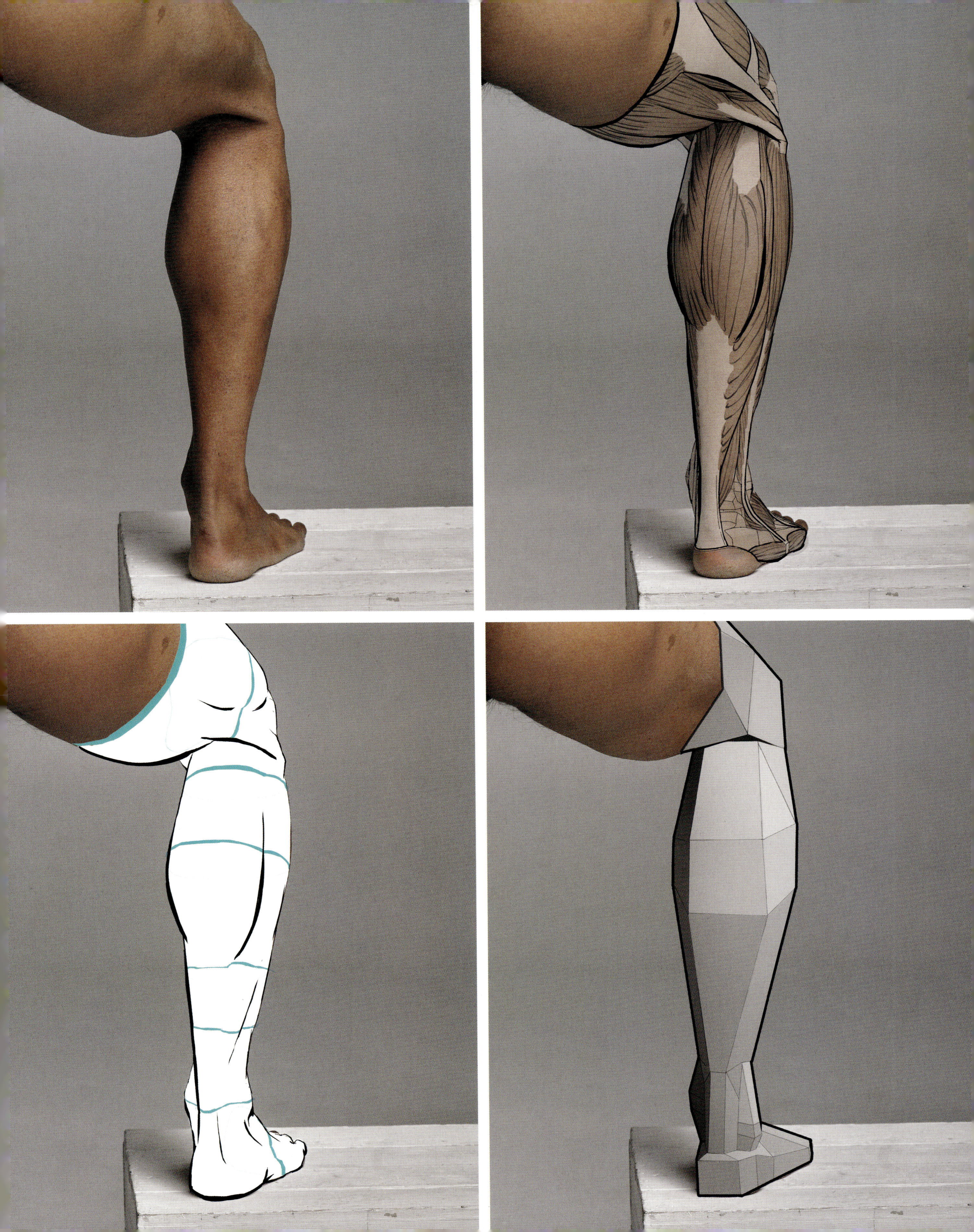

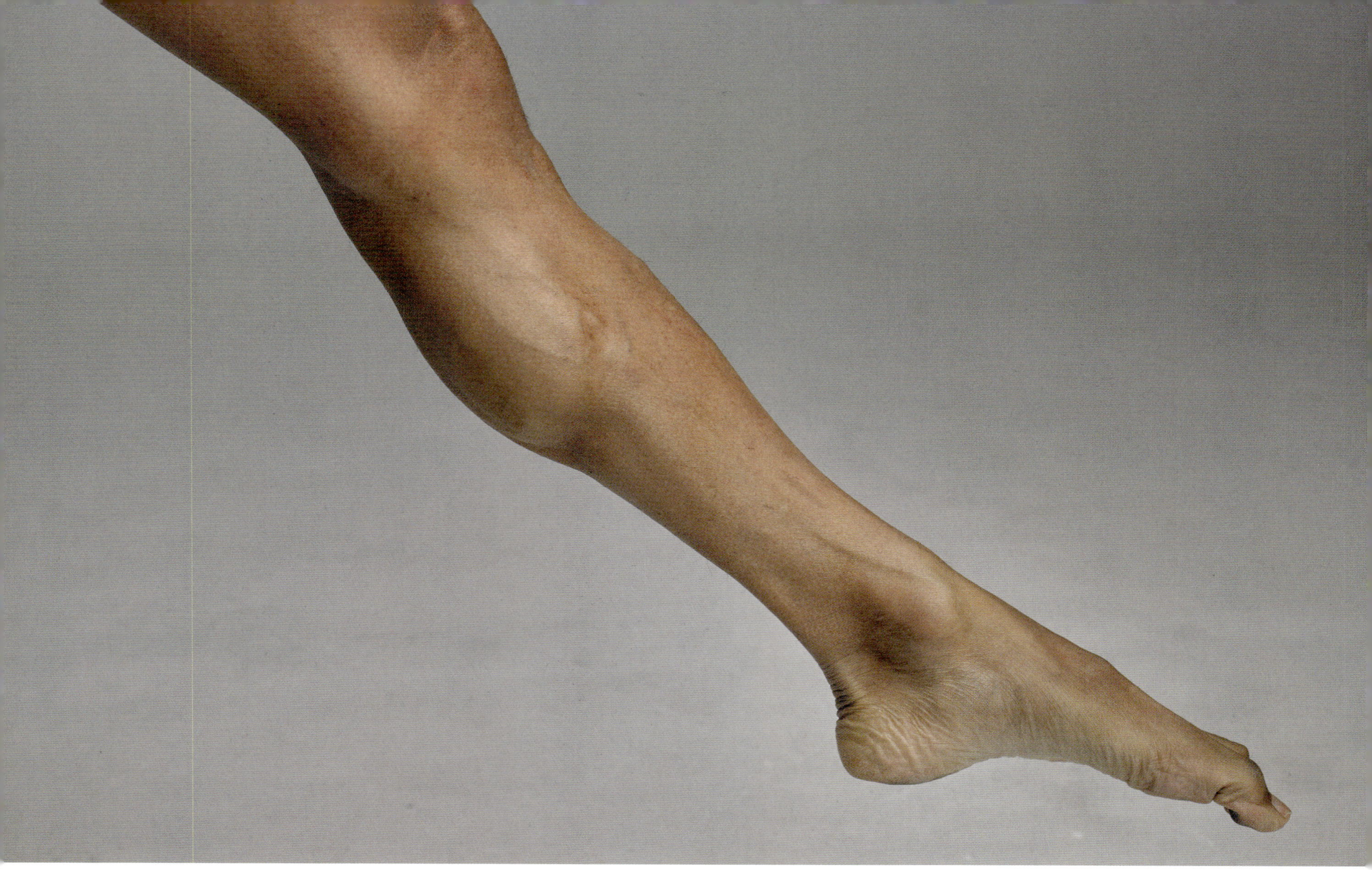

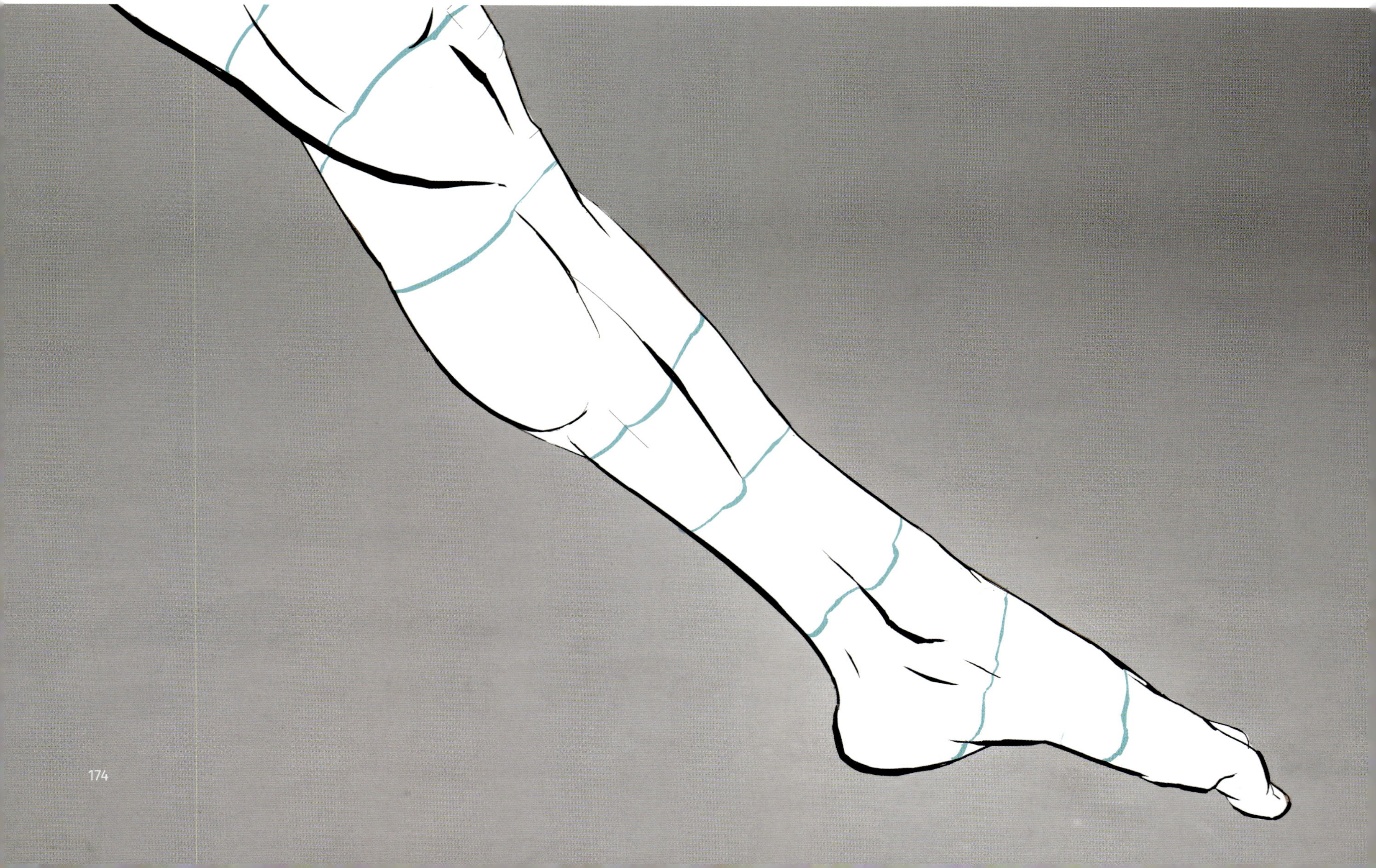

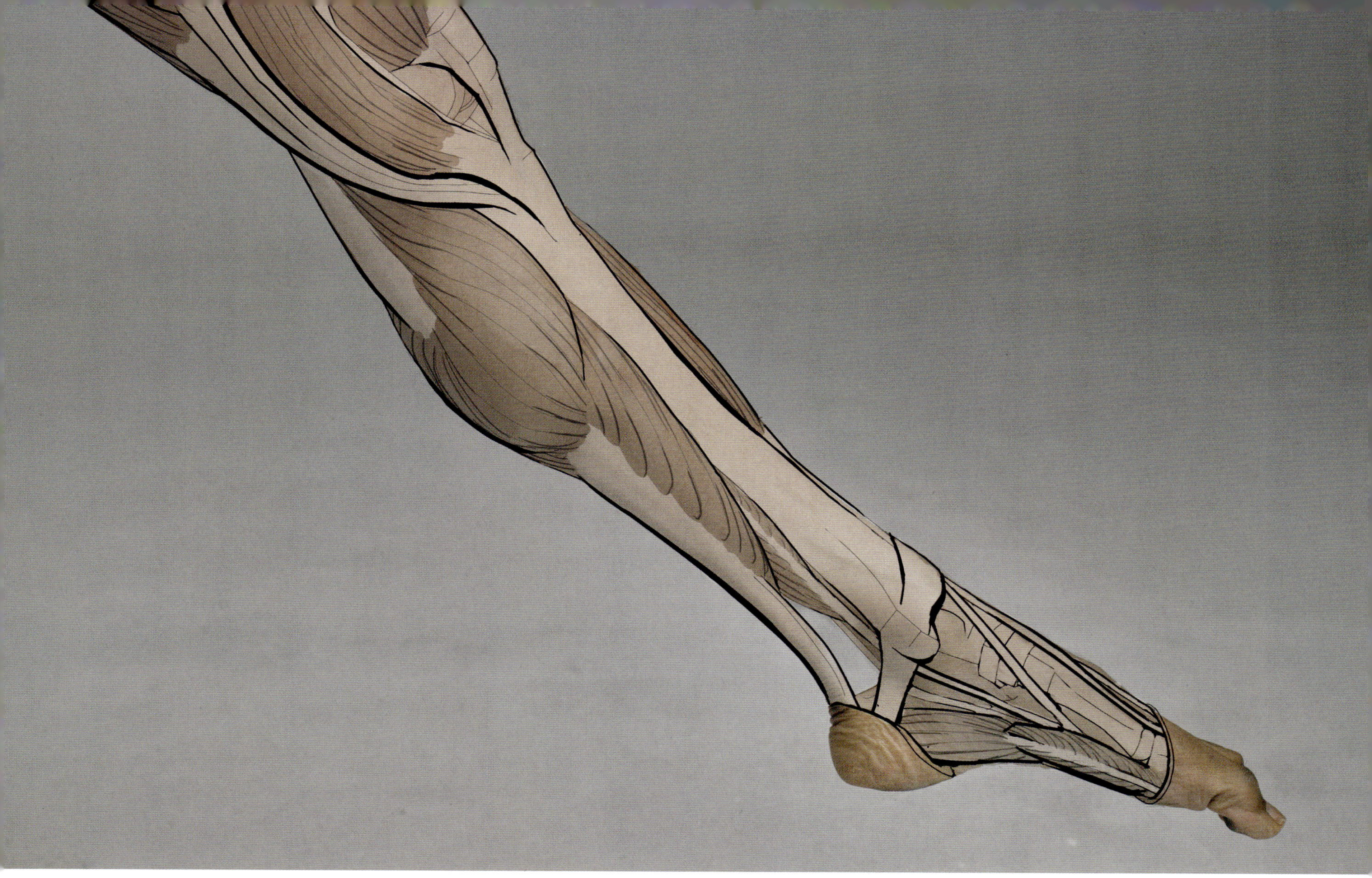

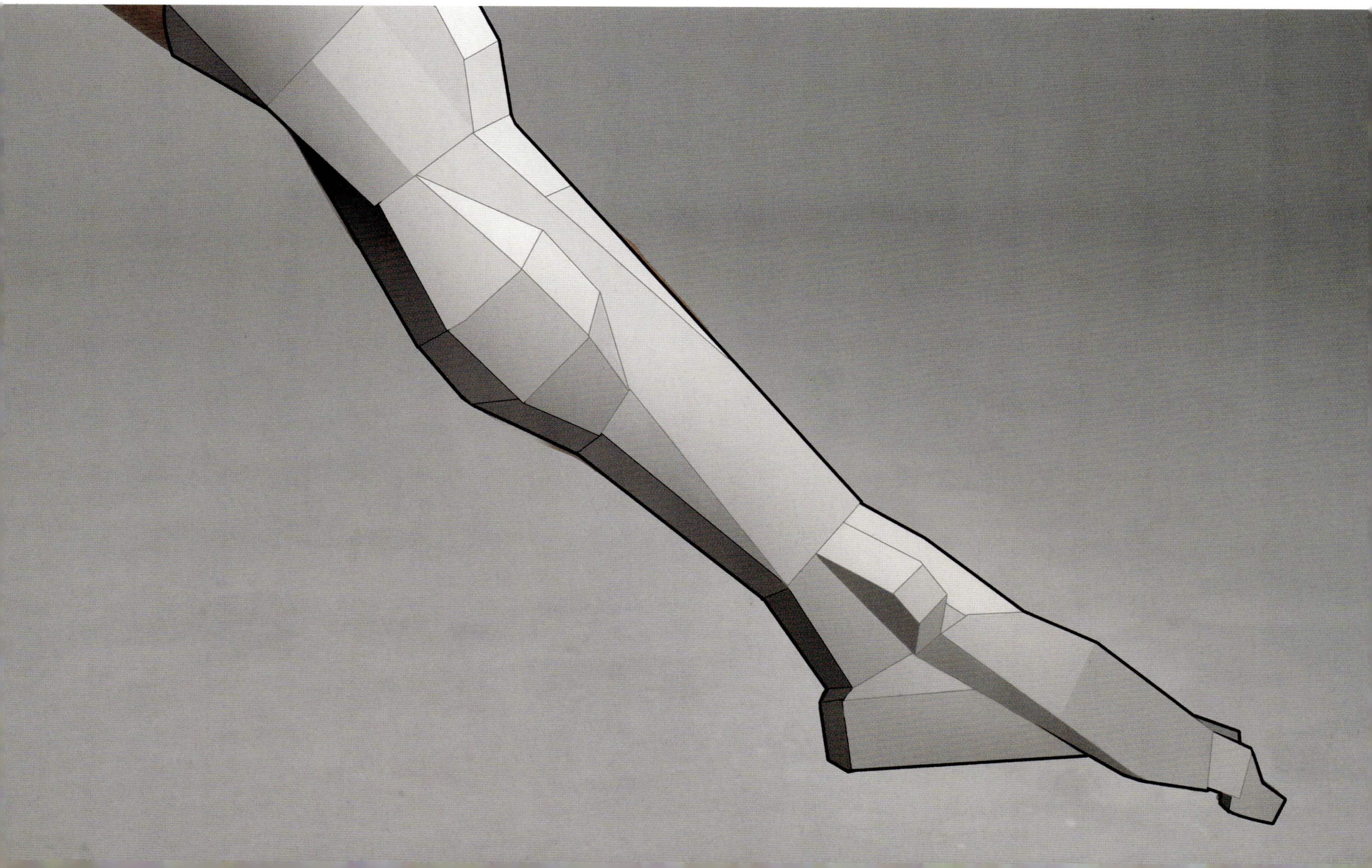

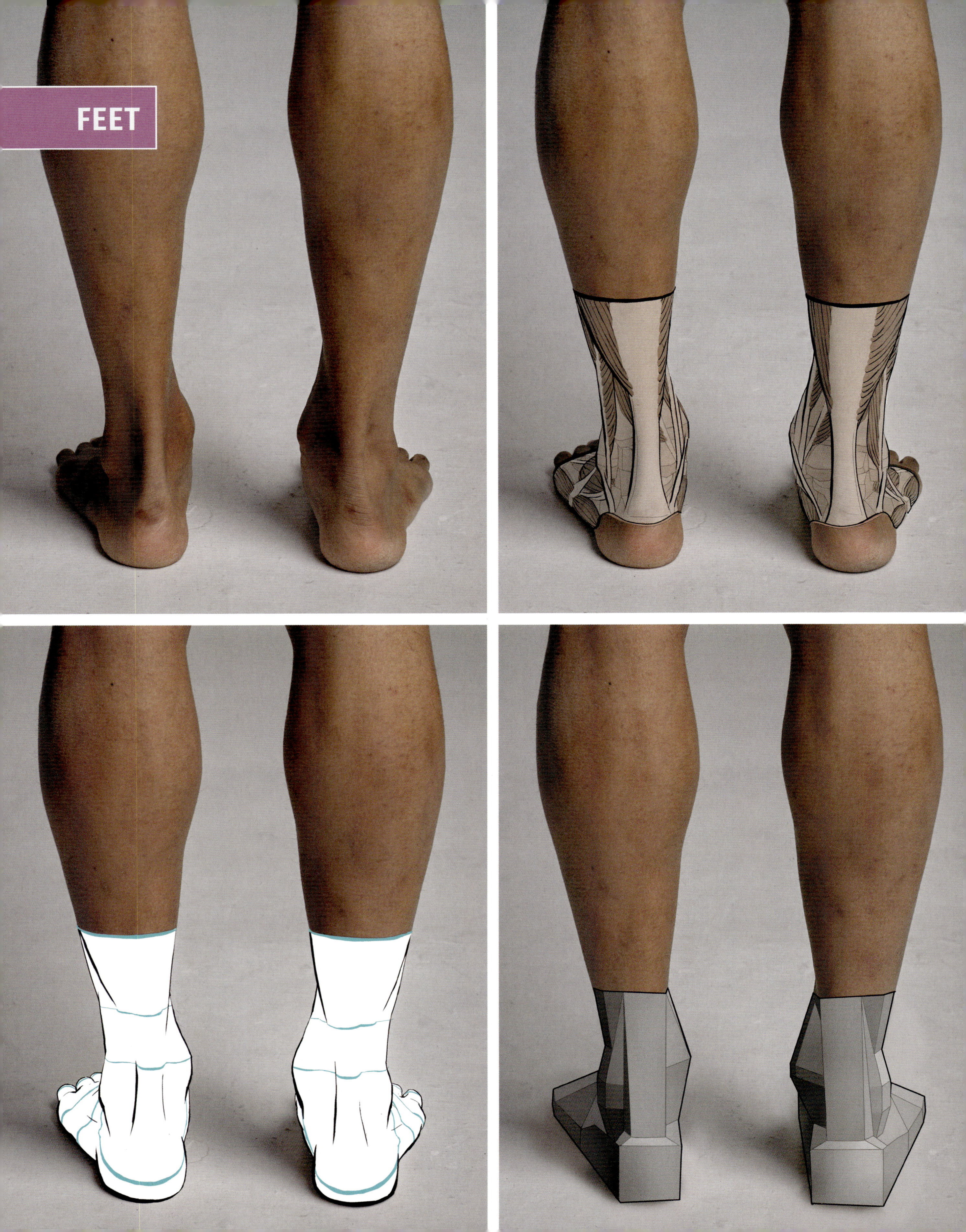

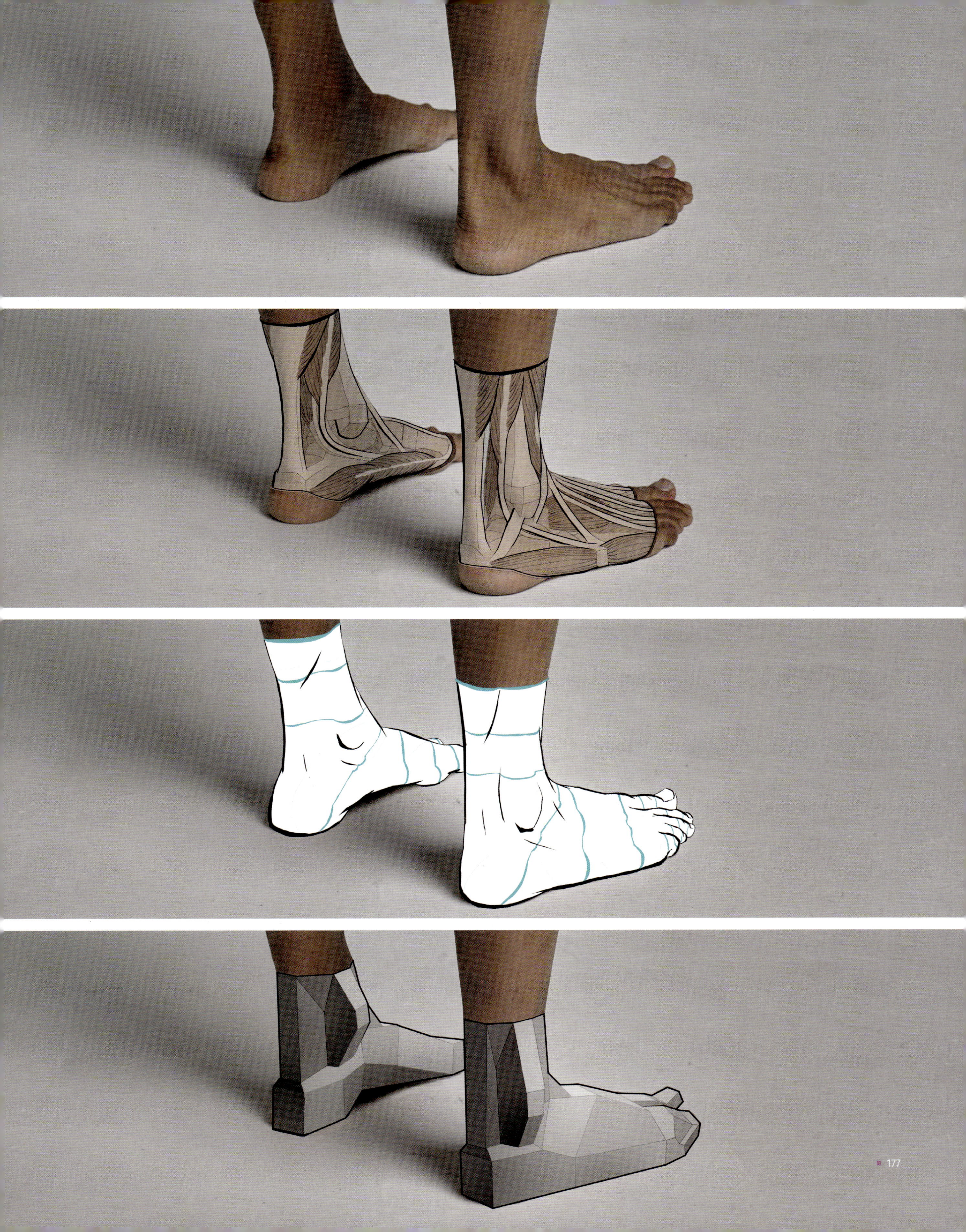

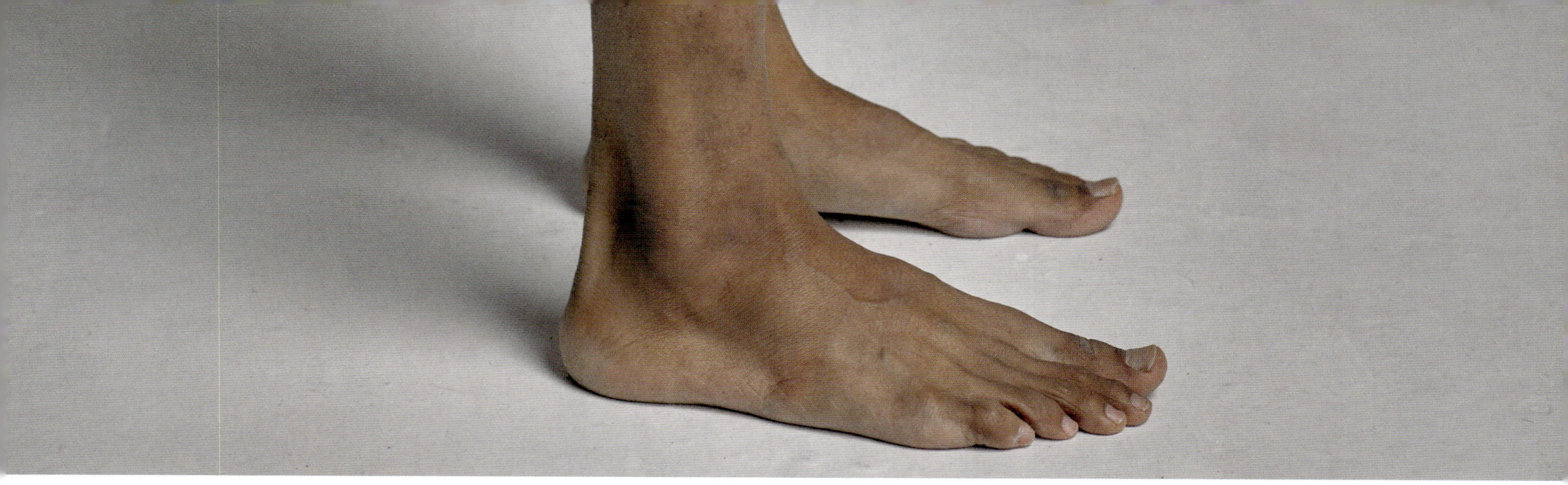
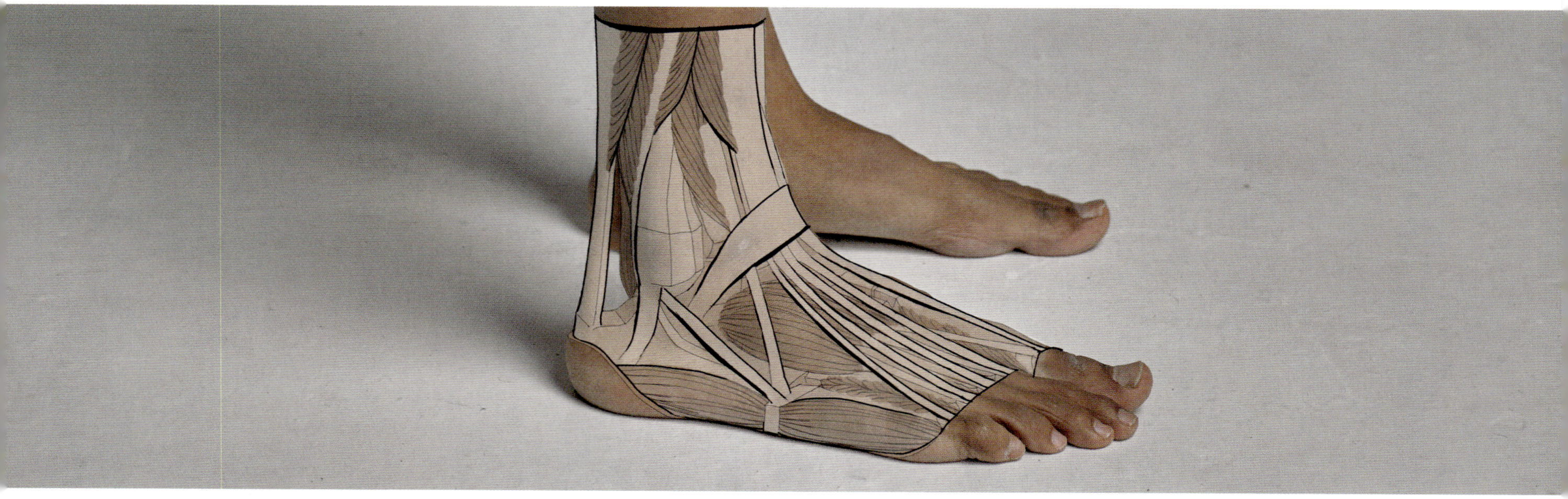
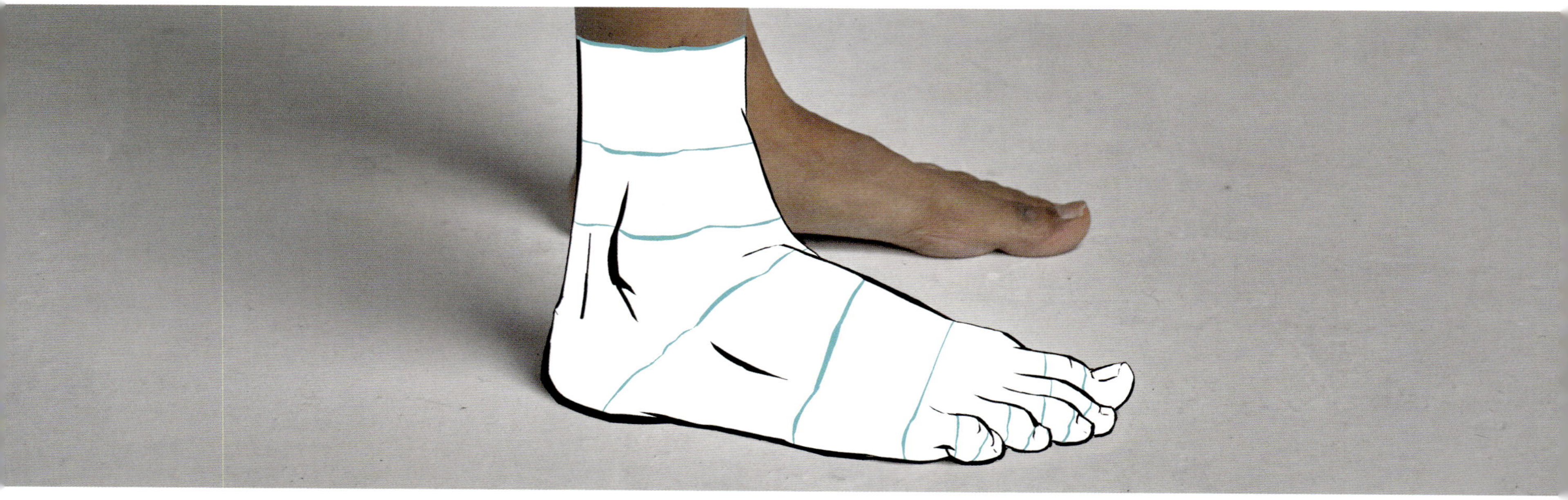
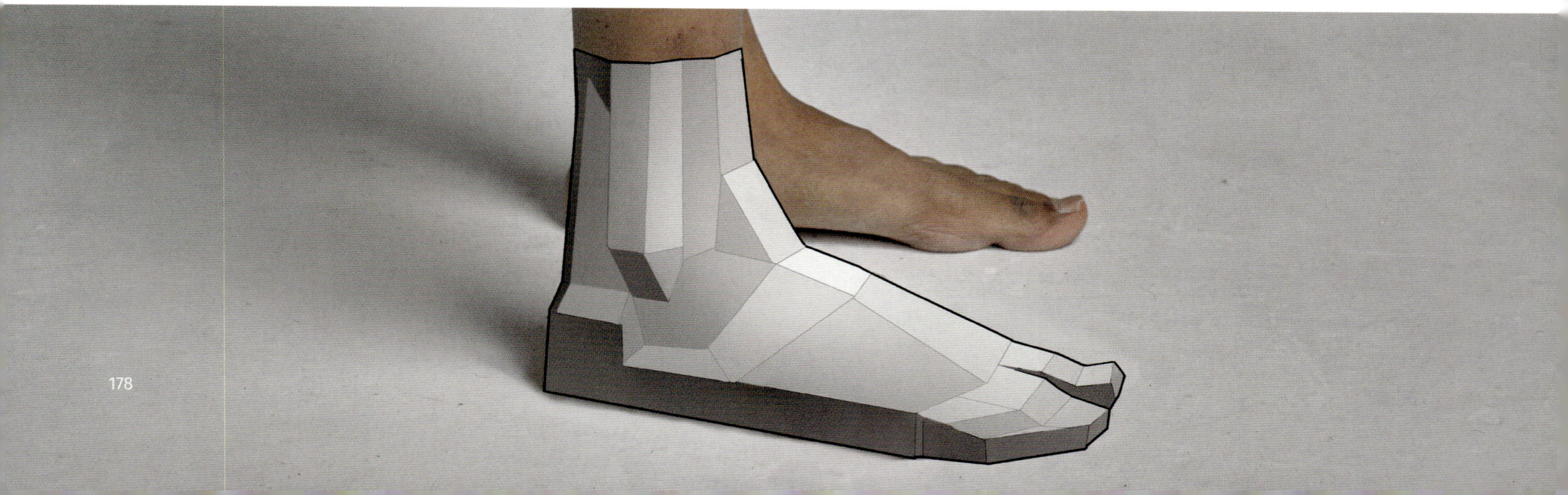

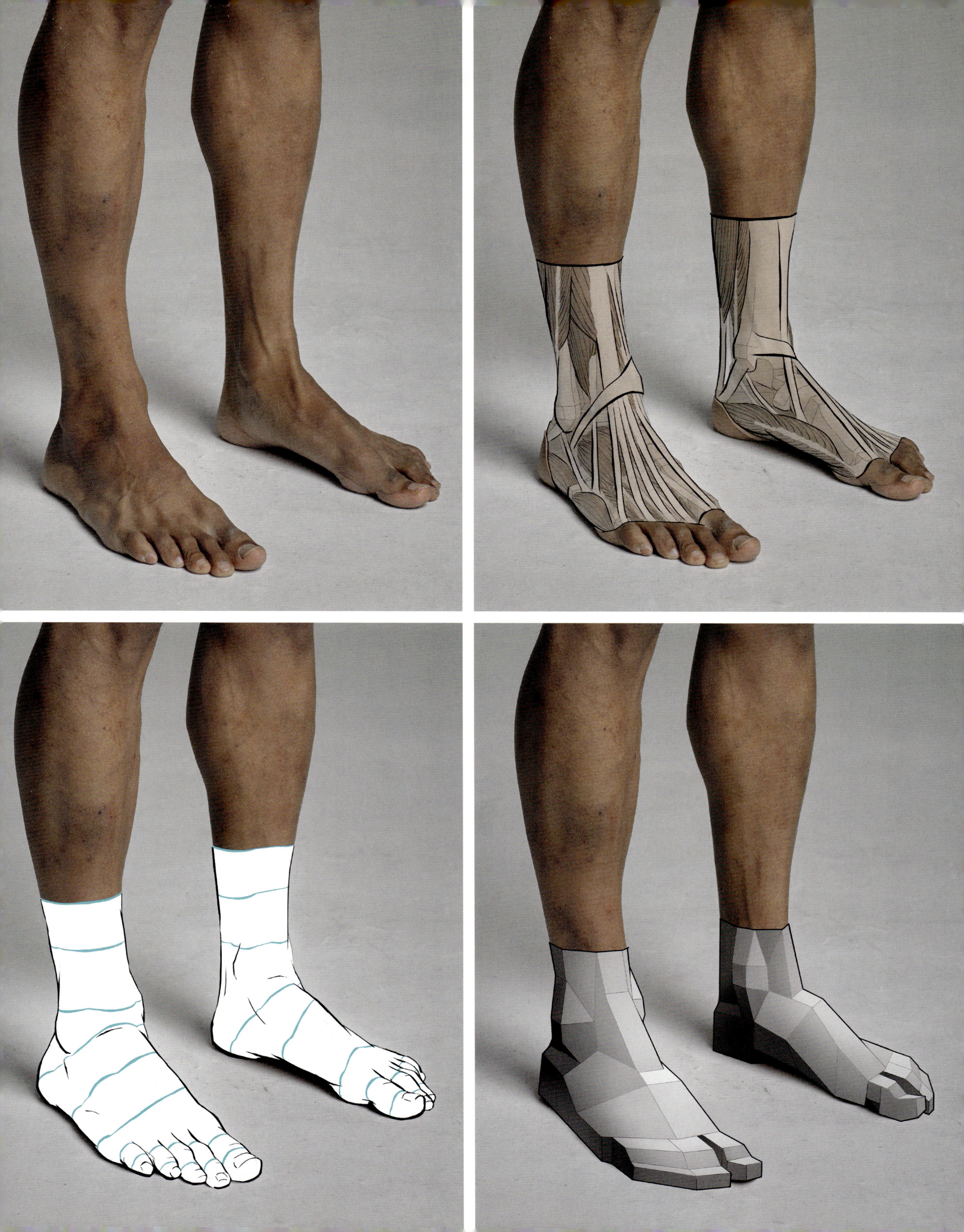

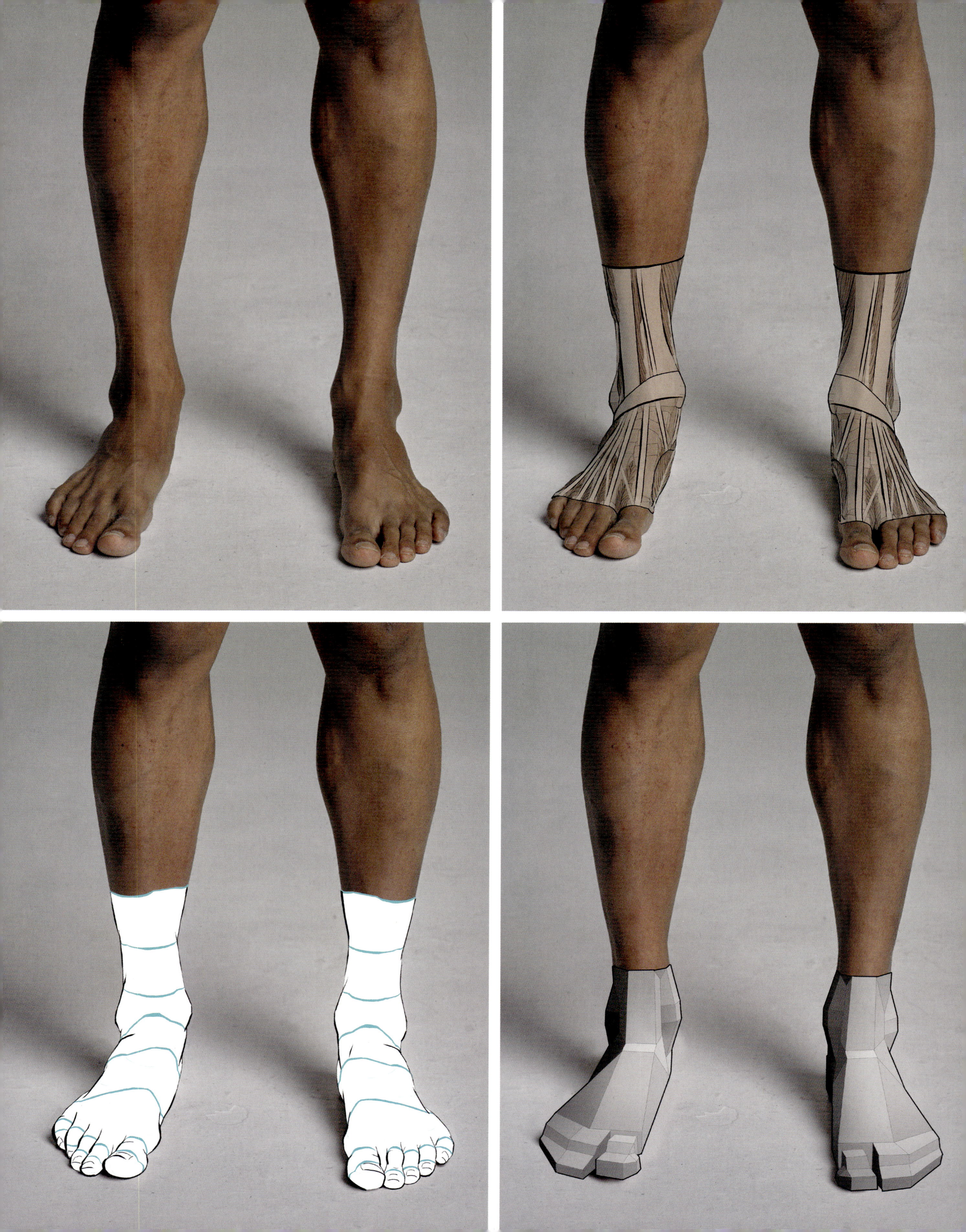

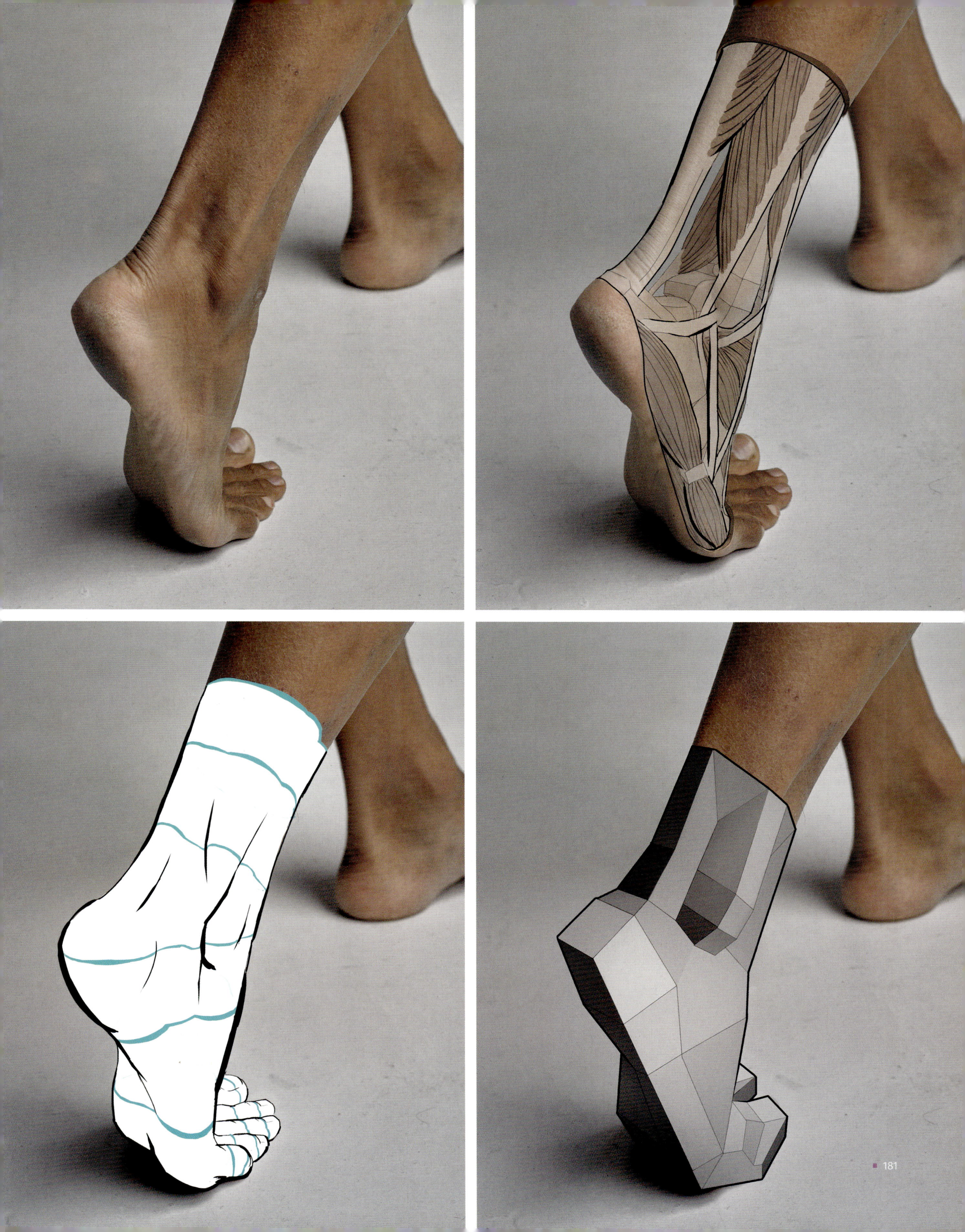

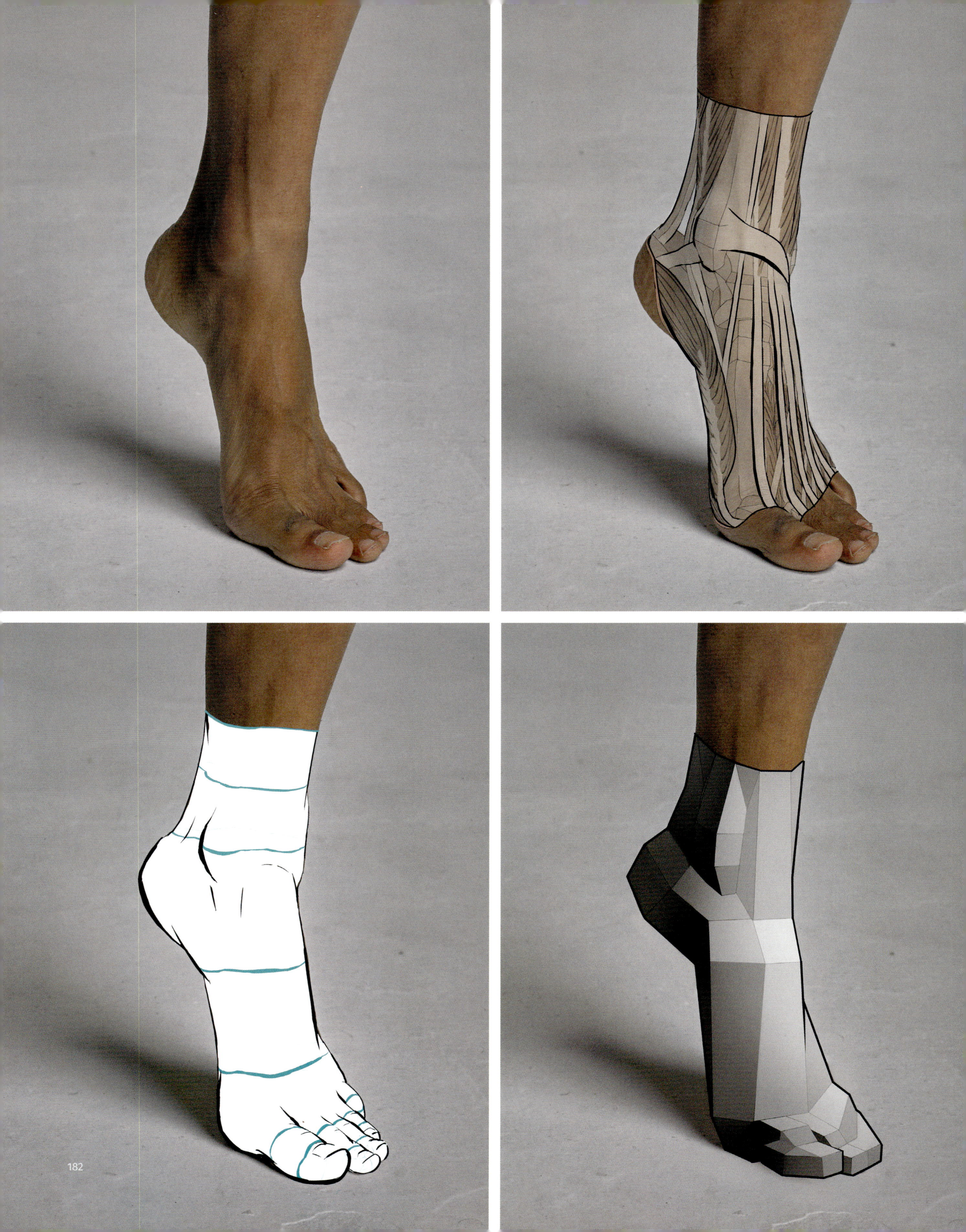

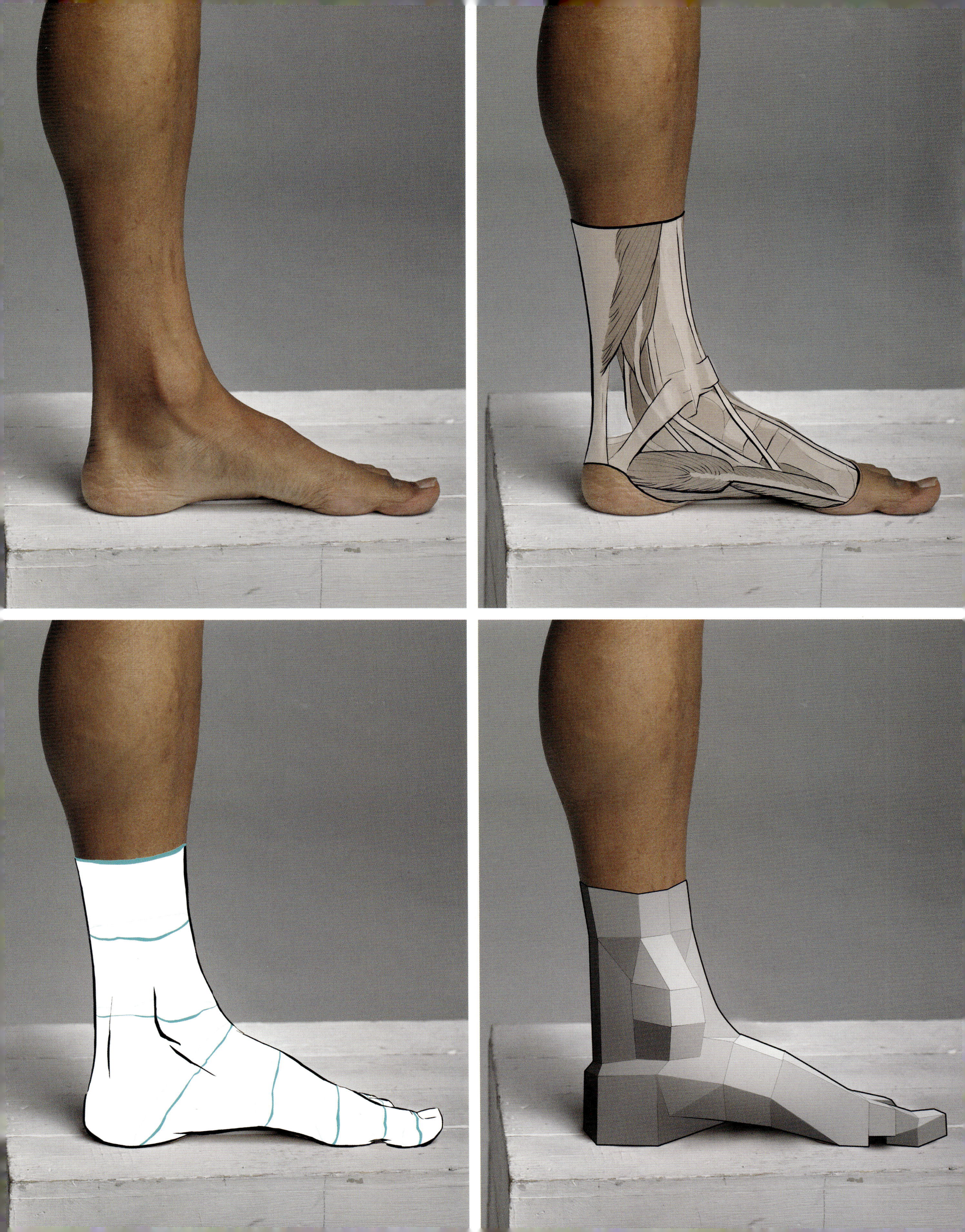

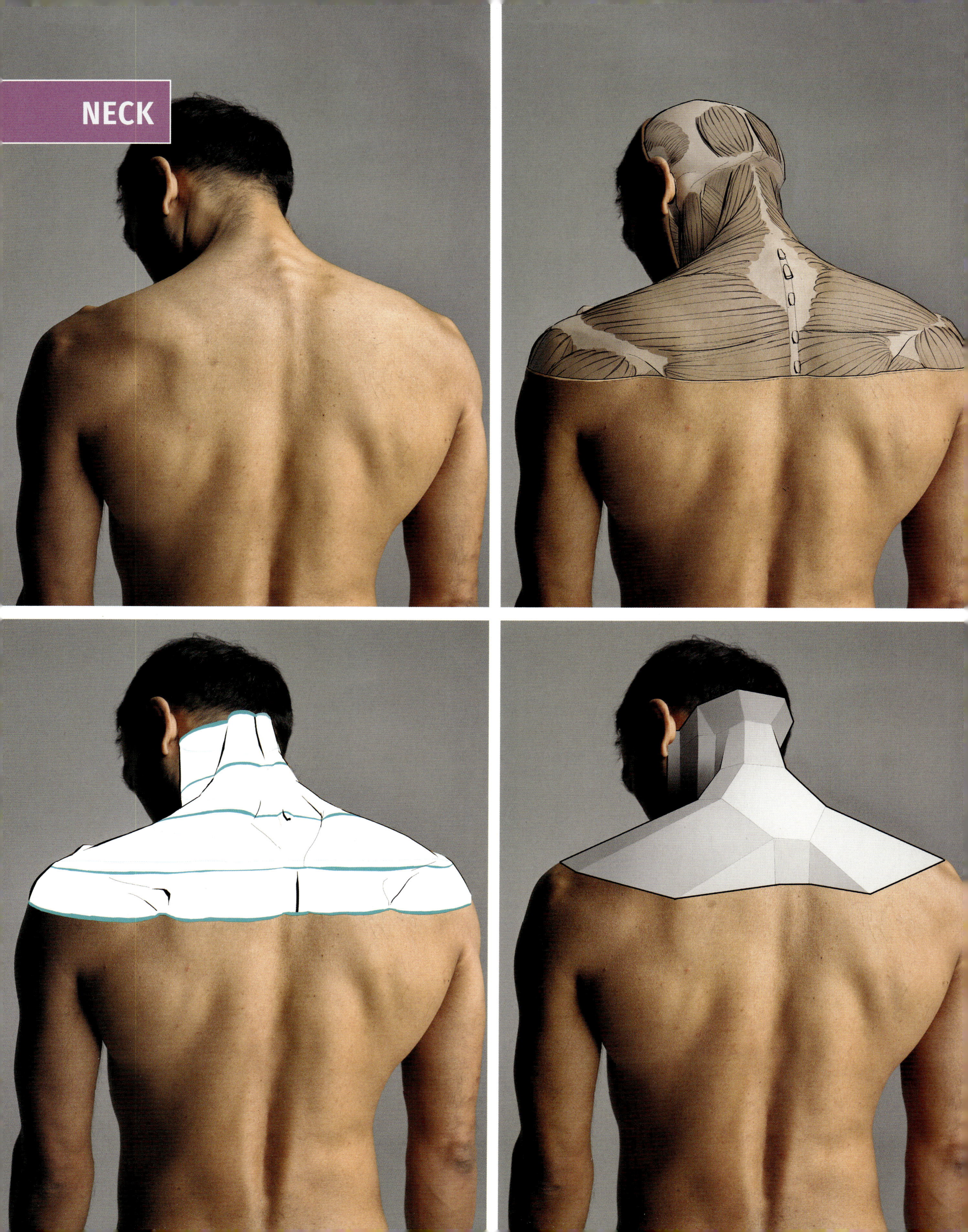

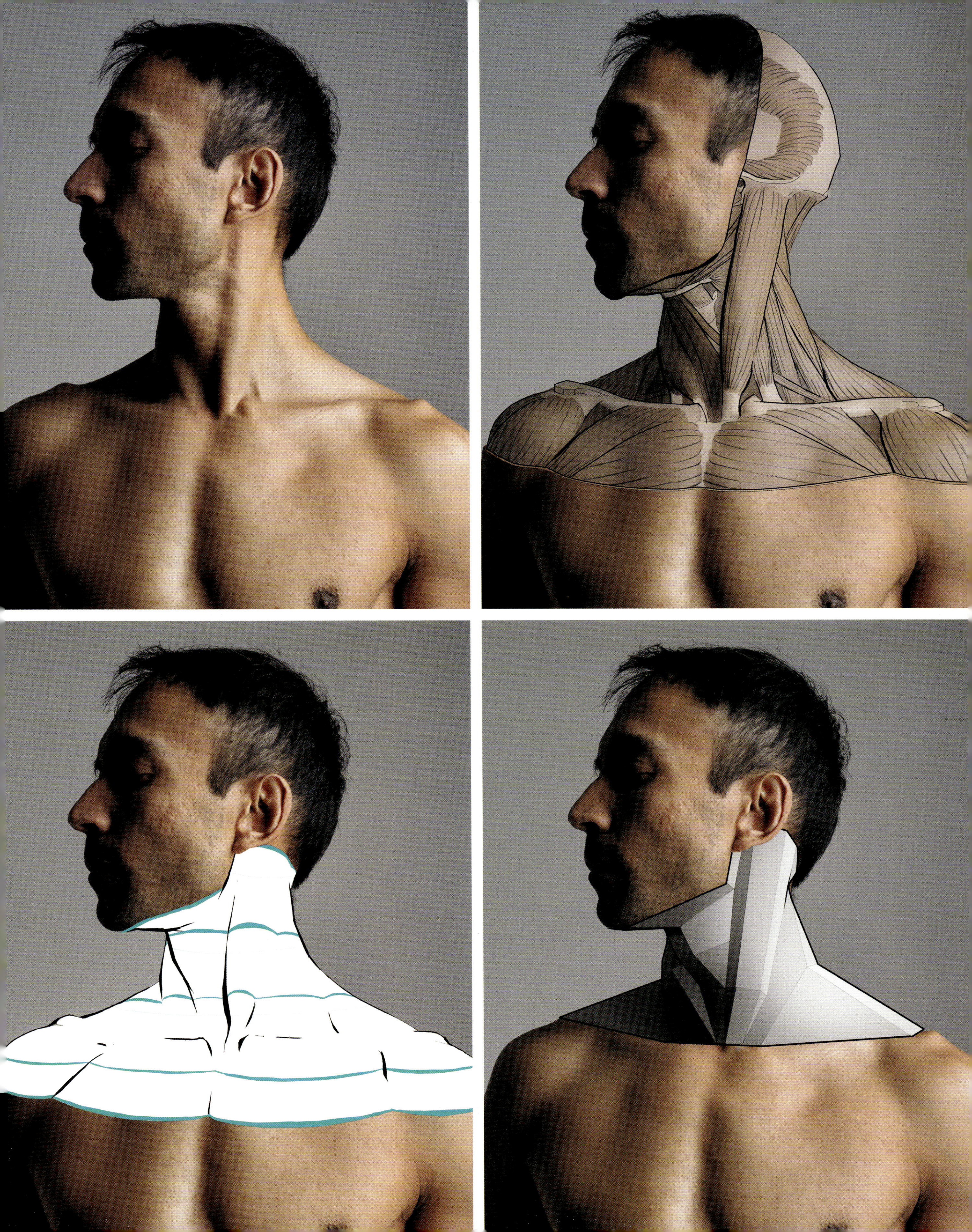

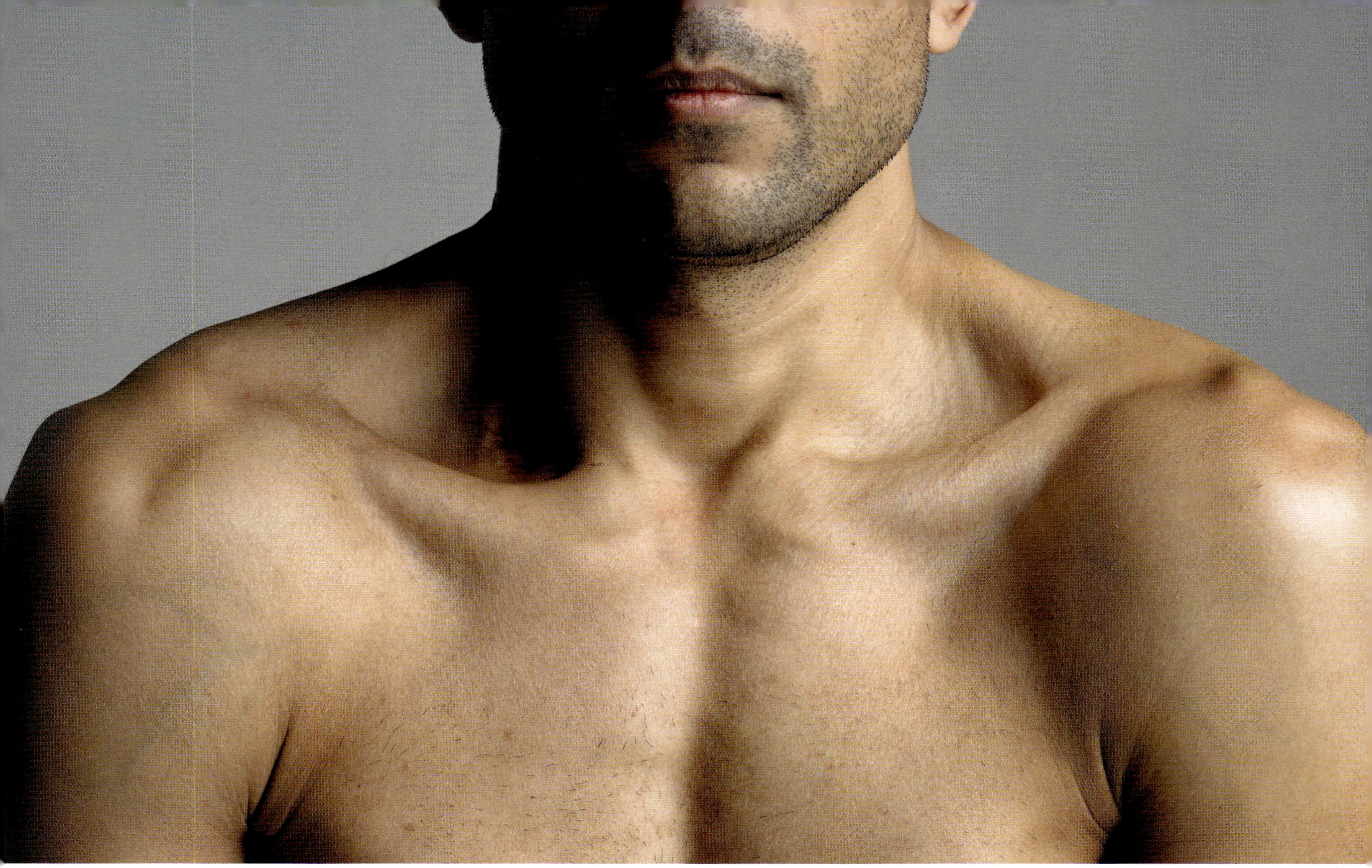

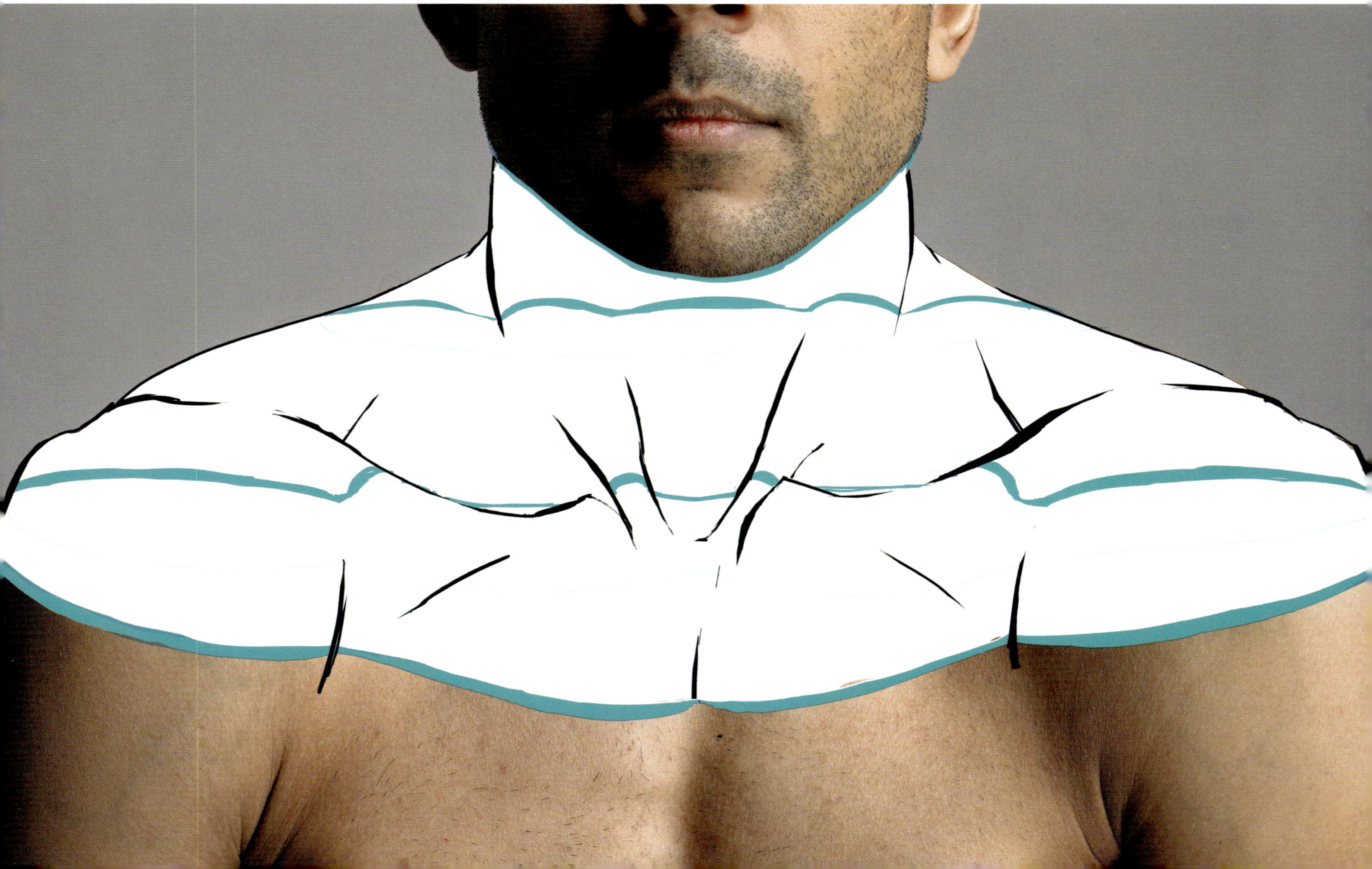

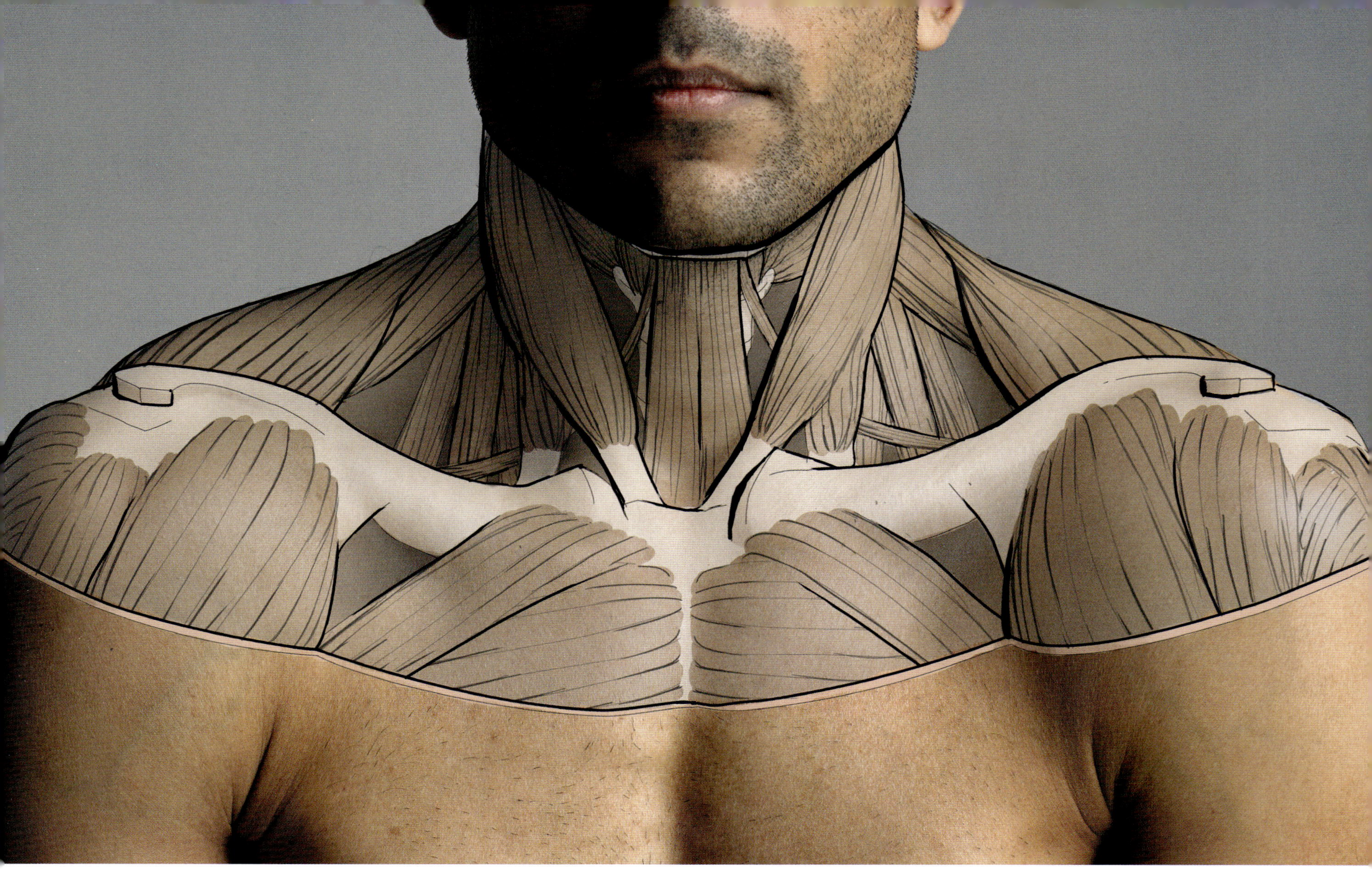

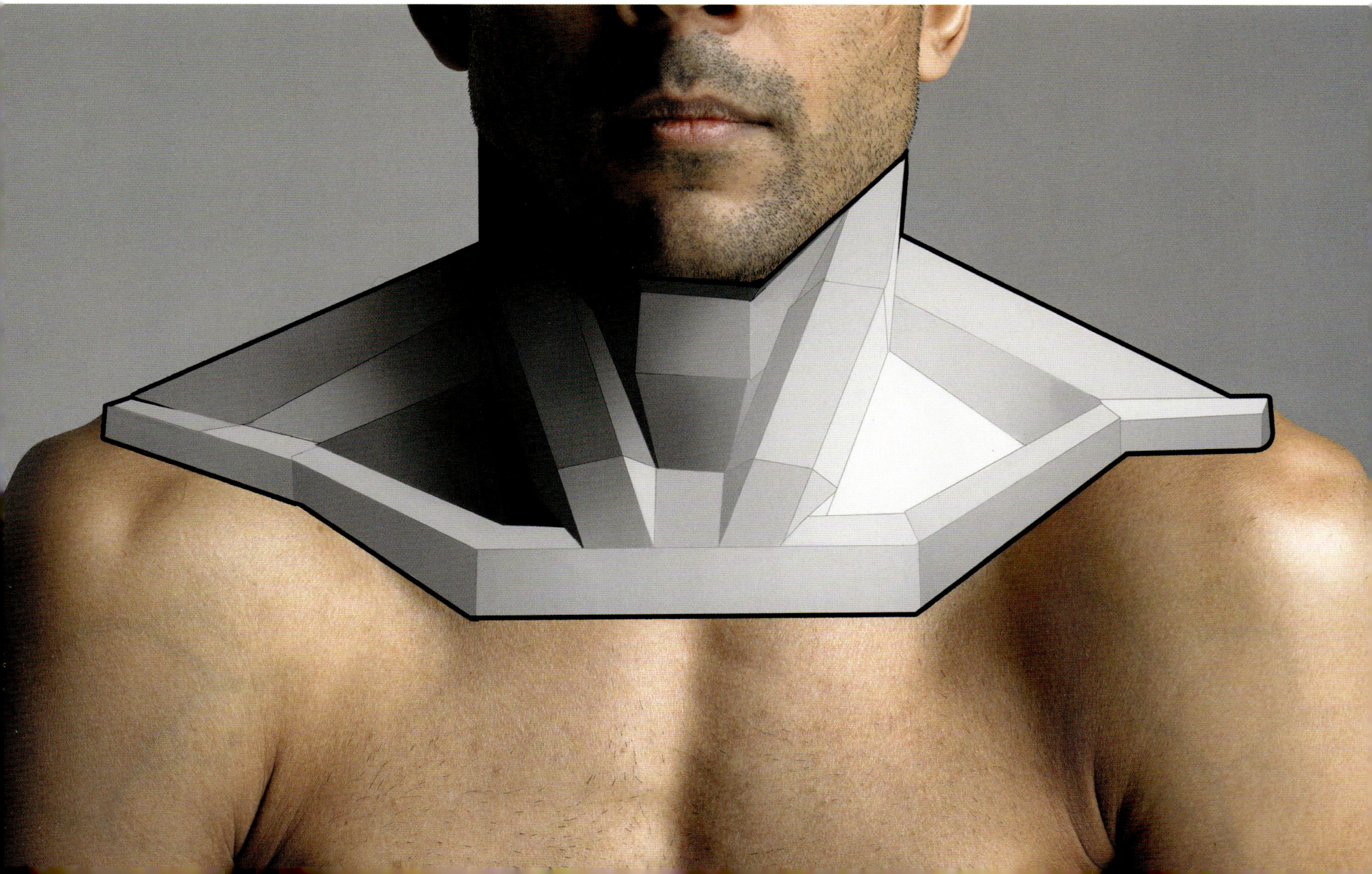

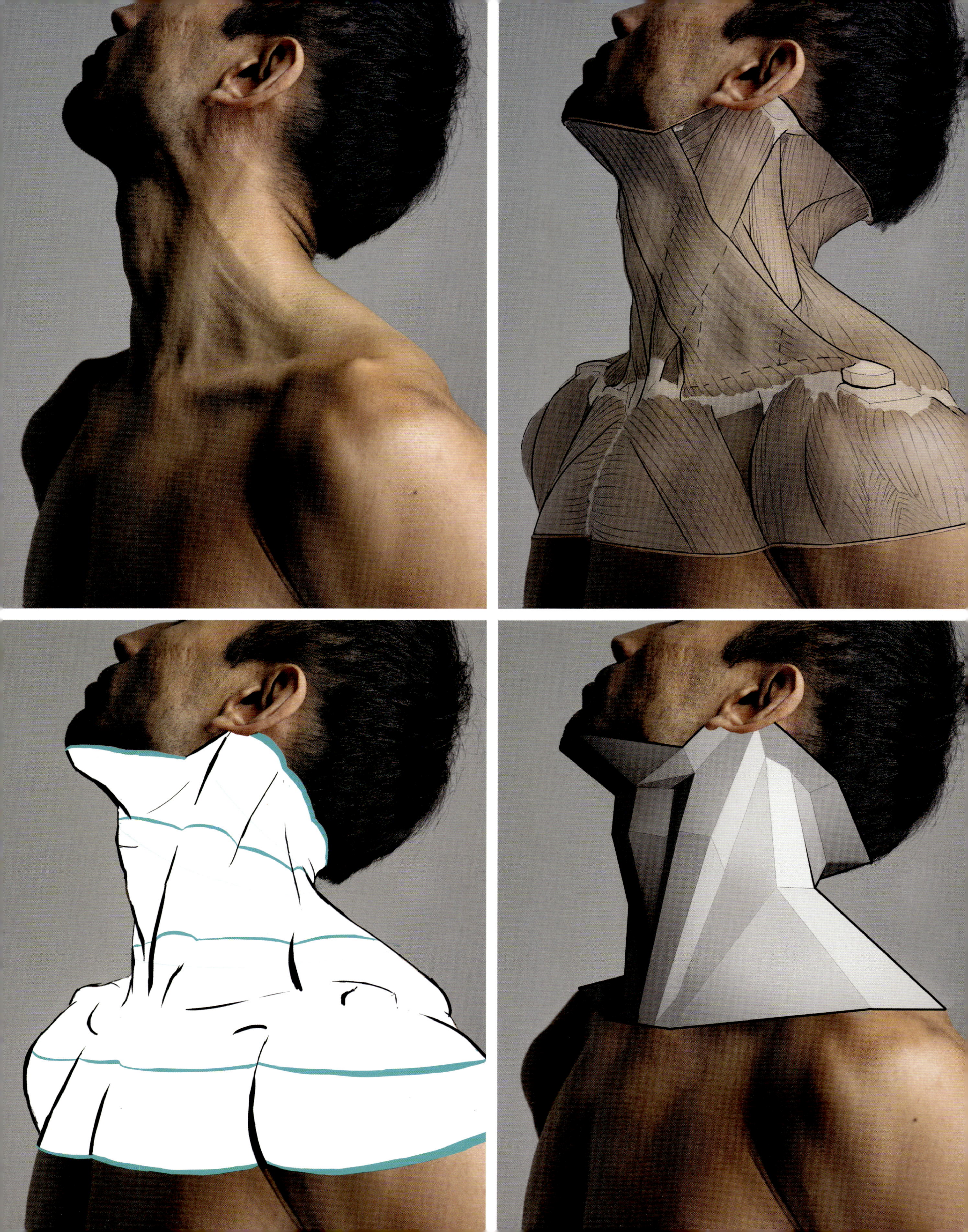

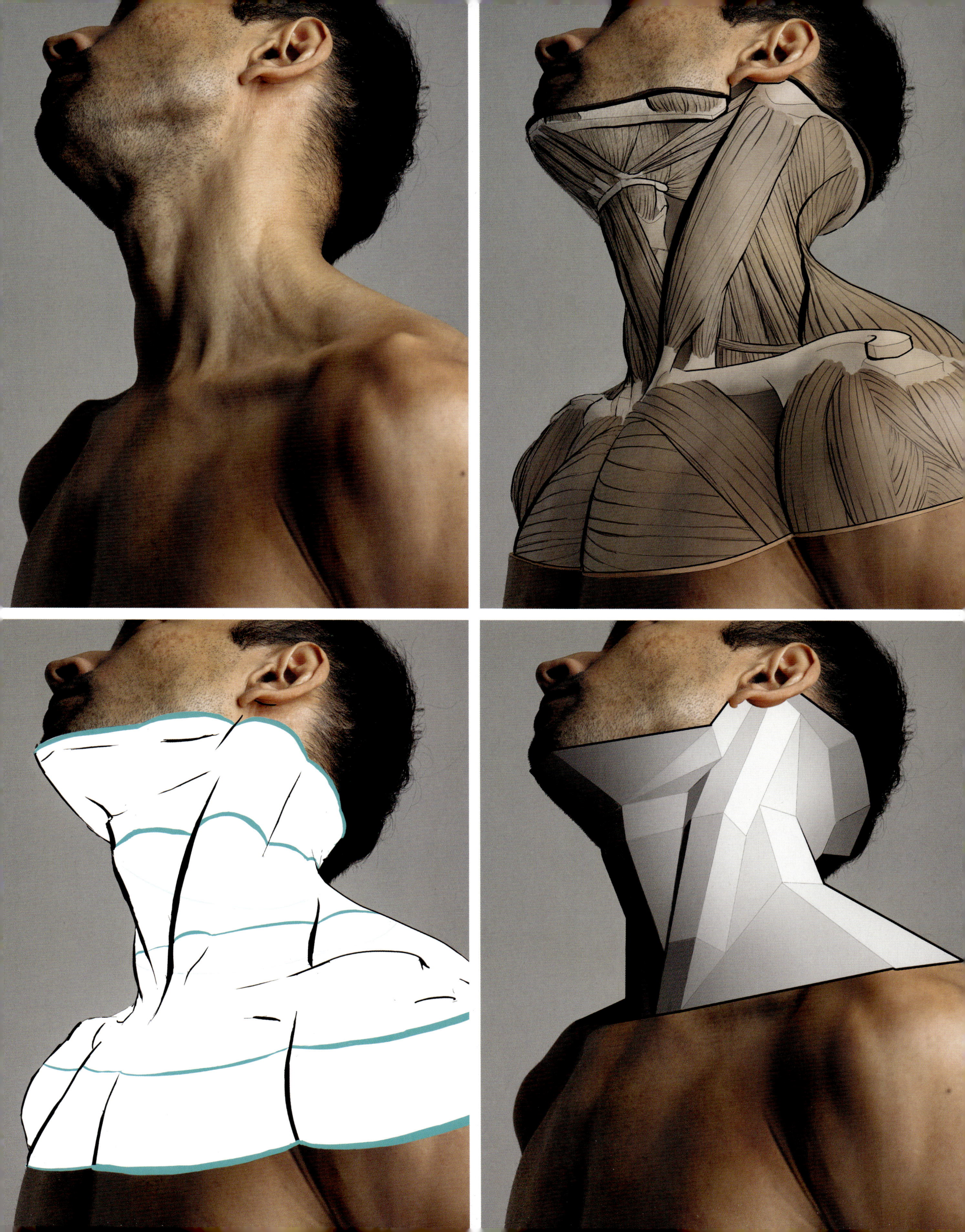

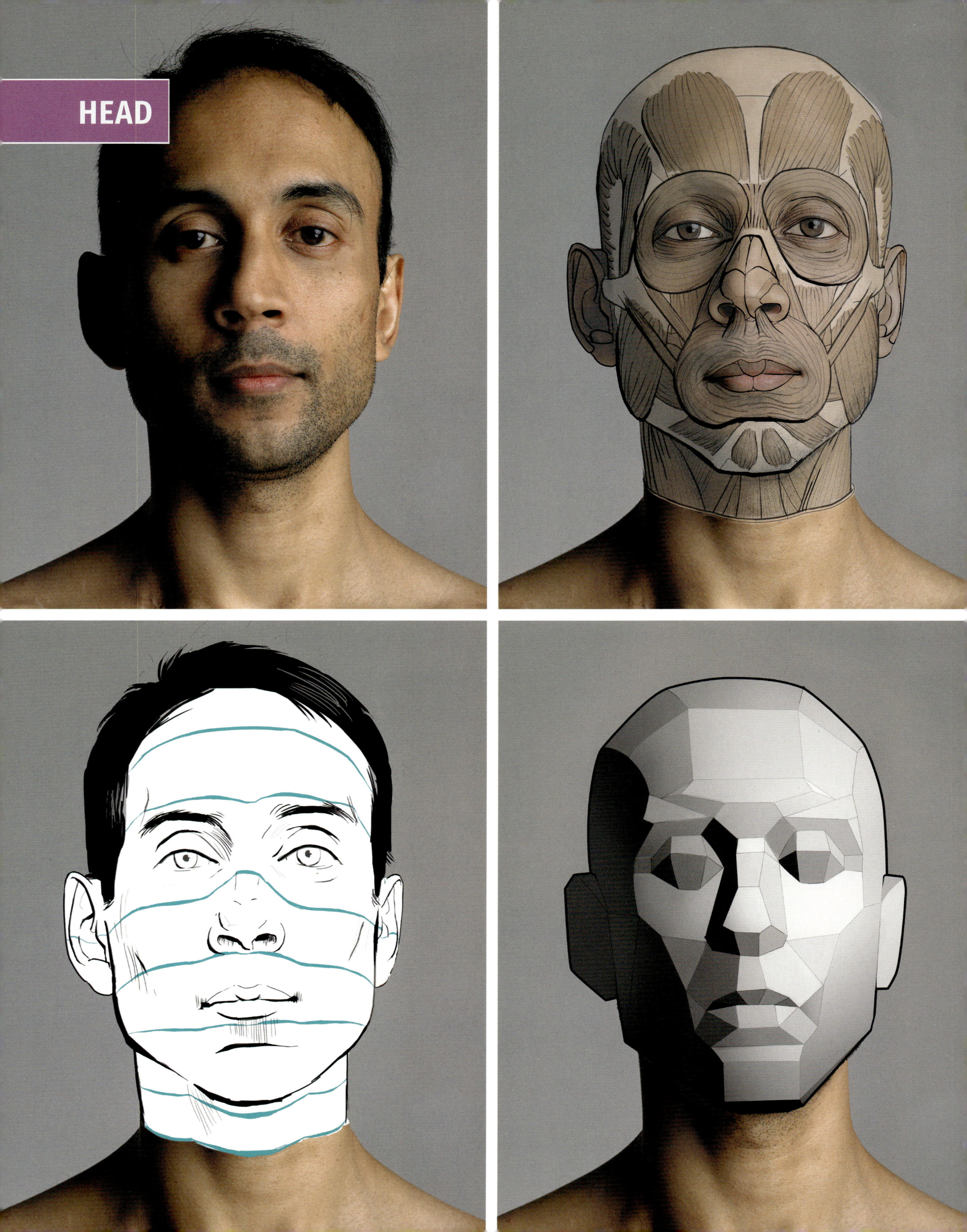

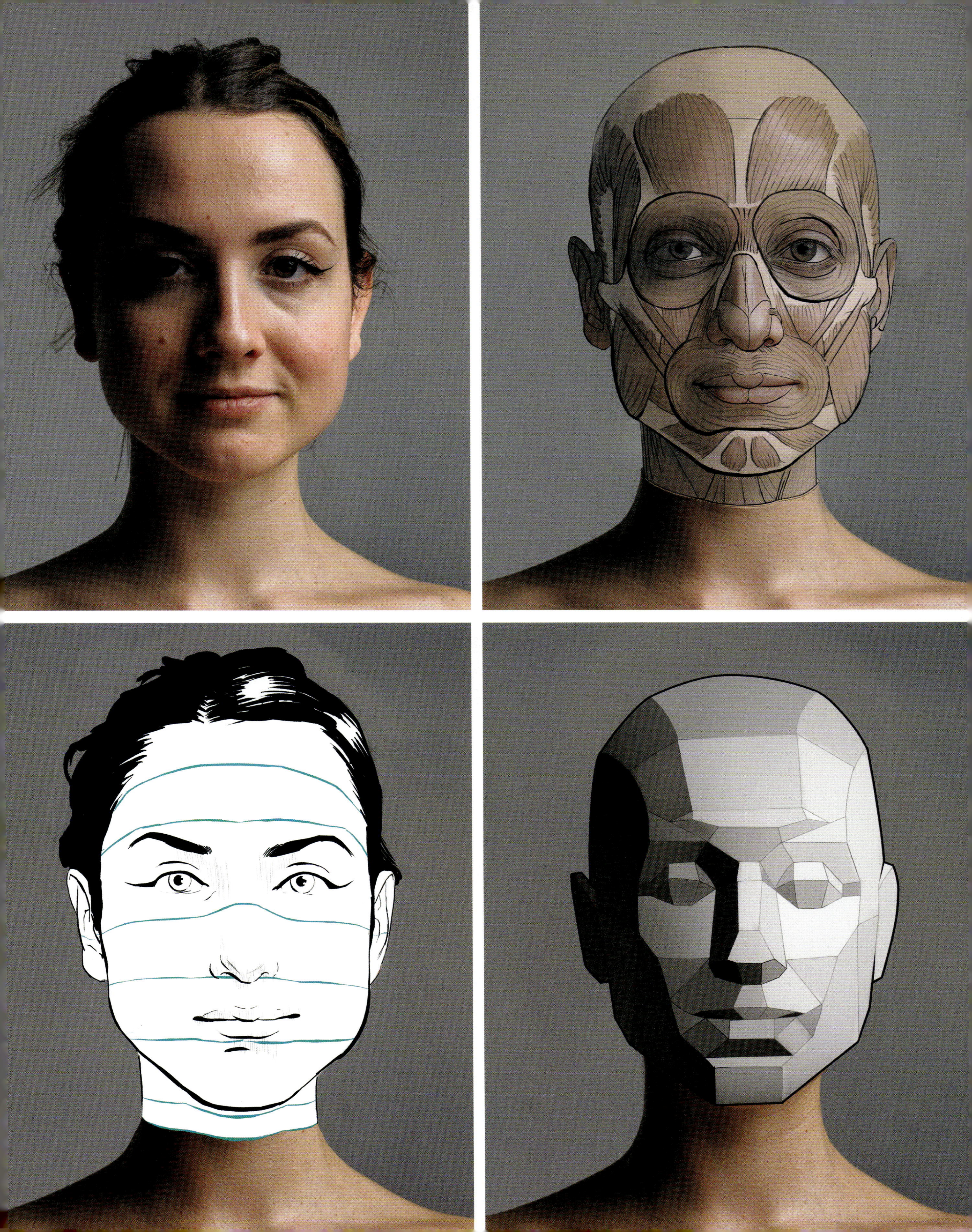

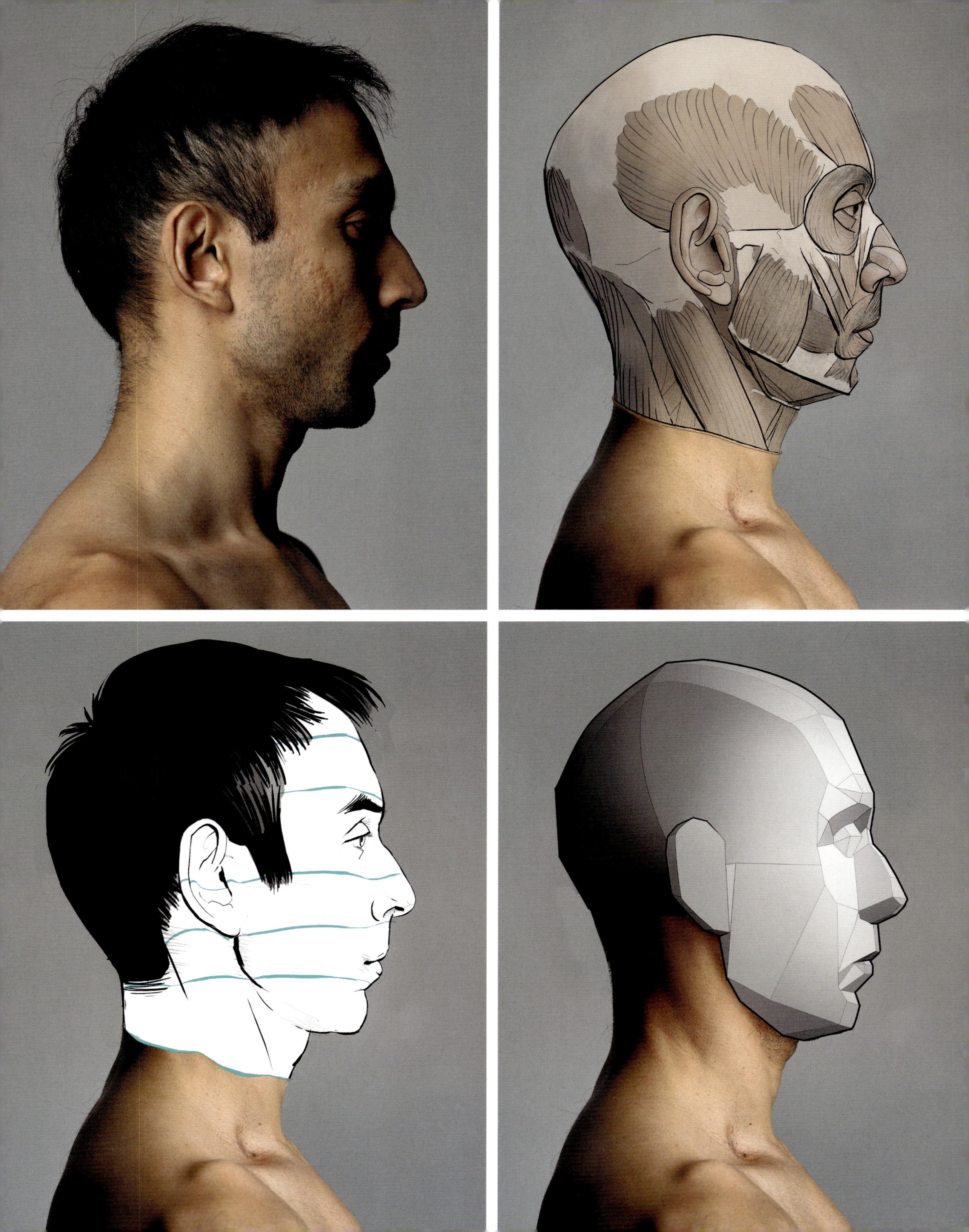

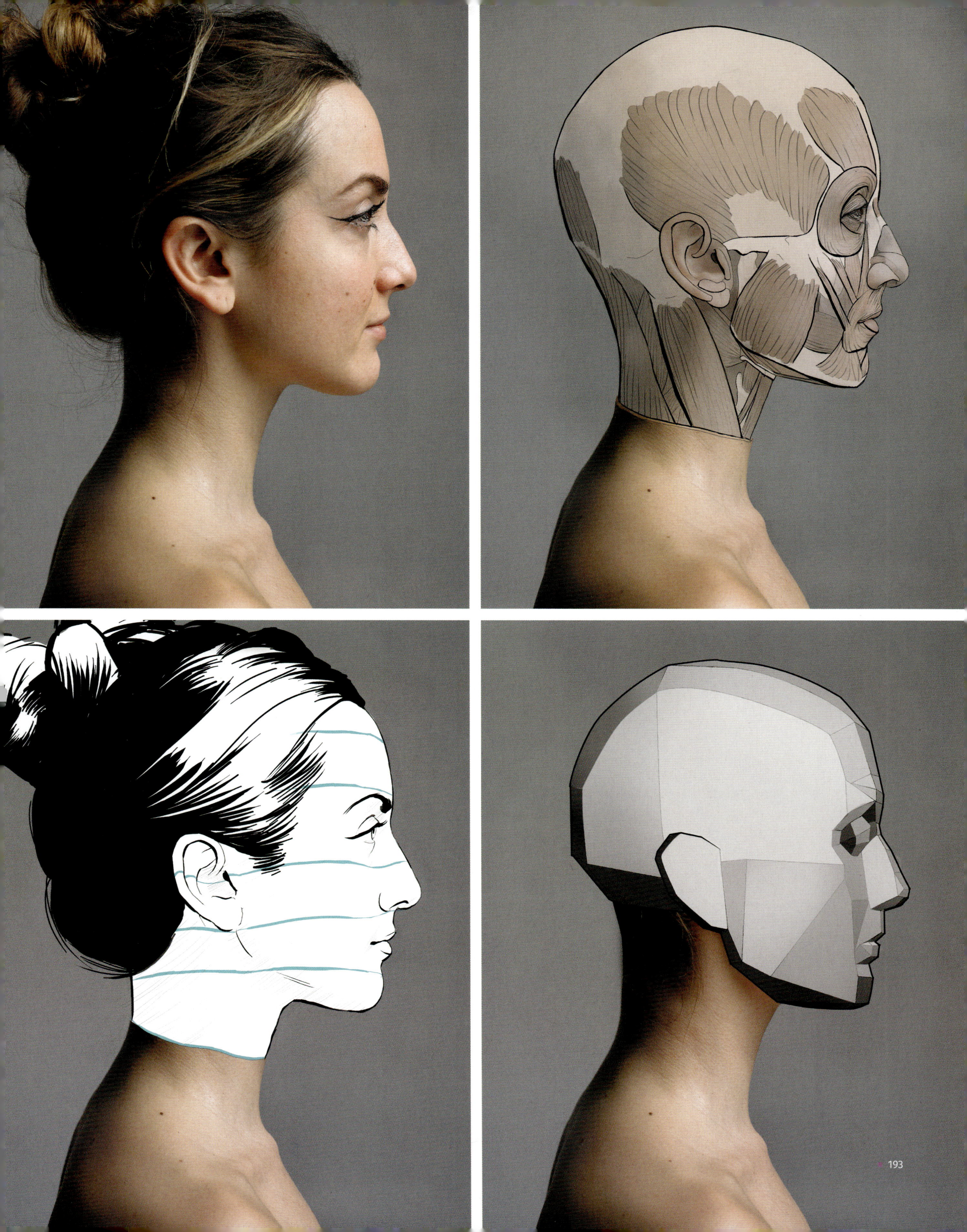

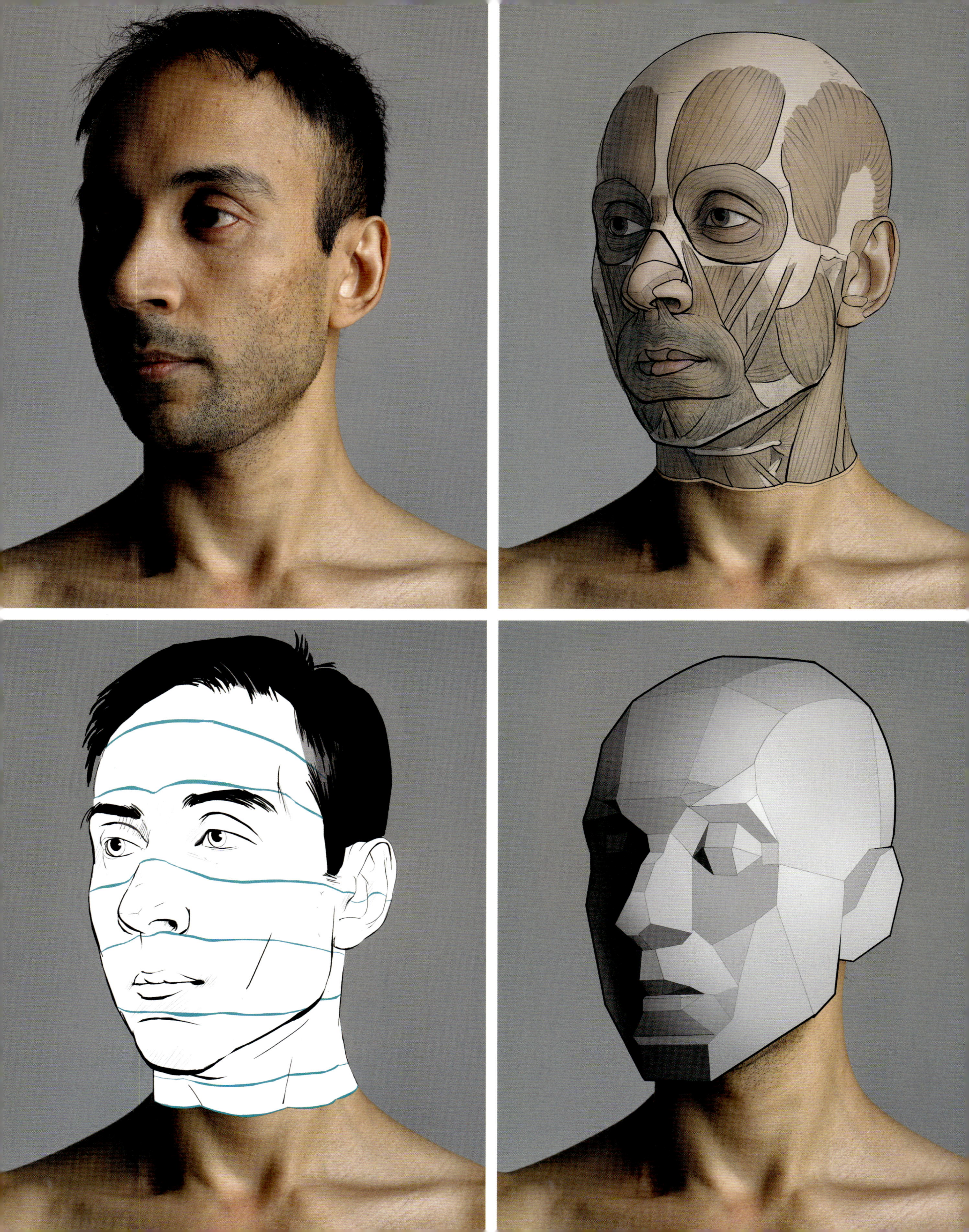

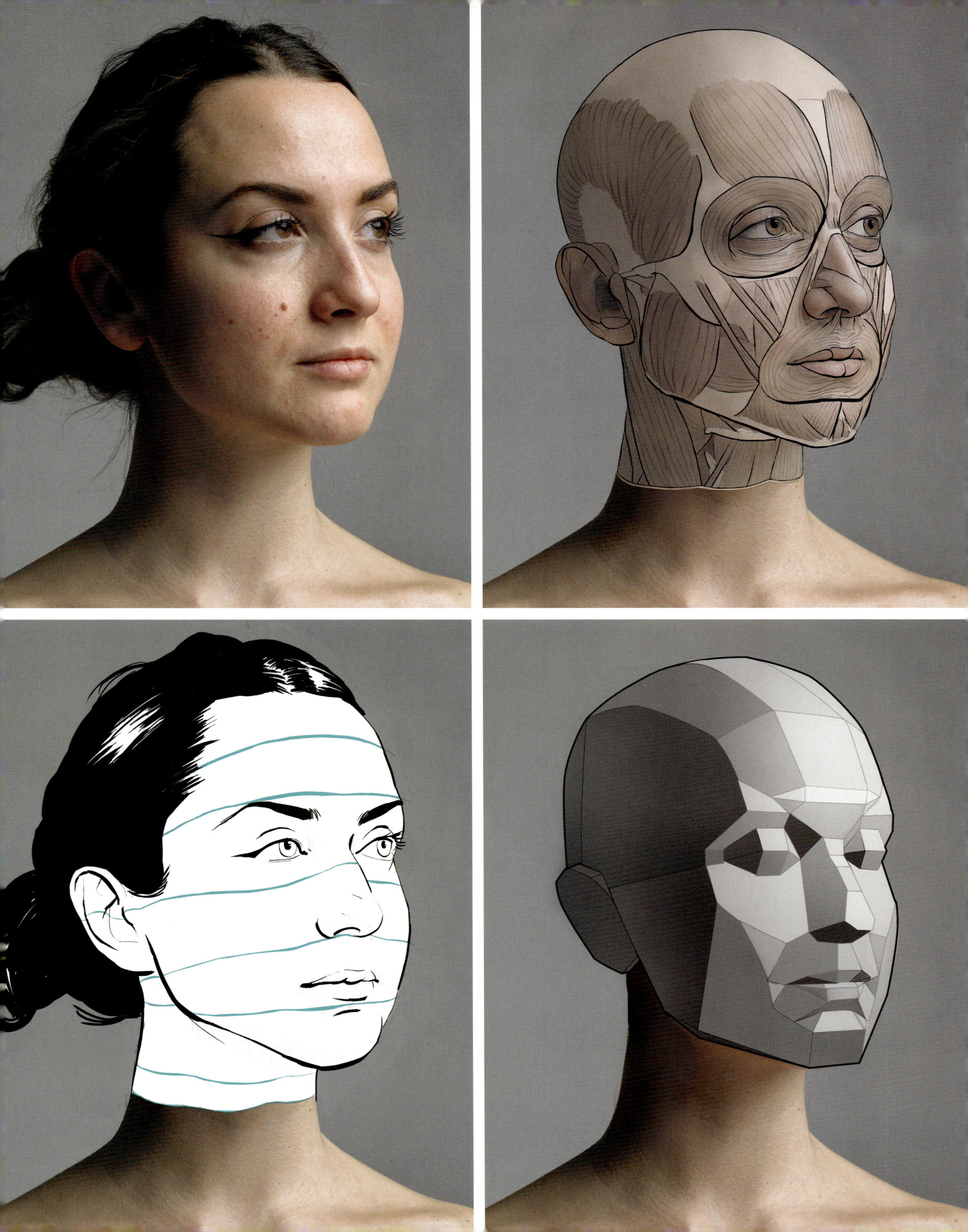

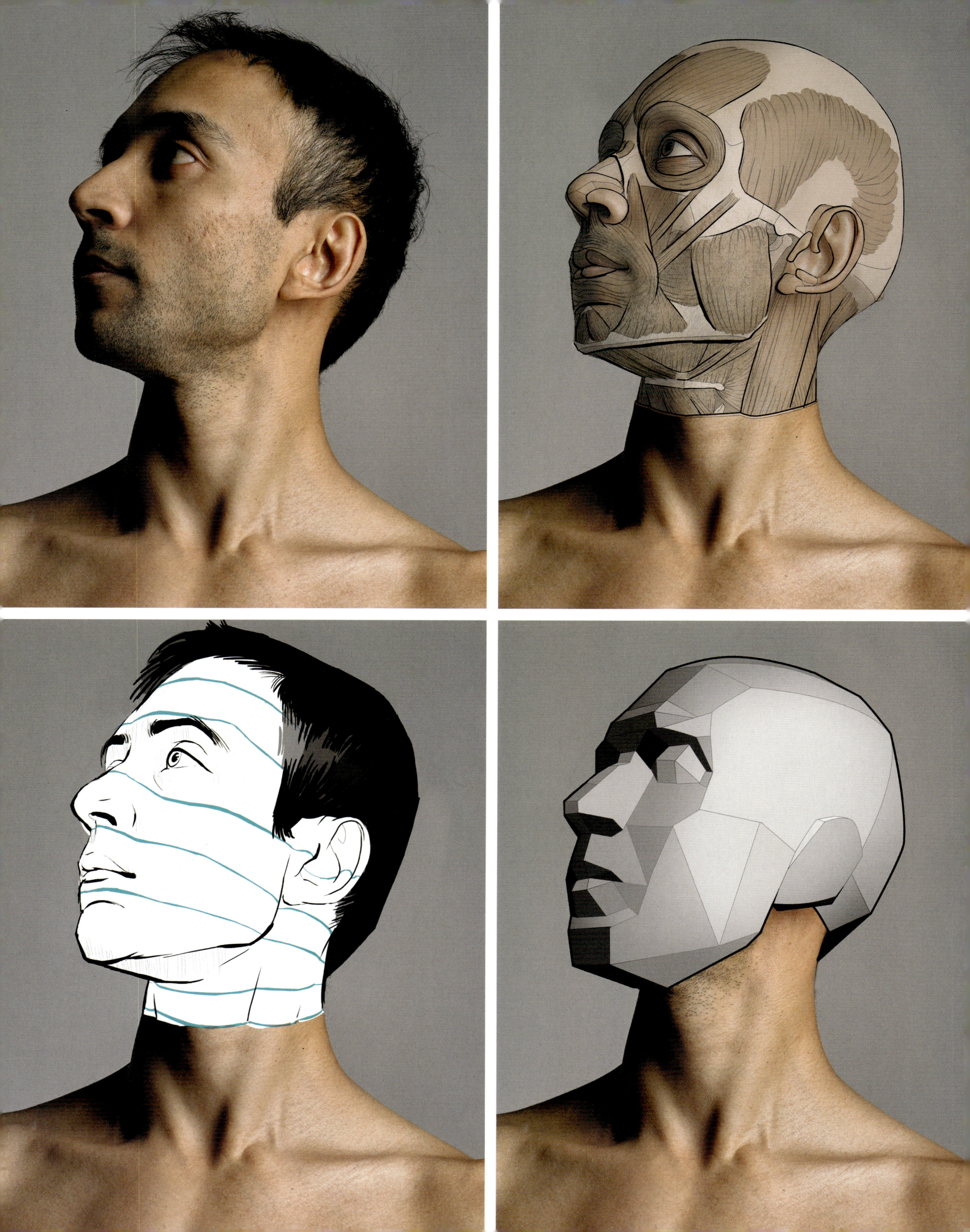

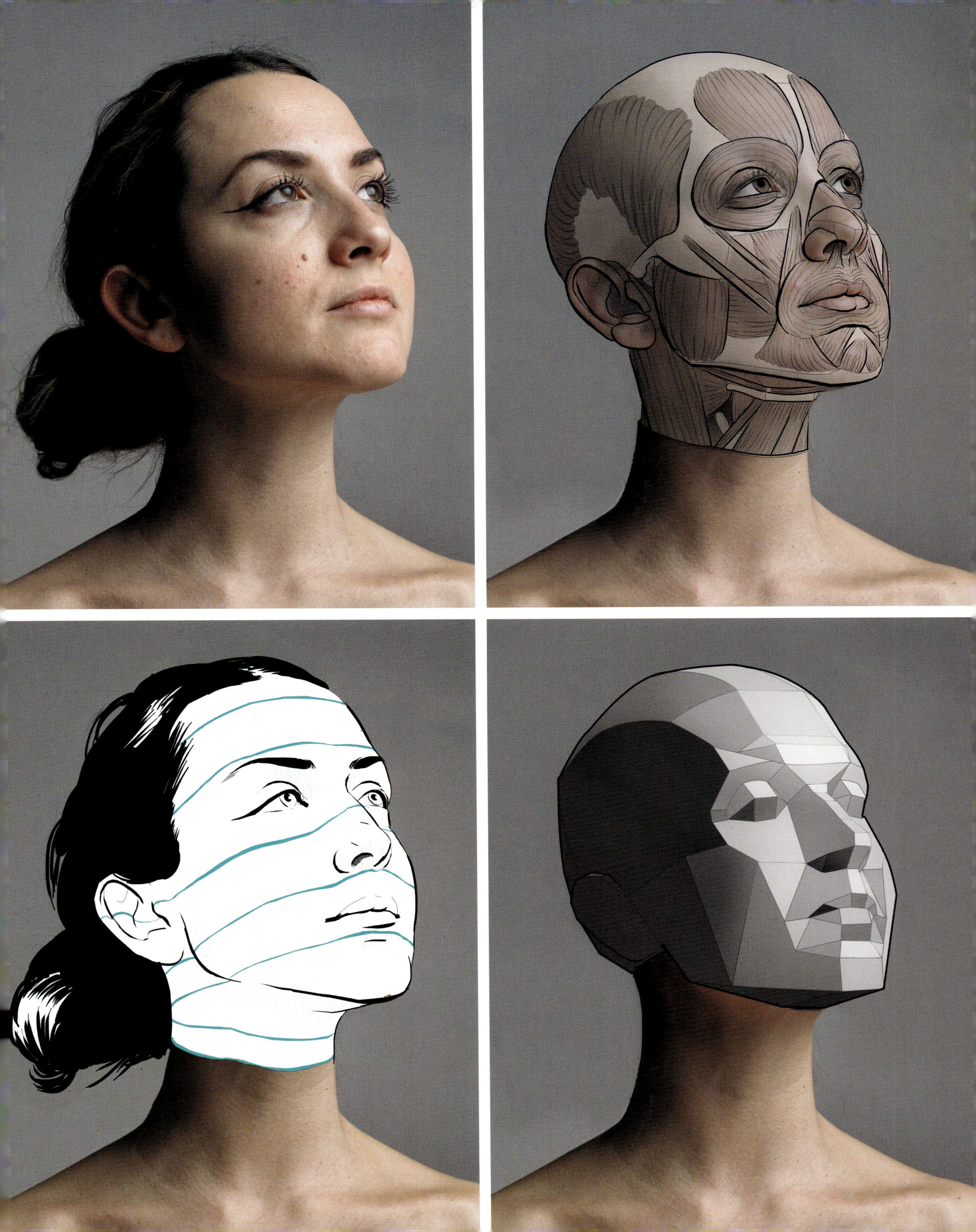

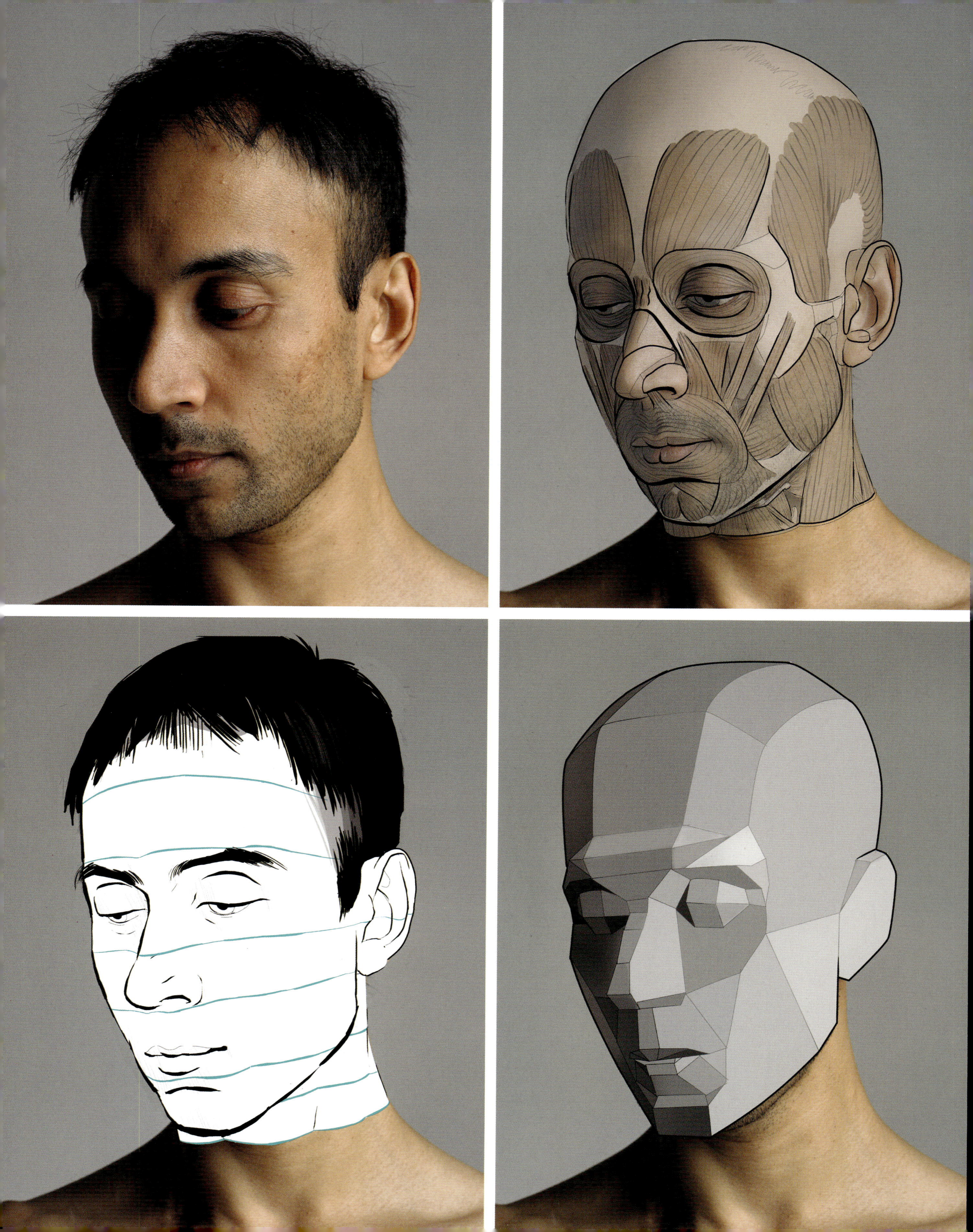

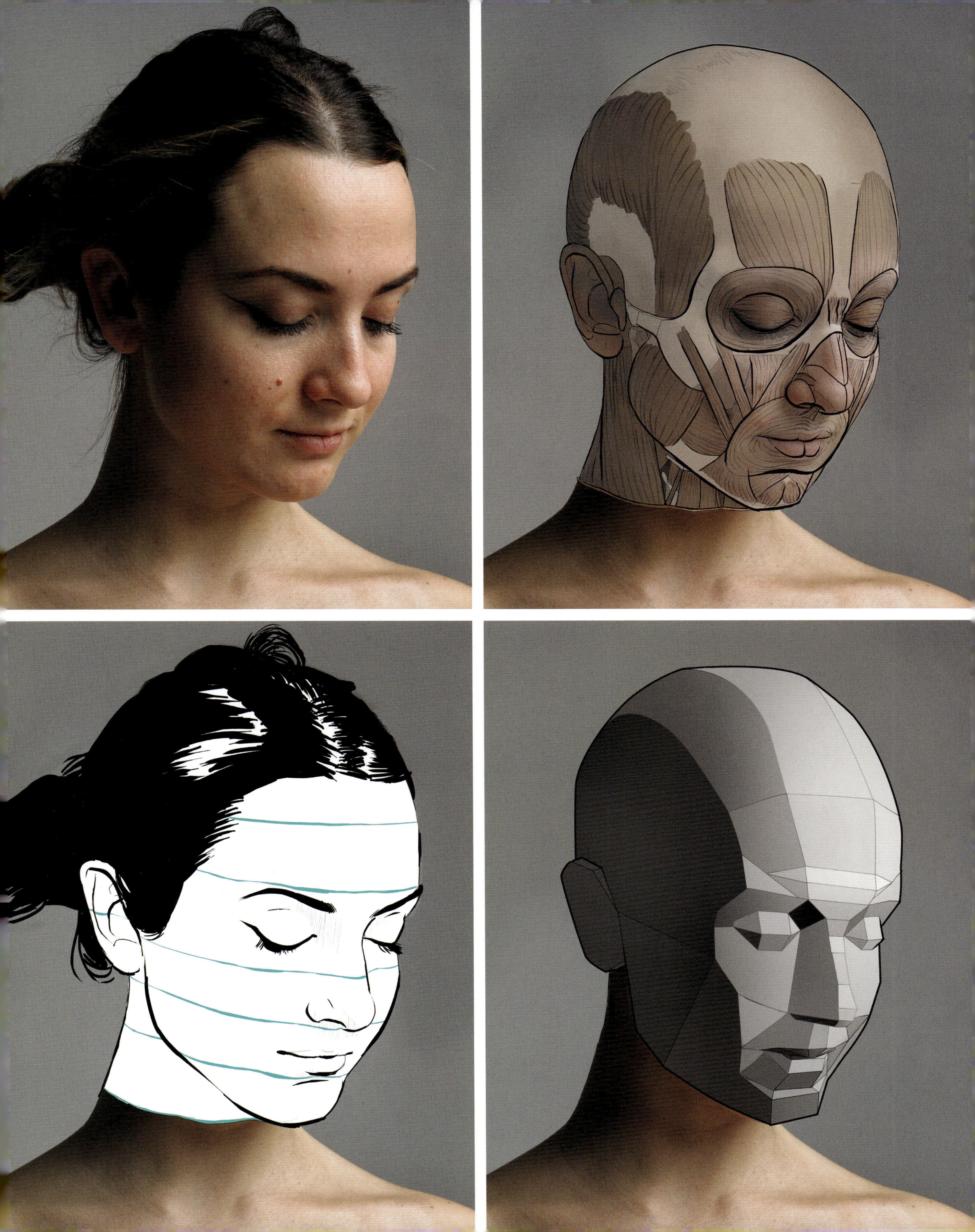

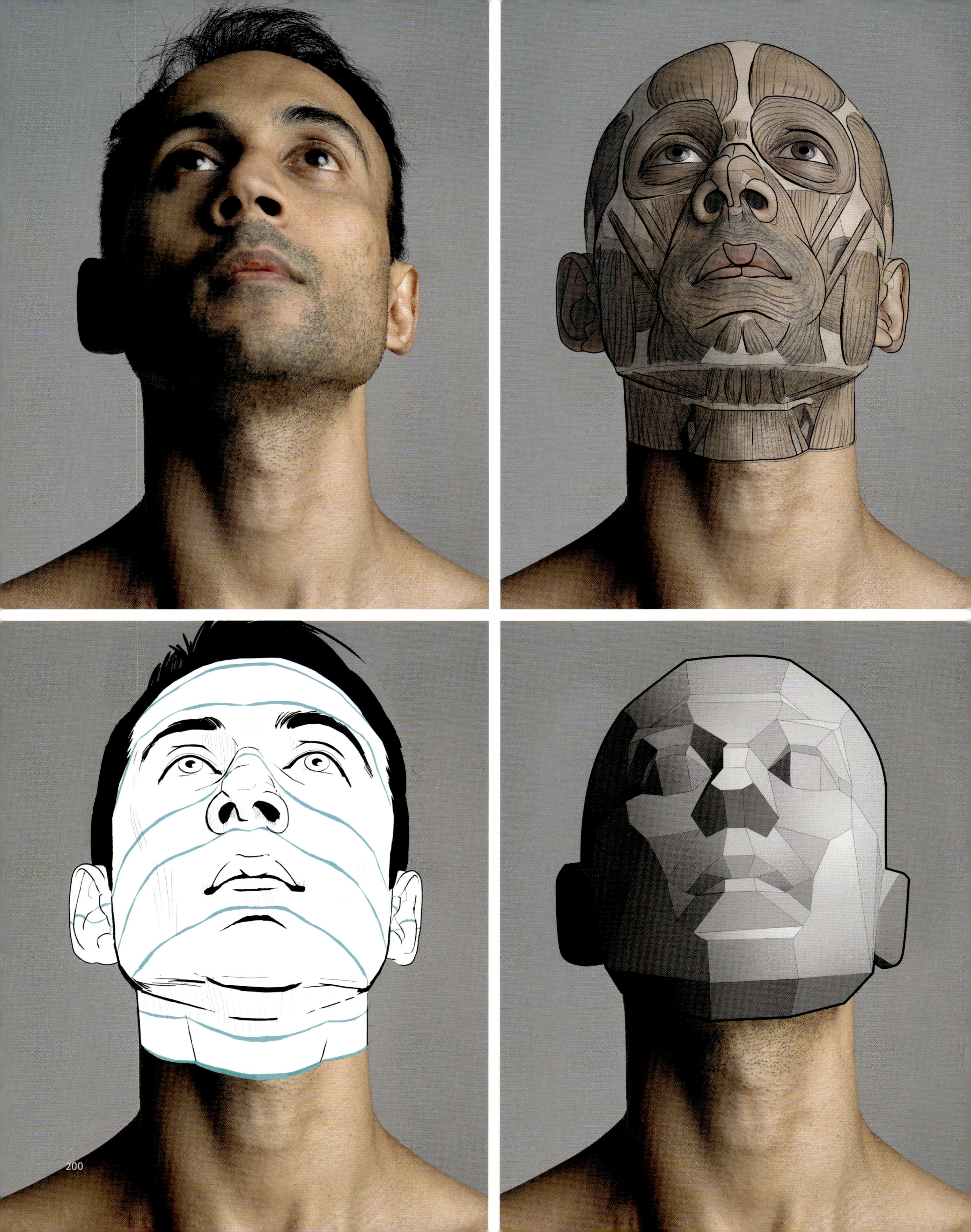

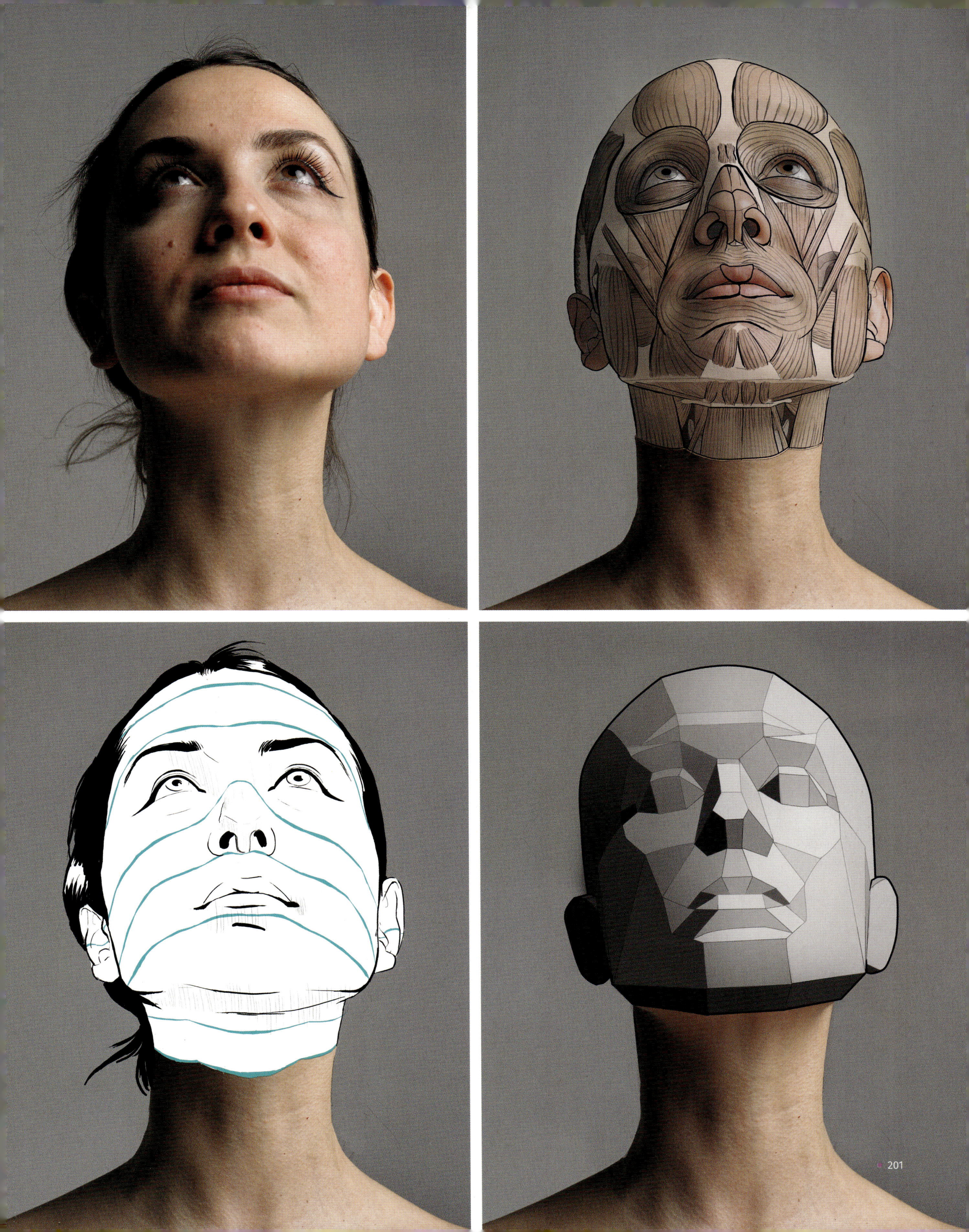

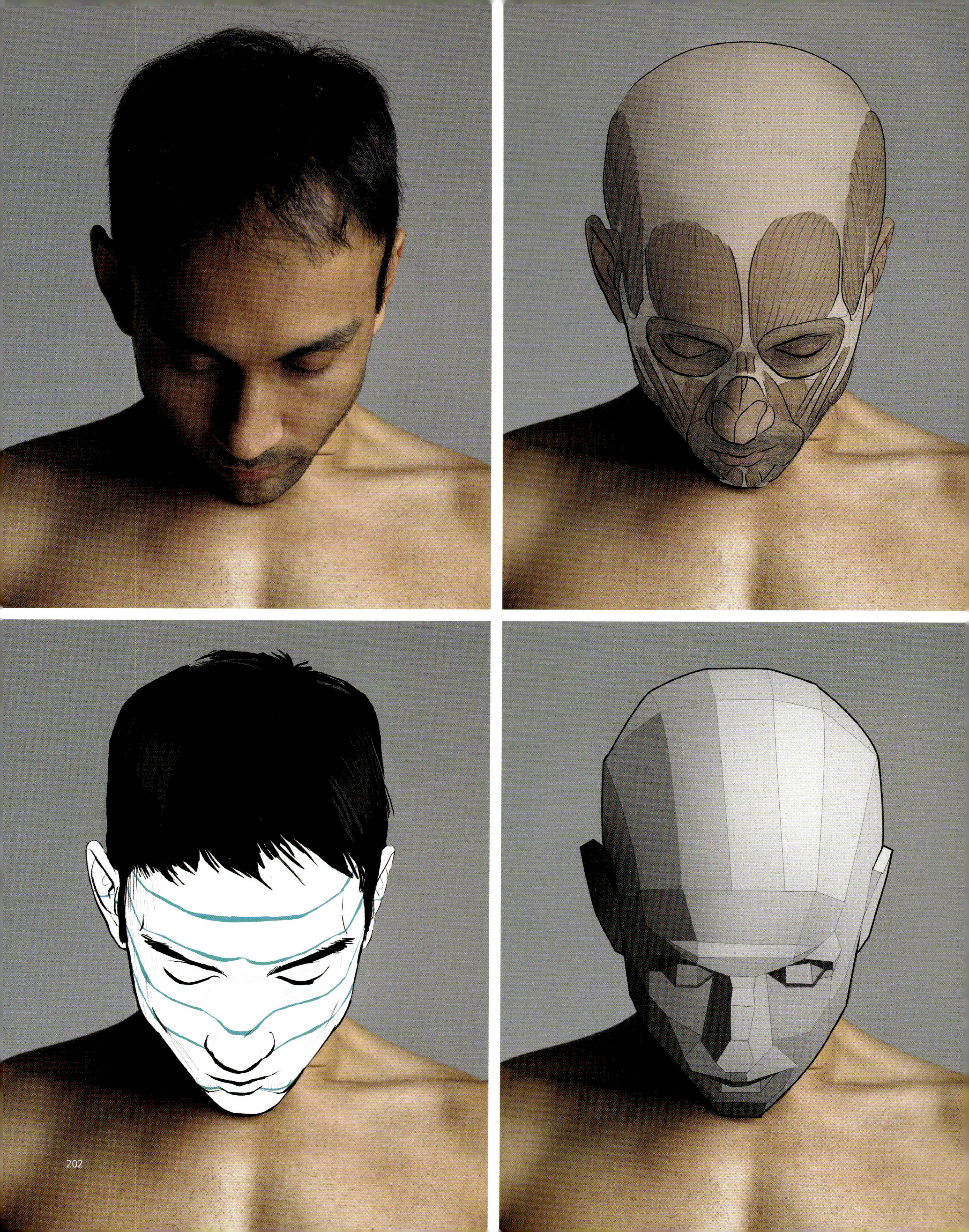

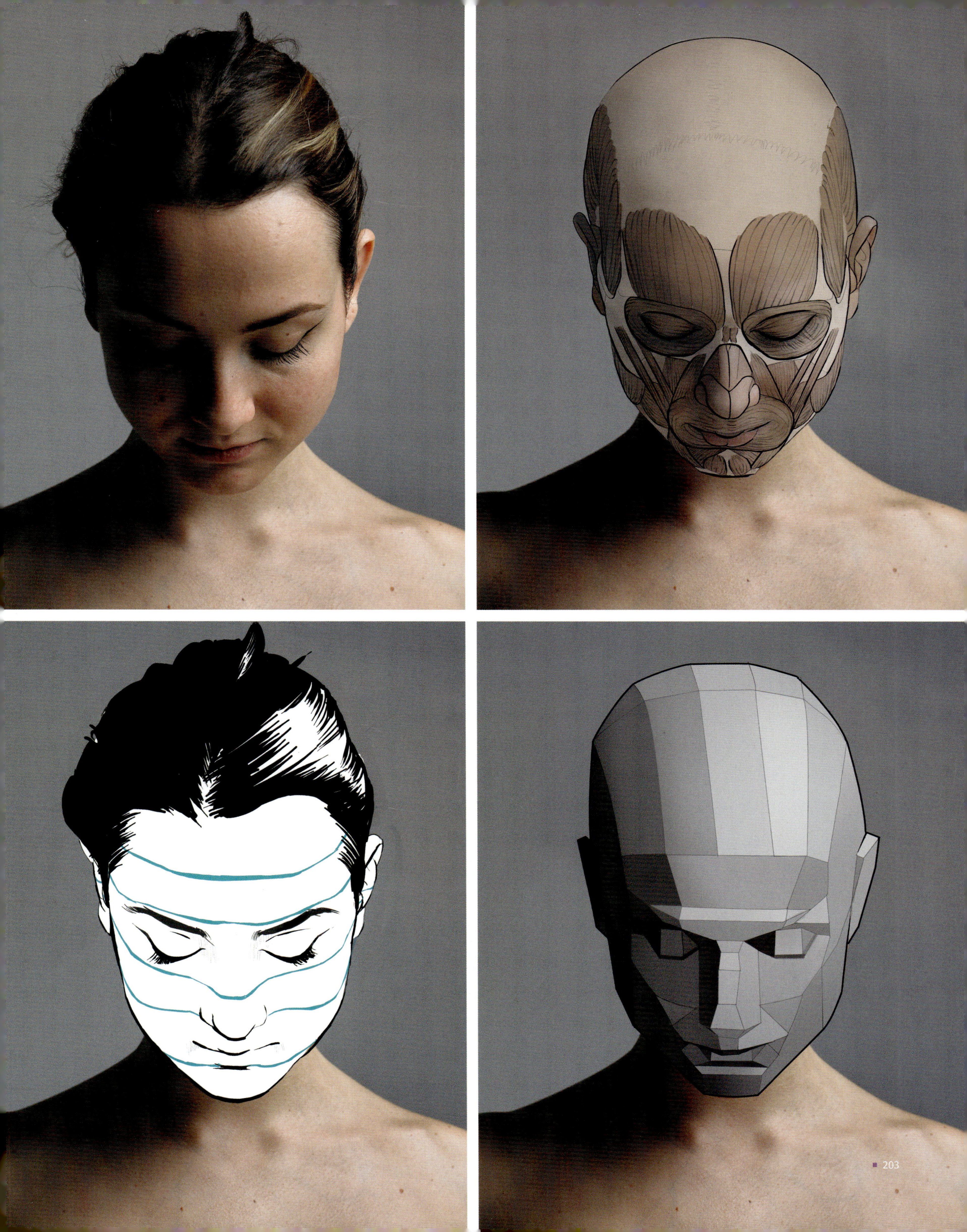

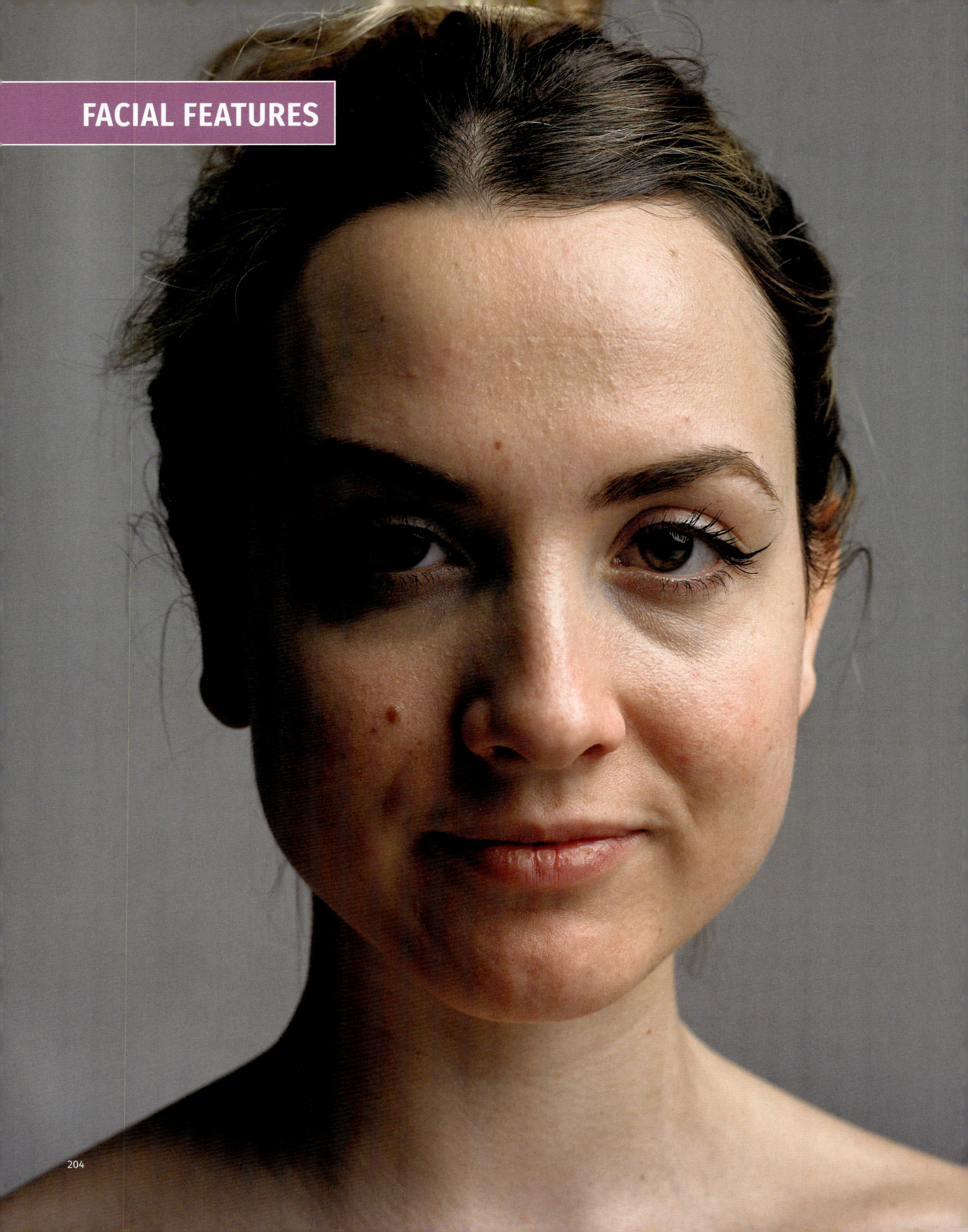

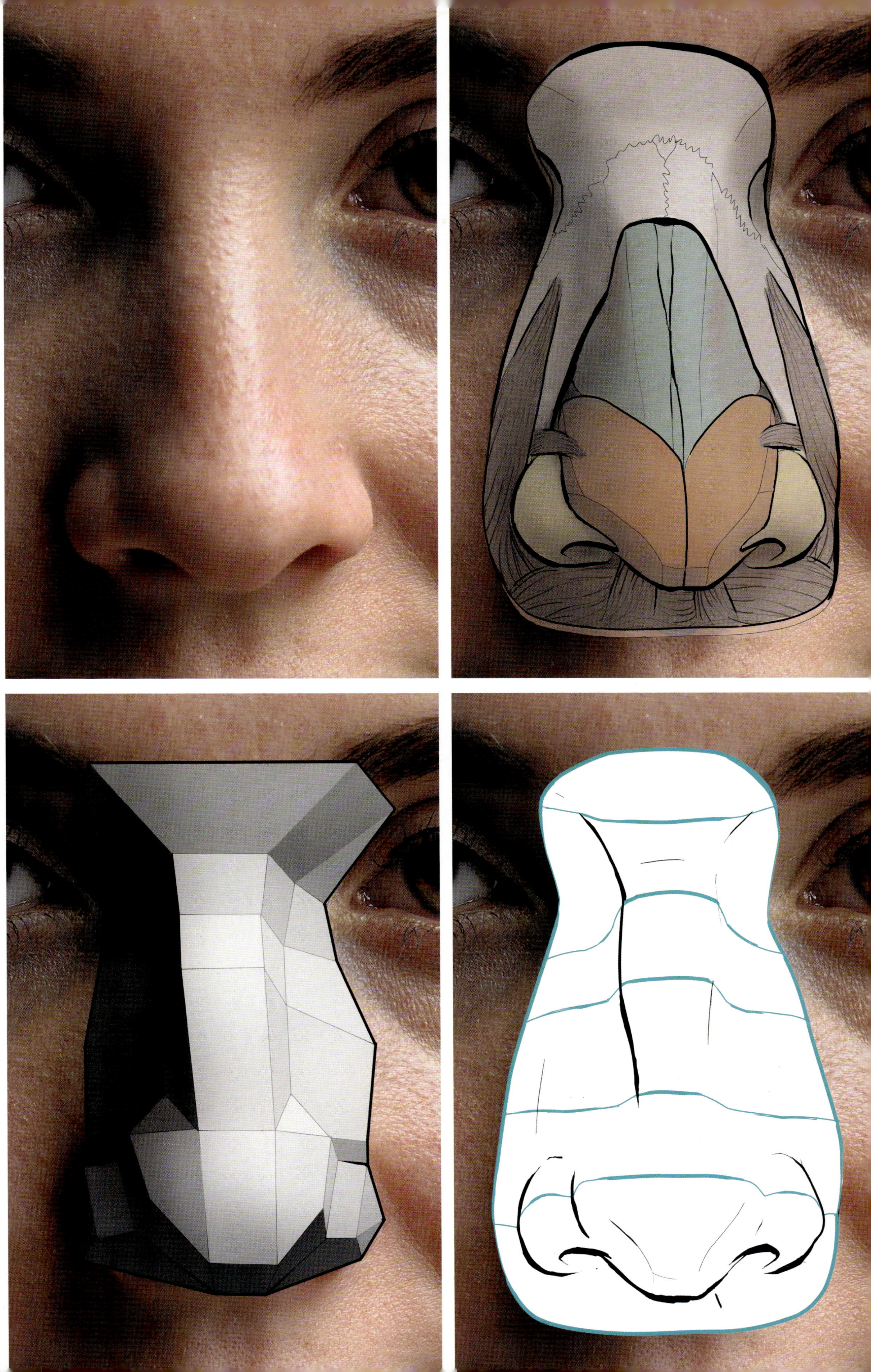

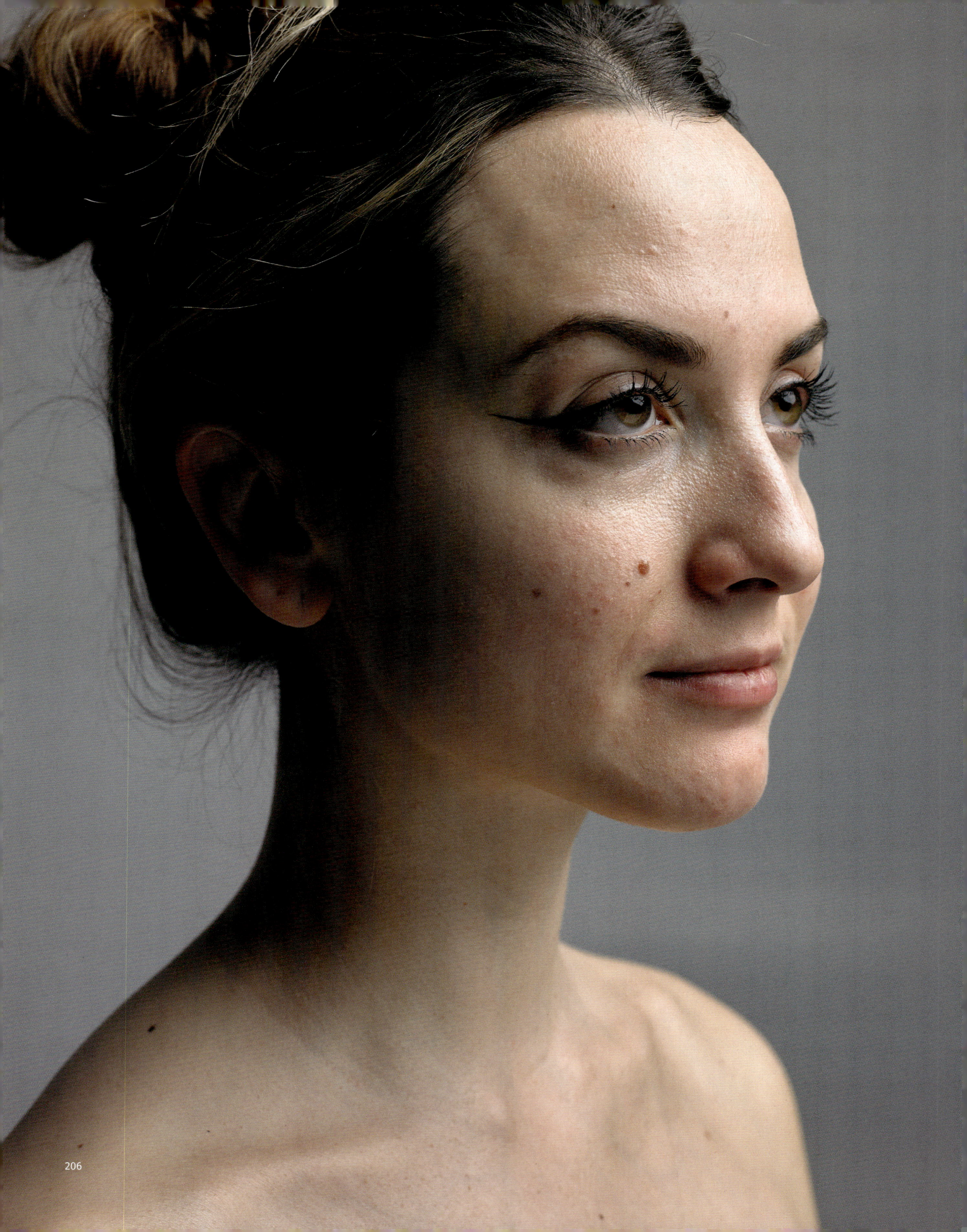

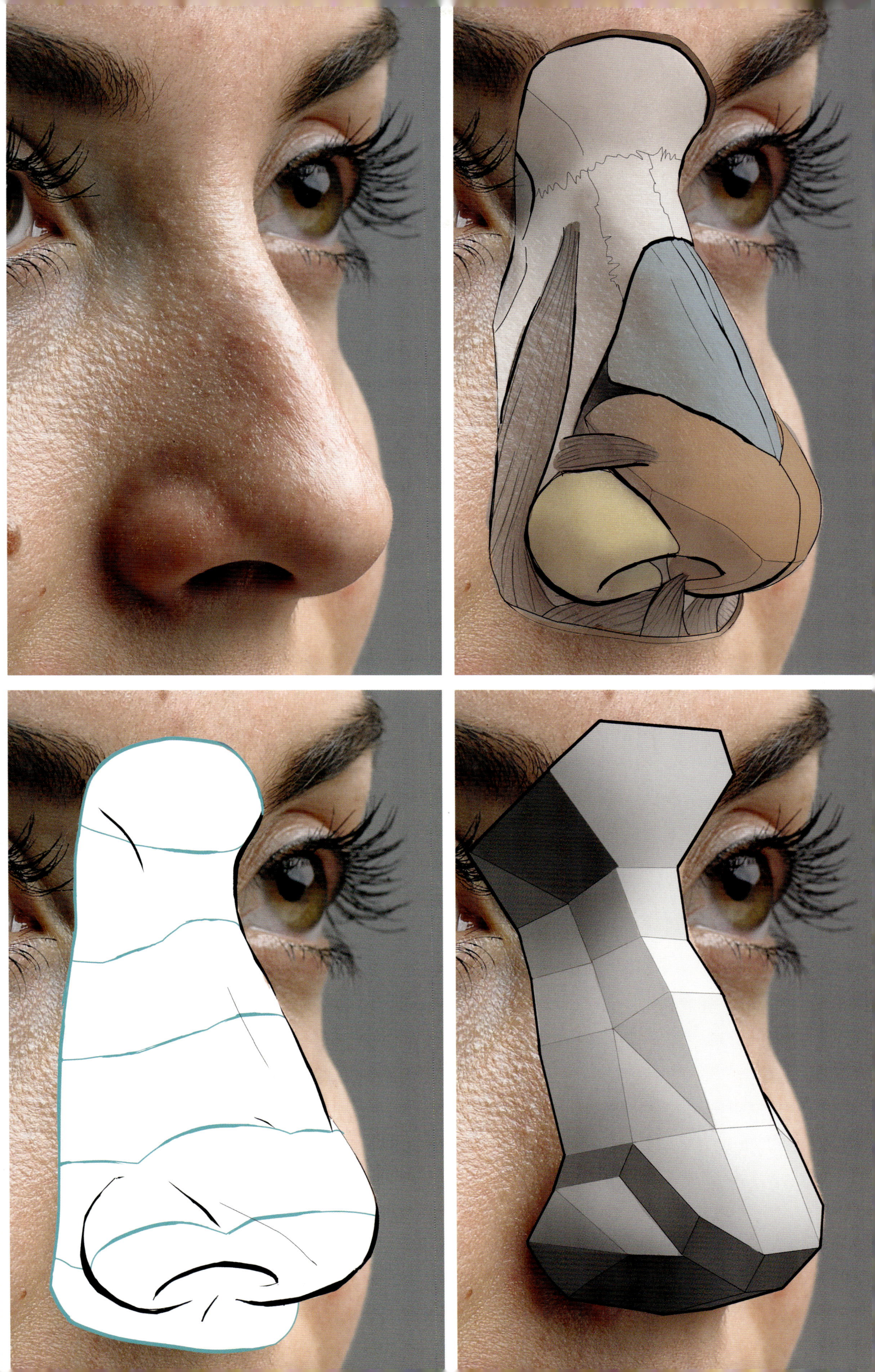

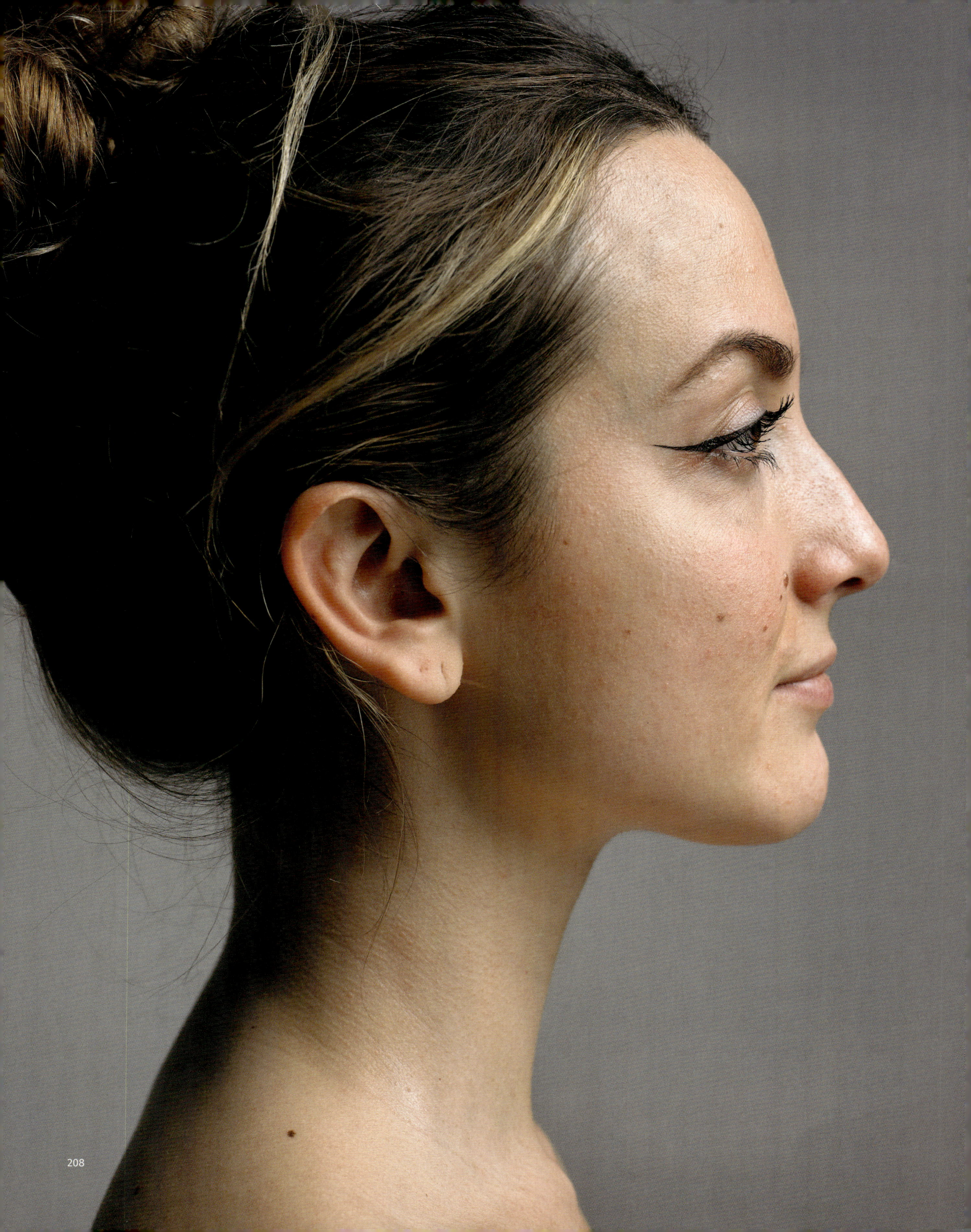

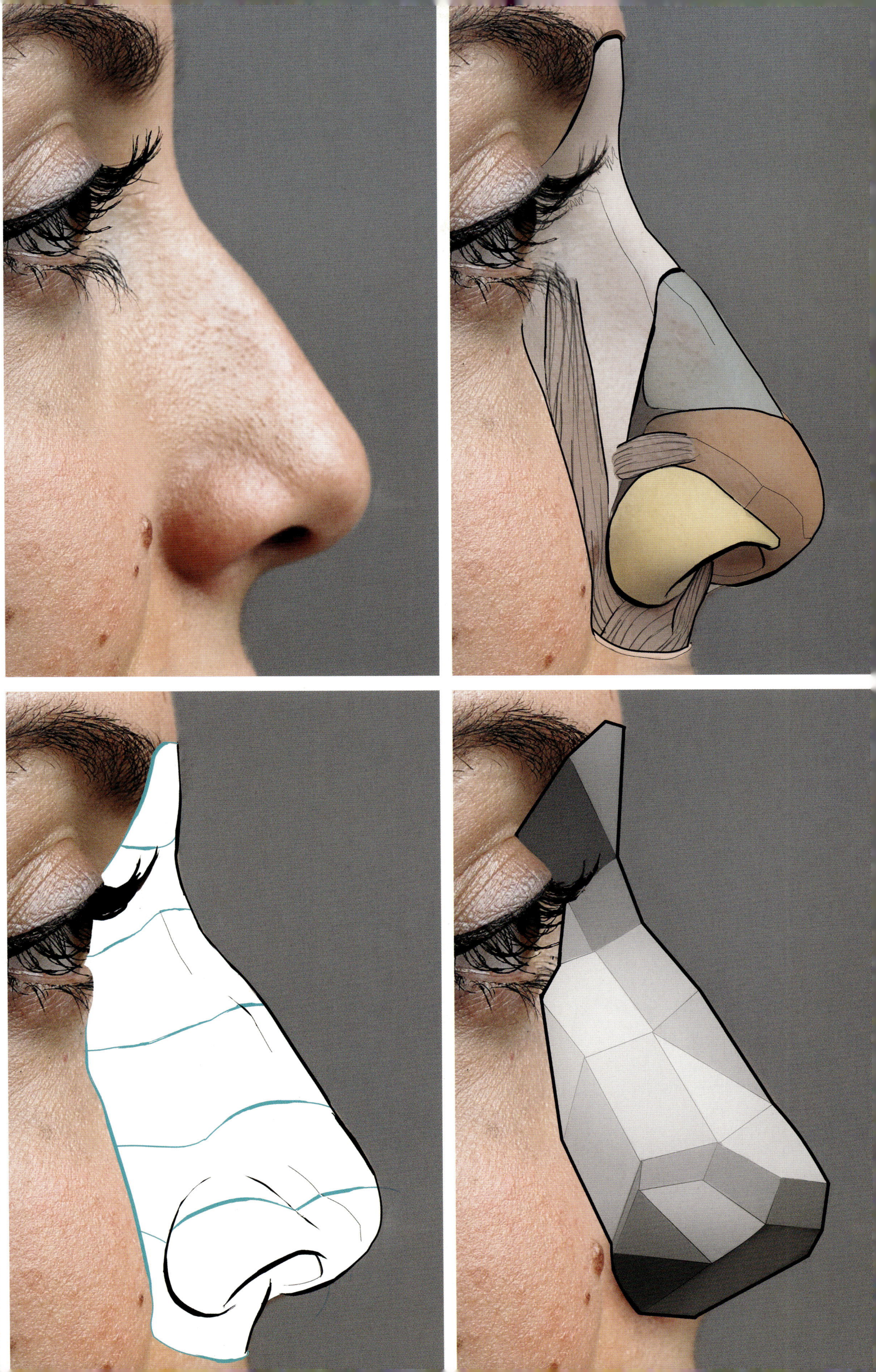

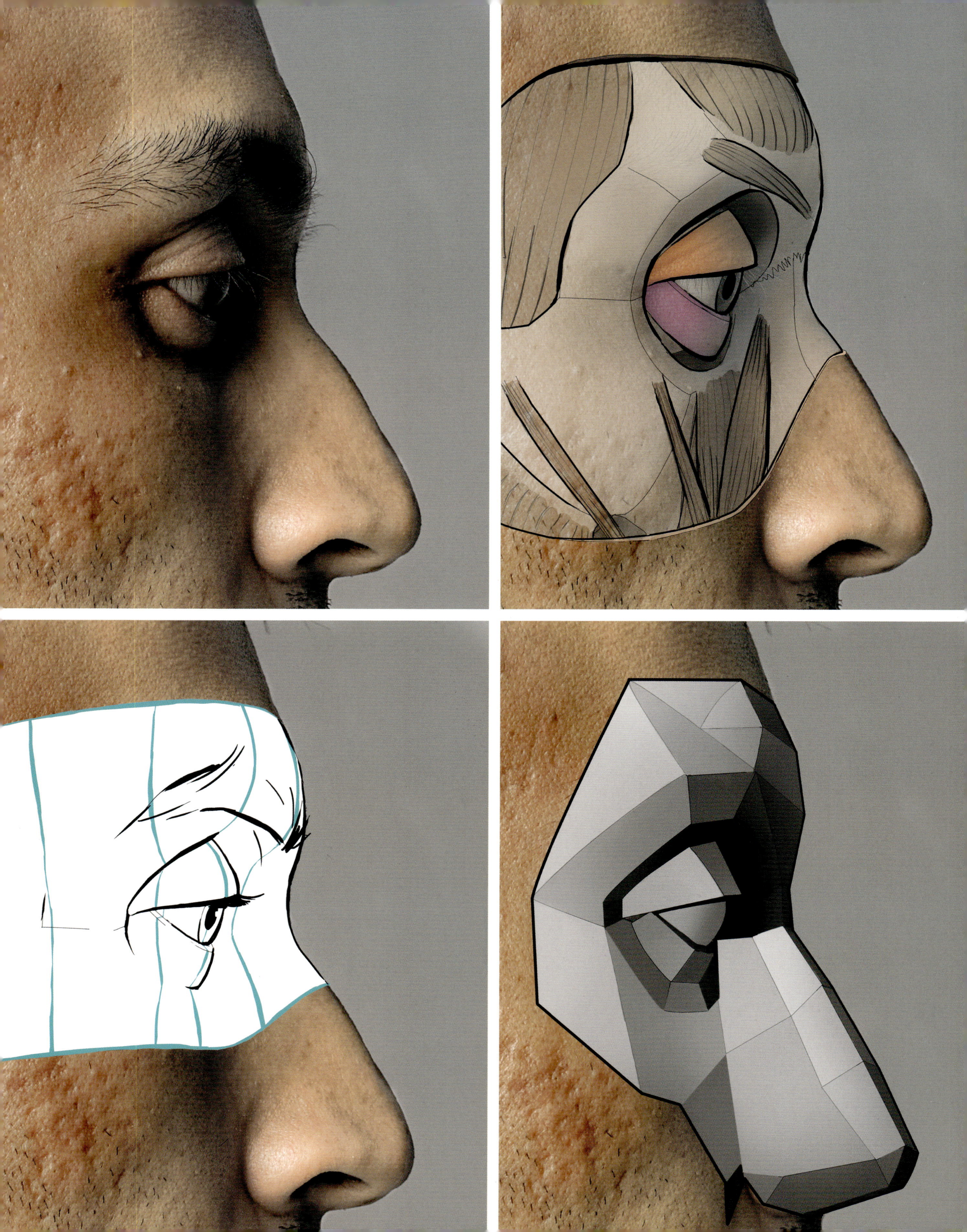

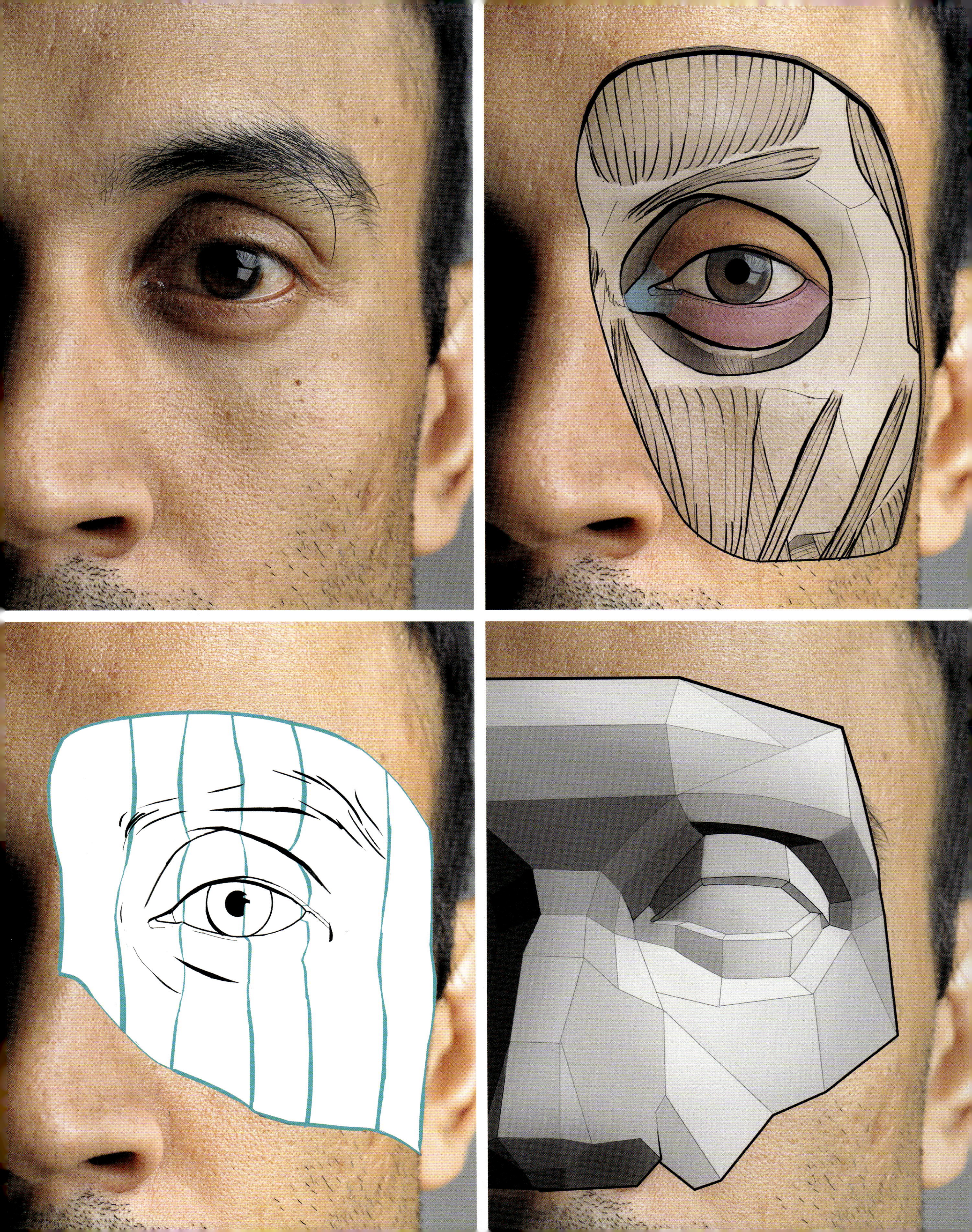

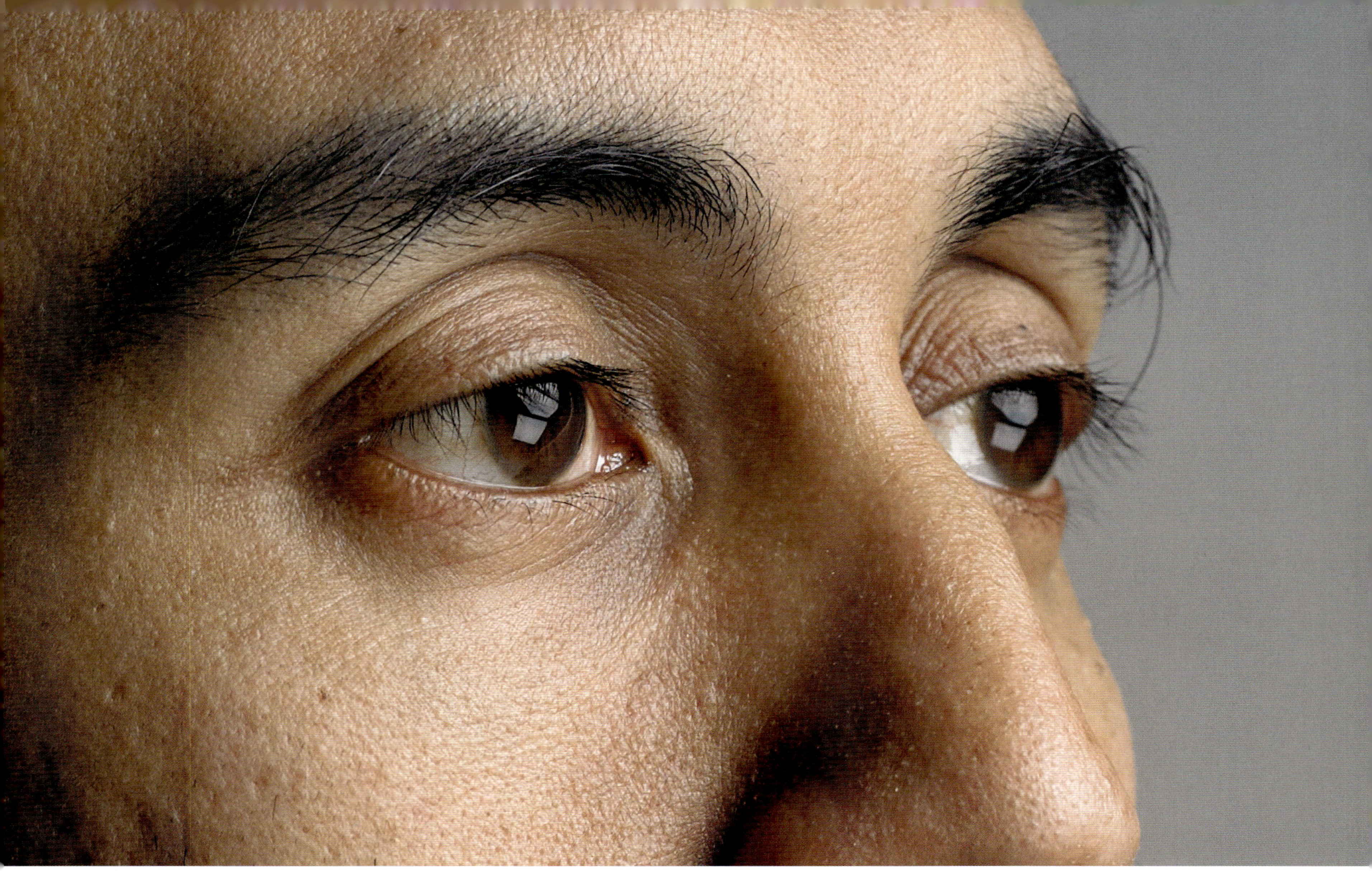

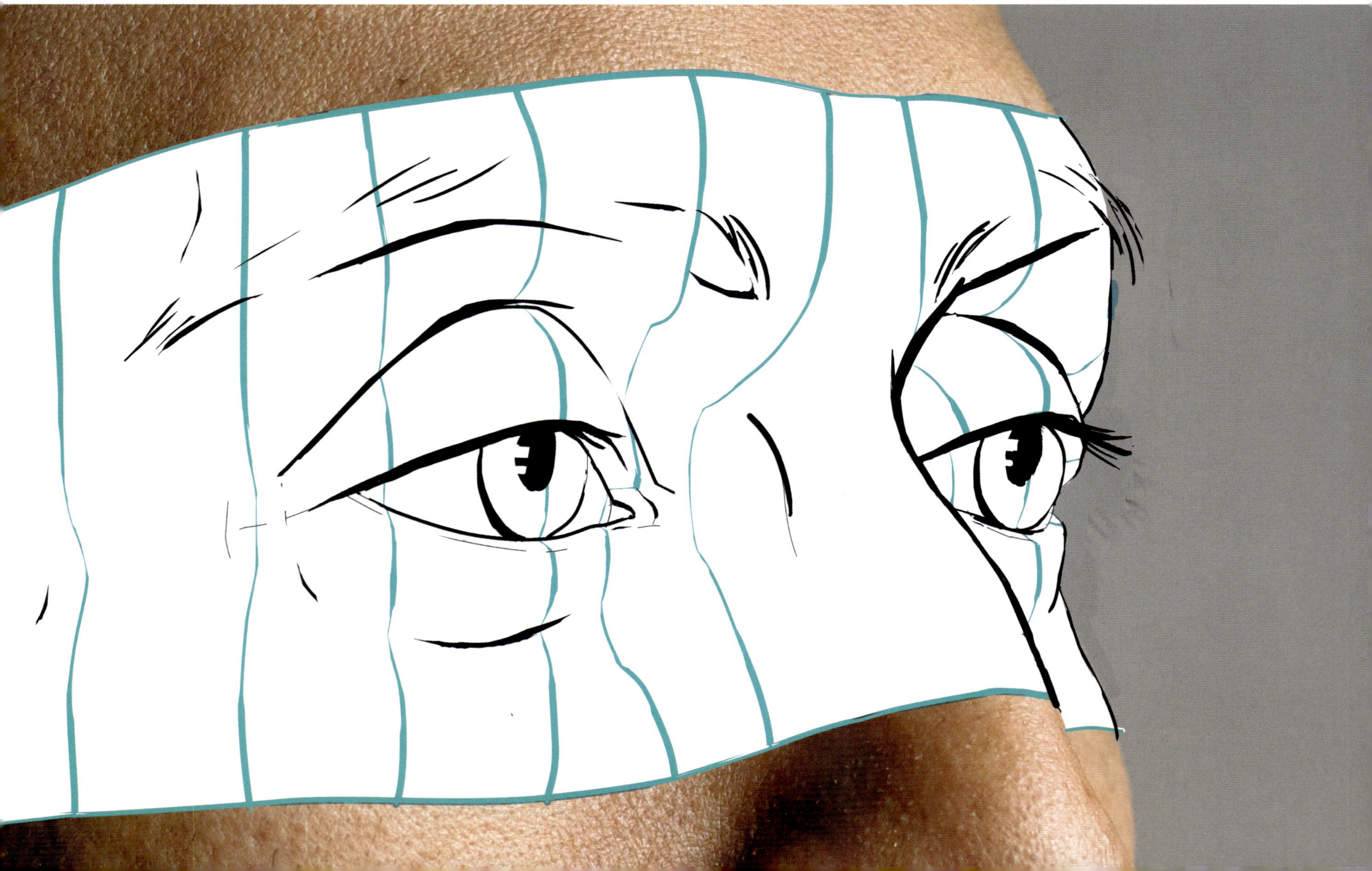

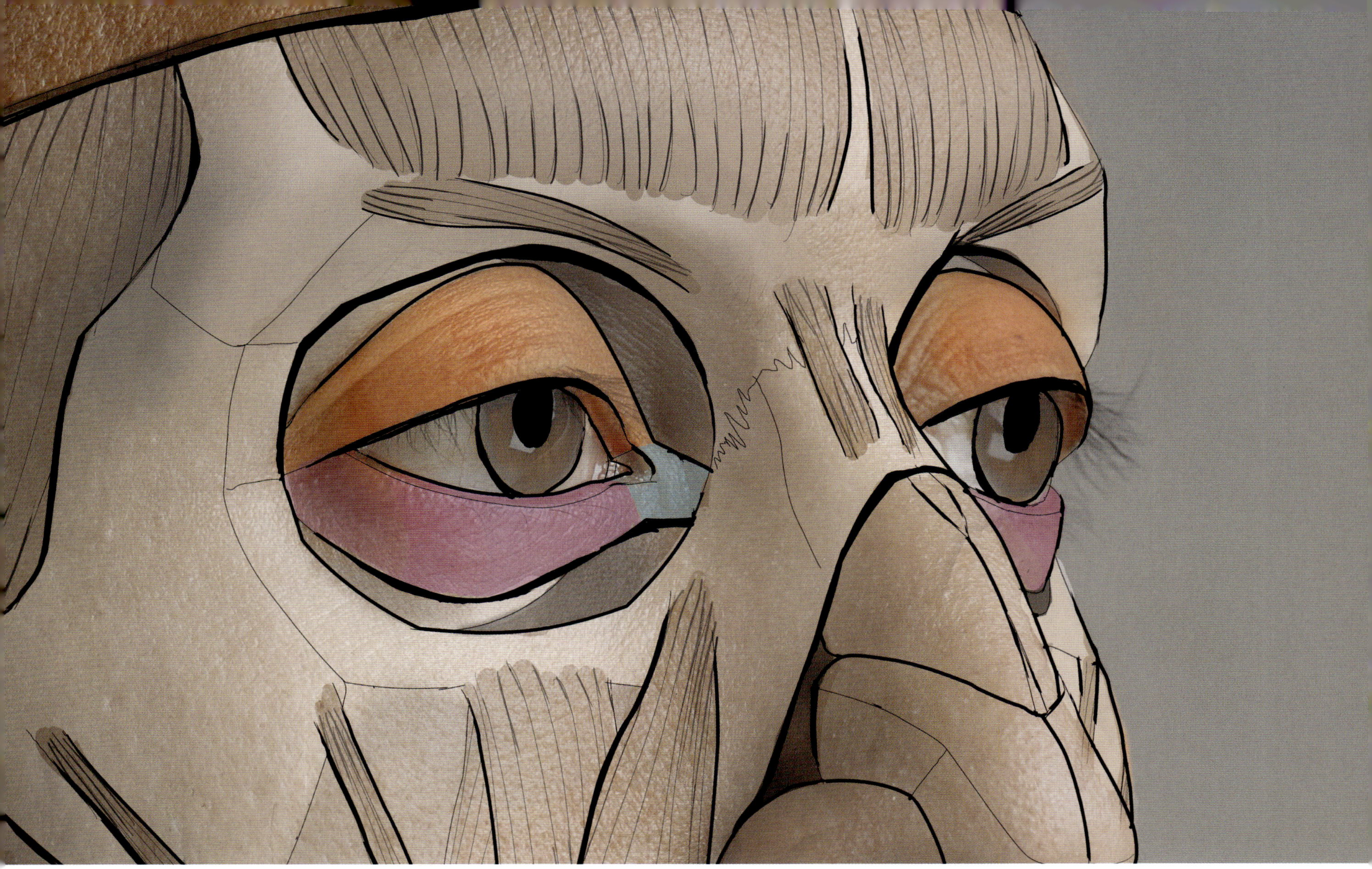

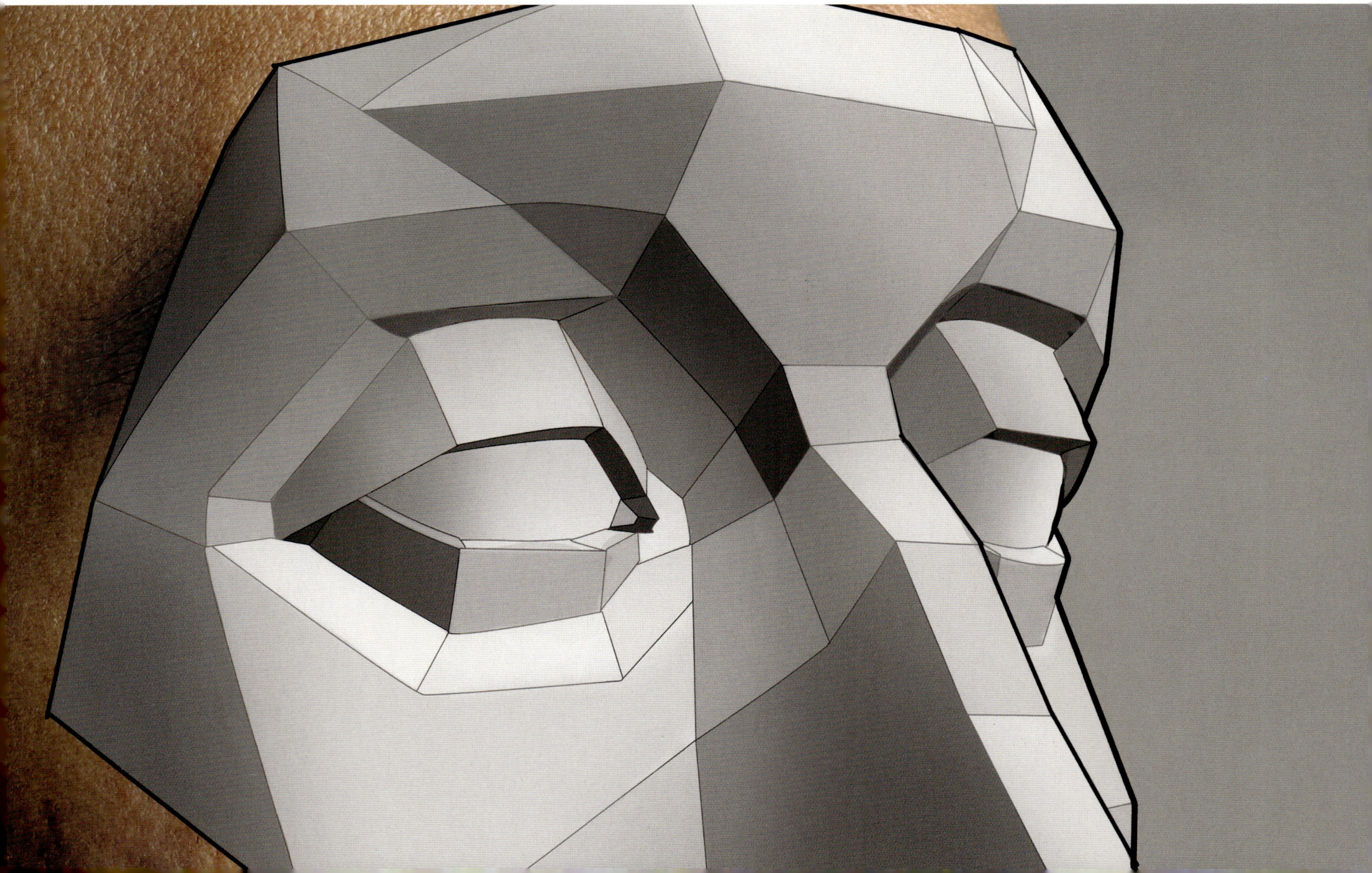

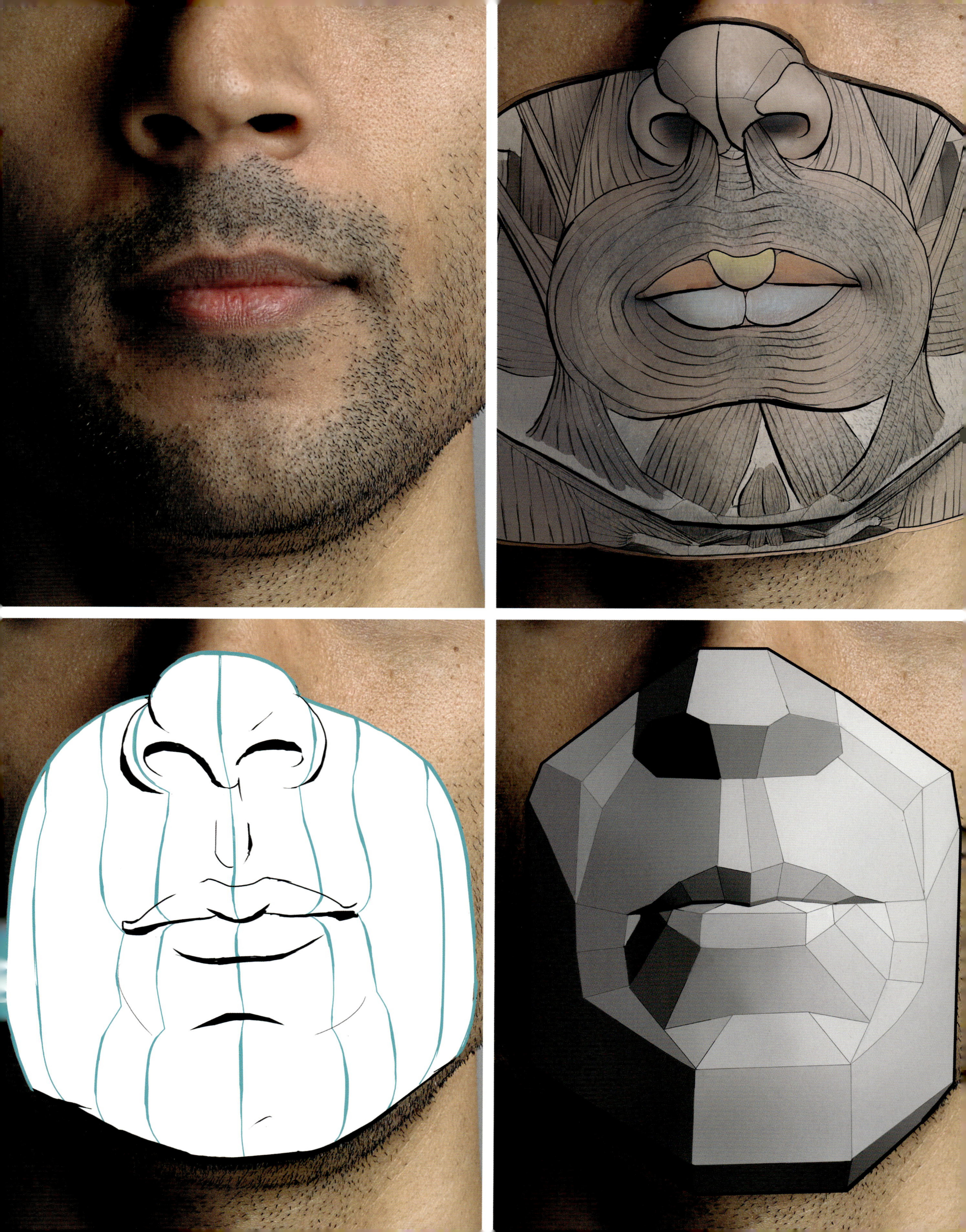

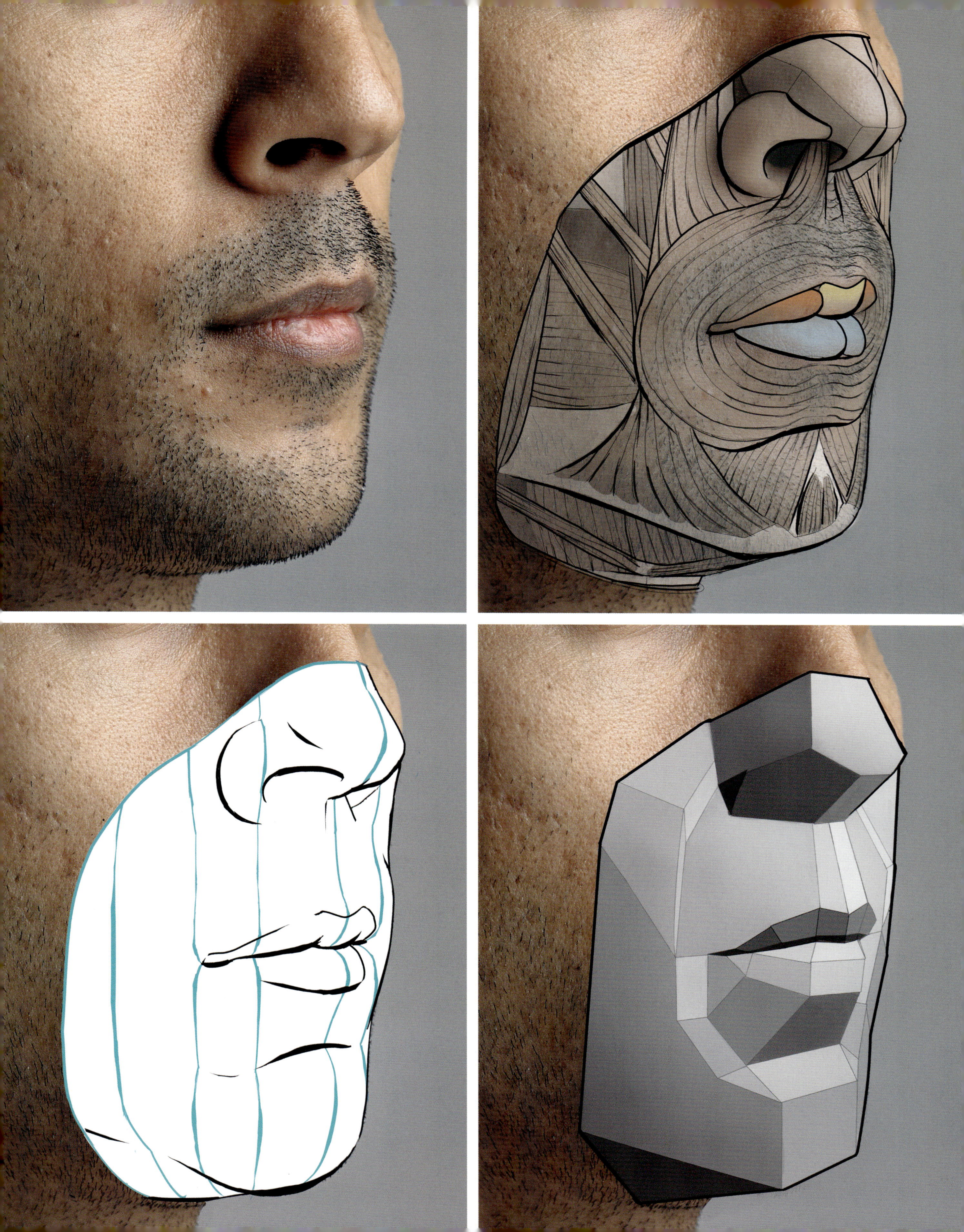

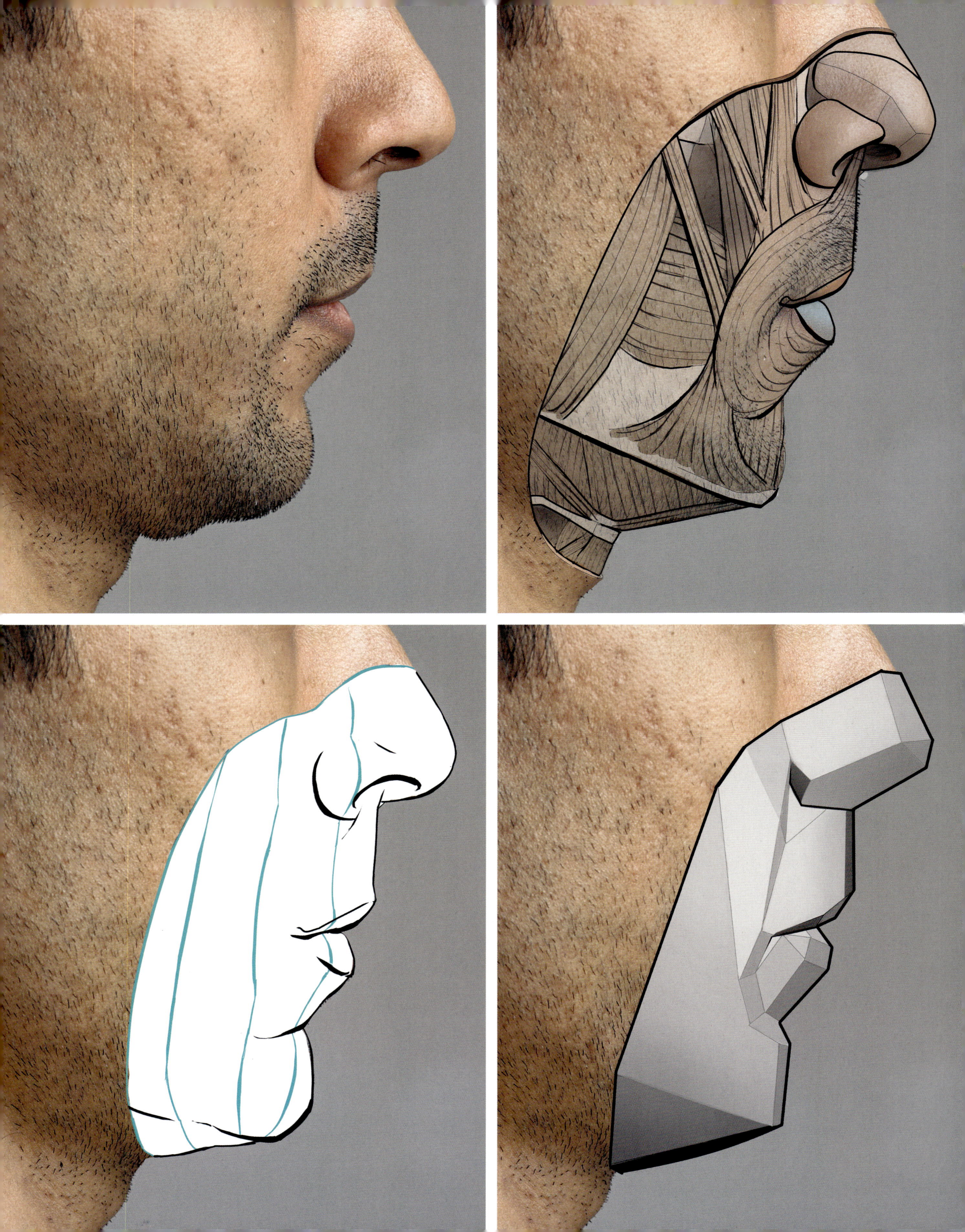

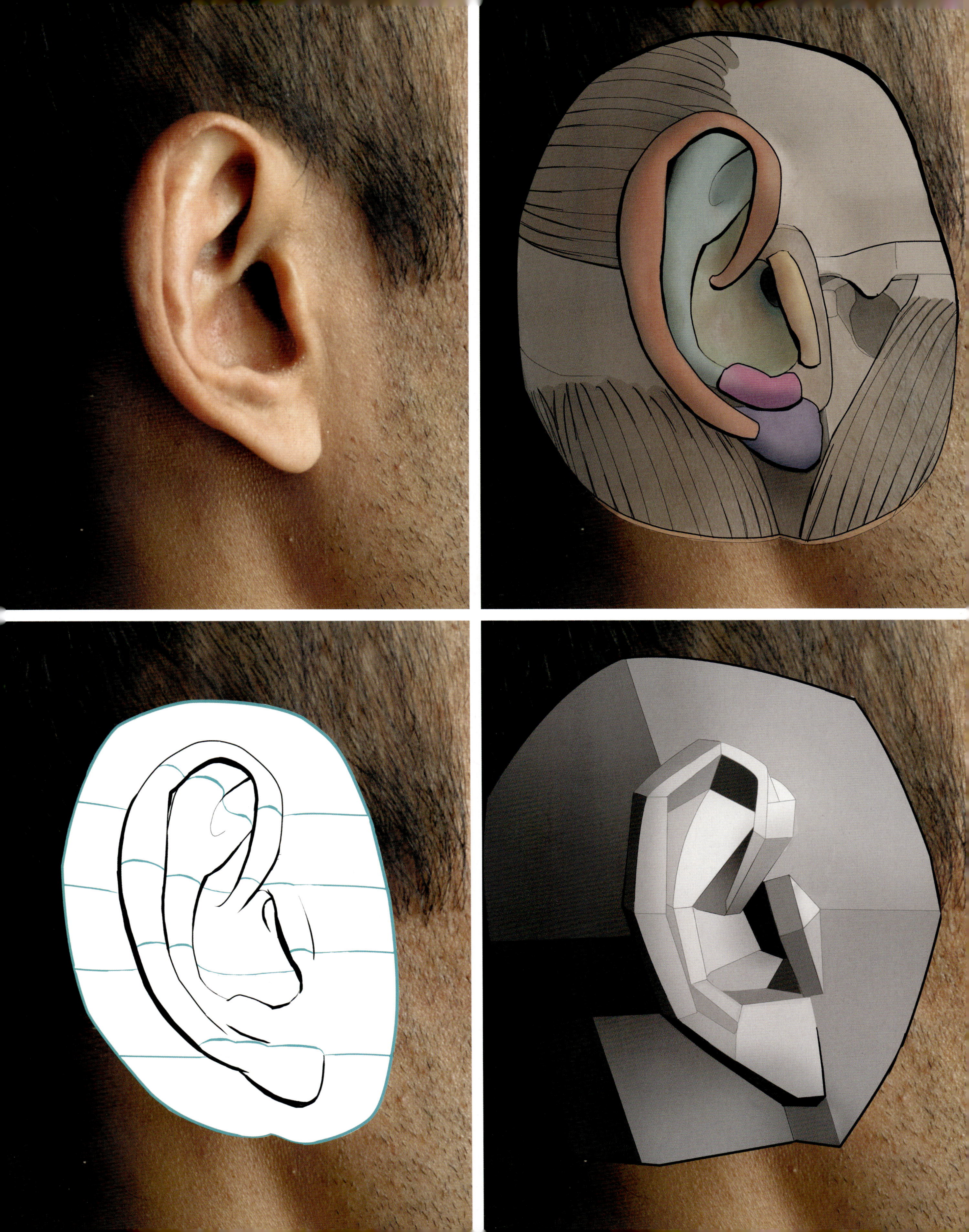

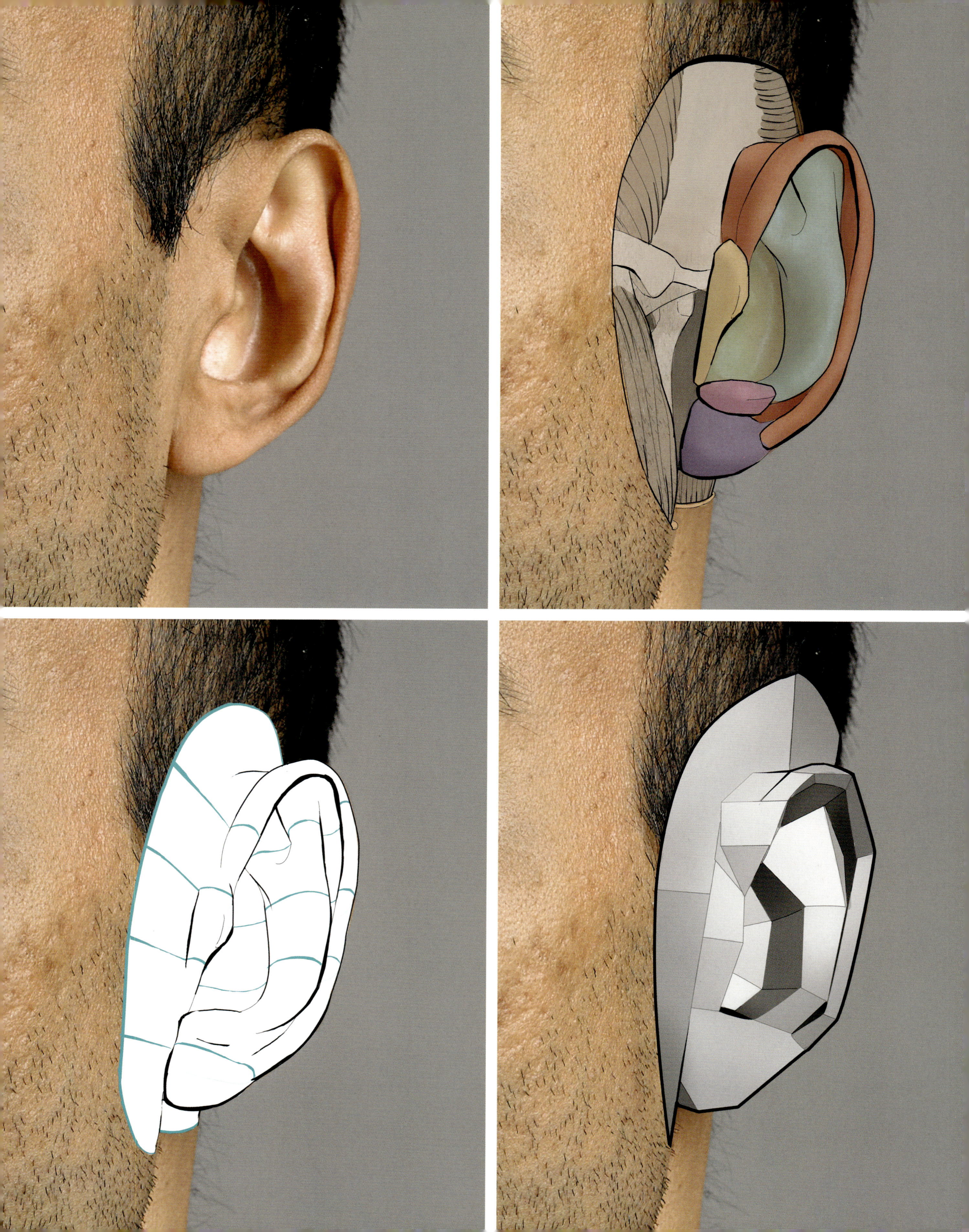

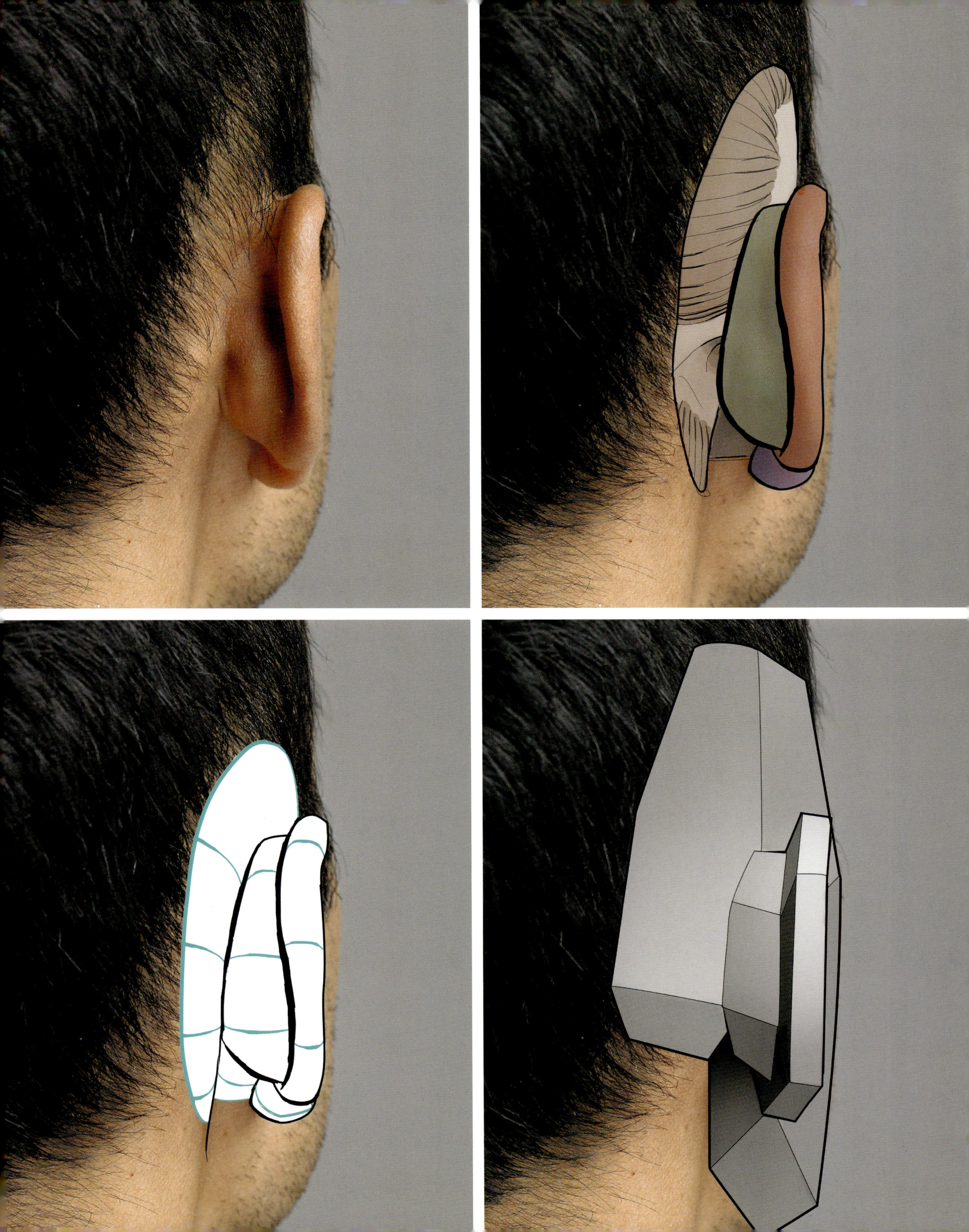

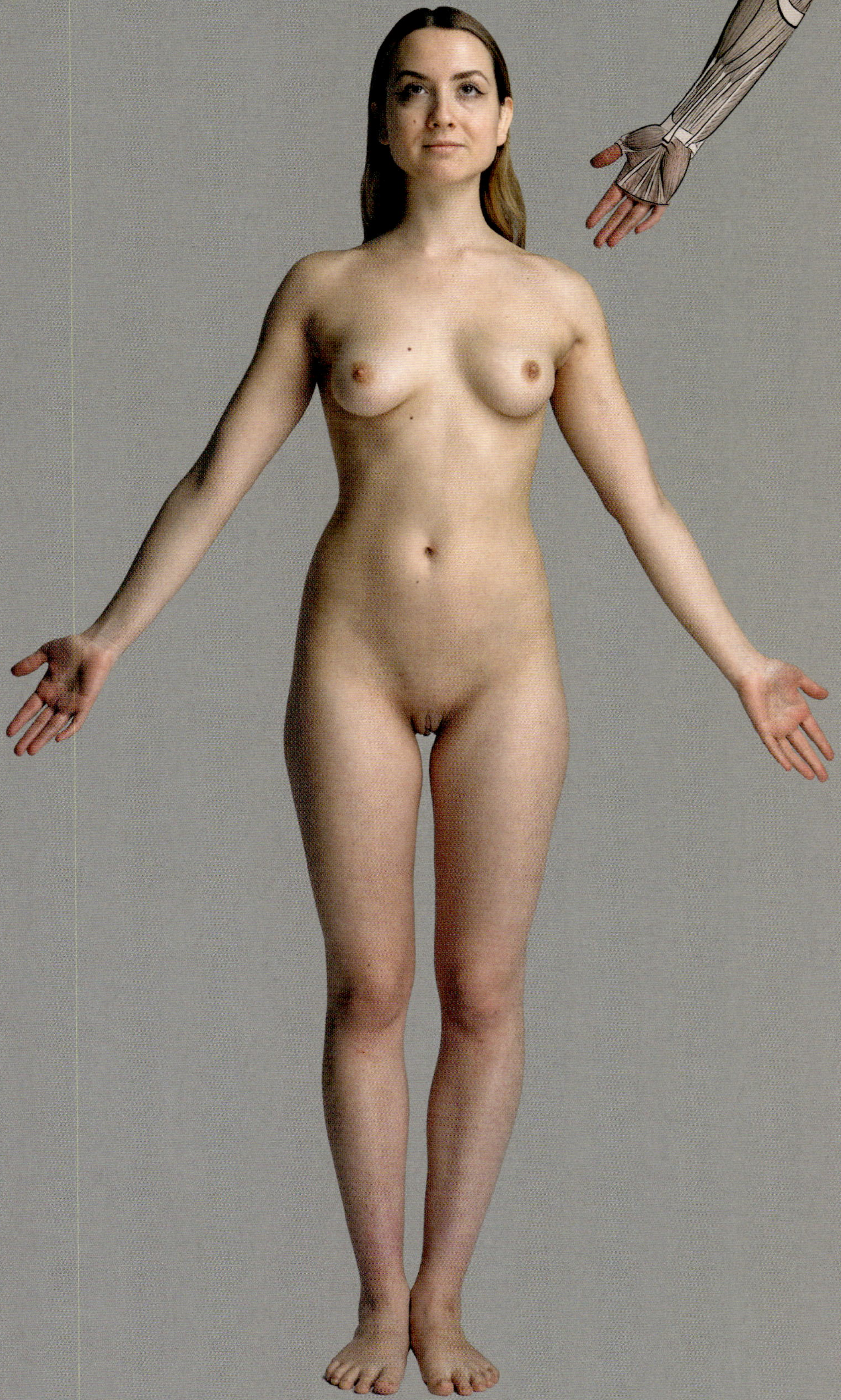

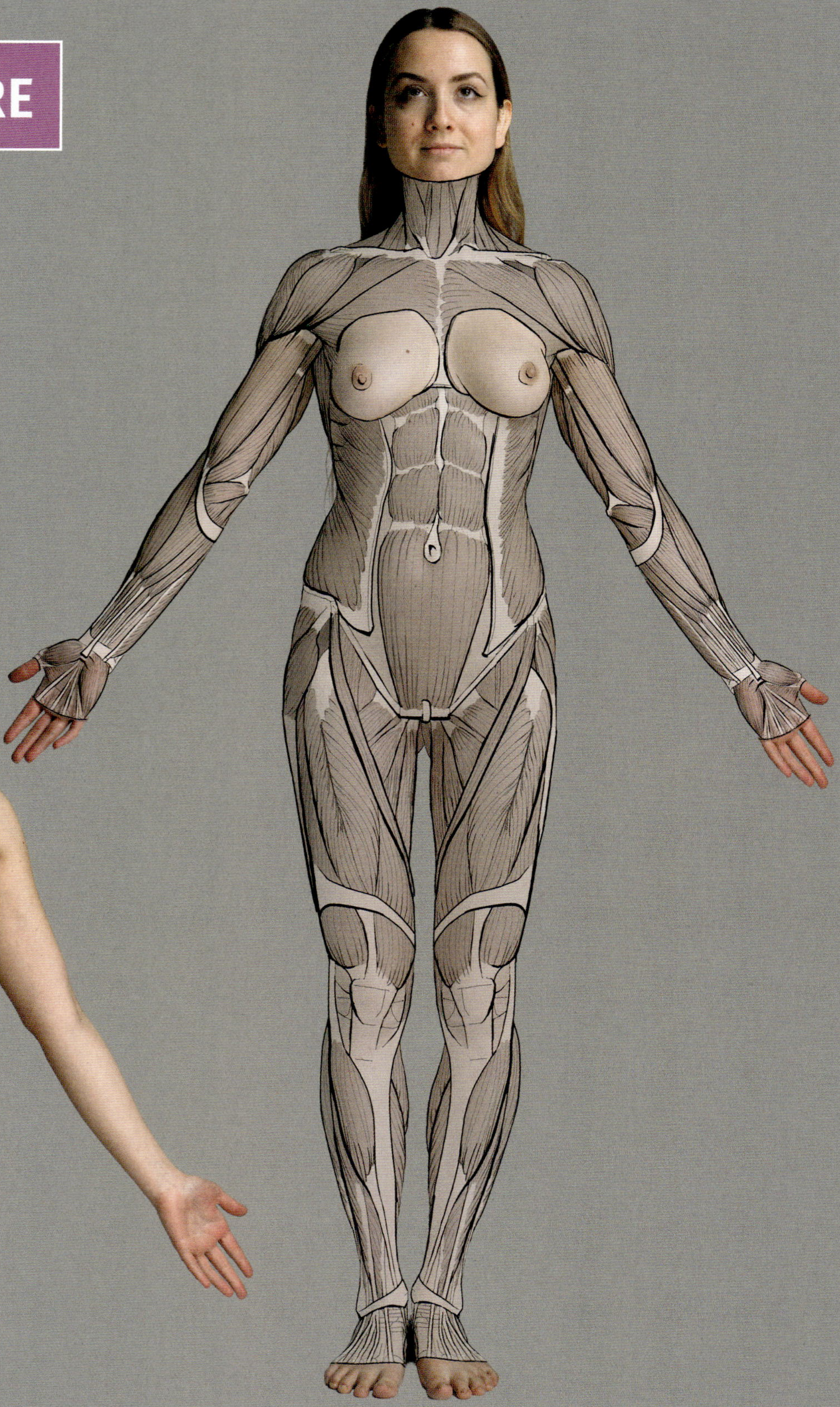

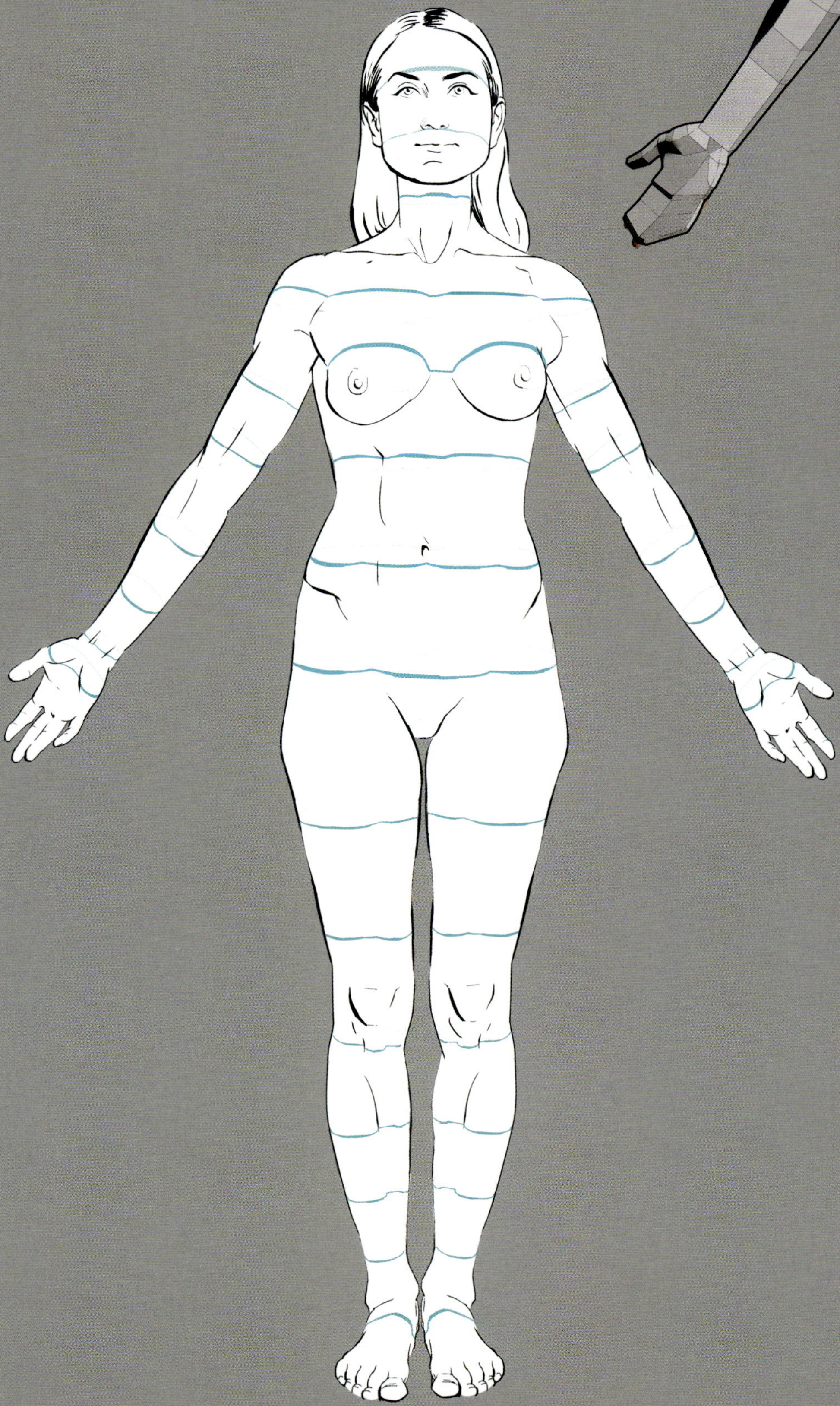

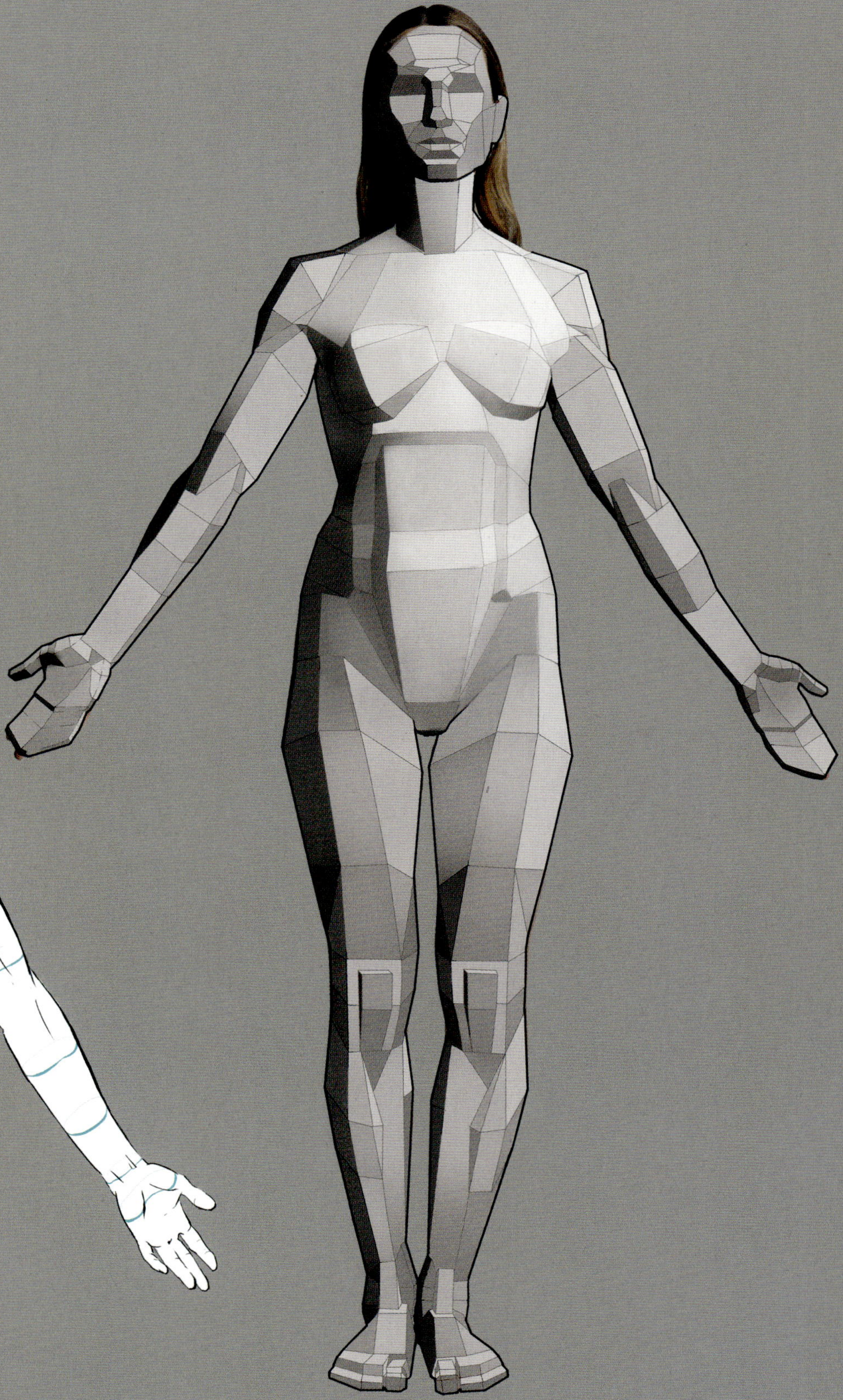

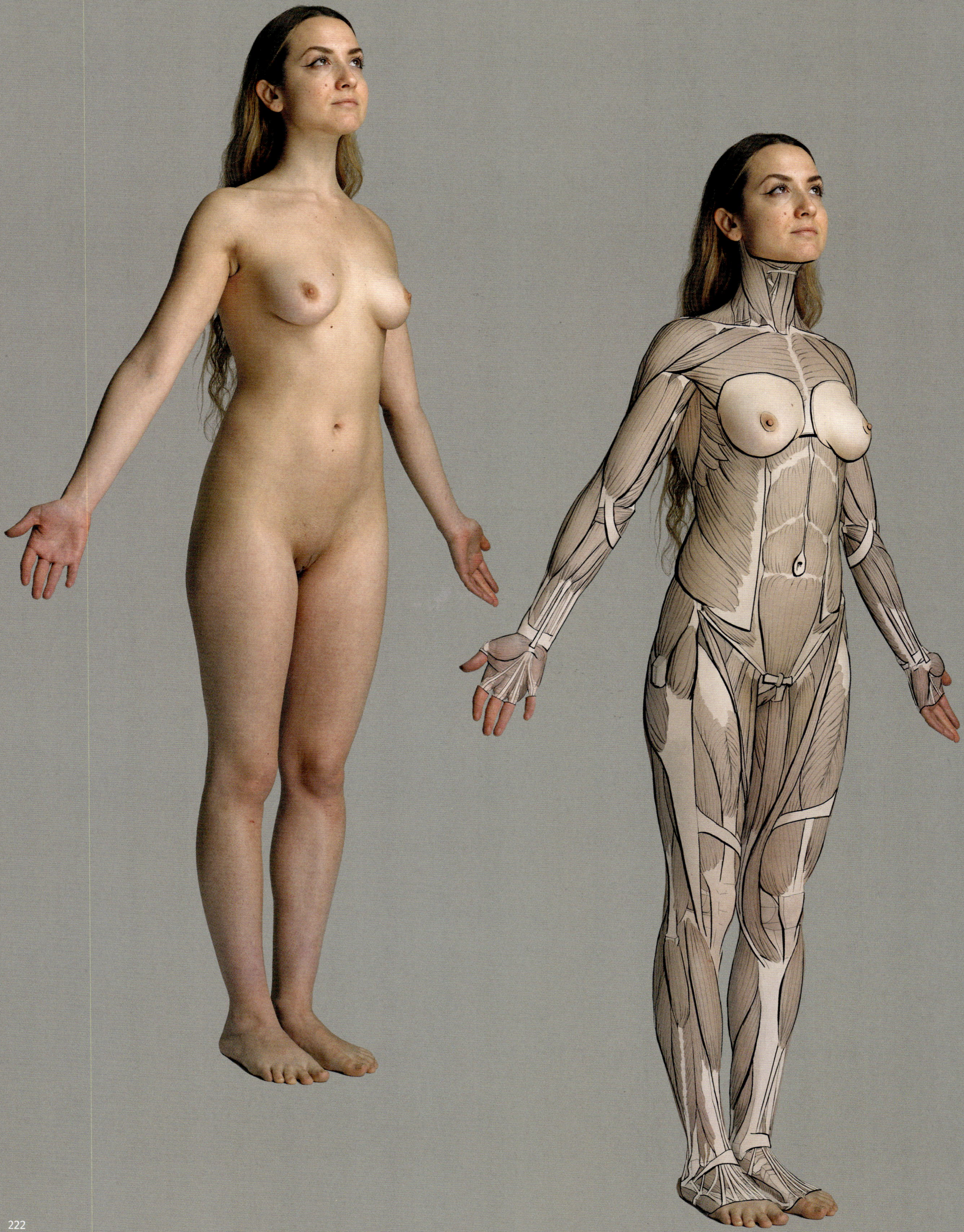

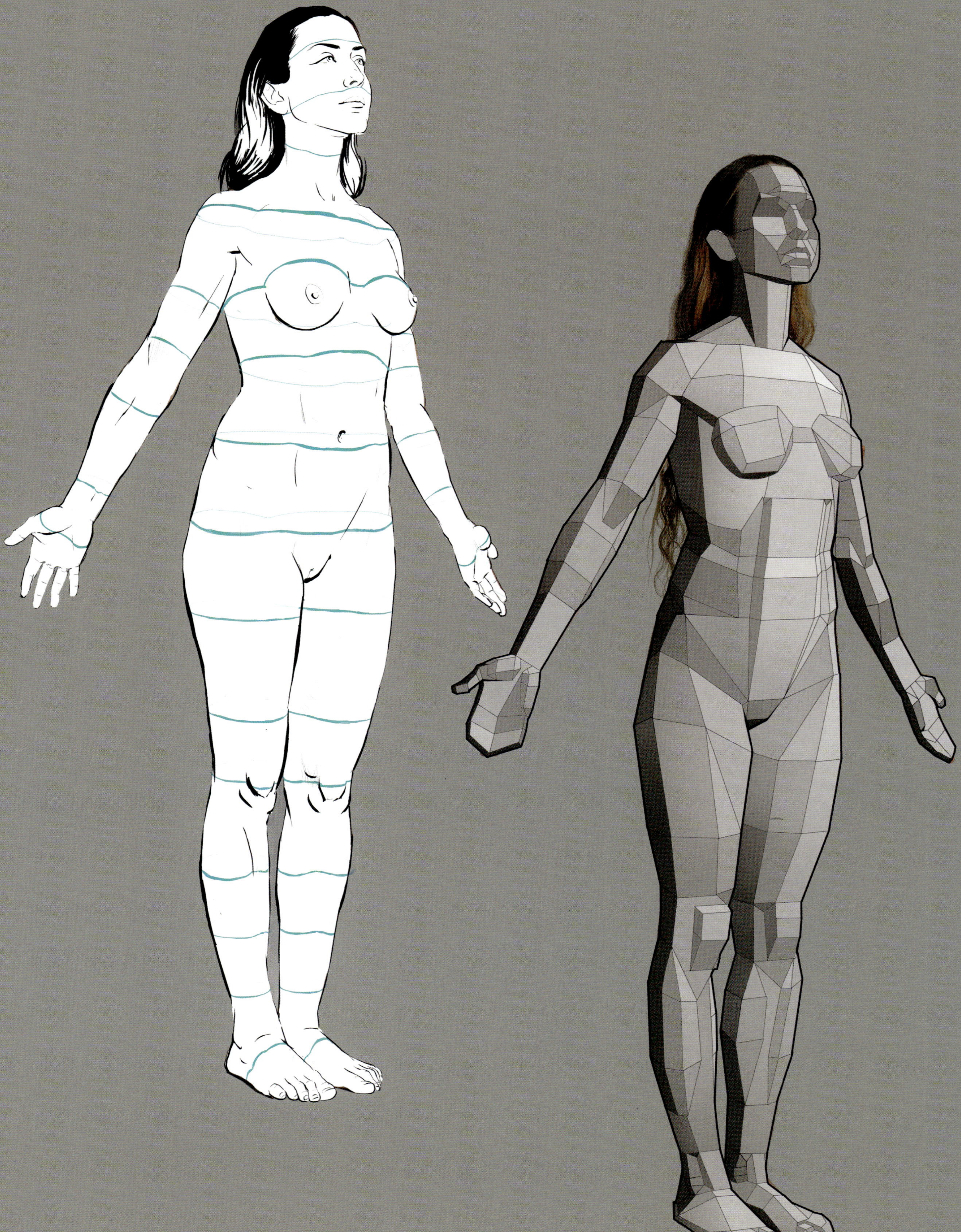

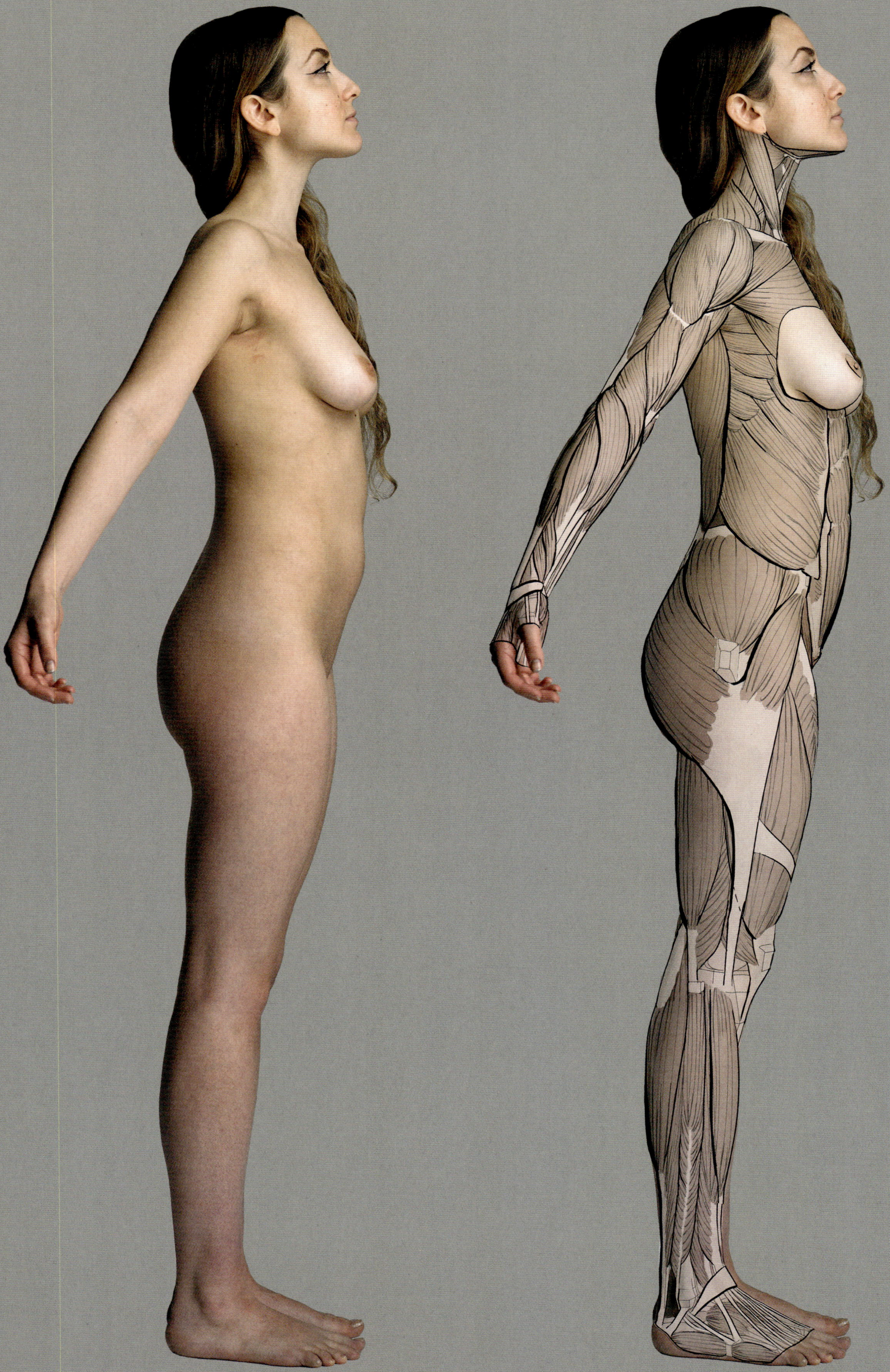

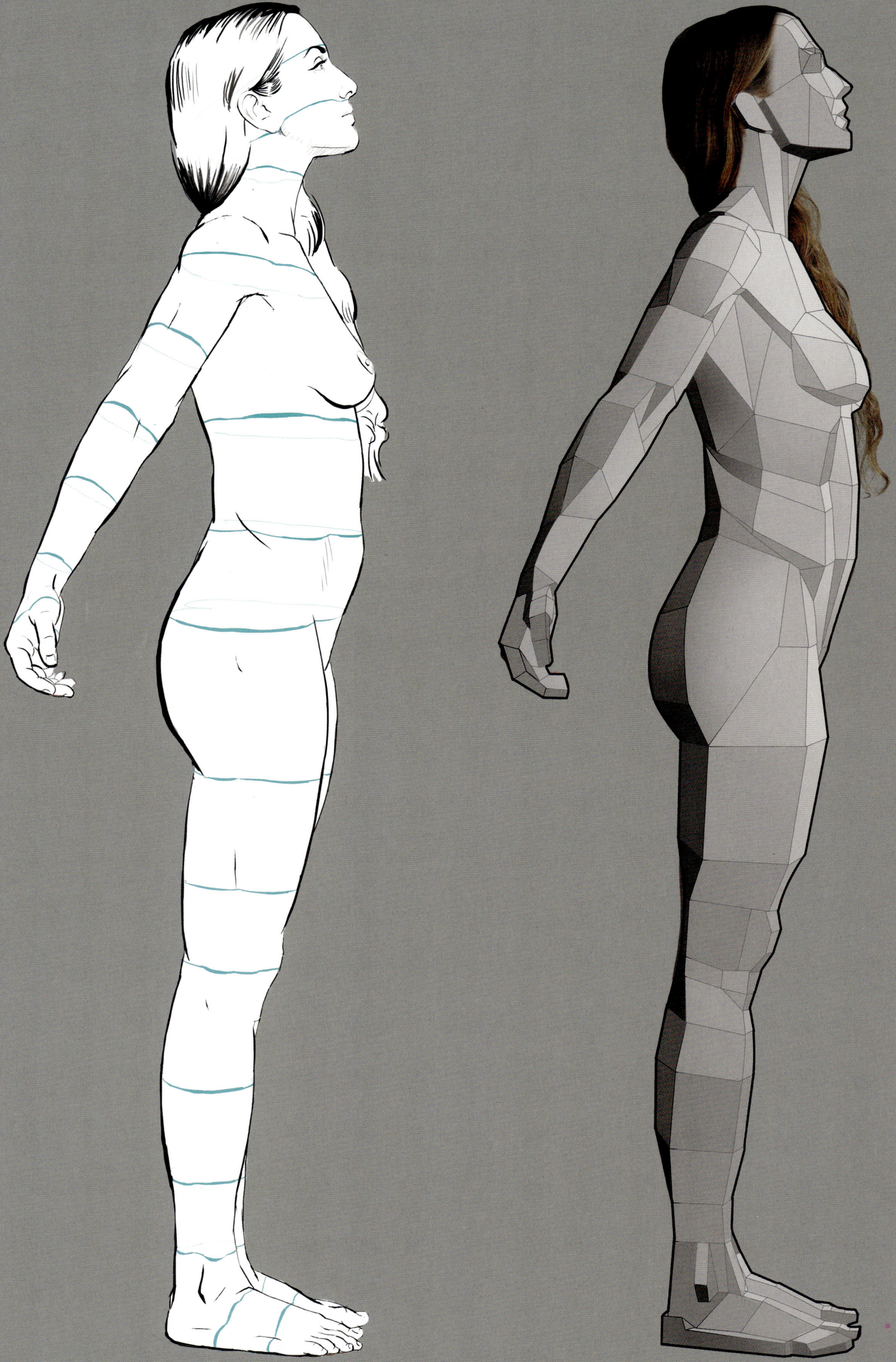

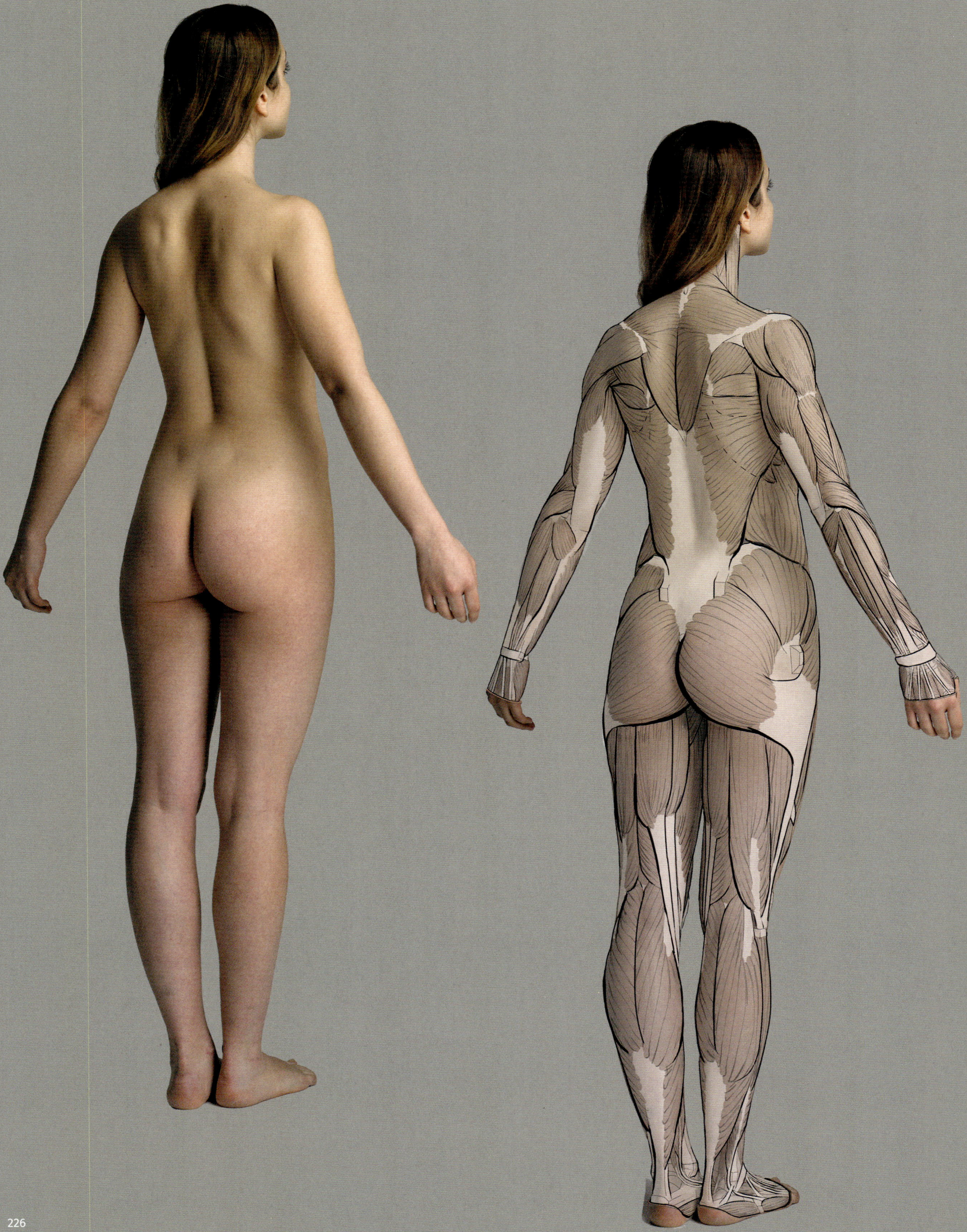

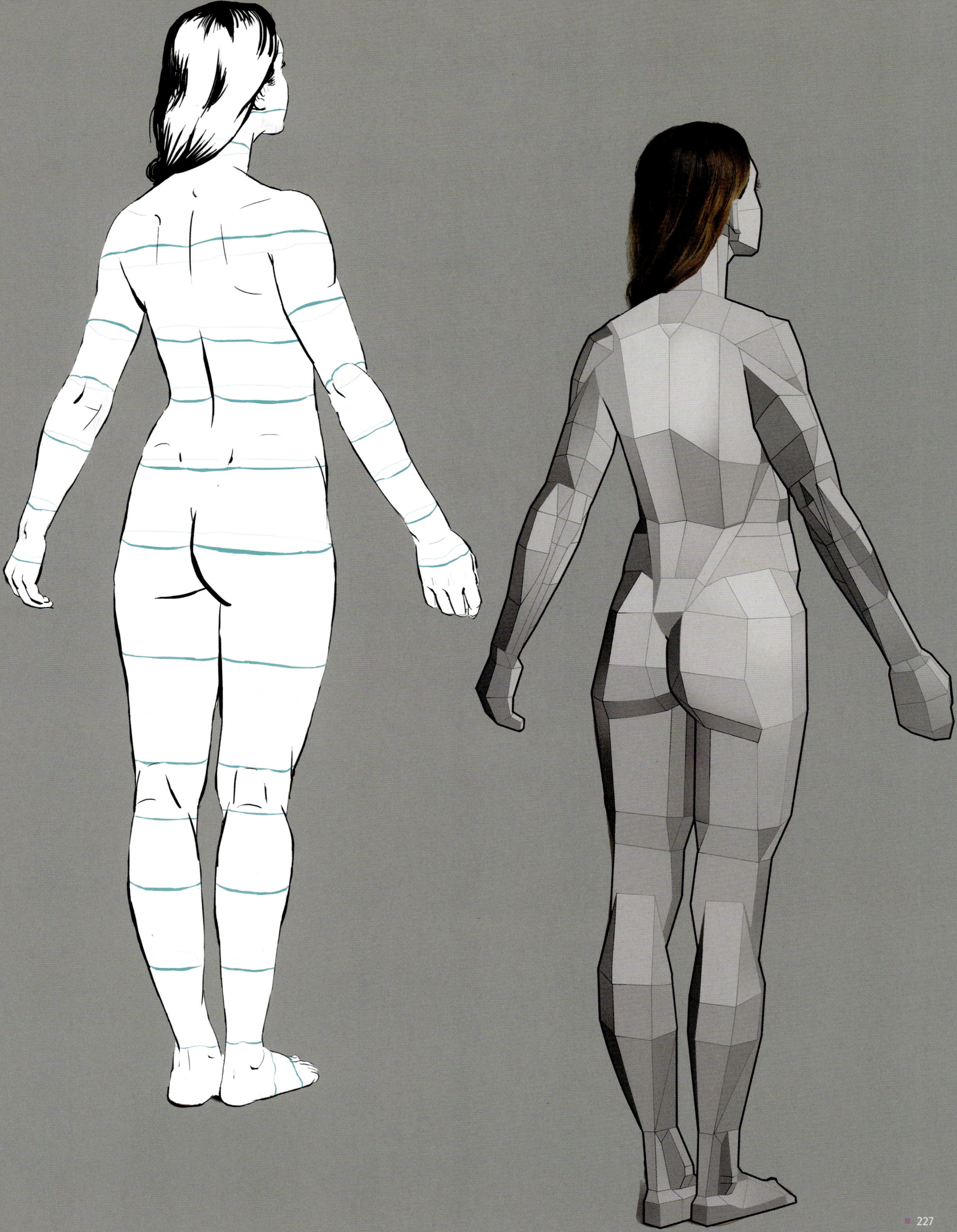

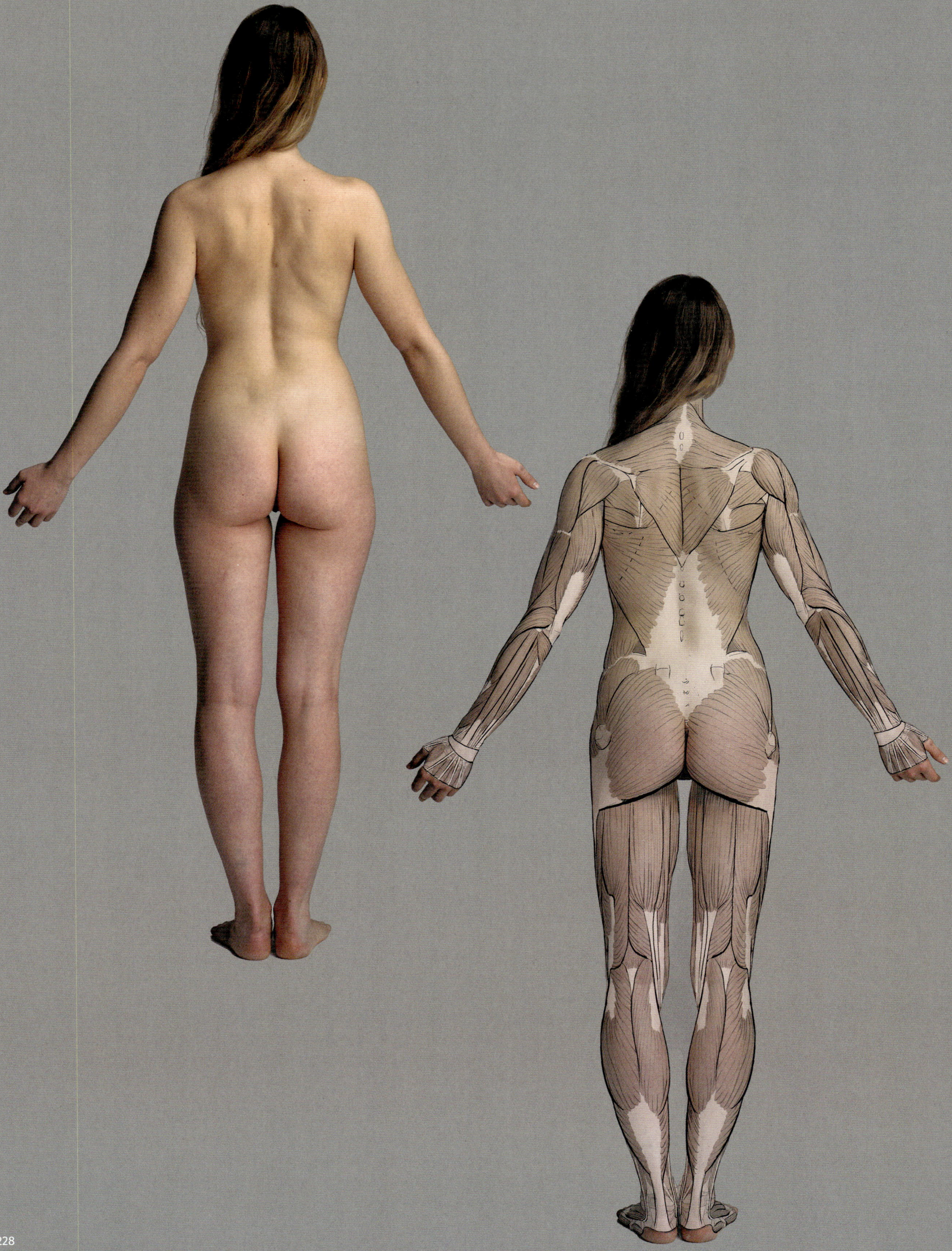

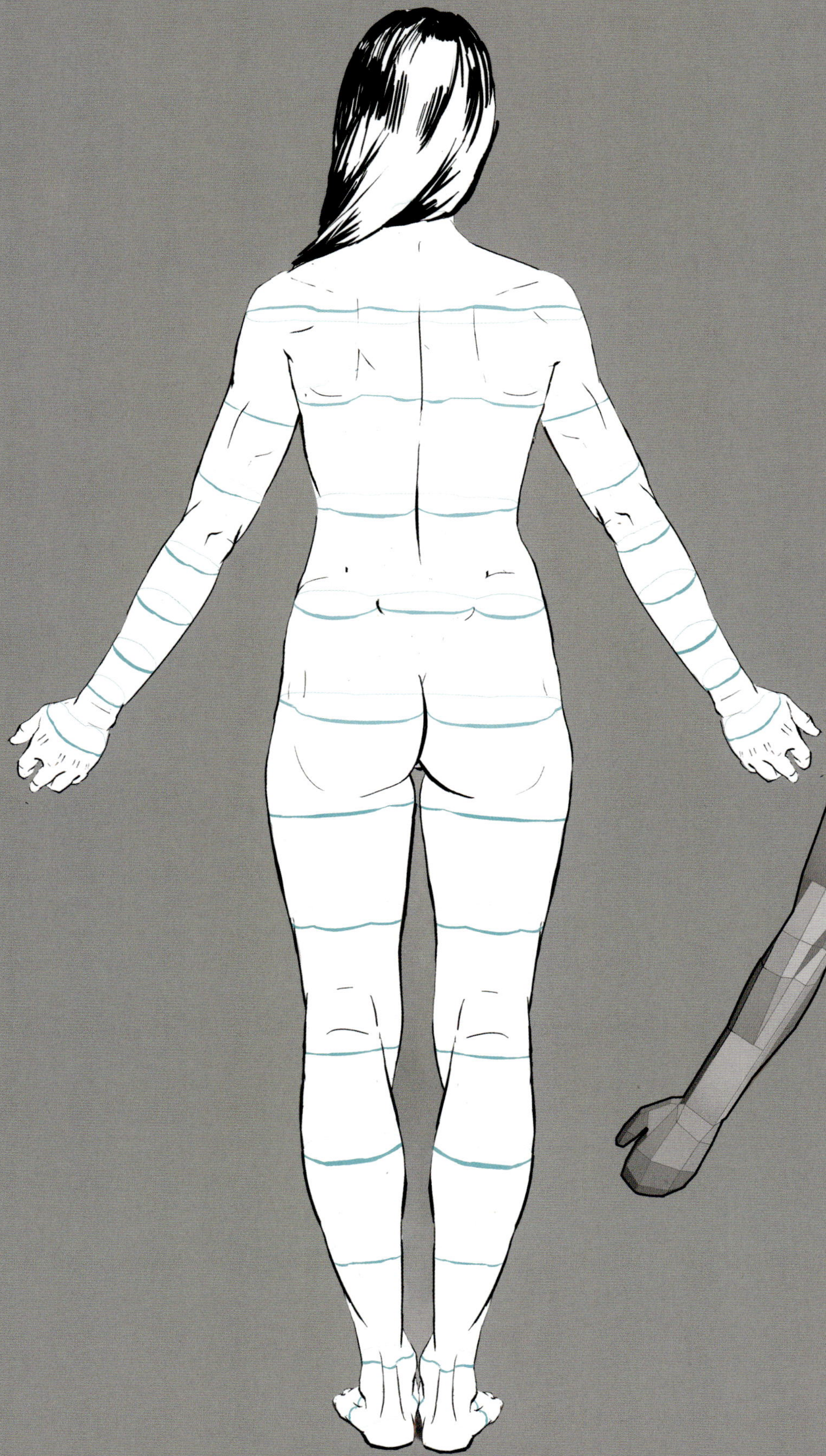

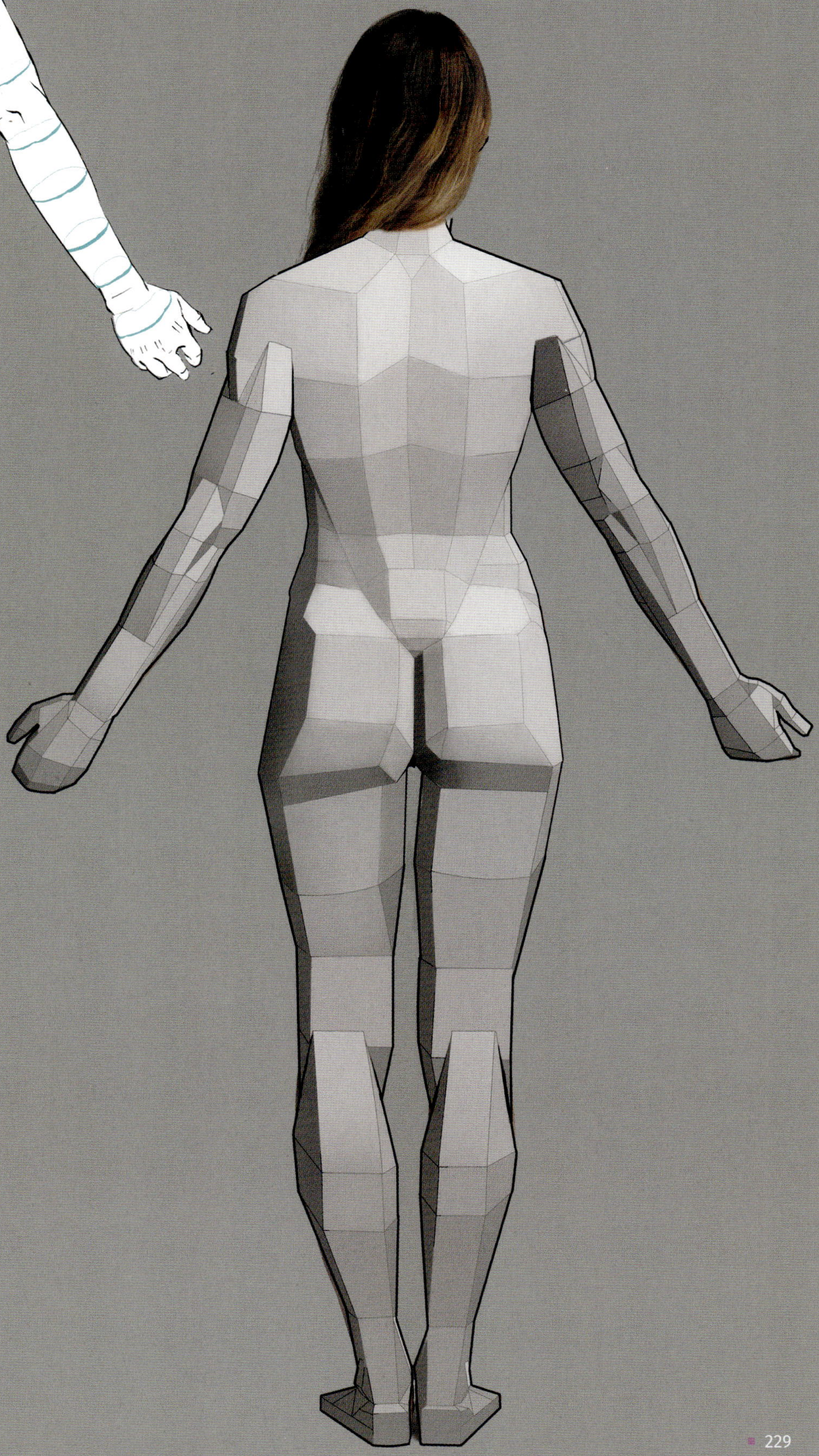

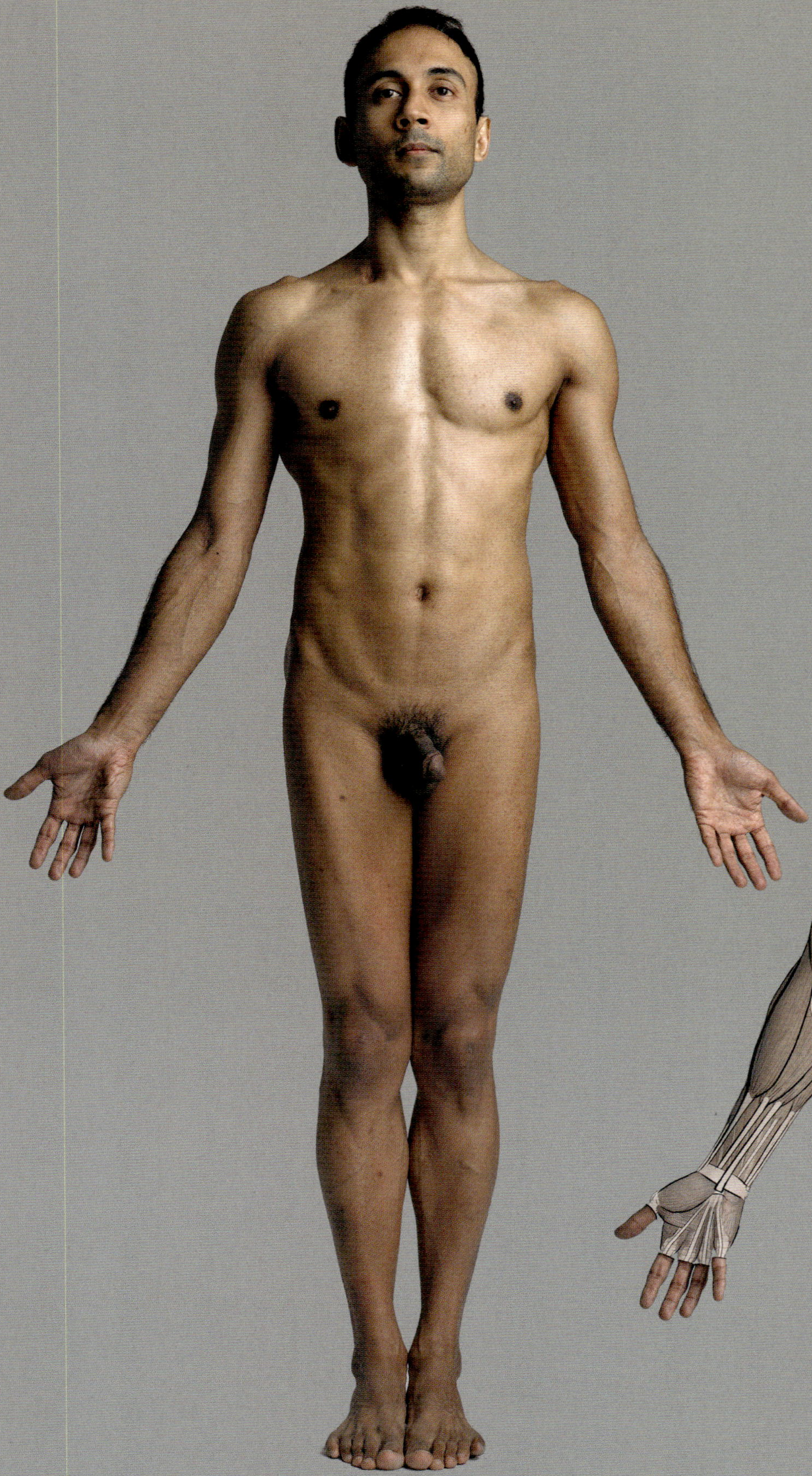

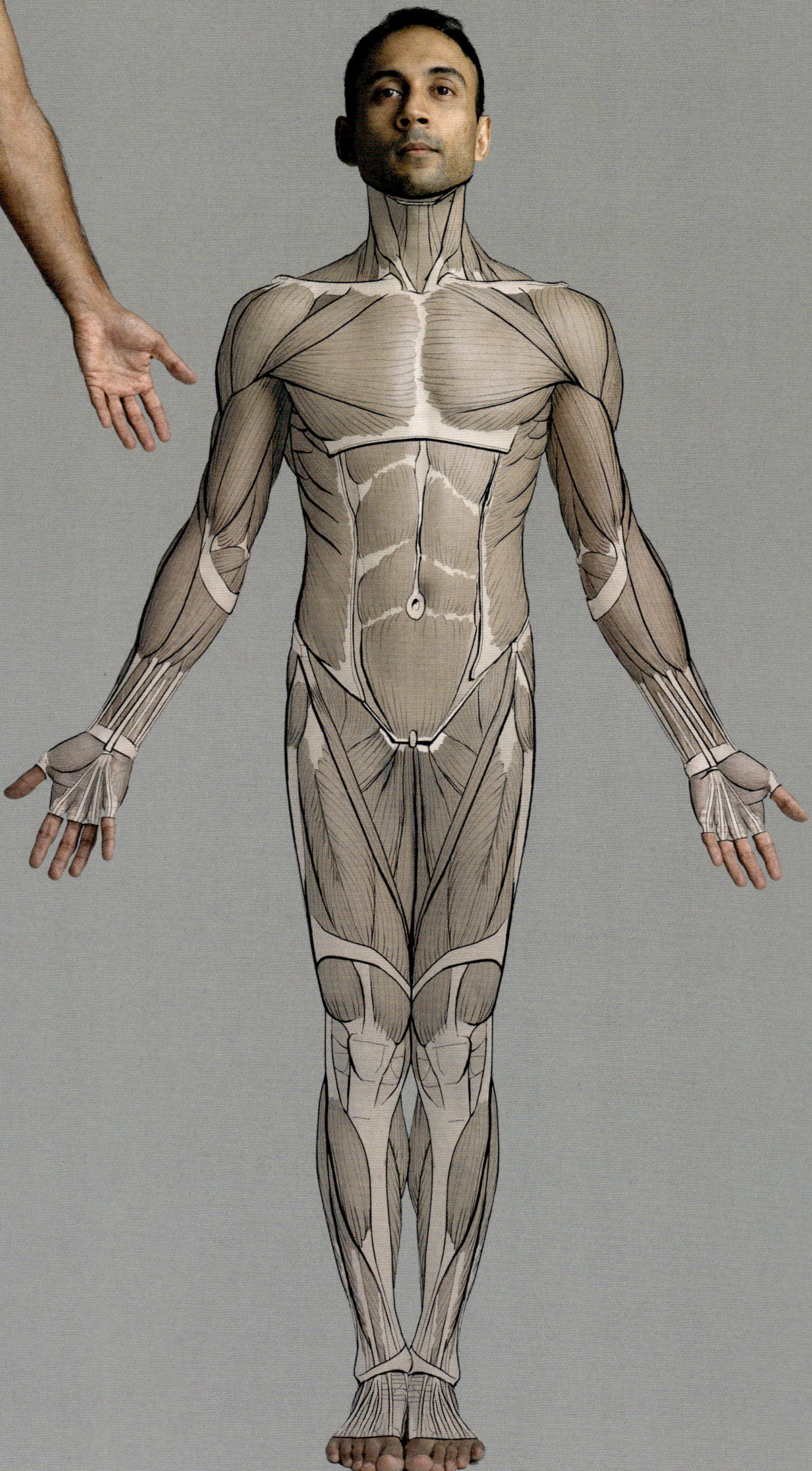

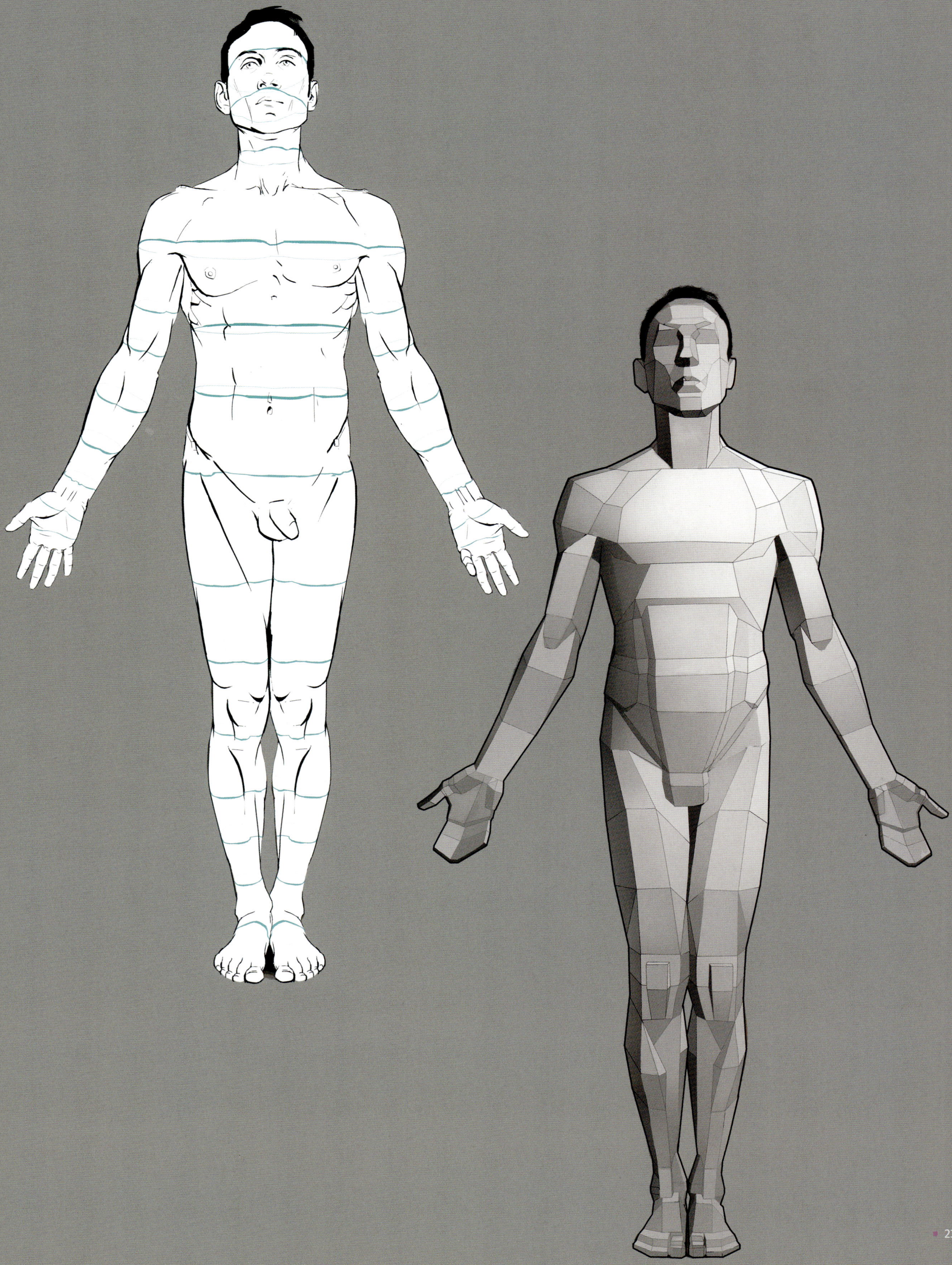

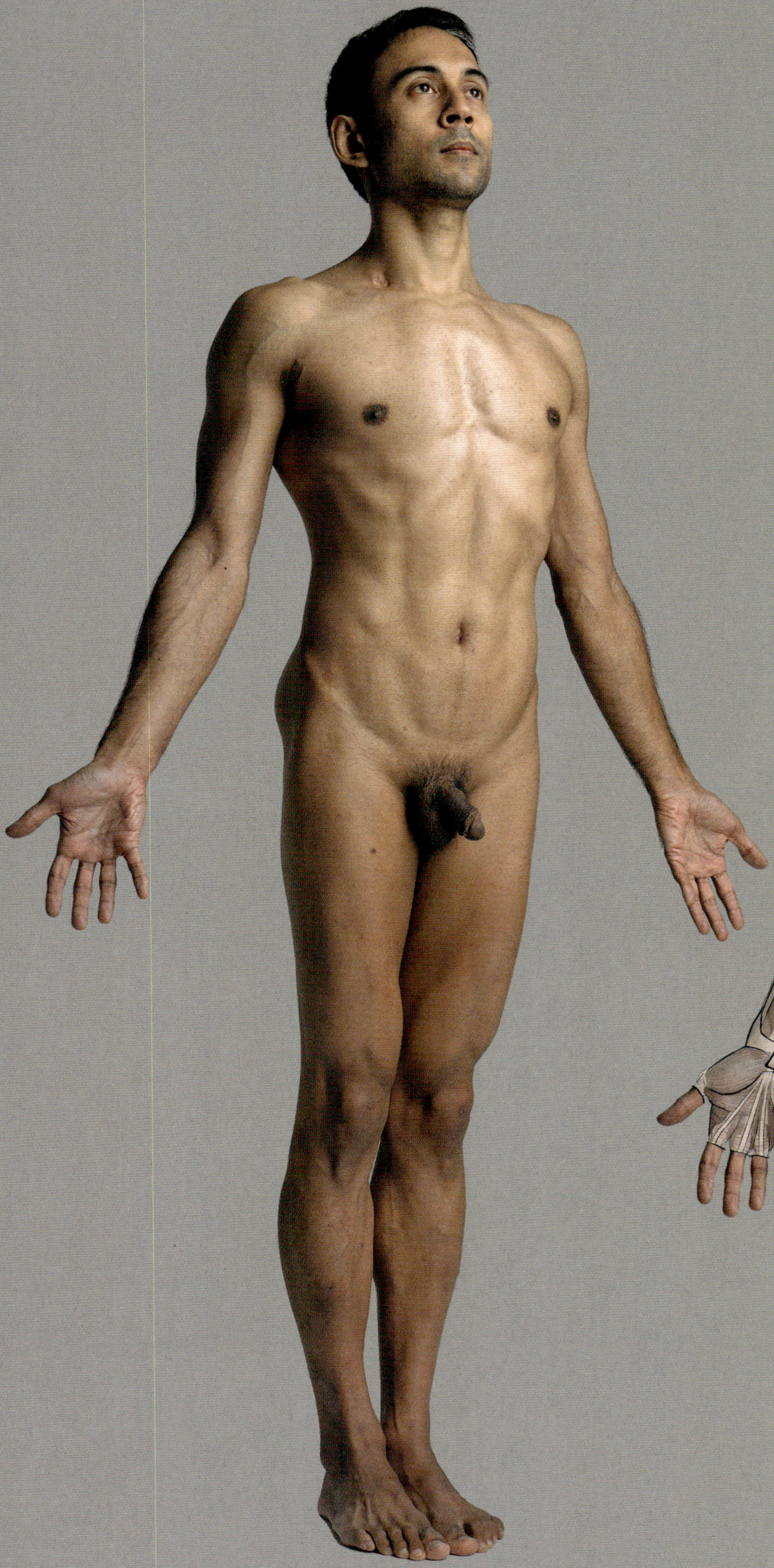

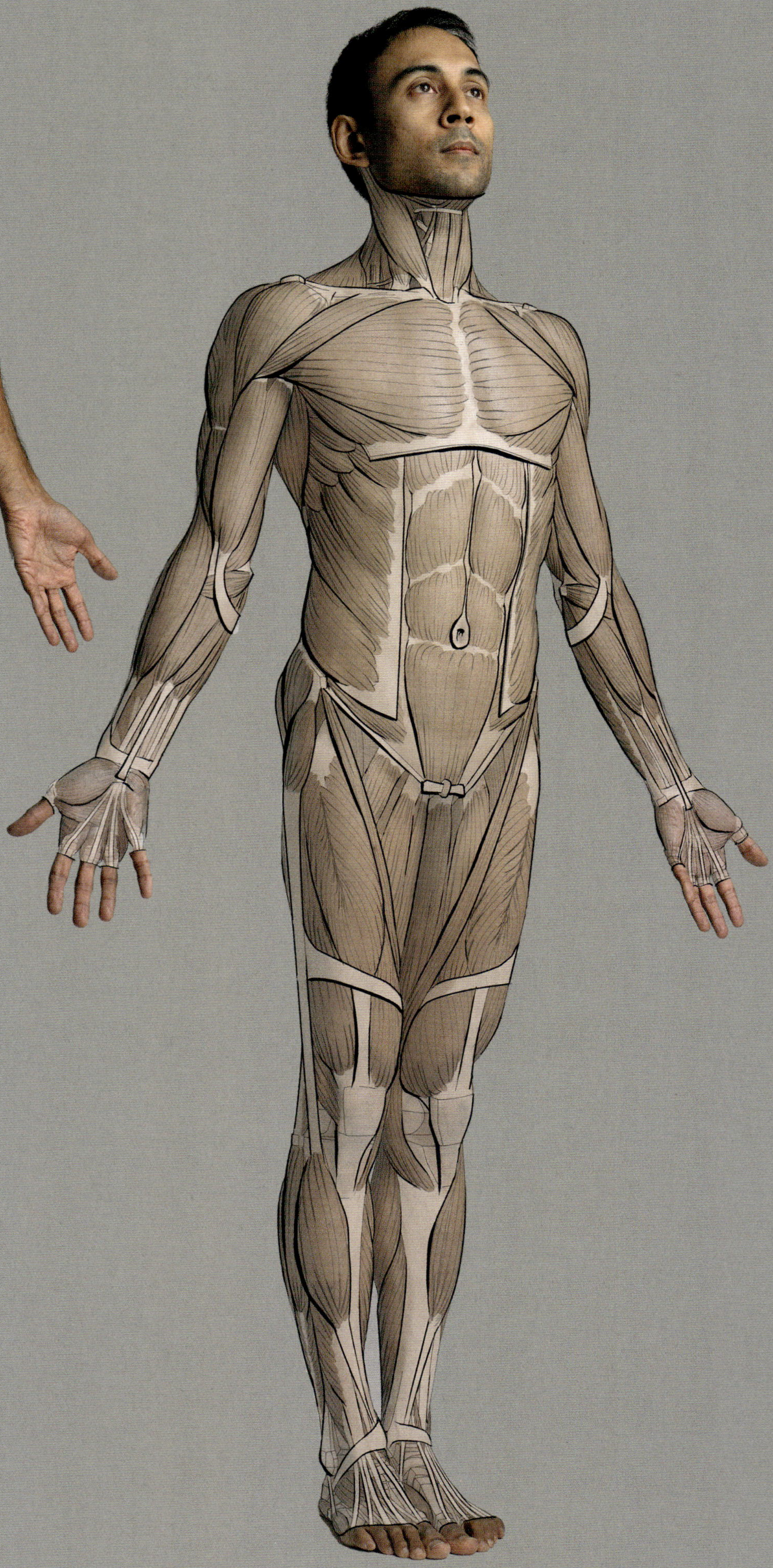

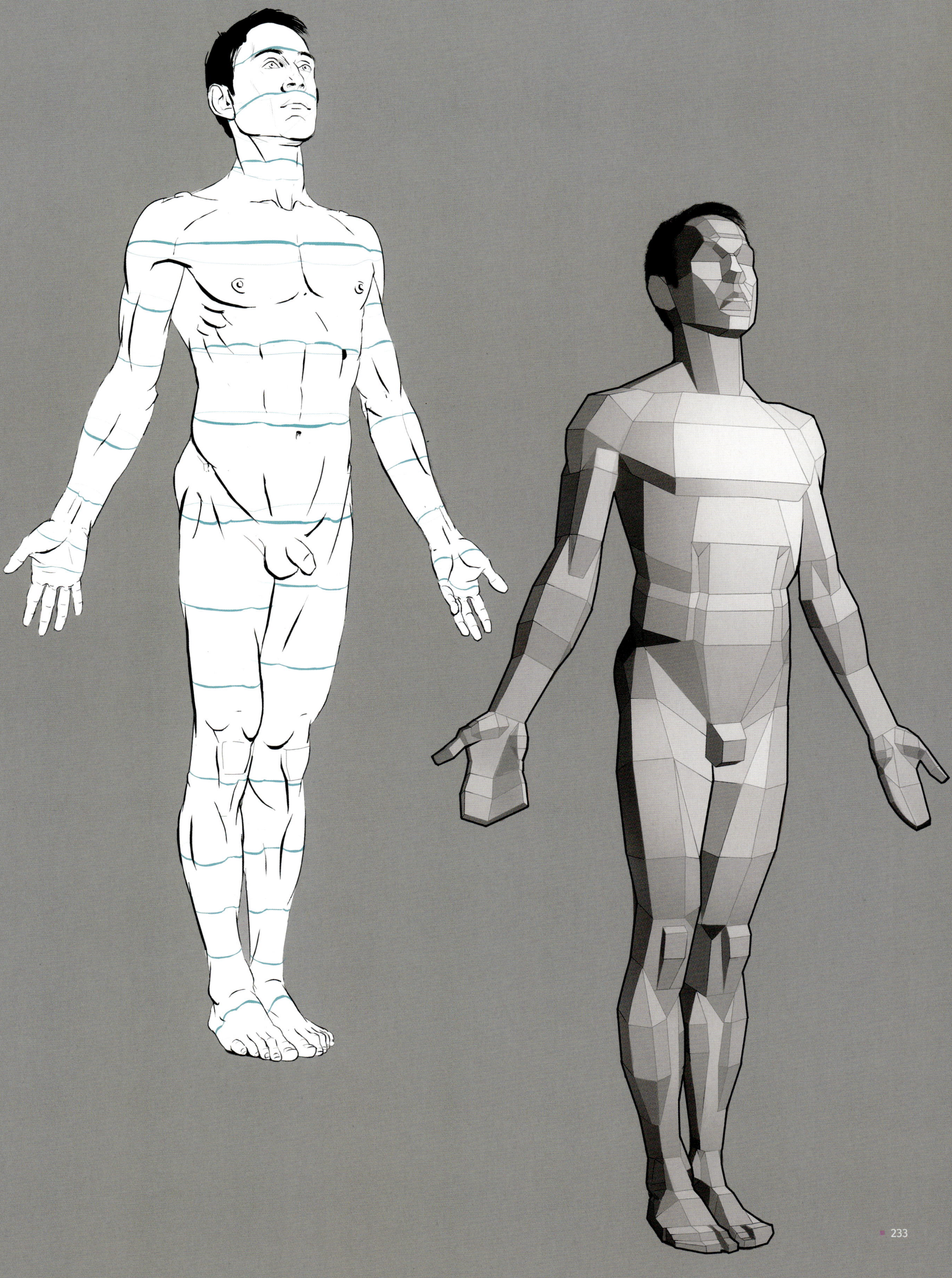

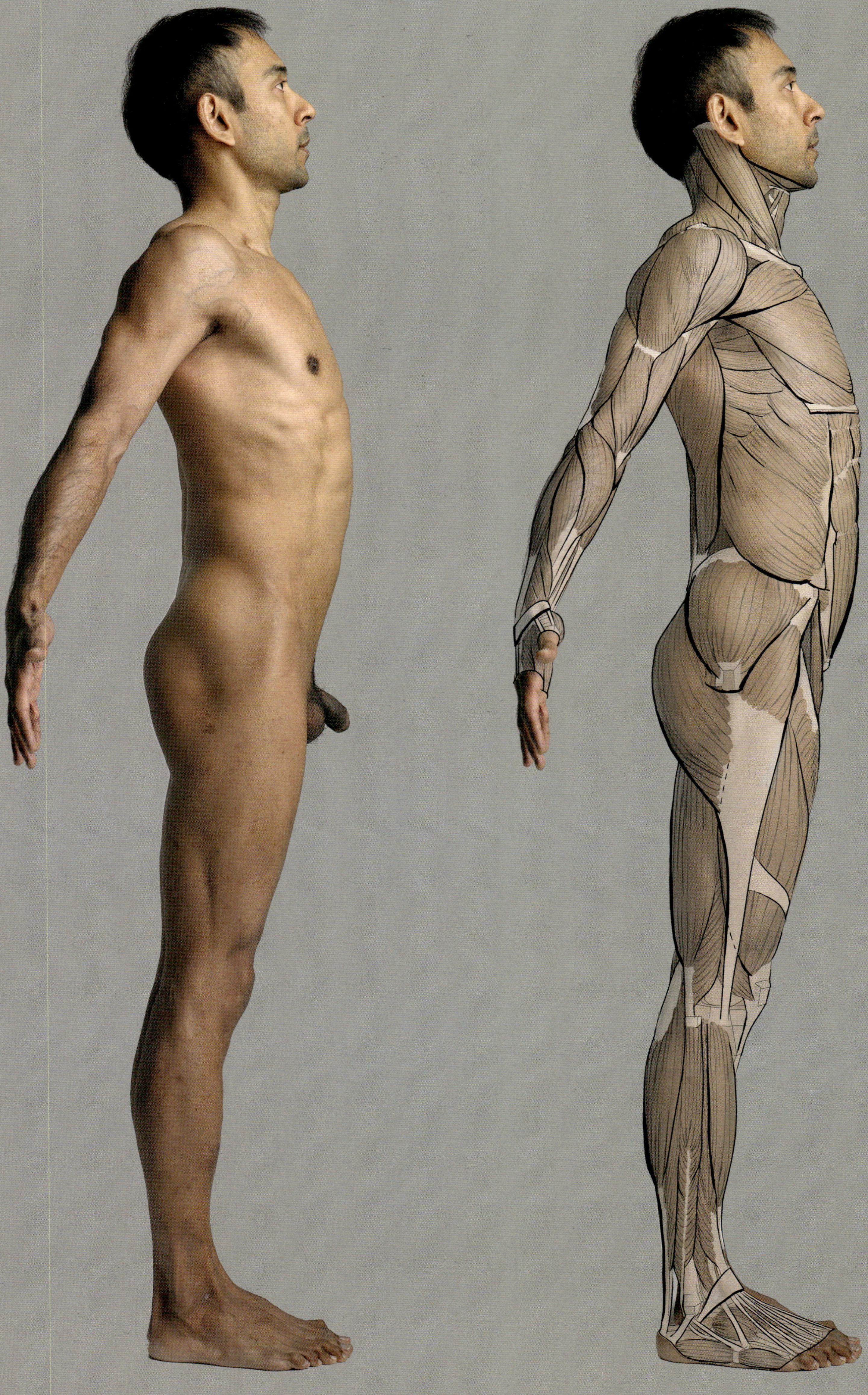

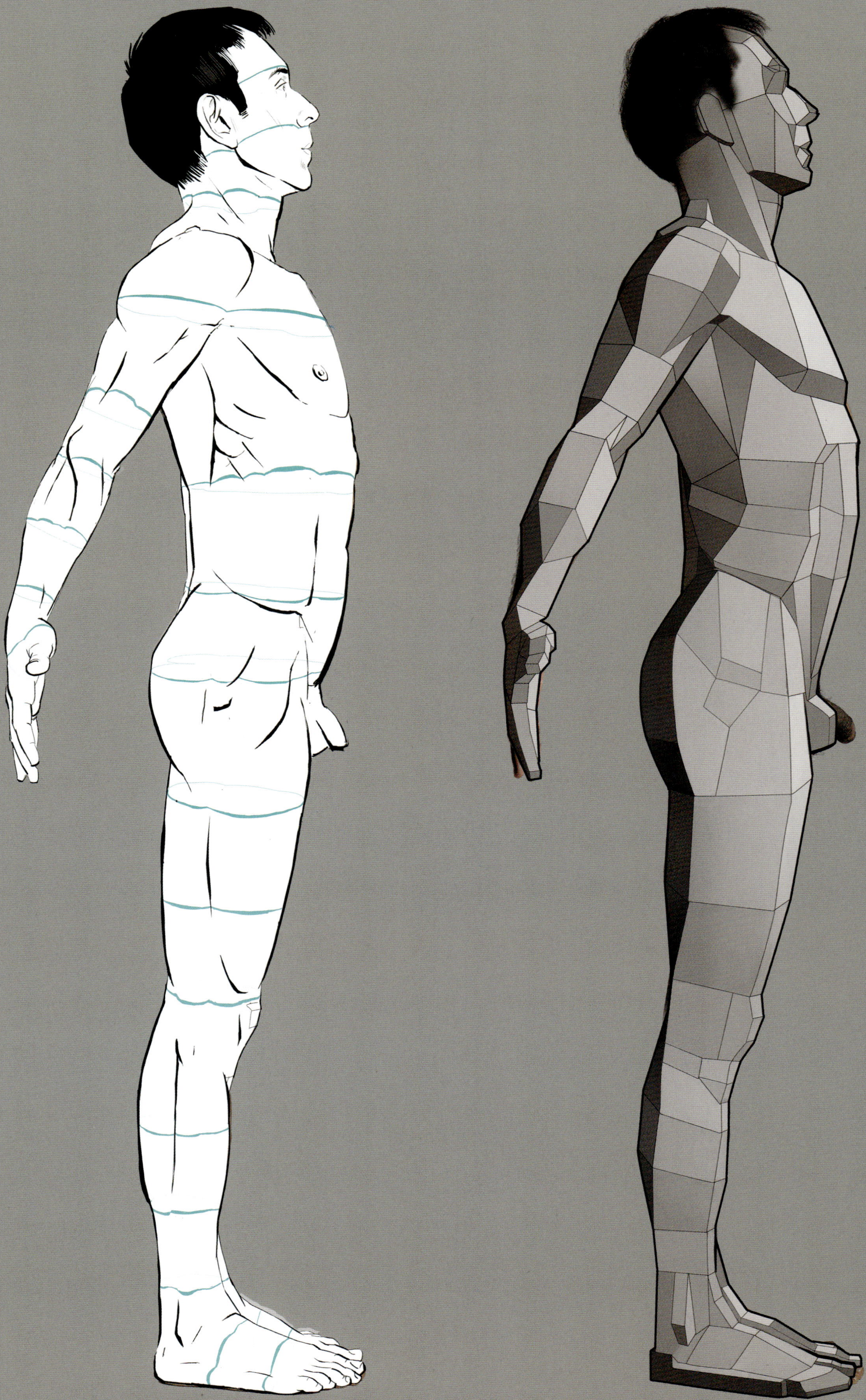

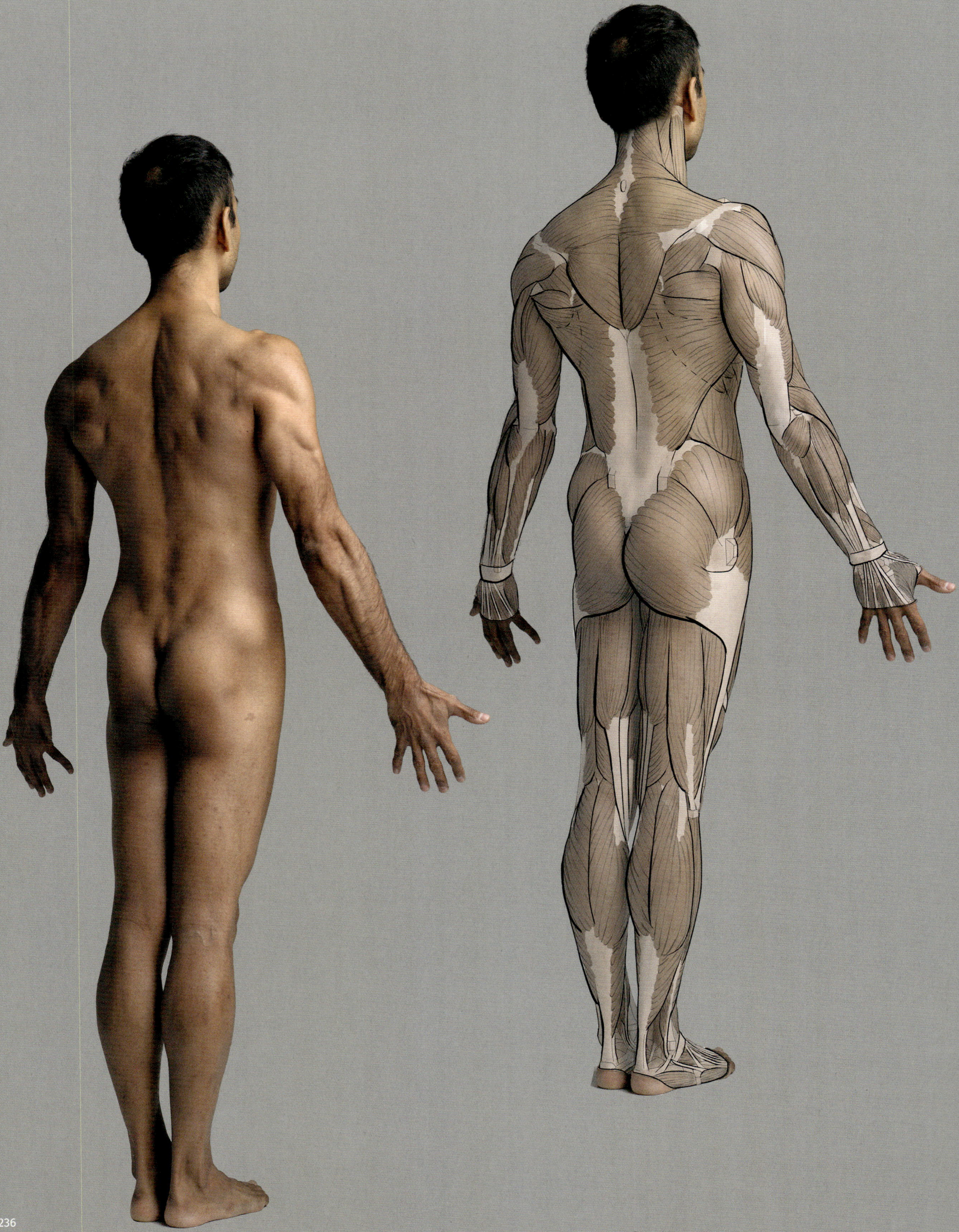

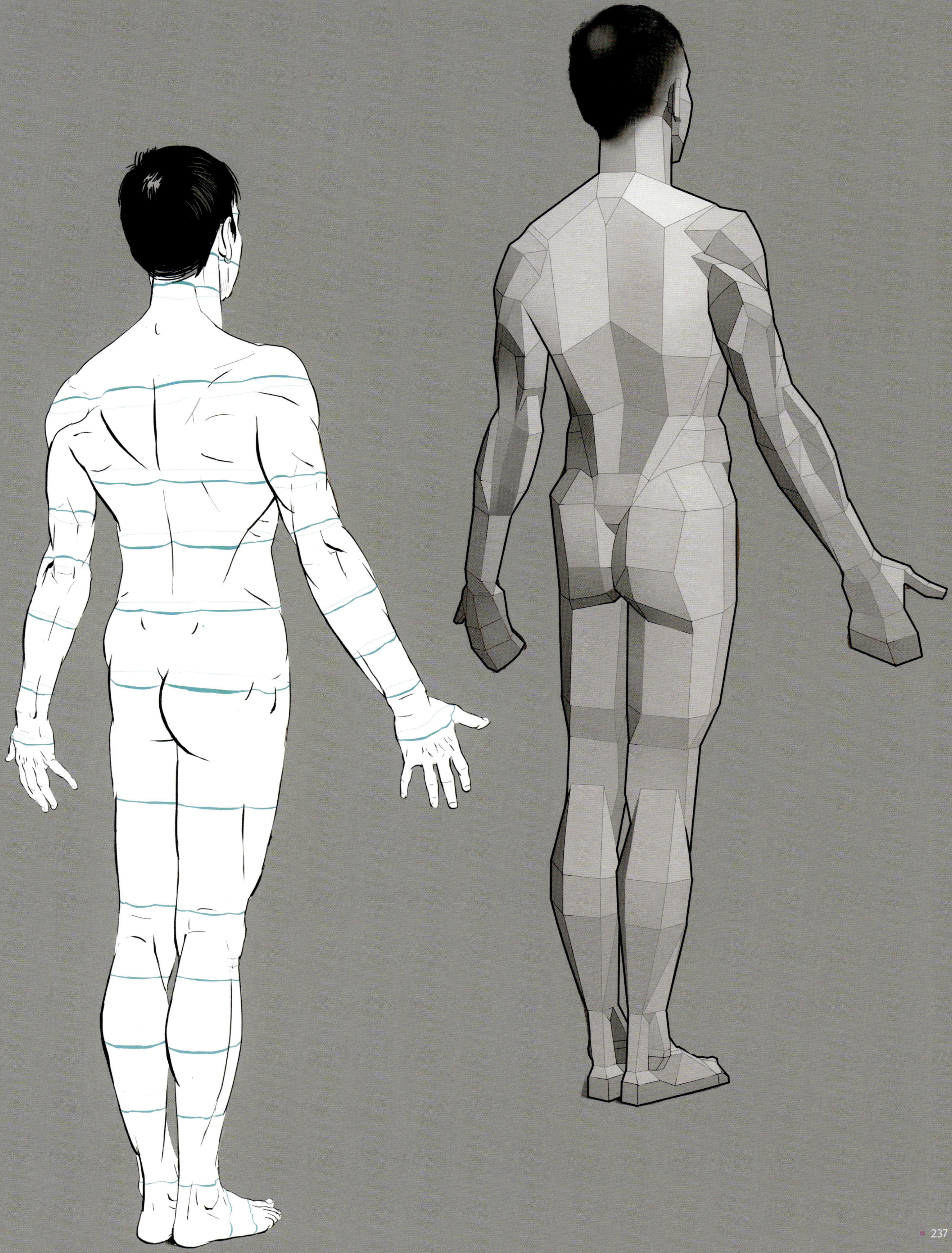

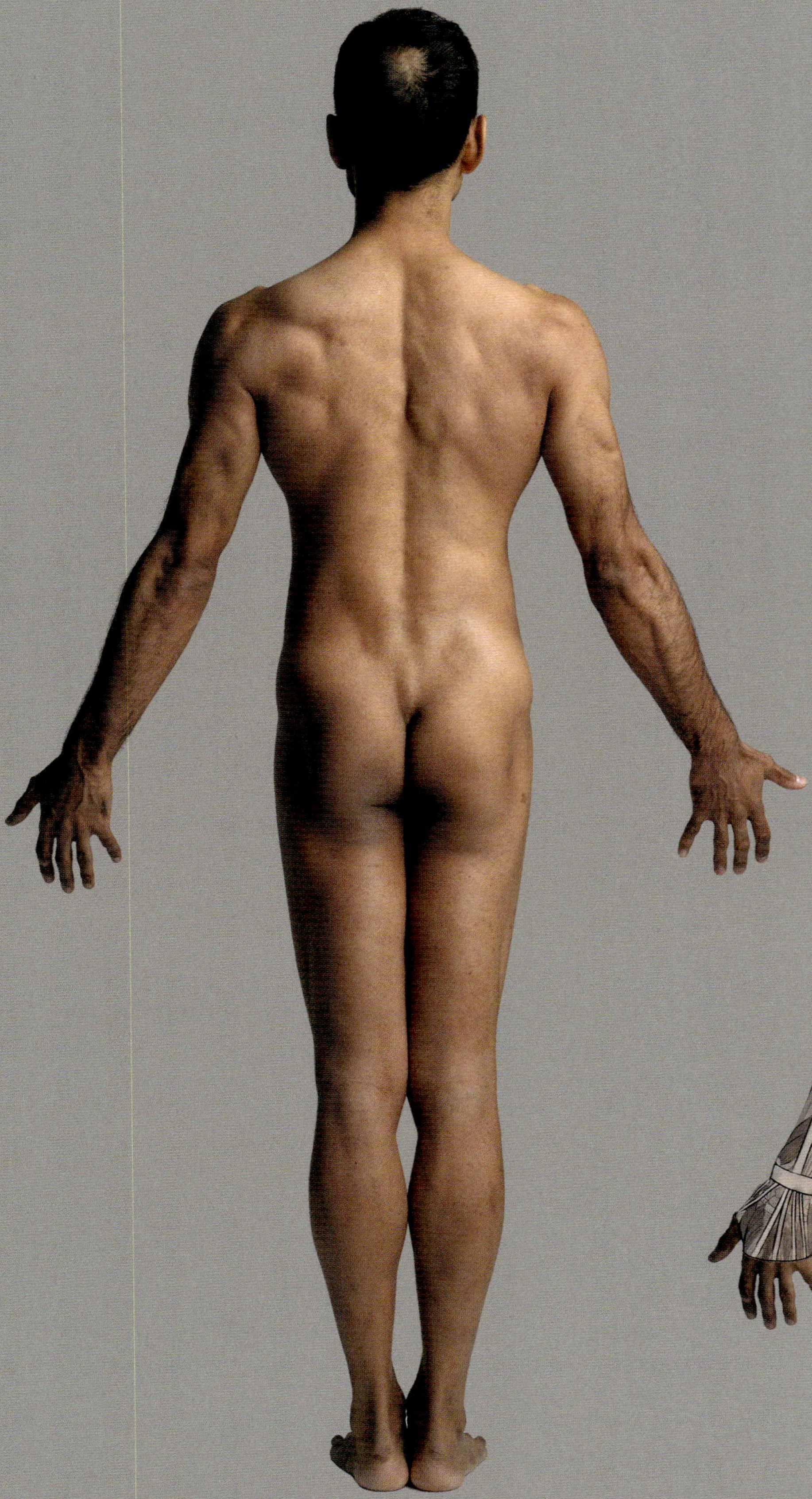

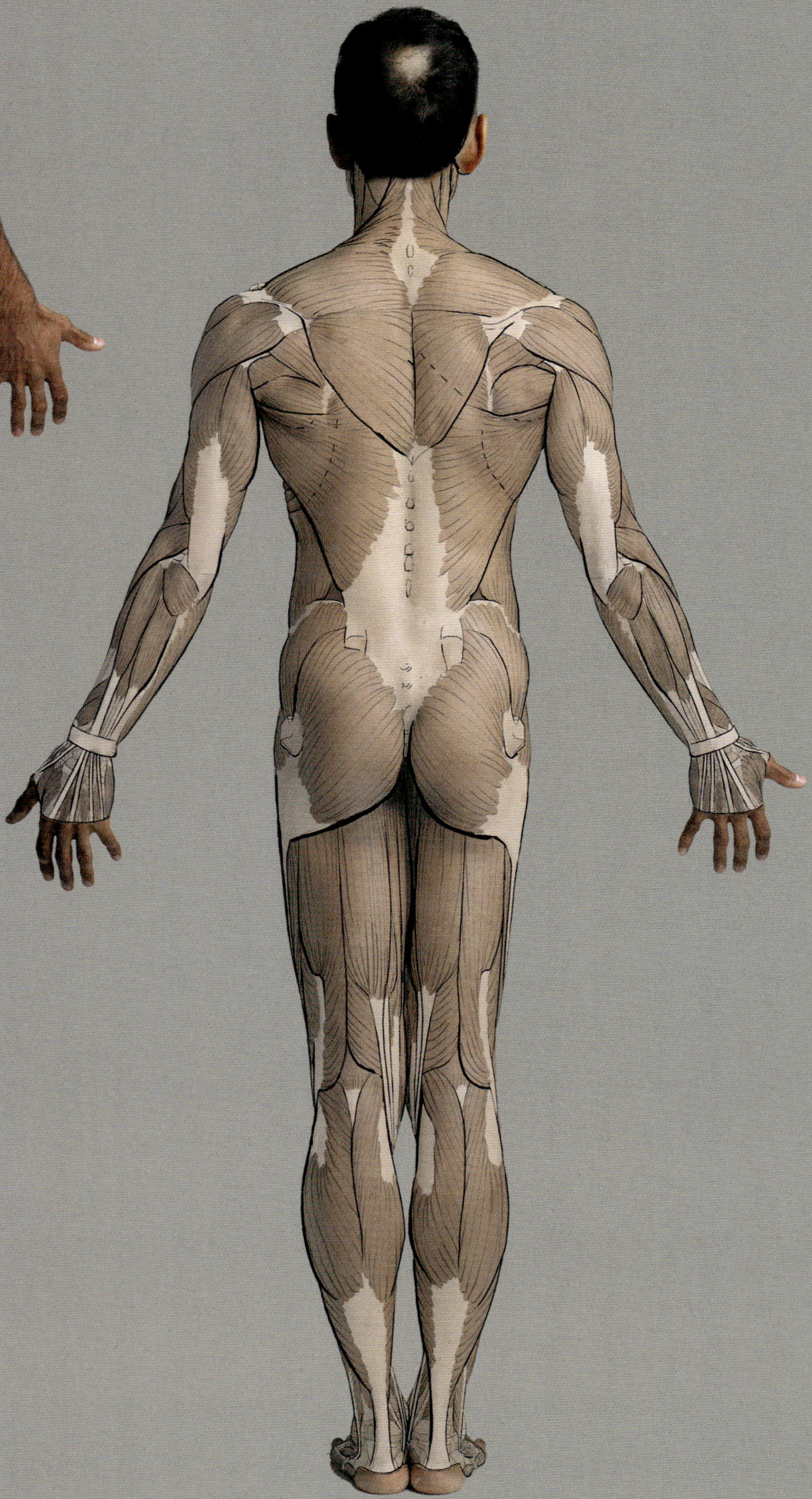

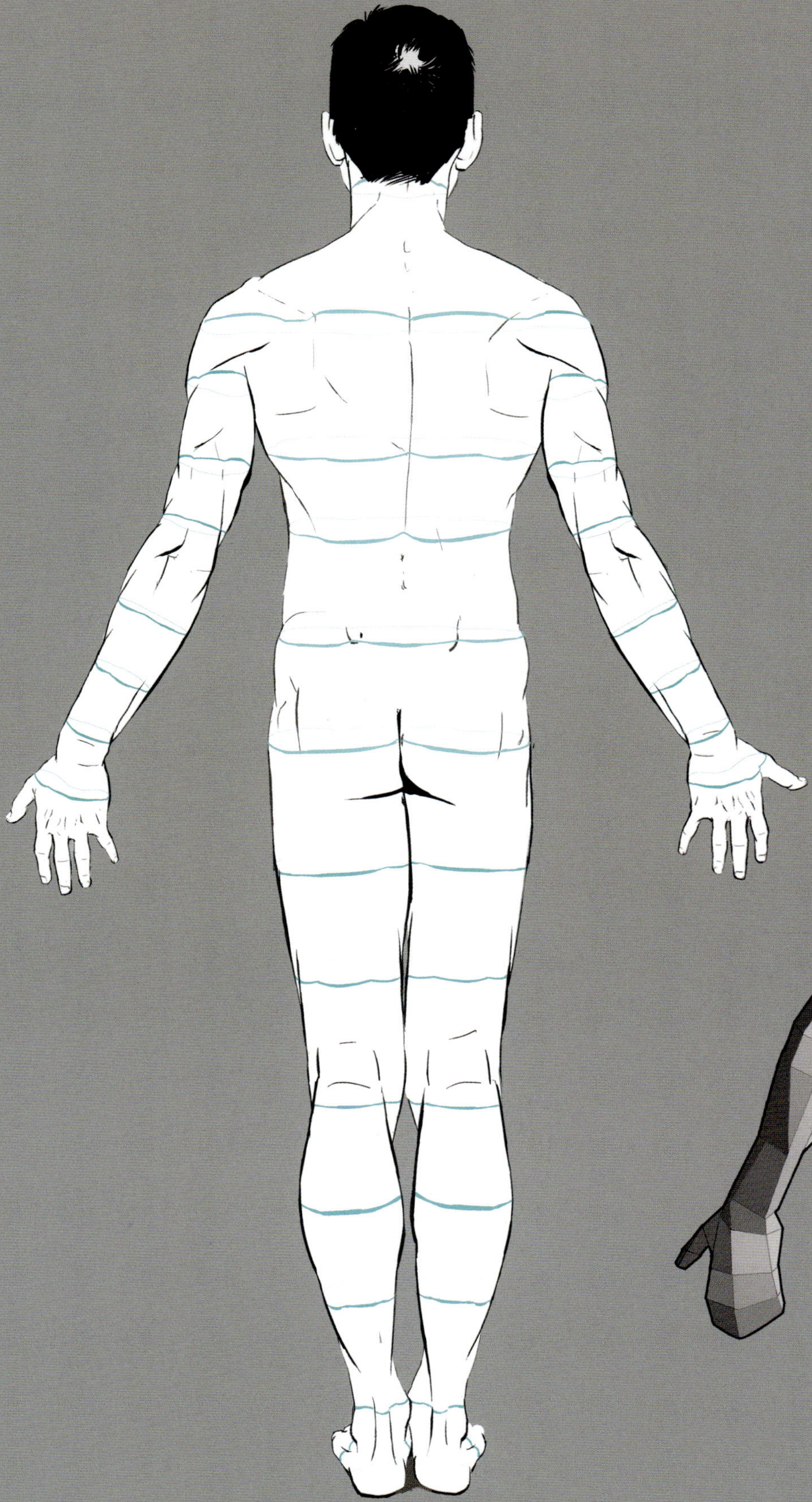

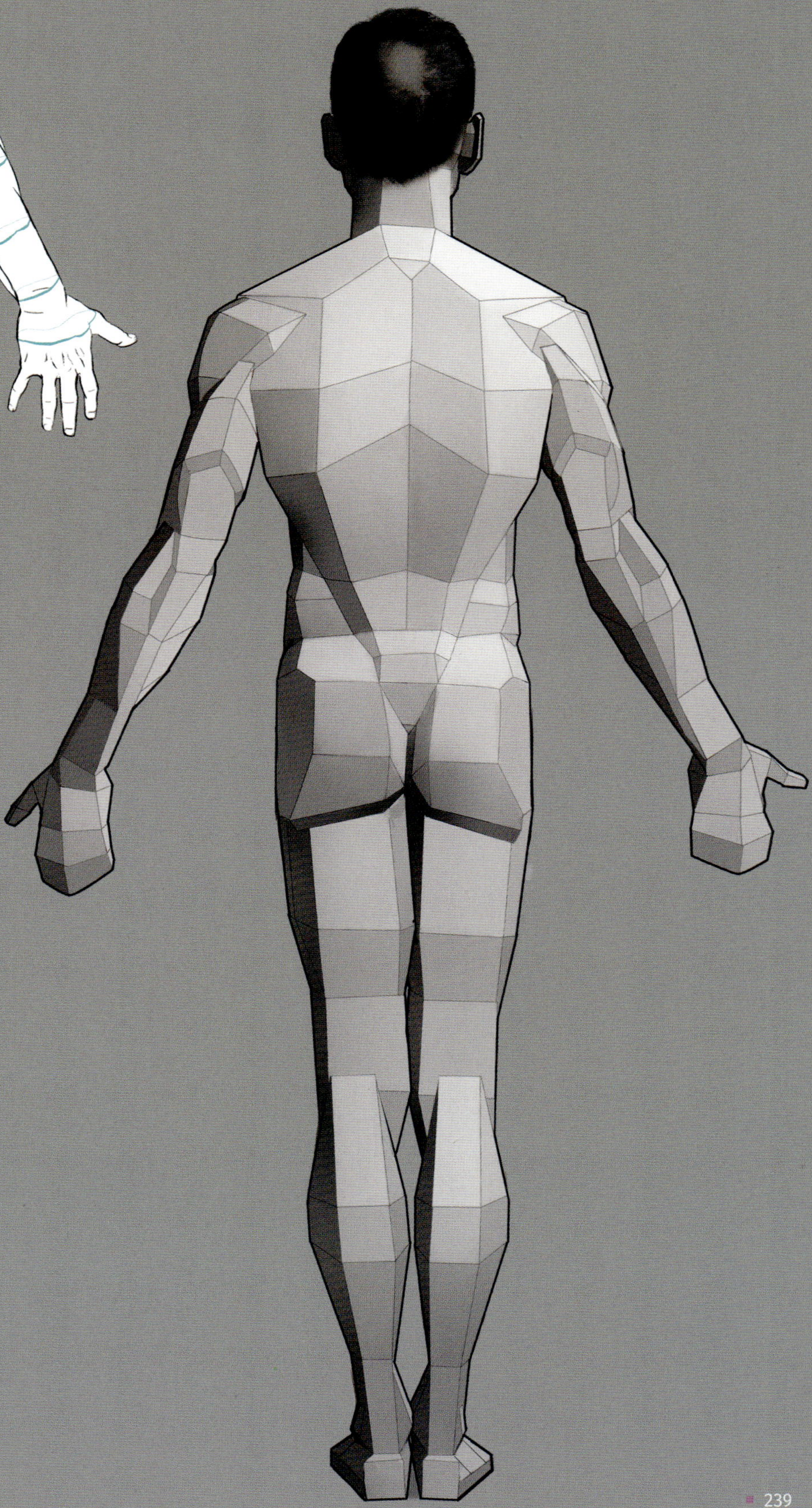

Creative poses

Artwork by Charlie Pickard

CLASSICAL STANDING POSES

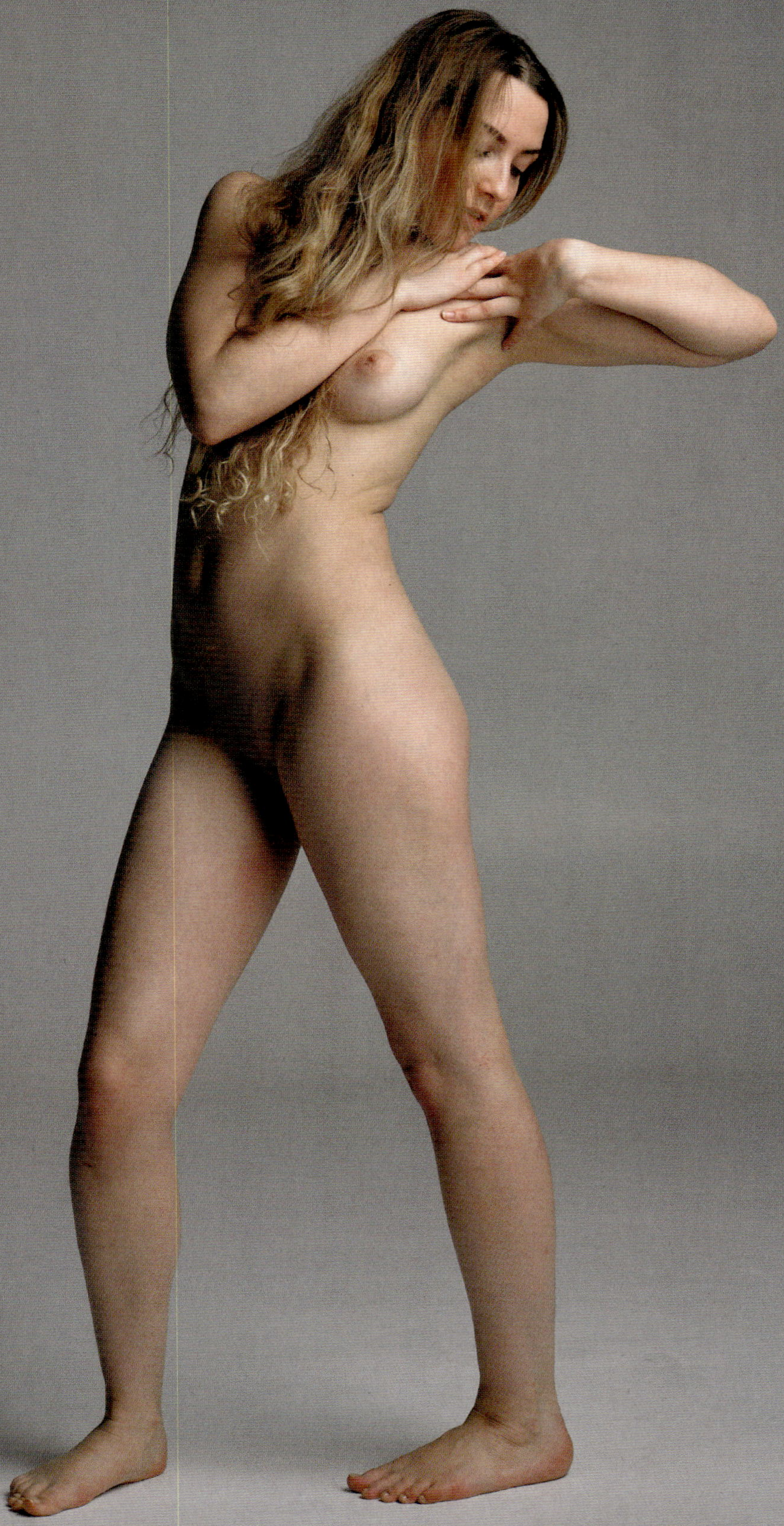

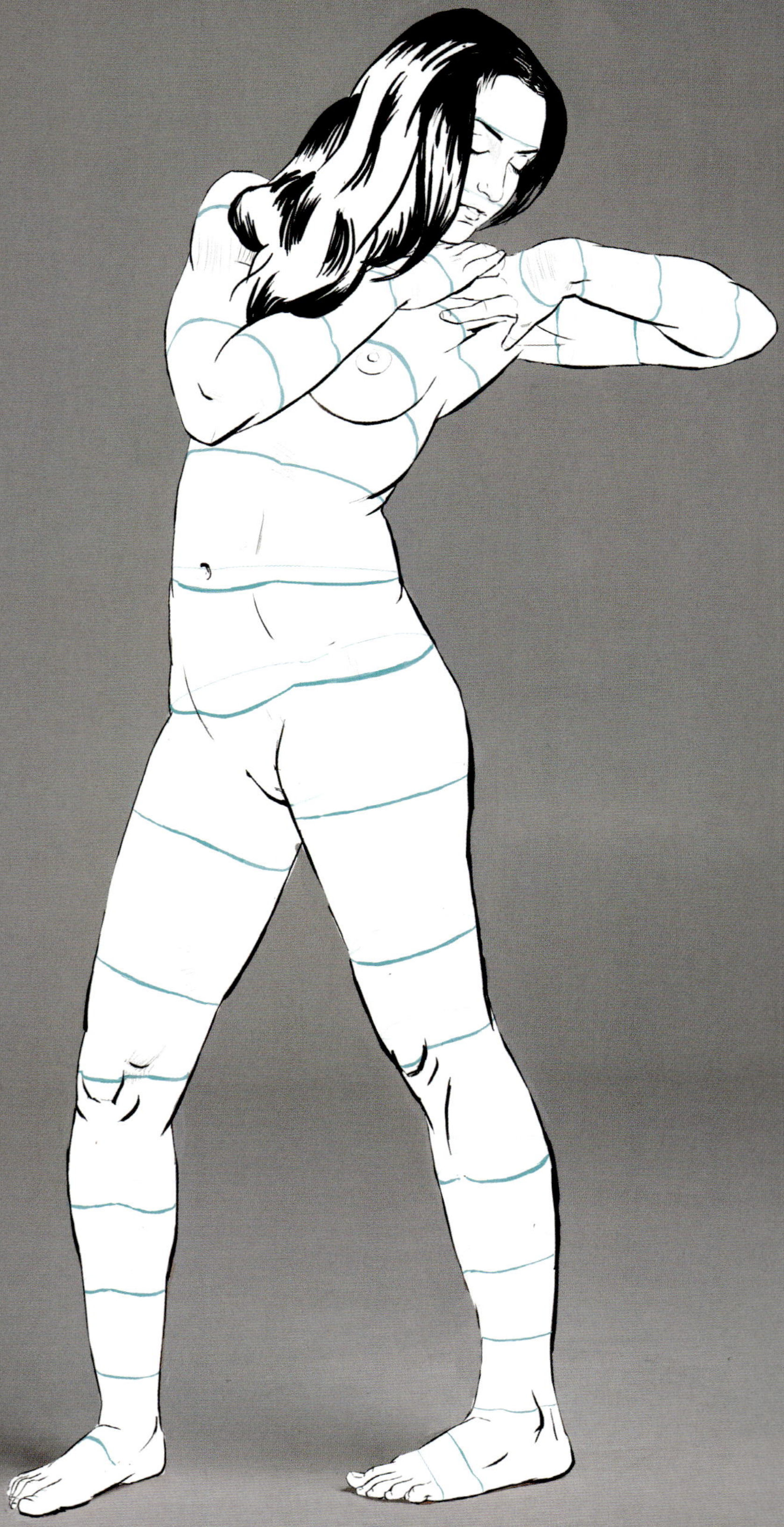

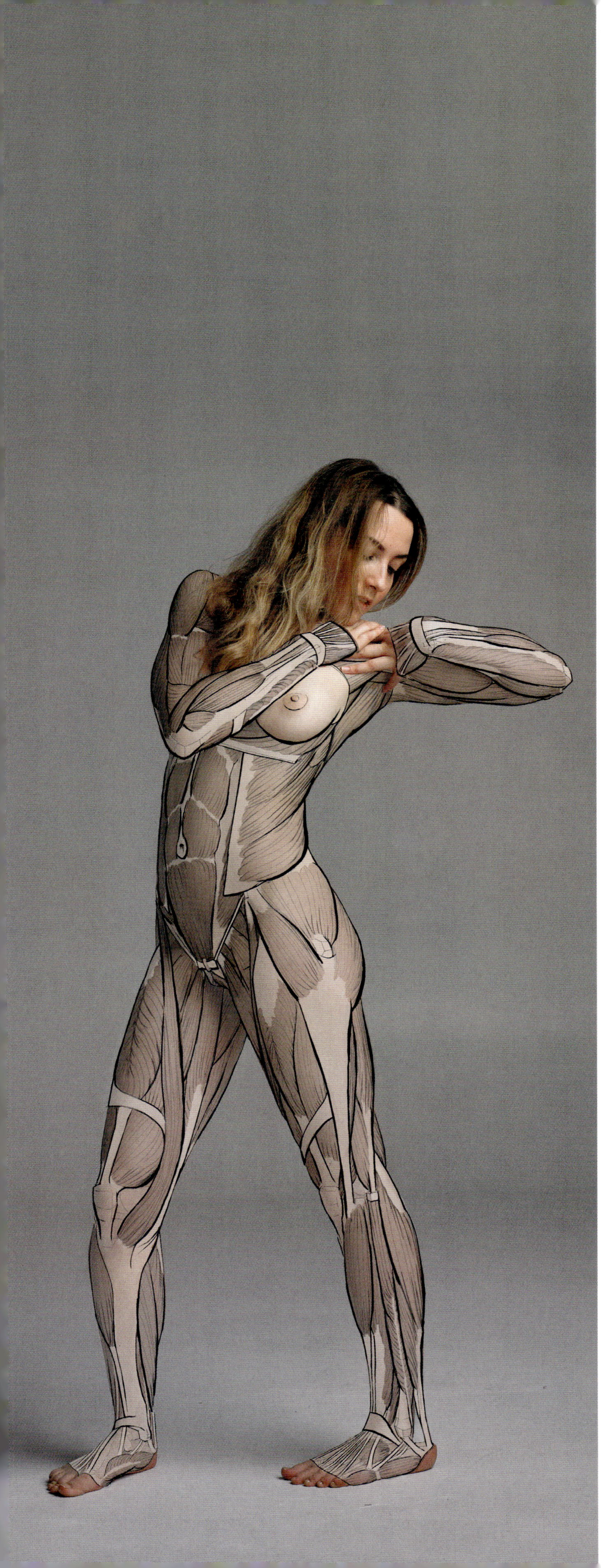

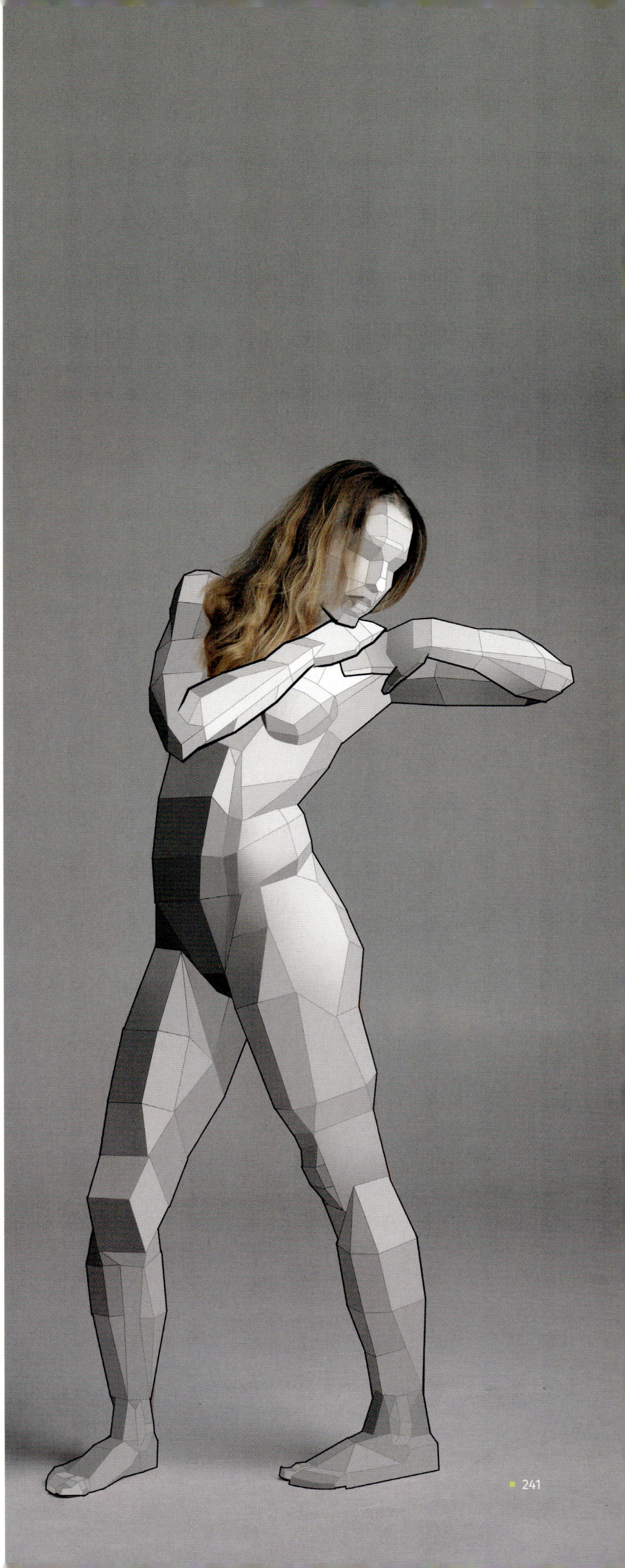

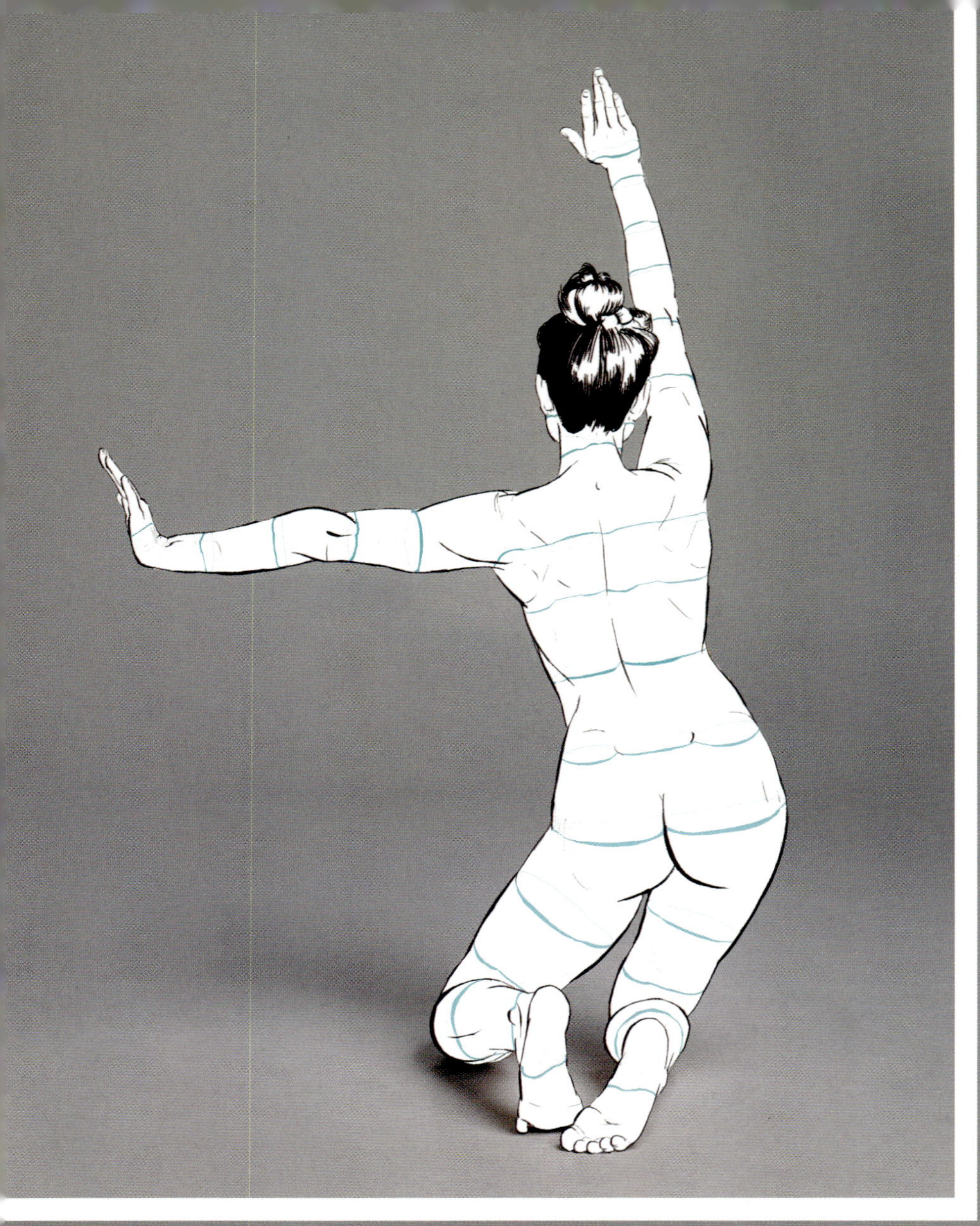

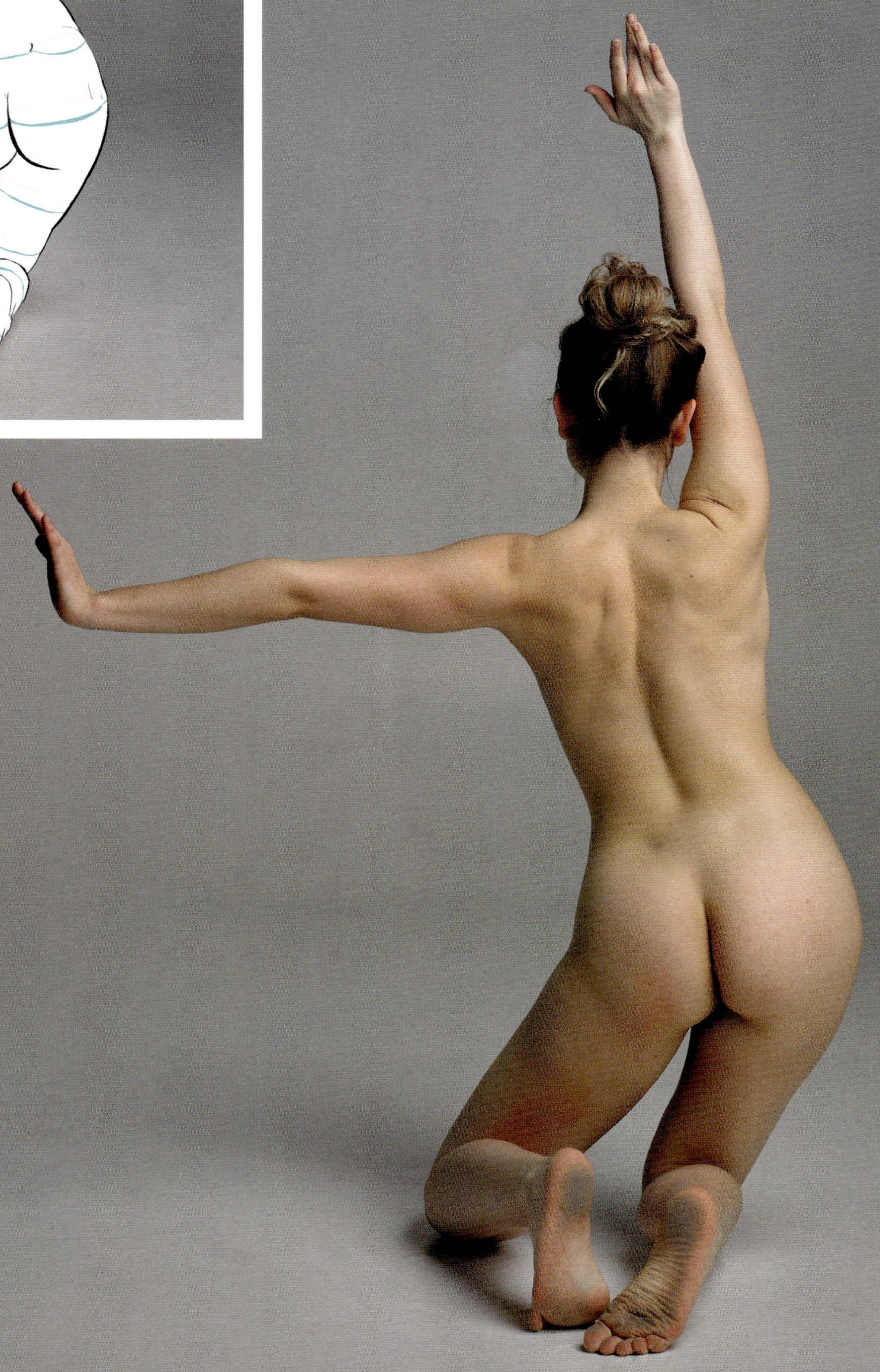

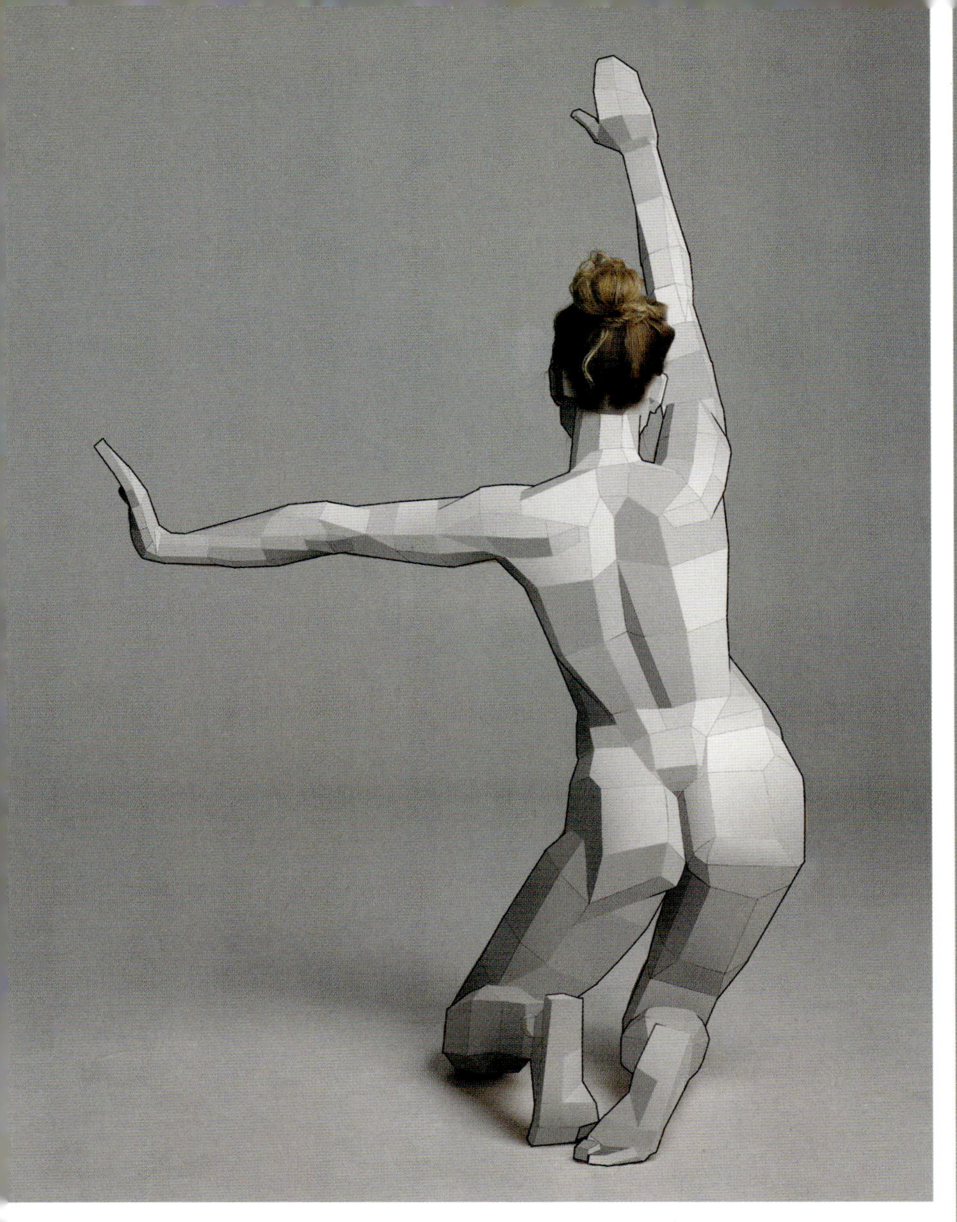

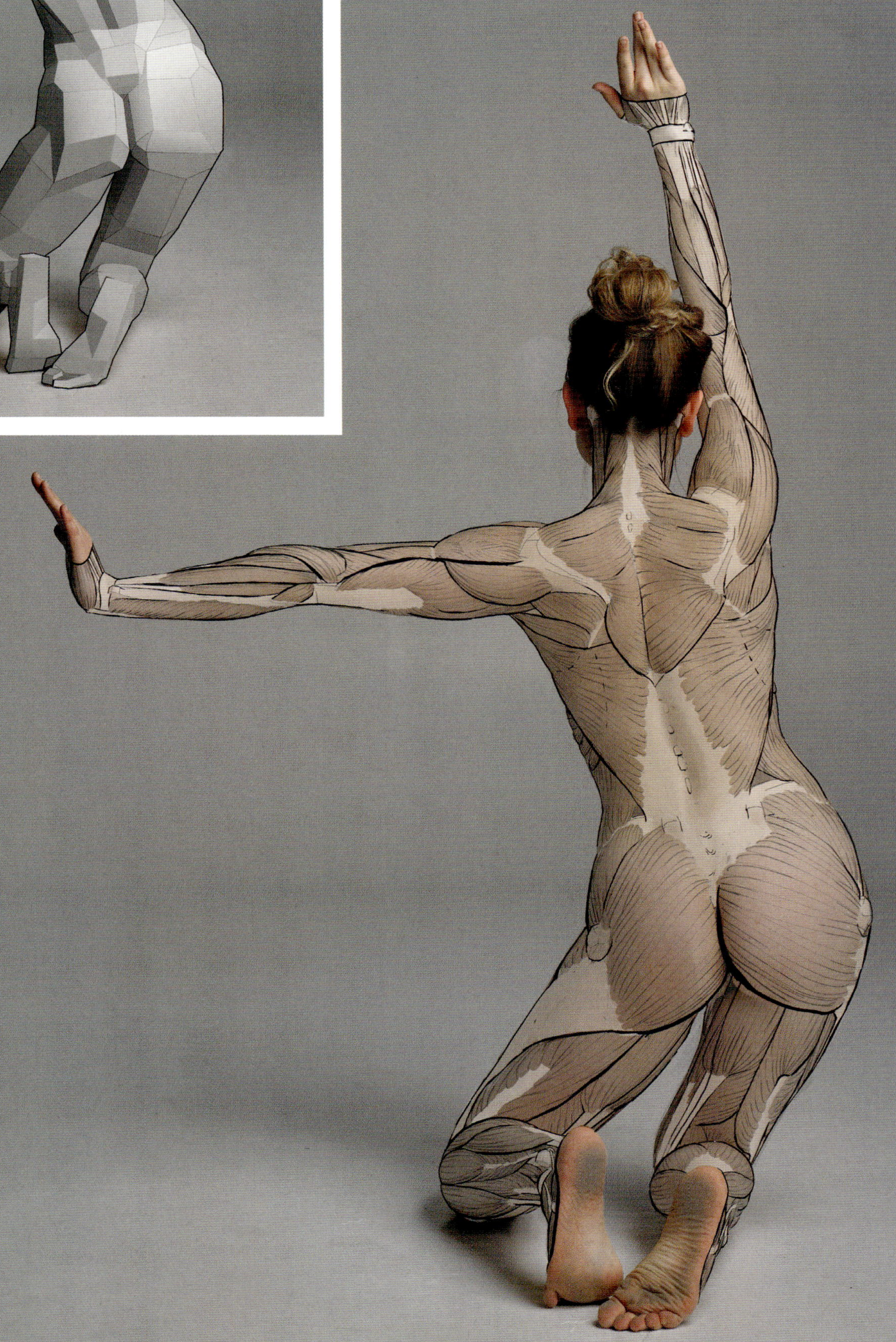

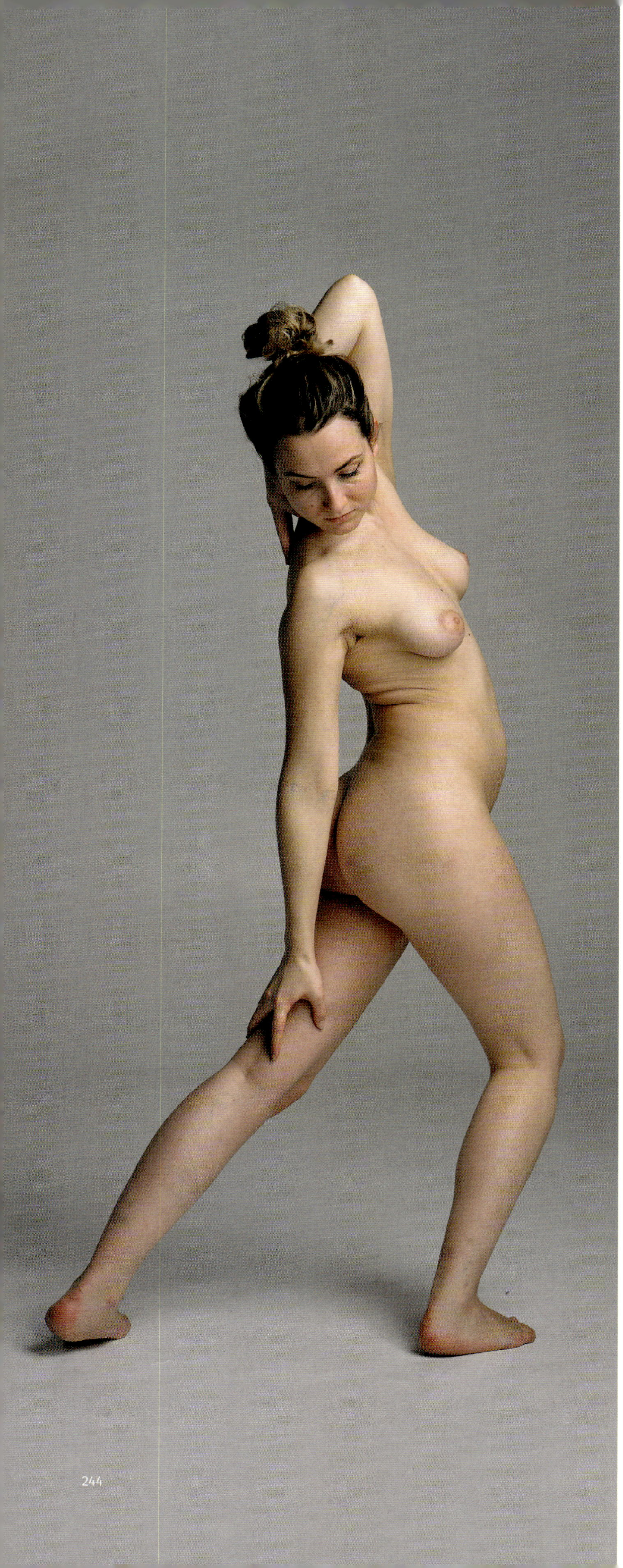

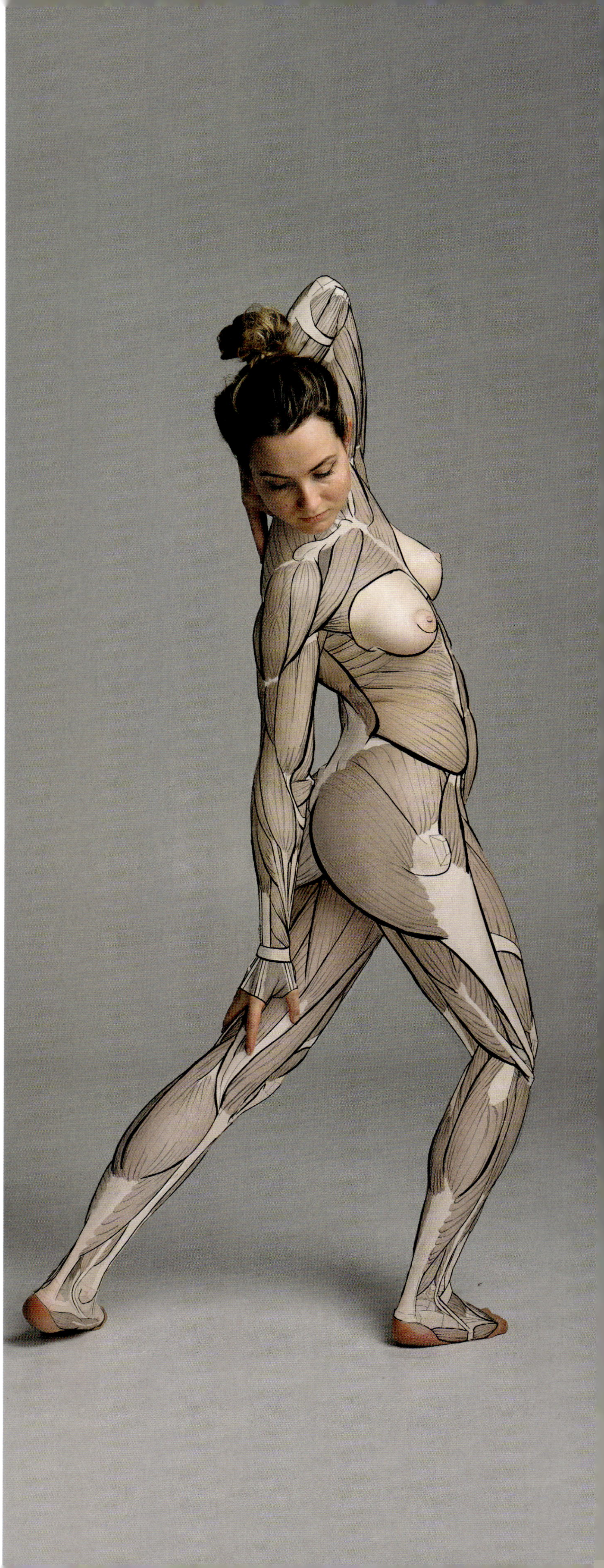

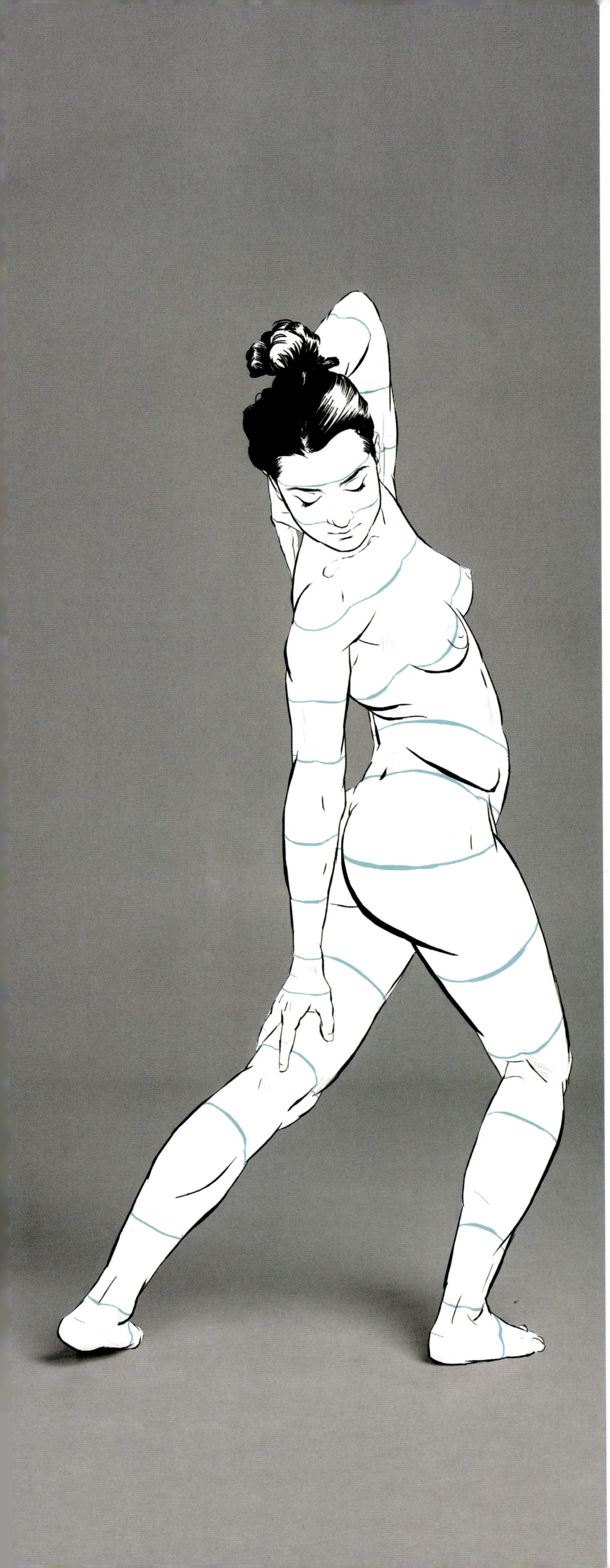

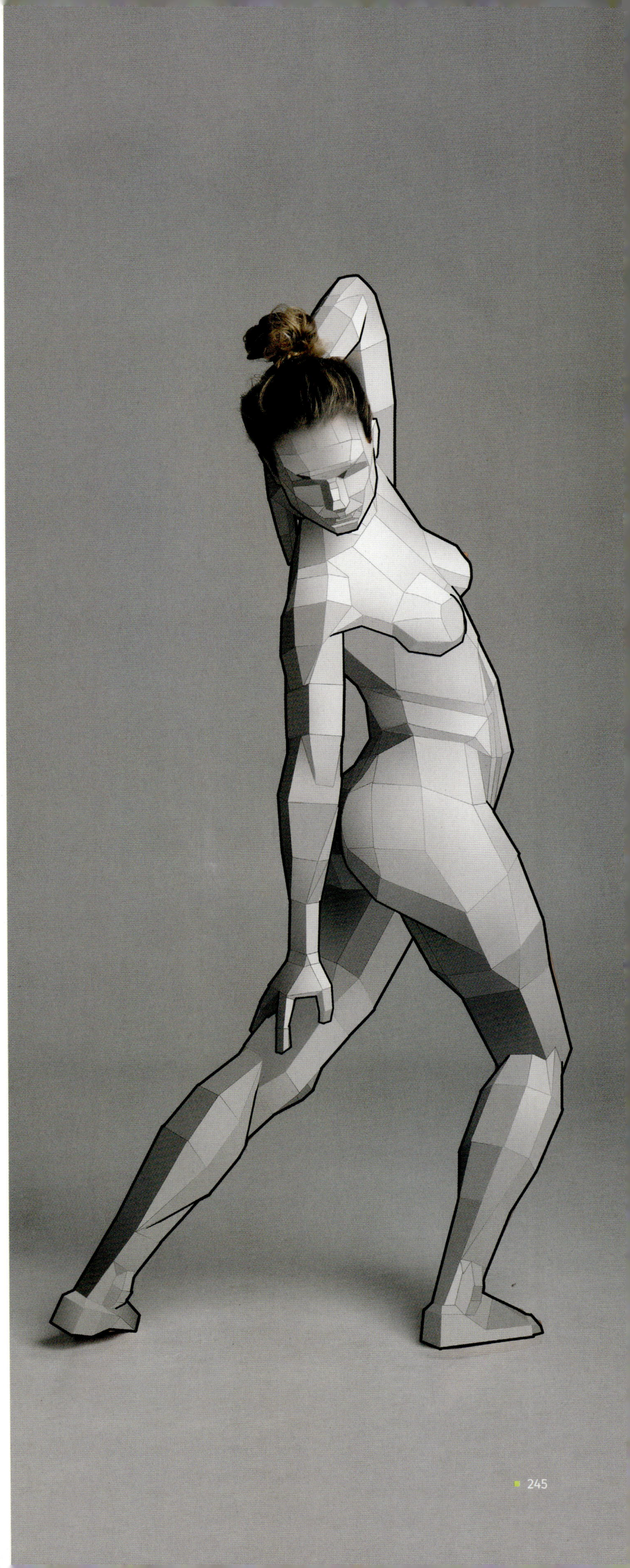

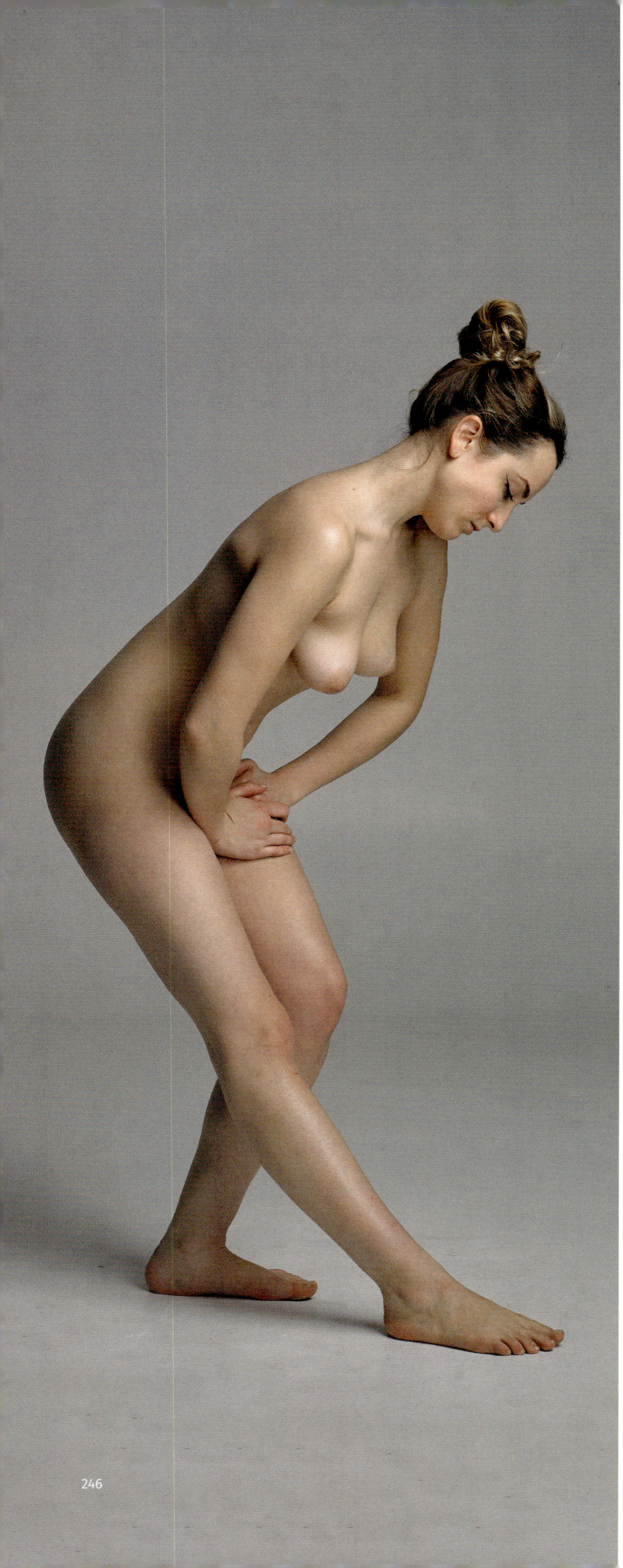

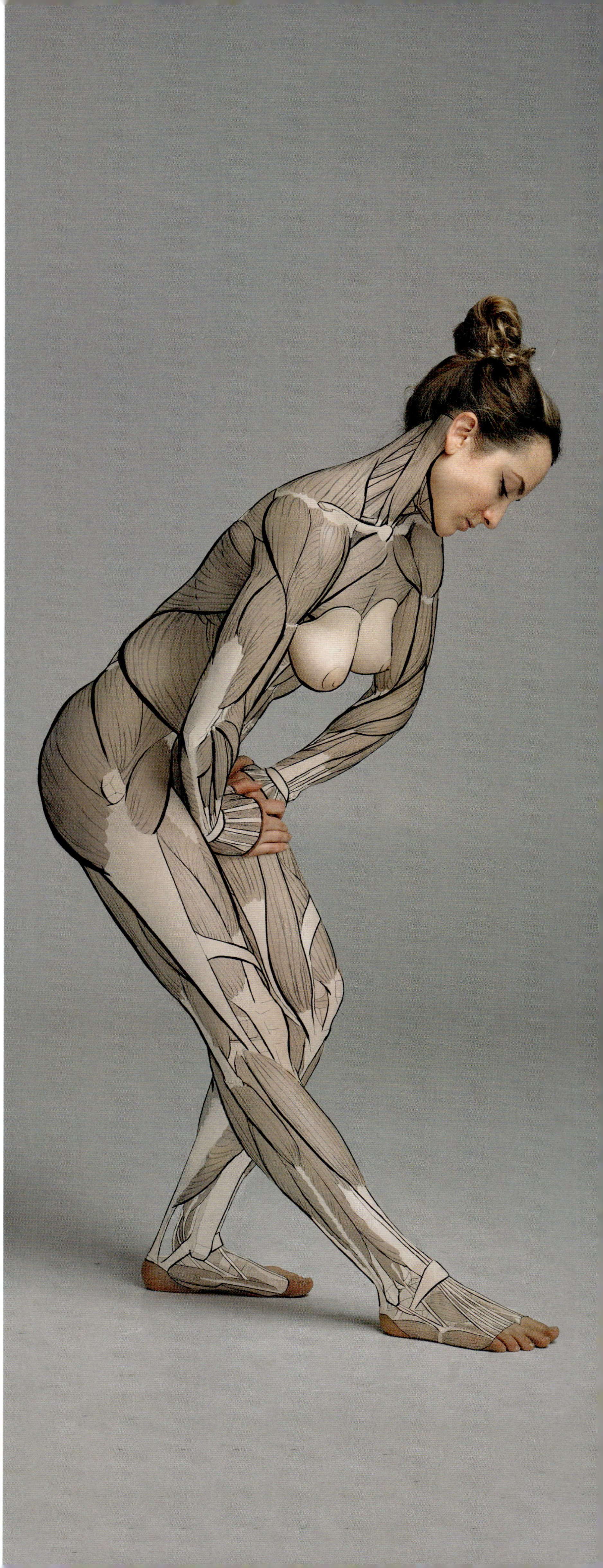

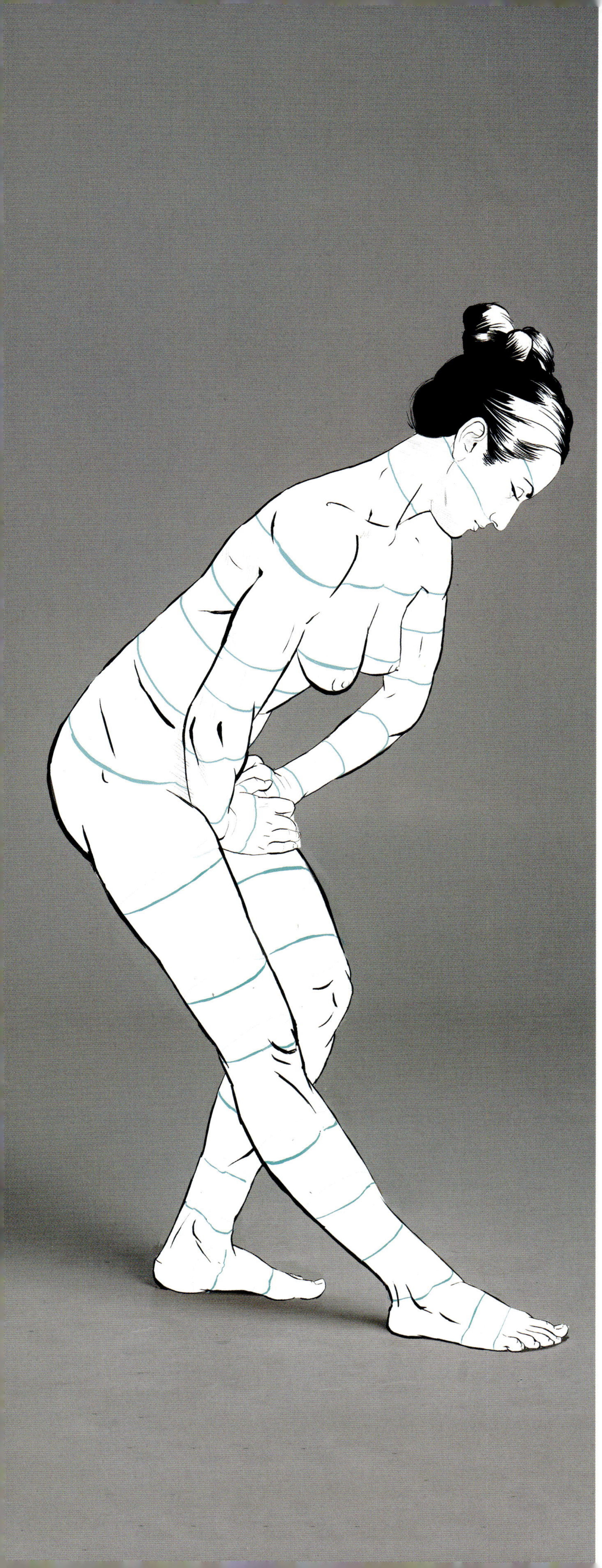

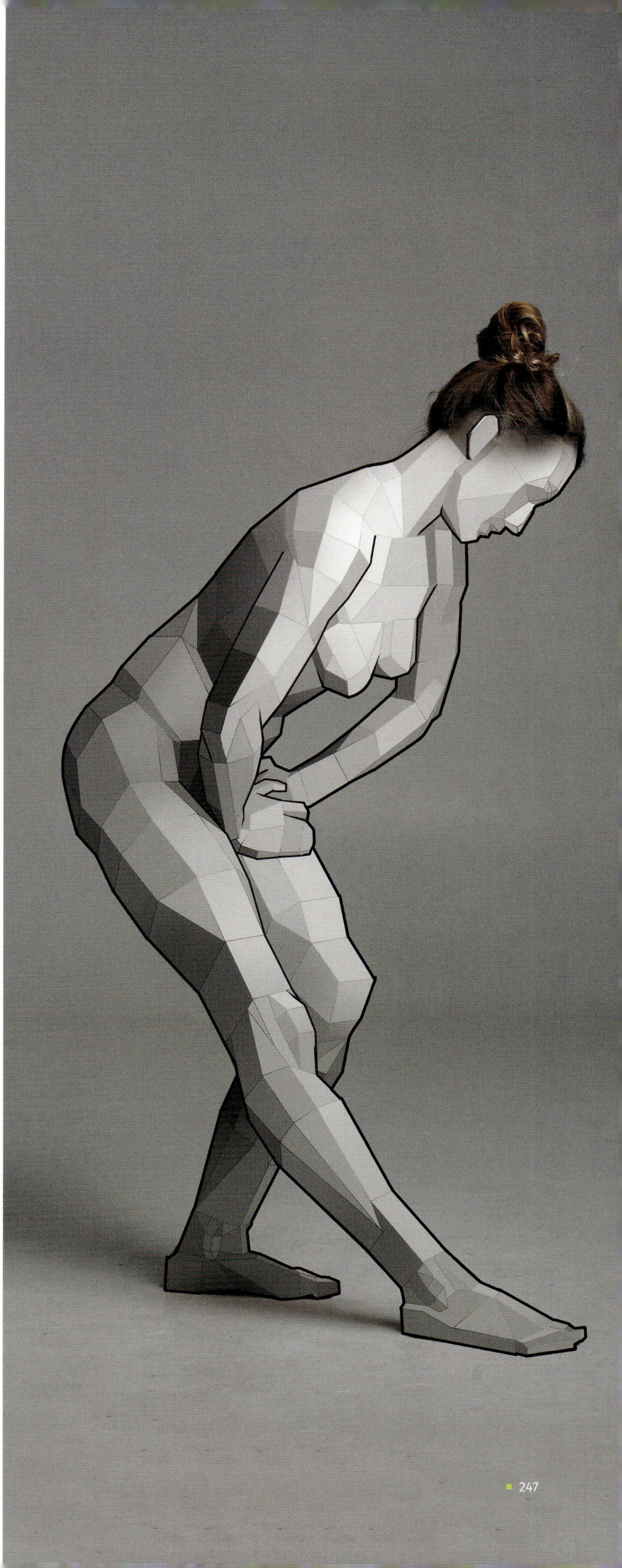

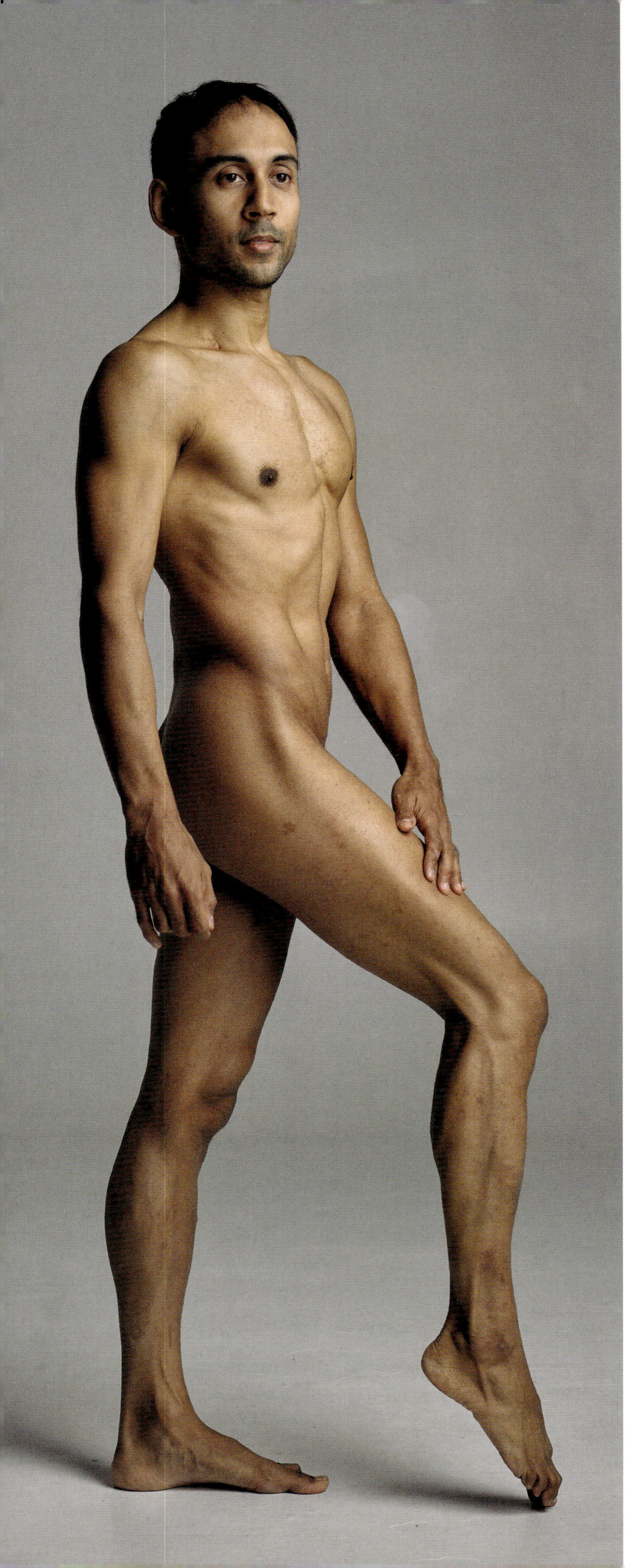

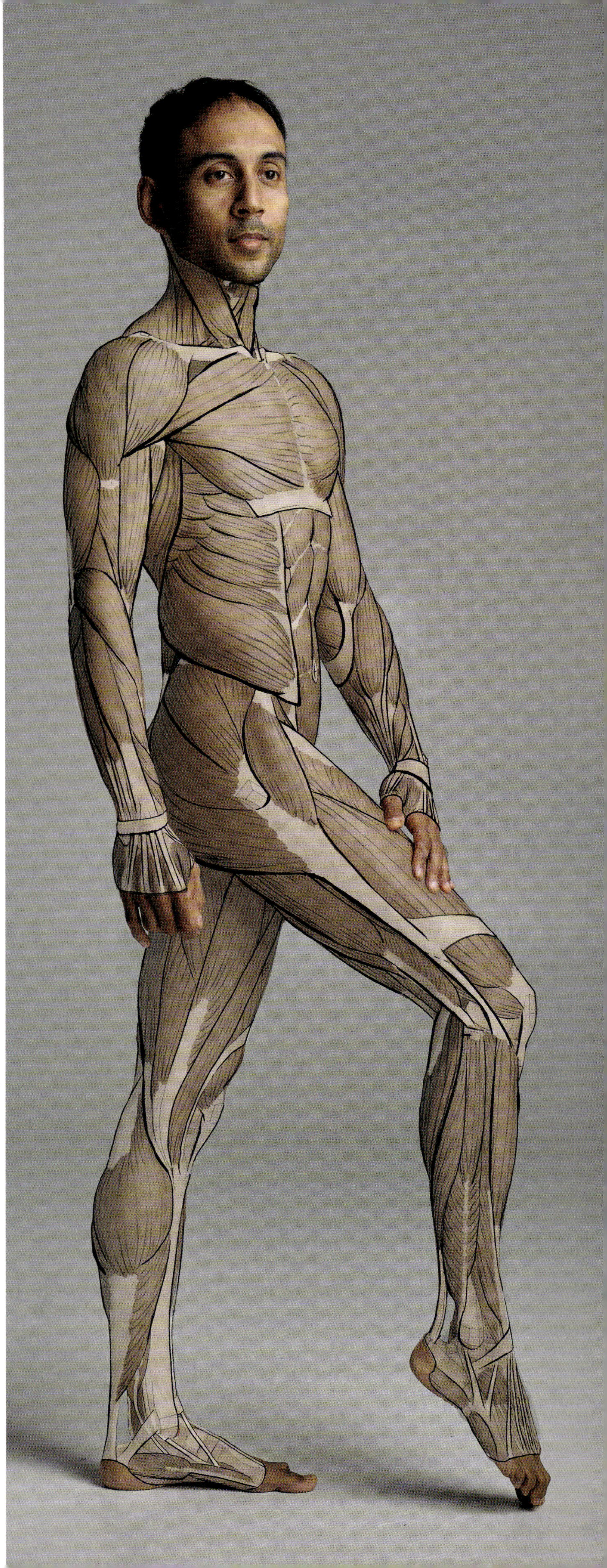

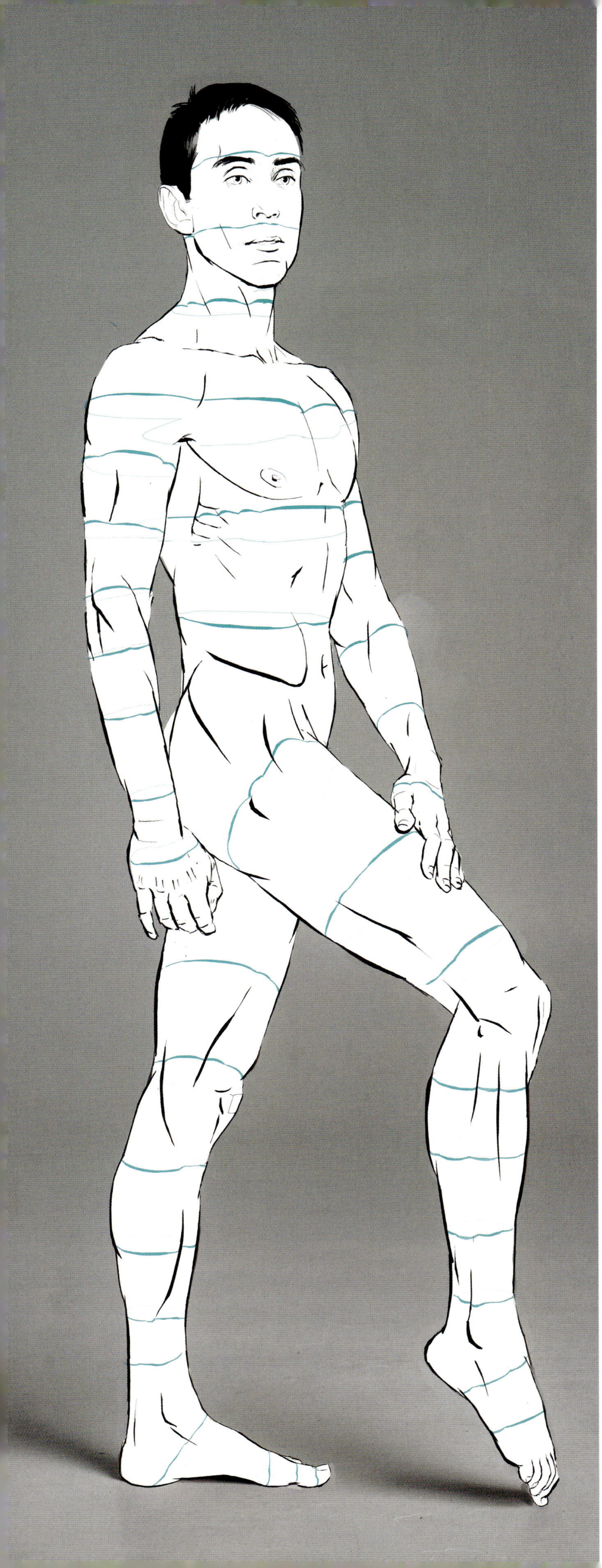
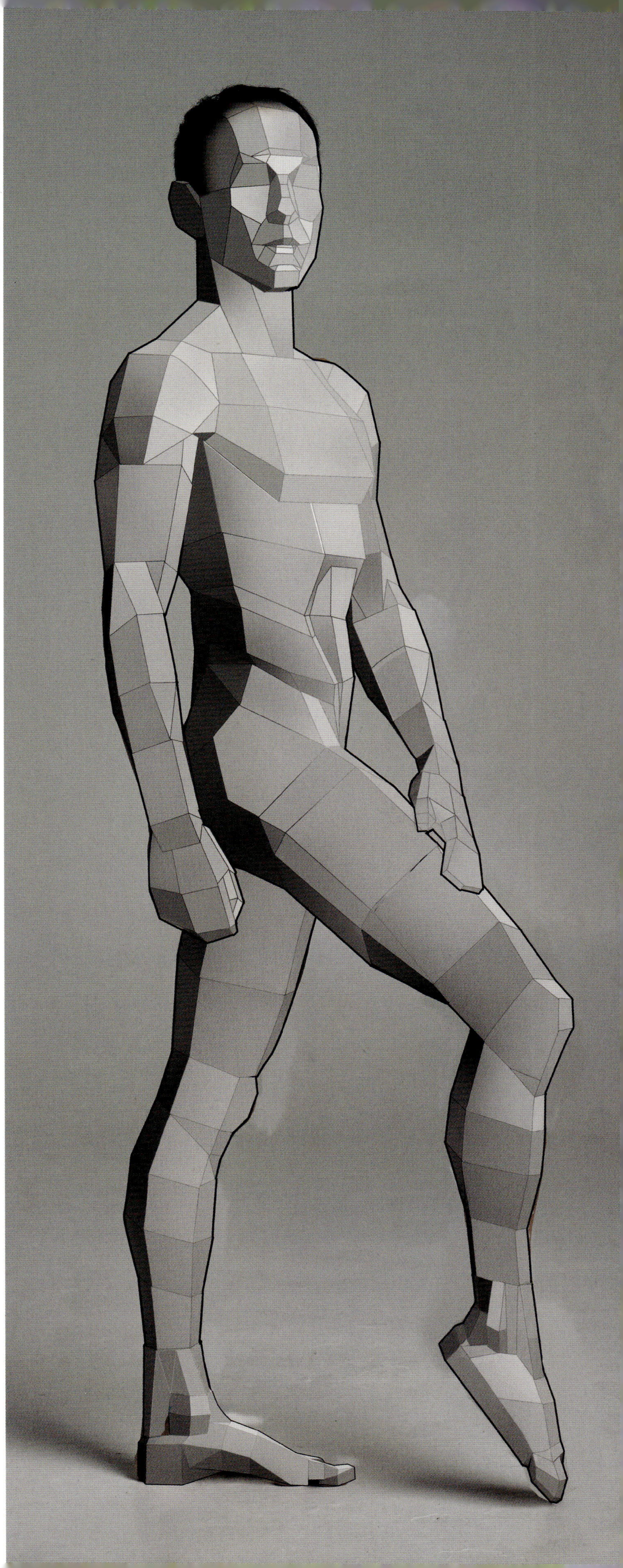

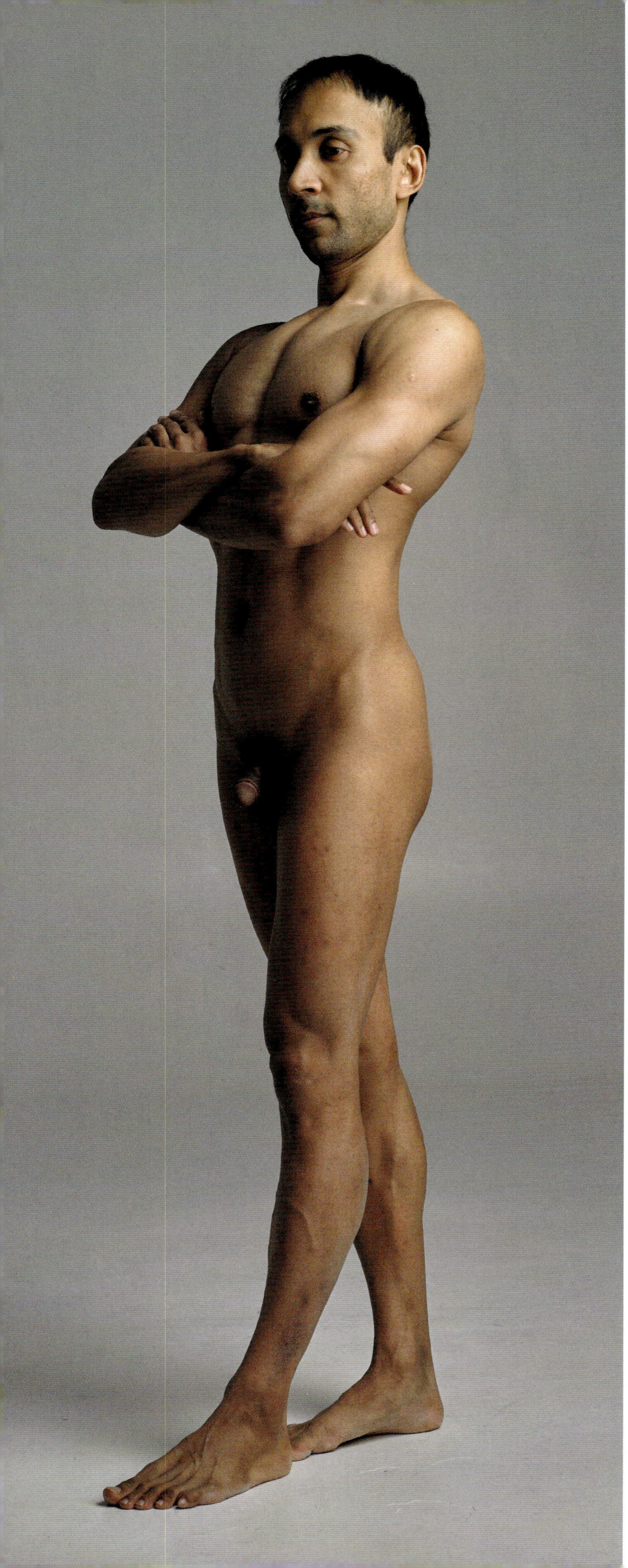
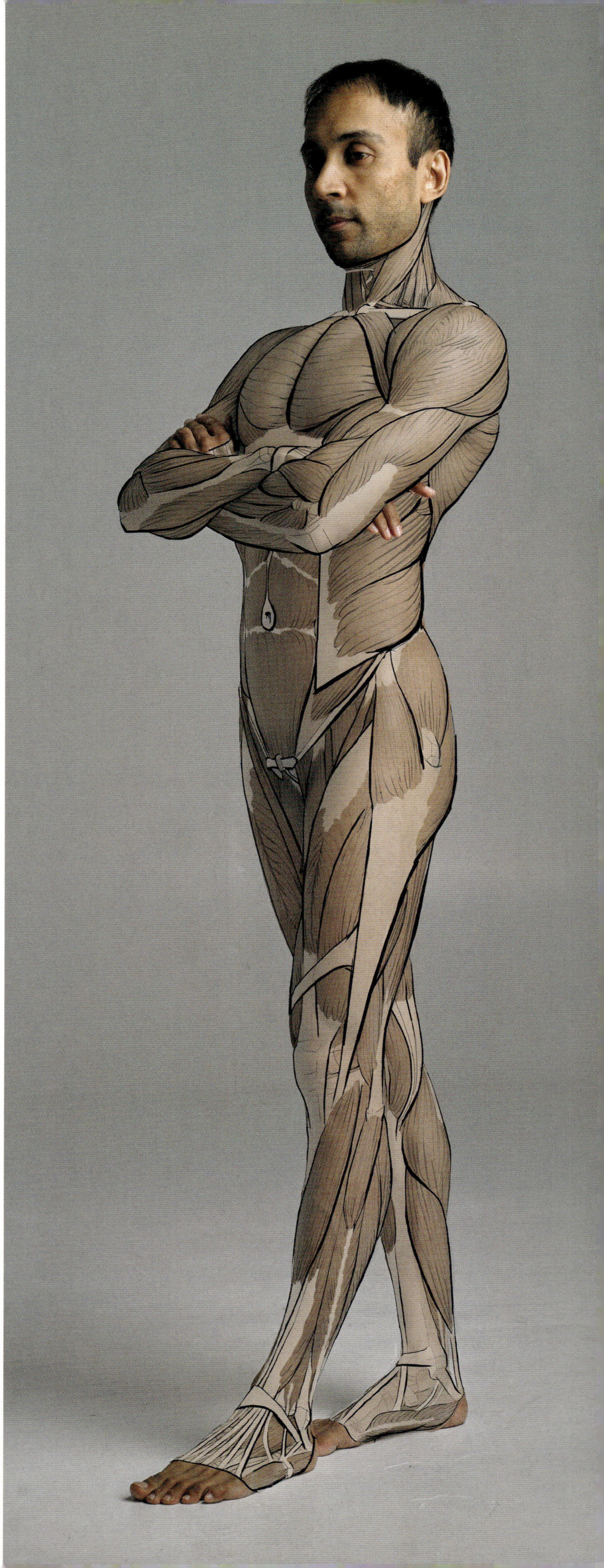

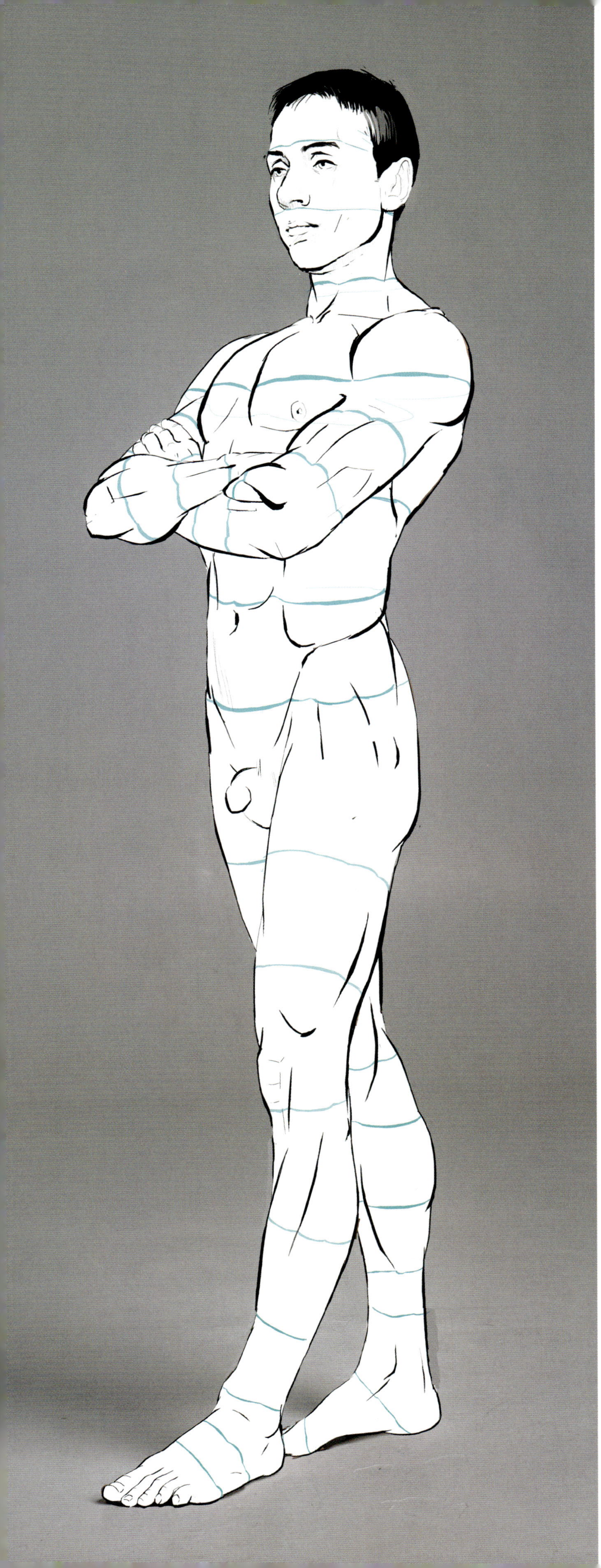

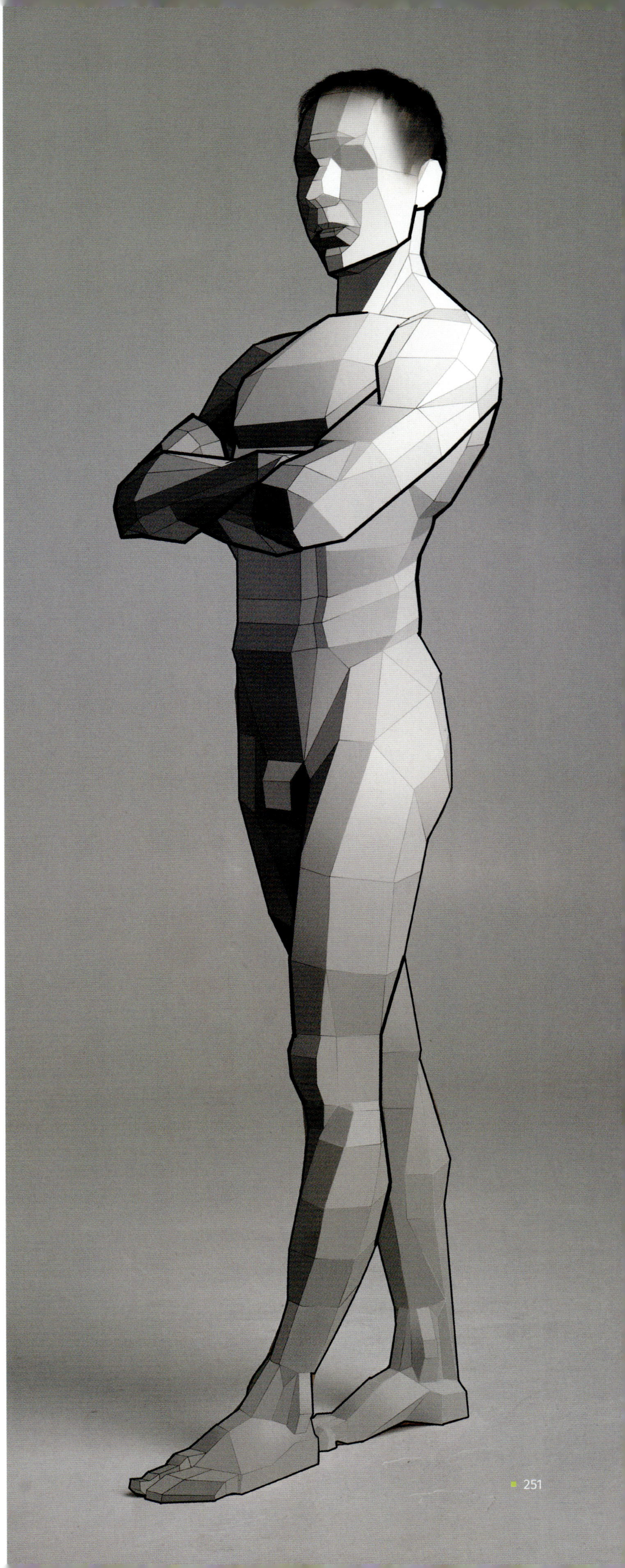

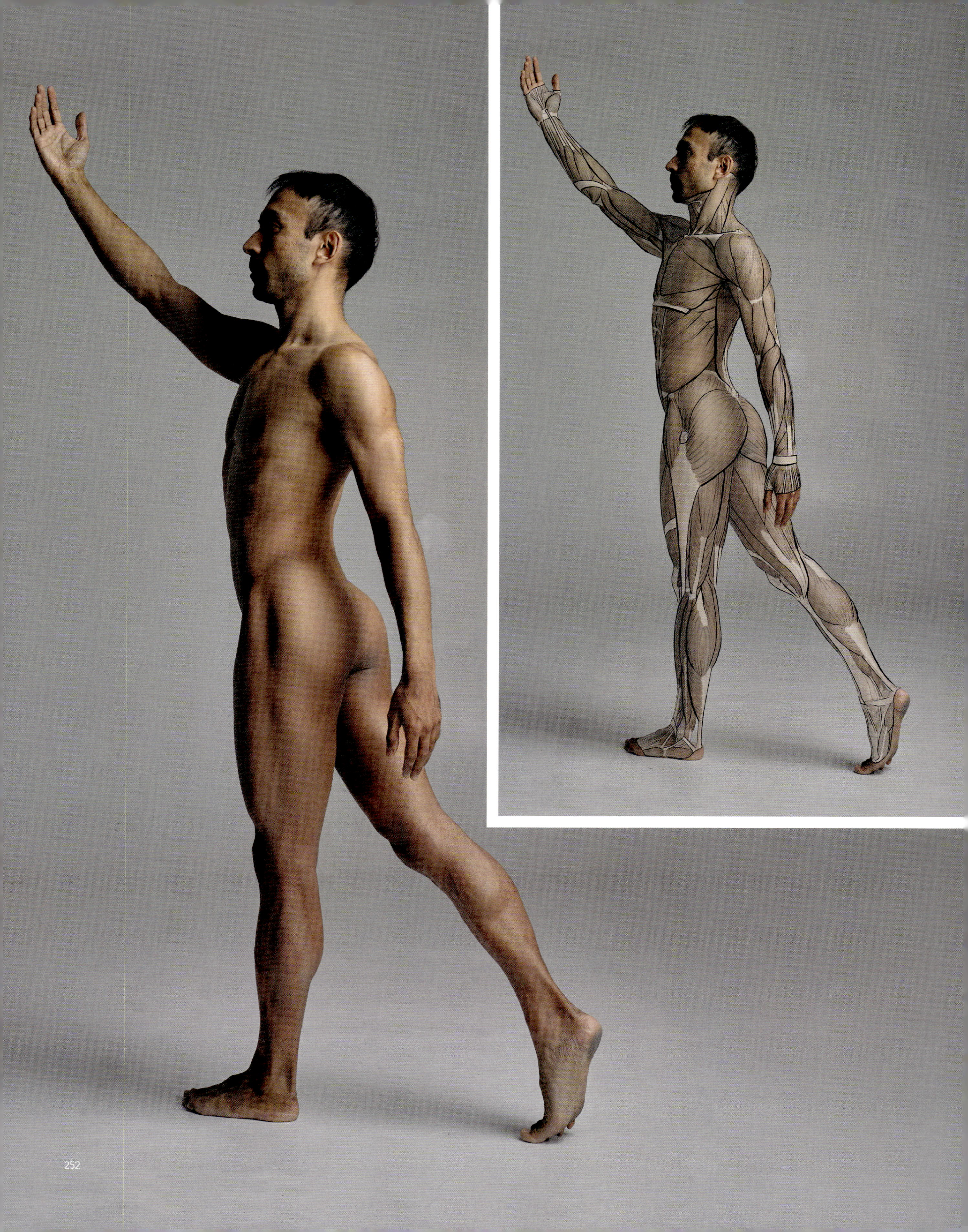

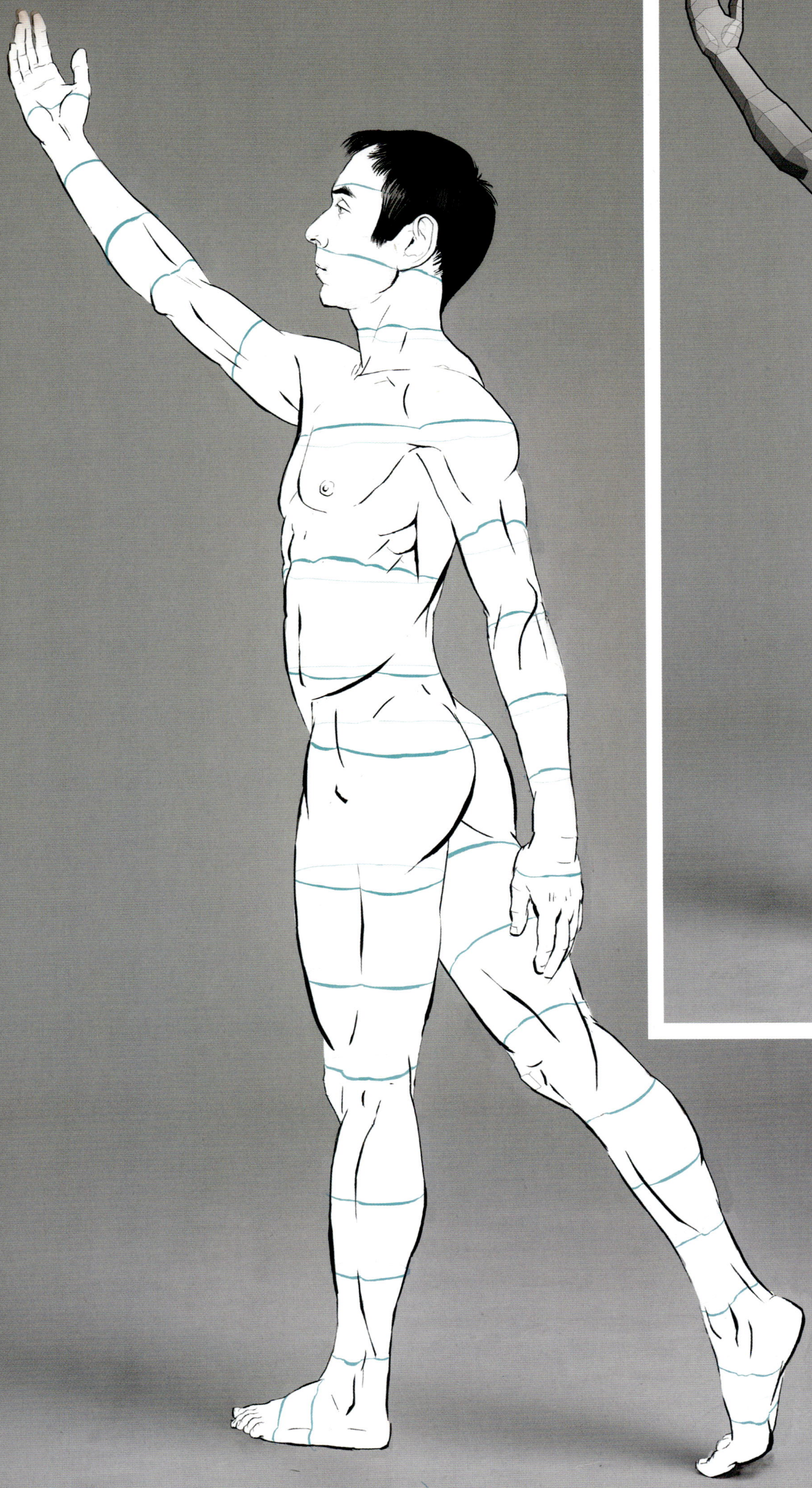

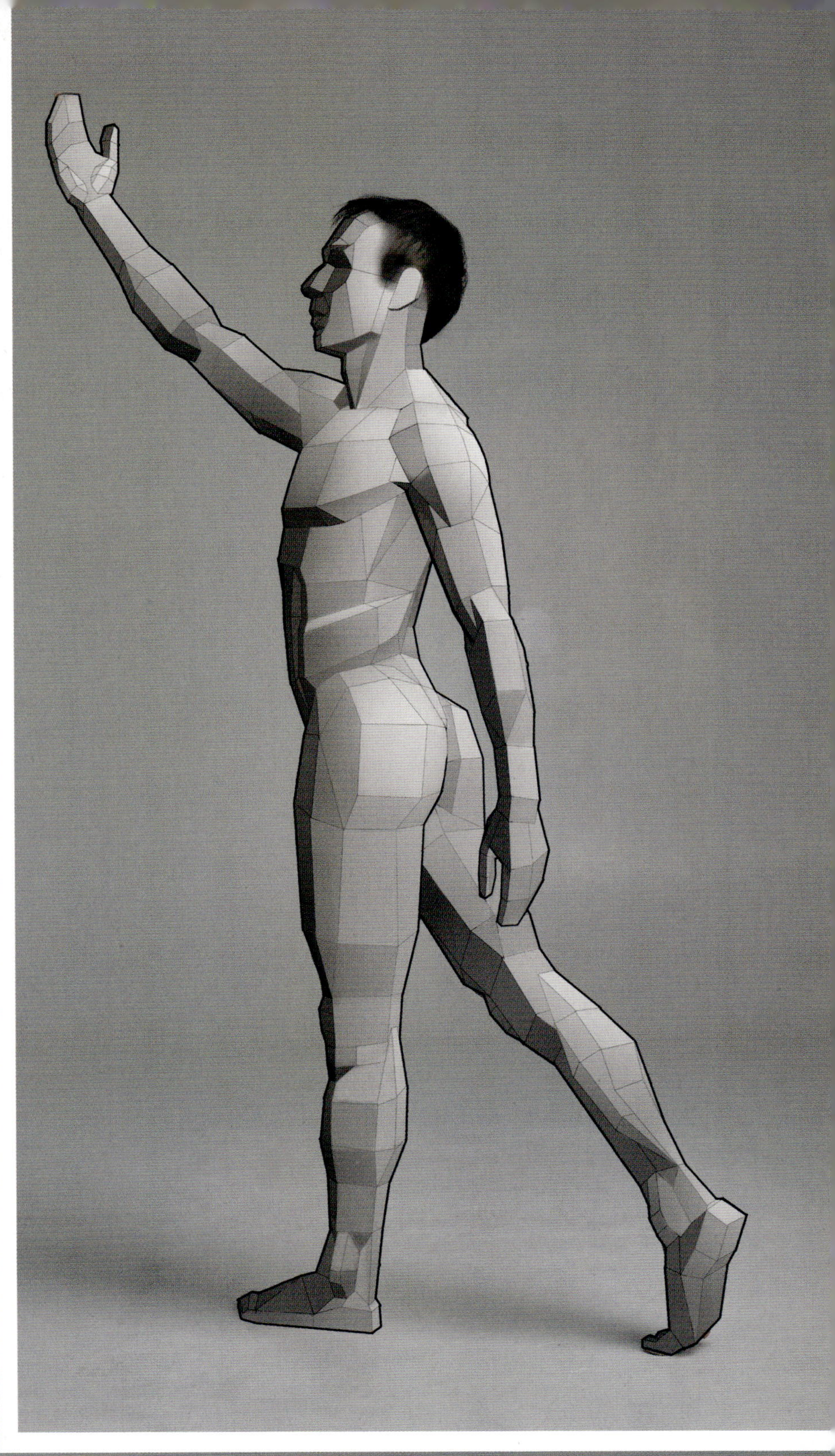

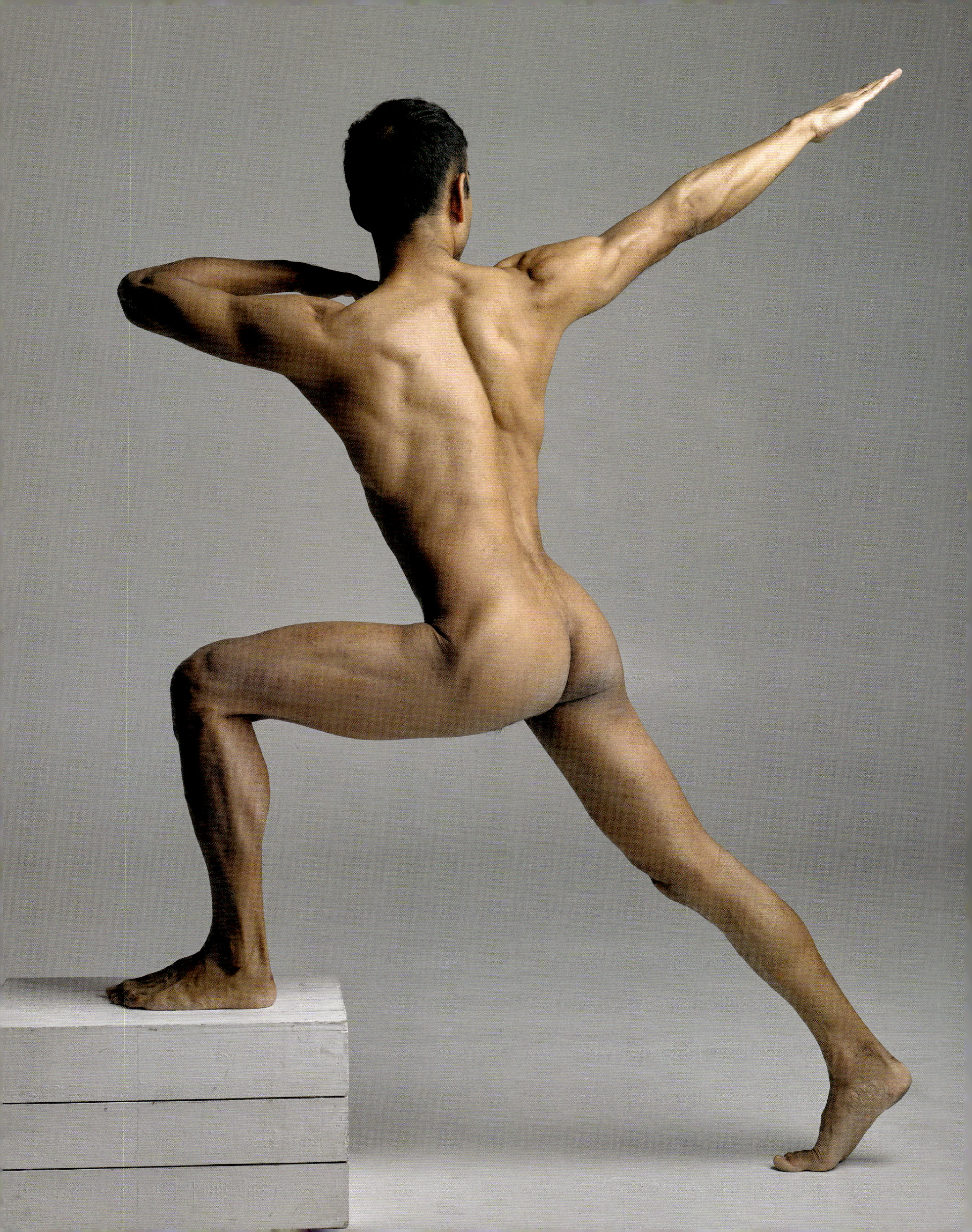

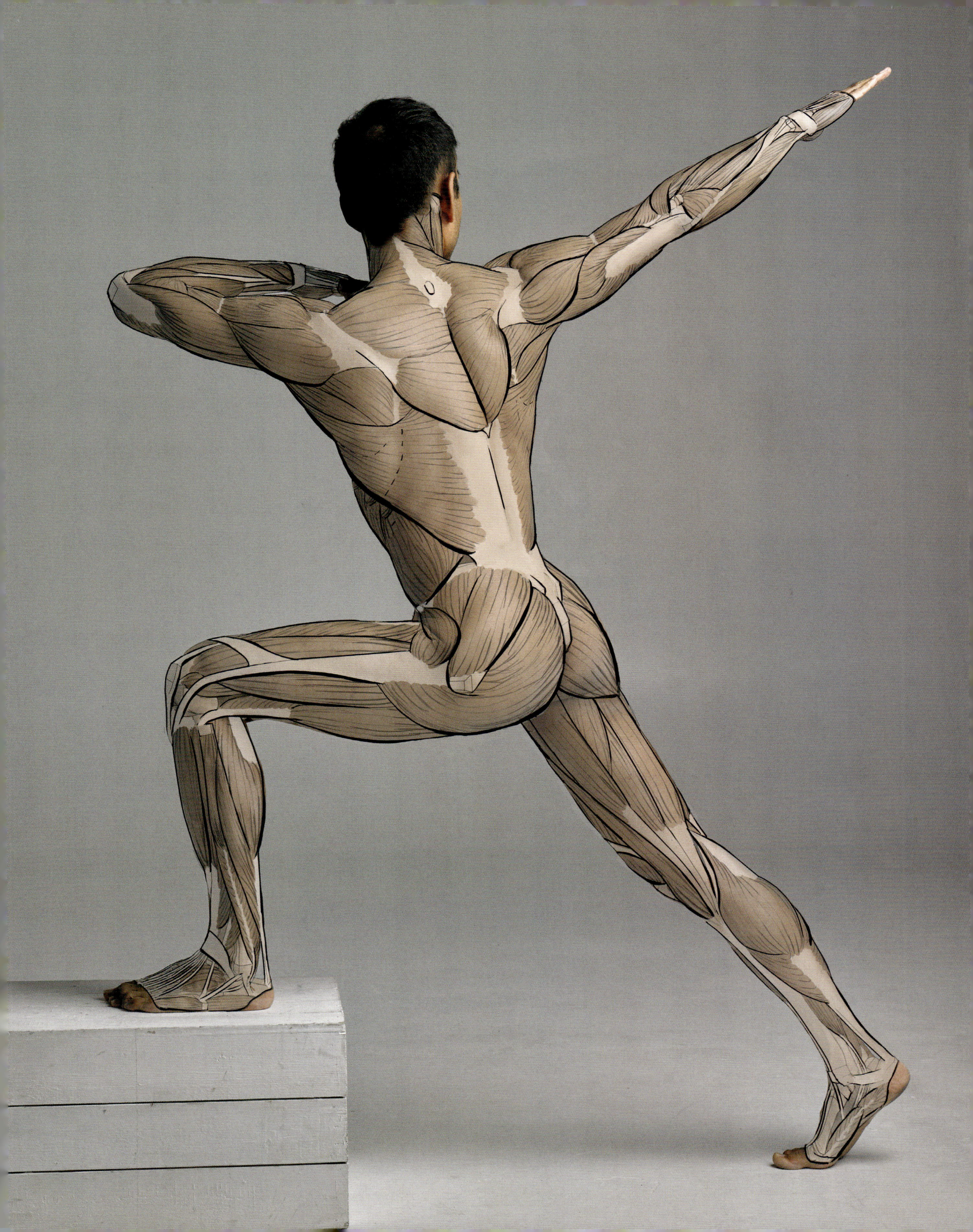

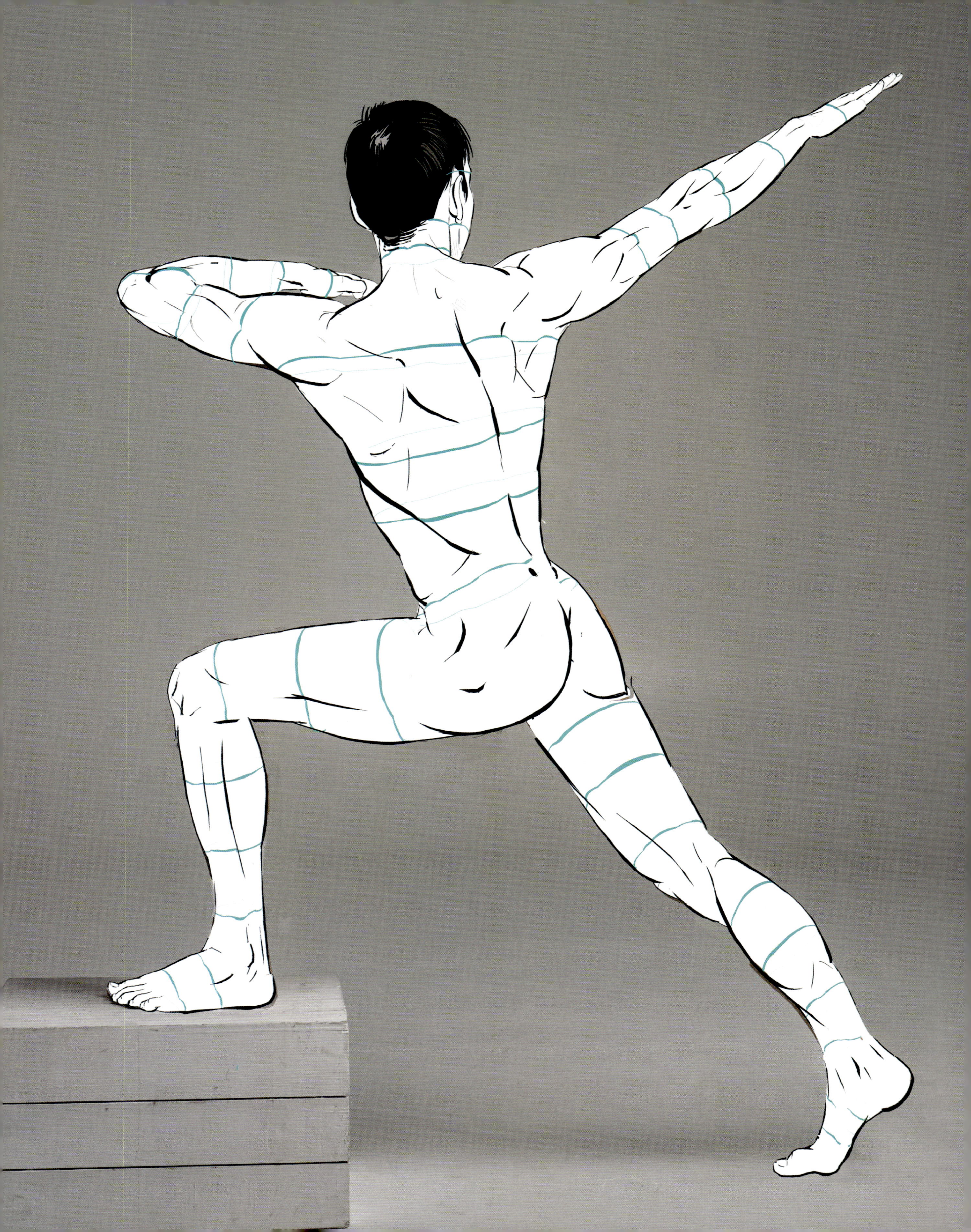

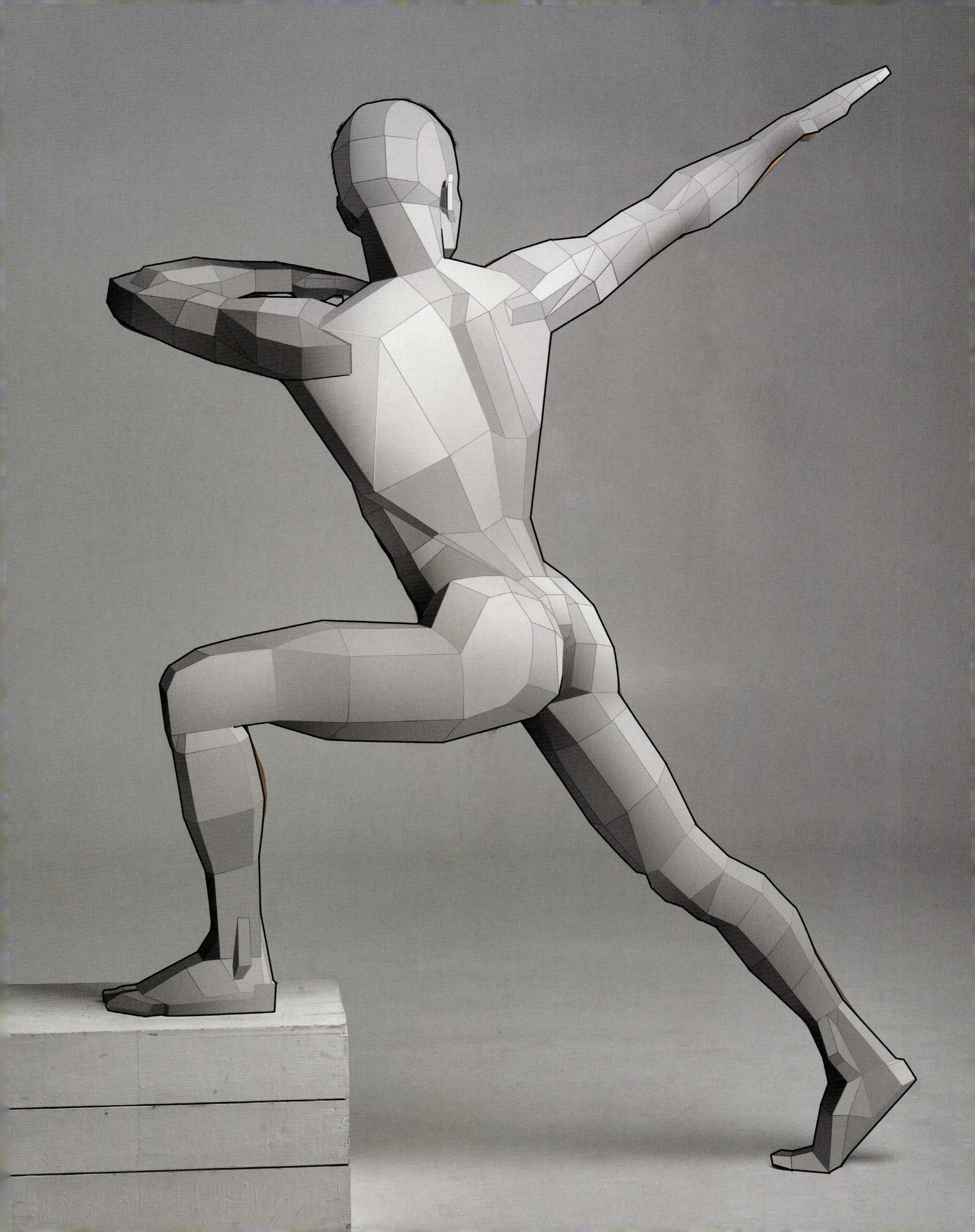

DYNAMIC ACTION POSES

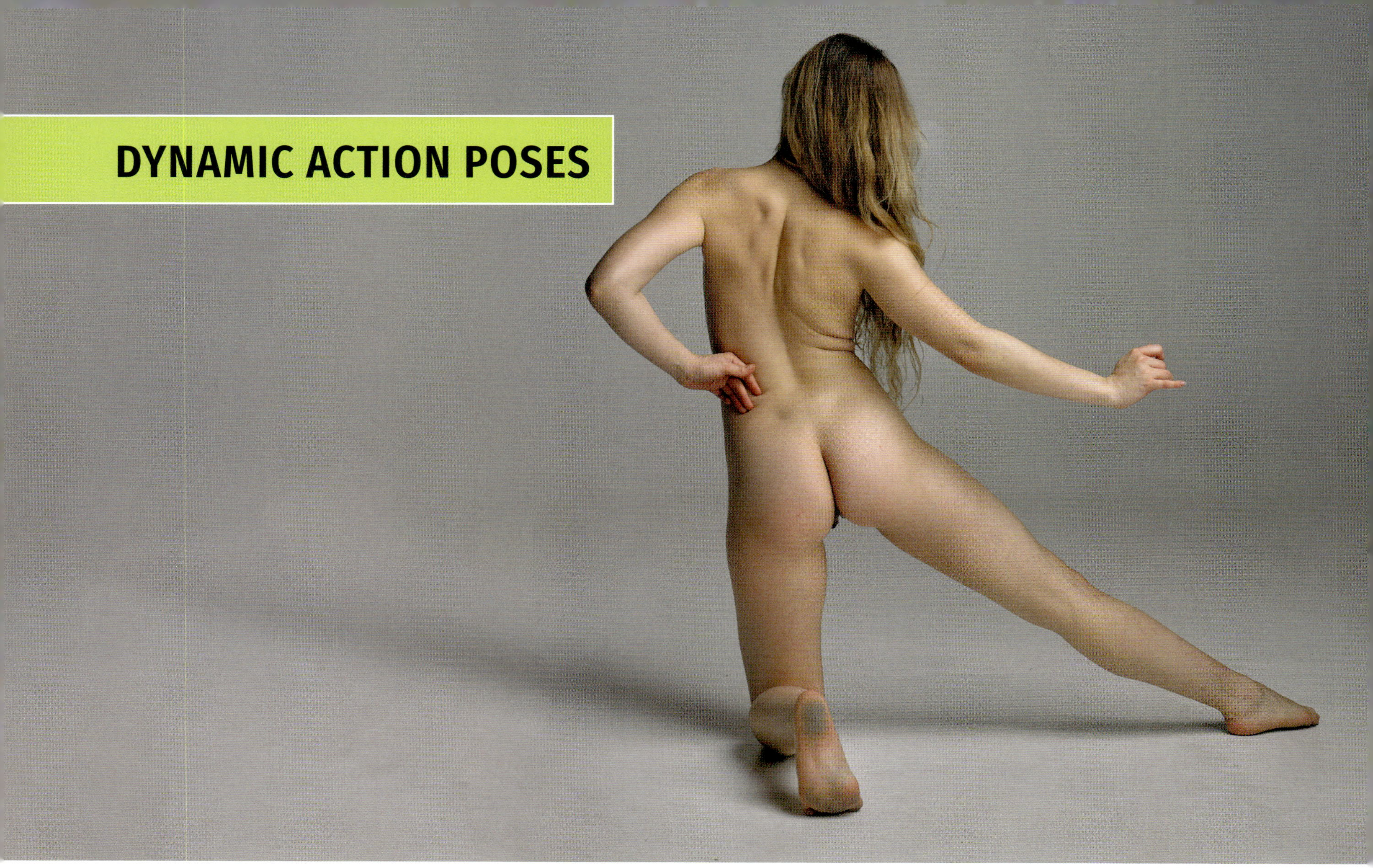

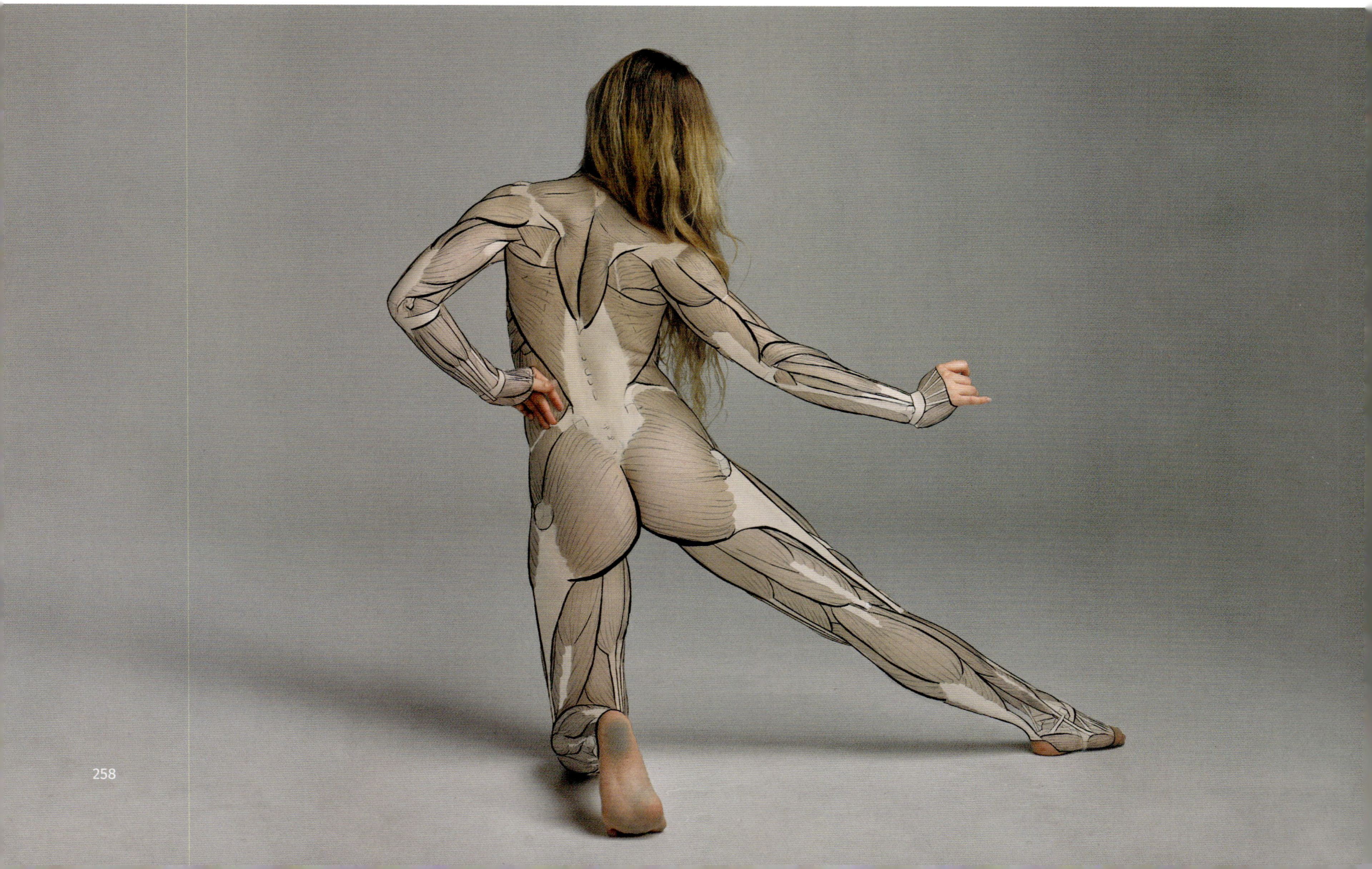

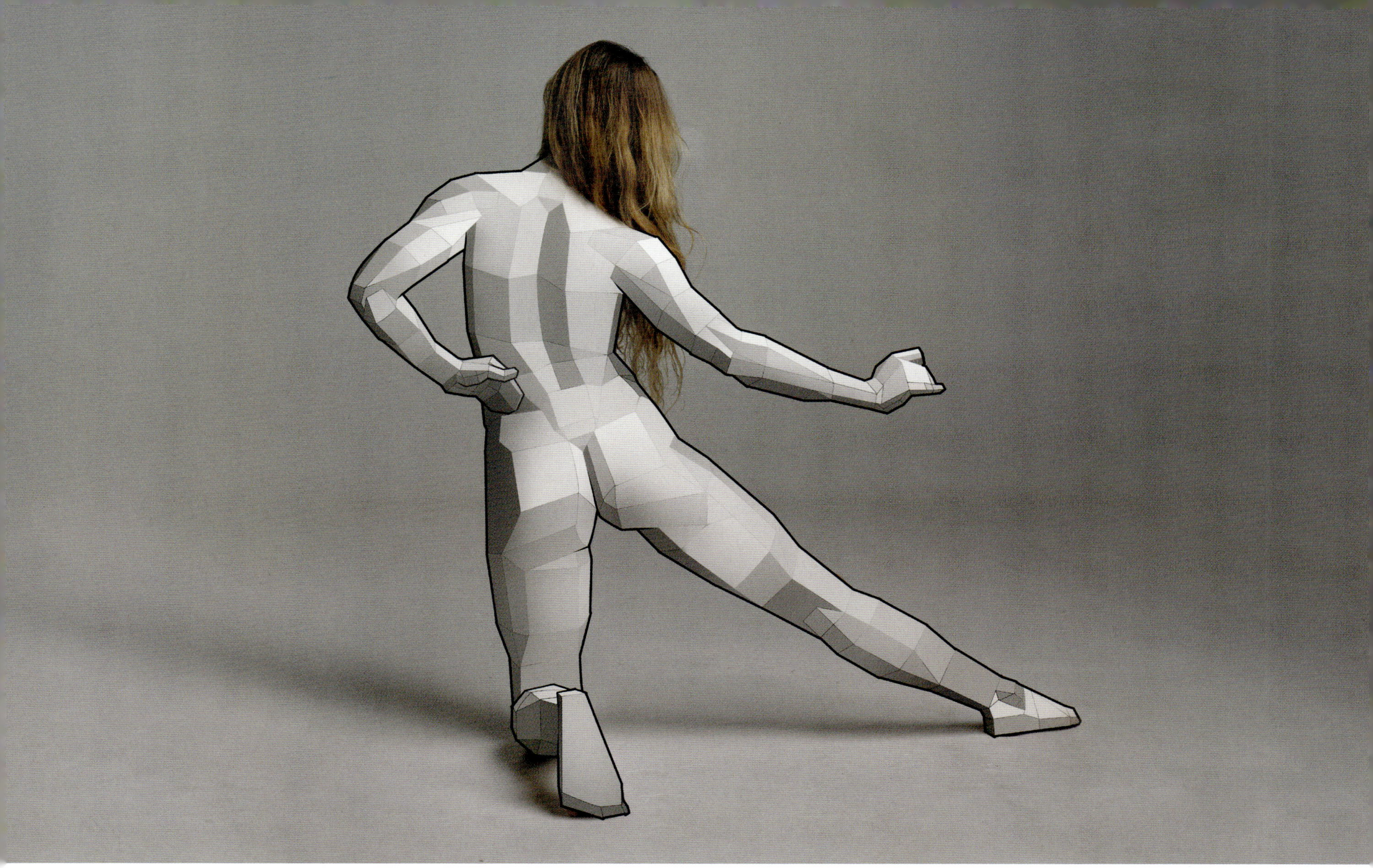

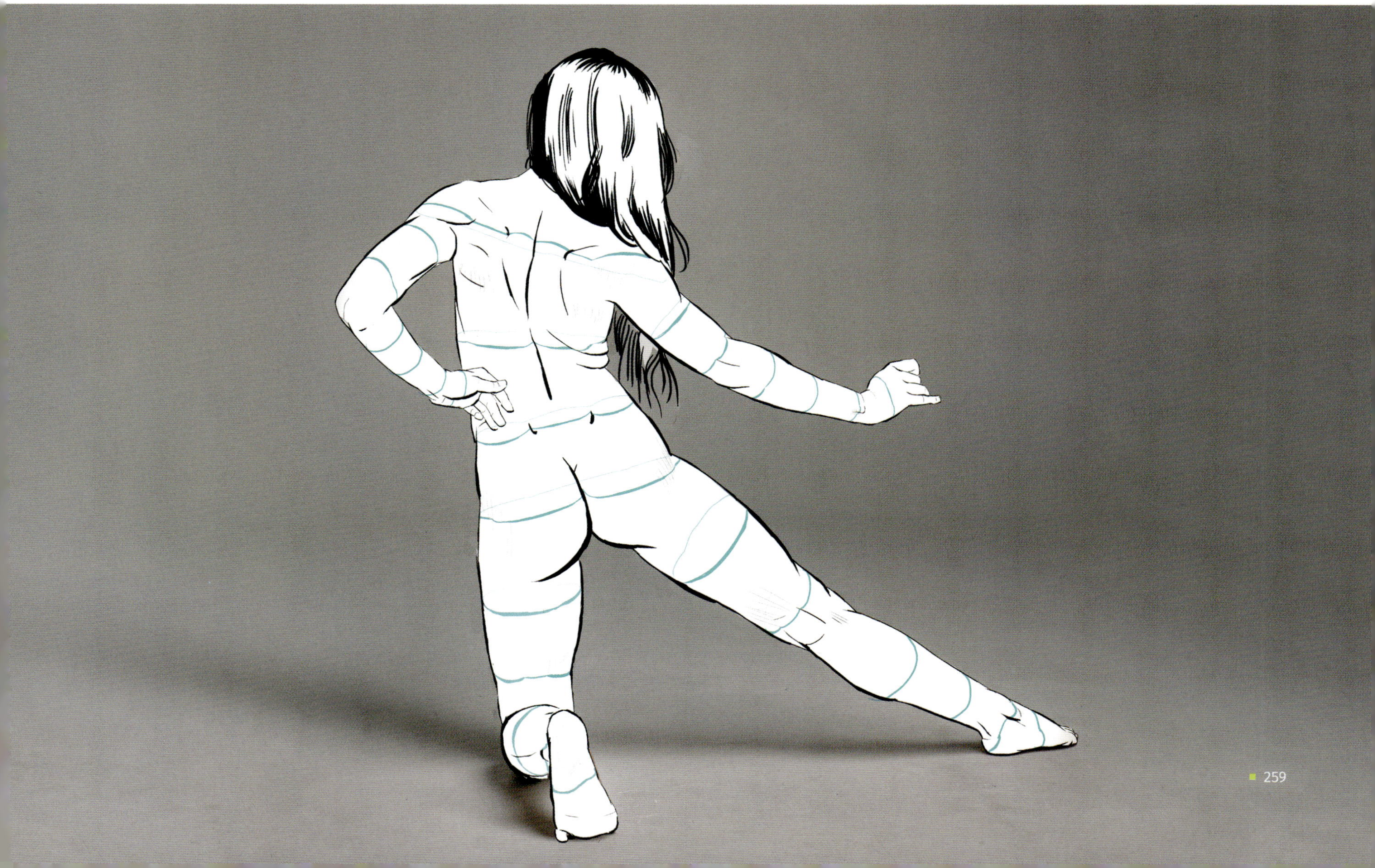

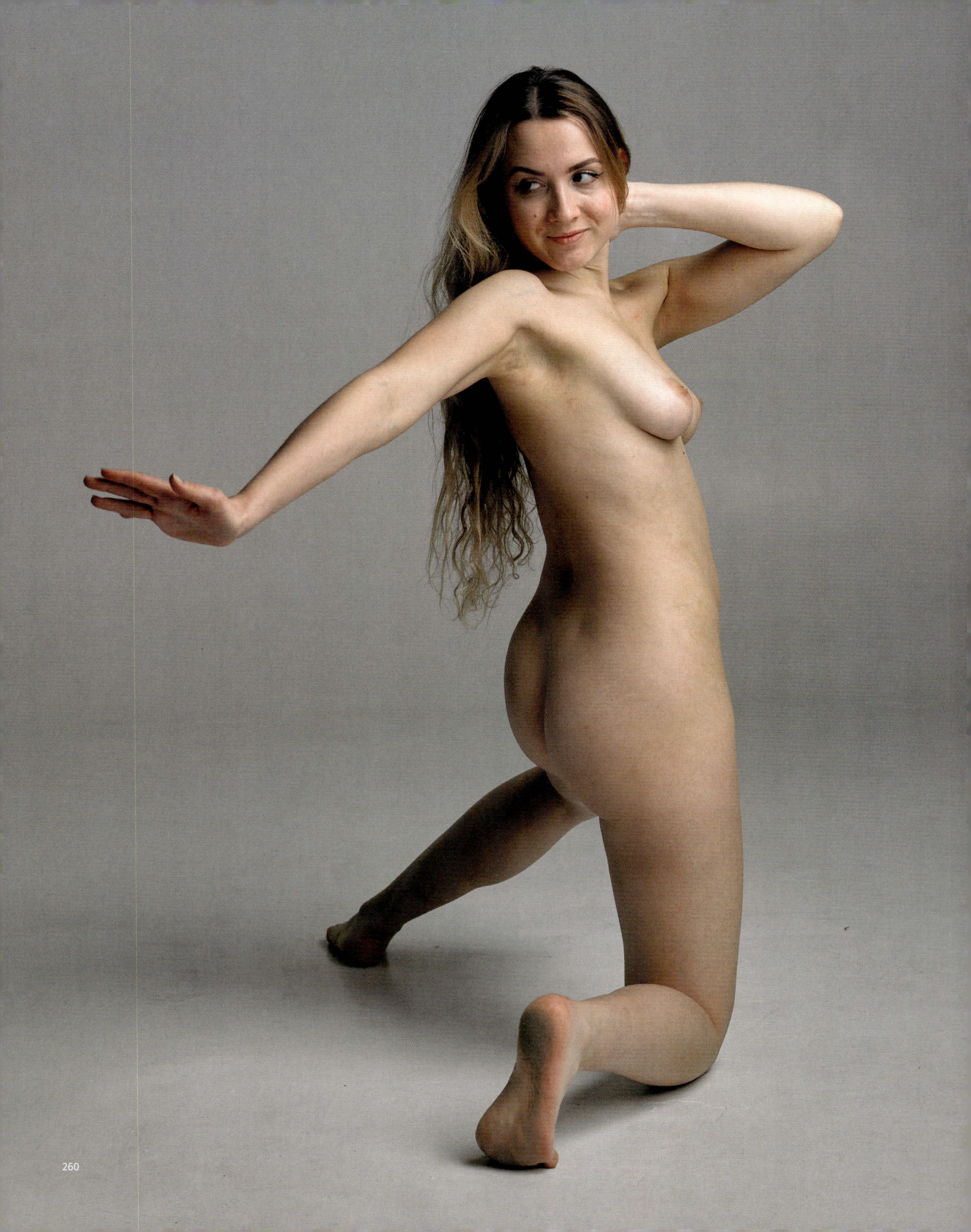

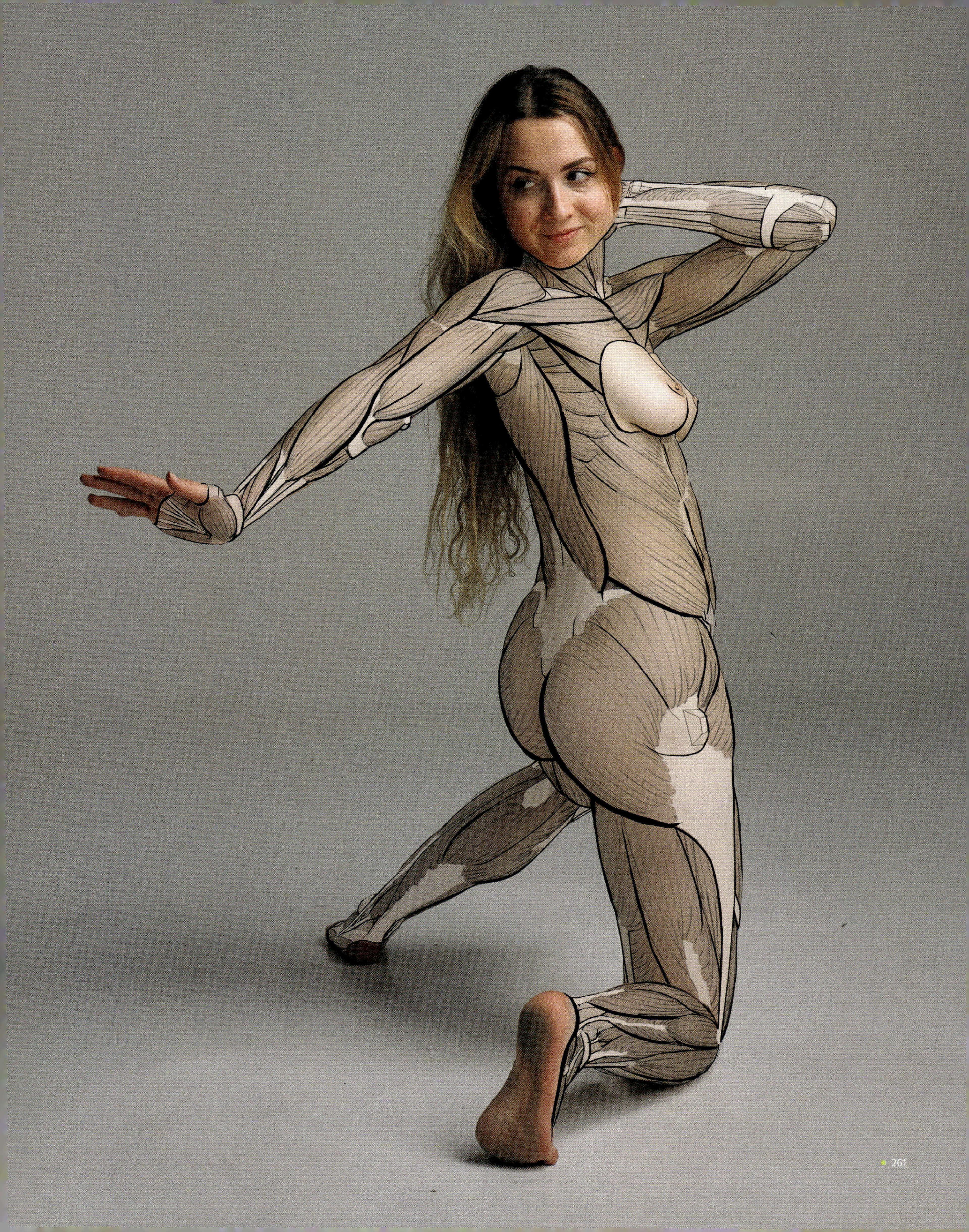

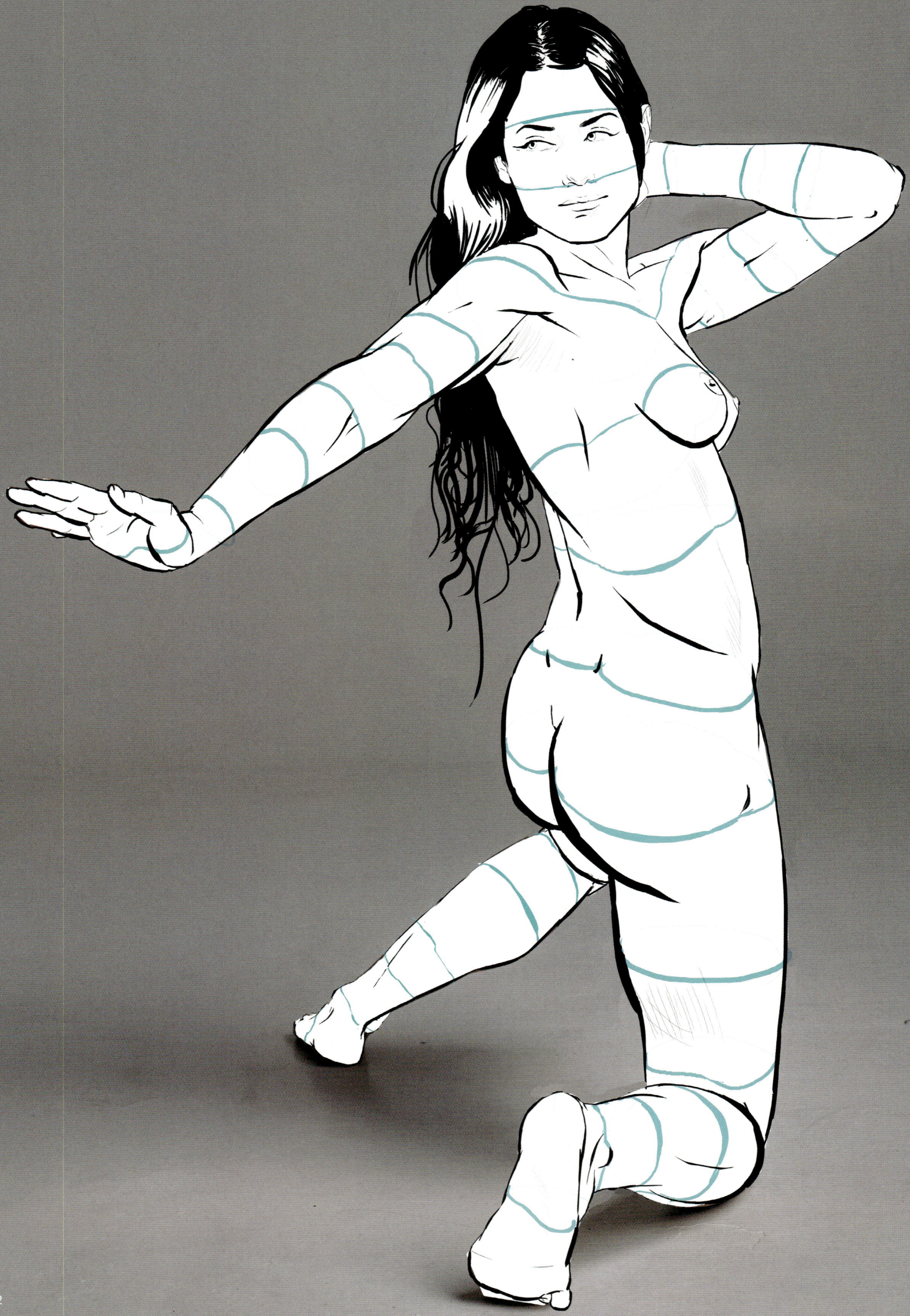

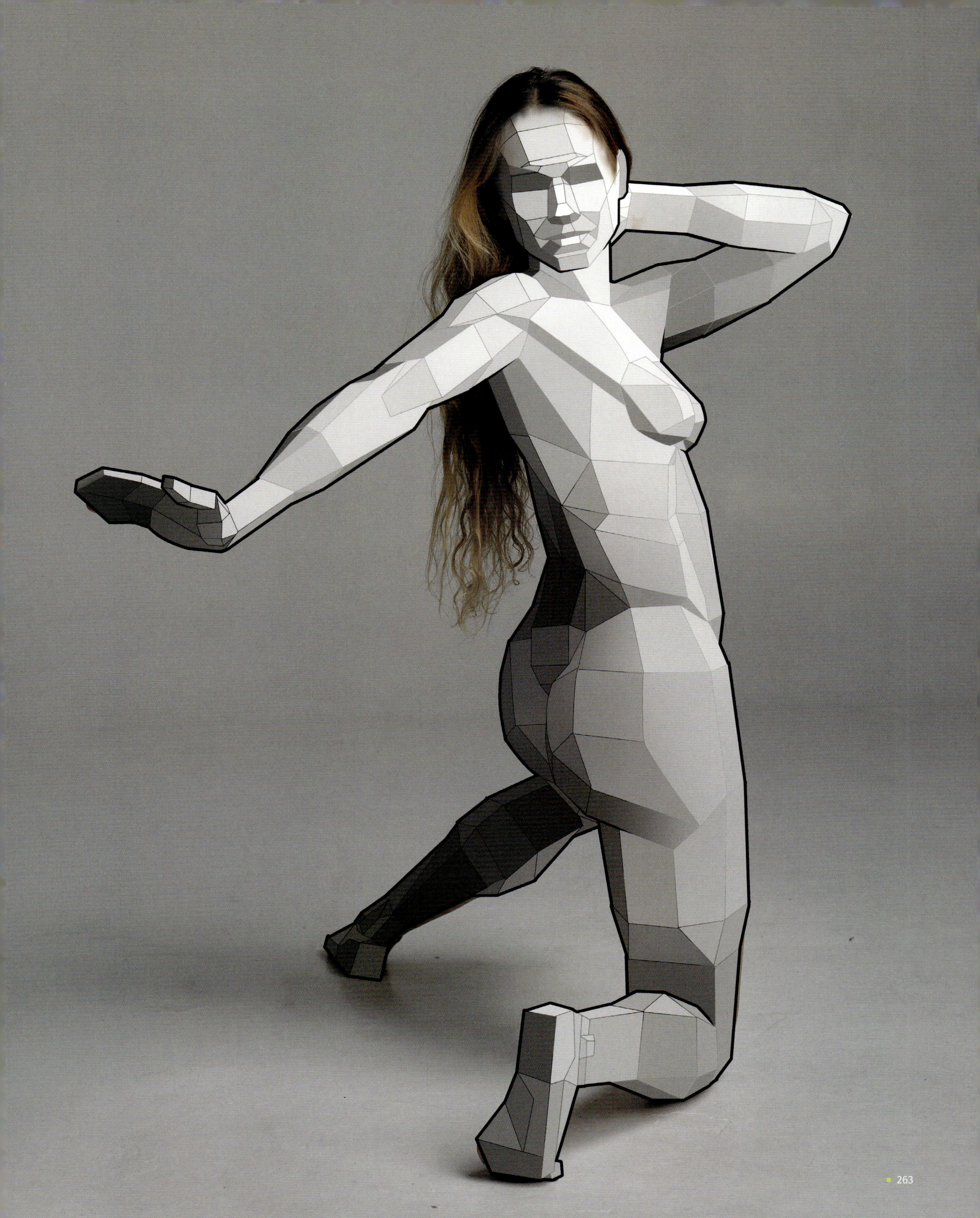

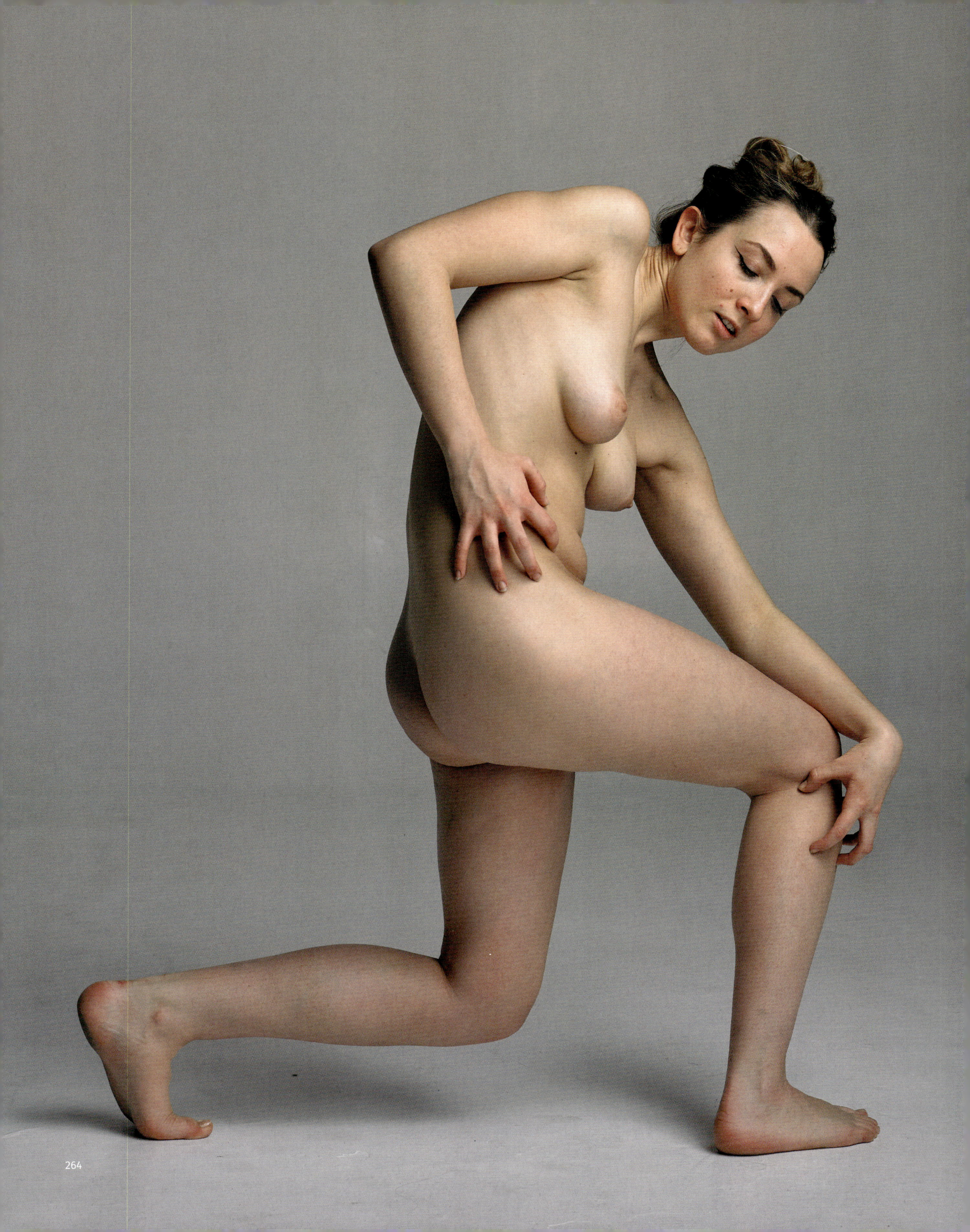

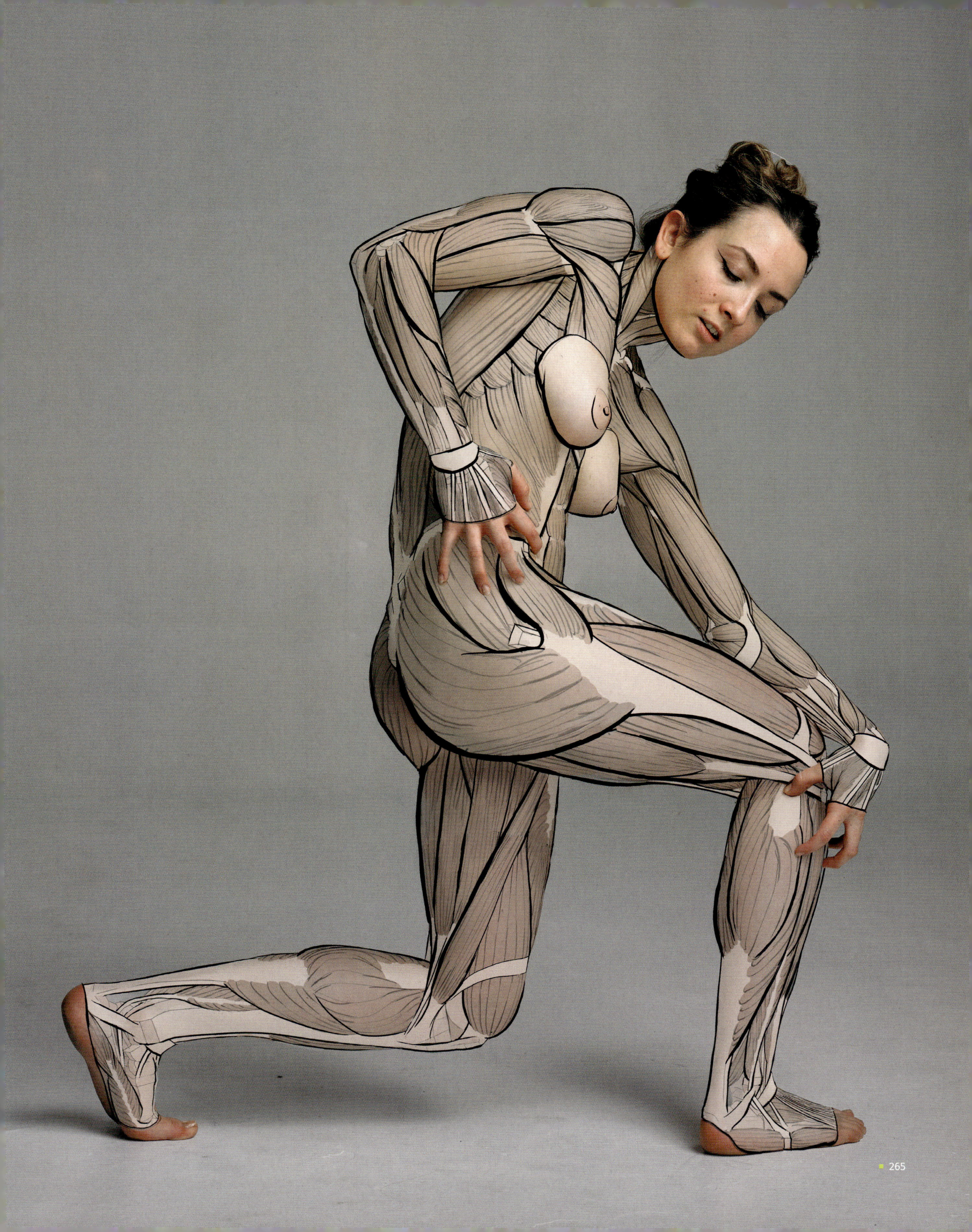

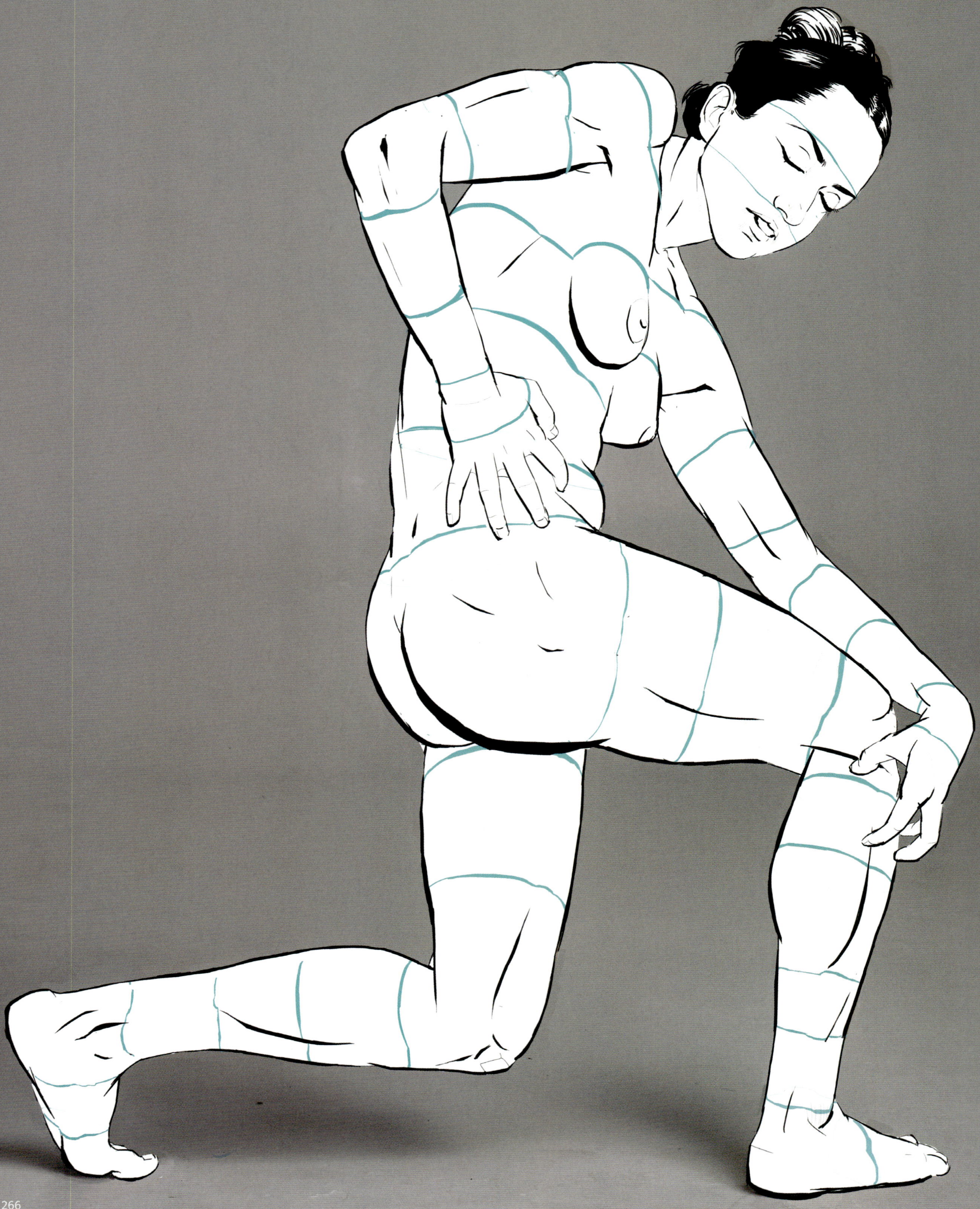

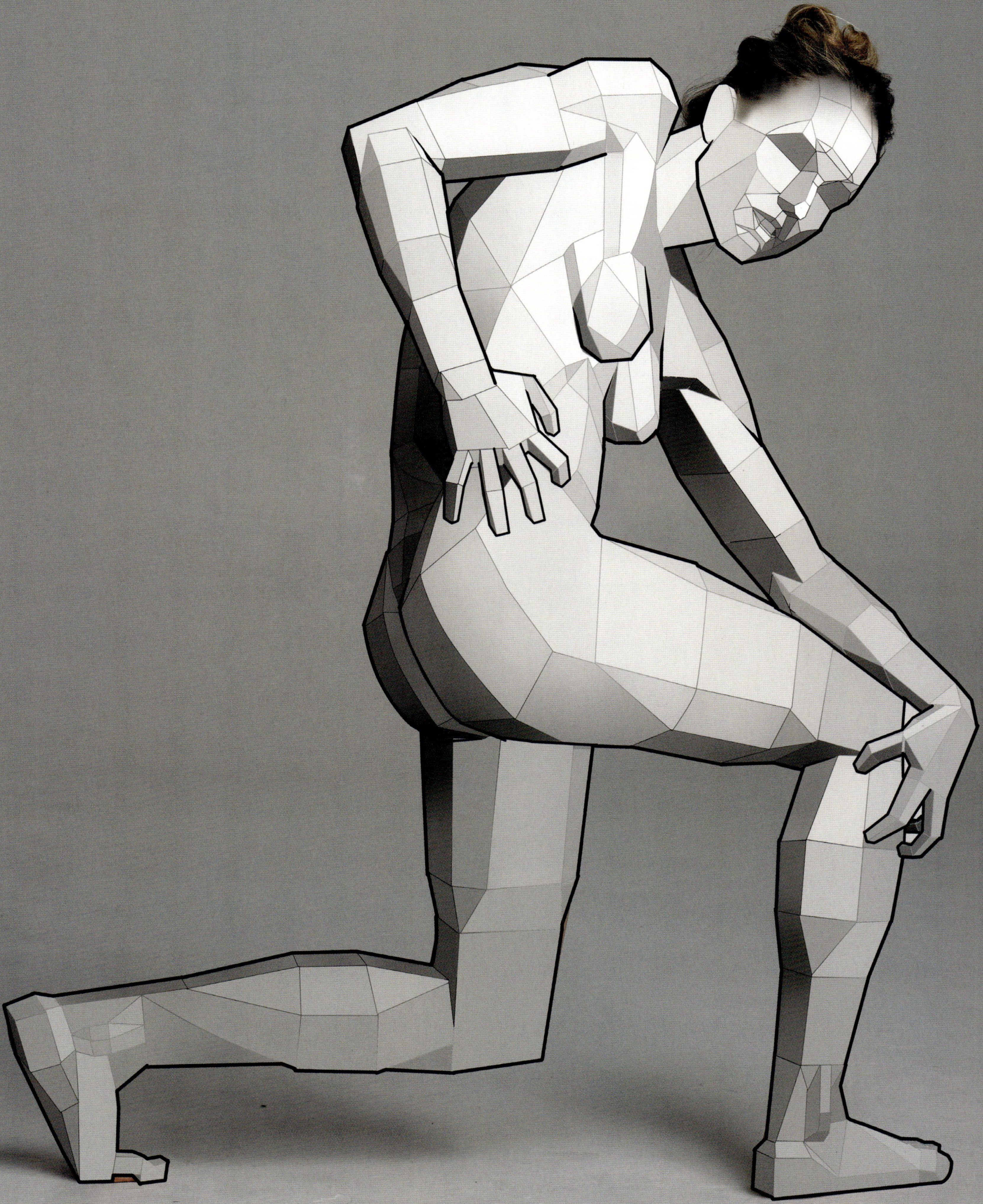

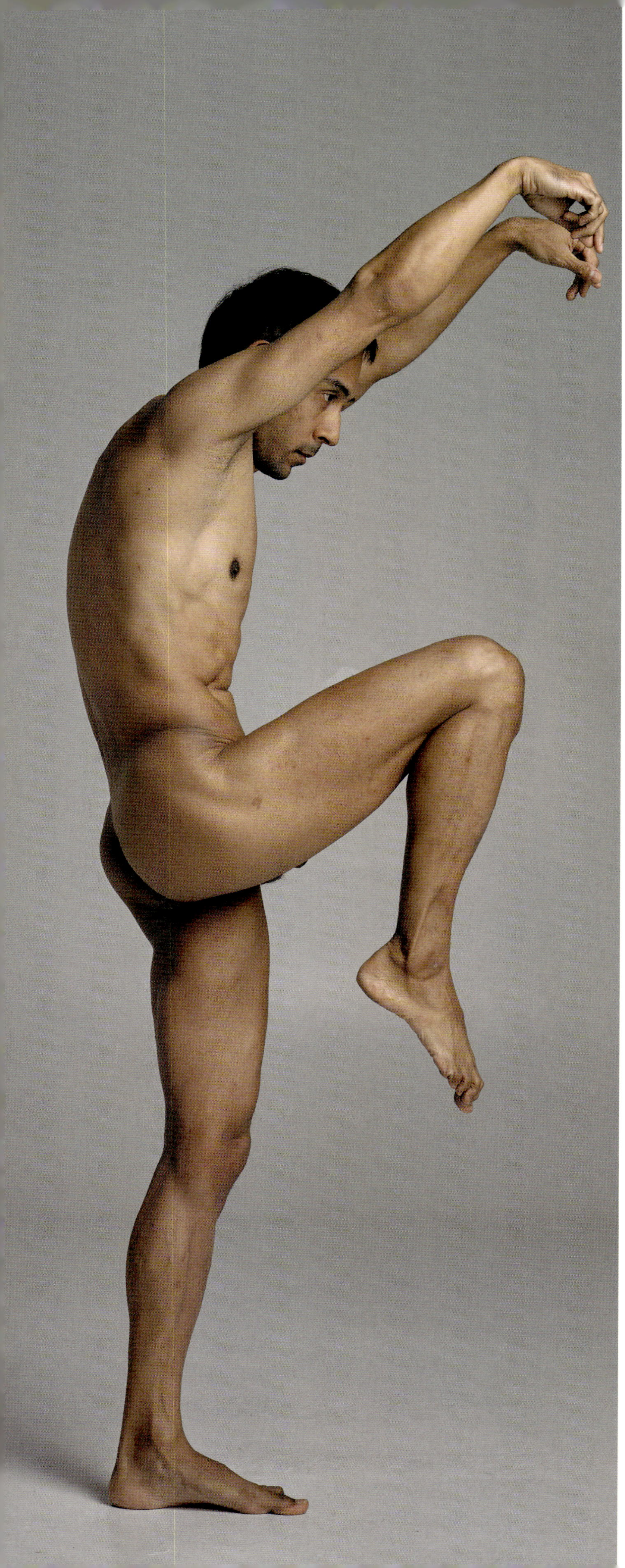
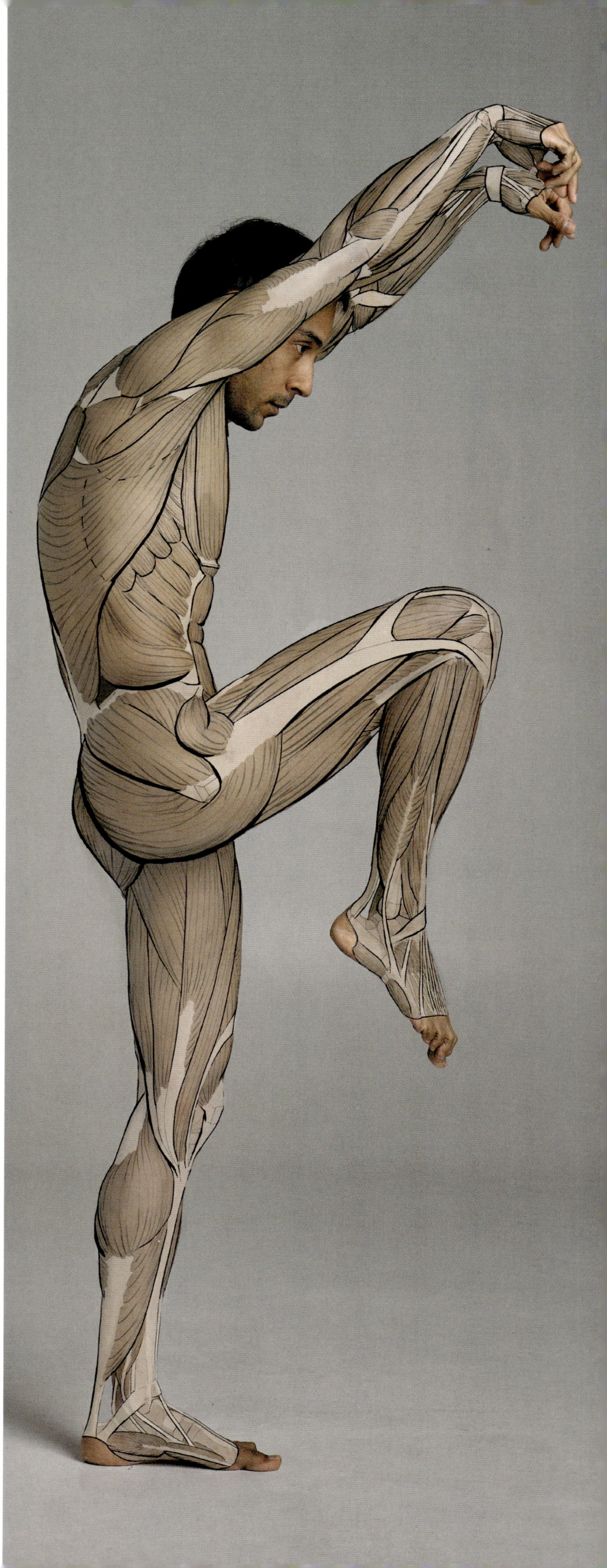

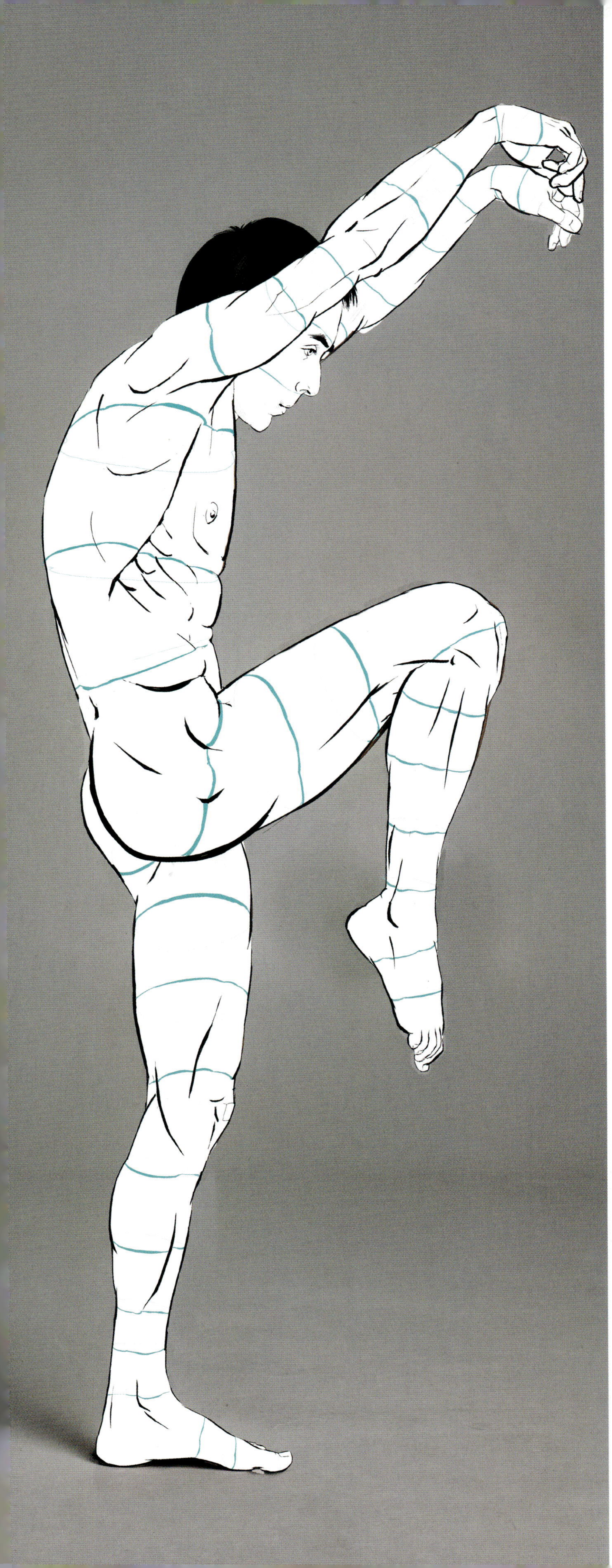

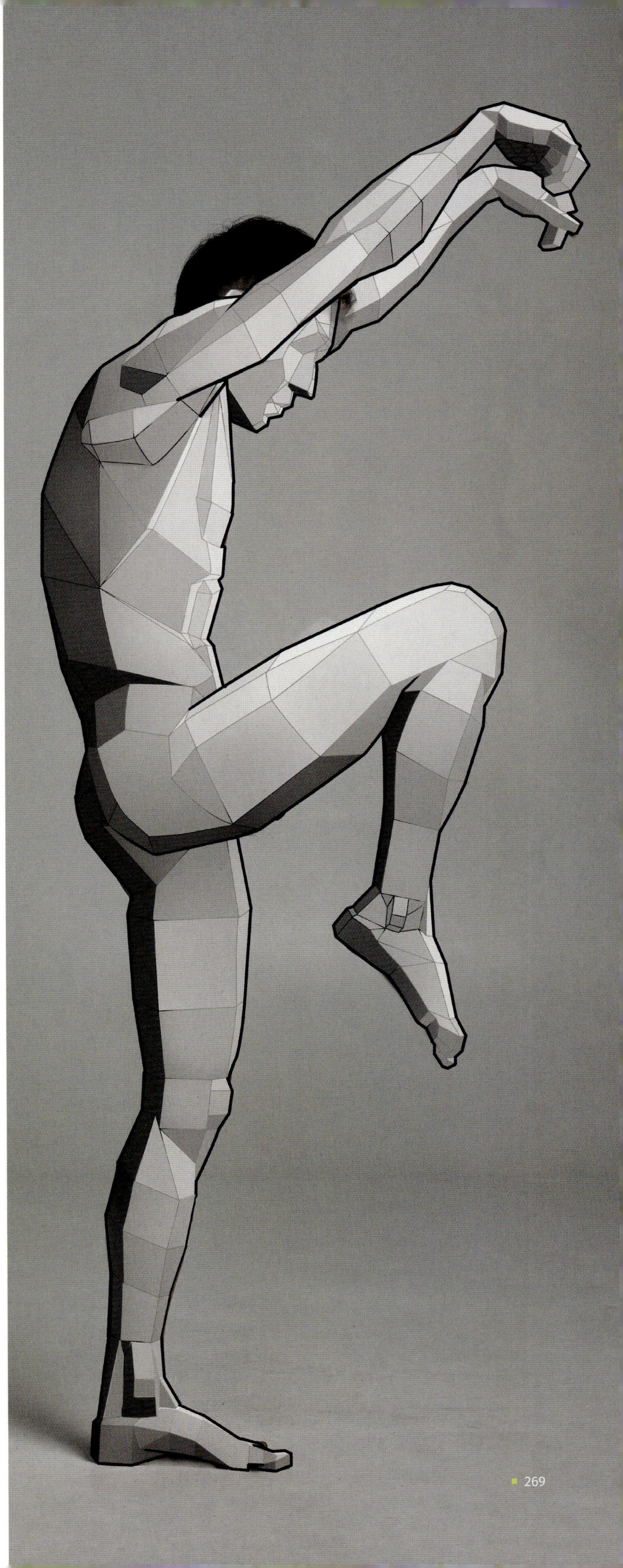

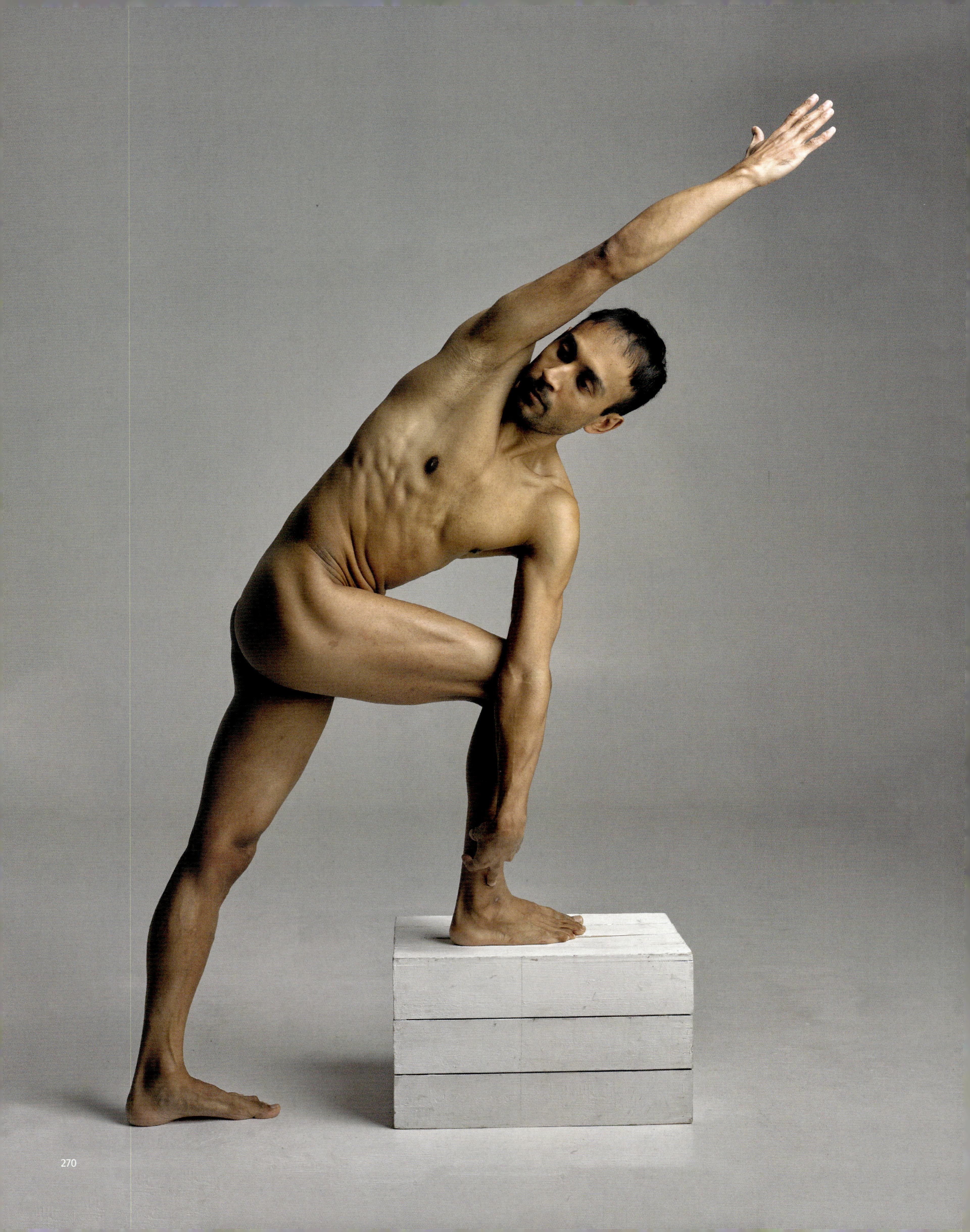

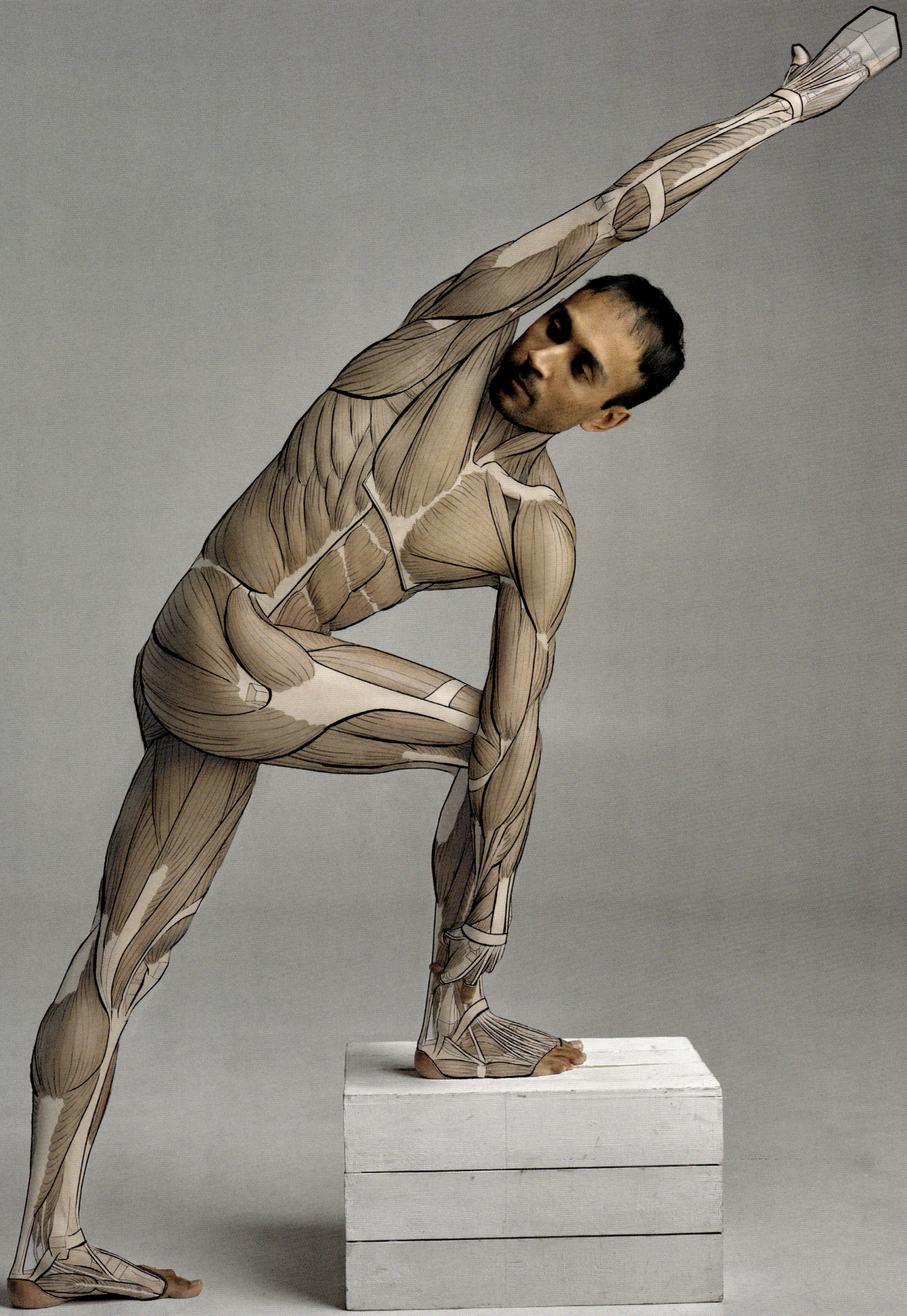

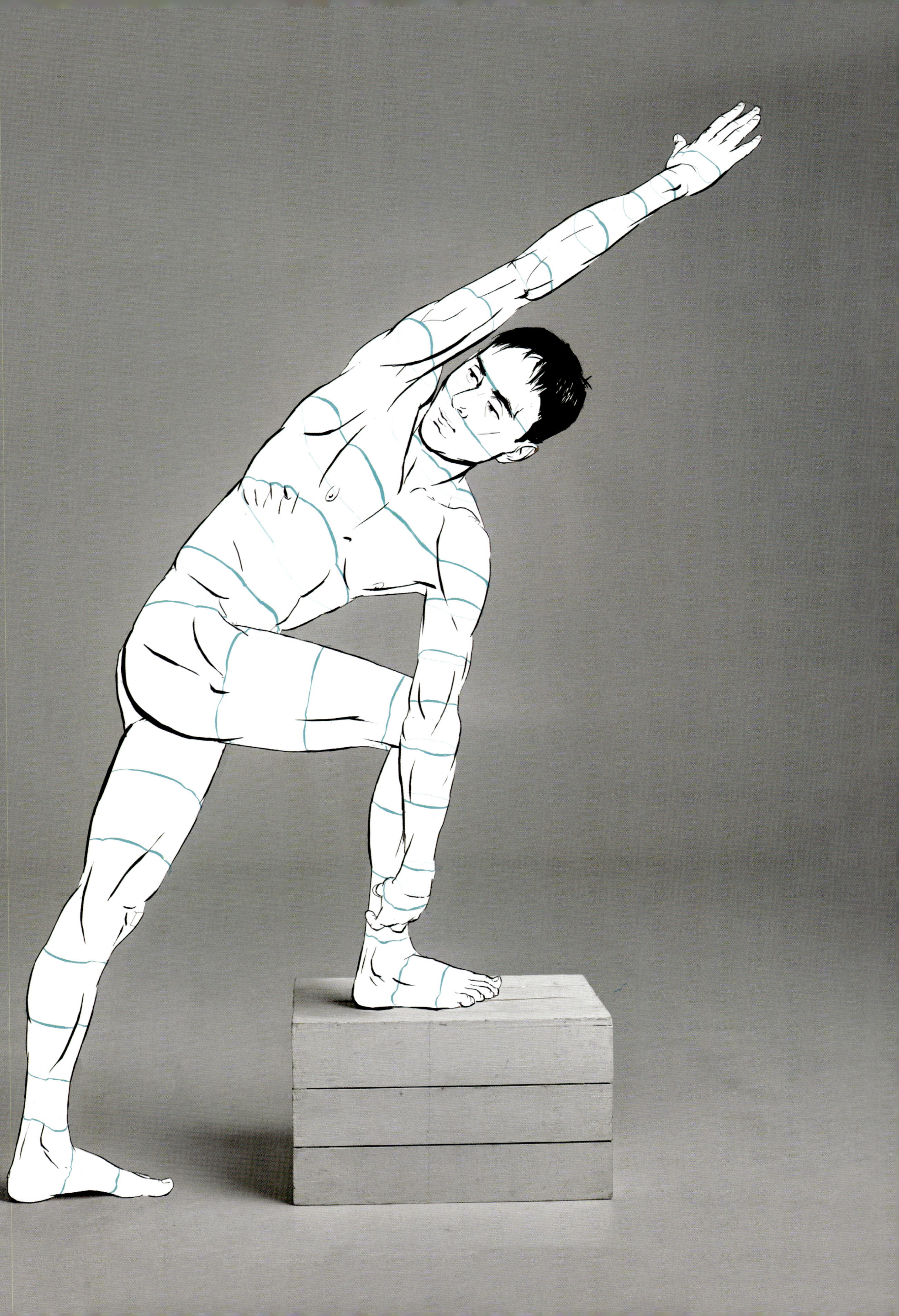

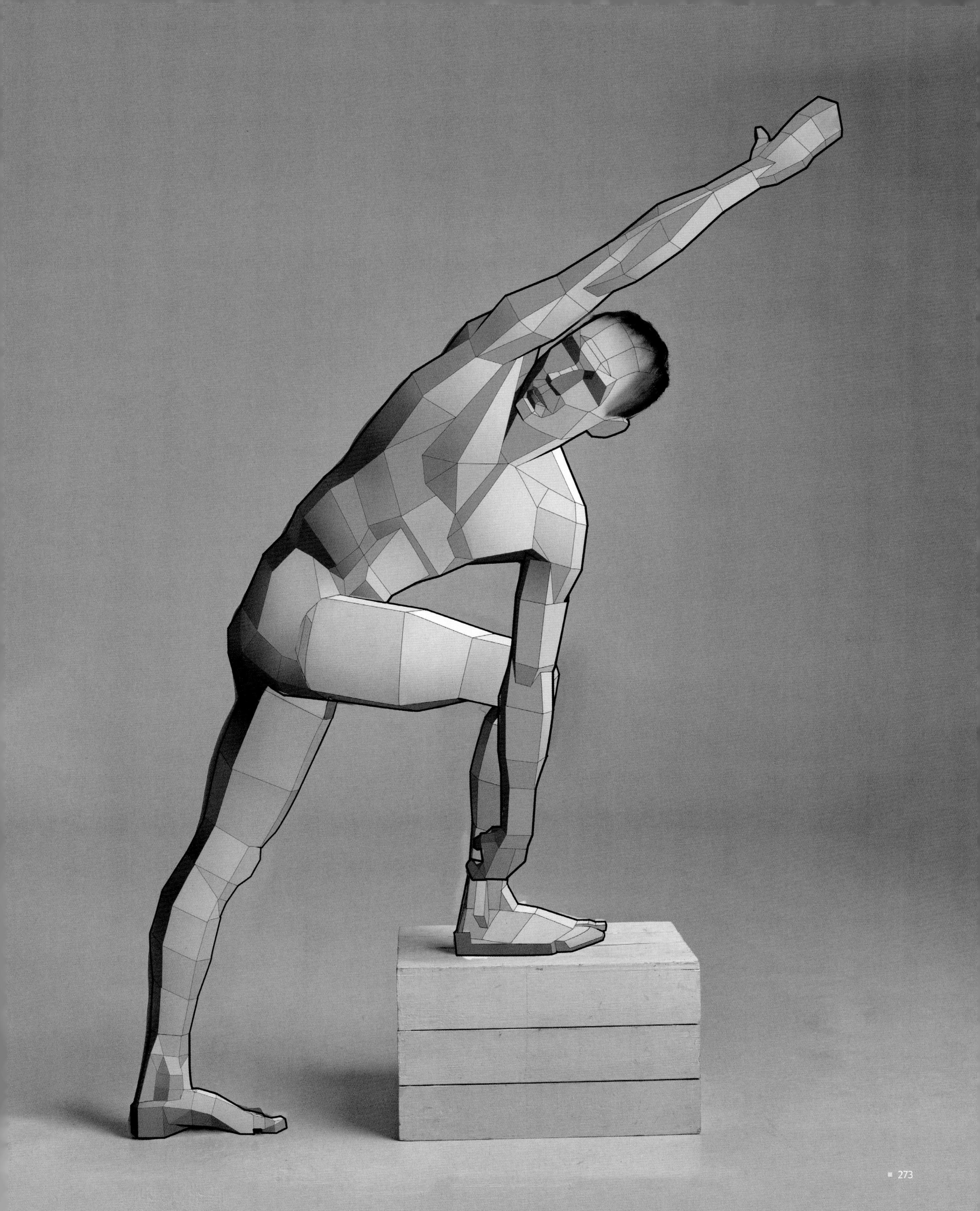

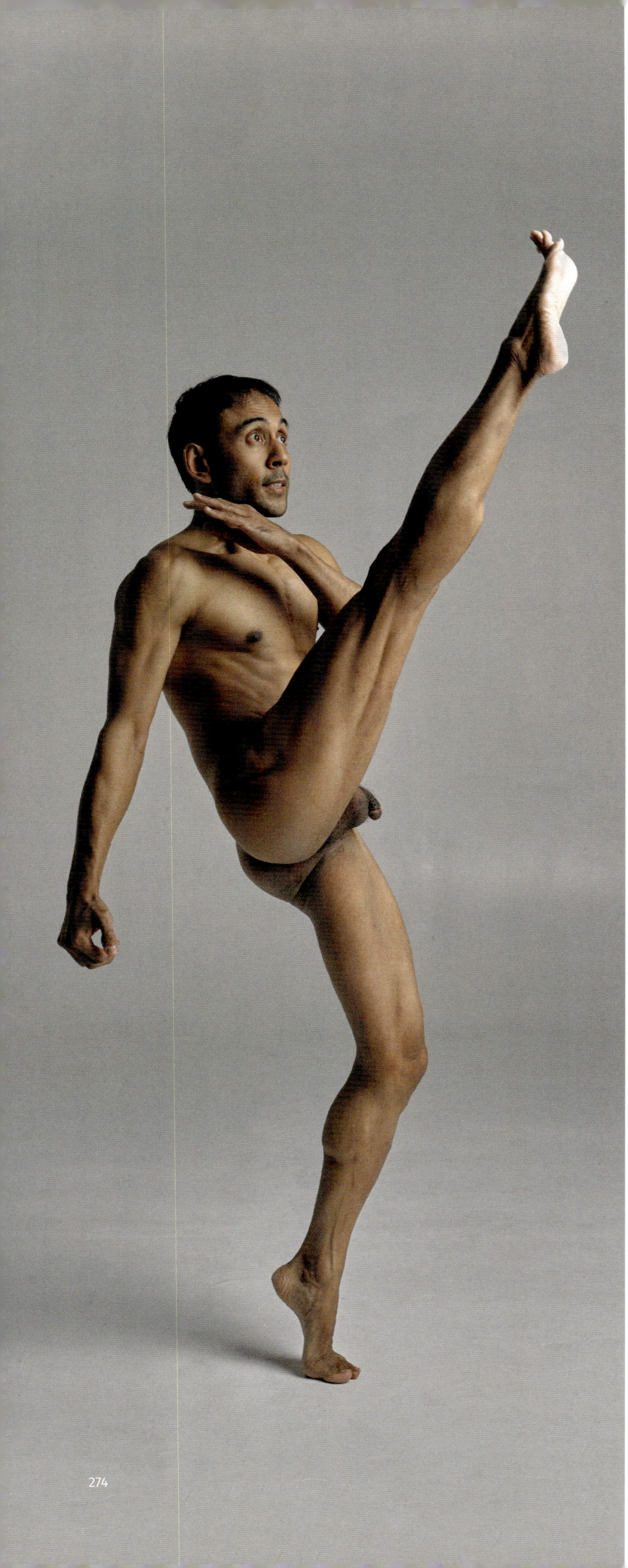

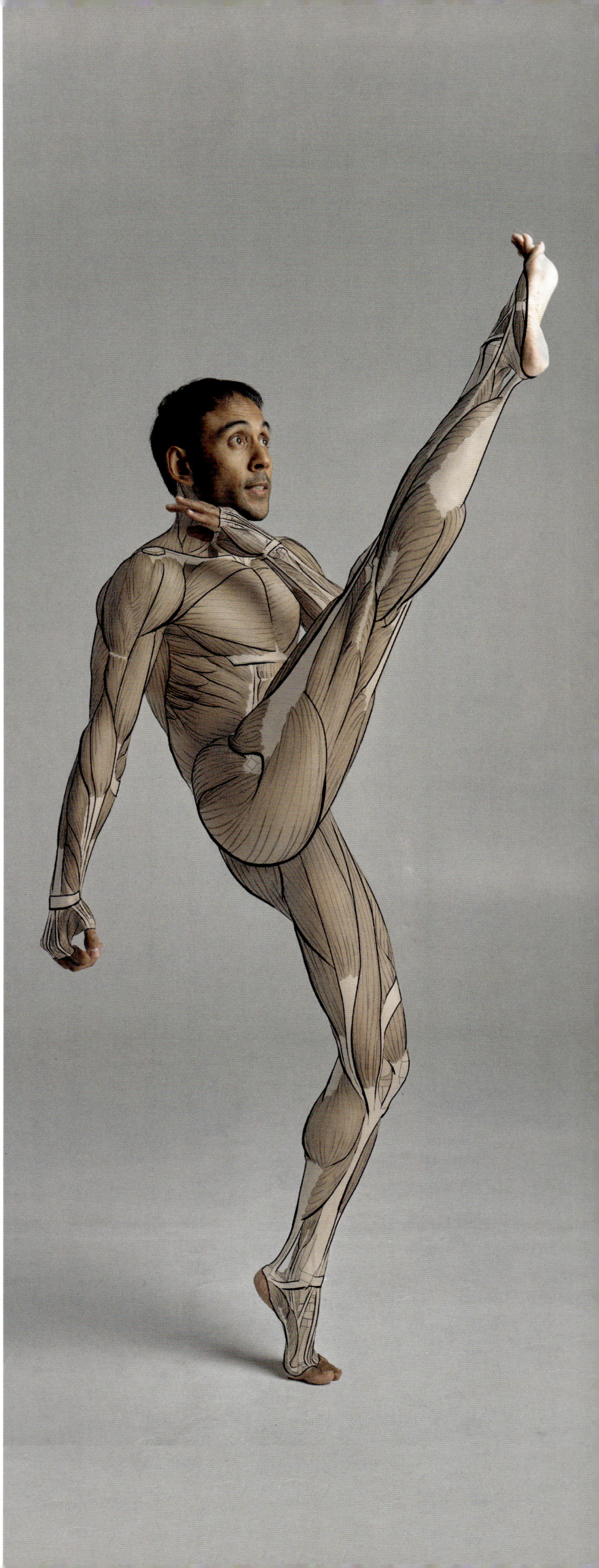

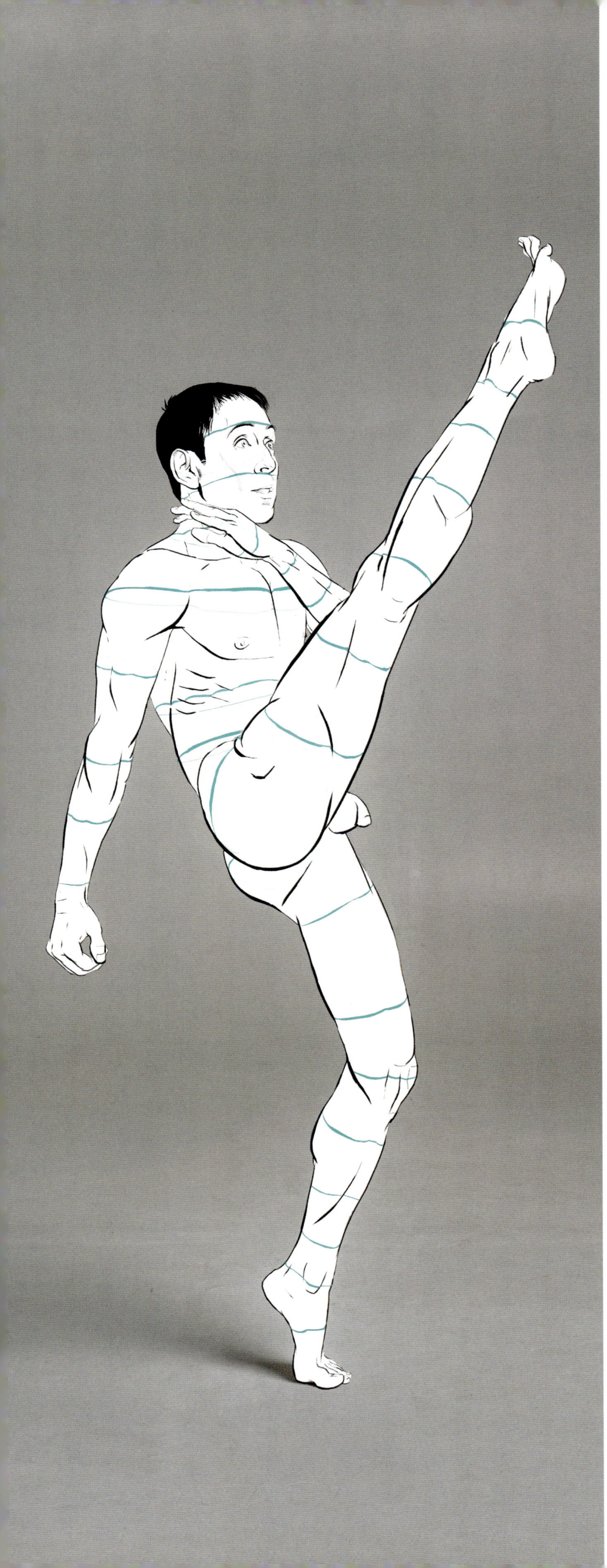

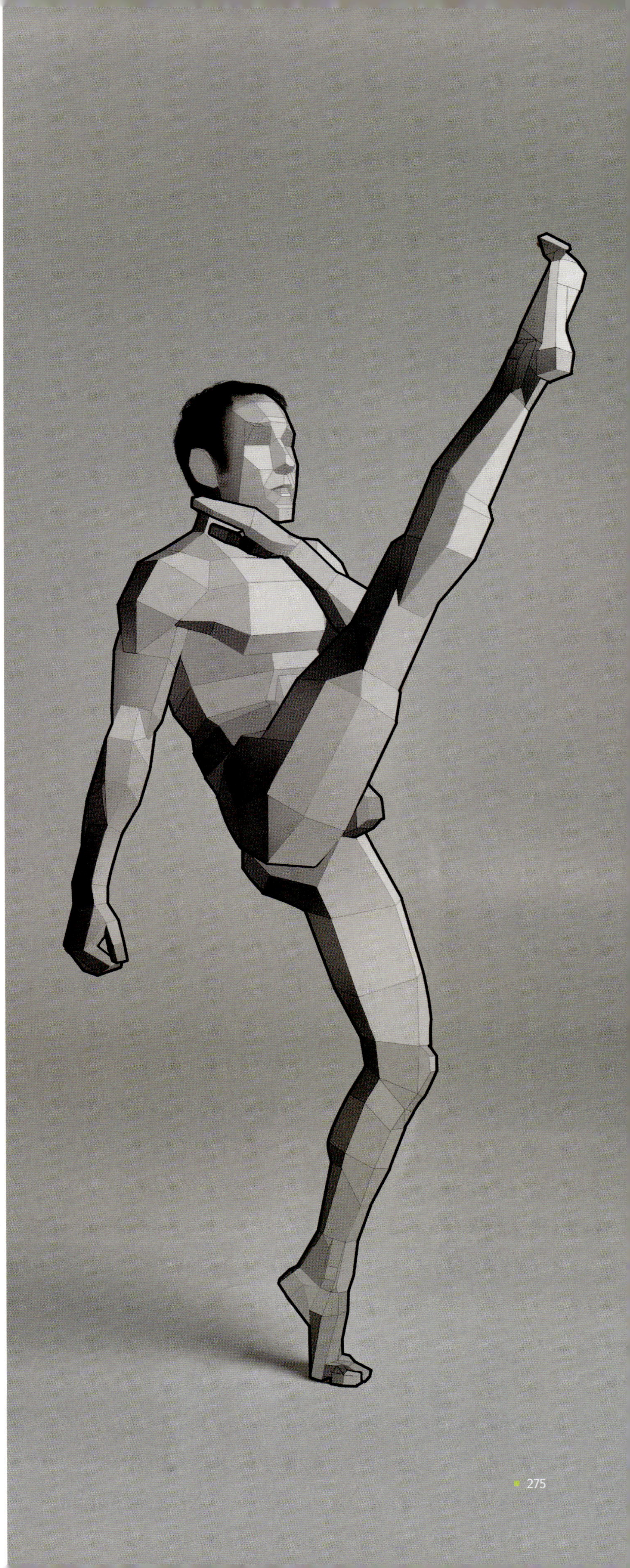

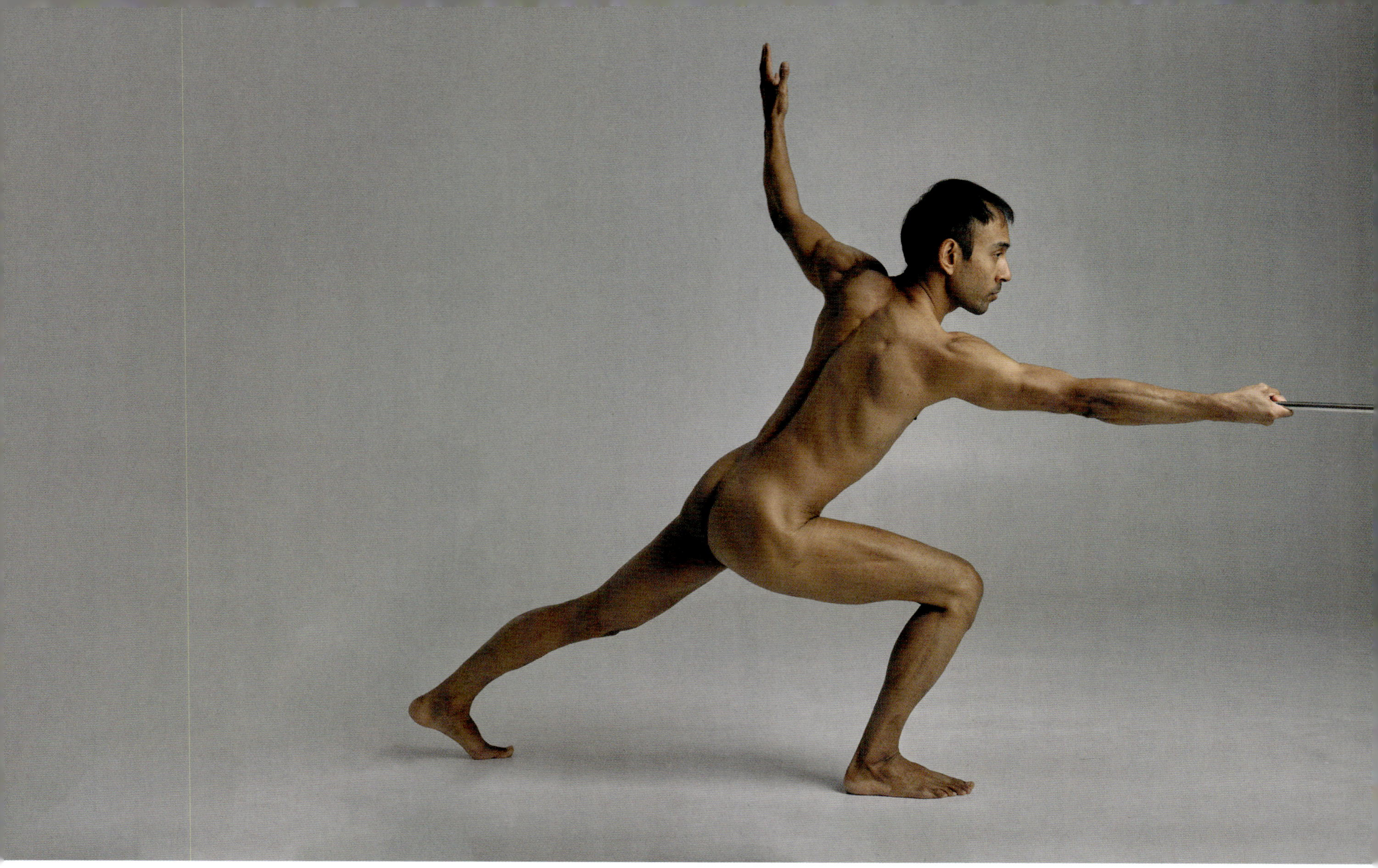

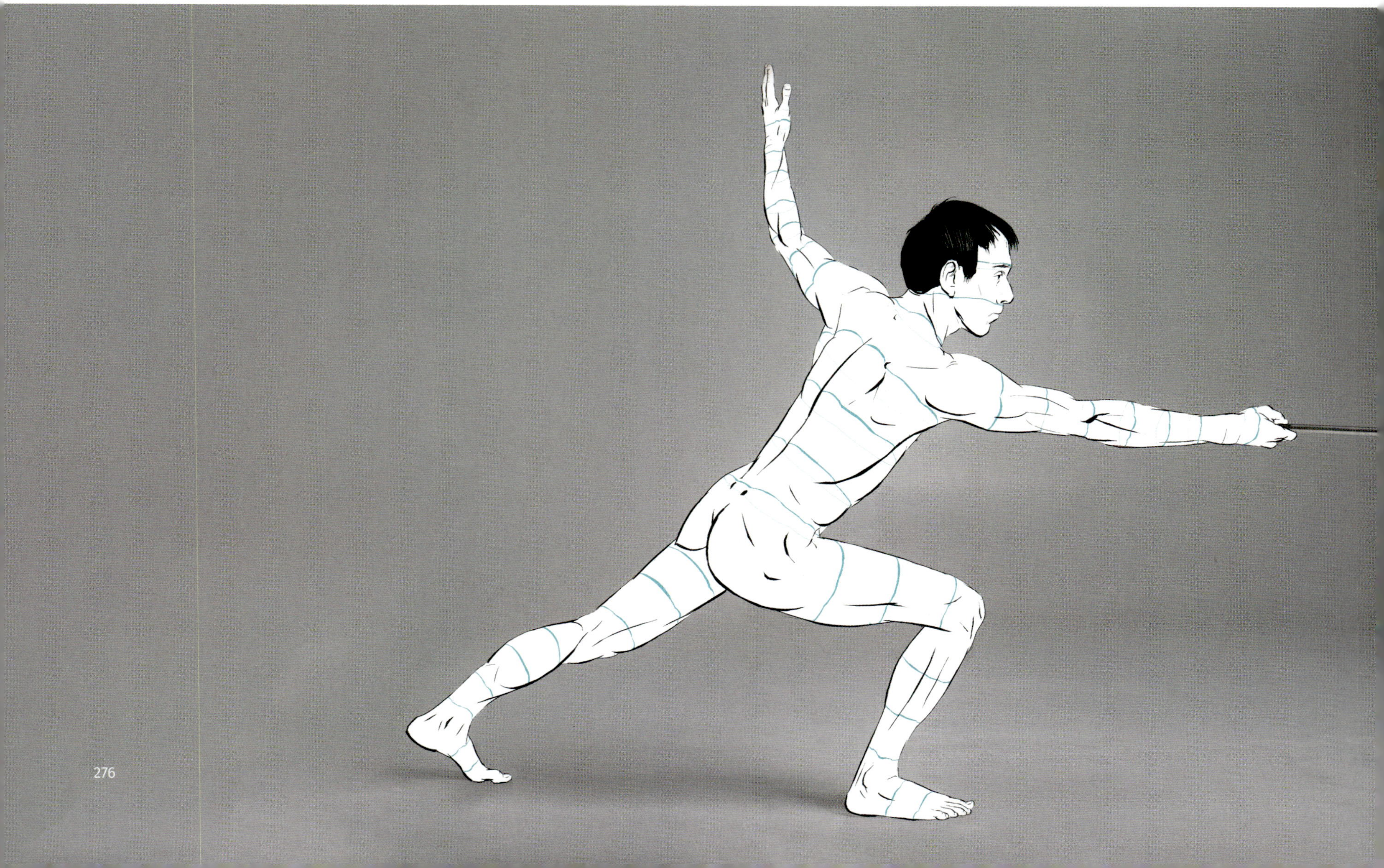

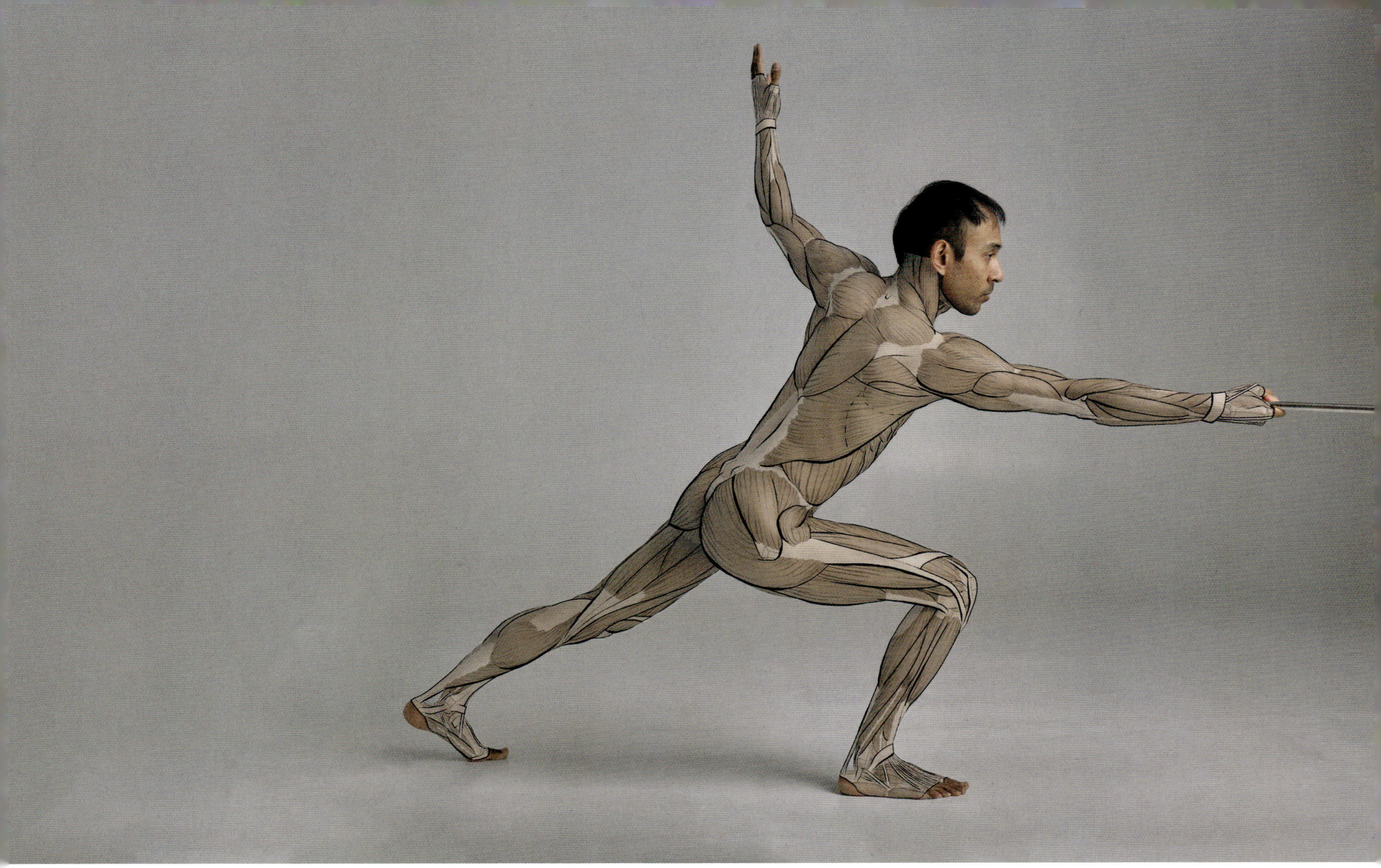

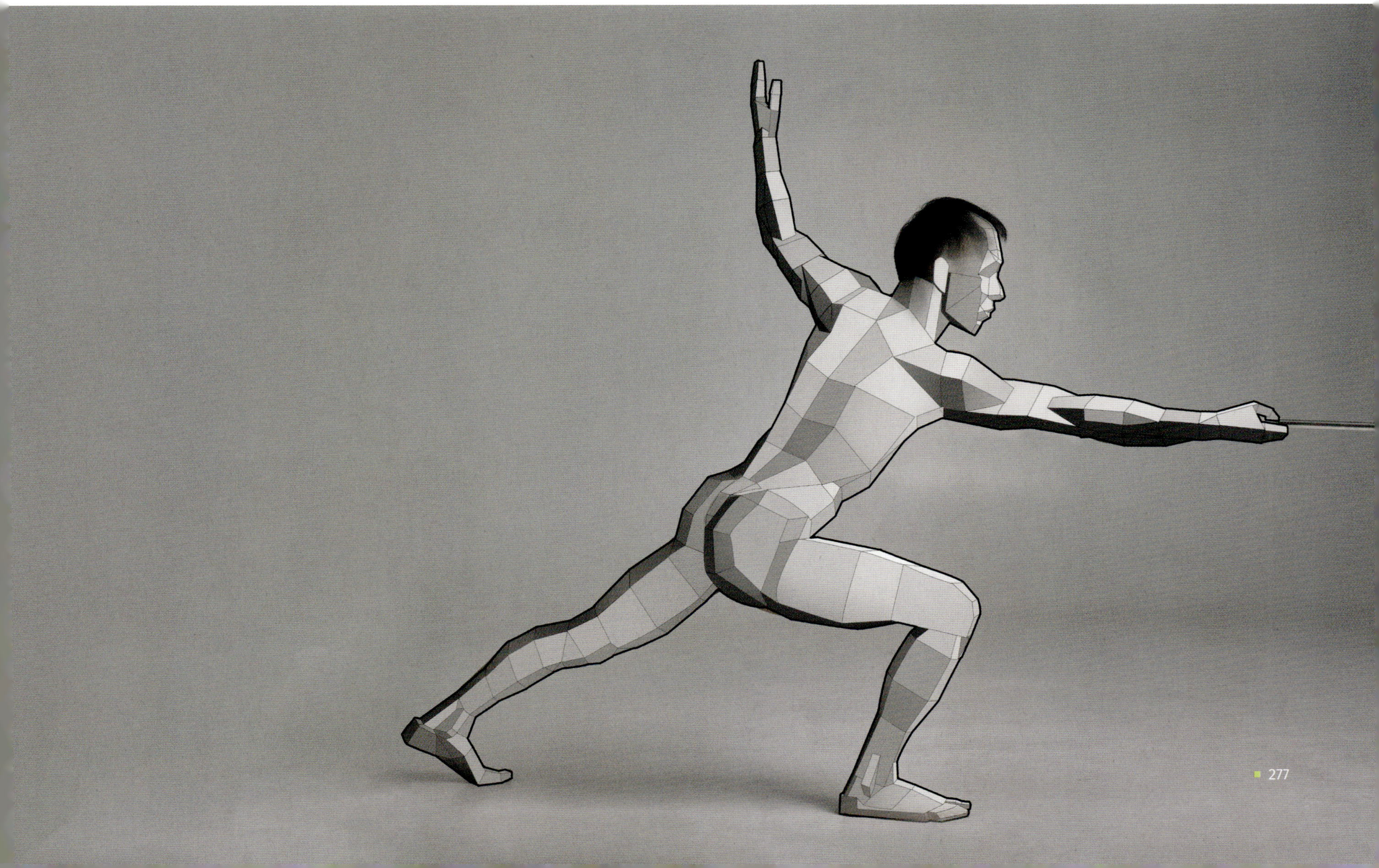

NARRATIVE POSES

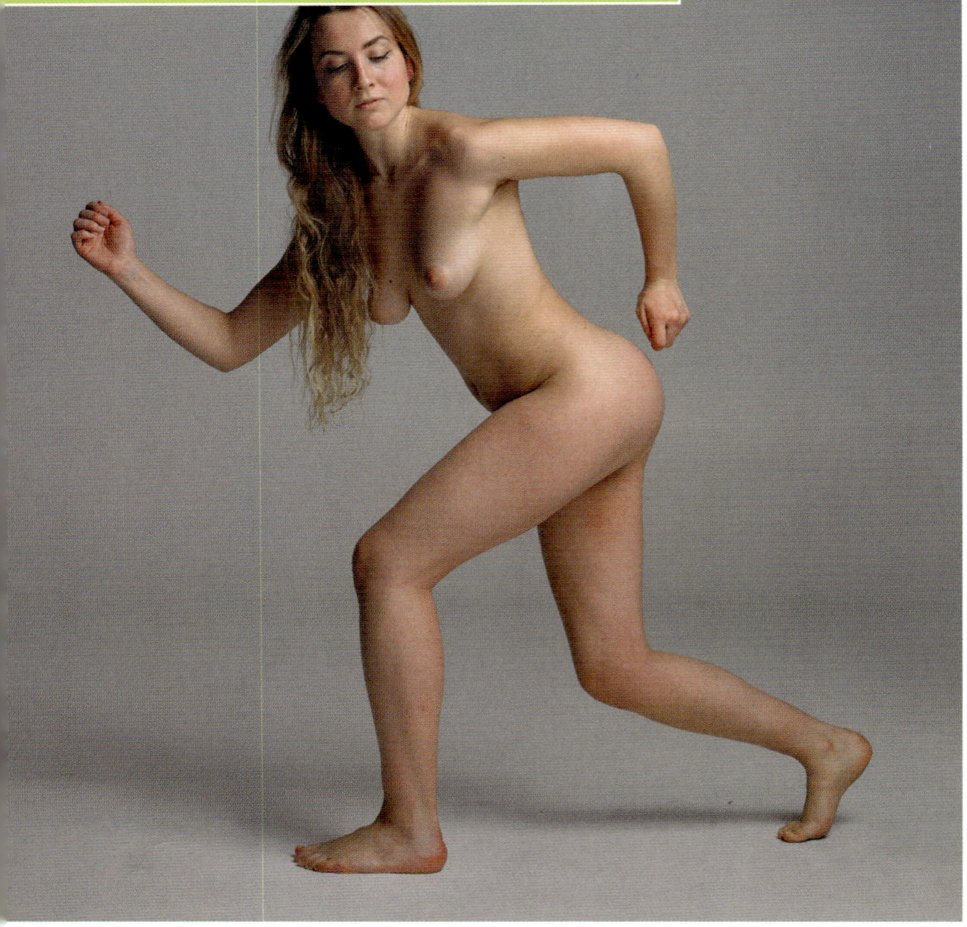

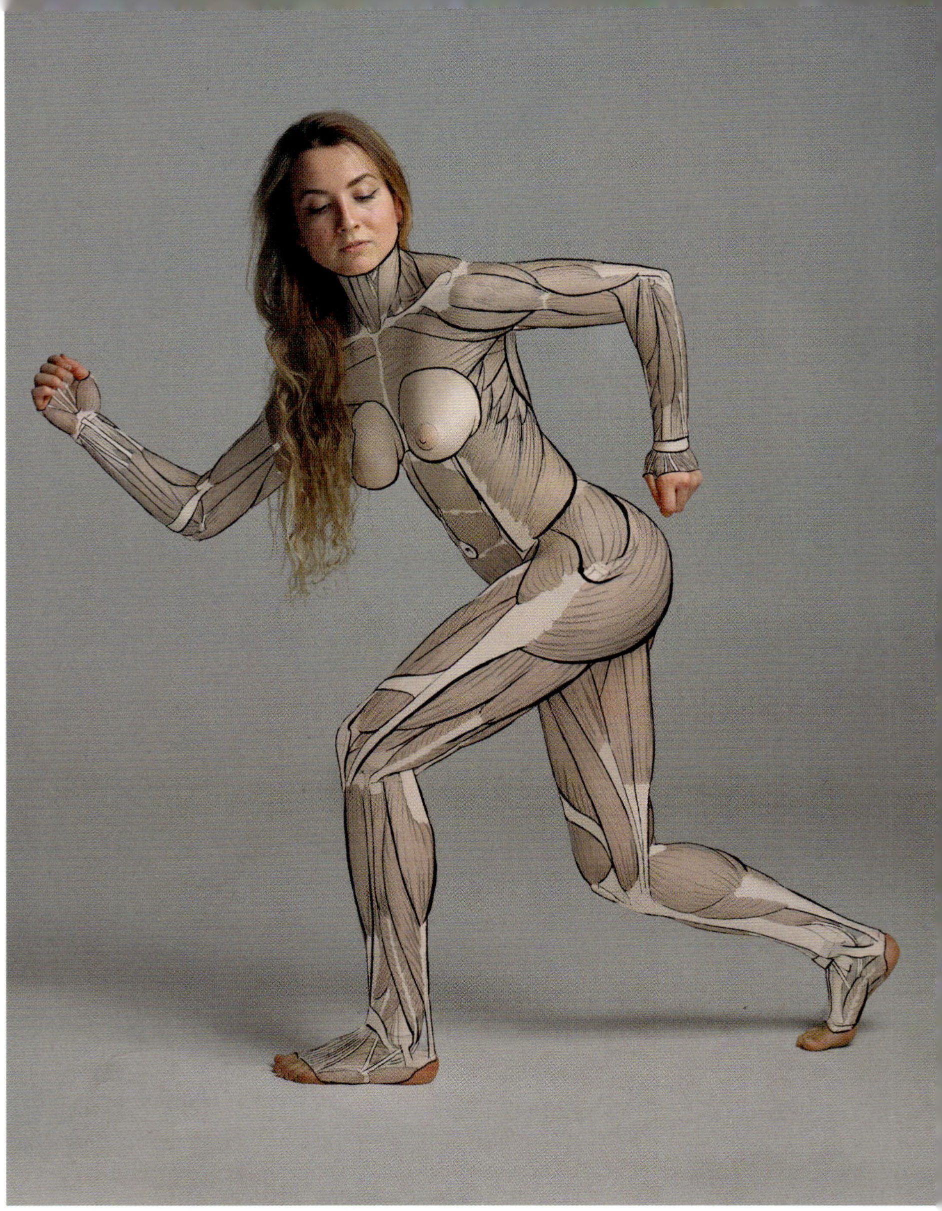

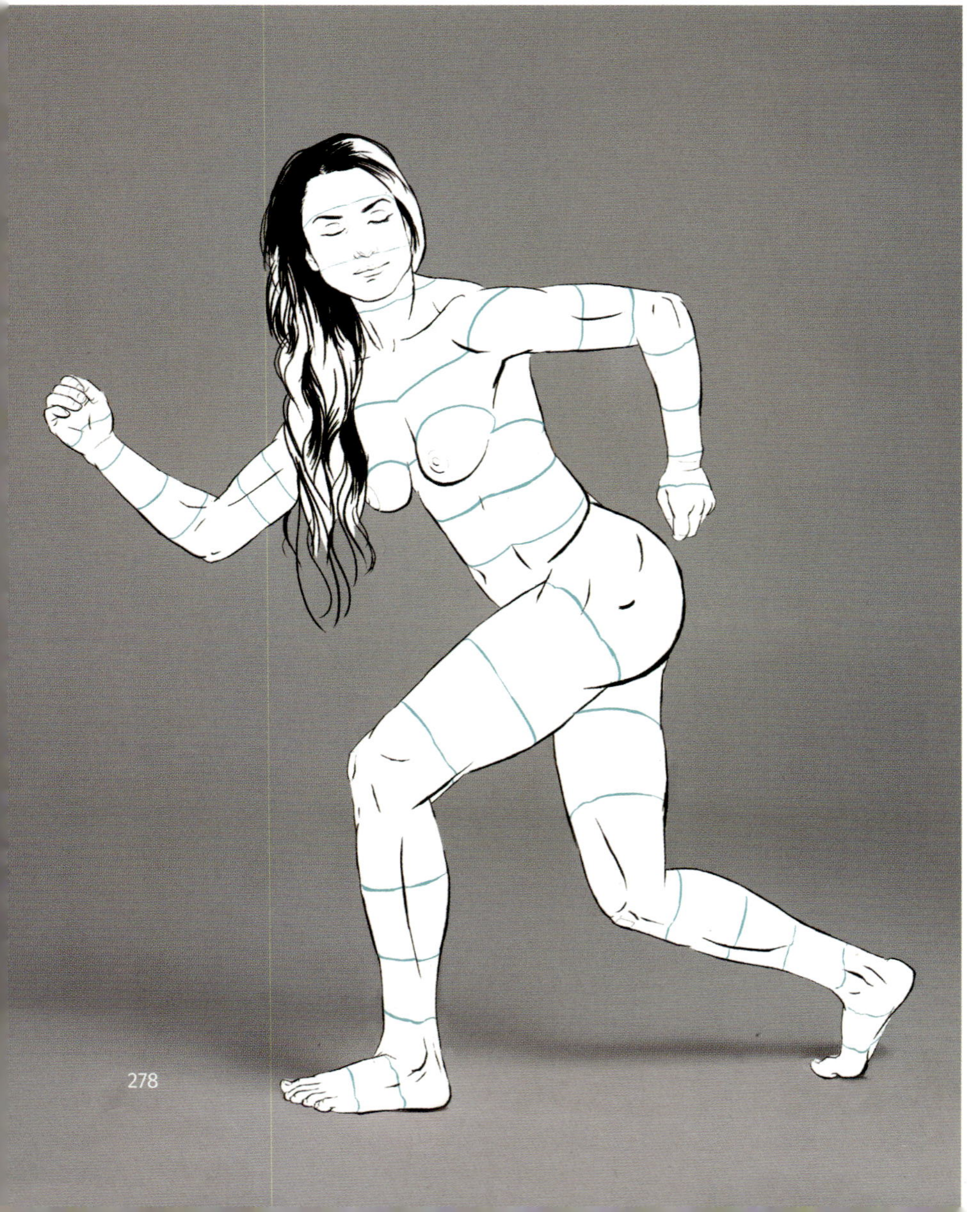

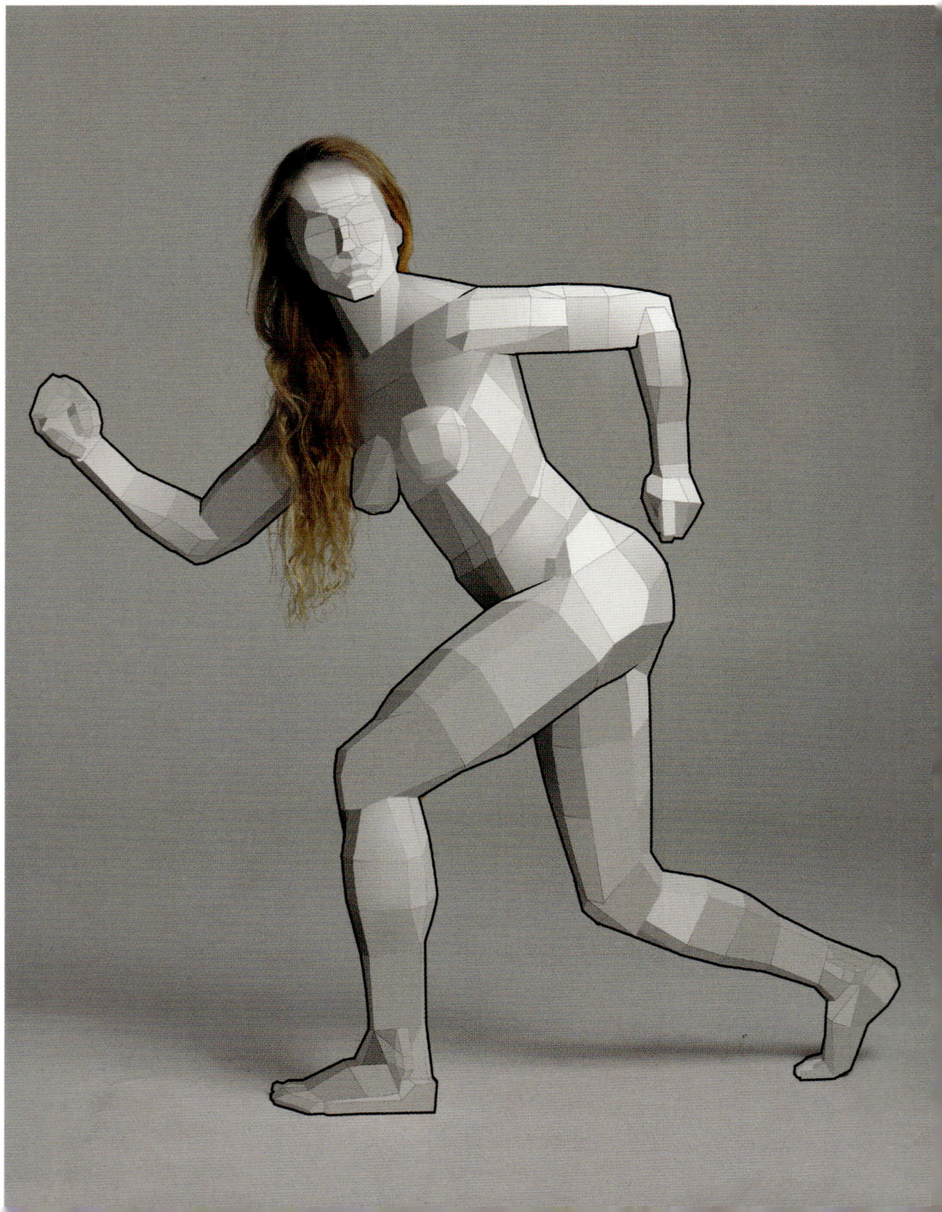

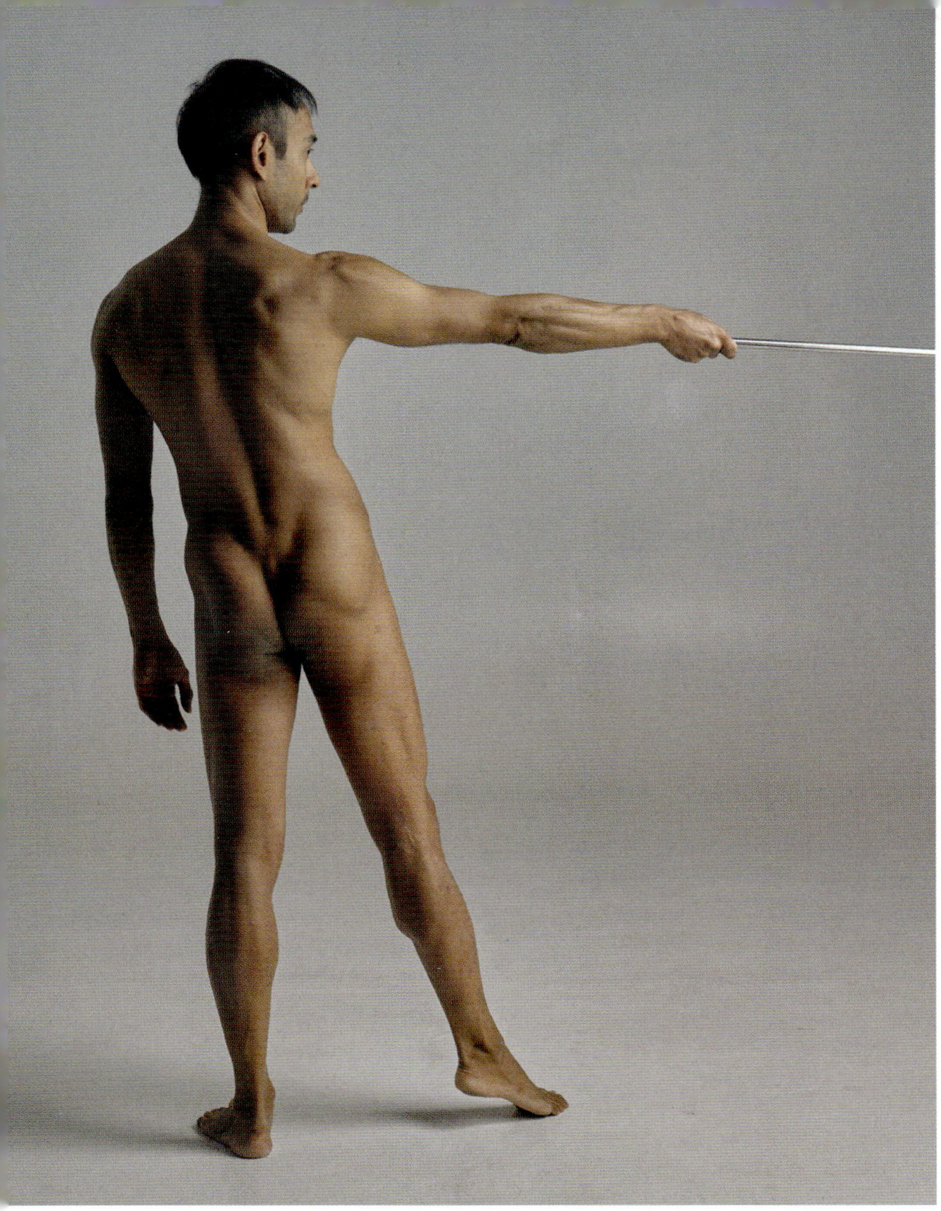

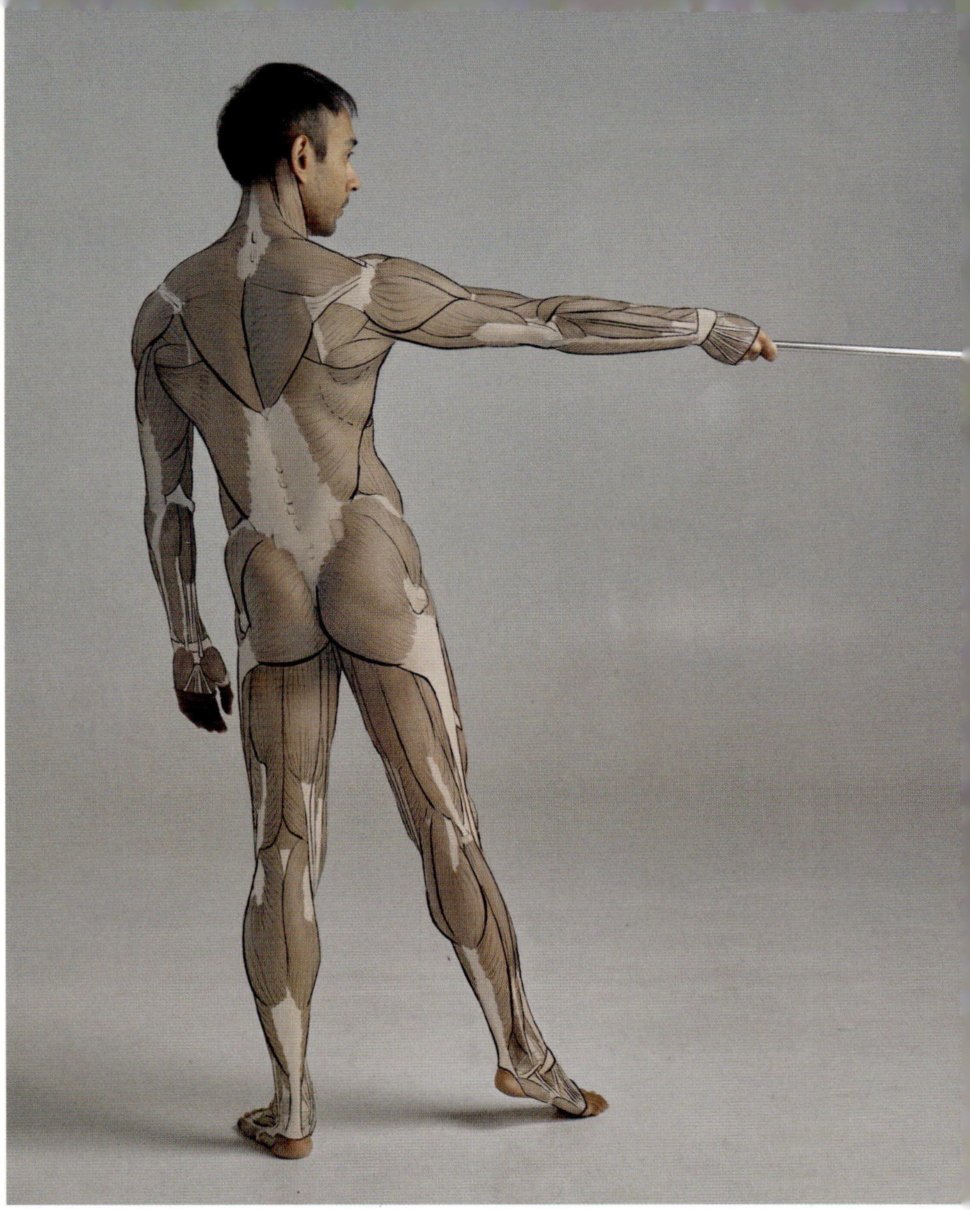

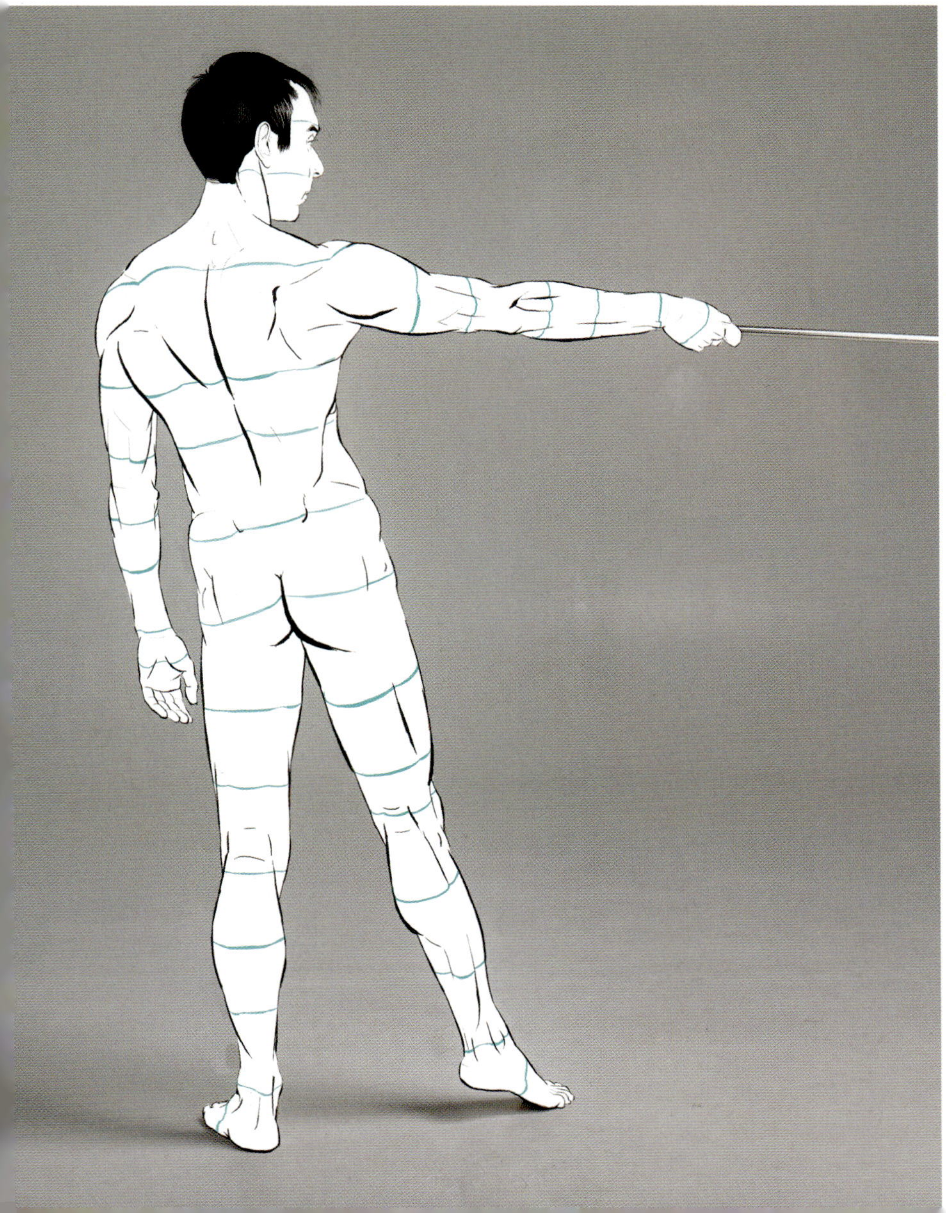

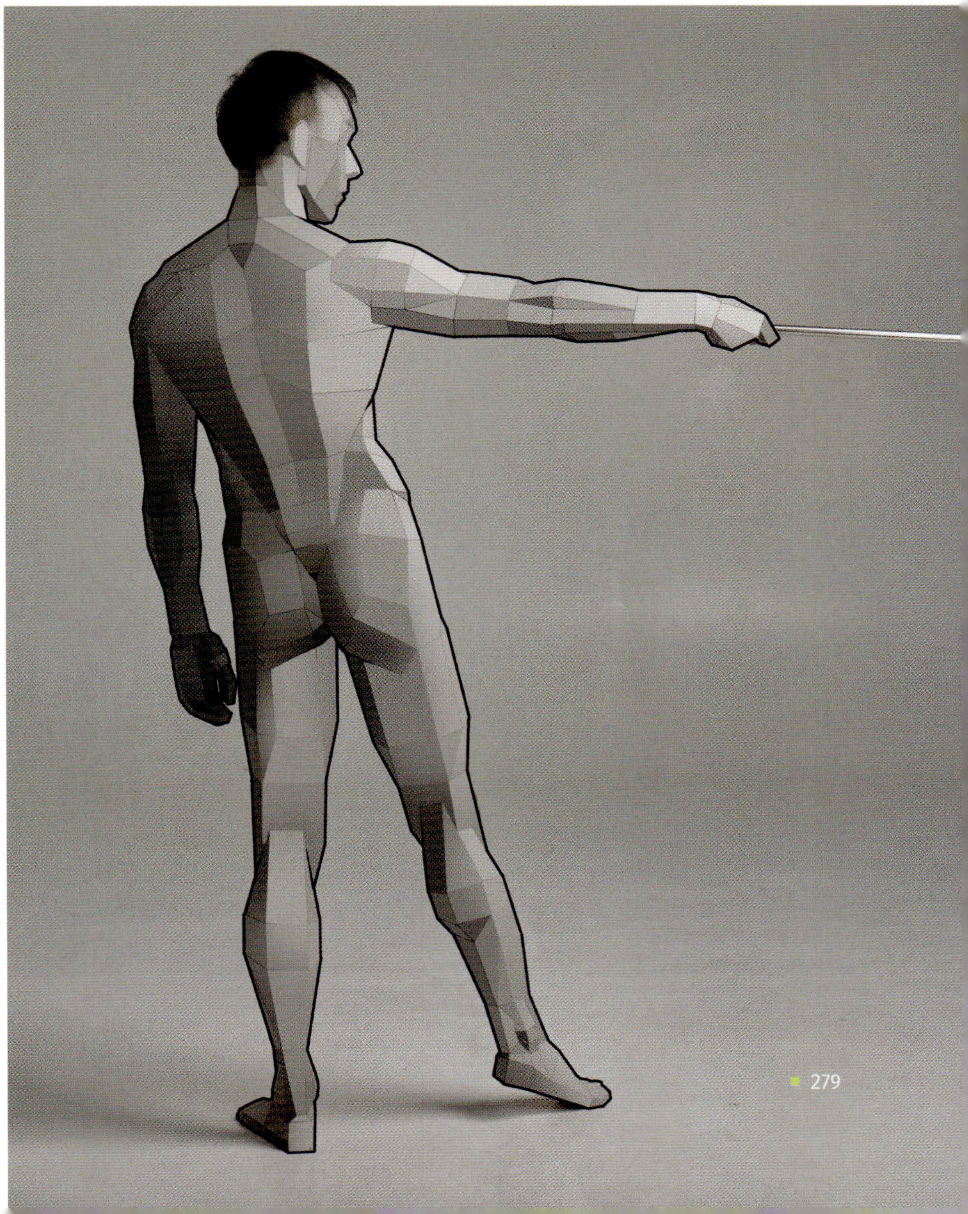

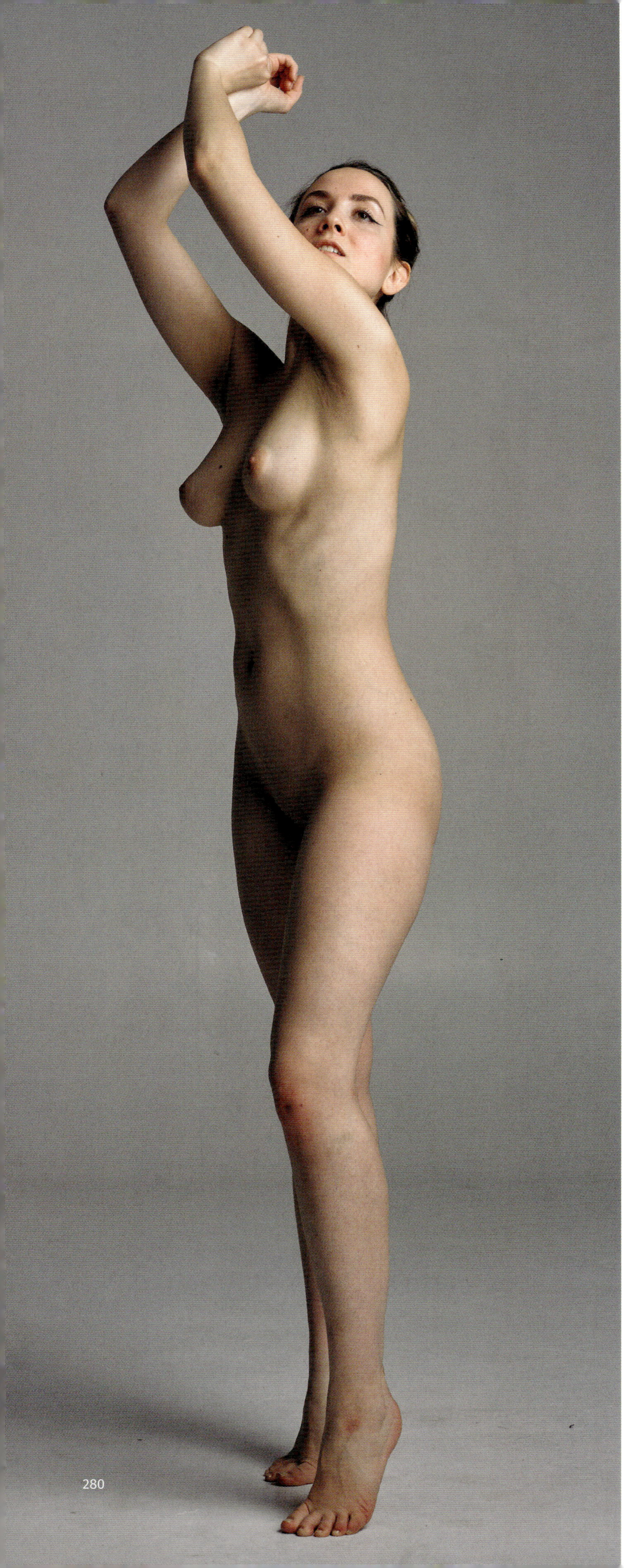

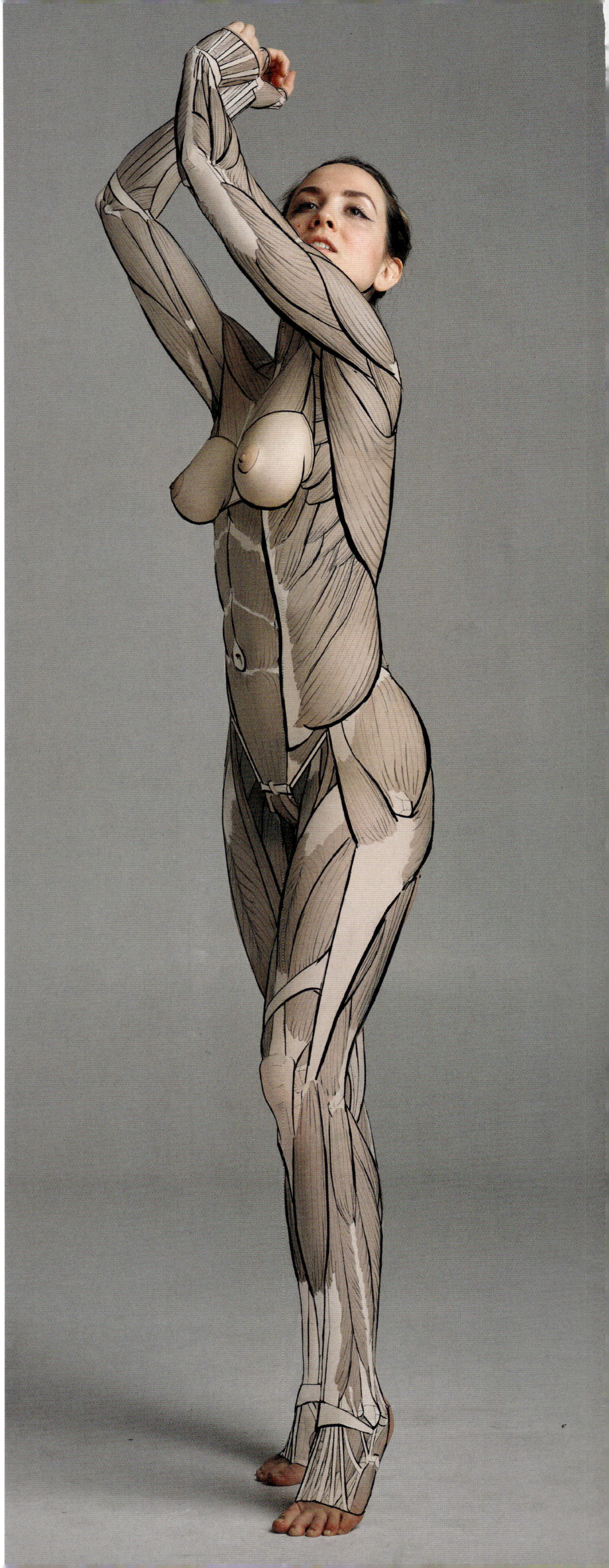

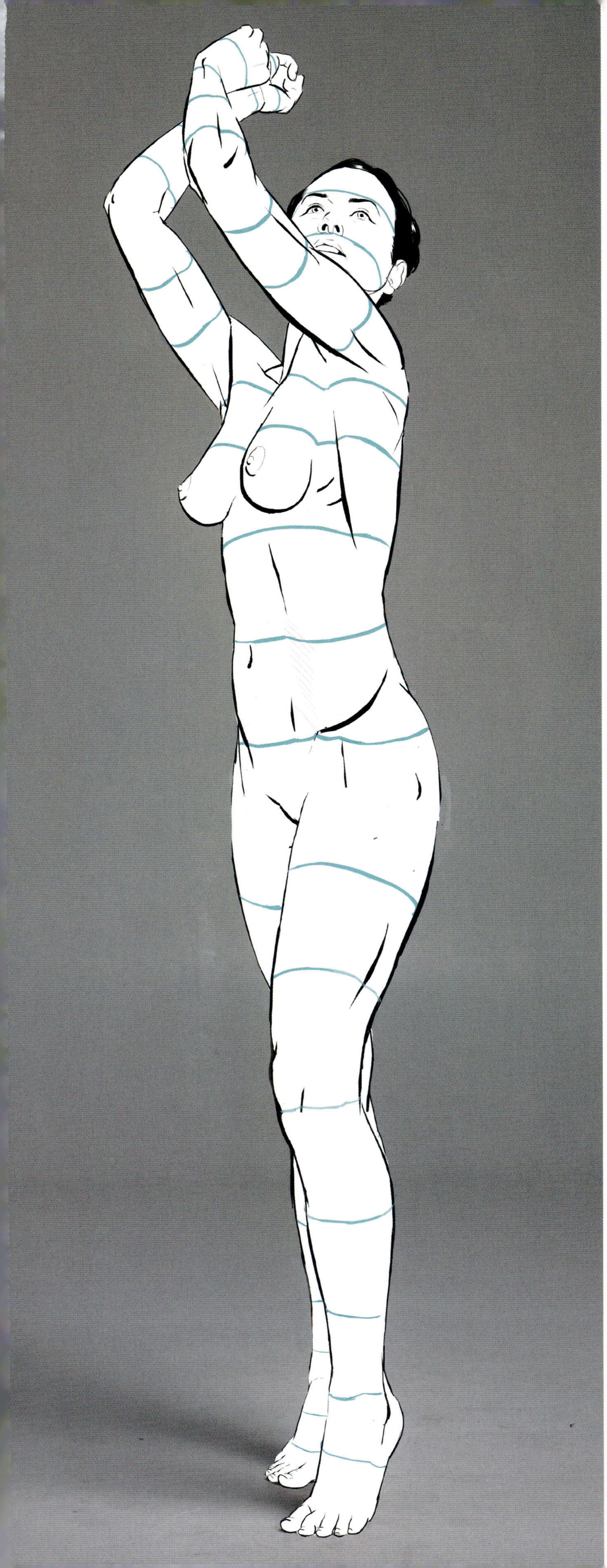

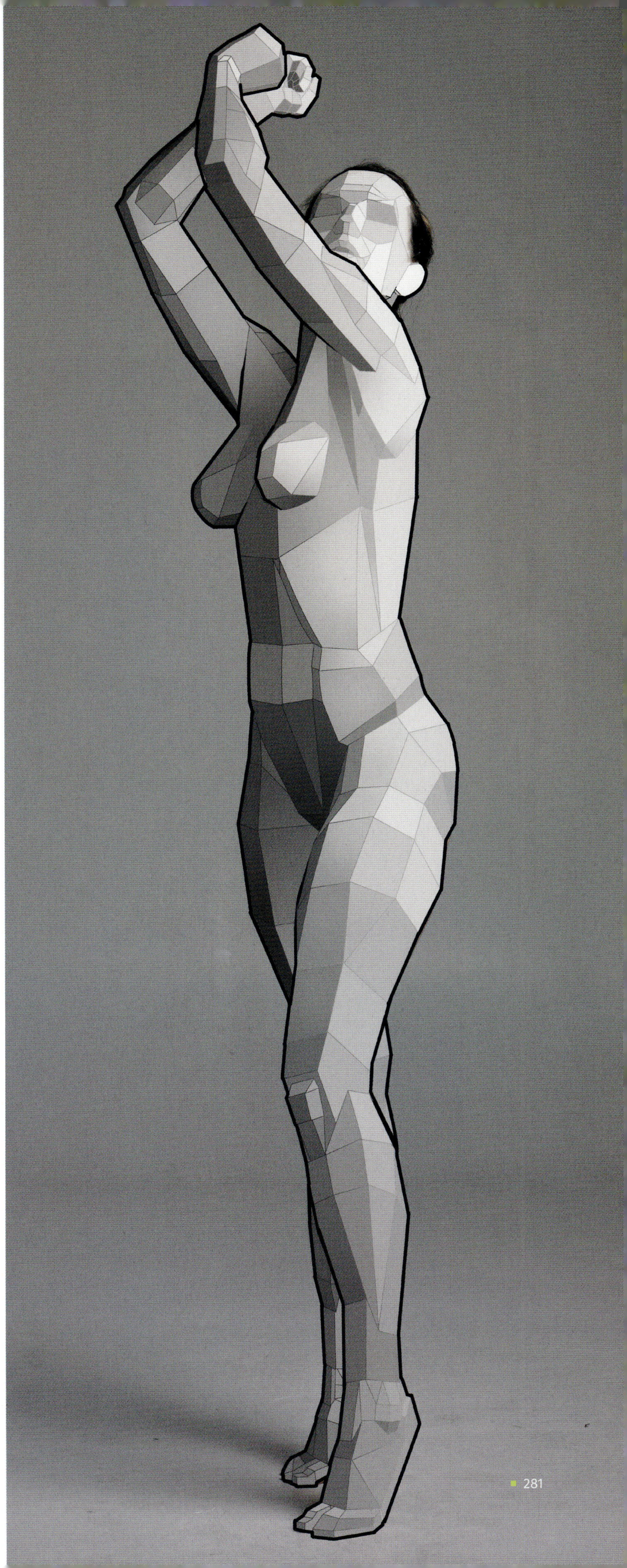

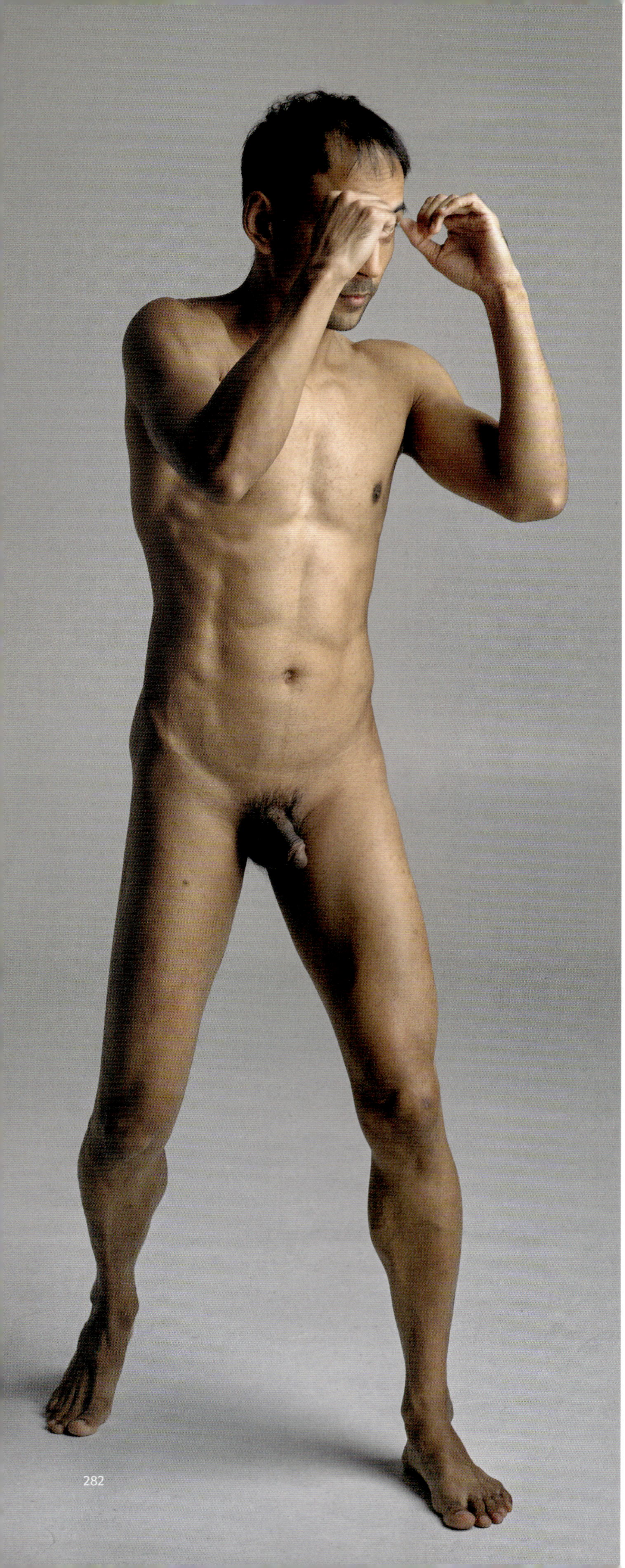

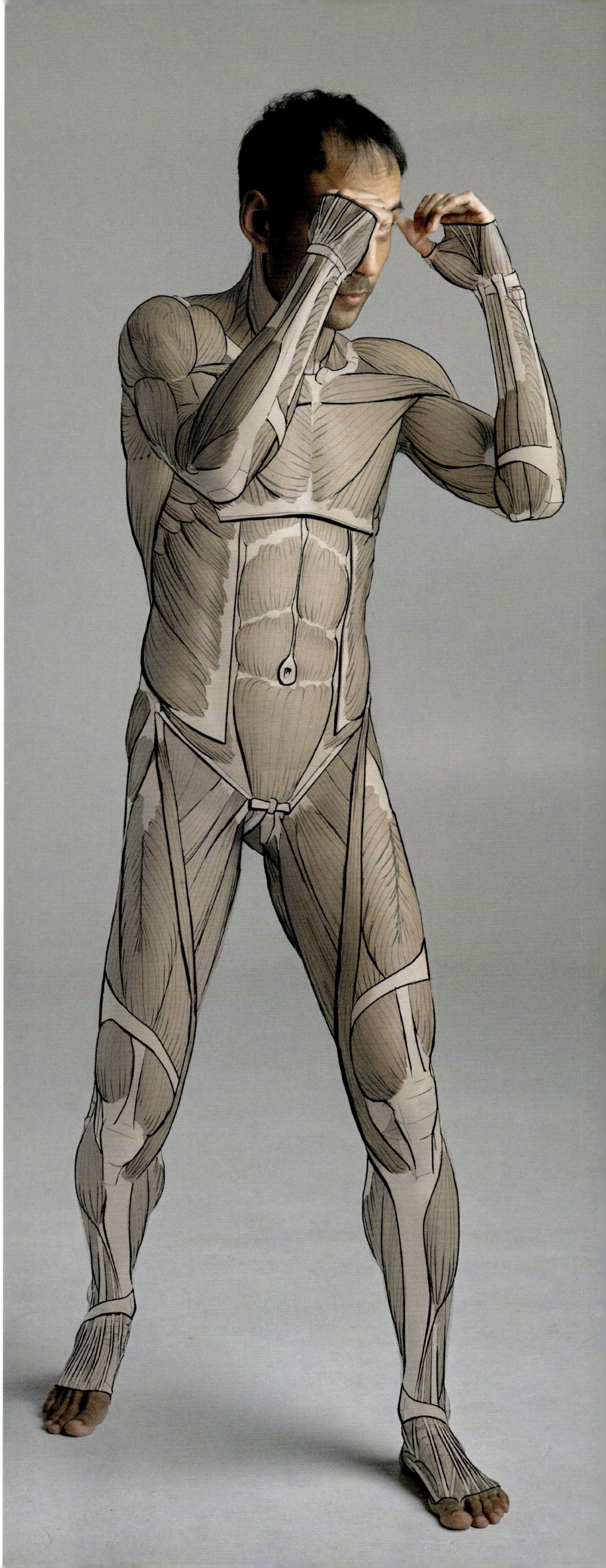

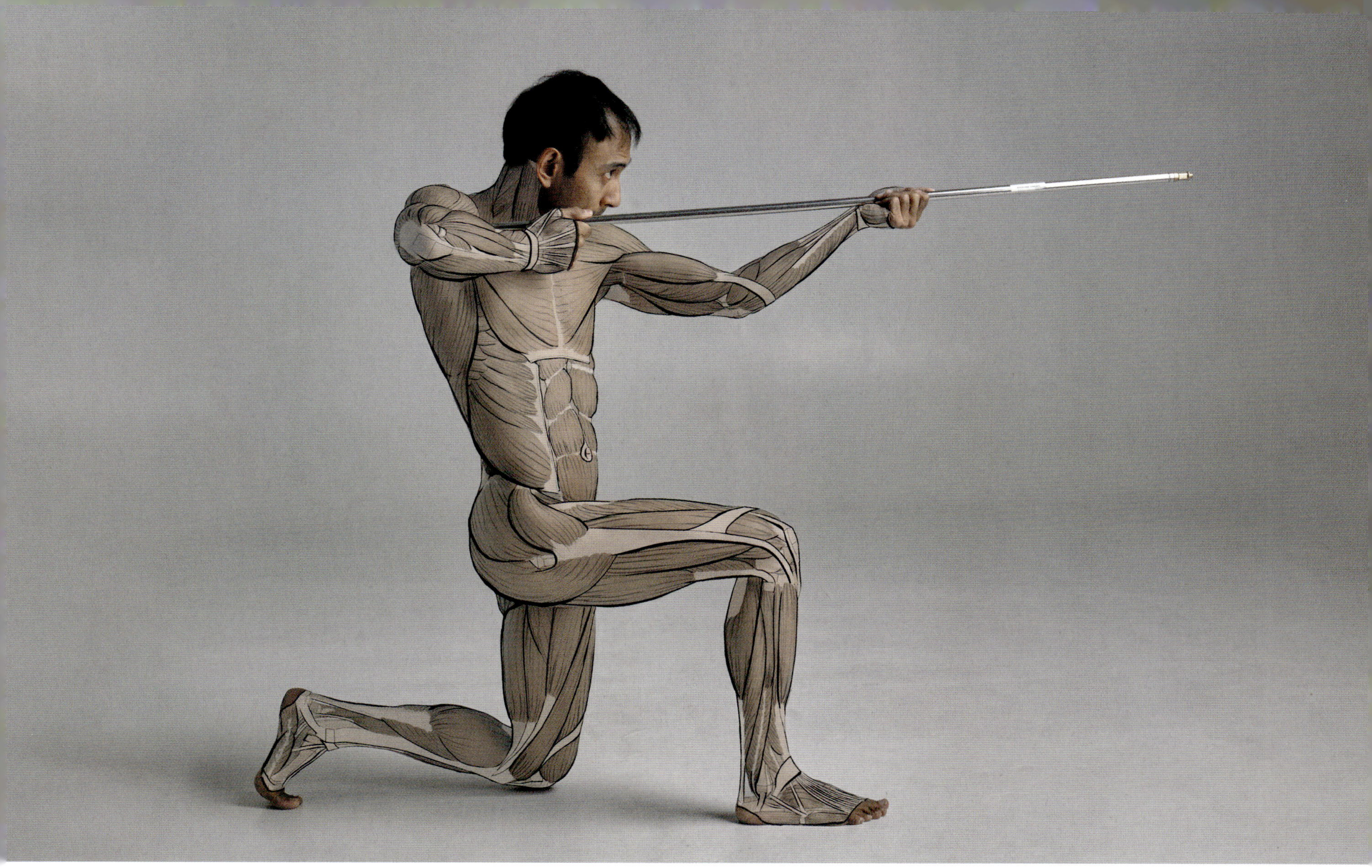

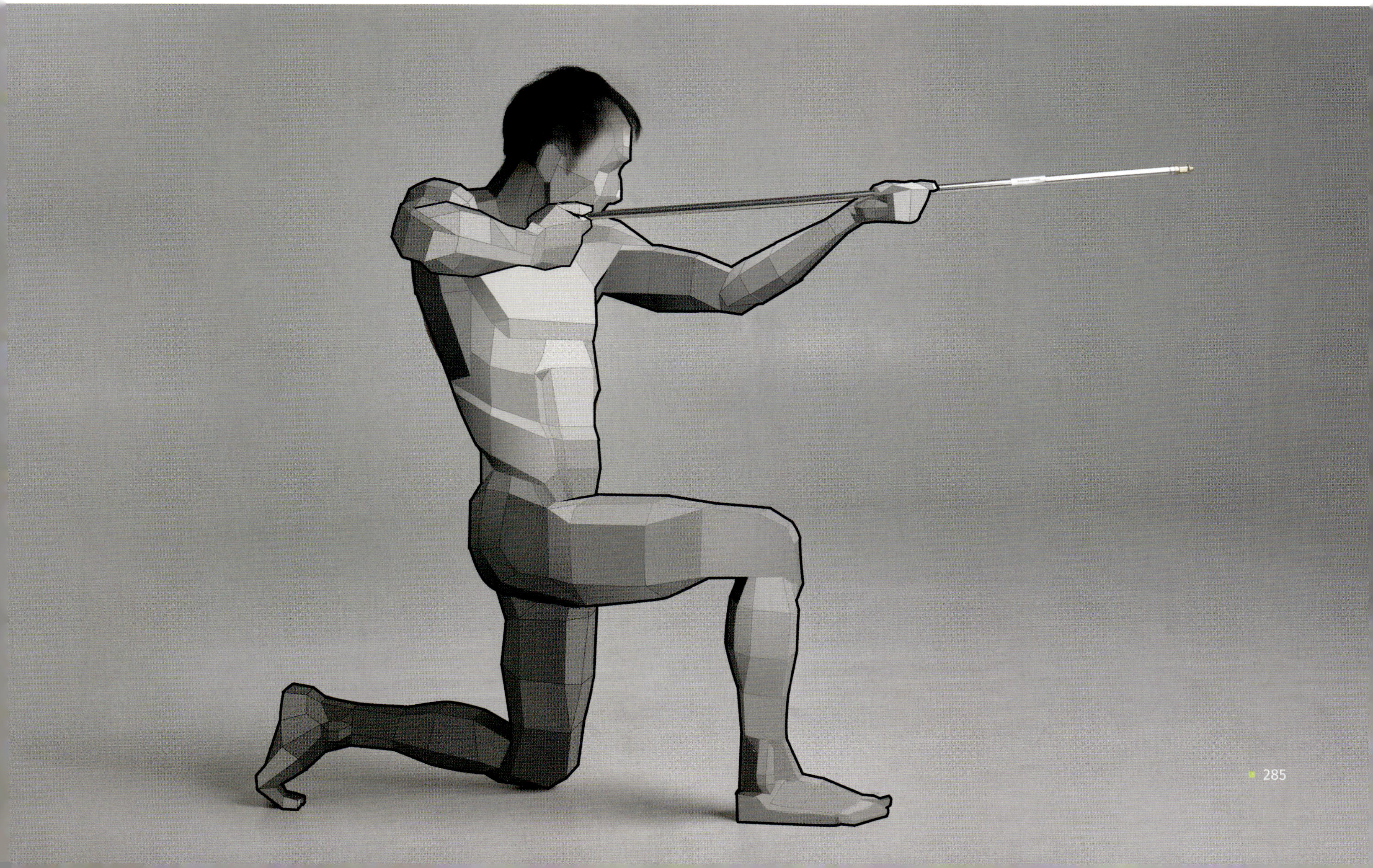

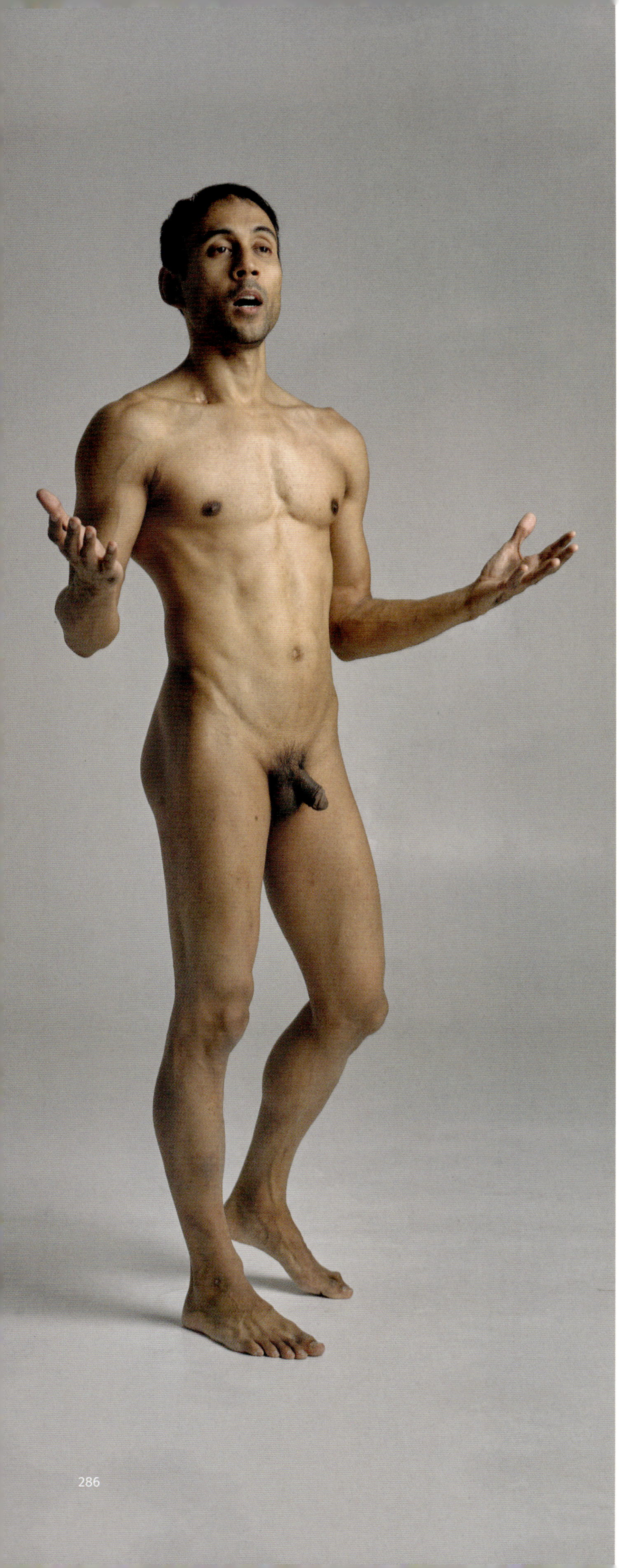

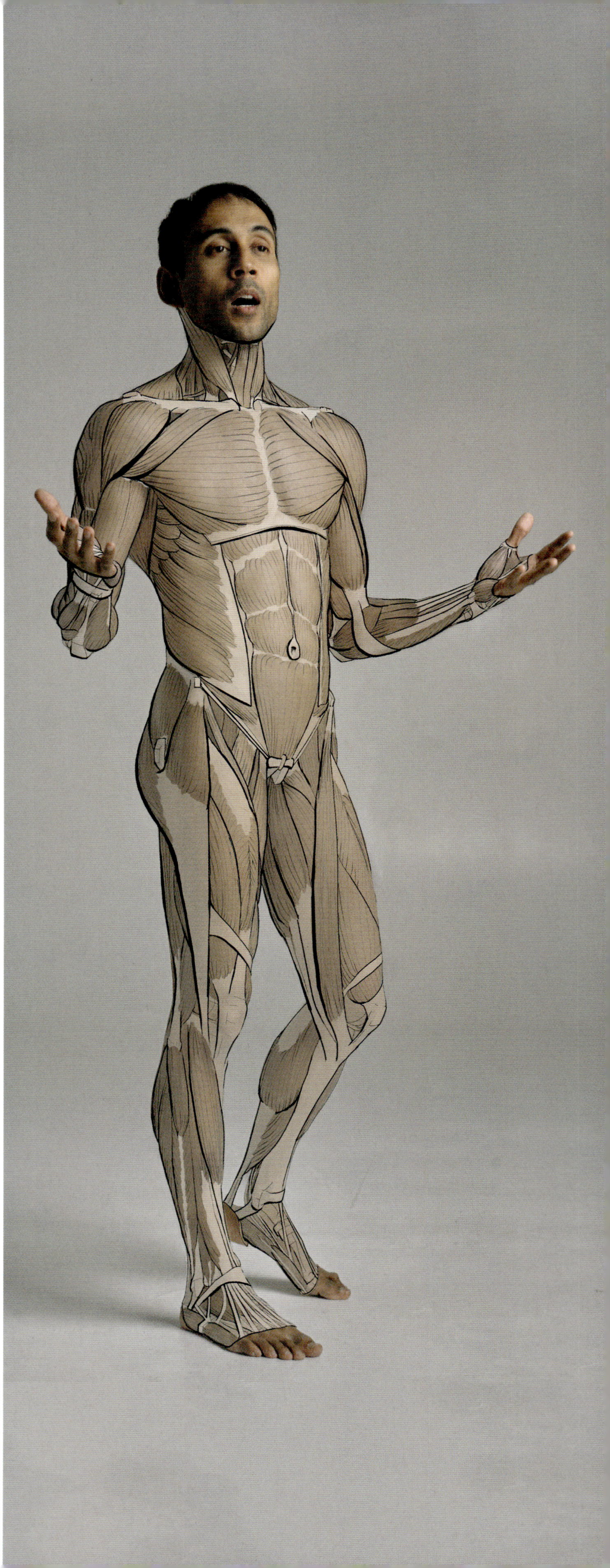

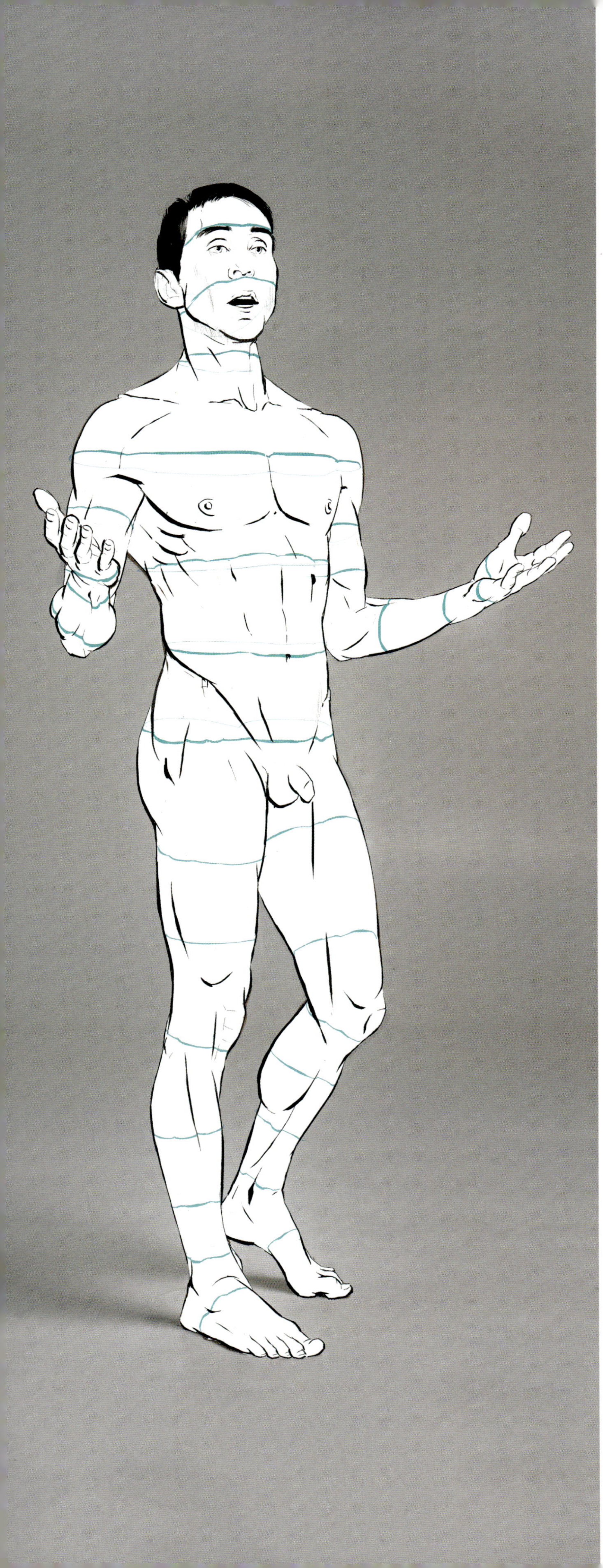

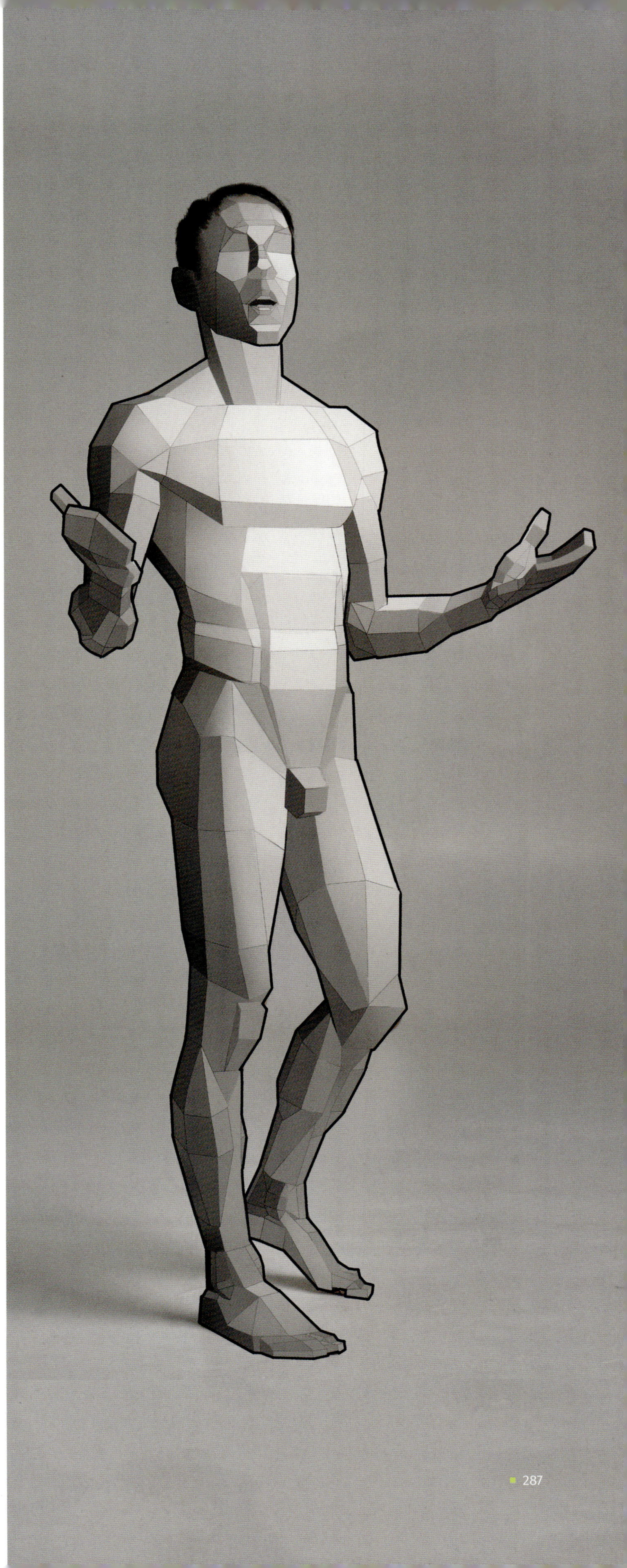

SEATED POSES

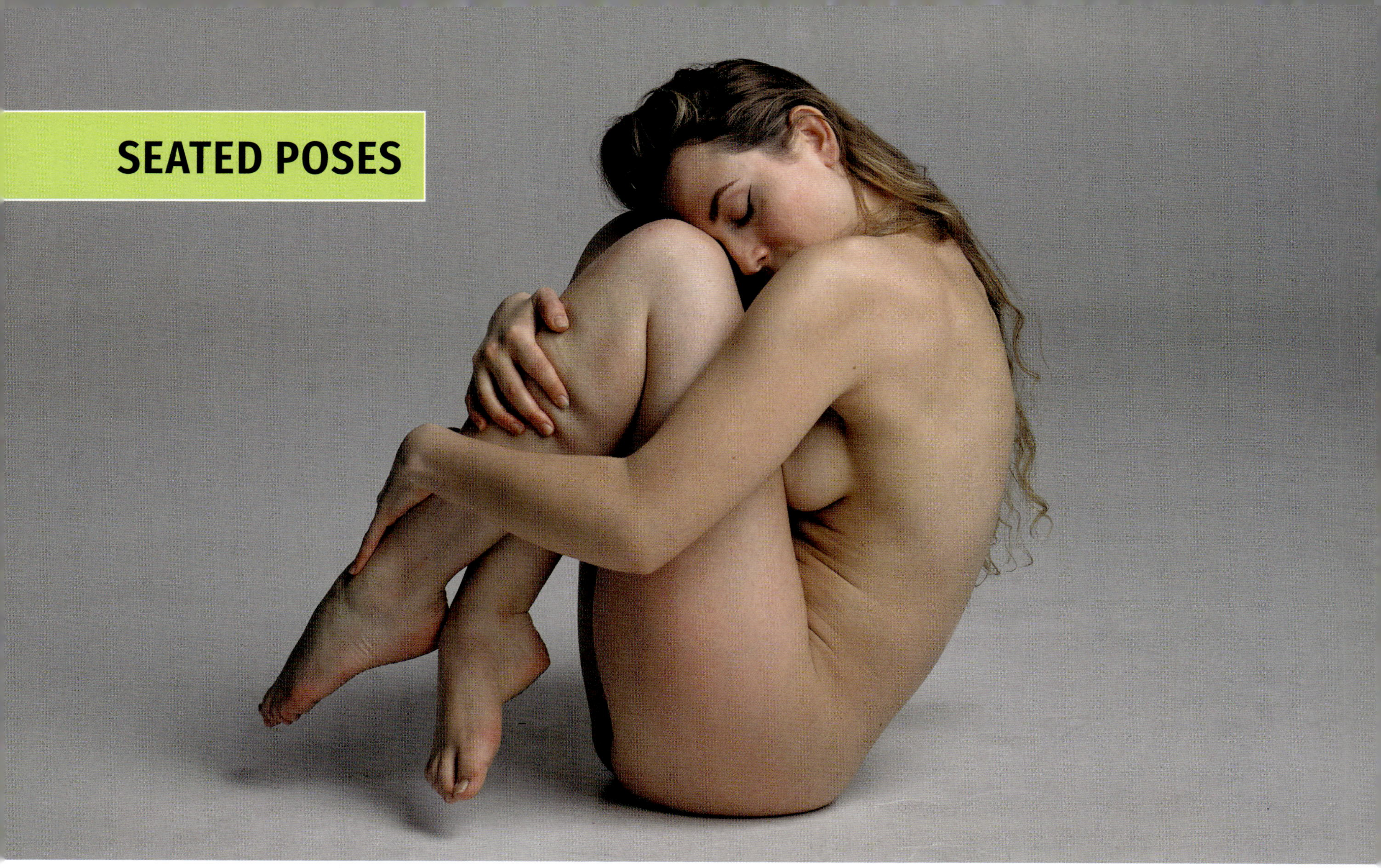

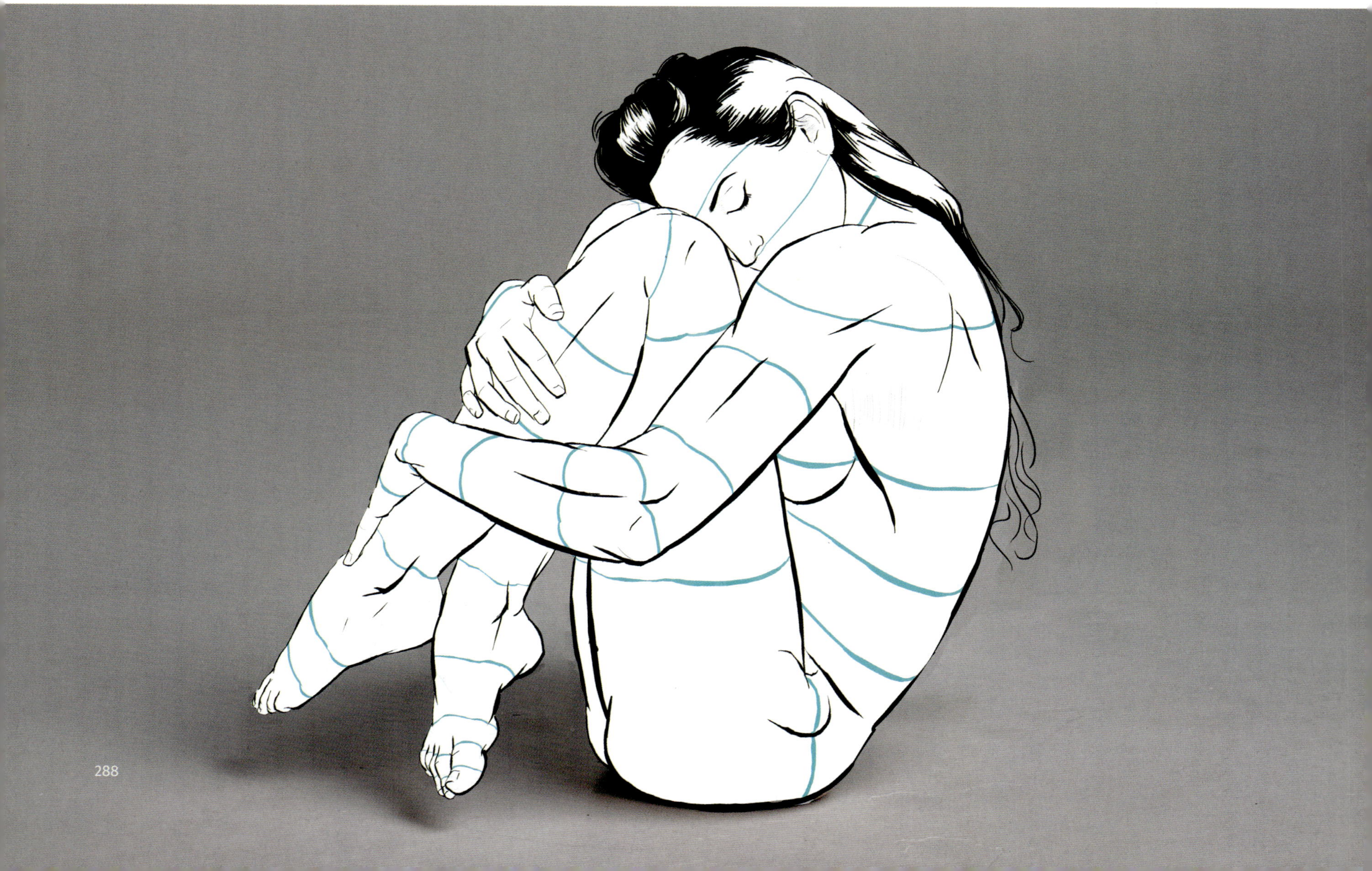

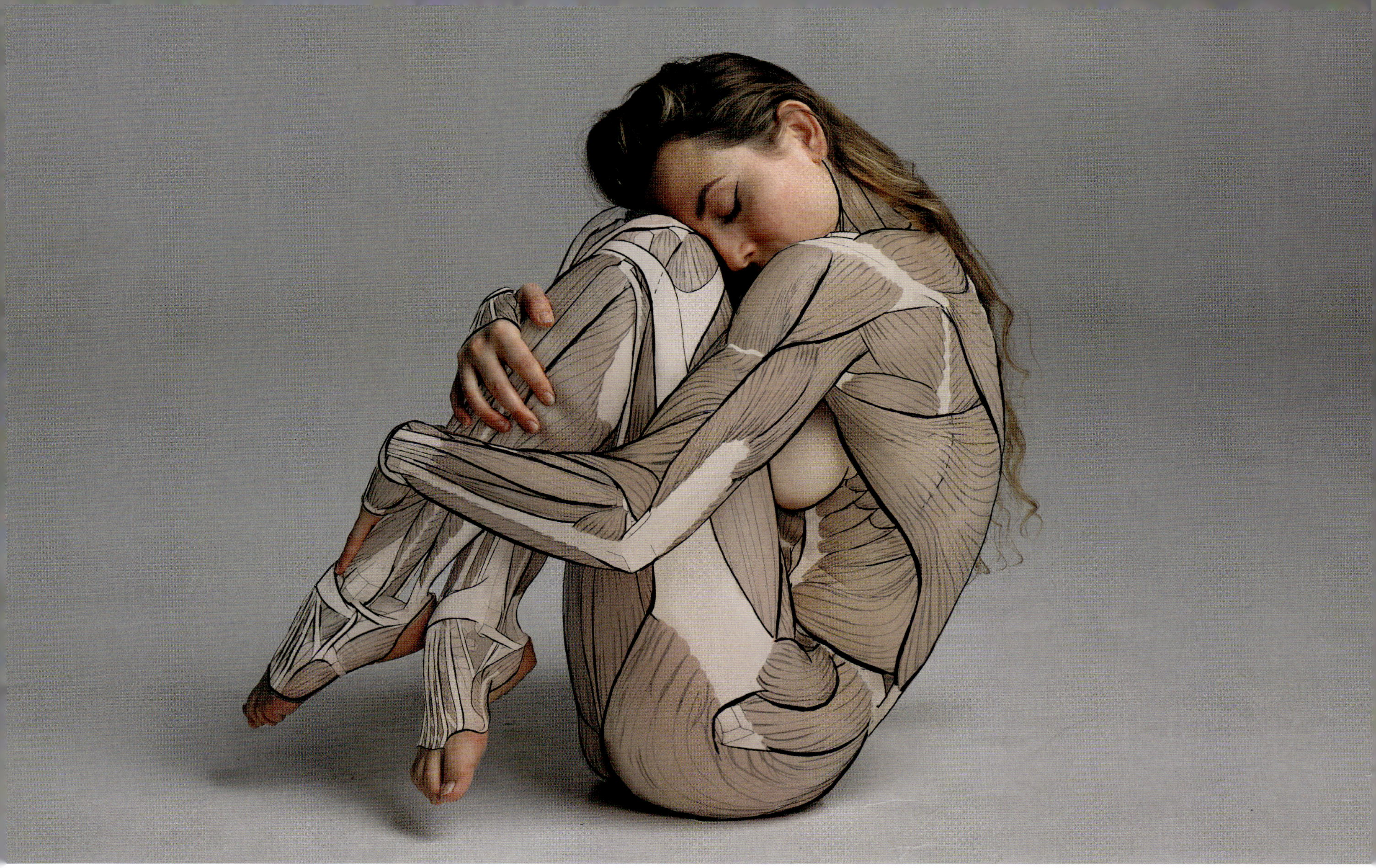

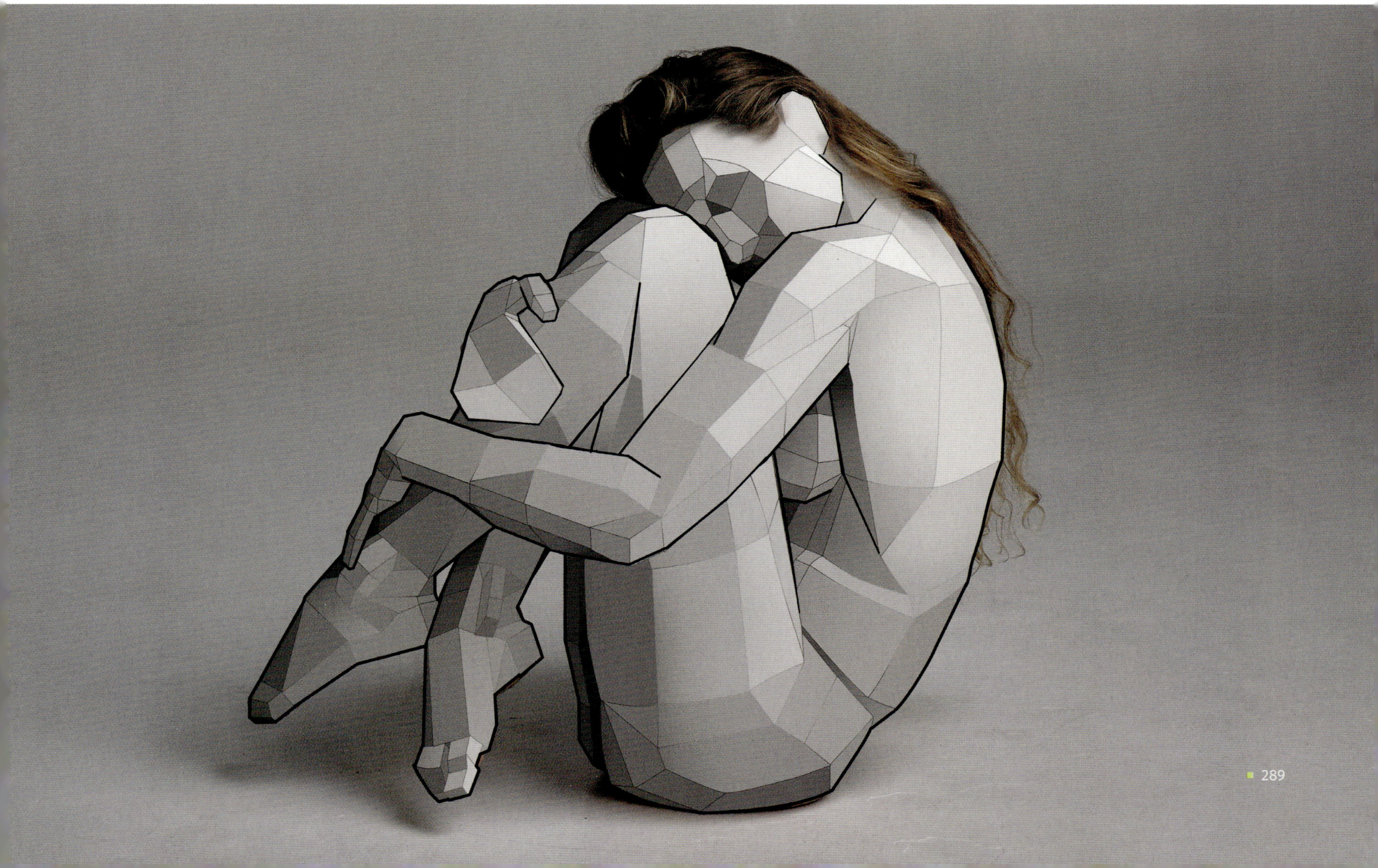

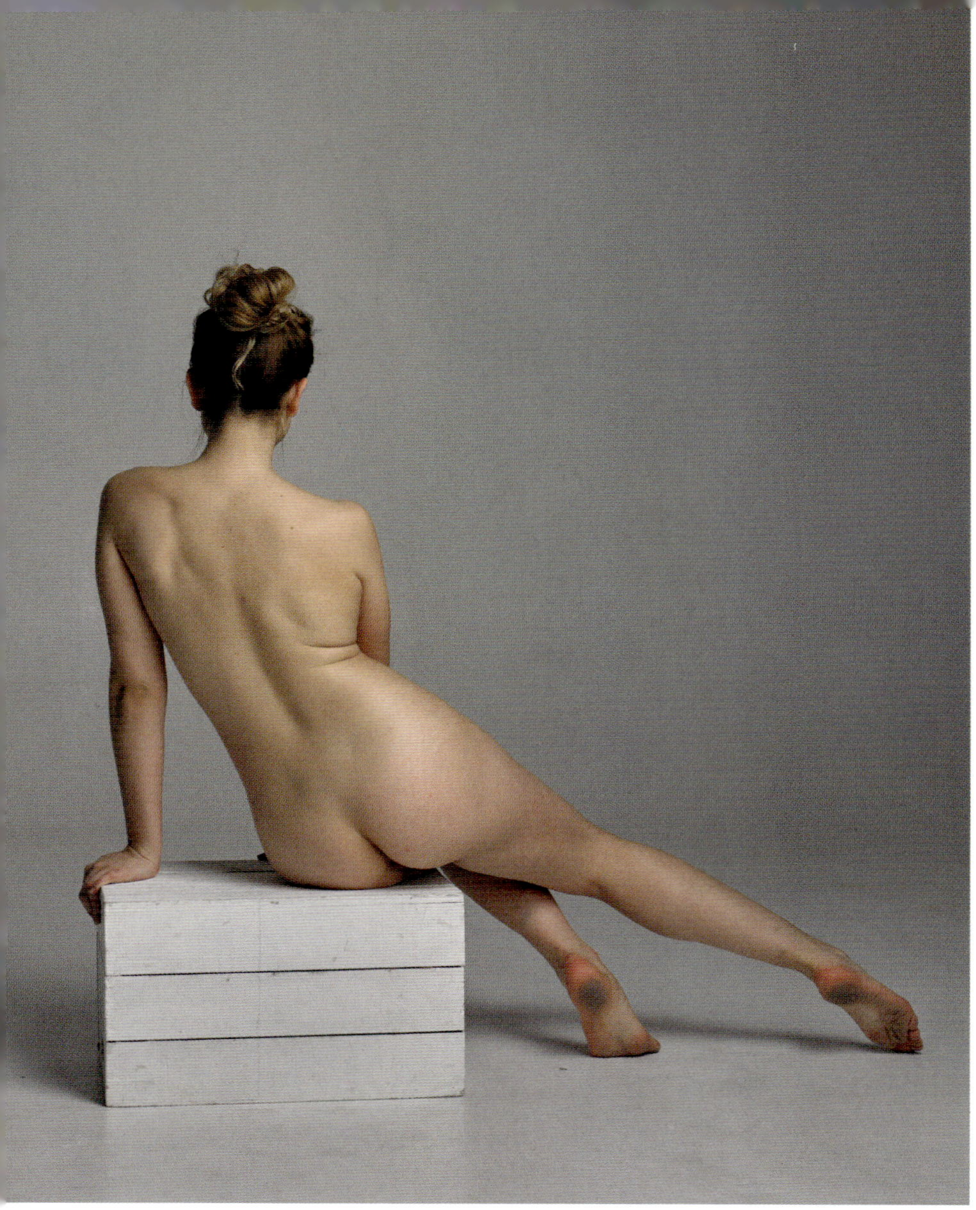
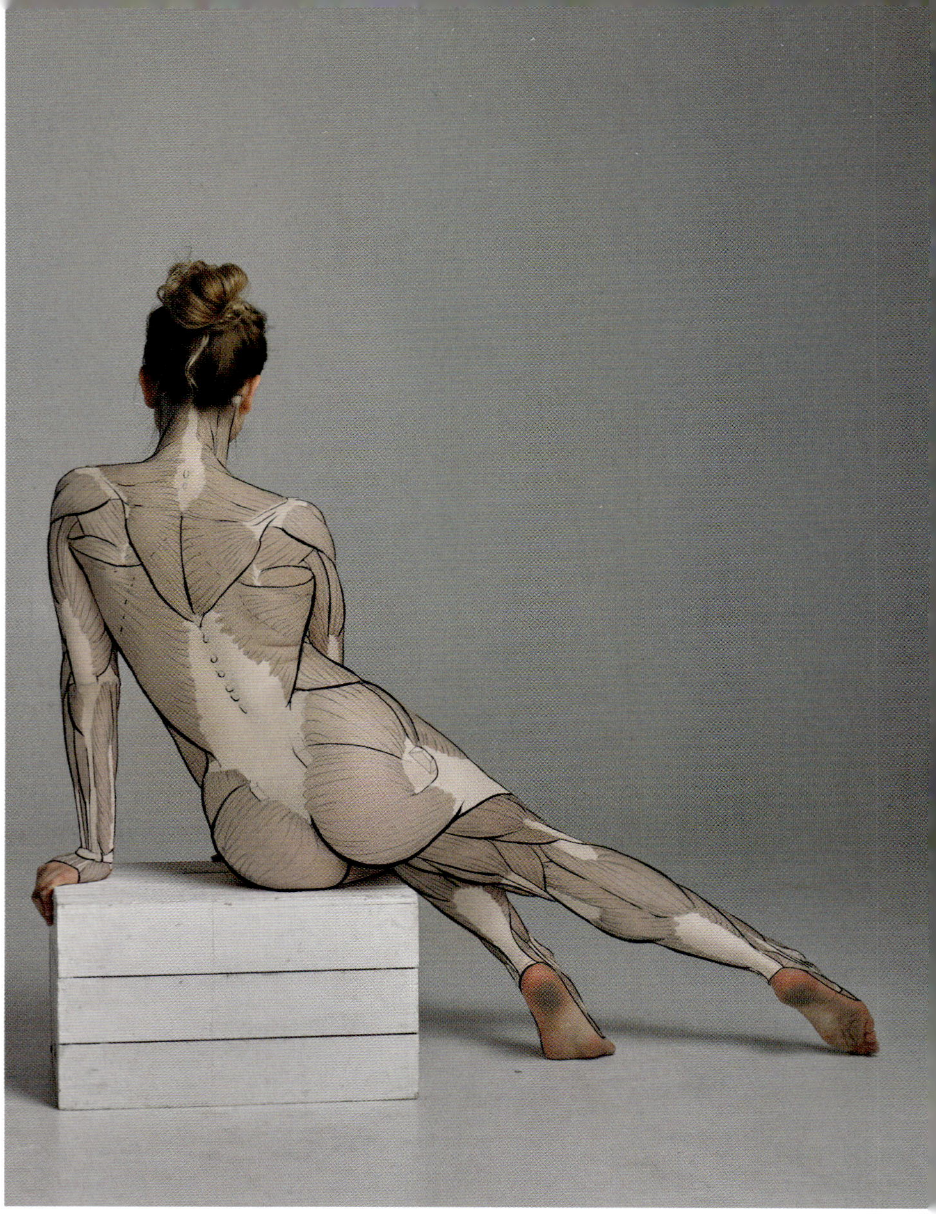
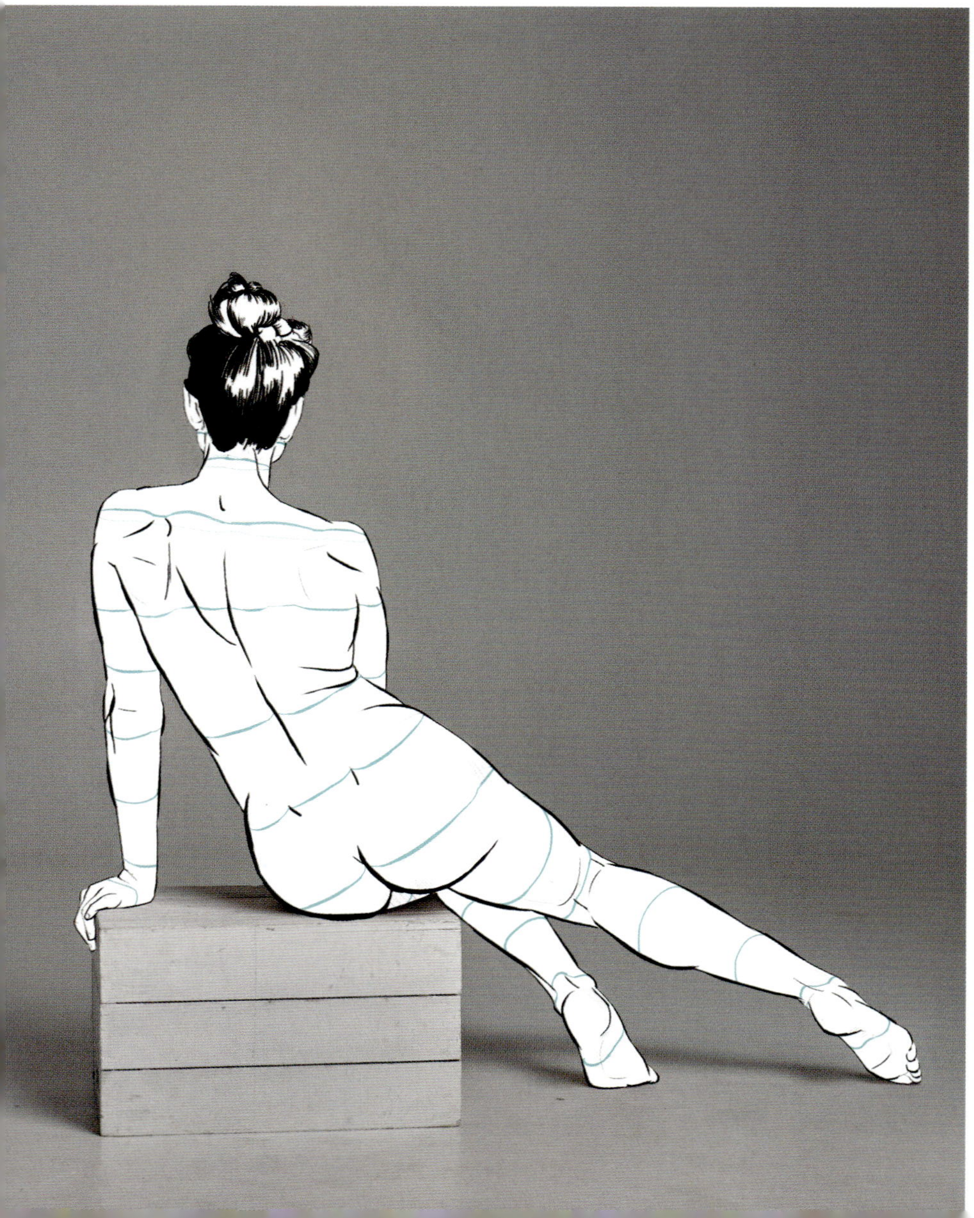
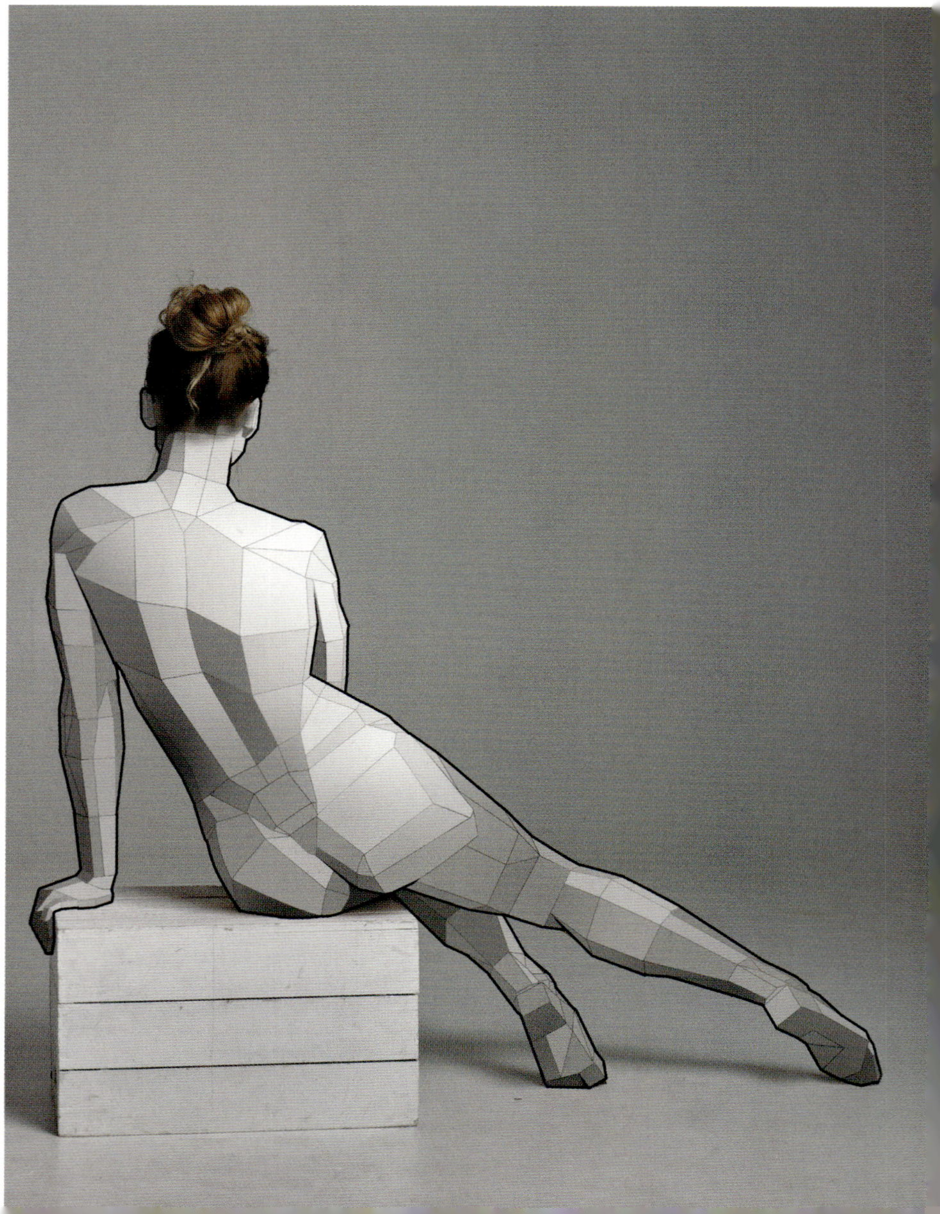

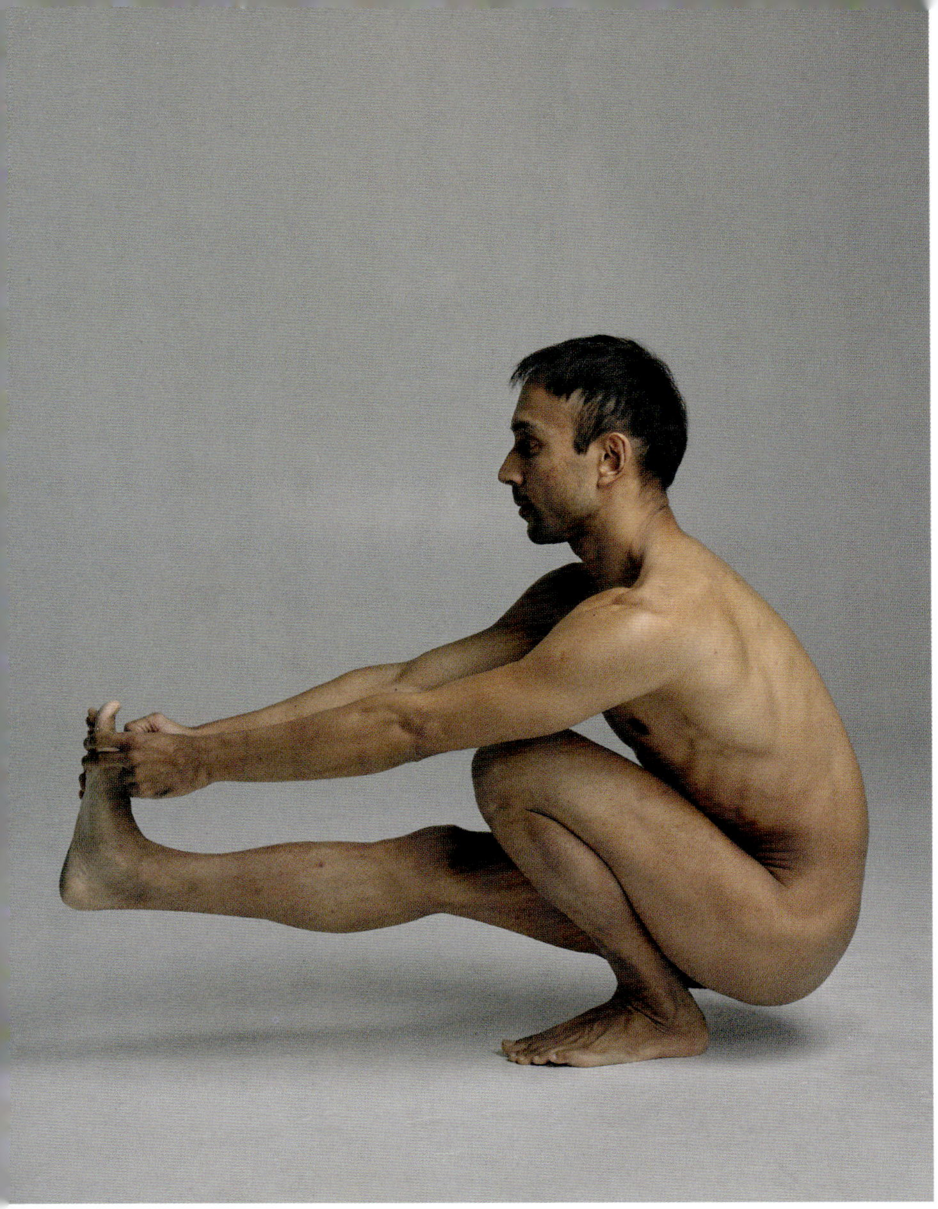
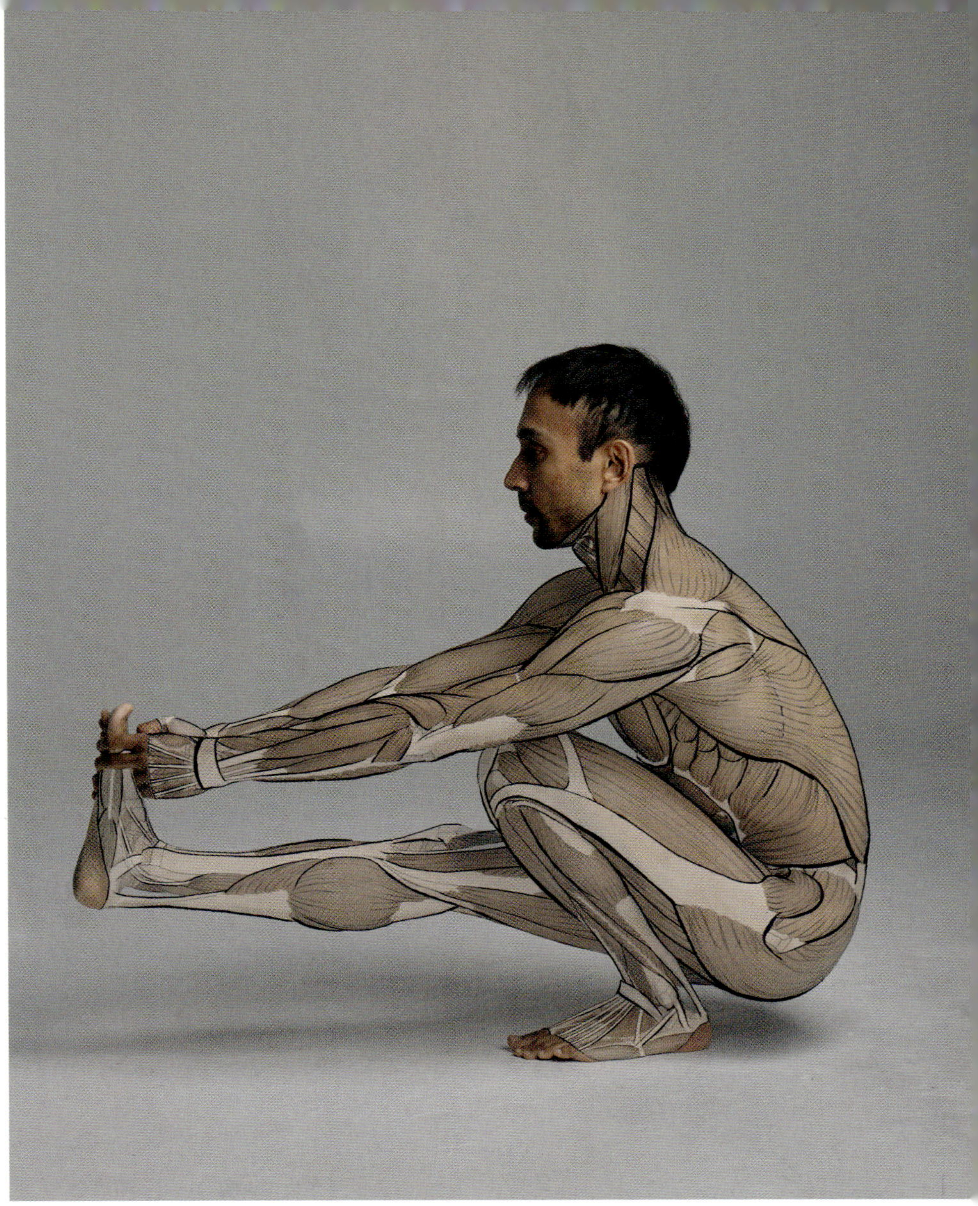
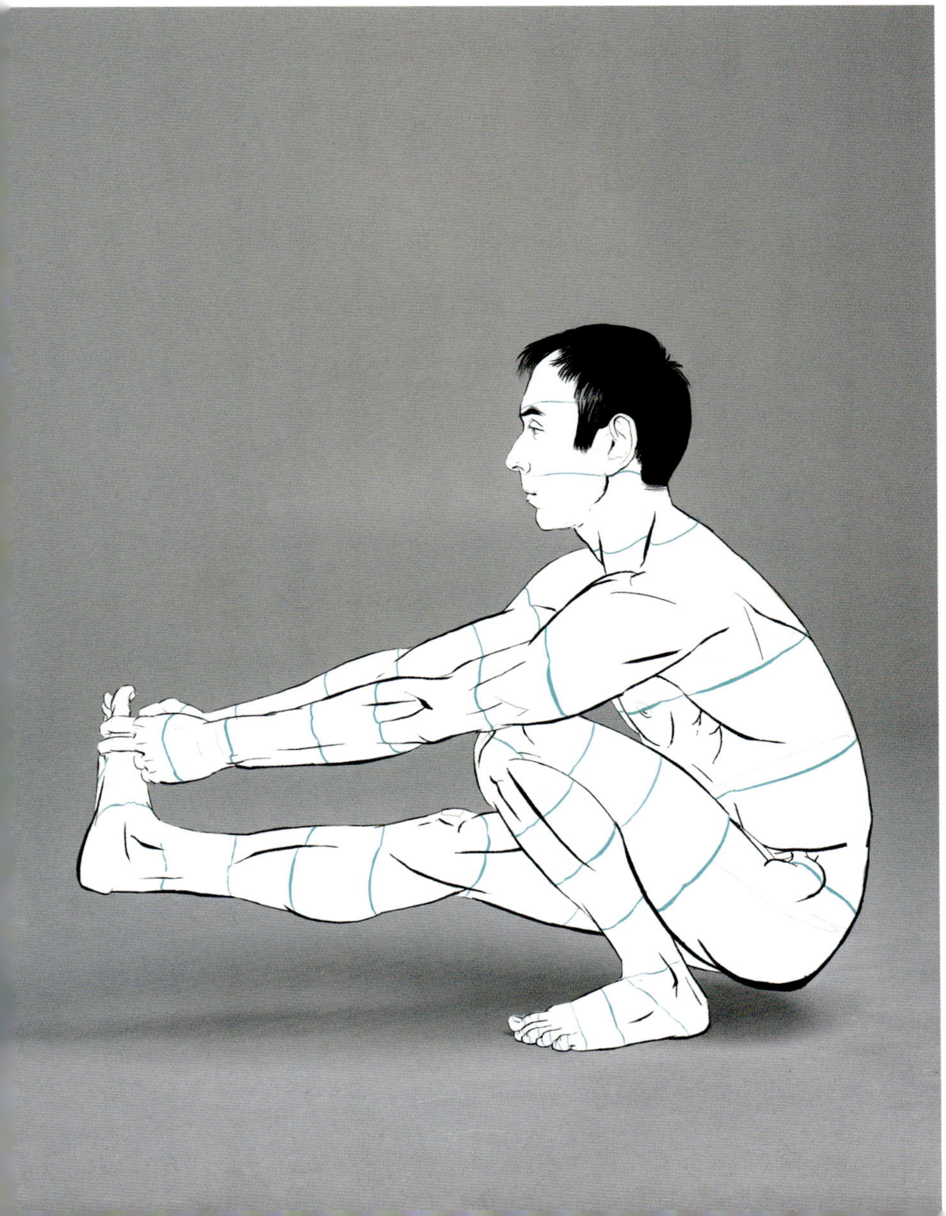
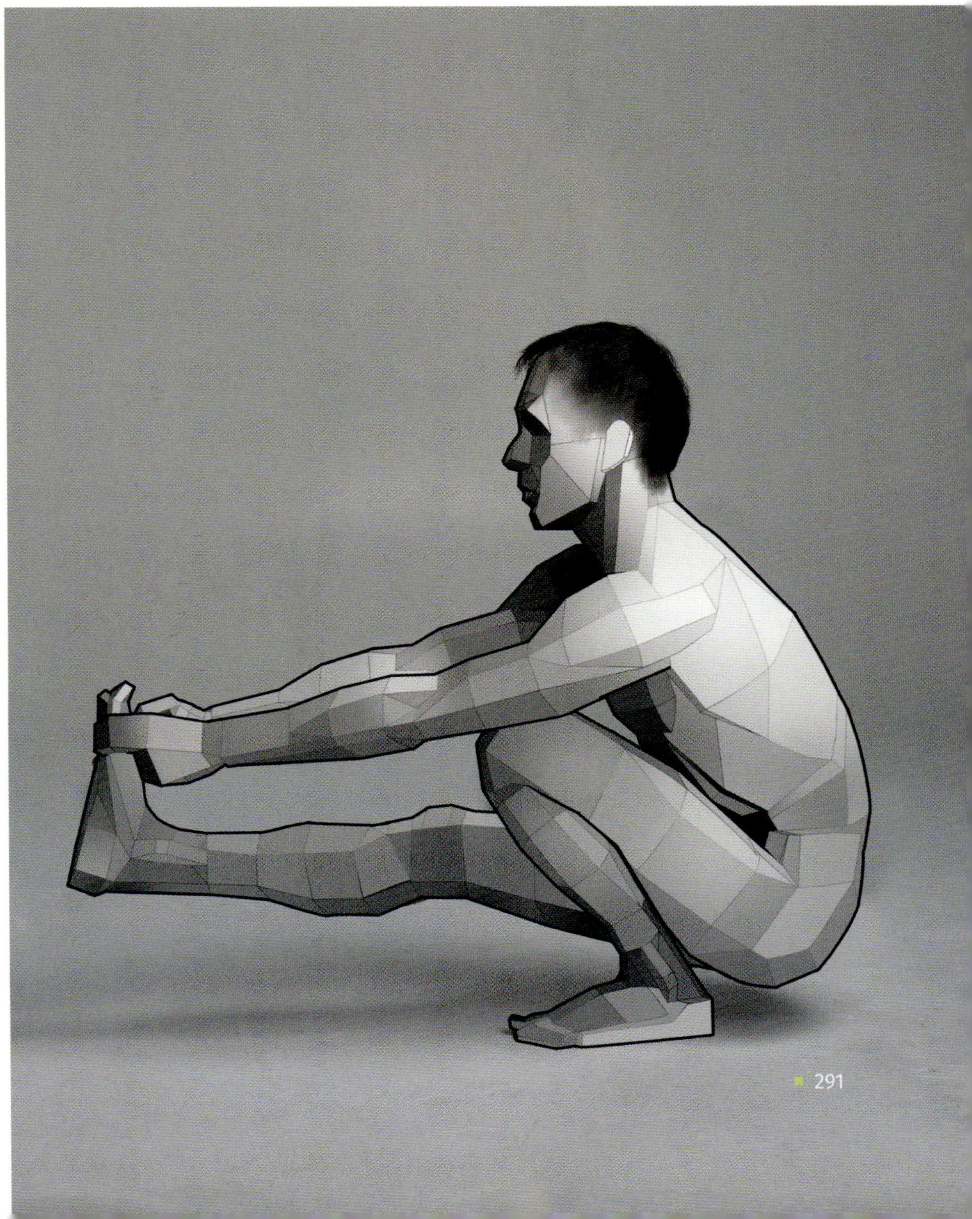

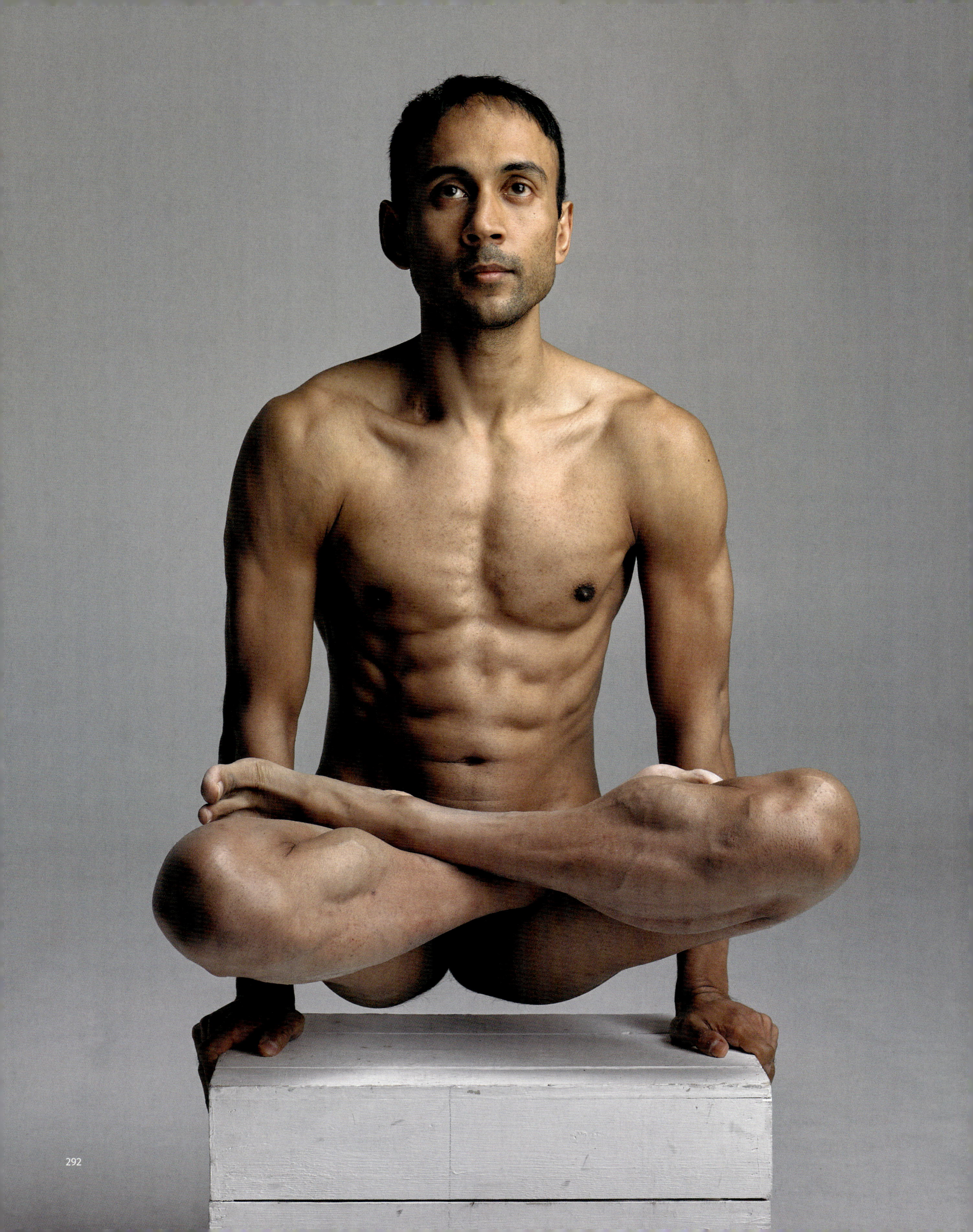

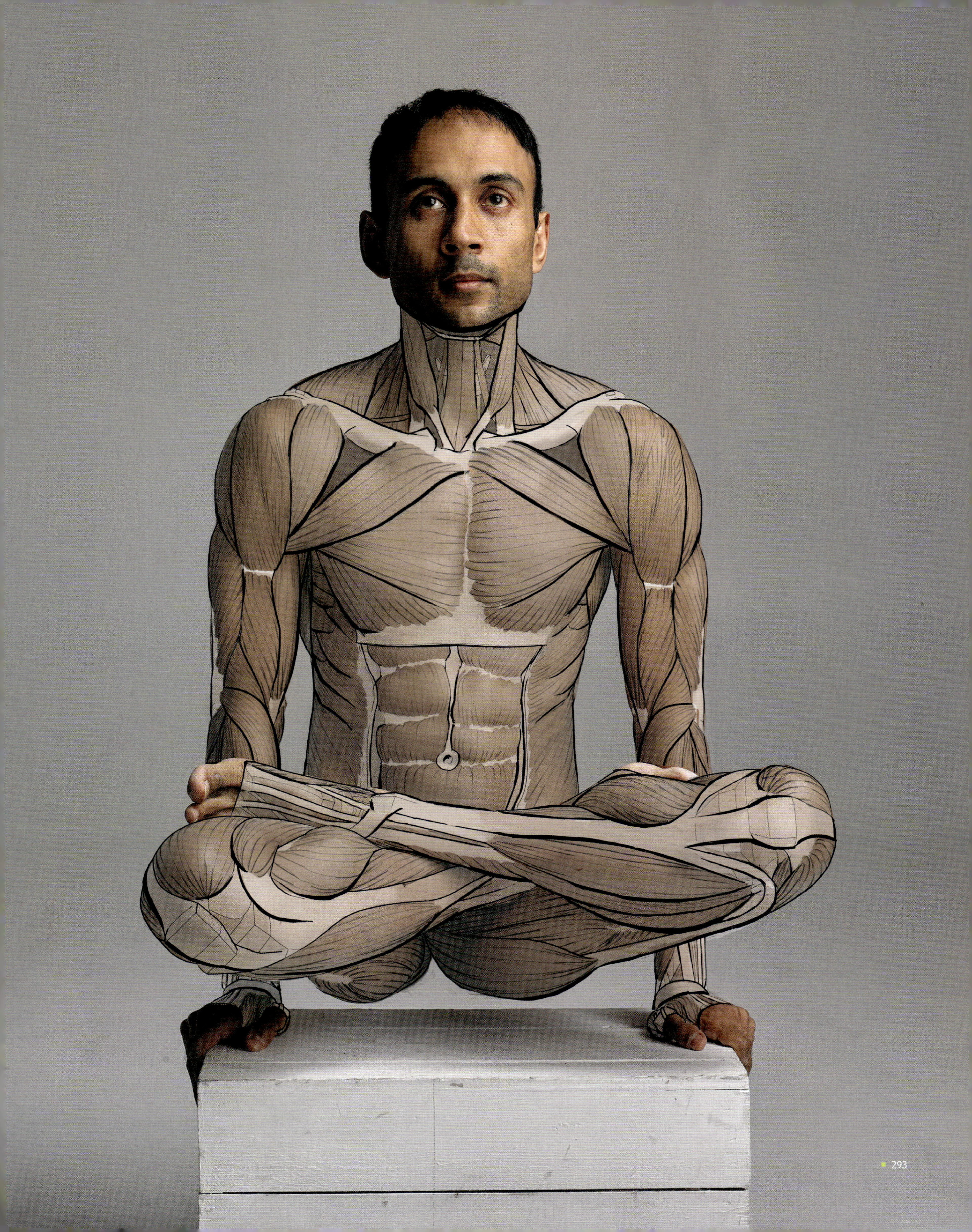

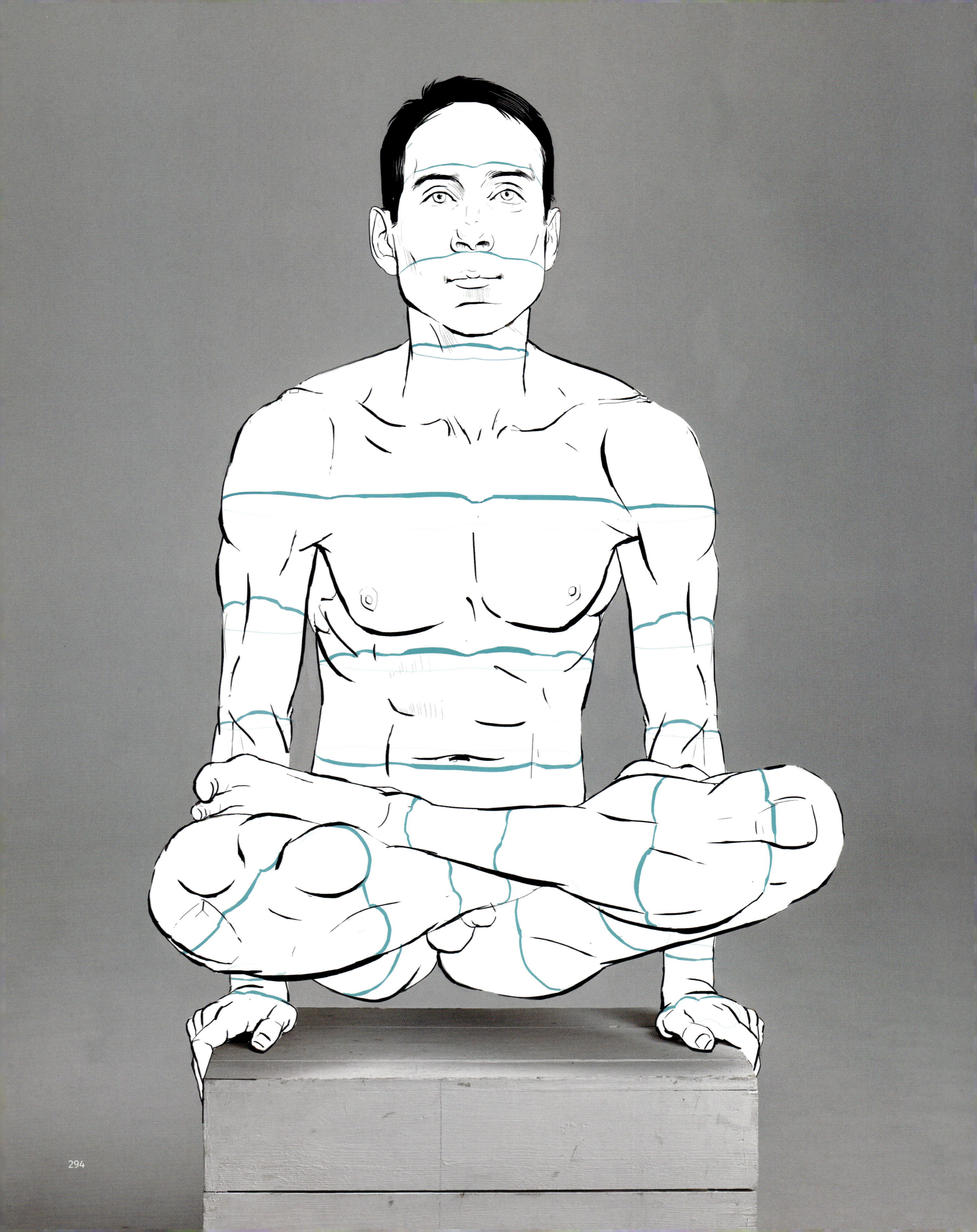

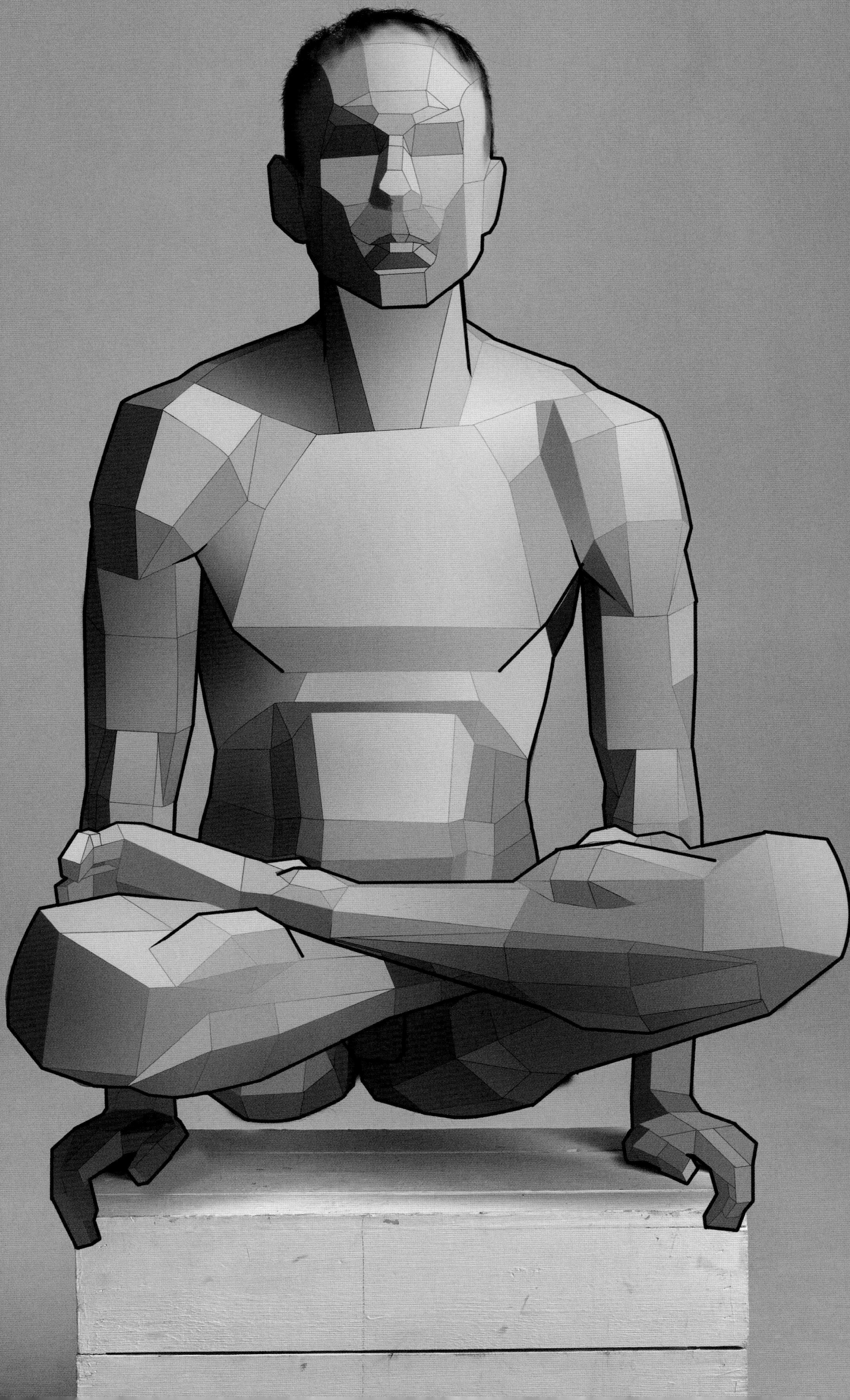

Glossary

Abdominal
Relating to the abdomen region.

Abduction
Moving away from the medial plane of the body. For example, raising the arm to the side.

Acromial
Relating to the shoulder region.

Adduction
Moving toward the medial plane of the body. For example, bringing the fingers together.

Agonist
The principle muscle(s) involved in the movement of an action. Part of an antagonistic pair of muscles.

Anatomical center
The point on the body where the frontal, horizontal, and median planes meet so that parts of the body can be referred to as anterior or posterior, or superior or inferior (for example) of this point.

Anatomy
The study of living things, from human to animal to plant. Translated from the Greek word *anatomē*, meaning "dissection."

Antagonists
The muscle(s) involved in a movement that oppose the agonist.

Anterior (or ventral)
Toward the front.

Appendicular skeleton
Part of the skeleton comprised of the shoulder girdle, the hip girdle, the upper extremity, and the lower extremity.

Axial skeleton
Part of the skeleton comprising the skull (cranial, facial, and auditory), the vertebral column (the cervical, thoracic, lumbar, sacrum, and coccyx), and the thoracic cage (the ribs and sternum).

Bone
Rigid living tissue that makes up the skeleton.

Bony landmark
An area on the surface of the skin where the underlying bone sits close to the surface and is palpable. These landmarks can be both felt and seen.

Brachial
Relating to the arm region.

Brevis
Short.

Carpal
Relating to the wrist region.

Cartilage
A tough but flexible tissue, which is the main type of connective tissue in the body.

Cephalic/cranial
Relating to the head region.

Circumduction
Circular motion created by a combination of flexion, extension, abduction, adduction, and medial and lateral movement.

Clavicular
Relating to the collarbone region.

Condyle
A condyle is a rounded articular area of bone where tendons, ligaments, or fascia attach to.

Cubital
Relating to the elbow region.

Deep
Further from the surface and covered.

Depression
The downward movement of part of the body.

Distal
Away from the trunk.

Dorsiflexion
Flexion of the foot at the ankle in the dorsal direction.

Elevation
The upward movement of part of the body.

Extension
Increasing the angle between two joints.

Fascia
A band or sheet of connective tissue beneath the skin that attaches, stabilizes, encloses, and separates muscles and organs.

Fixator
A muscle(s) that stabilizes the agonist muscle's origin.

Flexion
Decreasing the angle between two joints.

Fossa
A hollow or depression.

Frontal (or coronal) plane
This plane divides the body into front and back portions.

Horizontal (or transverse) plane
This is a horizontal plane. It runs perpendicular to both the frontal and the median plane.

Inferior (or caudal)
Toward the feet.

Insertion (in relation to muscle)
Where muscles insert to a part of the body, allowing motion when the muscles contract.

Joint
The meeting of two or more bones, allowing movement.

Lateral
Away from the median plane (away from the middle of the body).

Lateral rotation
Turning outward away from the medial plane.

Ligament
Fibrous tissue connecting bone to bone.

Longus
Long.

Lower extremity
The region consisting of the hip, thigh, leg, and foot.

Major
Large.

Mandible
The lower jawbone.

Mastication
The act of chewing. The muscles of mastication consist of the masseter, the temporalis, and the medial and lateral pterygoid.

Maxilla
The upper jawbone.

Medial
Toward the median plane (near the middle of the body).

Medial rotation
Turning inward toward the medial plane.

Median/medial (or midsagittal) plane
This plane divides the body into equal right and left halves.

Minor
Small.

Muscle
Soft tissue that functions to create movement.

Opposition
Bringing the tip of the thumb and fingers together.

Origin (relating to muscle)
Where muscles originate at a part of the body. Here there is little to no movement.

Palmarflexion
Movement of the hand so that the palm of the hand rotates closer to the forearm.

Palpable
At the surface and able to be felt.

Pelvic
Relating to the pelvic region.

Plantarflexion
Movement of the foot at the ankle away from the body.

Posterior (or dorsal)
Toward the back.

Pronation
Rotating the forearm so the palm faces downward.

Protraction
Moving forward along a plane.

Proximal
Near the trunk.

Pubic
Relating to the groin region.

Retraction
Moving backward along a plane.

Subcutaneous
Below the skin.

Superficial
Near or on the surface.

Superior (or cranial)
Toward the head.

Supination
Rotating the forearm so the palm faces upward.

Suture
A fibrous joint between the bones of the skull.

Synergist
Synergist muscles assist agonist muscles and can help with movement and stability.

Tendon
Fibrous tissue that connects muscle to bone.

Trunk
A person's body except for the head and limbs.

Upper extremity
The region consisting of the shoulder, arm, forearm, wrist, and hand.

Vertebrae
Bones of the spinal column.

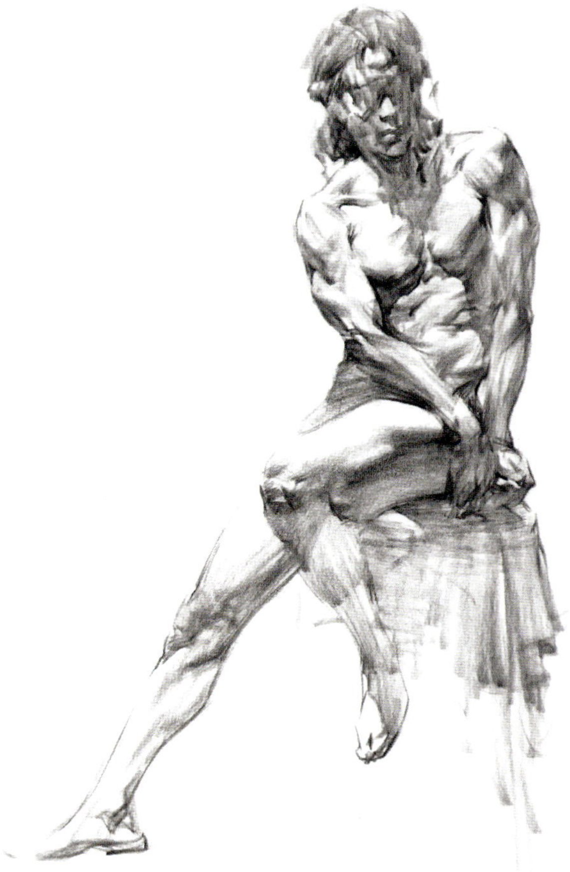

Artwork © Jacob Hankinson

Contributors

Jahirul Amin

VFX trainer
caveacademy.com

Jahirul is a computer animation and visual effects trainer, specializing in designing and delivering courses to create a range of solid and diverse production-ready skills.

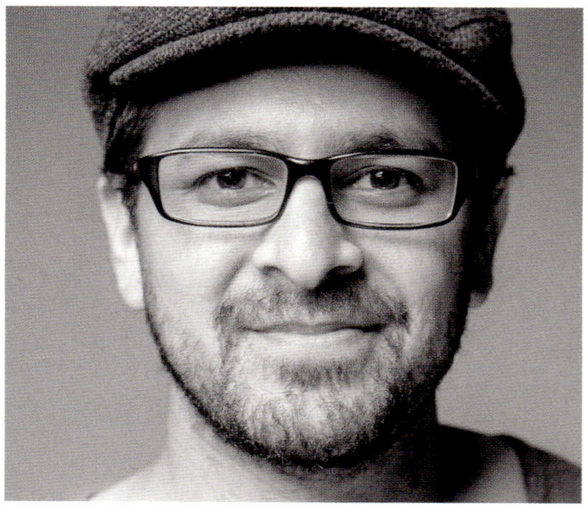

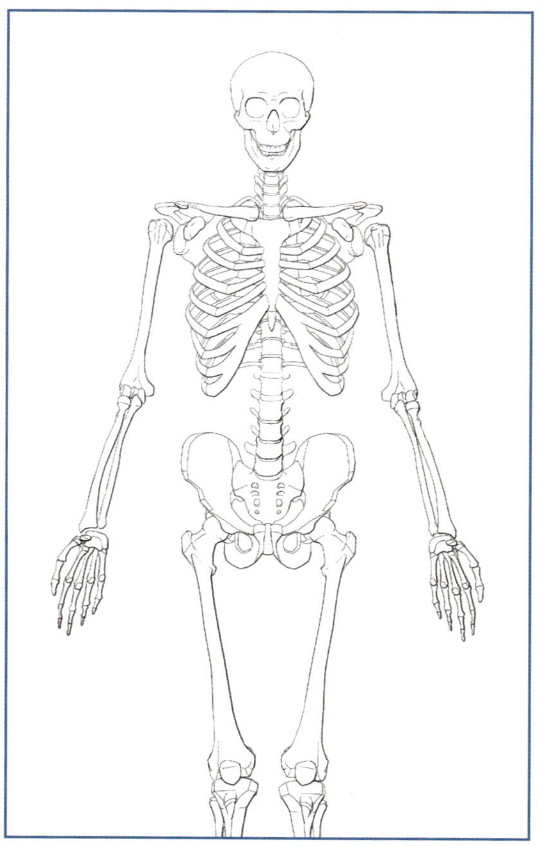

Robin Bharaj

Photographer
robinbharaj.com

Robin made his photography debut working in London's underground music scene, before moving into portraiture, fashion, and moving image. Recognized for his distinctive style, he works between personal, editorial, and commercial projects.

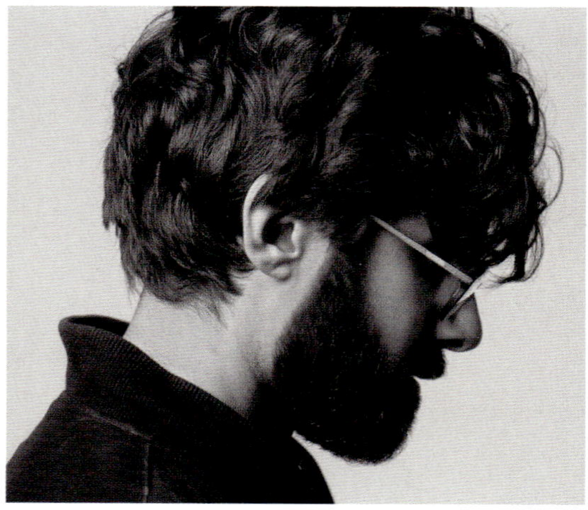

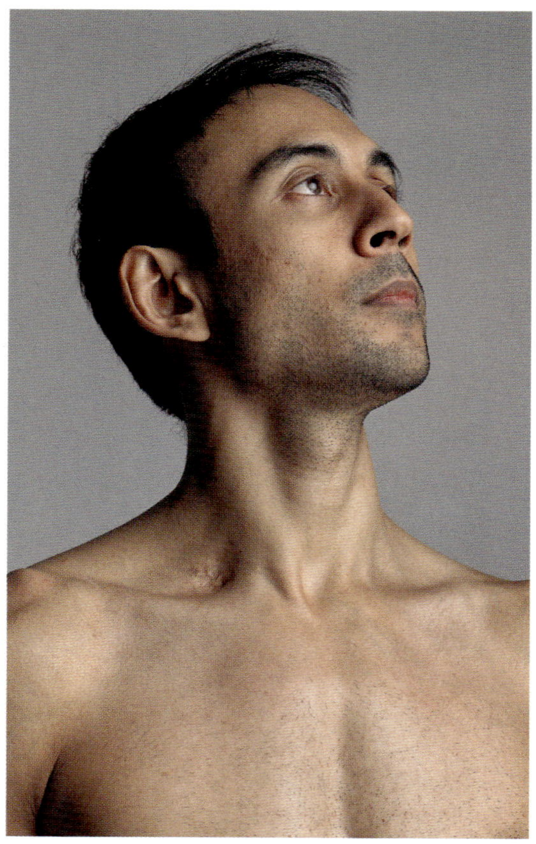

Charlie Pickard

Fine artist & illustrator
charliepickardart.com

Charlie is a classically trained fine artist and illustrator who was awarded the De Laszlo Foundation's Award for Excellence in 2020. He continues to work, exhibit, and teach out of his studio in London.

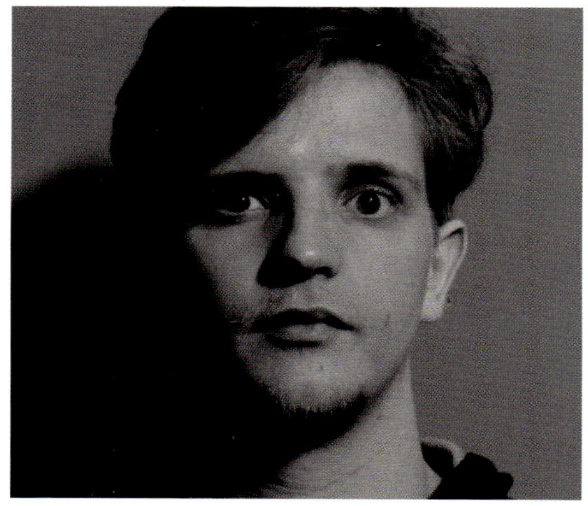

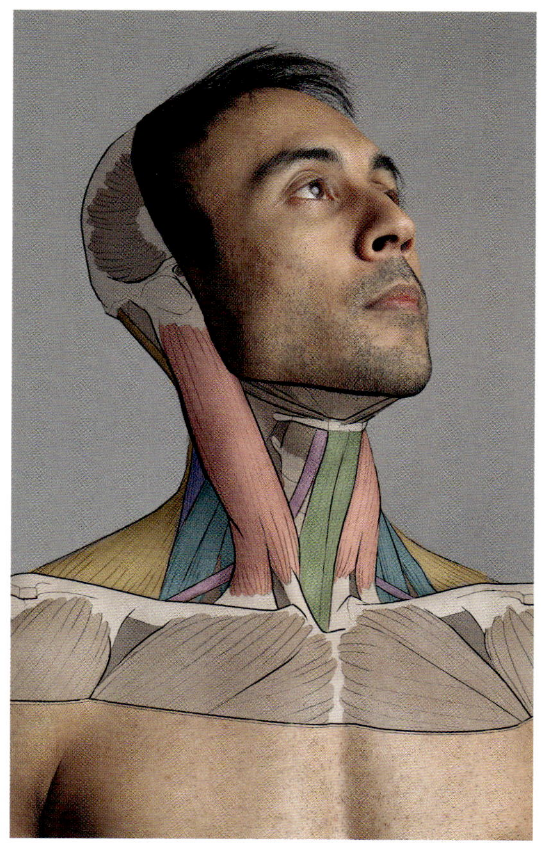

Index

G

H

I

J

K

L

M

N

O

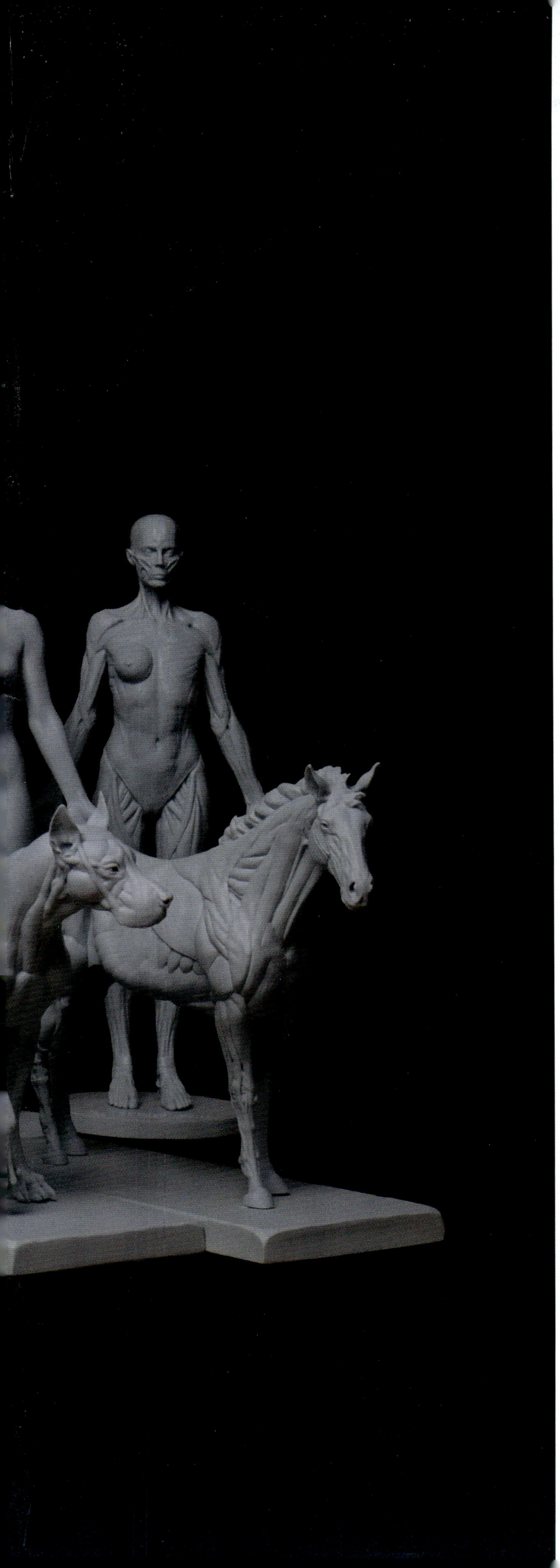

Art Fundamentals

2nd edition

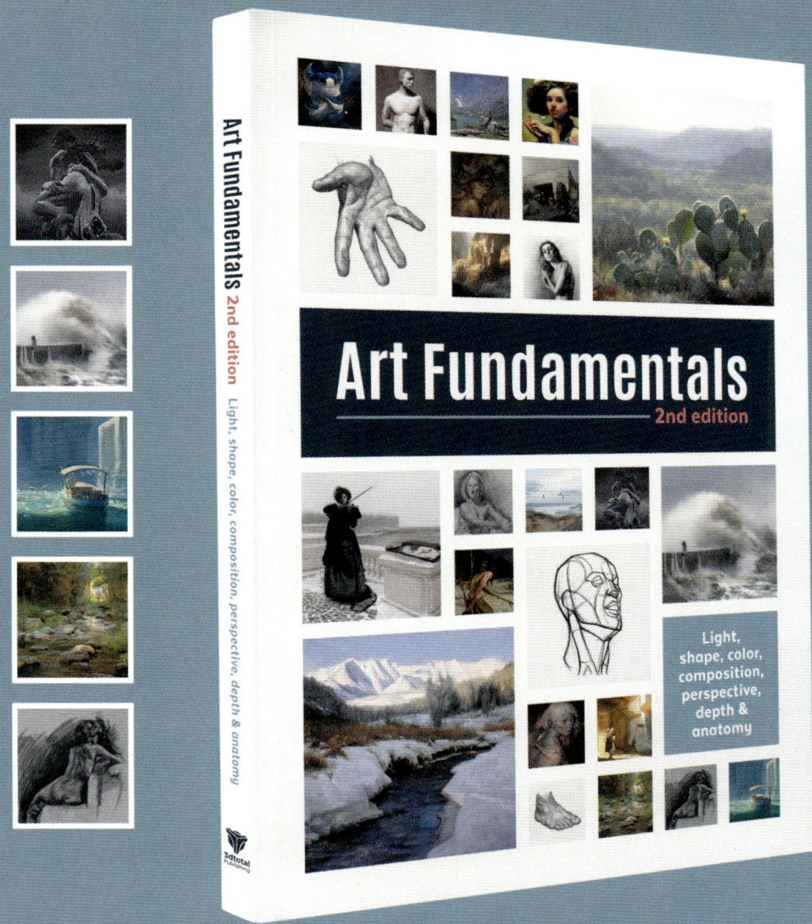

Even more expert advice, key techniques, and illuminating artwork upgrades 3dtotal's bestselling *Art Fundamentals*, the cornerstone of every artist's bookshelf.

Whether you work in a traditional or digital medium, understanding the foundations of art itself is essential for engaging and confident results. Real-world rules make concept art so much more believable, while a clear comprehension of time-honored principles can elevate a classic subject to new levels of accomplishment.

This must-have, updated edition of *Art Fundamentals* is written and illustrated by experts from a range of creative backgrounds. It demystifies the crucial elements of art, while specially selected artwork details how the fundamentals have been cleverly applied to the canvas by incredible professional artists.

288 pages
297mm x 210mm
£29.00 / $49.99
ISBN: 978-1-912843-07-7

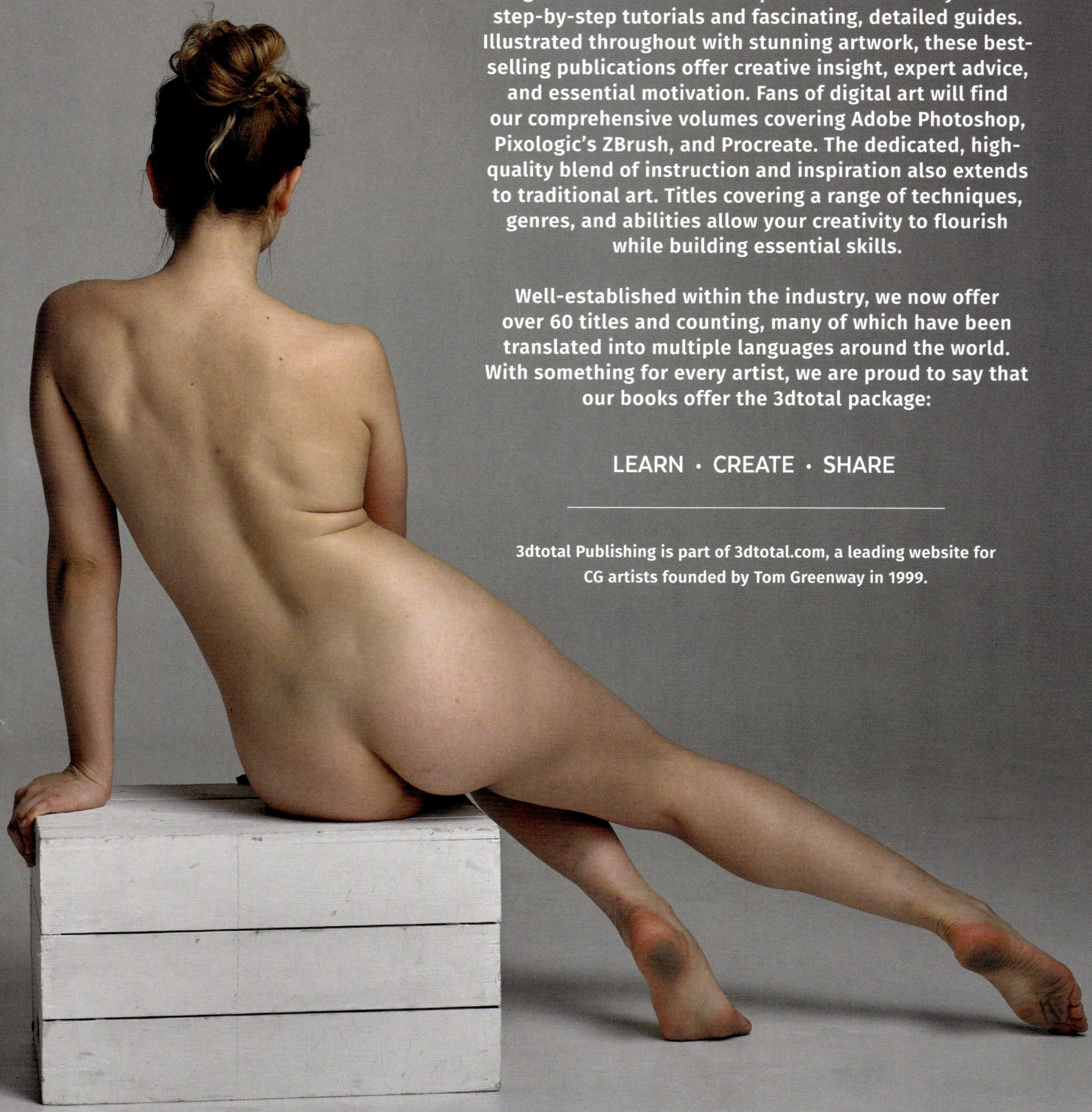

3dtotalPublishing

3dtotal Publishing is a trailblazing, creative publisher specializing in inspirational and educational resources for artists.

Our titles feature top industry professionals from around the globe who share their experience in skillfully written step-by-step tutorials and fascinating, detailed guides. Illustrated throughout with stunning artwork, these best-selling publications offer creative insight, expert advice, and essential motivation. Fans of digital art will find our comprehensive volumes covering Adobe Photoshop, Pixologic's ZBrush, and Procreate. The dedicated, high-quality blend of instruction and inspiration also extends to traditional art. Titles covering a range of techniques, genres, and abilities allow your creativity to flourish while building essential skills.

Well-established within the industry, we now offer over 60 titles and counting, many of which have been translated into multiple languages around the world. With something for every artist, we are proud to say that our books offer the 3dtotal package:

LEARN · CREATE · SHARE

3dtotal Publishing is part of 3dtotal.com, a leading website for CG artists founded by Tom Greenway in 1999.